6502 Assembly Language Subroutines

Lance A. Leventhal
Winthrop Saville

OSBORNE/McGraw-Hill
Berkeley, California

Disclaimer of Warranties and Limitation of Liabilities

The authors have taken due care in preparing this book and the programs in it, including research, development, and testing to ascertain their effectiveness. The authors and the publishers make no expressed or implied warranty of any kind with regard to these programs nor the supplementary documentation in this book. In no event shall the authors or the publishers be liable for incidental or consequential damages in connection with or arising out of the furnishing, performance, or use of any of these programs.

Apple II is a trademark of Apple Computer, Inc.

Published by
OSBORNE/McGraw-Hill
630 Bancroft Way
Berkeley, California 94710
U.S.A.

For information on translations and book distributors outside of the U.S.A., please write OSBORNE/McGraw-Hill at the above address.

6502 ASSEMBLY LANGUAGE SUBROUTINES

234567890 HCHC 8765432

ISBN 0-931988-59-4

Cover art by Jean Frega.

Text design by Paul Butzler.

Contents

Preface

This book is intended to serve as a source and a reference for the assembly language programmer. It contains an overview of assembly language programming for a particular microprocessor and a collection of useful routines. In writing the routines, we have used a standard format, documentation package, and parameter passing techniques. We have followed the rules of the original manufacturer's assembler and have described the purpose, procedure, parameters, results, execution time, and memory usage of each routine.

This overview of assembly language programming provides a summary for those who do not have the time or need for a complete textbook such as is provided already in the Assembly Language Programming series. Chapter 1 contains an introduction to assembly language programming for the particular processor and a brief summary of the major features that differentiate this processor from other microprocessors and minicomputers. Chapter 2 describes how to implement instructions and addressing modes that are not explicitly available. Chapter 3 discusses common errors that the programmer is likely to encounter.

The collection of routines emphasizes common tasks that occur in many applications such as code conversion, array manipulation, arithmetic, bit manipulation, shifting functions, string manipulation, summation, sorting, and searching. We have also provided examples of I/O routines, interrupt service routines, and initialization routines for common family chips such as parallel interfaces, serial interfaces, and timers. You should be able to use these routines as subroutines in actual applications and as guidelines for more complex programs.

We have aimed this book at the person who wants to use assembly language immediately, rather than just learn about it. The reader could be

- An engineer, technician, or programmer who must write assembly language programs for use in a design project.
- A microcomputer user who wants to write an I/O driver, a diagnostic program, or a utility or systems program in assembly language.

- A programmer or engineer with experience in assembly language who needs a quick review of techniques for a particular microprocessor.
- A system designer or programmer who needs a specific routine or technique for immediate use.
- A programmer who works in high-level languages but who must debug or optimize programs at the assembly level or must link a program written in a high-level language to one written in assembly language.
- A system designer or maintenance programmer who must quickly understand how specific assembly language programs operate.
- A microcomputer owner who wants to understand how the operating system works on a particular computer, or who wants to gain complete access to the computer's facilities.
- A student, hobbyist, or teacher who wants to see some examples of working assembly language programs.

This book can also serve as supplementary material for students of the Assembly Language Programming series.

This book should save the reader time and effort. There is no need to write, debug, test, or optimize standard routines, nor should the reader have to search through material with which he or she is thoroughly familiar. The reader should be able to obtain the specific information, routine, or technique that he or she needs with a minimum amount of effort. We have organized and indexed this book for rapid use and reference.

Obviously, a book with such an aim demands response from its readers. We have, of course, tested all the programs thoroughly and documented them carefully. If you find any errors, please inform the publisher. If you have suggestions for additional topics, routines, programming hints, index entries, and so forth, please tell us about them. We have drawn on our programming experience to develop this book, but we need your help to improve it. We would greatly appreciate your comments, criticisms, and suggestions.

NOMENCLATURE

We have used the following nomenclature in this book to describe the architecture of the 6502 processor, to specify operands, and to represent general values of numbers and addresses.

6502 Architecture

Byte-length registers include

A (accumulator)

F (flags, same as P)

P (status register)

S or SP (stack pointer)

X (index register X)

Y (index register Y)

Of these, the general purpose user registers are A, X, and Y. The stack pointer always contains the address of the next available stack location on page 1 of memory (addresses 0100_{16} through $01FF_{16}$). The P (status) or F (flag) register consists of a set of bits with independent functions and meanings, organized as shown in the following diagram:

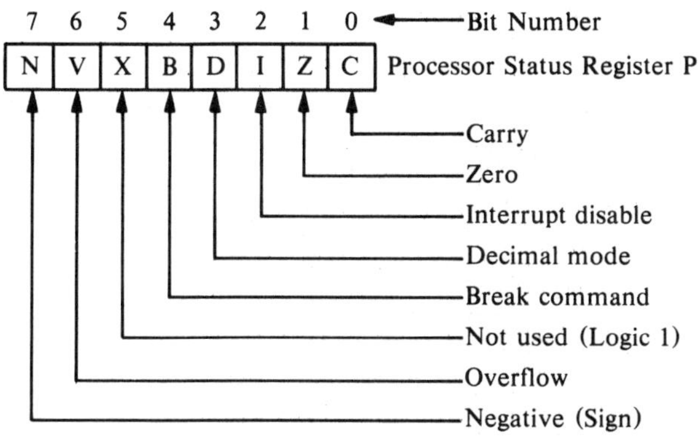

Word-length registers include

PC (program counter)

Note: Pairs of memory locations on page 0 may also be used as word-length registers to hold indirect addresses. The lower address holds the less significant byte and the higher address holds the more significant byte. Since the 6502 provides automatic wraparound, addresses $00FF_{16}$ and 0000_{16} form a rarely used pair.

Flags include

Break (B)

Carry (C)

Decimal Mode (D)

Interrupt Disable (I)

Negative or Sign (N)

Overflow (V)

Zero (Z)

These flags are arranged in the P or F register as shown previously.

6502 Assembler

Delimiters include

space	After a label or an operation code
,	Between operands in the operand (address) field
;	Before a comment
:	After a label (optional)
(,)	Around an indirect address

Pseudo-Operations include

.BLOCK	Reserve bytes of memory; reserve the specified number of bytes of memory for temporary storage
.BYTE	Form byte-length data; place the specified 8-bit data in the next available memory locations
.DBYTE	Form double-byte (word) length data with more significant byte first; place the specified 16-bit data in the next available memory locations with more significant byte first
.END	End of program
.EQU	Equate; define the attached label
.TEXT	Form string of ASCII characters; place the specified ASCII characters in the next available memory locations
.WORD	Form double-byte (word) length data with less significant byte first; place the specified 16-bit data in the next available memory locations with less significant byte first
*=	Set origin; assign the object code generated from the subsequent assembly language statements to memory addresses starting with the one specified
=	Equate; define the attached label

Designations include

Number systems:

$ (prefix) or H (suffix)	Hexadecimal
@ (prefix) or Q (suffix)	Octal
% (prefix) or B (suffix)	Binary

The default mode is decimal.

Others:

' (in front of character)	ASCII
*	Current value of location (program) counter

‘ ’ or “ ” (around a string of characters)	ASCII string
#	Immediate addressing
,x	Indexed addressing with index register X
,y	Indexed addressing with index register Y

The default addressing mode is absolute (direct) addressing.

General Nomenclature

ADDR	a 16-bit address in data memory
ADDRH	the more significant byte of ADDR
ADDRL	the less significant byte of ADDR
BASE	a constant 16-bit address
BASEH	the more significant byte of BASE
BASEL	the less signficant byte of BASE
DEST	a 16-bit address in program memory, the destination for a jump or branch instruction
NTIMES	an 8-bit data item
NTIMH	an 8-bit data item
NTIMHC	an 8-bit data item
NTIML	an 8-bit data item
NTIMLC	an 8-bit data item
OPER	a 16-bit address in data memory
OPER1	a 16-bit address in data memory
OPER2	a 16-bit address in data memory
PGZRO	an address on page 0 of data memory
PGZRO+1	the address one larger than PGZRO (with no carry to the more significant byte)
POINTER	a 16-bit address in data memory
POINTH	the more significant byte of POINTER
POINTL	the less significant byte of POINTER
RESLT	a 16-bit address in data memory

VAL16	a 16-bit data item
VAL16L	the less significant byte of VAL16
VAL16M	the more significant byte of VAL16
VALUE	an 8-bit data item
ZCOUNT	a 16-bit address in data memory

Chapter 1 General Programming Methods

This chapter describes general methods for writing assembly language programs for the 6502 and related microprocessors. It presents techniques for performing the following operations:

- Loading and saving registers
- Storing data in memory
- Arithmetic and logical functions
- Bit manipulation
- Bit testing
- Testing for specific values
- Numerical comparisons
- Looping (repeating sequences of operations)
- Array processing and manipulation
- Table lookup
- Character code manipulation
- Code conversion
- Multiple-precision arithmetic
- Multiplication and division
- List processing
- Processing of data structures.

Special sections discuss passing parameters to subroutines, writing I/O drivers and interrupt service routines, and making programs run faster or use less memory.

The operations described are required in applications such as instrumentation, test equipment, computer peripherals, communications equipment, industrial control, process control, aerospace and military systems, business equipment, and consumer products. Microcomputer users will make use of these operations in writing I/O drivers, utility programs, diagnostics, and systems software, and in understanding, debugging, or improving programs written in high-level languages. This chapter provides a brief guide to 6502 assembly language programming for those who have an immediate application in mind.

QUICK SUMMARY FOR EXPERIENCED PROGRAMMERS

For those who are familiar with assembly language programming on other processors, we provide here a brief review of the peculiarities of the 6502. Being aware of these unusual features can save you a great deal of time and trouble.

1. The Carry flag acts as an inverted borrow in subtraction. A Subtract (SBC) or Compare (CMP, CPX, or CPY) instruction clears the Carry if the operation requires a borrow and sets it if it does not. The SBC instruction accounts for this inversion by subtracting 1 − Carry from the usual difference. Thus, the Carry has the opposite meaning after subtraction (or comparison) on the 6502 than it has on most other computers.

2. The only Addition and Subtraction instructions are ADC (Add with Carry) and SBC (Subtract with Carry). If you wish to exclude the Carry flag, you must clear it before addition or set it before subtraction. That is, you can simulate a normal Add instruction with

```
CLC
ADC     MEMORY
```

and a normal Subtract instruction with

```
SEC
SBC     MEMORY
```

3. There are no 16-bit registers and no operations that act on 16-bit quantities. The lack of 16-bit registers is commonly overcome by using pointers stored on page 0 and the indirect indexed (postindexed) addressing mode. However, both initializing and changing those pointers require sequences of 8-bit operations.

4. There is no true indirect addressing except with JMP. For many other instructions, however, you can simulate indirect addressing by clearing index register Y and using indirect indexed addressing, or by clearing index register X and using indexed indirect addressing. Both of these modes are limited to indirect addresses stored on page 0.

5. The stack is always on page 1 of memory. The stack pointer contains the less significant byte of the next empty address. Thus, the stack is limited to 256 bytes of memory.

6. The JSR (Jump to Subroutine) instruction saves the address of its own third byte in the stack, that is, JSR saves the return address minus 1. RTS (Return from Subroutine) loads the program counter from the top of the stack and then adds 1 to it. You must remember this offset of 1 in debugging and using JSR or RTS for purposes other than ordinary calls and returns.

7. The Decimal Mode (D) flag is used to perform decimal arithmetic. When this flag is set, all additions and subtractions produce decimal results. Increments and decrements, however, produce binary results regardless of the mode. The problem with this approach is that you may not be sure of the initial or current state of the D flag (the processor does not initialize it on Reset). A simple way to avoid problems in programs that use Addition or Subtraction instructions is to save the original D flag in the stack, assign D the appropriate value, and restore the original value before exiting. Interrupt service routines, in particular, should always either set or clear D before executing any addition or subtraction instructions. The PHP (Store Status Register in Stack) and PLP (Load Status Register from Stack) instructions can be used to save and restore the D flag, if necessary. The overall system startup routine must initialize D (usually to 0, indicating binary mode, with CLD). Most 6502-based operating systems assume the binary mode as a default and always return to that mode as soon as possible.

A minor quirk of the 6502's decimal mode is that the Zero and Negative flags are no longer universally valid. These flags reflect only the binary result, not the decimal result; only the Carry flag always reflects the decimal result. Thus, for example, subtracting 80_{16} from 50_{16} in the decimal mode sets the Negative flag (since the binary result is $D0_{16}$), even though the decimal result (70_{16}) has a most significant bit of 0. Similarly, adding 50_{16} and 50_{16} in the decimal mode clears the Zero flag (since the binary result is $A0_{16}$), even though the decimal result is zero. Note that adding 50_{16} and 50_{16} in the decimal mode does set the Carry. Thus when working in the decimal mode, the programmer should use only branches that depend on the Carry flag or operations that do not depend on the mode at all (such as subtractions or comparisons followed by branches on the Zero flag).

8. Ordinary Load (or Pull from the Stack) and Transfer instructions (except TXS) affect the Negative (Sign) and Zero flags. This is not the case with the 8080, 8085, or Z-80 microprocessors. Storing data in memory does not affect any flags.

9. INC and DEC cannot be applied to the accumulator. To increment A, use

```
CLC
ADC     #1          ;INCREMENT ACCUMULATOR BY 1
```

To decrement A, use

```
SEC
SBC     #1          ;DECREMENT ACCUMULATOR BY 1
```

10. The index registers are only 8 bits long. This creates obvious problems in handling arrays or areas of memory that are longer than 256 bytes. To overcome this, use the indirect indexed (postindexed) addressing mode. This mode allows you to store the starting address of the array in two memory locations on page 0. Whenever the program completes a 256-byte section, it must add 1 to the more significant byte of the indirect address before proceeding to the next section. The processor knows that it has completed a section when index register Y returns to 0. A typical sequence is

```
INY                 ;PROCEED TO NEXT BYTE
BNE     LOOP        ;UNLESS A PAGE IS DONE
INC     INDR+1      ;IF ONE IS, GO ON TO THE NEXT PAGE
```

Memory location INDR+1 (on page 0) contains the most significant byte of the indirect address.

11. 16-bit counters may be maintained in two memory locations. Counting up is much easier than counting down since you can use the sequence

```
INC     COUNTL      ;COUNT UP LESS SIGNIFICANT BYTE
BNE     LOOP
INC     COUNTH      ;CARRYING TO MSB IF NECESSARY
JMP     LOOP
```

COUNTL contains the less significant byte of a 16-bit counter and COUNTH the more significant byte. Note that we check the Zero flag rather than the Carry flag since, as on most computers, Increment and Decrement instructions do not affect Carry.

12. The BIT instruction (logical AND with no result saved) has several unusual features. In the first place, it allows only direct addressing (absolute and zero page). If you want to test bit 3 of memory location ADDR, you must use the sequence

```
LDA     #%00001000
BIT     ADDR
```

BIT also loads the Negative and Overflow flags with the contents of bits 7 and 6 of the memory location, respectively, regardless of the value in the accumulator. Thus, you can perform the following operations without loading the accumulator at all. Branch to DEST if bit 7 of ADDR is 1

```
BIT     ADDR
BMI     DEST
```

Branch to DEST if bit 6 of ADDR is 0

```
BIT     ADDR
BVC     DEST
```

Of course, you should document the special use of the Overflow flag for later reference.

13. The processor lacks some common instructions that are available on the 6800, 6809, and similar processors. Most of the missing instructions are easy to simulate, although the documentation can become awkward. In particular, we should mention Clear (use load immediate with 0 instead), Complement (use logical EXCLUSIVE OR with the all 1s byte instead), and the previously mentioned Add (without carry) and Subtract (without borrow). There is also no direct way to load or store the stack pointer (this can be done through index register X), load or store the status register (this can be done through the stack), or perform operations between registers (one must be stored in memory). Other missing instructions include Unconditional Relative Branch (use jump or assign a value to a flag and branch on it having that value), Increment and Decrement Accumulator (use the Addition and Subtraction instructions), Arithmetic Shift (copy bit 7 into Carry and rotate), and Test zero or minus (use a comparison with 0 or an increment, decrement sequence). Weller[1] describes the definition of macros to replace the missing instructions.

14. The 6502 uses the following common conventions:

- 16-bit addresses are stored with the less significant byte first. The order of the bytes is the same as in the 8080, Z-80, and 8085 microprocessors, but opposite the order used in 6800 and 6809.
- The stack pointer contains the address (on page 1) of the next available location. This convention is also used in the 6800, but the obvious alternative (last occupied location) is used in the 8080, 8085, Z-80, and 6809 microprocessors. Instructions store data in the stack using postdecrementing (they subtract 1 from the stack pointer after storing each byte) and load data from the stack using preincrementing (they add 1 to the stack pointer before loading each byte).
- The I (Interrupt) flag acts as a disable. Setting the flag (with SEI) disables the maskable interrupt and clearing the flag (with CLI) enables the maskable interrupt. This convention is the same as in the 6800 and 6809 but the opposite of that used in the 8080, 8085, and Z-80.

THE REGISTER SET

The 6502 assembly language programmer's work is complicated considerably by the processor's limited register set. In particular, there are no address-length (16-bit) user registers. Thus, variable addresses must normally be stored in pairs of memory locations on page 0 and accessed indirectly using either preindexing (indexed indirect addressing) or postindexing (indirect indexed addressing). The lack of 16-bit registers also complicates the handling of arrays or blocks that occupy more than 256 bytes of memory.

If we consider memory locations on page 0 as extensions of the register set, we may characterize the registers as follows:

· The accumulator is the center of data processing and is used as a source and destination by most arithmetic, logical, and other data processing instructions.

· Index register X is the primary index register for non-indirect uses. It is the only register that normally has a zero page indexed mode (except for the LDX STX instructions), and it is the only register that can be used for indexing with single-operand instructions such as shifts, increment, and decrement. It is also the only register that can be used for preindexing, although that mode is not common. Finally, it is the only register that can be used to load or store the stack pointer.

· Index register Y is the primary index register for indirect uses, since it is the only register that can be used for postindexing.

· Memory locations on page 0 are the only locations that can be accessed with the zero page (direct), zero page indexed, preindexed, and postindexed addressing modes.

Tables 1-1 through 1-7 contain lists of instructions having particular features. Table 1-1 lists instructions that apply only to particular registers and Table 1-2 lists instructions that can be applied directly to memory locations. Tables 1-3 through 1-7 list instructions that allow particular addressing modes: zero page (Table 1-3), absolute (Table 1-4), zero page indexed (Table 1-5), absolute indexed (Table 1-6), and preindexing and postindexing (Table 1-7).

We may describe the special features of particular registers as follows:

· **Accumulator**. Source and destination for all arithmetic and logical instructions except CPX, CPY, DEC, and INC. Only register that can be shifted with a single instruction. Only register that can be loaded or stored using preindexed or postindexed addressing.

· **Index register X**. Can be incremented using INX or decremented using DEX. Only register that can be used as an index in preindexing. Only register that can be used to load or store the stack pointer.

· **Index register Y**. Can be incremented using INY or decremented using DEY. Only register that can be used as an index in postindexing.

· **Memory locations on page 0**. Only memory locations that can hold indirect addresses for use in postindexing or preindexing. Only memory locations that can be accessed using zero page or zero page indexed addressing.

· **Status register**. Can only be stored in the stack using PHP or loaded from the stack using PLP.

Table 1-1: Registers and Applicable Instructions

Register	Instructions
A	ADC, AND, ASL, BIT, CMP, EOR, LDA, LSR, ORA, PHA, PLA, ROL, ROR, SBC, STA, TAX, TAY, TXA, TYA
P (processor status)	PHP, PLP (CLC, CLD, CLV, SEC, and SED affect particular flags)
S (stack pointer)	JSR, PHA, PHP, PLA, PLP, RTS, TSX, TXS
X	CPX, DEX, INX, LDX, STX, TAX, TSX, TXA, TXS
Y	CPY, DEY, INY, LDY, STY, TAY, TYA

Table 1-2: Instructions That Can Be Applied Directly to Memory Locations

Instruction	Function
ASL	Arithmetic shift left
BIT	Bit test (test bits 6 and 7)
DEC	Decrement by 1
INC	Increment by 1
LSR	Logical shift right
ROL	Rotate left
ROR	Rotate right

Table 1-3: Instructions That Allow Zero Page Addressing

Instruction	Function
ADC	Add with Carry
AND	Logical AND
ASL	Arithmetic shift left
BIT	Bit test
CMP	Compare memory and accumulator
CPX	Compare memory and index register X
CPY	Compare memory and index register Y
DEC	Decrement by 1
EOR	Logical EXCLUSIVE OR
INC	Increment by 1
LDA	Load accumulator
LDX	Load index register X
LDY	Load index register Y
LSR	Logical shift right
ORA	Logical OR
ROL	Rotate left
ROR	Rotate right
SBC	Subtract with Carry
STA	Store accumulator
STX	Store index register X
STY	Store index register Y

Table 1-4: Instructions That Allow Absolute (Direct) Addressing

Instruction	Function
ADC	Add with Carry
AND	Logical AND
ASL	Arithmetic shift left
BIT	Logical bit test
CMP	Compare memory and accumulator
CPX	Compare memory and index register X
CPY	Compare memory and index register Y
DEC	Decrement by 1
EOR	Logical EXCLUSIVE OR
INC	Increment by 1
JMP	Jump unconditional
JSR	Jump to subroutine
LDA	Load accumulator
LDX	Load index register X
LDY	Load index register Y
LSR	Logical shift right
ORA	Logical OR
ROL	Rotate left
ROR	Rotate right
SBC	Subtract with Carry
STA	Store accumulator
STX	Store index register X
STY	Store index register Y

Table 1-5: Instructions That Allow Zero Page Indexed Addressing

	Instruction	Function
Index Register X	ADC	Add with Carry
	AND	Logical AND
	ASL	Arithmetic shift left
	CMP	Compare memory and accumulator
	DEC	Decrement by 1
	EOR	Logical EXCLUSIVE OR
	INC	Increment by 1
	LDA	Load accumulator
	LDY	Load index register Y
	LSR	Logical shift right
	ORA	Logical OR
	ROL	Rotate left
	ROR	Rotate right
	SBC	Subtract with Carry
	STA	Store accumulator
	STY	Store index register Y
Index Register Y	LDX	Load index register X
	STX	Store index register X

Table 1-6: Instructions That Allow Absolute Indexed Addressing

	Instruction	Function
Index Register X	ADC	Add with Carry
	AND	Logical AND
	ASL	Arithmetic shift left
	CMP	Compare memory and accumulator
	DEC	Decrement by 1
	EOR	Logical EXCLUSIVE OR
	INC	Increment by 1
	LDA	Load accumulator
	LDY	Load index register Y
	LSR	Logical shift right
	ORA	Logical OR
	ROL	Rotate left
	ROR	Rotate right
	SBC	Subtract with Carry
	STA	Store accumulator
Index Register Y	ADC	Add with Carry
	AND	Logical AND
	CMP	Compare memory and accumulator
	EOR	Logical EXCLUSIVE OR
	LDA	Load accumulator
	LDX	Load index register X
	ORA	Logical OR
	SBC	Subtract with Carry
	STA	Store accumulator

Table 1-7: Instructions That Allow Postindexing and Preindexing

Instruction	Function
ADC	Add with Carry
AND	Logical AND
CMP	Compare memory and accumulator
EOR	Logical EXCLUSIVE OR
LDA	Load accumulator
ORA	Logical OR
SBC	Subtract with Carry
STA	Store accumulator

· **Stack pointer**. Always refers to an address on page 1. Can only be loaded from or stored in index register X using TXS and TSX, respectively.

Note the following:

· Almost all data processing involves the accumulator, since it provides one operand for arithmetic and logical instructions and the destination for the result.

· Only a limited number of instructions operate directly on the index registers or on memory locations. An index register can be incremented by 1, decremented by 1, or compared to a constant or to the contents of an absolute address. The data in a memory location can be incremented by 1, decremented by 1, shifted left or right, or rotated left or right.

· The available set of addressing methods varies greatly from instruction to instruction. Note in particular the limited sets available with the instructions BIT, CPX, CPY, LDX, LDY, STX, and STY.

Register Transfers

Only a limited number of direct transfers between registers are provided. A single instruction can transfer data from an index register to the accumulator, from the accumulator to an index register, from the stack pointer to index register X, or from index register X to the stack pointer. The mnemonics for the transfer instructions have the form TSD, where "S" is the source register and "D" is the destination register as in the convention proposed in IEEE Standard 694.[2] The status (P) register may only be transferred to or from the stack using PHP or PLP.

LOADING REGISTERS FROM MEMORY

The 6502 microprocessor offers many methods for loading registers from memory. The following addressing modes are available: zero page (direct), absolute (direct), immediate zero page indexed, absolute indexed, postindexed, and preindexed. Osborne[3] describes all these modes in Chapter 6 of *An Introduction to Microcomputers: Volume 1 — Basic Concepts.*

Direct Loading of Registers

The accumulator, index register X, and index register Y can be loaded from memory using direct addressing. A special zero page mode loads registers from addresses on page 0 more rapidly than from addresses on other pages. Terminology for 6502 refers to zero page direct addressing as *zero page addressing* and to the more general direct addressing as *absolute addressing.*

Examples

1. LDA $40

This instruction loads the accumulator from memory location 0040_{16}. The special zero page addressing mode requires less time and memory than the more general absolute (direct) addressing.

2. LDX $C000

This instruction loads index register X from memory location $C000_{16}$. It uses absolute (direct) addressing.

Immediate Loading of Registers

This method can be used to load the accumulator, index register X, or index register Y with a specific value.

Examples

1. LDY #6

This instruction loads index register Y with the number 6. The 6 is an 8-bit data item, not a 16-bit address; do not confuse the number 6 with the address 0006_{16}.

2. LDA #$E3

This instruction loads the accumulator with the number $E3_{16}$.

Indexed Loading of Registers

The instructions LDA, LDX, and LDY can be used in the indexed mode. The limitations are that index register X cannot be loaded using X as an index; similarly, index register Y cannot be loaded using Y as an index. As with direct addressing, a special zero page mode is provided. Note, however, that the accumulator cannot be loaded in the zero page mode using Y as an index.

Examples

1. LDA $0340,X

This instruction loads the accumulator from the address obtained by indexing with index register X from the base address 0340_{16}; that is, the effective address is 0340_{16}+(X). This is the typical indexing described in *An Introduction to Microcomputers: Volume 1 — Basic Concepts.*[4]

2. LDX $40,Y

This instruction loads index register X from the address obtained by indexing with register Y from the base address 0040_{16}. Here the special zero page indexed mode saves time and memory.

Postindexed Loading of Registers

The instruction LDA can be used in the postindexed mode, in which the base address is taken from two memory locations on page 0. Otherwise, this mode is the same as regular indexing.

Example

LDA ($40),Y

This instruction loads the accumulator from the address obtained by indexing with index register Y from the base address in memory locations 0040_{16} and 0041_{16}. This mode is restricted to page 0 and index register Y. It also assumes that the indirect address is stored with its less significant byte first (at the lower address) in the usual 6502 manner.

Preindexed Loading of Registers

The instruction LDA can be used in the preindexed mode, in which the indexed address is itself used indirectly. This mode is restricted to page 0 and index register X. Note that it also assumes the existence of a table of 2-byte indirect addresses, so that only even values in X make sense.

Example

LDA ($40,X)

This instruction loads the accumulator from the indirect address obtained by indexing with register X from the base address 0040_{16}. The indirect address is in the two bytes of memory starting at $0040_{16} + (X)$. This mode is uncommon; one of its uses is to select from a table of device addresses for input/output.

Stack Loading of Registers

The instruction PLA loads the accumulator from the top of the stack and subtracts 1 from the stack pointer. The instruction PLP is similar, except that it loads the status (P) register. This is the only way to load the status register with a specific value. The index registers cannot be loaded directly from the stack, but they can be loaded via the accumulator. The required sequences are

(for index register X)

```
PLA                    ;TOP OF STACK TO A
TAX                    ;AND ON TO X
```

(for index register Y)

```
PLA                    ;TOP OF STACK TO A
TAY                    ;AND ON TO Y
```

The stack has the following special features:

- It is always located on page 1 of memory. The stack pointer contains only the less significant byte of the next available address.
- Data is stored in the stack using postdecrementing — the instructions decrement the stack pointer by 1 *after* storing each byte. Data is loaded from the stack using preincrementing — the instructions increment the stack pointer by 1 *before* loading each byte.
- As is typical with microprocessors, there are no overflow or underflow indicators.

STORING REGISTERS IN MEMORY

The same approaches that we used to load registers from memory can also be used to store registers in memory. The only differences between loading and storing registers are

- Store instructions do not allow immediate addressing. There is no way to directly store a number in memory. Instead, it must be transferred through a register.
- STX and STY allow only zero page indexed addressing. Neither allows absolute indexed addressing.
- As you might expect, the order of operations in storing index registers in the stack is the opposite of that used in loading them from the stack. The sequences are

(for index register X)

```
TXA                    ;MOVE X TO A
PHA                    ;AND THEN TO TOP OF STACK
```

(for index register Y)

```
TYA                    ;MOVE Y TO A
PHA                    ;AND THEN TO TOP OF STACK
```

Other storage operations operate in exactly the same manner as described in the discussion of loading registers.

Examples

1. STA $50

This instruction stores the accumulator in memory location 0050_{16}. The special zero page mode is both shorter and faster than the absolute mode, since the more significant byte of the address is assumed to be 0.

2. STX $17E8

This instruction stores index register X in memory location $17E8_{16}$. It uses the absolute addressing mode with a full 16-bit address.

3. STA $A000,Y

This instruction stores the accumulator in the effective address obtained by adding index register Y to the base address $A000_{16}$. The effective address is $A000_{16}+(Y)$.

4. STA ($50),Y

This instruction stores the accumulator in the effective address obtained by adding index register Y to the base address in memory locations 0050_{16} and 0051_{16}. The instruction obtains the base address indirectly.

5. STA ($43,X)

This instruction stores the accumulator in the effective address obtained indirectly by adding index register X to the base 0043_{16}. The indirect address is in the two bytes of memory starting at $0043_{16}+(X)$.

STORING VALUES IN RAM

The normal way to initialize RAM locations is through the accumulator, one byte at a time. The programmer can also use index registers X and Y for this purpose.

Examples

1. Store an 8-bit item (VALUE) in address ADDR.

```
LDA     #VALUE          ;GET THE VALUE
STA     ADDR            ;INITIALIZE LOCATION ADDR
```

We could use either LDX, STX or LDY, STY instead of the LDA, STA sequence. Note that the 6502 treats all values the same; there is no special CLEAR instruction for generating 0s.

2. Store a 16-bit item (POINTER) in addresses ADDR and ADDR+1 (MSB in ADDR+1).

We assume that POINTER consists of POINTH (more significant byte) and POINTL (less significant byte).

```
LDA     #POINTL      ;GET LSB
STA     ADDR         ;INITIALIZE LOCATION ADDR
LDA     #POINTH      ;GET MSB
STA     ADDR+1       ;INITIALIZE LOCATION ADDR+1
```

This method allows us to initialize indirect addresses on page 0 for later use with postindexing and preindexing.

ARITHMETIC AND LOGICAL OPERATIONS

Most arithmetic and logical operations (addition, subtraction, AND, OR, and EXCLUSIVE OR) can be performed only between the accumulator and an 8-bit byte in memory. The result replaces the operand in the accumulator. Arithmetic and logical operations may use immediate, zero page (direct), absolute (direct), indexed, zero page indexed, indexed indirect, or indirect indexed addressing.

Examples

1. Add memory location 0040_{16} to the accumulator with carry.

```
ADC     $40
```

This instruction adds the contents of memory location 0040_{16} and the contents of the Carry flag to the accumulator.

2. Logically OR the accumulator with the contents of an indexed address obtained using index register X and the base $17E0_{16}$.

```
ORA     $17E0,X
```

The effective address is $17E0_{16}+(X)$.

3. Logically AND the accumulator with the contents of memory location $B470_{16}$.

```
AND     $B470
```

Note the following special features of the 6502's arithmetic and logical instructions:

· The only addition instruction is ADC (Add with Carry). To exclude the Carry, you must clear it explicitly using the sequence

```
CLC                  ;MAKE CARRY ZERO
ADC     $40          ;ADD WITHOUT CARRY
```

· The only subtraction instruction is SBC (Subtract with Borrow). This instruction subtracts a memory location and the complemented Carry flag from the accumulator. SBC produces

(A) = (A) − (M) − (1−CARRY)

where M is the contents of the effective address. To exclude the Carry, you must set it explicitly using the sequence

```
SEC                     ;MAKE INVERTED BORROW ONE
SBC     $40             :SUBTRACT WITHOUT CARRY
```

Note that you must set the Carry flag before a subtraction, but clear it before an addition.

· Comparison instructions perform subtractions without changing registers (except for the flags in the status register). Here we have not only CMP (Compare Memory with Accumulator), but also CPX (Compare Memory with Index Register X) and CPY (Compare Memory with Index Register Y). Note the differences between CMP and SBC; CMP does not include the Carry in the subtraction, change the accumulator, or affect the Overflow flag.

· There is no explicit Complement instruction. However, you can complement the accumulator by EXCLUSIVE ORing it with a byte which contains all 1s (11111111_2 or FF_{16}). Remember, the EXCLUSIVE OR of two bits is 1 if they are different and 0 if they are the same. Thus, EXCLUSIVE ORing with a 1 will produce a result of 0 if the other bit is 1 and 1 if the other bit is 0, the same as a logical complement (NOT instruction).

Thus we have the instruction

```
EOR     #%11111111      ;COMPLEMENT ACCUMULATOR
```

· The BIT instruction performs a logical AND but does not return a result to the accumulator. It affects only the flags. You should note that this instruction allows only direct addressing (zero page or absolute); it does not allow immediate or indexed addressing. More complex operations require several instructions; typical examples are the following:

· Add memory locations OPER1 and OPER2, place result in RESLT

```
LDA     OPER1           ;GET FIRST OPERAND
CLC                     ;MAKE CARRY ZERO
ADC     OPER2           ;ADD SECOND OPERAND
STA     RESLT           ;SAVE SUM
```

Note that we must load the first operand into the accumulator and clear the Carry before adding the second operand.

• Add a constant (VALUE) to memory location OPER.

```
LDA     OPER          ;GET CURRENT VALUE
CLC                   ;MAKE CARRY ZERO
ADC     #VALUE        ;ADD VALUE
STA     OPER          ;STORE SUM BACK
```

If VALUE is 1, we can shorten this to

```
INC     OPER          ;ADD 1 TO CURRENT VALUE
```

Similarly, if VALUE is −1, we have

```
DEC     OPER          ;SUBTRACT 1 FROM CURRENT VALUE
```

BIT MANIPULATION

The programmer can set, clear, complement, or test bits by means of logical operations with appropriate masks. Shift instructions can rotate or shift the accumulator or a memory location. Chapter 7 contains additional examples of bit manipulation.

You may operate on individual bits in the accumulator as follows:

• Set them by logically ORing with 1s in the appropriate positions.

• Clear them by logically ANDing with 0s in the appropriate positions.

• Invert (complement) them by logically EXCLUSIVE ORing with 1s in the appropriate positions.

• Test them by logically ANDing with 1s in the appropriate positions.

Examples

1. Set bit 6 of the accumulator.

```
ORA     #%01000000    ;SET BIT 6 BY ORING WITH 1
```

2. Clear bit 3 of the accumulator.

```
AND     #%11110111    ;CLEAR BIT 3 BY ANDING WITH 0
```

3. Invert (complement) bit 2 of the accumulator.

```
EOR     #%00000100    ;INVERT BIT 2 BY XORING WITH 1
```

4. Test bit 5 of the accumulator. Clear the Zero flag if bit 5 is a logic 1 and set the Zero flag if bit 5 is a logic 0.

```
AND     #%00100000    ;TEST BIT 5 BY ANDING WITH 1
```

You can change more than one bit at a time by changing the masks.

5. Set bits 4 and 5 of the accumulator.

```
ORA     #%00110000    ;SET BITS 4 AND 5 BY ORING WITH 1
```

6. Invert (complement) bits 0 and 7 of the accumulator.

```
EOR     #%10000001   ;INVERT BITS 0 AND 7 BY XORING WITH 1
```

The only general way to manipulate bits in other registers or in memory is by moving the values to the accumulator.

· Set bit 4 of memory location 0040_{16}.

```
LDA     $40
ORA     $%00010000   ;SET BIT 4 BY ORING WITH 1
STA     $40
```

· Clear bit 1 of memory location $17E0_{16}$.

```
LDA     $17E0
AND     #%11111101   ;CLEAR BIT 1 BY ANDING WITH 0
STA     $17E0
```

An occasional, handy shortcut to clearing or setting bit 0 of a register or memory location is using an increment (INC, INX, or INY) to set it (if you know that it is 0) and a decrement (DEC, DEX, or DEY) to clear it (if you know that it is 1). If you do not care about the other bit positions, you can also use DEC or INC. These shortcuts are useful when you are storing a single 1-bit flag in a byte of memory.

The instruction LSR (ASL) shifts the accumulator or a memory location right (left) one position, filling the leftmost (rightmost) bit with a 0. Figures 1-1 and 1-2 describe the effects of these two instructions. The instructions ROL and ROR provide a circular shift (rotate) of the accumulator or a memory location as shown in Figures 1-3 and 1-4. Rotates operate as if the accumulator or memory location and the Carry flag formed a 9-bit circular register. You should note the following:

· Left shifts set the Carry to the value that was in bit position 7 and the Negative flag to the value that was in bit position 6.

· Right shifts set the Carry to the value that was in bit position 0.

· Rotates preserve all the bits, whereas LSR and ASL destroy the old Carry flag.

· Rotates allow you to move serial data between memory or the accumulator and the Carry flag. This is useful in performing serial I/O and in handling single bits of information such as Boolean indicators or parity.

Multibit shifts simply require the appropriate number of single-bit instructions.

Examples

1. Rotate accumulator right three positions.

```
ROR     A
ROR     A
ROR     A
```

Original contents of Carry flag and accumulator or memory location

C		B_7	B_6	B_5	B_4	B_3	B_2	B_1	B_0

After ASL (Arithmetic Shift Left)

B_7		B_6	B_5	B_4	B_3	B_2	B_1	B_0	0

Figure 1-1: The ASL (Arithmetic Shift Left) Instruction

Original contents of Carry flag and accumulator or memory location

C		B_7	B_6	B_5	B_4	B_3	B_2	B_1	B_0

After LSR (Logical Shift Right)

B_0		0	B_7	B_6	B_5	B_4	B_3	B_2	B_1

Figure 1-2: The LSR (Logical Shift Right) Instruction

Original contents of Carry flag and accumulator or memory location

Carry		Data							
C		B_7	B_6	B_5	B_4	B_3	B_2	B_1	B_0

After ROL (Rotate Left)

Carry		Data							
B_7		B_6	B_5	B_4	B_3	B_2	B_1	B_0	C

Figure 1-3: The ROL (Rotate Left) Instruction

Original contents of Carry flag and accumulator or memory location

Carry		Data							
C		B_7	B_6	B_5	B_4	B_3	B_2	B_1	B_0

After ROR (Rotate Right)

Carry		Data							
B_0		C	B_7	B_6	B_5	B_4	B_3	B_2	B_1

Figure 1-4: The ROR (Rotate Right) Instruction

2. Shift memory location 1700_{16} left logically four positions.

```
ASL     $1700
ASL     $1700
ASL     $1700
ASL     $1700
```

An alternative approach would be to use the accumulator; that is,

```
LDA     $1700
ASL     A
ASL     A
ASL     A
ASL     A
STA     $1700
```

The second approach is shorter (10 bytes rather than 12) and faster (16 clock cycles rather than 24), but it destroys the previous contents of the accumulator.

You can implement arithmetic shifts by using the Carry flag to preserve the current value of bit 7. Shifting right arithmetically is called *sign extension,* since it copies the sign bit to the right. A shift that operates in this manner preserves the sign of a two's complement number and can therefore be used to divide or normalize signed numbers.

Examples

1. Shift the accumulator right 1 bit arithmetically, preserving the sign (most significant) bit.

```
TAX                 ;SAVE THE ACCUMULATOR
ASL     A           ;MOVE BIT 7 TO CARRY
TXA                 ;RESTORE THE ACCUMULATOR
ROR     A           ;SHIFT THE ACCUMULATOR, COPYING BIT 7
```

When the processor performs ROR A, it moves the Carry (the old bit 7) to bit 7 and bit 7 to bit 6, thus preserving the sign of the original number.

2. Shift the accumulator left 1 bit arithmetically, preserving the sign (most significant) bit.

```
ASL     A           ;SHIFT A, MOVING BIT 7 TO CARRY
ROL     A           ;SAVE BIT 7 IN POSITION 0
TAX
LSR     A           ;CHANGE CARRY TO OLD BIT 7
TXA
ROR     A           ;SHIFT THE ACCUMULATOR, PRESERVING BIT 7
```

or

```
        ASL     A           ;SHIFT A, MOVING BIT 7 TO CARRY
        BCC     CLRSGN      ;WAS BIT 7 1?
        ORA     #%10000000  ;  YES, THEN KEEP IT 1
        BMI     EXIT
CLRSGN  AND     #%01111111  ;  NO, THEN KEEP IT ZERO
EXIT    NOP
```

BMI EXIT always forces a branch.

MAKING DECISIONS

We will now discuss procedures for making three types of decisions:

- Branching if a bit is set or cleared (a logic 1 or a logic 0).
- Branching if two values are equal or not equal.
- Branching if one value is greater than another or less than it.

The first type of decision allows the processor to sense the value of a flag, switch, status line, or other binary (ON/OFF) input. The second type of decision allows the processor to determine whether an input or a result has a specific value (e.g., an input is a specific character or terminator or a result is 0). The third type of decision allows the processor to determine whether a value is above or below a numerical threshold (e.g., a value is valid or invalid or is above or below a warning level or set point). Assuming that the primary value is in the accumulator and the secondary value (if needed) is in address ADDR, the procedures are as follows.

Branching Set or Cleared Bit

- Determine if a bit is set or cleared by logically ANDing the accumulator with a 1 in the appropriate bit position and 0s in the other bit positions. The Zero flag then reflects the bit value and can be used for branching (with BEQ or BNE).

Examples

1. Branch to DEST if bit 5 of the accumulator is 1.

```
AND     #%00100000  ;TEST BIT 5 OF A
BNE     DEST
```

The Zero flag is set to 1 if and only if bit 5 of the accumulator is 0. Note the inversion here.

If we assume that the data is in address ADDR, we can use the BIT instruction to produce an equivalent effect. To branch to DEST if bit 5 of ADDR is 1, we can use either

```
LDA     ADDR
AND     #%00100000
BNE     DEST
```

or

```
LDA     #%00100000
BIT     ADDR
BNE     DEST
```

We must reverse the order of the operations, since BIT does not allow immediate addressing. It does, however, leave the accumulator unchanged for later use.

2. Branch to DEST if bit 2 of the accumulator is 0.

```
AND    #%00000100   ;TEST BIT 2 OF A
BEQ    DEST
```

There are special short procedures for examining bit positions 0, 6, or 7. Bit 7 is available readily as the Negative flag after a Load or Transfer instruction; bit 0 can be moved to the Carry with LSR A or ROR A; bit 6 can be moved to the Negative flag with ASL A or ROL A.

3. Branch to DEST if bit 7 of memory location ADDR is 1.

```
LDA    ADDR         ;IS BIT 7 1?
BMI    DEST         ;YES, BRANCH
```

Note that LDA affects the Zero and Negative flags; so do transfer instructions such as TAX, TYA, TSX (but not TXS), and PLA. Store instructions (including PHA) do not affect any flags.

4. Branch to DEST if bit 6 of the accumulator is 0.

```
ASL    A            ;MOVE BIT 6 TO BIT 7
BPL    DEST
```

5. Branch to DEST if bit 0 of memory location ADDR is 1.

```
ROR    ADDR         ;MOVE BIT 0 OF ADDR TO CARRY
BCS    DEST         ;AND THEN TEST THE CARRY
```

The BIT instruction has a special feature that allows one to readily test bit 6 or bit 7 of a memory location. When the processor executes BIT, it sets the Negative flag to the value of bit 7 of the addressed memory location and the Overflow flag to the value of bit 6, regardless of the contents of the accumulator.

6. Branch to DEST if bit 7 of memory location ADDR is 0.

```
BIT    ADDR         ;TEST BIT 7 OF ADDR
BPL    DEST
```

This sequence does not affect or depend on the accumulator.

7. Branch to DEST if bit 6 of memory location ADDR is 1.

```
BIT    ADDR         ;TEST BIT 6 OF ADDR
BVS    DEST
```

This sequence requires careful documentation, since the Overflow flag is being used in a special way. Here again, the contents of the accumulator do not change or affect the sequence at all.

Branching Based on Equality

• Determine if the value in the accumulator is equal to another value by subtraction. The Zero flag will be set to 1 if the values are equal. The Compare instruction (CMP) is more useful than the Subtract instruction (SBC) because Compare does not change the accumulator or involve the Carry.

Examples

1. Branch to DEST if the accumulator contains the number VALUE.

```
CMP     #VALUE          ;IS DATA = VALUE?
BEQ     DEST            ;YES, BRANCH
```

We could also use index register X with CPX or index register Y with CPY.

2. Branch to DEST if the contents of the accumulator are not equal to the contents of memory location ADDR.

```
CMP     ADDR            ;IS DATA = VALUE IN MEMORY?
BNE     DEST            ;NO, BRANCH
```

3. Branch to DEST if memory location ADDR contains 0.

```
LDA     ADDR            ;IS DATA ZERO?
BEQ     DEST            ;YES, BRANCH
```

We can handle some special cases without using the accumulator.

4. Branch to DEST if memory location ADDR contains 0, but do not change the accumulator or either index register.

```
INC     ADDR            ;TEST MEMORY FOR ZERO
DEC     ADDR
BEQ     DEST            :BRANCH IF IT IS FOUND
```

5. Branch to DEST if memory location ADDR does not contain 1.

```
DEC     ADDR            ;SET ZERO FLAG IF ADDR IS 1
BNE     DEST
```

This sequence, of course, changes the memory location.

6. Branch to DEST if memory location ADDR contains FF_{16}.

```
INC     ADDR            ;SET ZERO FLAG IF ADDR IS FF
BEQ     DEST
```

INC does not affect the Carry flag, but it does affect the Zero flag. Note that you cannot increment or decrement the accumulator with INC or DEC.

Branching Based on Magnitude Comparisons

• Determine if the contents of the accumulator are greater than or less than some other value by subtraction. If, as is typical, the numbers are unsigned, the Carry flag indicates which one is larger. Note that the 6502's Carry flag is a negative borrow after comparisons or subtractions, unlike the true borrow produced by such processors as the 8080, Z-80, and 6800. In general,

- Carry = 1 if the contents of the accumulator are greater than or equal to the value subtracted from it. Carry = 1 if the subtraction does not require (generate) a borrow.
- Carry = 0 if the value subtracted is larger than the contents of the accumulator. That is, Carry = 0 if the subtraction does require a borrow.

Note that the Carry is the inverse of a normal borrow. If the two operands are equal, the Carry is set to 1, just as if the accumulator were larger. If, however, you want equal values to affect the Carry as if the other value were larger, all that you must do is reverse the identities of the operands, that is, you must subtract in reverse, saving the accumulator in memory and loading it with the other value instead.

Examples

1. Branch to DEST if the contents of the accumulator are greater than or equal to the number VALUE.

```
CMP     #VALUE        ;IS DATA ABOVE VALUE?
BCS     DEST          ;YES, BRANCH
```

The Carry is set to 1 if the unsigned subtraction does not require a borrow.

2. Branch to DEST if the contents of memory address OPER1 are less than the contents of memory address OPER2.

```
LDA     OPER1         ;GET FIRST OPERAND
CMP     OPER2         ;IS IT LESS THAN SECOND OPERAND?
BCC     DEST          ;YES, BRANCH
```

The Carry will be set to 0 if the subtraction requires a borrow.

3. Branch to DEST if the contents of memory address OPER1 are less than or equal to the contents of memory address OPER2.

```
LDA     OPER2         ;GET SECOND OPERAND
CMP     OPER1         ;IS IT GREATER THAN OR EQUAL TO FIRST?
BCS     DEST          ;YES, BRANCH
```

If we loaded the accumulator with OPER1 and compared to OPER2, we could branch only on the conditions

- OPER1 greater than or equal to OPER2 (Carry set)
- OPER1 less than OPER2 (Carry cleared)

Since neither of these is what we want, we must handle the operands in the opposite order.

If the values are signed, we must allow for the possible occurrence of two's complement overflow. This is the situation in which the difference between the numbers cannot be contained in seven bits and, therefore, changes the sign of the result. For example, if one number is +7 and the other is −125, the difference is

−132, which is beyond the capacity of eight bits (it is less than −128, the most negative number that can be contained in eight bits).

Thus, in the case of signed numbers, we must allow for the following two possibilities:

· The result has the sign (positive or negative, as shown by the Negative flag) that we want, and the Overflow flag indicates that the sign is correct.

· The result does not have the sign that we want, but the Overflow flag indicates that two's complement overflow has changed the real sign.

We have to look for both a true positive (the sign we want, unaffected by overflow) or a false negative (the opposite of the sign we want, but inverted by two's complement overflow).

Examples

1. Branch to DEST if the contents of the accumulator (a signed number) are greater than or equal to the number VALUE.

```
        SEC                 ;CLEAR INVERTED BORROW
        SBC     #VALUE      ;PERFORM THE SUBTRACTION
        BVS     FNEG
        BPL     DEST        ;TRUE POSITIVE, NO OVERFLOW
        BMI     DONE
FNEG    BMI     DEST        ;FALSE NEGATIVE, OVERFLOW
DONE    NOP
```

2. Branch to DEST if the contents of the accumulator (a signed number) are less than the contents of address ADDR.

```
        SEC                 ;CLEAR INVERTED BORROW
        SBC     ADDR        ;PERFORM THE SUBTRACTION
        BVS     FNEG
        BMI     DEST        ;TRUE POSITIVE, NO OVERFLOW
        BPL     DONE
FNEG    BPL     DEST        ;FALSE NEGATIVE, OVERFLOW
DONE    NOP
```

Note that we must set the Carry and use SBC, because CMP does not affect the Overflow flag.

Tables 1-8 and 1-9 summarize the common instruction sequences used to make decisions with the 6502 microprocessor. Table 1-8 lists the sequences that depend only on the value in the accumulator; Table 1-9 lists the sequences that depend on numerical comparisons between the contents of the accumulator and a specific value or the contents of a memory location. Tables 1-10 and 1-11 contain the sequences that depend on an index register or on the contents of a memory location alone.

Table 1-8: Decision Sequences Depending on the Accumulator Alone

Condition	Flag-Setting Instruction	Conditional Branch
Any bit of A = 0	AND #MASK (1 in bit position)	BEQ
Any bit of A = 1	AND #MASK (1 in bit position)	BNE
Bit 7 of A = 0	ASL A or ROL A	BCC
	CMP #0 (preserves A)	BPL
Bit 7 of A = 1	ASL A or ROL A	BCS
	CMP #0 (preserves A)	BMI
Bit 6 of A = 0	ASL A or ROL A	BPL
Bit 6 of A = 1	ASL A or ROL A	BMI
Bit 0 of A = 0	LSR A or ROR A	BCC
Bit 0 of A = 1	LSR A or ROR A	BCS
(A) = 0	LDA, PLA, TAX, TAY, TXA, or TYA	BEQ
(A) ≠ 0	LDA, PLA, TAX, TAY, TXA, or TYA	BNE
(A) positive (MSB = 0)	LDA, PLA, TAX, TAY, TXA, or TYA	BPL
(A) negative (MSB = 1)	LDA, PLA, TAX, TAY, TXA, or TYA	BMI

Table 1-9: Decision Sequences Depending on Numerical Comparisons

Condition	Flag-Setting Instruction	Conditional Branch
(A) = VALUE	CMP #VALUE	BEQ
(A) ≠ VALUE	CMP #VALUE	BNE
(A) ≥ VALUE (unsigned)	CMP #VALUE	BCS
(A) < VALUE (unsigned)	CMP #VALUE	BCC
(A) = (ADDR)	CMP ADDR	BEQ
(A) ≠ (ADDR)	CMP ADDR	BNE
(A) ≥ (ADDR) (unsigned)	CMP ADDR	BCS
(A) < (ADDR) (unsigned)	CMP ADDR	BCC

Table 1-10: Decision Sequences Depending on an Index Register

Condition	Flag-Setting Instruction	Conditional Branch
(X or Y) = VALUE	CPX or CPY #VALUE	BEQ
(X or Y) ≠ VALUE	CPX or CPY #VALUE	BNE
(X or Y) ≥ VALUE (unsigned)	CPX or CPY #VALUE	BCS
(X or Y) < VALUE (unsigned)	CPX or CPY #VALUE	BCC
(X or Y) = (ADDR)	CPX or CPY ADDR	BEQ
(X or Y) ≠ (ADDR)	CPX or CPY ADDR	BNE
(X or Y) ≥ (ADDR) (unsigned)	CPX or CPY ADDR	BCS
(X or Y) < (ADDR) (unsigned)	CPX or CPY ADDR	BCC

Table 1-11: Decision Sequences Depending on a Memory Location Alone

Condition	Flag-Setting Instruction(s)	Conditional Branch
Bit 7 = 0	BIT ADDR	BPL
	ASL ADDR or ROL ADDR	BCC
Bit 7 = 1	BIT ADDR	BMI
	ASL ADDR or ROL ADDR	BCS
Bit 6 = 0	BIT ADDR	BVC
	ASL ADDR or ROL ADDR	PBL
Bit 6 = 1	BIT ADDR	BVS
	ASL ADDR or ROL ADDR	BMI
(ADDR) = 0	INC ADDR, DEC ADDR	BEQ
(ADDR) ≠ 0	INC ADDR, DEC ADDR	BNE
Bit 0 = 0	LSR ADDR or ROR ADDR	BCC
Bit 0 = 1	LSR ADDR or ROR ADDR	BCS

LOOPING

The simplest way to implement a loop (that is, repeat a sequence of instructions) with the 6502 microprocessor is as follows:

1. Load an index register or memory location with the number of times the sequence is to be executed.
2. Execute the sequence.
3. Decrement the index register or memory location by 1.
4. Return to Step 2 if the result of Step 3 is not 0.

Typical programs look like this:

```
        LDX     #NTIMES      ;COUNT = NUMBER OF REPETITIONS
LOOP    .
        .
        .  instructions to be repeated
        .
        DEX
        BNE     LOOP
```

Nothing except clarity stops us from counting up (using INX, INY, or INC); of course, you must change the initialization appropriately. As we will see later, a 16-bit counter is much easier to increment than it is to decrement. In any case, the instructions to be repeated must not interfere with the counting of the repetitions. You can store the counter in either index register or any memory location. Index register X's special features are its use in preindexing and the wide availability of zero page indexed modes. Index register Y's special feature is its use in postindexing. As usual, memory locations on page 0 are shorter and faster to use than are memory locations on other pages.

Of course, if you use an index register or a single memory location as a counter, you are limited to 256 repetitions. You can provide larger numbers of repetitions by nesting loops that use a single register or memory location or by using a pair of memory locations as illustrated in the following examples:

· Nested loops

```
        LDX     #NTIMM       ;START OUTER COUNTER
LOOPO   LDY     #NTIML       ;START INNER COUNTER
LOOPI   .
        .
        .  instructions to be repeated
        .
        DEY                  ;DECREMENT INNER COUNTER
        BNE     LOOPI
        DEX                  ;DECREMENT OUTER COUNTER
        BNE     LOOPO
```

The outer loop restores the inner counter (index register Y) to its starting value

(NTIML) after each decrement of the outer counter (index register X). The nesting produces a multiplicative factor — the instructions starting at LOOPI are repeated NTIMM × NTIML times. Of course, a more general (and more reasonable) approach would use two memory locations on page 0 instead of two index registers.

- 16-bit counter in two memory locations

```
        LDA     #NTIMLC     ;INITIALIZE LSB OF COUNTER
        STA     COUNTL
        LDA     #NTIMHC     ;INITIALIZE MSB OF COUNTER
        STA     COUNTH
LOOP    .
        .   instructions to be repeated
        .
        INC     NTIMLC      ;INCREMENT LSB OF COUNTER
        BNE     LOOP
        INC     NTIMHC      ;AND CARRY TO MSB OF COUNTER IF NEEDED
        BNE     LOOP
```

The idea here is to increment only the less significant byte unless there is a carry to the more significant byte. Note that we can recognize a carry only by checking the Zero flag, since INC does not affect the Carry flag. Counting up is much simpler than counting down; the comparable sequence for decrementing a 16-bit counter is

```
        LDA     NTIML       ;IS LSB OF COUNTER ZERO?
        BNE     CNTLSB
        DEC     NTIMH       ;YES, BORROW FROM MSB
CNTLSB  DEC     NTIML       ;DECREMENT LSB OF COUNTER
        BNE     LOOP        ;CONTINUE IF LSB HAS NOT REACHED ZERO
        LDA     NTIMH       ;OR IF MSB HAS NOT REACHED ZERO
        BNE     LOOP
```

If we count up, however, we must remember to initialize the counter to the complement of the desired value (indicated by the names NTIMLC and NTIMHC in the program using INC).

ARRAY MANIPULATION

The simplest way to access a particular element of an array is by using indexed addressing. One can then

1. Manipulate the element by indexing from the starting address of the array.

2. Access the succeeding element (at the next higher address) by incrementing the index register using INX or INY, or access the preceding element (at the next lower address) by decrementing the index register using DEX or DEY. One

could also change the base; this is simple if the base is an absolute address, but awkward if it is an indirect address.

3. Access an arbitrary element by loading an index register with its index. Typical array manipulation procedures are easy to program if the array is one-dimensional, the elements each occupy 1 byte, and the number of elements is less than 256. Some examples are

· Add an element of an array to the accumulator. The base address of the array is a constant BASE. Update index register X so that it refers to the succeeding 8-bit element.

```
        ADC     BASE,X          ;ADD CURRENT ELEMENT
        INX                     ;ADDRESS NEXT ELEMENT
```

· Check to see if an element of an array is 0 and add 1 to memory location ZCOUNT if it is. Assume that the address of the array is a constant BASE and its index is in index register X. Update index register X so that it refers to the preceding 8-bit element.

```
        LDA     BASE,X          ;GET CURRENT ELEMENT
        BNE     UPDDT           ;IS ITS VALUE ZERO?
        INC     ZCOUNT          ;YES, ADD 1 TO COUNT OF ZEROS
UPDDT   DEX                     ;ADDRESS PRECEDING ELEMENT
```

· Load the accumulator with the 35th element of an array. Assume that the starting address of the array is BASE.

```
        LDX     #35             ;GET INDEX OF REQUIRED ELEMENT
        LDA     BASE,X          ;OBTAIN THE ELEMENT
```

The most efficient way to process an array is to start at the highest address and work backward. This is the best approach because it allows you to count the index register down to 0 and exit when the Zero flag is set. You must adjust the initialization and the indexed operations slightly to account for the fact that the 0 index is never used. The changes are

· Load the index register with the number of elements.

· Use the base address START−1, where START is the lowest address actually occupied by the array.

If, for example, we want to perform a summation starting at address START and continuing through LENGTH elements, we use the program

```
        LDX     #LENGTH         ;START AT THE END OF THE ARRAY
        LDA     #0              ;CLEAR THE SUM INITIALLY
ADBYTE  CLC
        ADC     START-1,X       ;ADD THE NEXT ELEMENT
        DEX
        BNE     ADBYTE          ;COUNT ELEMENTS
```

Manipulating array elements becomes more difficult if you need more than one element during each iteration (as in a sort that requires interchanging of elements), if the elements are more than one byte long, or if the elements are themselves addresses (as in a table of starting addresses). The basic problem is the lack of 16-bit registers or 16-bit instructions. The processor can never be instructed to handle more than 8 bits. Some examples of more general array manipulation are

· Load memory locations POINTH and POINTL with a 16-bit element of an array (stored LSB first). The base address of the array is BASE and the index of the element is in index register X. Update X so that it points to the next 16-bit element.

```
        LDA     BASE,X          ;GET LSB OF ELEMENT
        STA     POINTL
        INX
        LDA     BASE,X          ;GET MSB OF ELEMENT
        STA     POINTH
        INX                     ;ADDRESS NEXT ELEMENT
```

The single instruction LDA BASE+1,X loads the accumulator from the same address as the sequence

```
        INX
        LDA     BASE,X
```

assuming that X did not originally contain FF_{16}. If, however, we are using a base address indirectly, the alternatives are

```
        INC     PGZRO           ;INCREMENT BASE ADDRESS
        BNE     INDEX
        INC     PGZRO+1         ;WITH CARRY IF NECESSARY
INDEX   LDA     (PGZRO),Y
```

or

```
        INY
        LDA     (PGZRO),Y
```

The second sequence is much shorter, but the first sequence will handle arrays that are more than 256 bytes long.

· Exchange an element of an array with its successor if the two are not already in descending order. Assume that the elements are 8-bit unsigned numbers. The base address of the array is BASE and the index of the first number is in index register X.

```
        LDA     BASE,X          ;GET ELEMENT
        CMP     BASE+1,X        ;IS SUCCESSOR SMALLER?
        BCS     DONE            ;NO, NO INTERCHANGE NECESSARY
        PHA                     ;YES, SAVE ELEMENT
        LDA     BASE+1,X        :INTERCHANGE
        STA     BASE,X
        PLA
        STA     BASE+1,X
DONE    INX                     ;ACCESS NEXT ELEMENT
```

· Load the accumulator from the 12th indirect address in a table. Assume that the table starts at the address BASE.

```
        LDX     #24             ;GET DOUBLED OFFSET FOR INDEX
        LDA     BASE,X          ;GET LSB OF ADDRESS
        STA     PGZRO           ;SAVE ON PAGE ZERO
        INX
        LDA     BASE,X          ;GET MSB OF ADDRESS
        STA     PGZRO+1         ;SAVE ON PAGE ZERO
        LDY     #0
        LDA     (PGZRO),Y       ;LOAD INDIRECT BY INDEXING WITH ZERO
```

Note that you must double the index to handle tables containing addresses, since each 16-bit address occupies two bytes of memory.

If the entire table is on page 0, we can use the preindexed (indexed indirect) addressing mode.

```
        LDX     #24             ;GET DOUBLED OFFSET FOR INDEX
        LDA     (BASE,X)        ;LOAD FROM INDEXED INDIRECT ADDRESS
```

You still must remember to double the index. Here we must also initialize the table of indirect addresses in the RAM on page 0.

We can generalize array processing by storing the base address in two locations on page 0 and using the postindexed (indirect indexed) addressing mode. Now the base address can be a variable. This mode assumes the use of page 0 and index register Y and is available only for a limited set of instructions.

Examples

1. Add an element of an array to the accumulator. The base address of the array is in memory locations PGZRO and PGZRO+1. The index of the element is in index register Y. Update index register Y so that it refers to the succeeding 8-bit element.

```
CLC     ADC     (PGZRO),Y       ;ADD CURRENT ELEMENT
        INY                     ;ADDRESS NEXT ELEMENT
```

2. Check to see if an element of an array is 0 and add 1 to memory location ZCOUNT if it is. Assume that the base address of the array is in memory locations PGZRO and PGZRO+1. The index of the element is in index register Y. Update index register Y so that it refers to the preceding 8-bit element.

```
        LDA     (PGZRO),Y       ;GET CURRENT ELEMENT
        BNE     UPDDT           ;IS ITS VALUE ZERO?
        INC     ZCOUNT          ;YES, ADD 1 TO COUNT OF ZEROS
UPDDT   DEY                     ;ADDRESS PRECEDING ELEMENT
```

Postindexing also lets us handle arrays that occupy more than 256 bytes. As we noted earlier, the simplest approach to long counts is to keep a 16-bit complemented count in two memory locations. If the array is described by a base address on page 0, we can update that base whenever we update the more significant byte of the complemented count. For example, if we want to clear an area of memory described by a complemented count in memory locations COUNTH and COUNTL and an initial base address in memory locations PGZRO and PGZRO+1, we can use the following program:

```
        LDA     #0              ;DATA = ZERO
        TAY                     ;INDEX = ZERO
CLEAR   STA     (PGZRO),Y       ;CLEAR A BYTE
        INY                     ;MOVE TO NEXT BYTE
        BNE     CHKCNT
        INC     PGZRO + 1       ;AND TO NEXT PAGE IF NEEDED
CHKCNT  INC     COUNTL          ;COUNT BYTES
        BNE     CLEAR
        INC     COUNTH          ;WITH CARRY TO MSB
        BNE     CLEAR
```

The idea here is to proceed to the next page by incrementing the more significant byte of the indirect address when we finish a 256-byte section.

One can also simplify array processing by reducing the multiplications required in indexing to additions. In particular, one can handle arrays of two-byte elements by using ASL A to double an index in the accumulator.

Example

Load the accumulator from the indirect address indexed by the contents of memory location INDEX. Assume that the table starts at address BASE.

```
        LDA     INDEX           ;GET INDEX
        ASL     A               ;AND DOUBLE IT FOR 2-BYTE ENTRIES
        TAX
        LDA     BASE,X          ;GET LSB OF INDIRECT ADDRESS
        STA     PGZRO           ;SAVE ON PAGE ZERO
        INX
        LDA     BASE,X          ;GET MSB OF INDIRECT ADDRESS
        STA     PGZRO + 1       ;SAVE ON PAGE ZERO
        LDY     #0              ;PREINDEX WITH ZERO
        LDA     (PGZRO),Y
```

As before, if the entire table of indirect addresses is on page 0, we can use the preindexed (indexed indirect) addressing mode.

```
        LDA     INDEX           ;GET INDEX
        ASL     A               ;DOUBLE INDEX FOR 2-BYTE ENTRIES
        TAX
        LDA     (BASE,X)        ;LOAD FROM INDEXED INDIRECT ADDRESS
```

You can handle indexing into longer arrays by using the postindexed (indirect indexed) mode. Here we must construct a base address with an explicit addition before indexing, since the 6502's index registers are only 8 bits long.

Example

Load the accumulator from the element of an array defined by a starting address BASE (BASEH more significant byte, BASEL less significant byte) and a 16-bit index in memory locations INDEX and INDEX+1 (MSB in INDEX+1).

```
        LDA     #BASEL        ;MOVE LSB OF BASE TO PAGE ZERO
        STA     PGZRO
        LDA     #BASEH        ;ADD MSB'S OF BASE AND INDEX
        STA     POINTL
        CLC
        ADC     INDEX+1
        STA     PGZRO+1
        LDY     INDEX         ;USE LSB OF INDEX EXPLICITLY
        LDA     (PGZRO),Y     ;GET ELEMENT
```

TABLE LOOKUP

Table lookup can be handled by the same procedures as array manipulation. Some examples are

· Load the accumulator with an element from a table. Assume that the base address of the table is BASE (a constant) and the 8-bit index is in memory location INDEX.

```
        LDX     INDEX         ;GET INDEX
        LDA     BASE,X        ;GET THE ELEMENT
```

The problem is more complicated if INDEX is a 16-bit number.

· Load the accumulator with an element from a table. Assume that the base address of the table is BASE (a constant, made up of bytes BASEH and BASEL) and the 16-bit index is in memory locations INDEX and INDEX+1 (MSB in INDEX+1).

The procedure is the same one we just showed for an array. You must add the more significant byte of the index to the more significant byte of the base with an explicit addition. You can then use postindexing to obtain the element.

· Load memory locations POINTH and POINTL with a 16-bit element from a table. Assume that the base address of the table is BASE (a constant) and the index is in memory location INDEX.

```
        LDA     INDEX         ;GET THE INDEX
        ASL     A             ;DOUBLE IT FOR TWO-BYTE ENTRIES
        TAX
        LDA     BASE,X        ;GET LSB OF ELEMENT
        INX
        LDA     BASE,X        ;GET MSB OF ELEMENT
        STA     POINTH
```

We can also handle the case in which the base address is a variable in two memory locations on page 0 (PGZRO and PGZRO+1).

```
        LDA     INDEX         ;GET THE INDEX
        ASL     A             ;DOUBLE IT FOR TWO-BYTE ENTRIES
        TAY
        LDA     (PGZRO),Y     ;GET LSB OF ELEMENT
        STA     POINTL
        INY
        LDA     (PGZRO),Y     ;GET MSB OF ELEMENT
        STA     POINTH
```

We can revise the program further to handle an array with more than 128 entries.

```
        LDA     INDEX         ;GET THE INDEX
        ASL     A             ;DOUBLE IT FOR TWO-BYTE ENTRIES
        BCC     LDELEM
        INC     PGZRO+1       ;ADD CARRY TO INDIRECT ADDRESS
LDELEM  TAY
        LDA     (PGZRO),Y     ;GET LSB OF ELEMENT
        STA     POINTL
        INY
        LDA     (PGZRO),Y     ;GET MSB OF ELEMENT
        STA     POINTH
```

Still another extension handles a 16-bit index.

```
        LDA     INDEX         ;GET LSB OF INDEX
        ASL     A             ;DOUBLE IT
        TAY
        LDA     INDEX+1       ;GET MSB OF INDEX
        ROL     A             ;DOUBLE IT WITH CARRY
        ADC     PGZRO+1       ;AND ADD RESULT TO INDIRECT ADDRESS
        STA     PGZRO+1
        LDA     (PGZRO),Y     ;GET LSB OF ELEMENT
        STA     POINTL
        INY
        LDA     (PGZRO),Y     ;GET MSB OF ELEMENT
        STA     POINTH
```

· Transfer control (jump) to a 16-bit address obtained from a table. Assume that the base address of the table is BASE (a constant) and the index is in memory location INDEX.

Here there are two options: Store the address obtained from the table in two memory locations and use an indirect jump, or store the address obtained from the table in the stack and use the RTS (Return from Subroutine) instruction.

OPTION 1: Indirect Jump

```
        LDA     INDEX         ;GET INDEX
        ASL     A             ;DOUBLE IT FOR TWO-BYTE ENTRIES
        TAX
        LDA     BASE,X        ;GET LSB OF DESTINATION ADDRESS
        STA     TEMP          ;STORE LSB SOMEWHERE
        INX
```

```
        LDA     BASE,X          ;GET MSB OF DESTINATION ADDRESS
        STA     TEMP+1          ;STORE MSB IN NEXT BYTE
        JMP     (TEMP)          ;INDIRECT JUMP TO DESTINATION
```

JMP is the only 6502 instruction that has true indirect addressing. Note that TEMP and TEMP+1 can be anywhere in memory; they need not be on page 0.

OPTION 2: Jump Through the Stack

```
        LDA     INDEX           ;GET INDEX
        ASL     A               ;DOUBLE IT FOR TWO-BYTE ENTRIES
        TAX
        INX
        LDA     BASE,X          :GET MSB OF DESTINATION ADDRESS
        PHA                     ;SAVE MSB IN STACK
        DEX
        LDA     BASE,X          ;GET LSB OF DESTINATION ADDRESS
        PHA                     ;SAVE LSB IN STACK
        RTS                     ;TRANSFER CONTROL TO DESTINATION
```

This alternative is awkward for the following reasons:

· RTS adds 1 to the program counter after loading it from the stack. Thus, the addresses in the table must all be one less than the actual values to which you wish to transfer control. This offset evidently speeds the processor's execution of the JSR (Jump to Subroutine) instruction, but it also can confuse the programmer.

· You must remember that the stack is growing down in memory, toward lower addresses. To have the destination address end up in its normal order (less significant byte at lower address), we must push the more significant byte first. This is essentially a double negative; we store the address in the wrong order but it ends up right because the stack is growing down.

· The use of RTS is confusing. How can one *return* from a routine that one has never called? In fact, this approach uses RTS to call a subroutine. You should remember that RTS is simply a jump instruction that obtains the new value for the program counter from the top of the stack. While the common use of RTS is to transfer control from a subroutine back to a main program (hence, the mnemonic), there is no reason to limit it to that function. The mnemonic may confuse the programmer, but the microprocessor does exactly what it is supposed to do. Careful documentation can help calm the nerves if you feel uneasy about this procedure.

The common uses of jump tables are to implement CASE statements (for example, multiway branches as used in languages such as FORTRAN, Pascal, and PL/I) to decode commands from a keyboard, and to respond to function keys on a terminal.

CHARACTER MANIPULATION

The easiest way to manipulate characters is to treat them as unsigned 8-bit numbers. The letters and digits form ordered subsequences of the ASCII characters; for example, the ASCII representation of the letter A is one less than the ASCII representation of the letter B. Handling one character at a time is just like handling normal 8-bit unsigned numbers. Some examples are

- Branch to address DEST if the accumulator contains an ASCII E.

```
        CMP     #'E             ;IS DATA E?
        BEQ     DEST            ;YES, BRANCH
```

- Search a string starting at address STRNG until a non-blank character is found.

```
        LDX     #0              ;POINT TO START OF STRING
        LDA     #'              ;GET A BLANK FOR CHECKING
EXAMC   CMP     STRNG,X         ;IS NEXT CHARACTER A BLANK?
        BNE     DONE            ;NO, DONE
        INX                     ;YES,PROCEED TO NEXT CHARACTER
        JMP     EXAMC
DONE    NOP
```

or

```
        LDX     #$FF            ;POINT TO BYTE BEFORE START
        LDA     #'              ;GET A BLANK FOR COMPARISON
EXAMC   INX                     ;PROCEED TO NEXT CHARACTER
        CMP     STRNG,X         ;IS IT A BLANK?
        BEQ     EXAMC           ;YES, KEEP LOOKING
```

- Branch to address DEST if the accumulator contains a letter between C and F, inclusive.

```
        CMP     #'C             ;IS DATA BELOW C?
        BCC     DONE            ;YES, DONE
        CMP     #'G             ;IS DATA BELOW G?
        BCC     DEST            ;YES, MUST BE BETWEEN C AND F
DONE    NOP
```

Chapter 8 contains further examples of string manipulation.

CODE CONVERSION

You can convert data from one code to another using arithmetic or logical operations (if the relationship is simple) or lookup tables (if the relationship is complex).

Examples

1. Convert an ASCII digit to its binary-coded decimal (BCD) equivalent.

```
        SEC                     ;CLEAR THE INVERTED BORROW
        SBC     #'0             ;CONVERT ASCII TO BCD
```

Since the ASCII digits form an ordered subsequence, all you must do is subtract the offset (ASCII 0).

You can also clear bit positions 4 and 5 with the single instruction

```
        AND     #%11001111      :CONVERT ASCII TO BCD
```

Either the arithmetic sequence or the logical instruction will, for example, convert ASCII 0 (30_{16}) to decimal 0 (00_{16}).

2. Convert a binary-coded decimal (BCD) digit to its ASCII equivalent.

```
        CLC                     ;CLEAR THE CARRY
        ADC     #'0             ;CONVERT BCD TO ASCII
```

The inverse conversion is equally simple. You can also set bit positions 4 and 5 with the single instruction

```
        ORA     #%00110000      ;CONVERT BCD TO ASCII
```

Either the arithmetic sequence or the logical instruction will, for example, convert decimal 6 (06_{16}) to ASCII 6 (36_{16}).

3. Convert one 8-bit code to another using a lookup table. Assume that the lookup table starts at address NEWCD and is indexed by the value in the original code (for example, the 27th entry is the value in the new code corresponding to 27 in the original code). Assume that the data is in memory location CODE.

```
        LDX     CODE            ;GET THE OLD CODE
        LDA     NEWCD,X         ;CONVERT IT TO THE NEW CODE
```

Chapter 4 contains further examples of code conversion.

MULTIPLE-PRECISION ARITHMETIC

Multiple-precision arithmetic requires a series of 8-bit operations. One must

· Clear the Carry before starting addition or set the Carry before starting subtraction, since there is never a carry into or borrow from the least significant byte.

· Use the Add with Carry (ADC) or Subtract with Borrow (SBC) instruction to perform an 8-bit operation and include the carry or borrow from the previous operation.

A typical 64-bit addition program is

```
        LDX     #8            ;NUMBER OF BYTES = 8
        CLC                   ;CLEAR CARRY TO START
ADDB:   LDA     NUM1-1,X      ;GET A BYTE OF ONE OPERAND
        ADC     NUM2-1,X      ;ADD A BYTE OF THE OTHER OPERAND
        STA     NUM1-1,X      ;STORE THE 8-BIT SUM
        DEX
        BNE     ADDB          ;COUNT BYTE OPERATIONS
```

Chapter 6 contains further examples.

MULTIPLICATION AND DIVISION

Multiplication can be implemented in a variety of ways. One technique is to convert simple multiplications to additions or left shifts.

Examples

1. Multiply the contents of the accumulator by 2.

```
        ASL     A             ;DOUBLE A
```

2. Multiply the contents of the accumulator by 5.

```
        STA     TEMP
        ASL     A             ;A TIMES 2
        ASL     A             ;A TIMES 4
        ADC     TEMP          ;A TIMES 5
```

This approach assumes that shifting the accumulator left never produces a carry. This approach is often handy in determining the locations of elements of two-dimensional arrays. For example, let us assume that we have a set of temperature readings taken at four different positions in each of three different tanks. We organize the readings as a two-dimensional array T(I,J), where I is the tank number (1, 2, or 3) and J is the number of the position in the tank (1, 2, 3, or 4). We store the readings in the linear memory of the computer one after another as follows, starting with tank 1:

```
BASE        T(1,1)    Reading at tank 1, location 1
BASE+1      T(1,2)    Reading at tank 1, location 2
BASE+2      T(1,3)    Reading at tank 1, location 3
BASE+3      T(1,4)    Reading at tank 1, location 4
BASE+4      T(2,1)    Reading at tank 2, location 1
BASE+5      T(2,2)    Reading at tank 2, location 2
BASE+6      T(2,3)    Reading at tank 2, location 3
BASE+7      T(2,4)    Reading at tank 2, location 4
BASE+8      T(3,1)    Reading at tank 3, location 1
BASE+9      T(3,2)    Reading at tank 3, location 2
BASE+10     T(3,3)    Reading at tank 3, location 3
BASE+11     T(3,4)    Reading at tank 3, location 4
```

So, generally the reading T(I,J) is located at address BASE+4 × (I−1) + (J−1). If I is in memory location IND1 and J is in memory location IND2, we can load the accumulator with T(I,J) as follows:

```
LDA     IND1          ;GET I
SEC
SBC     #1            ;CALCULATE I - 1
ASL     A             ;2 X (I - 1)
ASL     A             ;4 X (I - 1)
SEC
SBC     #1            ;4 X (I - 1) - 1
CLC
ADC     IND2          ;4 X (I - 1) + J - 1
TAX
LDA     BASE,X        ;GET T(I,J)
```

We can extend this approach to handle arrays with more dimensions.

Obviously, the program is much simpler if we store I−1 in memory location IND1 and J−1 in memory location IND2. We can then load the accumulator with T(I,J) using

```
LDA     IND1          ;GET I - 1
ASL     A             ;2 X (I - 1)
ASL     A             ;4 X (I - 1)
CLC
ADC     IND2          ;4 X (I - 1) + (J - 1)
TAX
LDA     BASE,X        ;GET T(I.J)
```

· Simple divisions can also be implemented as right logical shifts.

Example

Divide the contents of the accumulator by 4.

```
LSR     A             ;DIVIDE BY 2
LSR     A             ;AND BY 2 AGAIN
```

If you are multiplying or dividing signed numbers, you must be careful to separate the signs from the magnitudes. You must replace logical shifts with arithmetic shifts that preserve the value of the sign bit.

· Algorithms involving shifts and additions (multiplication) or shifts and subtractions (division) can be used as described in Chapter 6.

· Lookup tables can be used as discussed previously in this chapter.

Chapter 6 contains additional examples of arithmetic programs.

LIST PROCESSING[5]

Lists can be processed like arrays if the elements are stored in consecutive addresses. If the elements are queued or chained, however, the limitations of the instruction set are evident in that

- No 16-bit registers or instructions are available.
- Indirect addressing is allowed only through pointers on page 0.
- No true indirect addressing is available except for JMP instructions.

Examples

1. Retrieve an address stored starting at the address in memory locations PGZRO and PGZRO+1. Place the retrieved address in memory locations POINTL and POINTH.

```
        LDY     #0            ;INDEX = ZERO
        LDA     (PGZRO),Y     ;GET LSB OF ADDRESS
        STA     POINTL
        INY
        LDA     (PGZRO),Y     ;GET MSB OF ADDRESS
        STA     POINTH
```

This procedure allows you to move from one element to another in a linked list.

2. Retrieve data from the address currently in memory locations PGZRO and PGZRO+1 and increment that address by 1.

```
        LDY     #0            ;INDEX = ZERO
        LDA     (PGZRO),Y     ;GET DATA USING POINTER
        INC     PGZRO         ;UPDATE POINTER BY 1
        BNE     DONE
        INC     PGZRO+1
DONE    NOP
```

This procedure allows you to use the address in memory as a pointer to the next available location in a buffer. Of course, you can also leave the pointer fixed and increment a buffer index. If that index is in memory location BUFIND, we have

```
        LDY     BUFIND        ;GET BUFFER INDEX
        LDA     (PGZRO),Y     ;GET DATA FROM BUFFER
        INC     BUFIND        :UPDATE BUFFER INDEX BY 1
```

3. Store an address starting at the address currently in memory locations PGZRO and PGZRO+1. Increment the address in memory locations PGZRO and PGZRO+1 by 2.

```
        LDY     #0            ;INDEX = ZERO
        LDA     #ADDRL        ;SAVE LSB OF ADDRESS
        STA     (PGZRO),Y
        LDA     #ADDRH        ;SAVE MSB OF ADDRESS
        INY
        STA     (PGZRO),Y
        CLC                   ;INCREMENT POINTER BY 2
        LDA     PGZRO
        ADC     #2
        STA     PGZRO
        BCC     DONE          ;WITH CARRY IF NECESSARY
        INC     PGZRO+1
DONE    NOP
```

This procedure lets you build a list of addresses. Such a list could be used, for example, to write threaded code in which each routine concludes by transferring control to its successor. The list could also contain the starting addresses of a series of test procedures or tasks or the addresses of memory locations or I/O devices assigned by the operator to particular functions. Of course, some lists may have to be placed on page 0 in order to use the 6502's preindexed or postindexed addressing modes.

GENERAL DATA STRUCTURES[6]

More general data structures can be processed using the procedures that we have described for array manipulation, table lookup, and list processing. The key limitations in the instruction set are the same ones that we mentioned in the discussion of list processing.

Examples

1. **Queues or linked lists**. Assume that we have a queue header consisting of the address of the first element in memory locations HEAD and HEAD+1 (on page 0). If there are no elements in the queue, HEAD and HEAD+1 both contain 0. The first two locations in each element contain the address of the next element or 0 if there is no next element.

· Add the element in memory locations PGZRO and PGZRO+1 to the head of the queue.

```
LDX     PGZRO           ;REPLACE HEAD, SAVING OLD VALUE
LDA     HEAD
STX     HEAD
PHA
LDA     PGZRO+1
LDX     HEAD+1
STA     HEAD+1
LDY     #0              ;INDEX = ZERO
PLA                     ;NEW HEAD'S LINK IS OLD HEAD
STA     (HEAD),Y
TXA
INY
STA     (HEAD),Y
```

· Remove an element from the head of the queue and set the Zero flag if no element is available.

```
LDY     #0              ;GET ADDRESS OF FIRST ELEMENT
LDA     (HEAD),Y        ;GET LESS SIGNIFICANT BYTE
STA     PGZRO
INY
LDA     (HEAD),Y        ;GET MORE SIGNIFICANT BYTE
```

```
         STA     PGZRO+1
         ORA     PGZRO        ;ANY ELEMENTS IN QUEUE?
         BEQ     DONE         ;NO, DONE (LINK = 0000)
         LDA     (PGZRO),Y    ;YES, MAKE NEXT ELEMENT NEW HEAD
         STA     (HEAD),Y
         DEY
         LDA     (PGZRO),Y
         STA     (HEAD),Y
         INY                  ;CLEAR ZERO FLAG BY MAKING Y 1
DONE     NOP
```

Note that we can use the sequence

```
         LDA     ADDR
         ORA     ADDR+1
```

to test the 16-bit number in memory locations ADDR and ADDR+1. The Zero flag is set only if both bytes are 0.

2. **Stacks**. Assume that we have a stack structure consisting of 8-bit elements. The address of the next empty location is in addresses SPTR and SPTR+1 on page 0. The lowest address that the stack can occupy is LOW and the highest address is HIGH.

· If the stack overflows, clear the Carry flag and exit. Otherwise, store the accumulator in the stack and increase the stack pointer by 1. Overflow means that the stack has exceeded its area.

```
         LDA     #HIGHL       :STACK POINTER GREATER THAN HIGH?
         CMP     SPTR
         LDA     #HIGHM
         SBC     SPTR+1
         BCC     EXIT         ;YES, CLEAR CARRY AND EXIT (OVERFLOW)
         LDY     #0           ;NO STORE ACCUMULATOR IN STACK
         STA     (SPTR),Y
         INC     SPTR         ;INCREMENT STACK POINTER
         BNE     EXIT
         INC     SPTR+1
EXIT     NOP
```

· If the stack underflows, set the Carry flag and exit. Otherwise, decrease the stack pointer by 1 and load the accumulator from the stack. Underflow means that there is nothing left in the stack.

```
         LDA     #LOWL        ;STACK POINTER AT OR BELOW LOW?
         CMP     SPTR
         LDA     #LOWM
         SBC     SPTR+1
         BCS     EXIT         ;YES, SET CARRY AND EXIT (UNDERFLOW)
         LDA     SPTR         ;NO, DECREMENT STACK POINTER
         BNE     NOBOR
         DEC     SPTR+1
NOBOR    DEC     SPTR
         LDY     #0           :LOAD ACCUMULATOR FROM STACK
         LDA     (SPTR),Y
EXIT     NOP
```

PARAMETER PASSING TECHNIQUES

The most common ways to pass parameters on the 6502 microprocessor are

1. **In registers**. Three 8-bit registers are available (A, X, and Y). This approach is adequate in simple cases but it lacks generality and can handle only a limited number of parameters. The programmer must remember the normal uses of the registers in assigning parameters. In other words,

- The accumulator is the obvious place to put a single 8-bit parameter.
- Index register X is the obvious place to put an index, since it is the most accessible and has the most instructions that use it for addressing. Index register X is also used in preindexing (indexed indirect addressing).
- Index register Y is used in postindexing (indirect indexed addressing).

This approach is reentrant as long as the interrupt service routines save and restore all the registers.

2. **In an assigned area of memory**. The easiest way to implement this approach is to place the starting address of the assigned area in two memory locations on page 0. The calling routine must store the parameters in memory and load the starting address into the two locations on page 0 before transferring control to the subroutine. This approach is general and can handle any number of parameters, but it requires a large amount of management. If you assign different areas of memory for each call or each routine, you are essentially creating your own stack. If you use a common area of memory, you lose reentrancy. In this method, the programmer is responsible for assigning areas of memory, avoiding interference between routines, and saving and restoring the pointers required to resume routines after subroutine calls or interrupts. The extra memory locations on page 0 must be treated like registers.

3. **In program memory immediately following the subroutine call**. If you use this approach, you must remember the following:

- The starting address of the memory area minus 1 is at the top of the stack. That is, the starting address is the normal return address, which is 1 larger than the address the 6502's JSR instruction saves in the stack. You can move the starting address to memory locations RETADR and RETADR+1 on page 0 with the following sequence:

```
        PLA                 ;GET LSB OF RETURN ADDRESS
        STA    RETADR
        PLA                 ;GET MSB OF RETURN ADDRESS
        STA    RETADR+1
        INC    RETADR       ;ADD 1 TO RETURN ADDRESS
        BNE    DONE
        INC    RETADR+1
DONE    NOP
```

Now we can access the parameters through the indirect address. That is, you can load the accumulator with the first parameter by using the sequence

```
LDY     #0           ;INDEX = ZERO
LDA     (RETADR),Y   ;LOAD FIRST PARAMETER
```

An obvious alternative is to leave the return address unchanged and start the index at 1. That is, we would have

```
PLA                  ;GET LSB OF RETURN ADDRESS
STA     RETADR
PLA                  ;GET MSB OF RETURN ADDRESS
STA     RETADR+1
```

Now we could load the accumulator with the first parameter by using the sequence

```
LDY     #1           ;INDEX = 1
LDA     (RETADR),Y   ;LOAD FIRST PARAMETER
```

- All parameters must be fixed for a given call, since the program memory is typically ROM.

- The subroutine must calculate the actual return address (the address of the last byte in the parameter area) and place it on top of the stack before executing a Return from Subroutine (RTS) instruction.

Example

Assume that subroutine SUBR requires an 8-bit parameter and a 16-bit parameter. Show a main program that calls SUBR and contains the required parameters. Also show the initial part of the subroutine that retrieves the parameters, storing the 8-bit item in the accumulator and the 16-bit item in memory locations PGZRO and PGZRO+1, and places the correct return address at the top of the stack.

Subroutine call

```
        JSR     SUBR         ;EXECUTE SUBROUTINE
        .BYTE   PAR8         ;8-BIT PARAMETER
        .WORD   PAR16        ;16-BIT PARAMETER
        ... next instruction ...
```

Subroutine

```
SUBR    PLA                  ;GET LSB OF PARAMETER ADDRESS
        STA     RETADR
        PLA                  ;GET MSB OF PARAMETER ADDRESS
        STA     RETADR+1
        LDY     #1           ;ACCESS FIRST PARAMETER
        LDA     (RETADR),Y   ;GET FIRST PARAMETER
        TAX
        INY
        LDA     (RETADR),Y   ;ACCESS LSB OF 16-BIT PARAMETER
        STA     PGZRO
        INY
        LDA     (RETADR),Y   ;GET MSB OF 16-BIT PARAMETER
```

```
        STA     PGZRO+1
        LDA     RETADR          ;CALCULATE ACTUAL RETURN ADDRESS
        CLC
        ADA     #3
        TAY
        BCC     STRMSB
        INC     RETADR+1
STRMSB  LDA     RETADR+1        ;PUT RETURN ADDRESS ON TOP OF STACK
        PHA
        TYA
        PHA
```

The initial sequence pops the return address from the top of the stack (JSR saved it there) and stores it in memory locations RETADR and RETADR+1. In fact, the return address does not contain an instruction; instead, it contains the first parameter. Remember that JSR actually saves the return address minus 1; that is why we must start the index at 1 rather than at 0. Finally, adding 3 to the return address and saving the sum in the stack lets a final RTS instruction transfer control back to the instruction following the parameters.

This approach allows parameters lists of any length. However, obtaining the parameters from memory and adjusting the return address is awkward at best; it becomes a longer and slower process as the number of parameters increases.

4. **In the stack**. If you use this approach, you must remember the following:

- JSR stores the return address at the top of the stack. The parameters that the calling routine placed in the stack begin at address 01ss + 3, where ss is the contents of the stack pointer. The 16-bit return address occupies the top two locations and the stack pointer itself always refers to the next empty address, not the last occupied one. Before the subroutine can obtain its parameters, it must remove the return address from the stack and save it somewhere.

- The only way for the subroutine to determine the value of the stack pointer is by using the instruction TSX. After TSX has been executed, you can access the top of the stack by indexing with register X from the base address 0101_{16}. The extra offset of 1 is necessary because the top of the stack is empty.

- The calling program must place the parameters in the stack before calling the subroutine.

- Dynamically allocating space on the stack is difficult at best. If you wish to reduce the stack pointer by NRESLT, two general approaches are

```
        TSX                     ;MOVE STACK POINTER TO A VIA X
        TXA
        SEC                     ;SUBTRACT NRESLT FROM POINTER
        SBC     #NRESLT
        TAX                     ;RETURN DIFFERENCE TO STACK POINTER
        TXS
```

or

```
         LDX     #NRESLT      ;COUNT = NRESLT
PUSHB    PHA                  ;MOVE STACK POINTER DOWN 1
         DEX
         BNE     PUSHB
```

Either approach leaves NRESLT empty locations at the top of the stack as shown in Figure 1-5. Of course, if NRESLT is 1 or 2, simply executing PHA the appropriate number of times will be much faster and shorter. The same approaches can be used to provide stack locations for temporary storage.

Example

Assume that subroutine SUBR requires an 8-bit parameter and a 16-bit parameter, and that it produces two 8-bit results. Show a call of SUBR, the removal of the return address from the stack, and the cleaning of the stack after the return. Figure 1-6 shows the appearance of the stack initially, after the subroutine call, and at the end. If you always use the stack for parameters and results, you will generally keep the parameters at the top of the stack in the proper order. Then you will not have to save the parameters or assign space in the stack for the results (they will replace some or all of the original parameters). You will, however, have to assign space on the stack for temporary storage to maintain generality and reentrancy.

Calling program

```
         TSX                  ;LEAVE ROOM ON STACK FOR RESULTS
         TXA                  ;A GENERAL WAY TO ADJUST SP
         CLC
         ADC     #2
         TAX
         TXS
         LDA     #PAR16H      ;MOVE 16-BIT PARAMETER TO STACK
         PHA
         LDA     #PAR16L
         PHA
         LDA     #PAR8        ;MOVE 8-BIT PARAMETER TO STACK
         PHA
         JSR     SUBR         ;EXECUTE SUBROUTINE
         TSX                  ;CLEAN PARAMETERS FROM STACK
         TXA
         CLC
         ADC     #3
         TAX
         TXS                  ;RESULT IS NOW AT TOP OF STACK
```

Subroutine

```
SUBR     PLA                  ;REMOVE RETURN ADDRESS FROM STACK
         STA     RETADR
         PLA
         STA     RETADR+1
```

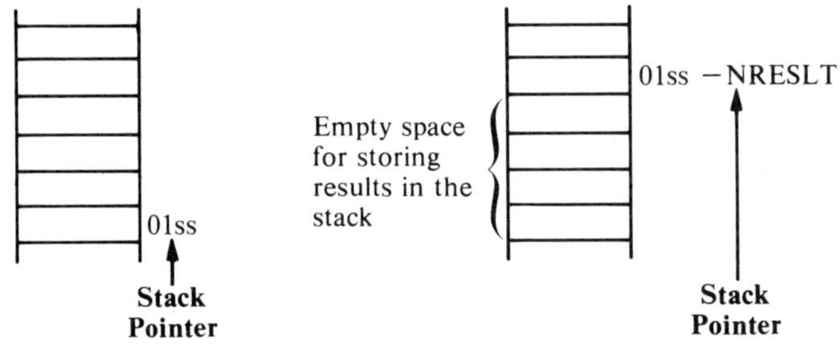

No values are placed in the locations.
The initial contents of the stack pointer are ss.

Figure 1-5: The Stack Before and After Assigning NRESLT Empty Locations for Results

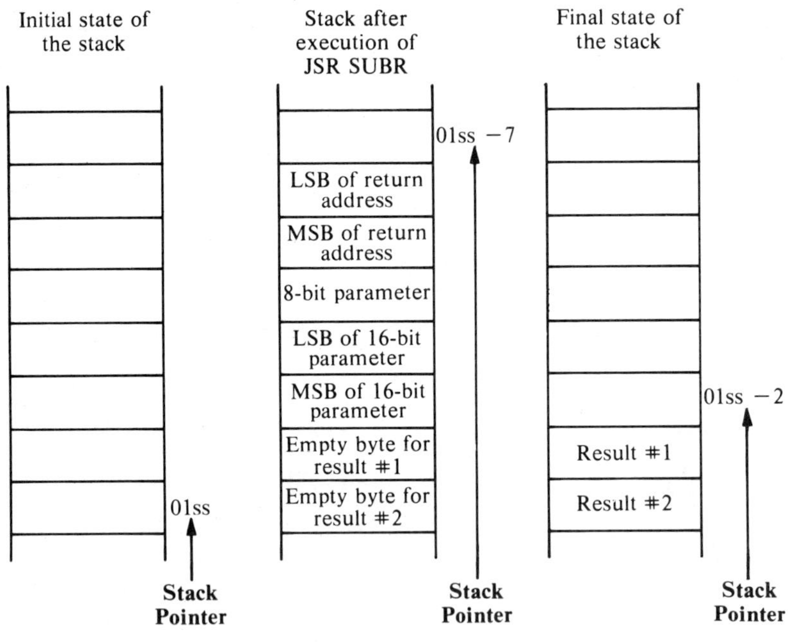

The initial contents of the stack pointer are ss.

Figure 1-6: The Effect of a Subroutine on the Stack

SIMPLE INPUT/OUTPUT

Simple input/output can be performed using any memory addresses and any instructions that reference memory. The most common instructions are the following:

- LDA (load accumulator) transfers eight bits of data from an input port to the accumulator.
- STA (store accumulator) transfers eight bits of data from the accumulator to an output port.

Other instructions can combine the input operation with arithmetic or logical operations. Typical examples are the following:

- AND logically ANDs the contents of the accumulator with the data from an input port.
- BIT logically ANDs the contents of the accumulator with the data from an input port but does not store the result anywhere. It does, however, load the Negative flag with bit 7 of the input port and the Overflow flag with bit 6, regardless of the contents of the accumulator.
- CMP subtracts the data at an input port from the contents of the accumulator, setting the flags but leaving the accumulator unchanged.

Instructions that operate on data in memory can also be used for input or output. Since these instructions both read and write memory, their effect on input and output ports may be difficult to determine. Remember, input ports cannot generally be written, nor can output ports generally be read. The commonly used instructions are the following:

- ASL shifts its data to the left, thus moving bit 7 to the Carry for possible serial input.
- DEC decrements its data. Among other effects, this inverts bit 0.
- INC increments its data. Among other effects, this inverts bit 0.
- LSR shifts its data to the right, thus moving bit 0 to the Carry for possible serial input.
- ROR rotates its data to the right, thus moving the old Carry to bit 7 and moving bit 0 to the Carry.
- ROL rotates its data to the left, thus moving the old Carry to bit 0 and moving bit 7 to the Carry.

The effects of these instructions on an input port are typically similar to their effects on a ROM location. The microprocessor can read the data, operate on it, and set the flags, but it cannot store the result back into memory. The effects on an output port are even stranger, unless the port is latched and buffered. If it is not, the data that the processor reads is system-dependent and typically has no connection with what was last stored there.

Examples

1. Perform an 8-bit input operation from the input port assigned to memory address $B000_{16}$.

```
        LDA     $B000           ;INPUT DATA
```

2. Perform an 8-bit output operation to the output port assigned to memory address $3A5E_{16}$.

```
        STA     $3A5E           ;OUTPUT DATA
```

3. Set the Zero flag if bit 5 of the input port assigned to memory address $75D0_{16}$ is 0.

```
        LDA     #%00100000      ;GET MASK
        AND     $75D0           ;SET FLAG IF BIT 5 IS ZERO
```

We can also use the sequence

```
        LDA     #%00100000      ;GET MASK
        BIT     $75D0           ;SET FLAG IF BIT 5 IS ZERO
```

If the bit position of interest is number 6, we can use the single instruction

```
        BIT     $75D0
```

to set the Overflow flag to its value.

4. Set the Zero flag if the data at the input port assigned to memory address 1700_{16} is $1B_{16}$.

```
        LDA     #$1B
        CMP     $1700
```

5. Load the Carry flag with the data from bit 7 of the input port assigned to memory address $33A5_{16}$.

```
        ASL     $33A5
```

Note that this instruction does not change the data in memory location $33A5_{16}$ unless that location is latched and buffered. If, for example, there are eight simple switches attached directly to the port, the instruction will surely have no effect on whether the switches are open or closed.

6. Place a logic 1 in bit 0 of the output port assigned to memory address $B070_{16}$.

```
        LDA     $B070
        ORA     #%00000001
        STA     $B070
```

If none of the other bits in address $B070_{16}$ are connected, we can use the sequence

```
        SEC
        ROL     $B070
```

If we know that bit 0 of address $B070_{16}$ is currently a logic 0, we can use the single instruction

```
        INC     $B070
```

All of these alternatives will have strange effects if memory address $B070_{16}$ cannot be read. The first two will surely make bit 0 a logic 1, but their effects on the other bits are uncertain. The outcome of the third alternative would be a total mystery, since we would have no idea what is being incremented. We can avoid the uncertainty by saving a copy of the data in RAM location TEMP. Now we can operate on the copy using

```
        LDA     TEMP            ;GET COPY OF OUTPUT DATA
        ORA     #%00000001      ;SET BIT 0
        STA     $B070           ;OUTPUT NEW DATA
        STA     TEMP            ;AND SAVE A COPY OF IT
```

LOGICAL AND PHYSICAL DEVICES

One way to select I/O devices by number is to use an I/O device table. An I/O device table assigns the actual I/O addresses (*physical devices*) to the device numbers (*logical devices*) to which a program refers. Using this method, a program written in a high-level language may refer to device number 2 for input and number 5 for output. For testing purposes, the operator may assign devices numbers 2 and 5 to be the input and output ports, respectively, of his or her terminal. For normal stand-alone operation, the operator may assign device number 2 to be an analog input unit and device number 5 the system printer. If the system is to be operated by remote control, the operator may assign devices numbers 2 and 5 to be communications units used for input and output.

One way to provide this distinction between logical and physical devices is to use the 6502's indexed indirect addressing or preindexing. This mode assumes that the device table is located on page 0 and is accessed via an index in register X. If we have a device number in memory location DEVNO, the following programs can be used:

- Load the accumulator from the device number given by the contents of memory location DEVNO.

```
        LDA     DEVNO           ;GET DEVICE NUMBER
        ASL     A               ;DOUBLE IT TO HANDLE DEVICE ADDRESSES
        TAX
        LDA     (DEVTAB,X)      ;GET DATA FROM DEVICE
```

- Store the accumulator in the device number given by the contents of memory location DEVNO.

```
PHA                     ;SAVE THE DATA
LDA     DEVNO           ;GET DEVICE NUMBER
ASL     A               ;DOUBLE IT TO HANDLE DEVICE ADDRESSES
TAX
PLA
STA     (DEVTAB,X)      ;SEND DATA TO DEVICE
```

In both cases, we assume that the I/O device table starts at address DEVTAB (on page 0) and consists of 2-byte addresses. Note that the 6502 provides an appropriate addressing method, but does not produce any error messages if the programmer uses that method improperly by accessing odd addresses or by indexing off the end of page 0 (the processor does provide automatic wraparound). In real applications (see Chapter 10), the device table will probably contain the starting addresses of I/O subroutines (*drivers*) rather than actual device addresses.

STATUS AND CONTROL

You can handle status and control signals like any other data. The only special problem is that the processor may not be able to read output ports; in that case, you must retain copies (in RAM) of the data sent to those ports.

Examples

1. Branch to address DEST if bit 3 of the input port assigned to memory address $A100_{16}$ is 1.

```
LDA     $A100           ;GET INPUT DATA
AND     #%00001000      ;MASK OFF BIT 3
BNE     DEST
```

2. Branch to address DEST if bits 4, 5, and 6 of the input port assigned to address STAT are 5 (101 binary).

```
LDA     STAT            ;GET STATUS
AND     #%01110000      ;MASK OFF BITS 4, 5, AND 6
CMP     #%01010000      ;IS STATUS FIELD 5?
BEQ     DEST            ;YES, BRANCH
```

3. Set bit 5 of address CNTL to 1.

```
LDA     CNTL            ;GET CURRENT DATA FROM PORT
ORA     #%00100000      ;SET BIT 5
STA     CNTL            ;RESTORE DATA TO PORT
```

If address CNTL cannot be read properly, we can use a copy in memory address TEMP.

```
LDA     TEMP            ;GET CURRENT DATA FROM PORT
ORA     #%00100000      ;SET BIT 5
STA     CNTL            ;RESTORE DATA TO PORT
STA     TEMP            ;UPDATE COPY OF DATA
```

You must update the copy every time you change the data.

4. Set bits 2, 3, and 4 of address CNTL to 6 (110 binary).

```
LDA    CNTL         ;GET CURRENT DATA FROM PORT
AND    #%11100011   ;CLEAR BITS 2, 3, AND 4
ORA    #%00011000   ;SET CONTROL FIELD TO 6
STA    CNTL         ;RESTORE DATA TO PORT
```

As in example 3, if address CNTL cannot be read properly, we can use a copy in memory address TEMP.

```
LDA    TEMP         ;GET CURRENT DATA FROM PORT
AND    #%11100011   ;CLEAR BITS 2, 3, AND 4
ORA    #%00011000   ;SET CONTROL FIELD TO 6
STA    CNTL         ;UPDATE PORT
STA    TEMP         ;UPDATE COPY OF DATA
```

Retaining copies of the data in memory (or using the values stored in a latched, buffered output port) allows you to change part of the data without affecting other parts that may have unrelated meanings. For example, you could change the state of one indicator light (for example, a light that indicated local or remote operation) without affecting other indicator lights attached to the same port. You could similarly change one control line (for example, a line that determined whether motion was in the positive or negative X-direction) without affecting other control lines attached to the same port.

PERIPHERAL CHIPS

The major peripheral chips in 6502-based microcomputers are the 6520 and 6522 parallel interfaces (known as the Peripheral Interface Adapter or PIA and the Versatile Interface Adapter or VIA, respectively), the 6551 and 6850 serial interfaces (known as Asynchronous Communications Interface Adapters or ACIAs), and the 6530 and 6532 multifunction devices (known as ROM-I/O-timers or RAM-I/O-timers or ROM-RAM-I/O-timers, abbreviated RIOT or RRIOT and sometimes called *combo* chips). All of these devices can perform a variety of functions, much like the microprocessor itself. Of course, peripheral chips perform fewer different functions than processors and the range of functions is limited. The idea behind programmable peripheral chips is that each contains many useful circuits; the designer selects the ones he or she wants to use by storing one or more selection codes in control registers, much as one selects a particular circuit from a Designer's Casebook by turning to a particular page. The advantages of programmable chips are that a single board containing such devices can handle many applications and changes, or, corrections can be made by changing selection codes rather than by redesigning circuit boards. The disadvantages of programmable chips are the lack of standards and the difficulty of determining how specific chips operate.

Chapter 10 contains typical initialization routines for the 6520, 6522, 6551, 6850, 6530, and 6532 devices. These devices are also discussed in detail in the *Osborne 4 and 8-Bit Microprocessor Handbook*[7]. We will provide only a brief overview of the 6522 device here, since it is the most widely used. 6522 devices are used, for example, in the Rockwell AIM-65, Synertek SYM-1, Apple, and other popular microcomputers as well as in add-on I/O boards and other functions available from many manufacturers.

6522 Parallel Interface (Versatile Interface Adapter)

A VIA contains two 8-bit parallel I/O ports (A and B), four status and control lines (CA1, CA2, CB1, and CB2 — two for each of the two ports), two 16-bit counter/timers (timer 1 and timer 2), an 8-bit shift register, and interrupt logic. Each VIA occupies 16 memory addresses. The RS (register select) lines choose the various internal registers as described in Table 1-12. The way that a VIA operates is determined by the values that the program stores in four registers.

· Data Direction Register A (DDRA) determines whether the pins on port A are inputs (0s) or outputs (1s). A data direction register determines only the direction in which traffic flows; you may compare it to a directional arrow that indicates which way traffic can move on a highway lane or railroad track. The data direction register does not affect what data flows or how often it changes; it only affects the direction. Each pin in the I/O port has a corresponding bit in the data direction register, and thus, each pin can be selected individually as either an input or an output. Of course, the most common choices are to make an entire 8-bit I/O port input or outport by storing 0s or 1s in all eight bits of the data direction register.

· Data Direction Register B (DDRB) similarly determines whether the pins in port B are inputs or outputs.

· The Peripheral Control Register (PCR) determines how the handshaking control lines (CA1, CB1, CA2, and CB2) operate. Figure 1-7 contains the bit assignments for this register. We will discuss briefly the purposes of these bits and their uses in common applications.

· The Auxiliary Control Register (ACR) determines whether the input data ports are latched and how the timers and shift register operate. Figure 1-8 contains the bit assignments for this register. We will also discuss briefly the purposes of these bits and their uses in common applications.

Table 1-12: Addressing the Internal Registers of the 6522 VIA

Label	Select Lines				Addressed Location
	RS3	RS2	RS1	RS0	
DEV	0	0	0	0	Output register for I/O Port B
DEV+1	0	0	0	1	Output register for I/O Port A, with handshaking
DEV+2	0	0	1	0	I/O Port B Data Direction register
DEV+3	0	0	1	1	I/O Port A Data Direction register
DEV+4	0	1	0	0	Read Timer 1 Counter low-order byte Write to Timer 1 Latch low-order byte
DEV+5	0	1	0	1	Read Timer 1 Counter high-order byte Write to Timer 1 Latch high-order byte and initiate count
DEV+6	0	1	1	0	Access Timer 1 Latch low-order byte
DEV+7	0	1	1	1	Access Timer 1 Latch high-order byte
DEV+8	1	0	0	0	Read low-order byte of Timer 2 and reset Counter interrupt Write to low-order byte of Timer 2 but do not reset interrupt
DEV+9	1	0	0	1	Access high-order byte of Timer 2, reset Counter interrupt on write
DEV+A	1	0	1	0	Serial I/O Shift register
DEV+B	1	0	1	1	Auxiliary Control register
DEV+C	1	1	0	0	Peripheral Control register
DEV+D	1	1	0	1	Interrupt Flag register
DEV+E	1	1	1	0	Interrupt Enable register
DEV+F	1	1	1	1	Output register for I/O Port A, without handshaking

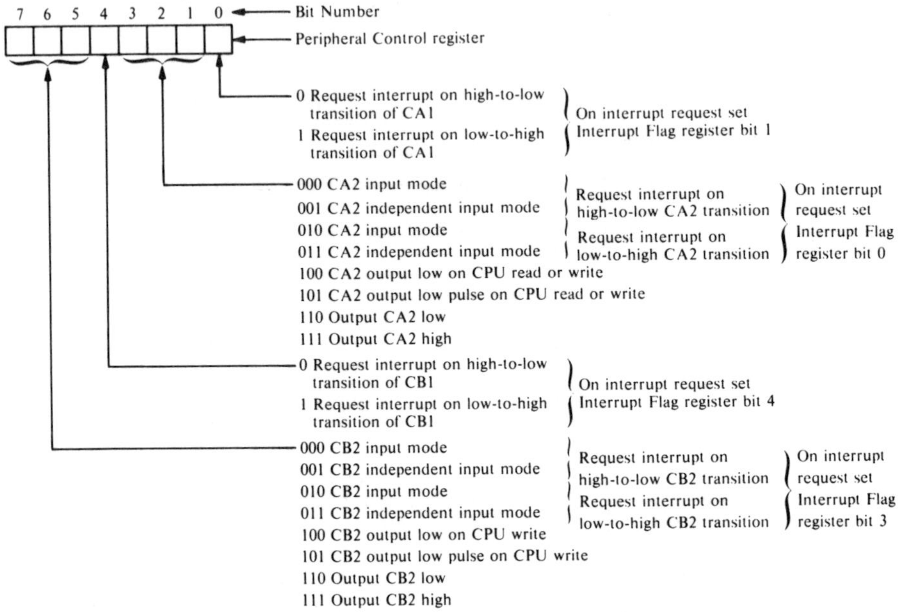

Figure 1-7: Bit Assignments for the 6522 VIA's Peripheral Control Register

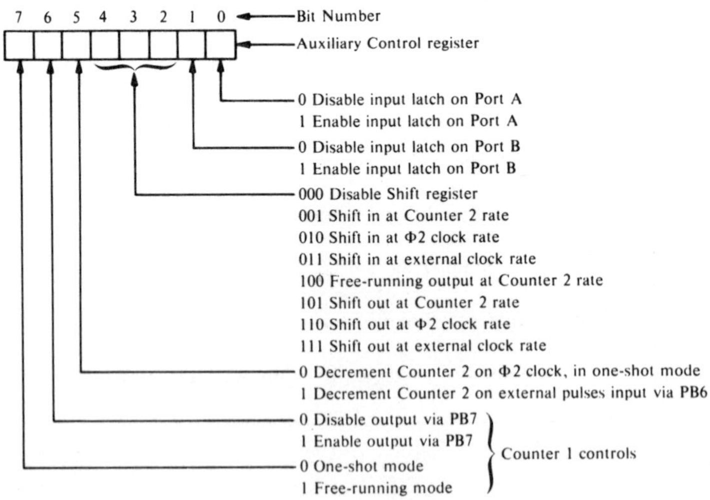

Figure 1-8: Bit Assignments for the 6522 VIA's Auxiliary Control Register

In order to initialize a VIA properly, we must know what its start-up state is. Reset clears all the VIA registers, thus making all the data and control lines inputs, disabling all latches, interrupts, and other functions, and clearing all status bits.

The data direction registers are easy to initialize. Typical routines are

- Make port A input.

```
LDA    #0
STA    DDRA
```

- Make port B output.

```
LDA    #%11111111
STA    DDRB
```

- Make bits 0 through 3 of port A input, bits 4 through 7 output.

```
LDA    #$11110000
STA    DDRA
```

- Make bit 0 of port B input, bits 1 through 7 output.

```
LDA    #$11111110
STA    DDRB
```

Bit 0 could, for example, be a serial input line.

The Peripheral Control Register is more difficult to initialize. We will briefly discuss the purposes of the control lines before showing some examples.

Control lines CA1, CA2, CB1, and CB2 are basically intended for use as handshaking signals. In a handshake, the sender indicates the availability of data by means of a transition on a serial line; the transition tells the receiver that new data is available to it on the parallel lines. Common names for this serial line are VALID DATA, DATA READY, and DATA AVAILABLE. In response to this signal, the receiver must accept the data and indicate its acceptance by means of a transition on another serial line. This transition tells the sender that the latest parallel data has been accepted and that another transmission sequence can begin. Common names for the other serial line are DATA ACCEPTED, PERIPHERAL READY, BUFFER EMPTY, and DATA ACKNOWLEDGE.

Typical examples of complete sequences are

- **Input from a keyboard**. When the operator presses a key, the keyboard produces a parallel code corresponding to the key and a transition on the DATA READY or VALID DATA line. The computer must determine that the transition has occurred, read the data, and produce a transition on the DATA ACCEPTED line to indicate that the data has been read.

- **Output to a printer**. The printer indicates to the computer that it is ready by means of a transition on a BUFFER EMPTY or PERIPHERAL READY line. Note that PERIPHERAL READY is simply the inverse of DATA ACCEPTED, since the peripheral obviously cannot be ready as long as it has not accepted the latest data. The computer must determine that the printer is ready, send the data, and produce a transition on the DATA READY line to indicate that new data is available. Of course, input and output are in some sense mirror images. In the input case, the peripheral is the sender and the computer is the receiver; in the output case, the computer is the sender and the peripheral is the receiver.

Thus, a chip intended for handshaking functions must provide the following functions:

- It must recognize the appropriate transitions on the DATA READY or PERIPHERAL READY lines.
- It must provide an indication that the transition has occurred in a form that is easy for the computer to handle.
- It must allow for the production of the response — that is, for the computer to indicate DATA ACCEPTED to an input peripheral or DATA READY to an output peripheral.

There are some obvious variations that the handshaking chip should allow for, including the following:

- The active transition may be either a high-to-low edge (a trailing edge) or a low-to-high edge (a leading edge). If the chip does not allow either one, we will need extra inverter gates in some situations, since both polarities are common.
- The response may require either a high-to-low edge or a low-to-high edge. In fact, it may require either a brief pulse or a long signal that lasts until the peripheral begins its next operation.

Experience has shown that the handshaking chip can provide still more convenience, at virtually no cost, in the following ways:

- It can latch the transitions on the DATA READY or PERIPHERAL READY lines, so that they are held until the computer is ready for them. The computer need not monitor the status lines continuously to avoid missing a transition.
- It can clear the status latches automatically when an input port is read or an output port is written, thus preparing them for the next operation.
- It can produce the response automatically when an input port is read or an output port is written, thus eliminating the need for additional instructions. This option is known as an *automatic mode.* The problem with any automatic mode, no matter how flexible the designers make it, is that it will never satisfy all applications. Thus, most chips also provide a mode in which the program retains control over the response; this mode is called a *manual mode.*
- In cases where the peripherals are simple switches or lights and do not need

any status or control signals, the chip should allow independent operation of the status lines. The designer can then use these lines (which would otherwise be wasted) for such purposes as threshold detection, zero-crossing detection, or clock inputs. In such cases, the designer wants the status and control signals to be entirely independent of the operations on the parallel port. We should not have any automatic clearing of latches or sending of responses. This is known as an *independent mode.*

The 6522 peripheral control register allows the programmer to provide any of these functions. Bits 0 through 3 govern the operation of port B and its control signals; bits 4 through 7 govern the operation of port A and its control signals. The status indicators are in the Interrupt flag register (see Figure 1-9). We may characterize the bits in the control register as follows:

- Bit 0 (for port A) and bit 4 (for port B) determine whether the active transition on control line 1 is high-to-low (0) or low-to-high (1). If control line 2 is an extra input, bit 2 (for port A) and bit 6 (for port B) has a similar function.

- If control line 2 is an extra input, bit 1 (for port A) and bit 5 (for port B) determine whether it operates independently of the parallel data port. This bit is 0 for normal handshaking and 1 for independent operation.

- Bit 3 (for port A) and bit 7 (for port B) determine whether control line 2 is an extra input line (0) or an output response (1).

- If control line 2 is an output response, bit 2 (for port A) and bit 6 (for port B) determine whether it operates in an automatic mode (0) or a manual mode (1).

- If control line 2 is being operated in the automatic mode, bit 1 (for port A) and bit 5 (for port B) determine whether the response lasts for one clock cycle (1) or until the peripheral produces another active transition on control line 1 (0).

- If control line 2 is being operated in the manual mode, bit 1 (for port A) and bit 5 (for port B) determine its level.

Some typical examples are

- The peripheral indicates DATA READY or PERIPHERAL READY with a high-to-low transition on control line 1. No response is necessary.

In the 4 bits controlling a particular port, the only requirement is that bit 0 must be 0 to allow recognition of a high-to-low transition on control line 1. The other bits are arbitrary, although our preference is to clear unused bits as a standard convention. Thus, the bits would be 0000.

- The peripheral indicates DATA READY or PERIPHERAL READY with a low-to-high transition on control line 1. No response is necessary. Bit 0 must be set to 1; the other bits are arbitrary. Bit 0 determines which edge the VIA recogizes.

7	6	5	4	3	2	1	0	← Bit Number
IRQ	T1	T2	CB1	CB2	SR	CA1	CA2	← Interrupt Flag register

Bit Number	Set by	Cleared by
0	Active transition of the signal on the CA2 pin.	Reading or writing the A Port Output register (ORA) using address 0001.
1	Active transition of the signal on the CA1 pin.	Reading or writing the A Port Output register (ORA) using address 0001.
2	Completion of eight shifts.	Reading or writing the Shift register.
3	Active transition of the signal on the CB2 pin.	Reading or writing the B Port Output register.
4	Active transition of the signal on the CB1 pin.	Reading or writing the B Port Output register.
5	Time-out of Timer 2.	Reading T2 low-order counter or writing T2 high-order counter.
6	Time-out of Timer 1.	Reading T1 low-order counter or writing T1 high-order latch.
7	Active and enabled interrupt condition.	Action which clears interrupt condition.
Bits 0, 1, 3, and 4 are the I/O handshake signals. Bit 7 (IRQ) is 1 if any of the interrupts is both active and enabled.		

Figure 1-9: The 6522 VIA's Interrupt Flag Register

· The peripheral indicates DATA READY or PERIPHERAL READY with a high-to-low transition on control line 1. The port must respond by producing a pulse on control line 2 that lasts one clock cycle after the processor reads the input or writes the output.

The required 4-bit sequence is

Bit 3 = 1 to make control line 2 an output
Bit 2 = 0 to operate control line 2 in the automatic mode.

The port therefore produces the response without processor intervention.

Bit 1 = 1 to make the response last one clock cycle.
Bit 0 = 0 to recognize a high-to-low transition on control line 1.

· The peripheral indicates DATA READY or PERIPHERAL READY with a low-to-high transition on control line 1. The port must respond by bringing control line 2 low until the peripheral becomes ready again.

The required 4-bit sequence is

Bit 3 = 1 to make control line 2 an output.
Bit 2 = 0 to operate control line 2 in the automatic mode.
Bit 1 = 0 to make the response last until the peripheral becomes ready again.
Bit 0 = 1 to recognize a low-to-high transition on control line 1 as the ready signal.

· The peripheral indicates DATA READY or PERIPHERAL READY with a low-to-high transition on control line 1. The processor must respond under program control.

The required 4-bit sequence is

Bit 3 = 1 to make control line 2 an output.
Bit 2 = 1 to operate control line 2 in the manual mode.
Bit 1 is the initial state for control line.
Bit 0 = 1 to recognize a low-to-high transition on control line 1 as the ready signal.

The following sequences can be used to produce the response

```
Make CA2 a logic 1:
        LDA     VIAPCR          ;READ THE PERIPHERAL REGISTER
        ORA     #%00000010      ;SET CONTROL LINE 2 TO 1
        STA     VIAPCR
Make CA2 a logic 0:
        LDA     VIAPCR          ;READ THE PERIPHERAL REGISTER
        AND     #%11111101      ;SET CONTROL LINE 2 TO 0
        STA     VIAPCR
Make CB2 a logic 1:
        LDA     VIAPCR          ;READ THE PERIPHERAL REGISTER
        ORA     #%00100000      ;SET CONTROL LINE 2 TO 1
        STA     VIAPCR
Make CB2 a logic 0:
        LDA     VIAPCR          ;READ THE PERIPHERAL REGISTER
        AND     #%11011111      ;SET CONTROL LINE 2 TO 0
        STA     VIAPCR
```

These sequences do not depend on the contents of the peripheral control register, since they do not change any of the bits except the one that controls the response.

Tables 1-13 and 1-14 summarize the operating modes for control lines CA2 and CB2. Note that the automatic output modes differ slightly in that port A produces a response after either read or write operations, whereas port B produces a response only after write operations.

Table 1-13: Operating Modes for Control Line CA2 of a 6522 VIA

PCR3	PCR2	PCR1	Mode
0	0	0	Input Mode — Set CA2 Interrupt flag (IFR0) on a negative transition of the input signal. Clear IFR0 on a read or write of the Peripheral A Output register.
0	0	1	Independent Interrupt Input Mode — Set IFR0 on a negative transition of the CA2 input signal. Reading or writing ORA does not clear the CA2 Interrupt flag.
0	1	0	Input Mode — Set CA2 Interrupt flag on a positive transition of the CA2 input signal. Clear IFR0 with a read or write of the Peripheral A Output register.
0	1	1	Independent Interrupt Input Mode — Set IFR0 on a positive transition of the CA2 input signal. Reading or writing ORA does not clear the CA2 Interrupt flag.
1	0	0	Handshake Output Mode — Set CA2 output low on a read or write of the Peripheral A Output register. Reset CA2 high with an active transition on CA1.
1	0	1	Pulse Output Mode — CA2 goes low for one cycle following a read or write of the Peripheral A Output register.
1	1	0	Manual Output Mode — The CA2 output is held low in this mode.
1	1	1	Manual Output Mode — The CA2 output is held high in this mode.

The auxiliary control register is less important than the peripheral control register. Its bits have the following functions (see Figure 1-8):

· Bits 0 and 1, if set, cause the VIA to latch the input data on port A (bit 0) or port B (bit 1) when an active transition occurs on control line 1. This option allows for the case in which the input peripheral provides valid data only briefly, and the data must be saved until the processor has time to handle it.

· Bits 2, 3, and 4 control the operations of the seldom-used shift register. This register provides a simple serial I/O capability, but most designers prefer either to use the serial I/O chips such as the 6551 or 6850 or to provide the entire serial interface in software.

· Bit 5 determines whether timer 2 generates a single time interval (the so-called one-shot mode) or counts pulses on line PB6 (pulse-counting mode).

· Bit 6 determines whether timer 1 generates one time interval (0) or operates continuously (1), reloading its counters from the latches after each interval elapses.

Table 1-14: Operating Modes for Control Line CB2 of a 6522 VIA

PCR7	PCR6	PCR5	Mode
0	0	0	Interrupt Input Mode — Set CB2 Interrupt flag (IFR3) on a negative transition of the CB2 input signal. Clear IFR3 on a read or write of the Peripheral B Output register.
0	0	1	Independent Interrupt Input Mode — Set IFR3 on a negative transition of the CB2 input signal. Reading or writing ORB does not clear the Interrupt flag.
0	1	0	Input Mode — Set CB2 Interrupt flag on a positive transition of the CB2 input signal. Clear the CB2 Interrupt flag on a read or write of ORB.
0	1	1	Independent Input Mode — Set IFR3 on a positive transition of the CB2 input signal. Reading or writing ORB does not clear the CB2 Interrupt flag.
1	0	0	Handshake Output Mode — Set CB2 low on a write ORB operation. Reset CB2 high on an active transition of the CB1 input signal.
1	0	1	Pulse Output Mode — Set CB2 low for one cycle following a write ORB operation.
1	1	0	Manual Output Mode — The CB2 output is held low in this mode.
1	1	1	Manual Output Mode — The CB2 output is held high in this mode.

• Bit 7 determines whether timer 1 generates output pulses on PB7 (a logic 1 generates pulses).

The uses of most of these functions are straightforward. They are not as common as the handshaking functions governed by the peripheral control register.

You can also operate a 6522 VIA in an interrupt-driven mode. Interrupts are enabled or disabled by setting bits in the interrupt enable register (see Figures 1-10 and 1-11) with bit 7 (the enable/disable flag) set (for enabling) or cleared (for disabling). Interrupts can be recognized by examining the interrupt flag register (see Figure 1-9). Table 1-15 summarizes the setting and clearing (resetting) of interrupt flags on the 6522 VIA.

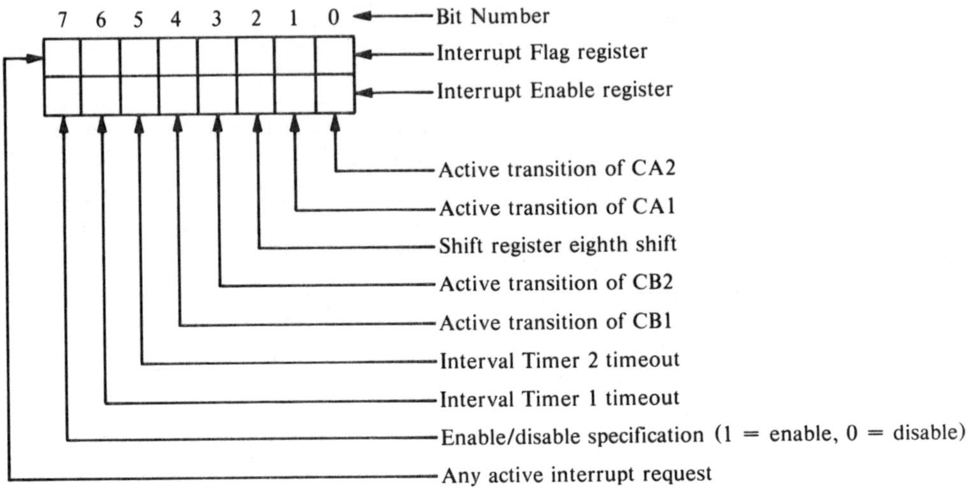

The Interrupt Flag register identifies those interrupts which are active. A 1 in any bit position indicates an active interrupt, whereas a 0 indicates an inactive interrupt.

Figure 1-10: The 6522 VIA's Interrupt Flag and Interrupt Enable Registers

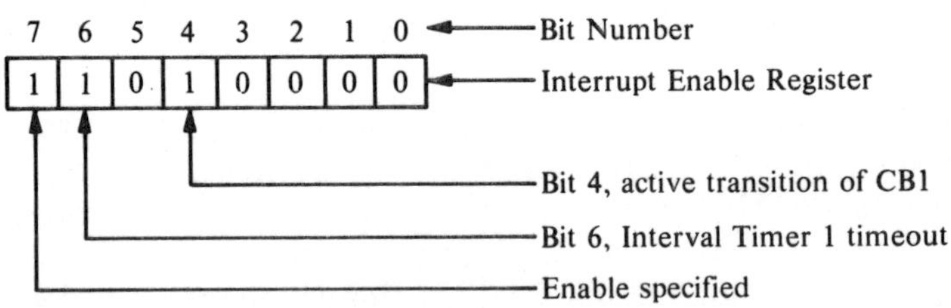

You can selectively enable or disable individual interrupts via the Interrupt Enable register. You enable individual interrupts by writing to the Interrupt Enable register with a 1 in bit 7. Thus you could enable "time out for Timer 1" and "active transitions of signal CB1" by storing $D0_{16}$ in the Interrupt Enable register:

Figure 1-11: A Typical Enabling Operation on the 6522 VIA's Interrupt Enable Register

Table 1-15: A Summary of Conditions for Setting and Resetting Interrupt Flags in the 6522 VIA

	Set by	Cleared by
6	Timeout of Timer 1	Reading Timer 1 Low-Order Counter or writing T1 High-Order Latch
5	Timeout of Timer 2	Reading Timer 2 Low-Order Counter or writing T2 High-Order Counter
4	Active transition of the signal on CB1	Reading from or writing to I/O Port B
3	Active transition of the signal on CB2 (input mode)	Reading from or writing to I/O Port B in input mode only
2	Completion of eight shifts	Reading or writing the Shift register
1	Active transition of the signal on CA1	Reading from or writing to I/O Port A using address 0001_2
0	Active transition of the signal on CA2 (input mode)	Reading from or writing to I/O Port A Output register (ORA) using address 0001_2 in input mode only

WRITING INTERRUPT- DRIVEN CODE

The 6502 microprocessor responds to an interrupt (either a nonmaskable interrupt, a maskable interrupt that is enabled, or a BRK instruction) as follows:

- By saving the program counter (more significant byte first) and the status register in the stack in the order shown in Figure 1-12. Note that the status register ends up on top of the program counter; the sequence PHP, JSR would produce the opposite order. The program counter value here is the address of the next instruction; there is no offset of 1 as there is with JSR.
- By disabling the maskable interrupt by setting the I flag in the status register.
- By fetching a destination address from a specified pair of memory addresses (see Table 1-16) and placing that destination in the program counter.

Thus, the programmer should consider the following guidelines when writing interrupt-driven code for the 6502:

- The accumulator and index registers must be saved and restored explicitly if the service routine changes them. Only the status register is saved automatically.

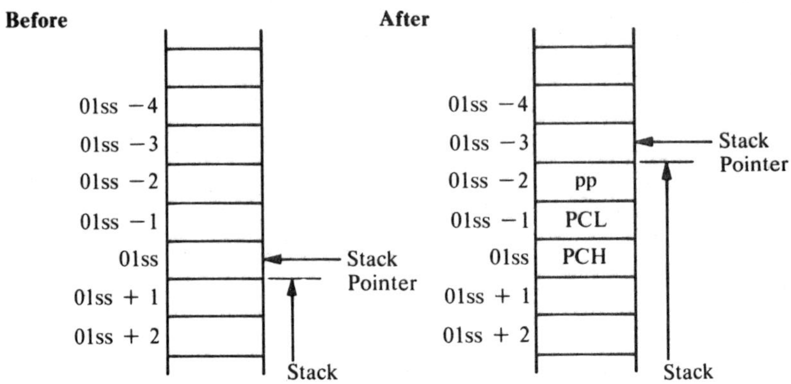

ss = Original contents of Stack Pointer
pp = Original contents of Status (P) register
PCH = Original contents of 8 higher order bits of Program Counter
PCL = Original contents of 8 lower order bits of Program Counter

Figure 1-12: The 6502 Microprocessor's Response to an Interrupt

The service routine must save the accumulator before it saves the index registers, since it can only transfer an index register to the stack via the accumulator. Typical saving and restoring sequences are

```
PHA                     ;SAVE ACCUMULATOR IN STACK
TXA                     ;SAVE INDEX REGISTER X
PHA
TYA                     ;SAVE INDEX REGISTER Y
PHA

PLA                     ;RESTORE INDEX REGISTER Y
TAY
PLA                     ;RESTORE INDEX REGISTER X
TAX
PLA                     ;RESTORE ACCUMULATOR FROM STACK
```

The order of the index registers does not matter, as long as the saving and restoring orders are opposites.

· The interrupt need not be reenabled explicitly, since the RTI (Return from Interrupt) instruction restores the old status register as part of its execution. This restores the original state of the Interrupt Disable flag. If you wish to return with interrupts disabled, you can set the Interrupt Disable flag in the stack with the sequence

```
PLA                     ;GET STATUS REGISTER
ORA     #%00000100      ;DISABLE INTERRUPT IN STACK
PHA                     ;PUT STATUS REGISTER BACK IN STACK
```

Table 1-16: Interrupt Vectors for the 6502 Microprocessor

Source	Address Used (Hexadecimal)
Interrupt Request ($\overline{\text{IRQ}}$) and BRK Instruction	FFFE and FFFF
Reset ($\overline{\text{RESET}}$)	FFFC and FFFD
Nonmaskable Interrupt ($\overline{\text{NMI}}$)	FFFA and FFFB

The addresses are stored in the usual 6502 fashion with the less significant byte at the lower address.

Note the convenience here of having the status register at the top, rather than underneath the return address.

• If you have code that the processor must execute with interrupts disabled, you can use SEI (Set Interrupt Disable) to disable maskable interrupts and CLI (Clear Interrupt Disable) to enable them afterward. If the section of code could be entered with interrupts either disabled or enabled, you must be sure to restore the original state of the Interrupt Disable flag. That is, you must save and restore the status register as follows:

```
PHP                 ;SAVE OLD INTERRUPT DISABLE
SEI                 ;DISABLE INTERRUPTS
.
.   CODE THAT MUST BE EXECUTED WITH INTERRUPTS DISABLED
.
PLP                 ;RESTORE OLD INTERRUPT DISABLE
```

The alternative (automatically reenabling the interrupts at the end) would cause a problem if the section were entered with the interrupts already disabled.

• If you want to allow the user to select the actual starting address of the service routine, place an indirect jump at the vectored address. That is, the routine starting at the vectored address is simply

```
JMP     (USRINT)     ;GO TO USER-SPECIFIED ADDRESS
```

This procedure increases the interrupt response time by the execution time of an indirect jump (five clock cycles).

• You must remember to save and restore incidental information that is essential for the proper execution of the interrupted program. Such incidental information may include memory locations on page 0, priority registers (particularly if they are write-only), and other status.

• To achieve general reentrancy, you must use the stack for all temporary storage beyond that provided by the registers. As we noted in the discussion of parameter passing, you can assign space on the stack (NPARAM bytes) with the sequence

```
TSX                   ;MOVE S OVER TO A
TXA
SEC                   ;ASSIGN NPARAM EMPTY BYTES
SBC     #NPARAM       ;A GENERAL WAY TO ADJUST SP
TAX
TXS
```

Later, you can remove the temporary storage area with the sequence

```
TSX                   ;MOVE S OVER TO A
TXA
CLC
ADC     #NPARAM       ;REMOVE NPARAM EMPTY BYTES
TAX
TXS
```

If NPARAM is only 1 or 2, you can replace these sequences with the appropriate number of push and pull instructions in which the data is ignored.

· The service routine should initialize the Decimal Mode flag with either CLD or SED if it uses ADC or SBC instructions. The old value of that flag is saved and restored automatically as part of the status register, but the service routine should not assume a particular value on entry.

MAKING PROGRAMS RUN FASTER

In general, you can make a program run substantially faster by first determining where it is spending its time. This requires that you determine which loops (other than delay routines) the processor is executing most often. Reducing the execution time of a frequently executed loop will have a major effect because of the multiplying factor. It is thus critical to determine how often instructions are being executed and to work on loops in the order of their frequency of execution.

Once you have determined which loops the processor executes most frequently, you can reduce their execution time with the following techniques:

· Eliminate redundant operations. These may include a constant that is being added during each iteration or a special case that is being tested for repeatedly. It may also include a constant value or a memory address that is being fetched each time rather than being stored in a register or used indirectly.

· Use page 0 for temporary data storage whenever possible.

· Reorganize the loop to reduce the number of jump instructions. You can often eliminate branches by changing the initial conditions, reversing the order of operations, or combining operations. In particular, you may find it helpful to start everything back one step, thus making the first iteration the same as all the others. Reversing the order of operations can be helpful if numerical comparisons are involved, since the equality case may not have to be handled separately. Reorganization may also allow you to combine condition checking inside the loop with the overall loop control.

· Work backward through arrays rather than forward. This allows you to count the index register down to 0 and use the setting of the Zero flag as an exit condition. No explicit comparison is then necessary. Note that you will have to subtract 1 from the base addresses, since 1 is the smallest index that is actually used.

· Increment 16-bit counters and indirect addresses rather than decrementing them. 16-bit numbers are easy to increment, since you can tell if a carry has occurred by checking the less significant byte for 0 afterward. In the case of a decrement, you must check for 0 first.

· Use in-line code rather than subroutines. This will save at least a JSR instruction and an RTS instruction.

· Watch the special uses of the index registers to avoid having to move data between them. The only register that can be used in indirect indexed addressing is register Y; the only register that can be used in indexed indirect addressing or in loading and storing the stack pointer is register X.

· Use the instructions ASL, DEC, INC, LSR, ROL, and ROR to operate directly on data in memory without moving it to a register.

· Use the BIT instruction to test bits 6 or 7 of a memory location without loading the accumulator.

· Use the CPX and CPY instructions to perform comparisons without using the accumulator.

A general way to reduce execution time is to replace long sequences of instructions with tables. A single table lookup can perform the same operation as a sequence of instructions if there are no special exits or program logic involved. The cost is extra memory, but that may be justified if the memory is readily available. If enough memory is available, a lookup table may be a reasonable approach even if many of its entries are repetitive — even if many inputs produce the same output. In addition to its speed, table lookup is easy to program, easy to change, and highly flexible.

MAKING PROGRAMS USE LESS MEMORY[8]

You can make a program use significantly less memory only by identifying common sequences of instructions and replacing those sequences with subroutine calls. The result is a single copy of each sequence. The more instructions you can place in subroutines, the more memory you save. The drawbacks of this approach are that JSR and RTS themselves require memory and take time to execute, and that the subroutines are typically not very general and may be difficult to understand or use. Some sequences of instructions may even be implemented as subroutines in a monitor or in other systems programs that are always resident. Then you can replace those sequences with calls to the systems program as long as the return is handled properly.

Some of the methods that reduce execution time also reduce memory usage. In particular, using page 0, reorganizing loops, working backward through arrays, incrementing 16-bit quantities, operating directly on memory, and using special instructions such as CPX, CPY, and BIT reduce both execution time and memory usage. Of course, using in-line code rather than loops and subroutines reduces execution time but increases memory usage.

Lookup tables generally use extra memory but save execution time. Some ways that you can reduce their memory requirements are by eliminating intermediate values and interpolating the results,[9,10] eliminating redundant values with special tests, and reducing the range of input values. Often you will find that a few prior tests or restrictions will greatly reduce the size of the required table.

REFERENCES

1. Weller, W.J., *Practical Microcomputer Programming: The 6502,* Northern Technology Books, Evanston, Ill., 1980.

2. Fischer, W.P., "Microprocessor Assembly Language Draft Standard," *IEEE Computer,* December 1979, pp. 96-109. Further discussions of the standard appear on pp. 79-80 of *IEEE Computer,* April 1980, and on pp. 8-9 of IEEE Computer, May 1981. See also Duncan, F.G., "Level-Independent Notation for Microcomputer Programs," *IEEE Micro,* May 1981, pp. 47-56.

3. Osborne, A. *An Introduction to Microcomputers: Volume 1 — Basic Concepts,* 2nd ed., Berkeley: Osborne/McGraw-Hill, 1980.

4. Ibid.

5. Shankar, K.S., "Data Structures, Types, and Abstractions," *IEEE Computer,* April 1980, pp. 67-77.

6. Ibid.

7. Osborne, A. and G. Kane, *4 and 8-Bit Microprocessor Handbook,* Berkeley: Osborne/McGraw-Hill, 1981, pp. 9-55 to 9-61 (6850 ACIA), Chapter 10 (6500 processors and associated chips).

8. Schember, K.A. and J.R. Rumsey, "Minimal Storage Sorting and Searching Techniques for RAM Applications," *Computer,* June 1977, pp. 92-100.

9. Seim, T.A., "Numerical Interpolation for Microprocessor-Based Systems," *Computer Design,* February 1978, pp. 111-16.

10. Abramovich, A. and T.R. Crawford, "An Interpolating Algorithm for Control Applications on Microprocessors," Proceedings of the 1978 Conference on Industrial Applications of Microprocessors, Philadelphia, Penn., pp. 195-201 (proceedings available from IEEE or IEEE Computer Society).

Two hobby magazines run many articles on 6502 assembly language programming; they are *Compute* (P.O. Box 5406, Greensboro, NC 27403) and *Micro* (P.O. Box 6502, Chelmsford, MA 01824).

Chapter 2 Implementing Additional Instructions And Addressing Modes

This chapter shows how to implement instructions and addressing modes that are not included in the 6502's instruction set. Of course, no instruction set can ever include all possible combinations. Designers must make choices based on how many operation codes are available, how easily an additional combination could be implemented, and how often it would be used. A description of additional instructions and addressing modes does not imply that the basic instruction set is incomplete or poorly designed.

We concentrate our attention on additional instructions and addressing modes that are

- Obvious parallels to those included in the instruction set
- Described in the draft Microprocessor Assembly Language Standard (IEEE Task P694)
- Discussed in Volume 1 of *An Introduction to Microcomputers*[1]
- Implemented on other microprocessors, especially ones that are closely related or partly compatible.[2, 3]

This chapter should be of particular interest to those who are familiar with the assembly languages of other computers.

INSTRUCTION SET EXTENSIONS

In describing extensions to the instruction set, we follow the organization suggested in the draft standard for IEEE Task P694.[4] We divide instructions into the following groups (listed in the order in which they are discussed): arithmetic, logical, data transfer, branch, skip, subroutine call, subroutine return, and miscellaneous. Within each type of instruction, we discuss operand types in the following order: byte (8-bit), word (16-bit), decimal, bit, nibble or digit, and multiple. In describing addressing modes, we use the following order: direct, indirect, immediate, indexed, register, autopreincrement, autopostincrement, autopredecrement, autopostdecrement, indirect preindexed (also called preindexed or indexed indirect), and indirect postindexed (also called postindexed or indirect indexed).

ARITHMETIC INSTRUCTIONS

In this group, we consider addition, addition with carry, subtraction, subtraction in reverse, subtraction with carry (borrow), increment, decrement, multiplication, division, comparison, two's complement (negate), and extension. Instructions that do not obviously fall into a particular category are repeated for convenience.

Addition Instructions (Without Carry)

1. Add memory location ADDR to accumulator.

```
CLC                     ;CLEAR CARRY
ADC     ADDR            ;(A) = (A) + (ADDR)
```

The same approach works for all addressing modes.

2. Add VALUE to accumulator.

```
CLC                     ;CLEAR CARRY
ADC     #VALUE          ;(A) = (A) + VALUE
```

3. Add Carry to accumulator.

```
ADC     #0              ;(A) = (A) + 0 + CARRY
```

4. Decimal add memory location ADDR to accumulator.

```
SED                     ;ENTER DECIMAL MODE
CLC                     ;CLEAR CARRY
ADC     ADDR            ;(A) = (A) + (ADDR) IN DECIMAL
CLD                     ;LEAVE DECIMAL MODE
```

A more general approach restores the original value of the D flag; that is,

```
PHP                     ;SAVE OLD D FLAG
SED                     ;ENTER DECIMAL MODE
CLC                     ;CLEAR CARRY
ADC     ADDR            ;(A) = (A) + (ADDR) IN DECIMAL
PLP                     ;RESTORE OLD D FLAG
```

Note that restoring the status register destroys the carry from the addition.

5. Decimal add VALUE to accumulator.

```
SED                     ;ENTER DECIMAL MODE
CLC                     ;CLEAR CARRY
ADC     #VALUE          ;(A) = (A) + VALUE IN DECIMAL
CLD                     ;LEAVE DECIMAL MODE
```

6. Decimal add Carry to accumulator.

```
SED                     ;ENTER DECIMAL MODE
ADC     #0              ;(A) = (A) + CARRY IN DECIMAL
CLD                     ;LEAVE DECIMAL MODE
```

7. Add index register to accumulator (using memory location ZPAGE).

```
STX     ZPAGE           ;SAVE INDEX REGISTER ON PAGE ZERO
CLC                     ;CLEAR CARRY
ADC     ZPAGE           ;(A) = (A) + (X)
```

This approach works for index register Y also.

8. Add the contents of memory locations ADDR and ADDR+1 (MSB in ADDR+1) to memory locations SUM and SUM+1 (MSB in SUM+1).

```
CLC                     ;CLEAR CARRY
LDA     SUM
ADC     ADDR            ;ADD LSB'S
STA     SUM
LDA     SUM+1           ;ADD MSB'S WITH CARRY
ADC     ADDR+1
STA     SUM+1
```

9. Add 16-bit number VAL16 (VAL16M more significant byte, VAL16L less significant byte) to memory locations SUM and SUM+1 (MSB in SUM+1).

```
CLC                     ;CLEAR CARRY
LDA     SUM             ;ADD LSB'S WITHOUT CARRY
ADC     #VAL16L
STA     SUM
LDA     SUM+1           ;ADD MSB'S WITH CARRY
ADC     #VAL16
STA     SUM+1
```

Addition Instructions (With Carry)

1. Add Carry to accumulator

```
ADC     #0              ;(A) = (A) + CARRY
```

2. Decimal add VALUE to accumulator with Carry.

```
SED                     ;ENTER DECIMAL MODE
ADC     #VALUE          ;(A) = (A) + VALUE + CARRY IN DECIMAL
CLD                     ;LEAVE DECIMAL MODE
```

3. Decimal add memory location ADDR to accumulator with Carry.

```
SED                     ;ENTER DECIMAL MODE
ADC     ADDR            ;(A) = (A) + (ADDR) + CARRY IN DECIMAL
CLD                     ;LEAVE DECIMAL MODE
```

4. Add the contents of memory locations ADDR and ADDR+1 (MSB in ADDR+1) to memory locations SUM and SUM+1 (MSB in SUM+1) with Carry.

```
LDA     SUM             ;ADD LSB'S WITH CARRY
ADC     ADDR
STA     SUM
LDA     SUM+1           ;ADD MSB'S WITH CARRY
ADC     ADDR+1
STA     SUM+1
```

5. Add 16-bit number VAL16 (VAL16M more significant byte, VAL16L less significant byte) to memory locations SUM and SUM+1 (MSB in SUM+1) with Carry.

```
LDA     SUM             ;ADD LSB'S WITH CARRY
ADC     VAL16L
STA     SUM
LDA     SUM+1           ;ADD MSB'S WITH CARRY
ADC     ADDR+1
STA     SUM+1
```

Subtraction Instructions (Without Borrow)

1. Subtract memory location ADDR from accumulator.

```
SEC                     ;SET INVERTED BORROW
SBC     ADDR            ;(A) = (A) - (ADDR)
```

The Carry flag acts as an inverted borrow, so it must be set to 1 if its value is to have no effect on the subtraction.

2. Subtract VALUE from accumulator.

```
SEC                     ;SET INVERTED BORROW
SBC     #VALUE          ;(A) = (A) - VALUE
```

3. Subtract inverse of borrow from accumulator.

```
SBC     #0              ;(A) = (A) - (1-CARRY)
```

The result is (A) − 1 if Carry is 0 and (A) if Carry is 1.

4. Decimal subtract memory location ADDR from accumulator.

```
SED                 ;ENTER DECIMAL MODE
SEC                 ;SET INVERTED BORROW
SBC     ADDR        ;(A) = (A) - (ADDR) IN DECIMAL
CLD                 ;LEAVE DECIMAL MODE
```

The Carry flag has the same meaning in the decimal mode as in the binary mode.

5. Decimal subtract VALUE from accumulator.

```
SED                 ;ENTER DECIMAL MODE
SEC                 ;SET INVERTED BORROW
SBC     #VALUE      ;(A) = (A) - VALUE IN DECIMAL
CLD                 ;LEAVE DECIMAL MODE
```

6. Subtract the contents of memory locations ADDR and ADDR + 1 (MSB in ADDR + 1) from memory locations DIFF and DIFF + 1 (MSB in DIFF + 1).

```
LDA     DIFF        ;SUBTRACT LSB'S WITH NO BORROW
SEC
SBC     ADDR
STA     DIFF
LDA     DIFF+1      ;SUBTRACT MSB'S WITH BORROW
SBC     ADDR+1
STA     DIFF+1
```

7. Subtract 16-bit number VAL16 (VAL16M more significant byte, VAL16L less significant byte) from memory locations DIFF and DIFF + 1 (MSB in DIFF + 1).

```
LDA     DIFF        ;SUBTRACT LSB'S WITH NO BORROW
SEC
SBC     #VAL16L
STA     DIFF
LDA     DIFF+1      ;SUBTRACT MSB'S WITH BORROW
SBC     #VAL16M
STA     DIFF+1
```

8. Decimal subtract inverse of borrow from accumulator.

```
SED                 ;ENTER DECIMAL MODE
SBC     #0          ;(A) = (A) - (1-CARRY) IN DECIMAL
CLD                 ;LEAVE DECIMAL MODE
```

Subtraction in Reverse Instructions

1. Subtract accumulator from VALUE and place difference in accumulator.

```
EOR     #$FF        ;ONE'S COMPLEMENT A
CLC
ADC     #1          ;TWO'S COMPLEMENT A
CLC
ADC     #VALUE      ;FORM -A + VALUE
```

or

```
STA     TEMP        ;SAVE A TEMPORARILY
LDA     #VALUE      ;FORM VALUE - A
SEC
SBC     TEMP
```

The Carry acts as an inverted borrow in either method; that is, the Carry is set to 1 if no borrow is necessary.

2. Subtract accumulator from the contents of memory location ADDR and place difference in accumulator.

```
EOR     #$FF        ;ONE'S COMPLEMENT A
CLC
ADC     #1          ;TWO'S COMPLEMENT A
CLC
ADC     ADDR        ;FORM -A + (ADDR)

STA     TEMP        ;SAVE A TEMPORARILY
LDA     ADDR        ;FORM (ADDR) - A
SEC
SBC     TEMP
```

3. Decimal subtract accumulator from VALUE and place difference in accumulator.

```
SED                 ;ENTER DECIMAL MODE
STA     TEMP        ;FORM VALUE - A
LDA     #VALUE
SEC
SBC     TEMP
CLD                 ;LEAVE DECIMAL MODE
```

4. Decimal subtract accumulator from the contents of memory location ADDR and place difference in accumulator.

```
SED                 ;ENTER DECIMAL MODE
STA     TEMP        ;FORM (ADDR) - A
LDA     ADDR
SEC
SBC     TEMP
CLD                 ;LEAVE DECIMAL MODE
```

Subtraction with Borrow (Carry) Instructions

1. Subtract inverse of borrow from accumulator.

```
SBC     #0              ;(A) = (A) - (1-CARRY)
```

2. Decimal subtract VALUE from accumulator with borrow.

```
SED                     ;ENTER DECIMAL MODE
SBC     #VALUE          ;(A) = (A) - VALUE - BORROW IN DECIMAL
CLD                     ;LEAVE DECIMAL MODE
```

3. Decimal subtract memory location ADDR from accumulator with borrow.

```
SED                     ;ENTER DECIMAL MODE
SBC     ADDR            ;(A) = (A) - VALUE - BORROW IN DECIMAL
CLD                     ;LEAVE DECIMAL MODE
```

4. Subtract the contents of memory locations ADDR and ADDR+1 (MSB in ADDR+1) from memory locations DIFF and DIFF+1 (MSB in DIFF+1) with borrow.

```
LDA     DIFF            ;SUBTRACT LSB'S WITH BORROW
SBC     ADDR
STA     DIFF
LDA     DIFF+1          ;SUBTRACT MSB'S WITH BORROW
SBC     ADDR+1
STA     DIFF+1
```

5. Subtract 16-bit number VAL16 (VAL16M more significant byte, VAL16L less significant byte) from memory locations DIFF and DIFF+1 (MSB in DIFF+1) with borrow.

```
LDA     DIFF            ;SUBTRACT LSB'S WITH BORROW
SBC     VAL16L
STA     DIFF
LDA     DIFF+1          ;SUBTRACT MSB'S WITH BORROW
SBC     VAL16M
STA     DIFF+1
```

Increment Instructions

1. Increment accumulator, setting the Carry flag if the result is zero.

```
CLC                     ;CLEAR CARRY
ADC     #1              ;INCREMENT BY ADDING 1
```

or

```
SEC                     ;SET CARRY
ADC     #0              ;INCREMENT BY ADDING 1
```

2. Increment accumulator without affecting the Carry flag.

```
        TAX                         ;MOVE A TO X
        INX                         ;INCREMENT X
        TXA
```

INX does not affect the Carry flag; it does, however, affect the Zero flag.

3. Increment stack pointer.

```
        TSX                         ;MOVE S TO X
        INX                         ;THEN INCREMENT X AND RETURN VALUE
        TXS
```

or

```
        TAX                         ;SAVE A
        PLA                         ;INCREMENT STACK POINTER
        TXA                         ;RESTORE A
```

Remember that PLA affects the Zero and Negative flags.

4. Decimal increment accumulator (add 1 to A in decimal).

```
        SED                         ;ENTER DECIMAL MODE
        CLC
        ADC     #1                  ;(A) = (A) + 1 DECIMAL
        CLD                         ;LEAVE DECIMAL MODE
```

Remember that INC and DEC produce binary results even when the D flag is set.

5. Increment contents of memory locations ADDR and ADDR+1 (MSB in ADDR+1).

```
        INC     ADDR                ;INCREMENT LSB
        BNE     DONE
        INC     ADDR+1              ;CARRY TO MSB IF LSB GOES TO ZERO
DONE    NOP
```

or

```
        LDA     ADDR                ;INCREMENT LSB
        CLC
        ADC     #1
        STA     ADDR
        LDA     ADDR+1              ;WITH CARRY TO MSB
        ADC     #0
        STA     ADDR+1
```

The first alternative is clearly much shorter.

6. Decimal increment contents of memory locations ADDR and ADDR+1 (MSB in ADDR+1).

```
        SED                         ;ENTER DECIMAL MODE
        LDA     ADDR                ;ADD 1 TO LSB
        CLC
        ADC     #1
```

```
        STA     ADDR
        BCC     DONE
        LDA     ADDR+1          ;CARRY TO MSB IF NECESSARY
        ADC     #0
        STA     ADDR+1
DONE    CLD                     ;LEAVE DECIMAL MODE
```

INC produces a binary result even when the Decimal Mode flag is set. Note that we could eliminate the BCC instruction from the program without affecting the result, but the change would increase the average execution time.

Decrement Instructions

1. Decrement accumulator, clearing the Carry flag if the result is FF_{16}.

```
        SEC                     ;SET INVERTED BORROW
        SBC     #1              ;DECREMENT BY SUBTRACTING 1
```

or

```
        CLC                     ;CLEAR INVERTED BORROW
        SBC     #0              ;DECREMENT BY SUBTRACTING 1
```

or

```
        CLC                     ;CLEAR CARRY
        ADC     #$FF            ;DECREMENT BY ADDING -1
```

2. Decrement accumulator without affecting the Carry flag.

```
        TAX                     ;MOVE A TO X
        DEX                     ;DECREMENT X
        TXA
```

DEX does not affect the Carry flag; it does, however, affect the Zero flag.

3. Decrement stack pointer.

```
        TSX                     ;MOVE S TO X
        DEX                     ;THEN DECREMENT X AND RETURN VALUE
        TXS
```

You can also decrement the stack pointer with PHA or PHP, neither of which affects any flags.

4. Decimal decrement accumulator (subtract 1 from A in decimal).

```
        SED                     ;ENTER DECIMAL MODE
        SEC
        SBC     #1              ;(A) = (A) - 1 DECIMAL
        CLD                     ;LEAVE DECIMAL MODE
```

5. Decrement contents of memory locations ADDR and ADDR+1 (MSB in ADDR+1).

```
        LDA    ADDR          ;IS LSB ZERO?
        BNE    DECLSB
        DEC    ADDR+1        ;YES, BORROW FROM MSB
DECLSB  DEC    ADDR          ;BEFORE DECREMENTING LSB
```

Decrementing a 16-bit number is significantly more difficult than incrementing one. In fact, incrementing is not only faster but also leaves the accumulator unchanged; of course, one could replace LDA with LDX, LDY, or the sequence INC, DEC. An alternative that uses no registers is

```
        INC    ADDR          ;IS LSB ZERO?
        DEC    ADDR
        BNE    DECLSB
        DEC    ADDR+1        ;YES, BORROW FROM MSB
DECLSB  DEC    ADDR          ;BEFORE DECREMENTING LSB
```

6. Decimal decrement contents of memory locations ADDR and ADDR+1 (MSB in ADDR+1).

```
        SED                  ;ENTER DECIMAL MODE
        LDA    ADDR          ;SUBTRACT 1 FROM LSB
        SEC
        SBC    #1
        STA    ADDR
        BCS    DONE
        LDA    ADDR+1        ;BORROW FROM MSB IF NECESSARY
        SBC    #0
        STA    ADDR+1
DONE    CLD                  ;LEAVE DECIMAL MODE
```

DEC produces a binary result even when the Decimal Mode flag is set. Note that we could eliminate the BCS instruction from the program without affecting the result, but the change would increase the average execution time.

Multiplication Instructions

1. Multiply accumulator by 2.

```
        ASL    A             ;MULTIPLY BY SHIFTING LEFT
```

The following version places the Carry (if any) in Y.

```
        LDY    #0            ;ASSUME MSB = 0
        ASL    A             ;MULTIPLY BY SHIFTING LEFT
        BCC    DONE
        INY                  ;AND MOVING CARRY TO Y
DONE    NOP
```

2. Multiply accumulator by 3 (using ADDR for temporary storage).

```
STA     ADDR            ;SAVE A
ASL     A               ;2 X A
ADC     ADDR            ;3 X A
```

3. Multiply accumulator by 4.

```
ASL     A               ;2 X A
ASL     A               ;4 X A
```

We can easily extend cases 1, 2, and 3 to multiplication by other small integers.

4. Multiply an index register by 2.

```
TAX                     ;MOVE TO A
ASL     A               ;MULTIPLY BY SHIFTING LEFT
TXA                     ;RETURN RESULT
```

5. Multiply the contents of memory locations ADDR and ADDR+1 (MSB in ADDR+1) by 2.

```
ASL     ADDR            ;MULTIPLY BY SHIFTING LEFT
ROL     ADDR+1          ;AND MOVING CARRY OVER TO MSB
```

6. Multiply the contents of memory locations ADDR and ADDR+1 (MSB in ADDR+1) by 4.

```
ASL     ADDR            ;MULTIPLY BY SHIFTING LEFT
ROL     ADDR+1          ;AND MOVING CARRY OVER TO MSB
ASL     ADDR            ;THEN MULTIPLY AGAIN
ROL     ADDR+1
```

Eventually, of course, moving one byte to the accumulator, shifting the accumulator, and storing the result back in memory becomes faster than leaving both bytes in memory.

Division Instructions

1. Divide accumulator by 2 unsigned.

```
LSR     A               ;DIVIDE BY SHIFTING RIGHT
```

2. Divide accumulator by 4 unsigned.

```
LSR     A               ;DIVIDE BY SHIFTING RIGHT
LSR     A
```

3. Divide accumulator by 2 signed.

```
TAX                     ;SAVE ACCUMULATOR
ASL     A               ;MOVE SIGN TO CARRY
TXA                     ;RESTORE ACCUMULATOR
ROR     A               ;SHIFT RIGHT BUT PRESERVE SIGN
```

The second instruction moves the original sign bit (bit 7) to the Carry flag, so the final rotate can preserve it. This is known as an *arithmetic shift,* since it preserves the sign of the number while reducing its magnitude. The fact that the sign bit is copied to the right is known as *sign extension.*

4. Divide the contents of memory locations ADDR and ADDR+1 (MSB in ADDR+1) by 2 unsigned.

```
        LSR    ADDR+1        ;DIVIDE BY SHIFTING RIGHT
        ROR    ADDR          ;AND MOVING CARRY OVER TO LSB
```

5. Divide the contents of memory locations ADDR and ADDR+1 (MSB in ADDR+1) by 2 signed.

```
        LDA    ADDR+1        ;MOVE SIGN TO CARRY
        ASL    A
        ROR    ADDR+1        ;DIVIDE BY SHIFTING RIGHT WITH SIGN
        ROR    ADDR          ;AND MOVING CARRY OVER TO LSB
```

Comparison Instructions

1. Compare VALUE with accumulator bit by bit, setting each bit position that is different.

```
        EOR    #VALUE
```

Remember, the EXCLUSIVE OR of two bits is 1, if and only if the two bits are different.

2. Compare memory locations ADR1 and ADR1+1 (MSB in ADR1+1) with memory locations ADR2 and ADR2+1 (MSB in ADR2+1). Set Carry if the first operand is greater than or equal to the second one (that is, if ADR1 and ADR1+1 contain a 16-bit unsigned number greater than or equal to the contents of ADR2 and ADR2+1). Clear Carry otherwise. Set the Zero flag if the two operands are equal and clear it otherwise.

```
        LDA    ADR1+1        ;COMPARE MSB'S
        CMP    ADR2+1
        BCC    DONE          ;CLEAR CARRY, ZERO IF 2ND IS LARGER
        BNE    DONE          ;SET CARRY, CLEAR ZERO IF 1ST LARGER
        LDA    ADR1          ;IF MSB'S EQUAL, COMPARE LSB'S
        CMP    ADR2          ;CLEAR CARRY IF 2ND IS LARGER
DONE    NOP
```

3. Compare memory locations ADR1 and ADR1+1 (MSB in ADR1+1) with the 16-bit number VAL16 (VAL16M more significant byte, VAL16L less significant byte). Set Carry if the contents of ADR1 and ADR1+1 are greater than or

equal to VAL16 in the unsigned sense. Clear Carry otherwise. Set the Zero flag if the contents of ADR1 and ADR1+1 are equal to VAL16, and clear it otherwise.

```
        LDA     ADR1+1          ;COMPARE MSB'S
        CMP     #VAL16M
        BCC     DONE            ;CLEAR CARRY, ZERO IF VAL16 LARGER
        BNE     DONE            ;SET CARRY, CLEAR ZERO IF DATA LARGER
        LDA     ADR1            ;IF MSB'S EQUAL, COMPARE LSB'S
        CMP     #VAL16L         ;CLEAR CARRY IF VAL16 LARGER
DONE    NOP
```

4. Compare memory locations ADR1 and ADR1+1 (MSB in ADR1+1) with memory locations ADR2 and ADR2+1 (MSB in ADR2+1). Set Carry if the first operand is greater than or equal to the second one in the unsigned sense.

```
        LDA     ADR1            ;COMPARE LSB'S
        CMP     ADR2
        LDA     ADR1+1          ;SUBTRACT MSB'S WITH BORROW
        SBC     ADR2+1
```

We use SBC on the more significant bytes in order to include the borrow from the less significant bytes. This sequence destroys the value in A and sets the Zero flag only from the final subtraction.

5. Compare memory locations ADR1 and ADR1+1 (MSB in ADR1+1) with the 16-bit number VAL16 (VAL16M more significant byte, VAL16L less significant byte). Set Carry if the contents of ADR1 and ADR1+1 are greater than or equal to VAL16 in the unsigned sense.

```
        LDA     ADR1            ;COMPARE LSB'S
        CMP     VAL16L
        LDA     ADR1+1          ;SUBTRACT MSB'S WITH BORROW
        SBC     VAL16M
```

If you want to set the Carry if the contents of ADR1 and ADR1+1 are greater than VAL16, perform the comparison with VAL16+1.

6. Compare stack pointer with the contents of memory location ADDR. Set Carry if the stack pointer is greater than or equal to the contents of the memory location in the unsigned sense. Clear Carry otherwise. Set the Zero flag if the two values are equal and clear it otherwise.

```
        TSX                     ;MOVE STACK POINTER TO X
        CPX     ADDR            ;AND THEN COMPARE
```

7. Compare stack pointer with the 8-bit number VALUE. Set Carry if the stack pointer is greater than or equal to VALUE in the unsigned sense. Clear Carry otherwise. Set the Zero flag if the two values are equal and clear it otherwise.

```
        TSX                     ;MOVE STACK POINTER TO X
        CPX     #VALUE          ;AND THEN COMPARE
```

8. Block comparison. Compare accumulator with memory bytes starting at address BASE and continuing until either a match is found (indicated by Carry=1) or until a byte counter in memory location COUNT reaches zero (indicated by Carry=0).

```
        LDY   COUNT     ;GET COUNT
        BEQ   NOTFND    ;EXIT IF COUNT IS ZERO
        LDX   #0        ;START INDEX AT ZERO
CMPBYT  CMP   BASE,X    ;CHECK CURRENT BYTE
        BEQ   DONE      ;DONE IF MATCH FOUND (CARRY = 1)
        INX             ;OTHERWISE, PROCEED TO NEXT BYTE
        DEY
        BNE   CMPBYT    ;IF ANY ARE LEFT
NOTFND  CLC             ;OTHERWISE, EXIT CLEARING CARRY
DONE    NOP
```

Remember, comparing two equal numbers sets the Carry flag.

Two's Complement (Negate) Instructions

1. Negate accumulator.

```
        EOR   #$FF      ;ONE'S COMPLEMENT
        CLC
        ADC   #1        ;TWO'S COMPLEMENT
```

The two's complement is the one's complement plus 1.

```
        STA   TEMP      ;ALTERNATIVE IS 0 - (A)
        LDA   #0
        SEC
        SBC   TEMP
```

2. Negate memory location ADDR.

```
        LDA   #0        ;FORM 0 - (ADDR)
        SEC
        SBC   ADDR
        STA   ADDR
```

3. Negate memory locations ADDR and ADDR+1 (MSB in ADDR+1).

```
        LDA   ADDR      ;ONE'S COMPLEMENT LSB
        EOR   #$FF
        CLC             ;ADD 1 FOR TWO'S COMPLEMENT
        ADC   #1
        STA   ADDR
        LDA   ADDR+1    ;ONE'S COMPLEMENT MSB
        EOR   #$FF
        ADC   #0        ;ADD CARRY FOR TWO'S COMPLEMENT
        STA   ADDR+1
```

or

```
LDA     #0          ;FORM 0 - (ADDR+1) (ADDR)
SEC
SBC     ADDR        ;SUBTRACT LSB'S WITHOUT BORROW
STA     ADDR
LDA     #0          ;SUBTRACT MSB'S WITH BORROW
SBC     ADDR+1
STA     ADDR+1
```

4. Nine's complement accumulator (that is, replace A with 99−A).

```
STA     TEMP        ;FORM 99-A
LDA     #$99
SEC
SBC     TEMP
```

There is no need to bother with the decimal mode, since 99−A is always a valid BCD number if A originally contained a valid BCD number.

5. Ten's complement accumulator (that is, replace A with 100−A).

```
SED                 ;ENTER DECIMAL MODE
STA     TEMP        ;FORM 100-A
LDA     #0
SEC
SBC     TEMP
CLD                 ;LEAVE DECIMAL MODE
```

Extend Instructions

1. Extend accumulator to a 16-bit unsigned number in memory locations ADDR and ADDR+1 (MSB in ADDR+1).

```
STA     ADDR        ;8-BIT MOVE
LDA     #0          ;EXTEND TO 16 BITS WITH 0'S
STA     ADDR+1
```

2. Extend accumulator to a 16-bit signed number in memory locations ADDR and ADDR+1 (MSB in ADDR+1).

```
STA     ADDR        ;8-BIT MOVE
ASL     A           ;MOVE SIGN BIT TO CARRY
LDA     #$FF        ;(A) = -1 + SIGN BIT
ADC     #0
EOR     #$FF        ;(A) = -SIGN BIT
STA     ADDR+1      ;SET MSB TO -SIGN BIT
```

The result of the calculation is −(−1+SIGN BIT)−1=−SIGN BIT. That is, (ADDR+1) = 00 if A was positive and FF_{16} if A was negative. An alternative is

```
        STA    ADDR        ;8-BIT MOVE
        LDX    #$FF        ;(X) = -1
        ASL    A
        BCS    STRSGN
        INX                ;(X) = -1+(1 - SIGN BIT) = -SIGN BIT
STRSGN  STX    ADDR+1      ;SET MSB TO -SIGN BIT
```

3. Extend bit 0 of accumulator across entire accumulator; that is, (A) = 00 if bit 0 = 0 and FF_{16} if bit 0 = 1.

```
        LSR    A           ;CARRY = BIT 0
        LDA    #$FF        ;(A) = -1 + BIT 0
        ADC    #0
        EOR    #$FF        ;(A) = -BIT 0
```

As in case 2, the result we want is −1 if the specified bit is 1 and 0 if the specified bit is 0. That is, we want the negative of the original bit value. The sequence LDA #$FF, ADC #0 obviously produces the result −1+Carry. The one's complement then gives us the negative of what we had minus 1 (or 1−Carry−1 = −Carry).

4. Sign function. Replace the value in the accumulator by 00 if it is positive and by FF_{16} if it is negative.

```
        ASL    A           ;MOVE SIGN BIT TO CARRY
        LDA    #$FF        ;(A) = -1 + SIGN BIT
        ADC    #0
        EOR    #$FF        ;(A) = -SIGN BIT
```

5. Sign function of a memory location. Set accumulator to 00 if memory location ADDR is positive and to FF_{16} if it is negative.

```
        LDX    #$FF        ;ASSUME NEGATIVE
        LDA    ADDR        ;IS (ADDR) POSITIVE?
        BMI    DONE
        INX                ;YES, SET SIGN TO ZERO
DONE    TXA
```

The approach shown in case 4 can also be used.

LOGICAL INSTRUCTIONS

In this group, we consider logical AND, logical OR, logical EXCLUSIVE OR, logical NOT (complement), shift, rotate, and test instructions.

Logical AND Instructions

1. Clear bit of accumulator.

```
AND     #MASK          ;CLEAR BIT BY MASKING
```

MASK has 0 bits in the positions to be cleared and 1 bits in the positions that are to be left unchanged. For example,

```
AND     #%11011011     ;CLEAR BITS 2 AND 5
```

Remember, logically ANDing a bit with 1 leaves it unchanged.

2. Bit test-set the flags according to the value of a bit of memory location ADDR.

Bits 0 through 5

```
LDA     #MASK
BIT     ADDR           ;TEST BIT OF ADDR
```

MASK should have a 1 in the position to be tested and 0s everywhere else. The Zero flag will be set to 1 if the bit tested is 0 and to 0 if the bit tested is 1.

Bits 6 or 7

```
BIT     ADDR           ;TEST BITS 6 AND 7 OF ADDR
```

This single instruction sets the Negative flag to bit 7 of ADDR and the Overflow flag to bit 6 of ADDR, regardless of the value in the accumulator. Note that the flags are not inverted as the Zero flag is in normal masking.

3. Logical AND immediate with condition codes (flags). Logically AND a byte of immediate data with the contents of the status register, clearing those flags that are logically ANDed with 0s. This instruction is implemented on the 6809 microprocessor.

```
PHP                    ;MOVE STATUS TO A
PLA
AND     #MASK          ;CLEAR FLAGS
PHA                    ;RETURN RESULT TO STATUS
PLP
```

Logical OR Instructions

1. Set bit of accumulator.

```
ORA     #MASK          ;SET BIT BY MASKING
```

MASK has 1 bits in the positions to be set and 0 bits in the positions that are to be left unchanged. For example,

```
ORA     #%00010010     ;SET BITS 1 AND 4
```

Remember, logically ORing a bit with 0 leaves it unchanged.

2. Test memory locations ADDR and ADDR+1 for 0. Set the Zero flag if both bytes are 0.

```
LDA     ADDR          ;TEST 16-BIT NUMBER FOR ZERO
ORA     ADDR+1
```

The Zero flag is set if and only if both bytes of the 16-bit number are 0. The other flags are also changed.

3. Logical OR immediate with condition codes (flags). Logically OR a byte of immediate data (MASK) with the contents of the status register, setting those flags that are logically ORed with 1s. This instruction is implemented on the 6809 microprocessor.

```
PHP                   ;MOVE STATUS TO A
PLA
ORA     #MASK         ;SET FLAGS
PHA                   ;RETURN RESULT TO STATUS
PLP
```

Logical EXCLUSIVE OR Instructions

1. Complement bit of accumulator.

```
EOR     #MASK         ;COMPLEMENT BIT BY MASKING
```

MASK has 1 bits in the positions to be complemented and 0 bits in the positions that are to be left unchanged. For example,

```
EOR     #%11000000    ;COMPLEMENT BITS 6 AND 7
```

Remember, logically EXCLUSIVE ORing a bit with 0 leaves it unchanged.

2. Complement accumulator, setting flags.

```
EOR     #%11111111    ;COMPLEMENT ACCUMULATOR
```

Logically EXCLUSIVE ORing the accumulator with all 1s inverts all the bits.

3. Compare memory location ADDR with accumulator bit by bit, setting each bit position that is different.

```
EOR     ADDR          ;BIT-BY-BIT COMPARISON
```

The EXCLUSIVE OR function is the same as a "not equal" function. Note that the Negative (Sign) flag is 1 if the two operands have different values in bit position 7.

4. Add memory location ADDR to accumulator logically (i.e., without any carries between bit positions).

```
EOR     ADDR            ;LOGICAL ADDITION
```

The EXCLUSIVE OR function is also the same as a bit by bit sum with no carries. Logical sums are often used to form checksums and error-detecting or error-correcting codes.

Logical NOT instructions

1. Complement accumulator, setting flags.

```
EOR     #$FF            ;COMPLEMENT ACCUMULATOR
```

Logically EXCLUSIVE ORing with all 1s inverts all the bits.

2. Complement bit of accumulator.

```
EOR     #MASK           ;COMPLEMENT BIT BY MASKING
```

MASK has 1 bits in the positions to be complemented and 0 bits in the positions that are to be left unchanged. For example,

```
EOR     #%01010001      ;COMPLEMENT BITS 0, 4, AND 6
```

Remember, logically EXCLUSIVE ORing a bit with 0 leaves it unchanged.

3. Complement a memory location.

```
LDA     ADDR
EOR     #$FF            ;COMPLEMENT
STA     ADDR
```

4. Complement bit 0 of a memory location.

```
INC     ADDR            ;COMPLEMENT BY INCREMENTING
```

or

```
DEC     ADDR            ;COMPLEMENT BY DECREMENTING
```

Either of these instructions may, of course, affect the other bits in the memory location. The final value of bit 0, however, will surely be 0 if it was originally 1 and 1 if it was originally 0.

5. Complement digit of accumulator.

- Less significant digit

```
EOR     #%00001111      ;COMPLEMENT LESS SIGNIFICANT 4 BITS
```

- More significant digit

```
EOR     #%11110000      ;COMPLEMENT MORE SIGNIFICANT 4 BITS
```

These procedures are useful if the accumulator contains a decimal digit in negative logic (e.g., the input from a typical ten-position rotary or thumbwheel switch).

6. Complement Carry flag.

```
        ROR    A              ;MOVE CARRY TO BIT 7 OF A
        EOR    #$FF           ;COMPLEMENT ALL OF A
        ROL    A              ;MOVE COMPLEMENTED CARRY BACK
```

Other combinations such as ROL, EOR, ROR, or ROR, EOR, ASL will work just as well. We could leave the accumulator intact by saving it in the stack originally and restoring it afterward.

An alternative that does not affect the accumulator is

```
        BCC    SETCAR
        CLC                   ;CLEAR CARRY IF IT WAS SET
        BCC    DONE
SETCAR  SEC                   ;SET CARRY IF IT WAS CLEARED
DONE    NOP
```

Shift Instructions

1. Shift accumulator right arithmetically, preserving the sign bit.

```
        TAX                   ;SAVE ACCUMULATOR
        ASL    A              ;MOVE SIGN BIT TO CARRY
        TXA
        ROR    A              ;SHIFT RIGHT, PRESERVING SIGN
```

We need a copy of the sign bit for an arithmetic shift. Of course, we could use a memory location for temporary storage instead of the index register.

2. Shift memory locations ADDR and ADDR+1 (MSB in ADDR+1) left logically.

```
        ASL    ADDR           ;SHIFT LSB LEFT LOGICALLY
        ROL    ADDR+1         ;AND MOVE CARRY OVER TO MSB
```

The key point here is that we must shift the more significant byte circularly (i.e., rotate it). The first 8-bit shift moves one bit (the least significant bit for a right shift and the most significant bit for a left shift) to the Carry. The 8-bit rotate then moves that bit from the Carry into the other half of the word.

3. Shift memory locations ADDR and ADDR+1 (MSB in ADDR+1) right logically.

```
        LSR    ADDR+1         ;SHIFT MSB RIGHT LOGICALLY
        ROR    ADDR           ;AND MOVE CARRY OVER TO LSB
```

4. Shift memory locations ADDR and ADDR+1 (MSB in ADDR+1) right arithmetically.

```
        LDA    ADDR+1        ;MOVE SIGN BIT TO CARRY
        ASL    A
        ROR    ADDR+1        ;SHIFT MSB RIGHT ARITHMETICALLY
        ROR    ADDR          ;AND MOVE CARRY OVER TO LSB
```

5. Digit shift memory locations ADDR and ADDR+1 (MSB in ADDR+1) left; that is, shift the 16-bit number left 4 bits logically.

```
        LDX    #4            ;NUMBER OF SHIFTS = 4
        LDA    ADDR          ;MOVE LSB TO A
SHFT1   ASL    A             ;SHIFT LSB LEFT LOGICALLY
        ROL    ADDR+1        ;AND MOVE CARRY OVER TO MSB
        DEX
        BNE    SHFT1         ;COUNT BITS
        STA    ADDR          ;RETURN LSB TO ADDR
```

A shorter but slower version that does not use the accumulator is

```
        LDX    #4            ;NUMBER OF SHIFTS = 4
SHFT1   ASL    ADDR          ;SHIFT LSB LEFT LOGICALLY
        ROL    ADDR+1        ;AND MOVE CARRY OVER TO MSB
        DEX
        BNE    SHFT1         ;COUNT SHIFTS
```

6. Digit shift memory locations ADDR and ADDR+1 (MSB in ADDR+1) right; that is, shift the 16-bit number right 4 bits logically.

```
        LDX    #4            ;NUMBER OF SHIFTS = 4
        LDA    ADDR          ;MOVE LSB TO A
SHFT1   LSR    ADDR+1        ;SHIFT MSB RIGHT LOGICALLY
        ROR    A             ;AND MOVE CARRY OVER TO LSB
        DEX
        BNE    SHFT1         ;COUNT SHIFTS
        STA    ADDR          ;RETURN LSB TO ADDR
```

A shorter but slower version that does not use the accumulator is

```
        LDX    #4            ;NUMBER OF SHIFTS = 4
SHFT1   LSR    ADDR+1        ;SHIFT MSB RIGHT LOGICALLY
        ROR    ADDR          ;AND MOVE CARRY OVER TO LSB
        DEX
        BNE    SHFT1         ;COUNT SHIFTS
```

7. Normalize memory locations ADDR and ADDR+1 (MSB in ADDR+1); that is, shift the 16-bit number left until the most significant bit is 1. Do not shift at all if the entire number is 0.

```
        LDA    ADDR+1        ;EXIT IF NUMBER ALREADY NORMALIZED
        BMI    DONE
        ORA    ADDR          ;OR IF ENTIRE NUMBER IS ZERO
        BEQ    DONE
        LDA    ADDR          ;MOVE LSB TO A
```

```
SHIFT    ASL    A           ;SHIFT LSB LEFT LOGICALLY 1 BIT
         ROL    ADDR+1      ;AND MOVE CARRY OVER TO MSB
         BPL    SHIFT       ;CONTINUE UNTIL MSB IS 1
         STA    ADDR        ;RETURN LSB TO ADDR
DONE     NOP
```

Rotate Instructions

A rotate through or with Carry acts as if the data were arranged in a circle with its least significant bit connected to its most significant bit through the Carry flag. A rotate without Carry differs in that it acts as if the least significant bit of the data were connected directly to the most significant bit.

1. Rotate memory locations ADDR and ADDR+1 (MSB in ADDR+1) right 1 bit position through Carry.

```
         ROR    ADDR+1      ;ROTATE BIT 8 TO CARRY
         ROR    ADDR        ;AND ON IN TO BIT 7
```

2. Rotate memory locations ADDR and ADDR+1 (MSB in ADDR+1) right 1 bit position without Carry.

```
         LDA    ADDR        ;CAPTURE BIT 0 IN CARRY
         ROR    A
         ROR    ADDR+1      ;ROTATE MSB WITH BIT 0 ENTERING AT LEFT
         ROR    ADDR        ;ROTATE LSB
```

3. Rotate memory locations ADDR and ADDR+1 (MSB in ADDR+1) left 1 bit position through Carry.

```
         ROL    ADDR        ;ROTATE BIT 7 TO CARRY
         ROL    ADDR+1      ;AND ON IN TO BIT 8
```

4. Rotate memory locations ADDR and ADDR+1 (MSB in ADDR+1) left 1 bit position without Carry.

```
         LDA    ADDR+1      ;CAPTURE BIT 15 IN CARRY
         ROL    A
         ROL    ADDR        ;ROTATE LSB WITH BIT 15 ENTERING AT RIGHT
         ROL    ADDR+1
```

Test Instructions

1. **Test accumulator**. Set flags according to the value in the accumulator without changing that value.

```
         TAX                ;MOVE AND SET FLAGS
```

or

```
         TAY                ;MOVE AND SET FLAGS
```

The following alternative does not affect either index register.

```
CMP     #0              ;TEST ACCUMULATOR
```

The instructions AND #$FF or ORA #0 would also do the job without affecting the Carry (CMP #0 sets the Carry flag).

2. **Test index register**. Set flags according to the value in an index register without changing that value.

```
CPX     #0              ;CHECK VALUE IN INDEX REGISTER
```

3. **Test memory location**. Set flags according to the value in memory location ADDR without changing that value.

```
INC     ADDR            ;CHECK VALUE IN MEMORY LOCATION
DEC     ADDR
```

4. **Test a pair of memory locations**. Set the Zero flag according to the value in memory locations ADDR and ADDR+1.

```
LDA     ADDR            ;TEST 16-BIT NUMBER FOR ZERO
ORA     ADDR+1
```

This sequence sets the Zero flag to 1 if and only if both bytes of the 16-bit number are 0. This procedure can readily be extended to handle numbers of any length.

5. **Test bit of accumulator**.

```
AND     #MASK           ;TEST BIT BY MASKING
```

MASK has a 1 bit in the position to be tested and 0 bits elsewhere. The instruction sets the Zero flag to 1 if the tested bit position contains 0 and to 0 if the tested bit position contains 1. For example,

```
AND     #%00001000      ;TEST BIT 3 BY MASKING
```

The result is 0 if bit 3 of A is 0 and 00001000 (binary) if bit 3 of A is 1. So the Zero flag ends up containing the logical complement of bit 3.

6. **Compare memory location ADDR with accumulator bit by bit.** Set each each bit position that is different.

```
EOR     ADDR            ;BIT-BY-BIT COMPARISON
```

The EXCLUSIVE OR function is the same as a "not equal" function.

DATA TRANSFER INSTRUCTIONS

In this group, we consider load, store, move, exchange, clear, and set instructions.

Load Instructions

1. Load accumulator indirect from address in memory locations PGZRO and PGZRO+1.

```
LDY     #0           ;AVOID INDEXING
LDA     (PGZRO),Y    ;LOAD INDIRECT INDEXED
```

The only instruction that has true indirect addressing is JMP. However, you can produce ordinary indirect addressing by using the postindexed (indirect indexed) addressing mode with index register Y set to 0.

An alternative approach is to clear index register X and use preindexing.

```
LDX     #0           ;AVOID INDEXING
LDA     (PGZRO,X)    ;LOAD INDEXED INDIRECT
```

The advantage of the first approach is that one can index from the indirect address with Y. For example, we could load addresses POINTL and POINTH indirectly from the address in memory locations PGZRO and PGZRO+1 as follows:

```
LDY     #0           ;AVOID INDEXING
LDA     (PGZRO),Y    ;GET LSB OF ADDRESS INDIRECTLY
STA     POINTL
INY                  ;GET MSB OF ADDRESS INDIRECTLY
LDA     (PGZRO),Y
STA     POINTH
```

2. Load index register X indirect from address in memory locations PGZRO and PGZRO+1.

```
LDY     #0           ;AVOID INDEXING
LDA     (PGZRO),Y    ;LOAD ACCUMULATOR INDIRECT INDEXED
TAX
```

Only the accumulator can be loaded using the indirect modes, but its contents can be transferred easily to an index register.

3. Load index register Y indirect from address in memory locations PGZRO and PGZRO+1.

```
LDX     #0           ;AVOID INDEXING
LDA     (PGZRO,X)    ;LOAD ACCUMULATOR INDEXED INDIRECT
TAY
```

4. Load stack pointer immediate with the 8-bit number VALUE.

```
LDX     #VALUE       ;INITIALIZE STACK POINTER
TXS
```

Only index register X can be transferred to or from the stack pointer.

5. Load stack pointer direct from memory location ADDR.

```
LDX     ADDR         ;INITIALIZE STACK POINTER
TXS
```

6. Load status register immediate with the 8-bit number VALUE.

```
LDA     #VALUE          ;GET THE VALUE
PHA                     ;TRANSFER IT THROUGH STACK
PLP
```

This procedure allows the user of a computer system to initialize the status register for debugging or testing purposes.

7. Load status register direct from memory location ADDR.

```
LDA     ADDR            ;GET THE INITIAL VALUE
PHA                     ;TRANSFER IT THROUGH STACK
PLP
```

8. Load index register from stack.

```
PLA                     ;TRANSFER STACK TO X THROUGH A
TAX
```

If you are restoring values from the stack, you must restore X and Y before A, since there is no direct path from the stack to X or Y.

9. Load memory locations PGZRO and PGZRO+1 (a pointer on page 0) with ADDR (ADDRH more significant byte, ADDRL less significant byte).

```
LDA     #ADDRL          ;INITIALIZE LSB
STA     PGZRO
LDA     #ADDRH          ;INITIALIZE MSB
STA     PGZRO+1
```

There is no simple way to initialize the indirect addresses that must be saved on page 0.

Store Instructions

1. Store accumulator indirect at address in memory locations PGZRO and PGZRO+1.

```
LDY     #0              ;AVOID INDEXING
STA     (PGZRO),Y       ;STORE INDIRECT INDEXED
```

or

```
LDX     #0              ;AVOID INDEXING
STA     (PGZRO,X)       ;STORE INDEXED INDIRECT
```

2. Store index register X indirect at address in memory locations PGZRO and PGZRO+1.

```
LDY     #0              ;AVOID INDEXING
TXA                     ;STORE X INDIRECT INDEXED THROUGH A
STA     (PGZRO),Y
```

3. Store index register Y indirect at address in memory locations PGZRO and PGZRO+1.

```
LDX     #0          ;AVOID INDEXING
TYA                 ;STORE Y INDEXED INDIRECT THROUGH A
STA     (PGZRO,X)
```

4. Store stack pointer in memory location ADDR.

```
TSX                 ;STORE S THROUGH X
STX     ADDR
```

5. Store status register in memory location ADDR.

```
PHP                 ;STORE P THROUGH STACK AND A
PLA
STA     ADDR
```

6. Store index register in stack.

```
TXA                 ;STORE X (OR Y) IN STACK VIA A
PHA
```

If you are saving values in the stack, you must save A before X or Y, since there is no direct path from X or Y to the stack.

Move Instructions

1. Transfer accumulator to status register.

```
PHA                 ;TRANSFER THROUGH STACK
PLP
```

2. Transfer status register to accumulator.

```
PHP                 ;TRANSFER THROUGH STACK
PLA
```

3. Transfer index register X to index register Y.

```
TXA                 ;TRANSFER THROUGH ACCUMULATOR
TAY
```

or without changing the accumulator

```
STX     TEMP        ;TRANSFER THROUGH MEMORY
LDY     TEMP
```

4. Transfer accumulator to stack pointer.

```
TAX                 ;TRANSFER THROUGH X REGISTER
TXS
```

5. Transfer stack pointer to accumulator.

```
TSX                 ;TRANSFER THROUGH X REGISTER
TXA
```

6. Move the contents of memory locations ADDR and ADDR+1 (MSB in ADDR+1) to the program counter.

```
         JMP    (ADDR)      ;JUMP INDIRECT
```

Note that JMP with indirect addressing loads the program counter with the contents of memory locations ADDR and ADDR+1; it acts more like LDA with direct addressing than like LDA with indirect (indexed) addressing.

7. Block move. Transfer data from addresses starting at the one in memory locations SORCE and SORCE+1 (on page 0) to addresses starting at the one in memory locations DEST and DEST+1 (on page 0). Register Y contains the number of bytes to be transferred.

```
MOVBYT  DEY                    ;TEST NUMBER OF BYTES
        LDA     (SORCE),Y      ;GET A BYTE FROM SOURCE
        STA     (DEST),Y       ;MOVE TO DESTINATION
        TYA
        BNE     MOVBYT
```

We assume here that the addresses do not overlap and that the initial value of Y is 1 or greater. Chapter 5 contains a more general block move.

The program becomes simpler if we reduce the base addresses by 1. That is, let memory locations SORCE and SORCE+1 contain an address one less than the lowest address in the source area, and let memory locations DEST and DEST+1 contain an address one less than the lowest address in the destination area. Now we can exit when Y is decremented to 0.

```
MOVBYT  LDA     (SORCE),Y      ;GET A BYTE FROM SOURCE
        STA     (DEST),Y       ;MOVE BYTE TO DESTINATION
        DEY
        BNE     MOVBYT         ;COUNT BYTES
```

The 0 index value is never used.

8. Move multiple (fill). Place the contents of the accumulator in memory locations starting at the one in memory locations PGZRO and PGZRO+1.

```
FILBYT  DEY
        STA     (PGZRO),Y      ;FILL A BYTE
        INY
        DEY
        BNE     FILBYT         ;COUNT BYTES
```

Chapter 5 contains a more general version.

Here again we can simplify the program by letting memory locations PGZRO and PGZRO+1 contain an address one less than the lowest address in the area to be filled. The revised program is

```
FILBYT  STA     (PGZRO),Y      ;FILL A BYTE
        DEY
        BNE     FILBYT         ;COUNT BYTES
```

Exchange Instructions

1. Exchange index registers X and Y.

```
STX     TEMP          ;SAVE X
TYA                   ;Y TO X
TAX
LDY     TEMP          ;X TO Y
```

or

```
TXA                   ;SAVE X
PHA
TYA                   ;Y TO X
TAX
PLA                   ;X TO Y
TAY
```

Both versions take the same number of bytes (assuming TEMP is on page 0). The second version is slower but reentrant.

2. Exchange memory locations ADDR1 and ADDR2.

```
LDA     ADDR1
LDX     ADDR2
STX     ADDR1
STA     ADDR2
```

3. Exchange accumulator and top of stack.

```
TAY                   ;SAVE A
PLA                   ;GET TOP OF STACK
TAX                   ;SAVE TOP OF STACK
TYA                   ;A TO TOP OF STACK
PHA
TXA                   ;TOP OF STACK TO A
```

Clear Instructions

1. Clear the accumulator.

```
LDA     #0
```

The 6502 treats 0 like any other number. There are no special clear instructions.

2. Clear an index register.

```
LDX     #0
```

or

```
LDY     #0
```

3. Clear memory location ADDR.

```
LDA     #0
STA     ADDR
```

Obviously, we could use X or Y as easily as A.

4. Clear memory locations ADDR and ADDR+1.

```
LDA     #0
STA     ADDR
STA     ADDR+1
```

5. Clear bit of accumulator.

```
AND     #MASK          ;CLEAR BIT BY MASKING
```

MASK has 0 bits in the positions to be cleared and 1 bits in the positions that are to be left unchanged. For example,

```
AND     #%10111110  ;CLEAR BITS 0 AND 6 OF A
```

Logically ANDing a bit with 1 leaves it unchanged.

Set Instructions

1. Set the accumulator to FF_{16} (all ones in binary).

```
LDA     #$FF
```

2. Set an index register to FF_{16}.

```
LDX     #$FF
```

or

```
LDY     #$FF
```

3. Set the stack pointer to FF_{16}.

```
LDX     #$FF
TXS
```

The next available location in the stack is at address $01FF_{16}$.

4. Set a memory location to FF_{16}.

```
LDA     #$FF
STA     ADDR
```

5. Set bit of accumulator.

```
ORA     #MASK          ;SET BIT BY MASKING
```

MASK has 1 bits in the positions to be set and 0 bits elsewhere. For example,

```
ORA     #%10000000  ;SET BIT 7 (SIGN BIT)
```

Logically ORing a bit with 0 leaves it unchanged.

BRANCH (JUMP) INSTRUCTIONS

Unconditional Branch Instructions

1. Unconditional branch relative to DEST.

```
CLC                     ;DELIBERATELY CLEAR CARRY
BCC     DEST            ;FORCE AN UNCONDITIONAL BRANCH
```

You can always force an unconditional branch by branching conditionally on a condition that is known to be true. Some obvious alternatives are

```
SEC
BCS     DEST
```

or

```
LDA     #0
BEQ     DEST
```

or

```
LDA     #1
BNE     DEST
```

2. Jump indirect to address at the top of the stack.

```
RTS
```

RTS is just an ordinary indirect jump in which the processor obtains the destination from the top of the stack. Be careful, however, of the fact that the processor adds 1 to the address before proceeding.

3. Jump indexed, assuming that the base of the address table is BASE and the index is in memory location INDEX. The addresses are arranged in the usual 6502 manner with the less significant byte first.[5]

- Using indirect addressing:

```
LDA     INDEX
ASL     A               ;DOUBLE INDEX FOR 2-BYTE ENTRIES
TAX
LDA     BASE,X          ;GET LSB OF DESTINATION
STA     INDIR
INX
LDA     BASE,X          ;GET MSB OF DESTINATION
STA     INDIR+1
JMP     (INDIR)         ;JUMP INDIRECT TO DESTINATION
```

- Using the stack:

```
LDA     INDEX
ASL     A               ;DOUBLE INDEX FOR 2-BYTE ENTRIES
TAX
LDA     BASE+1,X        ;GET MSB OF DESTINATION
PHA
```

```
LDA     BASE,X          ;GET LSB OF DESTINATION
PHA
RTS                     ;JUMP INDIRECT TO DESTINATION OFFSET 1
```

The second approach is faster but less straightforward. Note the following:

1. You must store the more significant byte first since the stack is growing toward lower addresses. Thus the bytes end up in their usual order.

2. Since RTS adds 1 to the program counter after loading it from the stack, the table entries must all be 1 less than the actual destination addresses for this method to work correctly.

3. Documentation is essential, since this method uses RTS for the rather surprising purpose of transferring control to a subroutine, rather than from it. The mnemonic may confuse the reader, but it obviously does not bother the microprocessor.

Conditional Branch Instructions

1. Branch if zero.

• Branch if accumulator contains zero.

```
TAX                     ;TEST ACCUMULATOR
BEQ     DEST
```

or

```
CMP     #0              ;TEST ACCUMULATOR
BEQ     DEST
```

Either AND #$FF or ORA #0 will set the Zero flag if (A)=0 without affecting the Carry flag (CMP #0 sets Carry).

• Branch if an index register contains 0.

```
CPX     #0              ;TEST INDEX REGISTER
BEQ     DEST
```

The instruction TXA or the sequence INX, DEX can be used to test the contents of index register X without affecting the Carry flag (CPX #0 sets the Carry). TXA, of course, changes the accumulator.

• Branch if a memory location contains 0.

```
INC     ADDR            ;TEST MEMORY LOCATION
DEC     ADDR
BEQ     DEST
```

or

```
LDA     ADDR            ;TEST MEMORY LOCATION
BEQ     DEST
```

· Branch if a pair of memory locations (ADDR and ADDR+1) both contain 0.

```
LDA     ADDR          ;TEST 16-BIT NUMBER FOR ZERO
ORA     ADDR+1
BEQ     DEST
```

· Branch if a bit of the accumulator is zero.

```
AND     #MASK         ;TEST BIT OF ACCUMULATOR
BEQ     DEST
```

MASK has a 1 bit in the position to be tested and 0s elsewhere. Note the inversion here; if the bit of the accumulator is a 0, the result is 0 and the Zero flag is set to 1. Special cases are

Bit position 7

```
ASL     A             ;MOVE BIT 7 TO CARRY
BCC     DEST
```

Bit position 6

```
ASL     A             ;MOVE BIT 6 TO NEGATIVE FLAG
BPL     DEST
```

Bit position 0

```
LSR     A             ;MOVE BIT 0 TO CARRY
BCC     DEST
```

· Branch if a bit of a memory location is 0.

```
LDA     #MASK
BIT     ADDR          ;TEST BIT OF MEMORY
BEQ     DEST
```

MASK has a 1 bit in the position to be tested and 0s elsewhere. Special cases are

Bit position 7

```
BIT     ADDR          ;TEST MEMORY
BPL     DEST          ;BRANCH ON BIT 7
```

Bit position 6

```
BIT     ADDR          ;TEST MEMORY
BVC     DEST          ;BRANCH ON BIT 6
```

The BIT instruction sets the Negative flag from bit 7 of the memory location and the Overflow flag from bit 6, regardless of the contents of the accumulator.

We can also use the shift instructions to test the bits at the ends, as long as we can tolerate changes in the memory locations.

Bit position 7

```
ASL     ADDR          ;TEST BIT 7
BCC     DEST
```

Bit position 6

```
ASL     ADDR          ;TEST BIT 6
BPL     DEST
```

Bit position 0

```
LSR     ADDR          ;TEST BIT 0
BCC     DEST
```

· Branch if the Interrupt Disable flag (bit 2 of the status register) is 0.

```
PHP                   ;MOVE STATUS TO A
PLA
AND     #%00000100    ;TEST INTERRUPT DISABLE
BEQ     DEST          ;BRANCH IF INTERRUPTS ARE ON
```

· Branch if the Decimal Mode flag (bit 3 of the status register) is 0.

```
PHP                   ;MOVE STATUS TO A
PLA
AND     #%00001000    ;TEST DECIMAL MODE FLAG
BEQ     DEST          ;BRANCH IF MODE IS BINARY
```

2. Branch if not 0.

· Branch if accumulator does not contain 0.

```
TAX                   ;TEST ACCUMULATOR
BNE     DEST
```

or

```
CMP     #0            ;TEST ACCUMULATOR
BNE     DEST
```

· Branch if an index register does not contain 0.

```
CPX     #0            ;TEST INDEX REGISTER
BNE     DEST
```

· Branch if a memory location does not contain 0.

```
INC     ADDR          ;TEST MEMORY LOCATION
DEC     ADDR
BNE     DEST
```

or

```
LDA     ADDR          ;TEST MEMORY LOCATION
BNE     DEST
```

· Branch if a pair of memory locations (ADDR and ADDR+1) do not both contain 0.

```
LDA     ADDR          ;TEST 16-BIT NUMBER FOR ZERO
ORA     ADDR+1
BNE     DEST
```

· Branch if a bit of the accumulator is 1.

```
AND     #MASK         ;TEST BIT OF ACCUMULATOR
BNE     DEST
```

MASK has a 1 bit in the position to be tested and 0s elsewhere. Note the inversion here; if the bit of the accumulator is a 1, the result is not 0 and the Zero flag is set to 0. Special cases are

Bit position 7

```
ASL     A               ;MOVE BIT 7 TO CARRY
BCS     DEST            ;AND TEST CARRY
```

Bit position 6

```
ASL     A               ;MOVE BIT 6 TO SIGN
BMI     DEST            ;AND TEST SIGN
```

Bit position 0

```
LSR     A               ;MOVE BIT 0 TO CARRY
BCS     DEST            ;AND TEST CARRY
```

- Branch if a bit of a memory location is 1.

```
LDA     #MASK
BIT     ADDR            ;TEST BIT OF MEMORY
BNE     DEST
```

MASK has a 1 bit in the position to be tested and 0s elsewhere. Special cases are

Bit position 7

```
BIT     ADDR            ;TEST BIT 7 OF MEMORY
BMI     DEST
```

Bit position 6

```
BIT     ADDR            ;TEST BIT 6 OF MEMORY
BVS     DEST
```

The BIT instruction sets the Negative flag from bit 7 of the memory location and the Overflow flag from bit 6, regardless of the contents of the accumulator.

We can also use the shift instructions to test the bits at the ends, as long as we can tolerate changes in the memory locations.

Bit position 7

```
ASL     ADDR            ;TEST BIT 7 OF MEMORY
BCS     DEST
```

This alternative is slower than BIT by 2 clock cycles, since it must write the result back into memory.

Bit position 6

```
ASL     ADDR            ;TEST BIT 6 OF MEMORY
BMI     DEST
```

Bit position 0

```
LSR     ADDR            ;TEST BIT 0 OF MEMORY
BCS     DEST
```

- Branch if the Interrupt Disable flag (bit 2 of the status register) is 1.

```
        PHP                  ;MOVE STATUS TO A THROUGH STACK
        PLA
        AND   #%00000100     ;TEST INTERRUPT DISABLE
        BNE   DEST           ;BRANCH IF INTERRUPTS ARE DISABLED
```

- Branch if the Decimal Mode flag (bit 3 of the status register) is 1.

```
        PHP                  ;MOVE STATUS TO A THROUGH STACK
        PLA
        AND   #%00001000     ;TEST DECIMAL MODE FLAG
        BNE   DEST           ;BRANCH IF MODE IS DECIMAL
```

3. Branch if Equal.
   - Branch if (A) = VALUE.

```
        CMP   #VALUE         ;COMPARE BY SUBTRACTING
        BEQ   DEST
```

- Branch if (X) = VALUE.

```
        CPX   #VALUE         ;COMPARE BY SUBTRACTING
        BEQ   DEST
```

Two special cases are
Branch if (X) = 1

```
        DEX
        BEQ   DEST
```

Branch if (X) = FF_{16}.

```
        INX
        BEQ   DEST
```

- Branch if (A) = (ADDR).

```
        CMP   ADDR           ;COMPARE BY SUBTRACTING
        BEQ   DEST
```

- Branch if (X) = (ADDR).

```
        CPX   ADDR           ;COMPARE BY SUBTRACTING
        BEQ   DEST
```

. Branch if the contents of memory locations PGZRO and PGZRO + 1 equal VAL16 (VAL16L less significant byte, VAL16M more significant byte).

```
        LDA   PGZRO+1        ;COMPARE MSB'S
        CMP   #VAL16M
        BNE   DONE
        LDA   PGZRO          ;AND LSB'S ONLY IF NECESSARY
        CMP   #VAL16L
        BEQ   DEST
DONE    NOP
```

- Branch if the contents of memory locations PGZRO and PGZRO + 1 equal those of memory locations LIML and LIMH.

```
        LDA     PGZRO+1         ;COMPARE MSB'S
        CMP     LIMH
        BNE     DONE
        LDA     PGZRO           ;AND LSB'S ONLY IF NECESSARY
        CMP     LIML
        BEQ     DEST
DONE    NOP
```

Note: Neither of the next two sequences should be used to test for stack overflow or underflow, since intervening instructions (for example, a single JSR or RTS) could change the stack pointer by more than 1.

- Branch if (S) = VALUE.

```
        TSX                     ;CHECK IF STACK IS AT LIMIT
        CPX     #VALUE
        BEQ     DEST
```

- Branch if (S) = (ADDR).

```
        TSX                     ;CHECK IF STACK IS AT LIMIT
        CPX     ADDR
        BEQ     DEST
```

4. Branch if Not Equal.

- Branch if (A) ≠ VALUE.

```
        CMP     #VALUE          ;COMPARE BY SUBTRACTING
        BNE     DEST
```

- Branch if (X) ≠ VALUE.

```
        CPX     #VALUE          ;COMPARE BY SUBTRACTING
        BNE     DEST
```

Two special cases are

Branch if (X) ≠ 1.

```
        DEX
        BNE     DEST
```

- Branch if (X) ≠ FF_{16}.

```
        INX
        BNE     DEST
```

- Branch if (A) ≠ (ADDR).

```
        CMP     ADDR            ;COMPARE BY SUBTRACTING
        BNE     DEST
```

- Branch if (X) ≠ (ADDR).

```
        CPX     ADDR            ;COMPARE BY SUBTRACTING
        BNE     DEST
```

- Branch if the contents of memory locations PGZRO and PGZRO+1 are not equal to VAL16 (VAL16L less significant byte, VAL16M more significant byte).

```
LDA     PGZRO+1       ;COMPARE MSB'S
CMP     #VAL16M
BNE     DEST
LDA     PGZRO         ;AND LSB'S ONLY IF NECESSARY
CMP     #VAL16L
BNE     DEST
```

· Branch if the contents of memory locations PGZRO and PGZRO + 1 are not equal to those of memory locations LIML and LIMH.

```
LDA     PGZRO+1       ;COMPARE MSB'S
CMP     LIMH
BNE     DEST
LDA     PGZRO         ;COMPARE LSB'S ONLY IF NECESSARY
CMP     LIML
BNE     DEST
```

Note: Neither of the next two sequences should be used to test for stack overflow or underflow, since intervening instructions (for example, a single JSR or RTS) could change the stack pointer by more than 1.

· Branch if (S) ≠ VALUE.

```
TSX                   ;CHECK IF STACK IS AT LIMIT
CPX     #VALUE
BNE     DEST
```

· Branch if (S) ≠ (ADDR).

```
TSX                   ;CHECK IF STACK IS AT LIMIT
CPX     ADDR
BNE     DEST
```

5. Branch if Positive.

· Branch if contents of accumulator are positive.

```
TAX                   ;TEST ACCUMULATOR
BPL     DEST
```

or

```
CMP     #0            ;TEST ACCUMULATOR
BPL     DEST
```

· Branch if contents of index register X are positive.

```
TXA                   ;TEST REGISTER X
BPL     DEST
```

or

```
CPX     #0            ;TEST INDEX REGISTER X
BPL     DEST
```

· Branch if contents of a memory location are positive.

```
LDA     ADDR          ;TEST A MEMORY LOCATION
BPL     DEST
```

or

```
BIT     ADDR
BPL     DEST
```

· Branch if 16-bit number in memory locations ADDR and ADDR+1 (MSB in ADDR+1) is positive.

```
        BIT     ADDR+1          ;TEST MSB
        BPL     DEST
```

Remember that BIT sets the Negative flag from bit 7 of the memory location, regardless of the contents of the accumulator.

6. Branch if Negative.

· Branch if contents of accumulator are negative.

```
        TAX                     ;TEST ACCUMULATOR
        BMI     DEST
```

or

```
        CMP     #0              ;TEST ACCUMULATOR
        BMI     DEST
```

· Branch if contents of index register X are negative.

```
        TXA                     ;TEST REGISTER X
        BMI     DEST
```

or

```
        CPX     #0              ;TEST INDEX REGISTER X
        BMI     DEST
```

· Branch if contents of a memory location are negative.

```
        BIT     ADDR            ;TEST A MEMORY LOCATION
        BMI     DEST
```

or

```
        LDA     ADDR            ;TEST A MEMORY LOCATION
        BMI     DEST
```

· Branch if 16-bit number in memory locations ADDR and ADDR+1 (MSB in ADDR+1) is negative.

```
        BIT     ADDR+1          ;TEST MSB
        BMI     DEST
```

Remember that BIT sets the Negative flag from bit 7 of the memory location, regardless of the contents of the accumulator.

7. Branch if Greater Than (Signed).

· Branch if (A) > VALUE.

```
        CMP     #VALUE          ;COMPARE BY SUBTRACTING
        BEQ     DONE            ;NO BRANCH IF EQUAL
        BVS     CHKOPP          ;DID OVERFLOW OCCUR?
        BPL     DEST            ;NO, THEN BRANCH ON POSITIVE
        BMI     DONE
CHKOPP  BMI     DEST            ;YES, THEN BRANCH ON NEGATIVE
DONE    NOP
```

The idea here is to branch if the result is greater than zero and overflow did not occur, or if the result is less than zero and overflow did occur. Overflow makes the apparent sign the opposite of the real sign.

- Branch if (A) > (ADDR).

```
         CMP    ADDR          ;COMPARE BY SUBTRACTING
         BEQ    DONE          ;NO BRANCH IF EQUAL
         BVS    CHKOPP        ;DID OVERFLOW OCCUR?
         BPL    DEST          ;NO, THEN BRANCH ON POSITIVE
         BMI    DONE
CHKOPP   BMI    DEST          ;YES, THEN BRANCH ON NEGATIVE
DONE     NOP
```

8. Branch if Greater Than or Equal To (Signed)

- Branch if (A) $\geq$ VALUE.

```
         CMP    #VALUE        ;COMPARE BY SUBTRACTING
         BVS    CHKOPP        ;DID OVERFLOW OCCUR?
         BPL    DEST          ;NO, THEN BRANCH ON POSITIVE
         BMI    DONE
CHKOPP   BMI    DEST          ;YES, THEN BRANCH ON NEGATIVE
DONE     NOP
```

The idea here is to branch if the result is greater than or equal to 0 and overflow did not occur, or if the result is less than 0 and overflow did occur.

- Branch if (A) $\geq$ (ADDR).

```
         CMP    ADDR          ;COMPARE BY SUBTRACTING
         BVS    CHKOPP        ;DID OVERFLOW OCCUR?
         BPL    DEST          ;NO, THEN BRANCH ON POSITIVE
         BMI    DONE
CHKOPP   BMI    DEST          ;YES, THEN BRANCH ON NEGATIVE
DONE     NOP
```

9. Branch if Less Than (Signed)

- Branch if (A) < VALUE (signed).

```
         CMP    #VALUE        ;COMPARE BY SUBTRACTING
         BVS    CHKOPP        ;DID OVERFLOW OCCUR?
         BMI    DEST          ;NO, THEN BRANCH ON NEGATIVE
         BPL    DONE
CHKOPP   BPL    DEST          ;YES, THEN BRANCH ON POSITIVE
DONE     NOP
```

The idea here is to branch if the result is negative and overflow did not occur, or if the result is positive but overflow did occur.

- Branch if (A) < (ADDR) (signed).

```
         CMP    ADDR          ;COMPARE BY SUBTRACTING
         BVS    CHKOPP        ;DID OVERFLOW OCCUR?
         BMI    DEST          ;NO, THEN BRANCH ON NEGATIVE
         BPL    DONE
CHKOPP   BPL    DEST          ;YES, THEN BRANCH ON POSITIVE
DONE     NOP
```

10. Branch if Less Than or Equal (Signed).

- Branch if (A) ≤ VALUE (signed).

```
        CMP     #VALUE          ;COMPARE BY SUBTRACTING
        BEQ     DEST            ;BRANCH IF EQUAL
        BVS     CHKOPP          ;DID OVERFLOW OCCUR?
        BMI     DEST            ;NO, THEN BRANCH ON NEGATIVE
        BPL     DONE
CHKOPP  BPL     DEST            ;YES, THEN BRANCH ON POSITIVE
DONE    NOP
```

The idea here is to branch if the result is 0, negative without overflow, or positive with overflow.

- Branch if (A) ≤ (ADDR) (signed).

```
        CMP     ADDR            ;COMPARE BY SUBTRACTING
        BEQ     DEST            ;BRANCH IF EQUAL
        BVS     CHKOPP          ;DID OVERFLOW OCCUR?
        BMI     DEST            ;NO, THEN BRANCH ON NEGATIVE
        BPL     DONE
CHKOPP  BPL     DEST            ;YES, THEN BRANCH ON POSITIVE
DONE    NOP
```

11. Branch if Higher (Unsigned). That is, branch if the unsigned comparison is nonzero and does not require a borrow.

- Branch if (A) > VALUE (unsigned).

```
        CMP     #VALUE          ;COMPARE BY SUBTRACTING
        BEQ     DONE            ;NO BRANCH IF EQUAL
        BCS     DEST            ;BRANCH IF NO BORROW NEEDED
DONE    NOP
```

or

```
        CMP     #VALUE+1        ;COMPARE BY SUBTRACTING VALUE + 1
        BCS     DEST            ;BRANCH IF NO BORROW NEEDED
```

It is shorter and somewhat more efficient to simply compare to a number one higher than the actual threshold. Then we can use BCS, which causes a branch if the contents of the accumulator are greater than or equal to VALUE+1 (unsigned).

- Branch if (A) > (ADDR) (unsigned).

```
        CMP     ADDR            ;COMPARE BY SUBTRACTING
        BEQ     DONE            ;NO BRANCH IF EQUAL
        BCS     DEST            ;BRANCH IF NO BORROW NEEDED
DONE    NOP
```

- Branch if (X) > VALUE (unsigned).

```
        CPX     #VALUE+1        ;COMPARE BY SUBTRACTING VALUE+1
        BCS     DEST
```

• Branch if (X) > (ADDR) (unsigned).

```
        CPX     ADDR            ;COMPARE BY SUBTRACTING
        BEQ     DONE            ;NO BRANCH IF EQUAL
        BCS     DEST            ;BRANCH IF NO BORROW NEEDED
DONE    NOP
```

• Branch if the contents of memory locations PGZRO and PGZRO+1 (MSB in PGZRO+1) are larger (unsigned) than VAL16 (VAL16L less significant byte, VAL16M more significant byte).

```
        LDA     #VAL16L         ;GENERATE BORROW BY COMPARING LSB'S
        CMP     PGZRO
        LDA     #VAL16M         ;COMPARE MSB'S WITH BORROW
        SBC     PGZRO+1
        BCC     DEST            ;BRANCH IF BORROW GENERATED
```

• Branch if the contents of memory locations PGZRO and PGZRO+1 (MSB in PGZRO+1) are larger (unsigned) than the contents of memory locations LIML and LIMH (MSB in LIMH).

```
        LDA     LIML            ;GENERATE BORROW BY COMPARING LSB'S
        CMP     PGZRO
        LDA     LIMH            ;COMPARE MSB'S WITH BORROW
        SBC     PGZRO+1
        BCC     DEST            ;BRANCH IF BORROW GENERATED
```

• Branch if (S) > VALUE (unsigned).

```
        TSX                     ;CHECK IF STACK BEYOND LIMIT
        CPX     #VALUE
        BEQ     DONE            ;NO BRANCH IF EQUAL
        BCS     DEST            ;BRANCH IF NO BORROW NEEDED
DONE    NOP
```

or

```
        TSX                     ;CHECK IF STACK BEYOND LIMIT
        CPX     #VALUE+1        ;COMPARE BY SUBTRACTING VALUE + 1
        BCS     DEST            ;BRANCH IF NO BORROW NEEDED
```

• Branch if (S) > (ADDR) (unsigned).

```
        TSX                     ;CHECK IF STACK BEYOND LIMIT
        BEQ     DONE            ;NO BRANCH IF EQUAL
        BCS     DEST            ;BRANCH IF NO BORROW NEEDED
DONE    NOP
```

12. Branch if Not Higher (Unsigned). Branch if the unsigned comparison is 0 or requires a borrow.

Branch if (A) $\leq$ VALUE (unsigned).

```
        CMP     #VALUE          ;COMPARE BY SUBTRACTING
        BCC     DEST            ;BRANCH IF BORROW NEEDED
        BEQ     DEST            ;BRANCH IF EQUAL
```

If the two values are the same, CMP sets the Carry to indicate that no borrow was necessary.

or

```
CMP     #VALUE+1      ;COMPARE BY SUBTRACTING VALUE + 1
BCC     DEST          ;BRANCH IF BORROW NEEDED
```

- Branch if (A) ≤ (ADDR) (unsigned).

```
CMP     ADDR          ;COMPARE BY SUBTRACTING
BCC     DEST          ;BRANCH IF BORROW NEEDED
BEQ     DEST          ;BRANCH IF EQUAL
```

- Branch if (X) ≤ VALUE (unsigned).

```
CPX     #VALUE        ;COMPARE BY SUBTRACTING
BCC     DEST          ;BRANCH IF BORROW NEEDED
BEQ     DEST          ;BRANCH IF EQUAL
```

or

```
CPX     #VALUE+1      ;COMPARE BY SUBTRACTING VALUE + 1
BCC     DEST          ;BRANCH IF BORROW NEEDED
```

- Branch if (X) ≤ (ADDR) (unsigned).

```
CPX     ADDR          ;COMPARE BY SUBTRACTING
BCC     DEST          ;BRANCH IF BORROW NEEDED
BEQ     DEST          ;BRANCH IF EQUAL
```

- Branch if the contents of memory locations PGZRO and PGZRO+1 (MSB in PGZRO+1) are less than or equal to (unsigned) VAL16 (VAL16M more significant byte, VAL16L less significant byte).

```
LDA     #VAL16L       ;GENERATE BORROW BY COMPARING LSB'S
CMP     PGZRO
LDA     #VAL16M       ;COMPARE MSB'S WITH BORROW
SBC     PGZRO+1
BCS     DEST          ;BRANCH IF NO BORROW GENERATED
```

- Branch if the contents of memory locations PGZRO and PGZRO+1 (MSB in PGZRO+1) are less than or equal to (unsigned) the contents of memory locations LIML and LIMH (MSB in LIMH).

```
LDA     LIML          ;GENERATE BORROW BY COMPARING LSB'S
CMP     PGZRO
LDA     LIMH          ;COMPARE MSB'S WITH BORROW
SBC     PGZRO+1
BCS     DEST          ;BRANCH IF NO BORROW GENERATED
```

- Branch if (S) ≤ VALUE (unsigned).

```
TSX                   ;CHECK IF STACK AT OR BELOW LIMIT
CPX     #VALUE
BCC     DEST          ;BRANCH IF BORROW NEEDED
BEQ     DEST          ;BRANCH IF EQUAL
```

or

```
TSX                 ;CHECK IF STACK AT OR BELOW LIMIT
CPX     #VALUE+1    ;COMPARE BY SUBTRACTING VALUE + 1
BCC     DEST
```

· Branch if (S) ≤ (ADDR) (unsigned).

```
TSX                 ;CHECK IF STACK AT OR BELOW LIMIT
CPX     ADDR
BCC     DEST        ;BRANCH IF BORROW NEEDED
BEQ     DEST        ;BRANCH IF EQUAL
```

13. Branch if Lower (Unsigned). That is, branch if the unsigned comparison requires a borrow.

· Branch if (A) < (unsigned).

```
CMP     #VALUE      ;COMPARE BY SUBTRACTING
BCC     DEST        ;BRANCH IF BORROW GENERATED
```

The Carry flag is set to 0 if the subtraction generates a borrow.

· Branch if (A) < (ADDR) (unsigned).

```
CMP     ADDR        ;COMPARE BY SUBTRACTING
BCC     DEST        ;BRANCH IF BORROW GENERATED
```

· Branch if (X) < VALUE (unsigned).

```
CPX     #VALUE      ;COMPARE BY SUBTRACTING
BCC     DEST        ;BRANCH IF BORROW GENERATED
```

· Branch if (X) < (ADDR) (unsigned).

```
CPX     ADDR        ;COMPARE BY SUBTRACTING
BCC     DEST        ;BRANCH IF BORROW GENERATED
```

· Branch if the contents of memory locations PGZRO and PGZRO+1 (MSB in PGZRO+1) are less than (unsigned) VAL16 (VAL16L less significant byte, VAL16M more significant byte).

```
LDA     PGZRO       ;GENERATE BORROW BY COMPARING LSB'S
CMP     #VAL16L
LDA     PGZRO+1     ;COMPARE MSB'S WITH BORROW
SBC     #VAL16M
BCC     DEST        ;BRANCH IF BORROW GENERATED
```

· Branch if the contents of memory locations PGZRO and PGZRO+1 (MSB in PGZRO+1) are less than (unsigned) the contents of memory locations LIML and LIMH (MSB in LIMH).

```
LDA     PGZRO       ;GENERATE BORROW BY COMPARING LSB'S
CMP     LIML
LDA     PGZRO+1     ;COMPARE MSB'S WITH BORROW
SBC     LIMH
BCC     DEST        ;BRANCH IF BORROW GENERATED
```

· Branch if (S) < VALUE (unsigned).

```
TSX                    ;CHECK IF STACK BELOW LIMIT
CPX     #VALUE
BCC     DEST           ;BRANCH IF BORROW NEEDED
```

· Branch if (S) < (ADDR) (unsigned).

```
TSX                    ;CHECK IF STACK BELOW LIMIT
CPX     ADDR
BCC     DEST           ;BRANCH IF BORROW NEEDED
```

14. Branch if Not Lower (Unsigned). That is, branch if the unsigned comparison does not require a borrow.

· Branch if (A) ≥ VALUE (unsigned).

```
CMP     #VALUE         ;COMPARE BY SUBTRACTING
BCS     DEST           ;BRANCH IF NO BORROW GENERATED
```

The Carry flag is set to one if the subtraction does not generate a borrow.

· Branch if (A) ≥ (ADDR) (unsigned).

```
CMP     ADDR           ;COMPARE BY SUBTRACTING
BCS     DEST
```

· Branch if (X) ≥ VALUE (unsigned).

```
CPX     #VALUE         ;COMPARE BY SUBTRACTING
BCS     DEST           ;BRANCH IF NO BORROW GENERATED
```

· Branch if (X) ≥ (ADDR) (unsigned).

```
CPX     ADDR           ;COMPARE BY SUBTRACTING
BCS     DEST
```

· Branch if the contents of memory locations PGZRO and PGZRO+1 (MSB in PGZRO+1) are greater than or equal to (unsigned) VAL16 (VAL16L less significant byte, VAL16M more significant byte).

```
LDA     PGZRO          ;GENERATE BORROW BY COMPARING LSB'S
CMP     #VAL16L
LDA     PGZRO+1        ;COMPARE MSB'S WITH BORROW
SBC     #VAL16M
BCS     DEST           ;BRANCH IF NO BORROW GENERATED
```

· Branch if the contents of memory locations PGZRO and PGZRO+1 (MSB in PGZRO+1) are greater than or equal to (unsigned) the contents of memory locations LIML and LIMH (MSB in LIMH).

```
LDA     PGZRO          ;GENERATE BORROW BY COMPARING LSB'S
CMP     LIML
LDA     PGZRO+1        ;COMPARE MSB'S WITH BORROW
SBC     LIMH
BCS     DEST           ;BRANCH IF NO BORROW GENERATED
```

- Branch if (S) $\geq$ VALUE (unsigned).

```
TSX                 ;CHECK IF STACK AT OR ABOVE LIMIT
CPX     #VALUE
BCS     DEST        ;BRANCH IF NO BORROW NEEDED
```

- Branch if (S) $\geq$ (ADDR) (unsigned).

```
TSX                 ;CHECK IF STACK AT OR ABOVE LIMIT
CPX     ADDR
BCS     DEST        ;BRANCH IF NO BORROW NEEDED
```

SKIP INSTRUCTIONS

You can implement skip instructions on the 6502 microprocessor by using branch or jump instructions with the proper destination. That destination should be one instruction beyond the one that the processor would execute sequentially after the branch. Note that skip instructions are awkward to implement on most microprocessors, because their instructions vary in length and it is difficult to determine how long a jump is required to skip an instruction.

SUBROUTINE CALL INSTRUCTIONS

Unconditional Call Instructions

You can implement an indirect call on the 6502 microprocessor by calling a routine that performs an ordinary indirect jump. A RETURN FROM SUBROUTINE (RTS) instruction at the end of the subroutine will then transfer control back to the original calling point. The main program performs

```
JSR     TRANS
```

where TRANS is the subroutine that actually transfers control using a jump instruction. Note that TRANS ends with a jump, not with a return. Typical TRANS routines are:

- To address in memory locations INDIR and INDIR+1 (MSB in INDIR+1).

```
JMP     (INDIR)
```

- To address in table starting at memory location BASE and using index in memory location INDEX.

```
        LDA     INDEX
        ASL     A               ;DOUBLE INDEX FOR 2-BYTE ENTRIES
        TAX
        LDA     BASE,X          ;GET LSB OF DESTINATION
        STA     INDIR
        INX
        LDA     BASE,X          ;GET MSB OF DESTINATION
        STA     INDIR+1
        JMP     (INDIR)         ;JUMP INDIRECT TO DESTINATION
```

or

```
        LDA     INDEX
        ASL     A               ;DOUBLE INDEX FOR 2-BYTE ENTRIES
        TAX
        LDA     BASE+1,X        ;GET MSB OF DESTINATION
        PHA
        LDA     BASE,X          ;GET LSB OF DESTINATION
        PHA
        RTS                     ;JUMP TO DESTINATION PLUS 1
```

In the second approach, the table must contain the actual destination addresses minus 1, since RTS adds 1 to the program counter after loading it from the stack.

Conditional Call Instructions

You can implement a conditional call on the 6502 microprocessor by branching on the opposite condition around the call. For example, you could provide CALL ON CARRY CLEAR with the sequence

```
        BCS     NEXT            ;BRANCH AROUND IF CARRY SET
        JSR     SUBR            ;CALL IF CARRY CLEAR
NEXT    NOP
```

RETURN INSTRUCTIONS

Unconditional Return Instructions

The RTS instruction returns control automatically to the address saved at the top of the stack (plus 1). If the return address is saved elsewhere (i.e., in two memory locations), you can return control to it by performing an indirect jump. Note that you must add 1 to the return address to simulate RTS.

The following sequence pops the return address from the top of the stack, adds 1 to it, and stores the adjusted value in memory locations RETADR and RETADR+1.

```
        PLA                     ;POP LSB OF RETURN ADDRESS
        CLC                     ;ADD 1 TO LSB
        ADC     #1
        STA     RETADR
        PLA                     ;POP MSB OF RETURN ADDRESS
        ADC     #0              ;ADD CARRY TO MSB
        STA     RETADR+1
```

A final JMP (RETADR) will now transfer control to the proper place.

Conditional Return Instructions

You can implement conditional returns on the 6502 microprocessor by using the conditional branches (on the opposite condition) to branch around an RTS instruction. That is, for example, you could provide RETURN ON NOT ZERO with the sequence

```
        BEQ     NEXT            ;BRANCH AROUND IF ZERO
        RTS                     ;RETURN ON NOT ZERO
NEXT    NOP
```

Return with Skip Instructions

· Return control to the address at the top of the stack after it has been incremented by an offset NUM. This sequence allows you to transfer control past parameters, data, or other nonexecutable items.

```
        PLA                     ;POP RETURN ADDRESS
        CLC
        ADC     #NUM+1          ;INCREMENT BY NUM
        STA     RETADR
        PLA
        ADC     #0              ;WITH CARRY IF NECESSARY
        STA     RETADR+1
        JMP     (RETADR)
```

or

```
        TSX                     ;MOVE STACK POINTER TO INDEX REGISTER
        LDA     $0101,X         ;INCREMENT RETURN ADDRESS BY NUM
        CLC
        ADC     #NUM
        STA     $0101,X
        BCC     DONE
        INC     $0102,X         ;WITH CARRY IF NECESSARY
DONE    RTS
```

· Change the return address to RETPT. Assume that the return address is stored currently at the top of the stack. RETPT consists of RETPTH (MSB) and RETPTL (LSB).

```
TSX
LDA     #RETPTL
STA     $0101,X
LDA     #RETPT
STA     $0102,X
RTS
```

The actual return point is RETPT + 1.

Return from Interrupt Instructions

If the initial portion of the interrupt service routine saves all the registers with the sequence.

```
PHA                     ;SAVE ACCUMULATOR
TXA                     ;SAVE INDEX REGISTER X
PHA
TYA                     ;SAVE INDEX REGISTER Y
PHA
```

A standard return sequence is

```
PLA                     ;RESTORE INDEX REGISTER Y
TAY
PLA                     ;RESTORE INDEX REGISTER X
TAX
PLA                     ;RESTORE ACCUMULATOR
```

MISCELLANEOUS INSTRUCTIONS

In this category, we include push and pop instructions, halt, wait, break, decimal adjust, enabling and disabling of interrupts, translation (table lookup), and other instructions that do not fall into any of the earlier categories.

1. Push Instructions.

· Push index register X.

```
TXA                     ;SAVE X IN STACK VIA A
PHA
```

· Push index register Y.

```
TYA                     ;SAVE Y IN STACK VIA A
PHA
```

· Push memory location ADDR.

```
LDA     ADDR            ;SAVE MEMORY LOCATION IN STACK
PHA
```

ADDR could actually be an external priority register or a copy of it.

· Push memory locations ADDR and ADDR+1 (ADDR+1 most significant).

```
        LDA     ADDR+1          ;SAVE 16-BIT NUMBER IN STACK
        PHA
        LDA     ADDR
        PHA
```

Since the stack is growing toward lower addresses, the 16-bit number ends up stored in its usual 6502 form.

2. Pop (pull) instructions.

· Pop index register X.

```
        PLA                     ;RESTORE X FROM STACK VIA A
        TAX
```

· Pop index register Y.

```
        PLA                     ;RESTORE Y FROM STACK VIA A
        TAY
```

· Pop memory location ADDR.

```
        PLA                     ;RESTORE MEMORY LOCATION FROM STACK
        STA     ADDR
```

ADDR could actually be an external priority register or a copy of it.

· Pop memory locations ADDR and ADDR+1 (ADDR+1 most significant byte).

```
        PLA                     ;RESTORE 16-BIT NUMBER FROM STACK
        STA     ADDR
        PLA
        STA     ADDR+1
```

We assume that the 16-bit number is stored in the usual 6502 form with the less significant byte at the lower address.

Wait Instructions

The simplest way to implement a wait on the 6502 microprocessor is to use an endless loop such as:

```
HERE    JMP     HERE
```

The processor will continue executing the instruction until it is interrupted and will resume executing it after the interrupt service routine returns control. Of course, maskable interrupts must have been enabled or the processor will execute the loop endlessly. The nonmaskable interrupt can interrupt the processor at any time.

Another alternative is a sequence that waits for a high-to-low transition on the Set Overflow input. Such a transition sets the Overflow (V) flag. So the required sequence is

```
        CLV                 ;CLEAR THE OVERFLOW FLAG
WAIT    BVC     WAIT        ;AND WAIT FOR A TRANSITION TO SET IT
```

This sequence is essentially a "Wait for Input Transition" instruction.

Adjust Instructions

1. Branch if accumulator does not contain a valid decimal (BCD) number.

```
        STA     TEMP        ;SAVE ACCUMULATOR
        SED                 ;ENTER DECIMAL MODE
        CLC                 ;ADD 0 IN DECIMAL MODE
        ADC     #0
        CLD                 ;LEAVE DECIMAL MODE
```

2. Decimal increment accumulator (add 1 to A in decimal).

```
        SED                 ;ENTER DECIMAL MODE
        CLC
        ADC     #1          ;ADD 1 DECIMAL
        CLD                 ;LEAVE DECIMAL MODE
```

3. Decimal decrement accumulator (subtract 1 from A in decimal).

```
        SED                 ;ENTER DECIMAL MODE
        SEC
        SBC     #1          ;SUBTRACT 1 DECIMAL
        CLD                 ;LEAVE DECIMAL MODE
```

4. Enter decimal mode but save the old Decimal Mode flag.

```
        PHP                 ;SAVE OLD DECIMAL MODE FLAG
        SED                 ;ENTER DECIMAL MODE
```

A final PLP instruction will restore the old value of the Decimal Mode flag (and the rest of the status register as well).

5. Enter binary mode but save the old Decimal Mode flag.

```
        PHP                 ;SAVE OLD DECIMAL MODE FLAG
        CLD                 ;ENTER BINARY MODE
```

A final PLP instruction will restore the old value of the Decimal Mode flag (and the rest of the status register as well).

Enable and Disable Interrupt Instructions

1. Enable interrupts but save previous value of I flag.

```
PHP                     ;SAVE OLD I FLAG
CLI                     ;ENABLE INTERRUPTS
```

After a sequence that must run with interrupts enabled, a PLP instruction will restore the previous state of the interrupt system (and the rest of the status register as well).

2. Disable interrupts but save previous value of I flag.

```
PHP                     ;SAVE OLD I FLAG
SEI                     ;DISABLE INTERRUPTS
```

After a sequence that must run with interrupts disabled, a PLP instruction will restore the previous state of the interrupt system (and the rest of the status register as well).

Translate Instructions

1. Translate the operand in A to a value obtained from the corresponding entry in a table starting at the address in memory locations PGZRO and PGZRO+1 (MSB in PGZRO+1).

```
TAY
LDA     (PGZRO),Y     ;REPLACE OPERAND WITH TABLE ENTRY
```

This procedure can be used to convert data from one code to another.

2. Translate the operand in A to a 16-bit value obtained from the corresponding entry in a table starting at the address in memory locations PGZRO and PGZRO+1 (MSB in PGZRO+1). Store the entry in memory locations TEMPL and TEMPH (MSB in TEMPH).

```
ASL     A             ;DOUBLE INDEX FOR 2-BYTE ENTRIES
TAY
LDA     (PGZRO),Y     ;GET LSB OF ENTRY
STA     TEMPL
INY
LDA     (PGZRO),Y     ;GET MSB OF ENTRY
STA     TEMPH
```

ADDITIONAL ADDRESSING MODES

- **Indirect Addressing**. You can provide indirect addressing on the 6502 processor (for addresses on page 0) by using the postindexed (indirect indexed) addressing mode with register Y set to 0. A somewhat less powerful alternative (because you cannot index from the indirect address) is to use preindexing (indexed indirect addressing) with register X set to 0. Otherwise, indirect addressing is available only for the JMP instruction. Note that with JMP, the indirect address may be located anywhere in memory; it is not restricted to page 0.

Examples

1. Load the accumulator indirectly from the address in memory locations PGZRO and PGZRO+1.

```
LDY     #0            ;SET INDEX TO ZERO
LDA     (PGZRO),Y     ;LOAD INDIRECT INDEXED
```

b. Store the accumulator indirectly at the address in memory locations PGZRO and PGZRO+1.

```
LDY     #0            ;SET INDEX TO ZERO
STA     (PGZRO),Y     ;STORE INDIRECT INDEXED
```

In the case of instructions that lack the indirect indexed mode (such as ASL, DEC, INC, LSR, ROL, ROR), you must move the data to the accumulator, operate on it there, and then store it back in memory.

3. Increment the data at the address in memory locations PGZRO and PGZRO+1.

```
LDY     #0            ;SET INDEX TO ZERO
LDA     (PGZRO),Y     ;GET THE DATA
CLC
ADC     #1            ;INCREMENT THE DATA
STA     (PGZRO),Y     ;STORE THE RESULT BACK
```

4. Logically shift right the data at the address in memory locations PGZRO and PGZRO+1.

```
LDY     #0            ;SET INDEX TO ZERO
LDA     (PGZRO),Y     ;GET THE DATA
LSR     A             ;SHIFT IT RIGHT
STA     (PGZRO),Y     ;STORE THE RESULT BACK
```

5. Clear the address in memory locations PGZRO and PGZRO+1.

```
LDY     #0            ;SET INDEX TO ZERO
TYA                   ;DATA = ZERO
STA     (PGZRO),Y     ;CLEAR THE INDIRECT ADDRESS
```

The only way to provide indirect addressing for other pages is to move the indirect address to page 0 first.

6. Clear the address in memory locations INDIR and INDIR+1 (not on page 0).

```
LDA     INDIR        ;MOVE INDIRECT ADDRESS TO PAGE ZERO
STA     PGZRO
LDA     INDIR+1
STA     PGZRO+1
LDY     #0           ;SET INDEX TO ZERO
TYA                  ;DATA = ZERO
STA     (PGZRO),Y    ;CLEAR THE INDIRECT ADDRESS
```

· **Indexed Addressing**. Indexed addressing is available for most instructions in the 6502 set. We will discuss briefly the handling of the few for which it is not available and we will then discuss the handling of indexes that are larger than 256.

No indexing is available for BIT, CPX, CPY, JMP, and JSR. Only page 0 indexing is available for STX and STY. We can overcome these limitations as follows:

1. BIT

BIT indexed can be simulated by saving the accumulator, using AND, and restoring the accumulator. You should note that restoring the accumulator with LDA, PHA, TXA, or TYA will affect the Zero and Negative flags. A typical sequence without restoring the accumulator is:

```
PHA                  ;SAVE A
AND     BASE,X       ;LOGICAL AND INDEXED
```

The Zero flag is set as if an indexed BIT had been executed and the contents of A are available at the top of the stack.

2. CPX or CPY

CPX or CPY indexed can be simulated by moving the index register to A and using CMP. That is, CPX indexed with Y can be simulated by the sequence:

```
TXA                  ;MOVE X TO A
CMP     BASE,Y       ;THEN COMPARE INDEXED
```

3. JMP

JMP indexed can be simulated by calculating the required indexed address, storing it in memory, and using either JMP indirect or RTS to transfer control. The sequences are:

```
LDA     INDEX
ASL     A            ;DOUBLE INDEX FOR 2-BYTE ENTRIES
TAX
LDA     BASE,X       ;GET LSB OF DESTINATION
STA     INDIR
INX
LDA     BASE,X       ;GET MSB OF DESTINATION
STA     INDIR+1
JMP     (INDIR)      ;JUMP INDIRECT TO DESTINATION
```

or

```
LDA     INDEX
ASL     A               ;DOUBLE INDEX FOR 2-BYTE ENTRIES
TAX
LDA     BASE+1,X        ;GET MSB OF DESTINATION
PHA
LDA     BASE,X          ;GET LSB OF DESTINATION
PHA
RTS                     ;JUMP INDIRECT TO DESTINATION OFFSET 1
```

The second approach requires that the table contain entries that are all 1 less than the actual destinations, since RTS adds 1 to the program counter after restoring it from the stack.

4. JSR

JSR indexed can be simulated by calling a transfer program that executes JMP indexed as shown above. The ultimate return address remains at the top of the stack and a final RTS instruction will transfer control back to the original calling program. That is, the main program contains:

```
JSR     TRANS
```

TRANS performs an indexed jump and thus transfers control to the actual subroutine.

5. STX or STY

STX or STY indexed can be simulated by moving the index register to A and using STA. That is, we can simulate STX indexed with Y by using the sequence:

```
TXA                     ;MOVE X TO A
STA     BASE,Y          ;THEN STORE INDEXED
```

BASE can be anywhere in memory, not just on page 0.

We can handle indexes that are larger than 256 by performing an explicit addition on the more significant bytes and using the indirect indexed addressing mode. That is, if the base address is in memory locations PGZRO and PGZRO+1 and the index is in memory locations INDEX and INDEX+1, the following sequence will place the corrected base address in memory locations TEMP and TEMP+1 (on page 0).

```
LDA     PGZRO           ;SIMPLY MOVE LSB
STA     TEMP
LDA     PGZRO+1         ;ADD MSB'S
CLC
ADC     INDEX+1
STA     TEMP+1
```

TEMP and TEMP+1 now contain a base address that can be used (in conjunction with INDEX) in the indirect indexed mode.

Examples

1. Load accumulator indexed.

```
        LDY     INDEX           ;GET LSB OF INDEX
        LDA     (TEMP),Y        ;LOAD A INDIRECT INDEXED
```

2. Store accumulator indexed, assuming that we have saved A at the top of the stack.

```
        LDY     INDEX           ;GET LSB OF INDEX
        PLA                     ;RESTORE A
        STA     (TEMP),Y        ;STORE A INDIRECT INDEXED
```

· **Autopreincrementing**. Autopreincrementing means that the contents of the index register are incremented automatically before they are used. You can provide autopreincrementing on the 6502 processor either by using INX or INY on an index register or by using the 16-bit methods to increment a base address in memory.

Examples

· Load the accumulator from address BASE using autopreincrementing on index register X.

```
        INX                     ;AUTOPREINCREMENT X
        LDA     BASE,X
```

We assume that the array contains fewer than 256 elements.

· Load the accumulator from the address in memory locations PGZRO and PGZRO + 1 using autopreincrementing on the contents of memory locations INDEX and INDEX + 1.

```
        INC     INDEX           ;AUTOPREINCREMENT INDEX
        BNE     DONE
        INC     INDEX+1         ;WITH CARRY IF NECESSARY
DONE    LDA     PGZRO           ;MOVE LSB
        STA     TEMP
        LDA     PGZRO+1         ;ADD MSB'S
        CLC
        ADC     INDEX+1
        STA     TEMP+1
        LDY     INDEX           ;GET LSB OF INDEX
        LDA     (TEMP),Y        ;LOAD ACCUMULATOR
```

If you must autoincrement by 2 (as in handling arrays of addresses) use the sequence

```
        LDA     INDEX           ;AUTOINCREMENT INDEX BY 2
        CLC
        ADC     #2
        STA     INDEX
        BCC     DONE
        INC     INDEX+1         ;CARRY TO MSB IF NECESSARY
DONE    NOP
```

· **Autopostincrementing**. Autopostincrementing means that the contents of the index register are incremented automatically after they are used. You can provide autopreincrementing on the 6502 processor either by using INX or INY on an index register or by using the 16-bit methods to increment an index in memory.

Examples

· Load the accumulator from address BASE using autopostincrementing on index register Y.

```
        LDA     BASE,Y          ;AUTOPOSTINCREMENT Y
        INY
```

· Load the accumulator from the address in memory locations PGZRO and PGZRO + 1 using autopostincrementing on the contents of memory locations INDEX and INDEX + 1.

```
        LDA     PGZRO           ;MOVE LSB OF BASE
        STA     TEMP
        LDA     PGZRO+1         ;ADD MSB'S OF BASE AND INDEX
        CLC
        ADC     INDEX+1
        STA     TEMP+1
        LDY     INDEX           ;GET LSB OF INDEX
        LDA     (TEMP),Y        ;LOAD ACCUMULATOR
        INC     INDEX           ;AUTOPOSTINCREMENT INDEX
        BNE     DONE
        INC     INDEX+1         ;WITH CARRY IF NECESSARY
DONE    NOP
```

· **Autopredecrementing**. Autopredecrementing means that the contents of the index register are decremented automatically before they are used. You can provide autopredecrementing on the 6502 processor either by using DEX or DEY on an index register or by using the 16-bit methods to decrement a base address or index in memory.

Examples

· Load the accumulator from address BASE using autopredecrementing on index register X.

```
        DEX                     ;AUTOPREDECREMENT X
        LDA     BASE,X
```

We assume that the array contains fewer than 256 elements.

· Load the accumulator from the address in memory locations PGZRO and PGZRO + 1 using autopredecrementing on the contents of memory locations INDEX and INDEX + 1.

```
        LDA     INDEX       ;AUTOPREDECREMENT INDEX
        BNE     DECLSB
        DEC     INDEX+1     ;BORROWING FROM MSB IF NECESSARY
DECLSB  DEC     INDEX
        LDA     PGZRO       ;MOVE LSB OF BASE
        STA     TEMP
        LDA     PGZRO+1     ;ADD MSB'S OF BASE AND INDEX
        CLC
        ADC     INDEX+1
        STA     TEMP+1
        LDY     INDEX       ;GET LSB OF INDEX
        LDA     (TEMP),Y    ;LOAD ACCUMULATOR
```

If you must autodecrement by 2 (as in handling arrays of addresses), use the sequence:

```
        LDA     INDEX       ;AUTODECREMENT INDEX BY 2
        SEC
        SBC     #2
        STA     INDEX
        BCS     DONE
        DEC     INDEX+1     ;BORROWING FROM MSB IF NECESSARY
DONE    NOP
```

· **Autopostdecrementing**. Autopostdecrementing means that the contents of the index register are decremented automatically after they are used. You can provide autopostdecrementing on the 6502 processor by using either DEX or DEY on an index register or by using the 16-bit methods to decrement an index in memory.

Examples

· Load the accumulator from address BASE using autopostdecrementing on index register Y.

```
        LDA     BASE,Y      ;AUTOPOSTDECREMENT Y
        DEY
```

· Load the accumulator from the address in memory locations PGZRO and PGZRO + 1 using autopostdecrementing on the contents of memory locations INDEX and INDEX + 1.

```
        LDA     PGZRO       ;MOVE LSB OF BASE
        STA     TEMP
        LDA     PGZRO+1     ;ADD MSB'S OF BASE AND INDEX
        CLC
        ADC     INDEX+1
        STA     TEMP+1
        LDY     INDEX       ;GET LSB OF INDEX
        LDA     (TEMP),Y    ;LOAD ACCUMULATOR
        CPY     #0          ;AUTOPOSTDECREMENT INDEX
        BNE     DECLSB
        DEC     INDEX+1     ;BORROWING FROM MSB IF NECESSARY
DECLSB  DEC     INDEX
```

· **Indexed indirect addressing (preindexing)**. The 6502 processor provides preindexing for many instructions. We can simulate preindexing for the instructions that lack it by moving the data to the accumulator using preindexing, operating on it, and (if necessary) storing the result back into memory using preindexing.

Examples

1. Rotate right the data at the preindexed address obtained by indexing with X from base address PGZRO.

```
LDA     (PGZRO,X)    ;GET THE DATA
ROR     A            ;ROTATE DATA RIGHT
STA     (PGZRO,X)    ;STORE RESULT BACK IN MEMORY
```

2. Clear the preindexed address obtained by indexing with X from base address PGZRO.

```
LDA     #0           ;DATA = ZERO
STA     (PGZRO,X)    ;CLEAR PREINDEXED ADDRESS
```

Note that if the calculation of an effective address in preindexing produces a result too large for eight bits, the excess is truncated and no error warning occurs. That is, the processor provides an automatic wraparound on page 0.

· **Indirect indexed addressing (postindexing)**. The 6502 processor provides postindexing for many instructions. We can simulate postindexing for the instructions that lack it by moving the data to the accumulator using postindexing, operating on it, and (if necessary) storing the result back into memory using postindexing.

Examples

1. Decrement the data at the address in memory locations PGZRO and PGZRO+1 using Y as an index.

```
LDA     (PGZRO),Y    ;GET THE DATA
SEC
SBC     #1           ;DECREMENT DATA BY 1
STA     (PGZRO),Y    ;STORE RESULT BACK IN MEMORY
```

2. Rotate left the data at the address in memory locations PGZRO and PGZRO+1 using Y as an index.

```
LDA     (PGZRO),Y    ;GET THE DATA
ROL     A            ;ROTATE DATA LEFT
STA     (PGZRO),Y    ;STORE RESULT BACK IN MEMORY
```

REFERENCES

1. Osborne, A. *An Introduction to Microcomputers, Volume 1: Basic Concepts,* 2nd ed. Berkeley: Osborne/McGraw-Hill, 1980.

2. Leventhal, L.A. *6800 Assembly Language Programming.* Berkeley: Osborne/ McGraw-Hill, 1978.

3. Leventhal, L.A. *6809 Assembly Language Programming.* Berkeley: Osborne/ McGraw-Hill, 1981.

4. Fischer, W.P. "Microprocessor Assembly Language Draft Standard," *IEEE Computer,* December 1979, pp. 96-109.

5. Scanlon, L.J. *6502 Software Design,* Howard W. Sams, Indianapolis, Ind., 1980, pp. 111-13.

Chapter 3 Common Programming Errors

This chapter describes common errors in 6502 assembly language programs. The final section describes common errors in input/output drivers and interrupt service routines. Our aims here are the following:

- To warn programmers of potential trouble spots and sources of confusion.
- To indicate likely causes of programming errors.
- To emphasize some of the techniques and warnings presented in Chapters 1 and 2.
- To inform maintenance programmers where to look for errors and misinterpretations.
- To provide the beginner with a starting point in the difficult process of locating and correcting errors.

Of course, no list of errors can be complete. We have emphasized the most common ones in our work, but we have not attempted to describe the rare, subtle, or occasional errors that frustrate even the experienced programmer. However, most errors are remarkably simple once you uncover them and this list should help you debug most programs.

CATEGORIZATION OF PROGRAMMING ERRORS

We may generally divide common 6502 programming errors into the following categories:

- Using the Carry improperly. Typical errors include forgetting to clear the Carry before addition or set it before subtraction, and interpreting it incorrectly after comparisons (it acts as an inverted borrow).

· Using the other flags improperly. Typical errors include using the wrong flag (such as Negative instead of Carry), branching after instructions that do not affect a particular flag, inverting the branch conditions (particularly when the Zero flag is involved), and changing a flag accidentally before branching.

· Confusing addresses and data. Typical errors include using immediate instead of direct addressing, or vice versa, and confusing memory locations on page 0 with the addresses accessed indirectly through those locations.

· Using the wrong formats. Typical errors include using BCD (decimal) instead of binary, or vice versa, and using binary or hexadecimal instead of ASCII.

· Handling arrays incorrectly. Typical problems include accidentally overrunning the array at one end or the other (often by 1) and ignoring page boundaries when the array exceeds 256 bytes in length.

· Ignoring implicit effects. Typical errors include using the contents of the accumulator, index register, stack pointer, flags, or page 0 locations without considering the effects of intermediate instructions on these contents. Most errors arise from instructions that have unexpected, implicit, or indirect effects.

· Failing to provide proper initial conditions for routines or for the microcomputer as a whole. Most routines require the initialization of counters, indirect addresses, indexes, registers, flags, and temporary storage locations. The microcomputer as a whole requires the initialization of the Interrupt Disable and Decimal Mode flags and all global RAM addresses (note particularly indirect addresses and other temporary storage on page 0).

· Organizing the program incorrectly. Typical errors include skipping or repeating initialization routines, failing to update indexes, counters, or indirect addresses, and forgetting to save intermediate or final results.

A common source of errors, one that is beyond the scope of our discussion, is conflict between user programs and systems programs. A simple example is a user program that saves results in temporary storage locations that operating systems or utility programs need for their own purposes. The results thus disappear mysteriously even though a detailed trace of the user program does not reveal any errors.

More complex sources of conflict may include the interrupt system, input/output ports, the stack, or the flags. After all, the systems programs must employ the same resources as the user programs. (Systems programs generally attempt to save and restore the user's environment, but they often have subtle or unexpected effects.) Making an operating system transparent to the user is a problem comparable to devising a set of regulations, laws, or tax codes that have no loopholes or side effects.

USING THE CARRY IMPROPERLY

The following instructions and conventions are the most common sources of errors:

- CMP, CPX, and CPY affect the Carry as if it were an inverted borrow, that is, they set the Carry if the subtraction of the memory location from the register did not require a borrow, and they clear the Carry if it did. Thus, Carry = 1 if no borrow was necessary and Carry = 0 if a borrow was required. This is contrary to the sense of the Carry in most other microprocessors (the 6800, 6809, 8080, 8085, or Z-80).

- SBC subtracts the inverted Carry flag from the normal subtraction of the memory location from the accumulator. That is, it produces the result (A) − (M) − (1 − Carry). If you do not want the Carry flag to affect the result, you must set it with SEC. Like comparisons, SBC affects the Carry as if it were an inverted borrow; Carry = 0 if the subtraction requires a borrow and 1 if it does not.

- ADC always includes the Carry in the addition. This produces the result (A) = (A) + (M) + Carry. If you do not want the Carry flag to affect the result, you must clear it with CLC. Note that the Carry has its normal meaning after ADC.

Examples

1. CMP ADDR

This instruction sets the flags as if the contents of memory location ADDR had been subtracted from the accumulator. The Carry flag is set if the subtraction does not require a borrow and cleared if it does. Thus

Carry = 1 if (A) ≥ (ADDR)
Carry = 0 if (A) < (ADDR)

We are assuming that both numbers are unsigned. Note that the Carry is set (to 1) if the numbers are equal.

2. SBC #VALUE

This instruction subtracts VALUE and 1−Carry from the accumulator. It sets the flags just like a comparison. To subtract VALUE alone from the accumulator, you must use the sequence

```
SEC                     ;SET INVERTED BORROW
SBC     #VALUE          ;SUBTRACT VALUE
```

This sequence produces the result (A) = (A) − VALUE. If VALUE = 1, the sequence is equivalent to a Decrement Accumulator instruction (remember, DEC cannot be applied to A).

3. ADC #VALUE

This instruction adds VALUE and Carry to the accumulator. To add VALUE alone to the accumulator, you must use the sequence

```
CLC                     ;CLEAR CARRY
ADC     #VALUE          ;ADD VALUE
```

This sequence produces the result (A) = (A) + VALUE. If VALUE = 1, the sequence is equivalent to an Increment Accumulator instruction (remember, INC cannot be applied to A).

USING THE OTHER FLAGS INCORRECTLY

Instructions for the 6502 generally have expected effects on the flags. The only special case is BIT. Situations that require some care include the following:

- Store instructions (STA, STX, and STY) do not affect the flags, so the flags do not necessarily reflect the value that was just stored. You may need to test the register by transferring it to another register or comparing it with 0. Note that load instructions (including PHA) and transfer instructions (excluding TXS) affect the Zero and Negative flags.

- After a comparison (CMP, CPX, or CPY), the Zero flag indicates whether the operands are equal. The Zero flag is set if the operands are equal and cleared if they are not. There is some potential confusion here — BEQ means *branch if the result is equal to 0;* that is, *branch if the Zero flag is 1.* Be careful of the difference between the result being 0 and the Zero flag being 0. These two conditions are opposites; the Zero flag is 0 if the result is not 0.

- In comparing unsigned numbers, the Carry flag indicates which number is larger. CMP, CPX, or CPY clears the Carry if the register's contents are greater than or equal to the other operand and sets the Carry if the register's contents are less. Note that comparing equal operands sets the Carry. If these alternatives *(greater than or equal* and *less than)* are not what you need (you want the alternatives to be *greater than* and *less than or equal*), you can reverse the subtraction, subtract 1 from the accumulator, or add 1 to the other operand.

- In comparing signed numbers, the Negative flag indicates which operand is larger unless two's complement overflow has occurred. We must first look at the Overflow flag. If that flag is 0, the Negative flag indicates which operand is larger; if that flag is 1, the sense of the Negative flag is inverted.

After a comparison (if no overflow occurs), the Negative flag is set if the register's contents are less than the other operand, and cleared if the register's contents are greater than or equal to the other operand. Note that comparing equal operands clears the Negative flag. As with the Carry, you can handle the equality case in the opposite way by adjusting either operand or by reversing the subtraction.

· If a condition holds and you wish the computer to do something, a common procedure is to branch around a section of the program on the opposite condition. For example, to increment memory location OVFLW if the Carry is 1, use the sequence

```
        BCC     NEXT
        INC     OVFLW
NEXT    NOP
```

The branch condition is the opposite of the condition under which the section should be executed.

· Increment and decrement instructions do not affect the Carry flag. This allows the instructions to be used for counting in loops that perform multiple-byte arithmetic (the Carry is needed to transfer carries or borrows between bytes). Increment and decrement instructions do, however, affect the Zero and Negative flags; you can use the effect on the Zero flag to determine whether an increment has produced a carry. Note the following typical sequences:

1. 16-bit increment of memory locations INDEX and INDEX+1 (MSB in INDEX+1)

```
        INC     INDEX       ;INCREMENT LSB
        BNE     DONE
        INC     INDEX+1     ;AND CARRY TO MSB IF NECESSARY
DONE    NOP
```

We determine if a carry has been generated by examining the Zero flag after incrementing the less significant byte.

2. 16-bit decrement of memory locations INDEX and INDEX+1 (MSB in INDEX+1)

```
        LDA     INDEX       ;CHECK LSB
        BNE     DECLSB
        DEC     INDEX+1     ;BORROW FROM MSB IF NECESSARY
DECLSB  DEC     INDEX       ;DECREMENT MSB
```

We determine if a borrow will be generated by examining the less significant byte before decrementing it.

· The BIT instruction has rather unusual effects on the flags. It places bit 6 of the memory location in the Overflow flag and bit 7 in the Negative flag, regardless of the value in the accumulator. Thus, only the Zero flag actually reflects the logical ANDing of the accumulator and the memory location.

· Only a few instructions affect the Carry or Overflow flags. The instructions that affect Carry are arithmetic (ADC, SBC), comparisons (CMP, CPX, and CPY), and shifts (ASL, LSR, ROL, and ROR), besides the obvious CLC and SEC. The only instructions that affect Overflow are ADC, BIT, CLV, and SBC; comparison and shift instructions do not affect the Overflow flag, unlike the situation in the closely related 6800 and 6809 microprocessors.

Examples

1. The sequence

```
        STA     $1700
        BEQ     DONE
```

will have unpredictable results, since STA does not affect any flags. Sequences that will produce a jump if the value stored is 0 are

```
        STA     $1700
        CMP     #0              ;TEST ACCUMULATOR
        BEQ     DONE
```

or

```
        STA     $1700
        TAX                     ;TEST ACCUMULATOR
        BEQ     DONE
```

2. The instruction CMP #$25 sets the Zero flag as follows:

Zero = 1 if the contents of A are 25_{16}
Zero = 0 if the contents of A are not 25_{16}

Thus, if you want to increment memory location COUNT, if (A) = 25_{16}, use the sequence

```
        CMP     #$25            ;IS A 25?
        BNE     DONE
        INC     COUNT           ;YES, INCREMENT COUNT
DONE    NOP
```

Note that we use BNE to branch around the increment if the condition (A = 25_{16}) does not hold. It is obviously easy to err by inverting the branch condition.

3. The instruction CPX #$25 sets the Carry flag as follows:

Carry = 0 if the contents of X are between 00 and 24_{16}
Carry = 1 if the contents of X are between 25_{16} and FF_{16}

Thus, the Carry flag is cleared if X contains an unsigned number less than the other operand and set if X contains an unsigned number greater than or equal to the other operand.

If you want to clear the Carry if the X register contains 25_{16}, use CPX #$26 instead of CPX #$25. That is, we have

```
CPX     #$25
BCC     LESS            ;BRANCH IF (X) LESS THAN 25
```

or

```
CPX     #$26
BCC     LESSEQ          ;BRANCH IF (X) 25 OR LESS
```

4. The sequence SEC, SBC #$40 sets the Negative (Sign) flag as follows:

Negative = 0 if A is between 40_{16} and $7F_{16}$ (normal signed arithmetic) or if A is between 80_{16} and $C0_{16}$ (because of two's complement overflow)

Negative = 1 if A is between 00_{16} and $3F_{16}$ or between $C1_{16}$ and FF_{16} (normal signed arithmetic)

Two's complement overflow occurs if A contains a number between 80_{16} (-128_{10} in two's complement) and $C0_{16}$ (-64_{10} in two's complement). Then subtracting 40_{16} (64_{10}) produces a result less than -128_{10}, which is beyond the range of an 8-bit signed number. The setting of the Overflow flag indicates this out-of-range condition.

The following sequence will thus produce a branch if A contains a signed number less than 40_{16}.

```
SEC                     ;SET INVERTED BORROW
SBC     #$40            ;SUBTRACT 40 HEX
BVS     DEST            ;BRANCH IF OVERFLOW IS SET
BMI     DEST            ;OR IF DIFFERENCE IS NEGATIVE
```

Note that we cannot use CMP here, since it does not affect the Overflow flag. We could, however, use the sequence

```
CMP     #0              ;BRANCH IF A IS NEGATIVE
BMI     DEST
CMP     #$40            ;OR IF A IS POSITIVE BUT BELOW 40 HEX
BCC     DEST
```

We eliminate the possibility of overflow by handling negative numbers separately.

5. The sequence

```
INC     ADDR
BCS     NXTPG
```

will have unpredictable results, since INC does not affect the Carry flag. A sequence that will produce a jump, if the result of the increment is 00 (thus implying the production of a carry), is illustrated below.

```
INC     ADDR
BEQ     NXTPG
```

We can tell when an increment has produced a carry, but we cannot tell when a decrement has required a borrow since the result then is FF_{16}, not 0. Thus, it is much simpler to increment a multibyte number than to decrement it.

6. The sequence

```
BIT     ADDR
BVS     DEST
```

produces a branch if bit 6 of ADDR is 1. The contents of the accumulator do not affect it. Similarly, the sequence

```
BIT     ADDR
BPL     DEST
```

produces a branch if bit 7 of ADDR is 0. The contents of the accumulator do not affect it. The only common sequence with BIT in which the accumulator matters is

```
LDA     #MASK
BIT     ADDR
```

This sequence sets the Zero flag if logically ANDing MASK and the contents of ADDR produces a result of 0. A typical example using the Zero flag is

```
LDA     #%00010000
BIT     ADDR
BNE     DEST            ;BRANCH IF BIT 4 OF ADDR IS 1
```

This sequence forces a branch if the result of the logical AND is nonzero, that is, if bit 4 of ADDR is 1.

The effects of BIT on the Overflow and Negative flags do not generally cause programming errors since there are no standard, widely used effects that might cause confusion. These effects do, however, create documentation problems since the approach is unique and those unfamiliar with the 6502 cannot be expected to guess what is happening.

7. The sequence

```
CMP     #VALUE
BVS     DEST
```

produces unpredictable results, since CMP does not affect the Overflow flag. Instead, to produce a branch if the subtraction results in two's complement overflow, use the sequence

```
SEC                     ;SET INVERTED BORROW
SBC     #VALUE          ;SUBTRACT VALUE
BVS     DEST            ;BRANCH IF OVERFLOW OCCURS
```

CONFUSING ADDRESSES AND DATA

The rules to remember are

· The immediate addressing mode requires the actual data as an operand. That is, LDA #$40 loads the accumulator with the number 40_{16}.

. The absolute and zero page (direct) addressing modes require the address of the data as an operand. That is, LDA $40 loads the accumulator with the contents of memory location 0040_{16}.

· The indirect indexed and indexed indirect addressing modes obtain the indirect address from two memory locations on page 0. The indirect address is in two memory locations starting at the specified address; it is stored *upside-down,* with its less significant byte at the lower address. Fortunately, the indexed indirect (preindexed) mode is rarely used and is seldom a cause of errors. The meaning of addressing modes with JMP and JSR can be confusing, since these instructions use addresses as if they were data. The assumption is that one could not transfer control to a number, so a jump with immediate addressing would be meaningless. However, the instruction JMP $1C80 loads $1C80_{16}$ into the program counter, just like a load with immediate addressing, even though we conventionally say that the instruction uses absolute addressing. Similarly, the instruction JMP (ADDR) loads the program counter with the address from memory locations ADDR and ADDR+1; it thus acts like a load instruction with absolute (direct) addressing.

Examples

1. LDX#$20 loads the number 20_{16} into index register X. LDX $20 loads the contents of memory location 0020_{16} into index register X.

2. LDA ($40),Y loads the accumulator from the address obtained by indexing with Y from the base address in memory locations 0040_{16} and 0041_{16} (MSB in 0041_{16}). Note that if LDA ($40),Y makes sense, then LDA ($41),Y generally does not, since it uses the base address in memory locations 0041_{16} and 0042_{16}. Thus, the indirect addressing modes generally make sense only if the indirect addresses are aligned properly on word boundaries; however, the 6502 does not check this alignment in the way that many computers (particularly IBM machines) do. The programmer must make sure that all memory locations used indirectly contain addresses with the bytes arranged properly.

Confusing addresses and their contents is a frequent problem in handling data structures. For example, the queue of tasks to be executed by a piece of test equipment might consist of a block of information for each task. That block might contain

· The starting address of the test routine.

- The number of seconds for which the test is to run.
- The address in which the result is to be saved.
- The upper and lower thresholds against which the result is to be compared.
- The address of the next block in the queue.

Thus, the block contains data, direct addresses, and indirect addresses. Typical errors that a programmer could make are

- Transferring control to the memory locations containing the starting address of the test routine, rather than to the actual starting address.
- Storing the result in the block rather than in the address specified in the block.
- Using a threshold as an address rather than as data.
- Assuming that the next block starts within the current block, rather than at the address given in the current block.

Jump tables are another common source of errors. The following are alternative implementations:

- Form a table of jump instructions and transfer control to the correct element (for example, to the third jump instruction).
- Form a table of destination addresses and transfer control to the contents of the correct element (for example, to the address in the third element).

You will surely have problems if you try to use the jump instructions as indirect addresses or if you try to execute the indirect addresses.

FORMAT ERRORS

The rules you should remember are

- A $ in front of a number (or an H at the end) indicates hexadecimal to the assembler and a % in front or a B at the end indicates binary. Be careful — some assemblers use different symbols.
- The default mode of most assemblers is decimal; that is, most assemblers assume all numbers to be decimal unless they are specifically designated as something else. A few assemblers (such as Apple's miniassembler and the mnemonic entry mode in Rockwell's AIM-65) assume hexadecimal as a default.
- ADC and SBC instructions produce decimal results if the Decimal Mode flag is 1 and binary results if the Decimal Mode flag is 0. All other instructions, including DEC, DEX, DEY, INC, INX, and INY, always produce binary results.

You should make special efforts to avoid the following common errors:

- Omitting the hexadecimal designation ($ or H) from a hexadecimal data item or address. The assembler will assume the item to be a decimal number if it contains no letter digits. It will treat the item as a name if it is valid (it must start with a letter in most assemblers). The assembler will indicate an error only if the item cannot be interpreted as a decimal number or a name.
- Omitting the binary designation (% or B) from a binary data item. The assembler will assume it to be a decimal number.
- Confusing decimal (BCD) representations with binary representations. Remember, ten is not an integral power of two, so the binary and BCD representations are not the same beyond nine. Standard BCD constants must be designated as hexadecimal numbers, not as decimal numbers.
- Confusing binary or decimal representations with ASCII representations. An ASCII input device produces ASCII characters and an ASCII output device responds to ASCII characters.

Examples

1. LDA 2000

This instruction loads the accumulator from memory address 2000_{10} ($07D0_{16}$), not address 2000_{16}. The assembler will not produce an error message, since 2000 is a valid decimal number.

2. AND #00000011

This instruction logically ANDs the accumulator with the decimal number 11 (1011_2), not with the binary number 11 (3_{10}). The assembler will not produce an error message, since 00000011 is a valid decimal number despite its unusual form.

3. ADC #40

This instruction adds 40_{10} (not $40_{16} = 64_{10}$) and the Carry to the accumulator. Note that 40_{10} is not the same as 40 BCD, which is 40_{16}; $40_{10} = 28_{16}$. The assembler will not produce an error message, since 40 is a valid decimal number.

4. LDA #3

This instruction loads the accumulator with the number 3. If this value is now sent to an ASCII output device, it will respond as if it had received the character ETX (03_{16}), not the character 3 (33_{16}). The correct version is

```
LDA     #'3           ;GET AN ASCII 3
```

5. If memory location 0040_{16} contains a single digit, the sequence

```
LDA     $40
STA     PORT
```

will not print that digit on an ASCII output device. The correct sequence is

```
LDA     $40             ;GET DECIMAL DIGIT
CLC
ADC     #'0             ;ADJUST TO ASCII
STA     PORT
```

or

```
LDA     $40             ;GET DECIMAL DIGIT
ORA     #%00110000      ;ADJUST TO ASCII
STA     PORT
```

6. If input port IPORT contains a single ASCII decimal digit, the sequence

```
LDA     IPORT
STA     $40
```

will not store the actual digit in memory location 0040_{16}. Instead, it will store the ASCII version, which is the actual digit plus 30_{16}. The correct sequence is

```
LDA     IPORT           ;GET ASCII DIGIT
SEC
SBC     #'0             ;ADJUST TO DECIMAL
STA     $40
```

or

```
LDA     IPORT           ;GET ASCII DIGIT
AND     #%11001111      ;ADJUST TO DECIMAL
STA     $40
```

Handling decimal arithmetic on the 6502 microprocessor is simple, since the processor has a Decimal Mode (D) flag. When that flag is set (by SED), all additions and subtractions produce decimal results. So, the following sequences implement decimal addition and subtraction:

- Decimal addition of memory location ADDR to the accumulator

```
SED                     :ENTER DECIMAL MODE
CLC
ADC     ADDR            ;ADD DECIMAL
CLD                     :LEAVE DECIMAL MODE
```

- Decimal subtraction of memory location ADDR from the accumulator

```
SED                     :ENTER DECIMAL MODE
SEC
SBC     ADDR            ;SUBTRACT DECIMAL
CLD                     ;LEAVE DECIMAL MODE
```

Since increment and decrement instructions always produce binary results, we must use the following sequences (assuming the D flag is set).

Increment memory location 0040_{16} in the decimal mode

```
LDA     $40
CLC
ADC     #1
STA     $40
```

Decrement memory location 0040_{16} in the decimal mode

```
LDA     $40
SEC
SBC     #1
STA     $40
```

The problem with the decimal mode is that it has implicit effects. That is, the same ADC and SBC instructions with the same data will produce different results, depending on the state of the Decimal Mode flag. The following procedures will reduce the likelihood of the implicit effects causing unforeseen errors:

- Initialize the Decimal Mode flag (with CLD) as part of the regular system initialization. Note that RESET has no effect on the Decimal Mode flag.
- Clear the Decimal Mode flag as soon as you are through performing decimal arithmetic.
- Initialize the Decimal Mode flag in interrupt service routines that include ADC or SBC instructions. That is, such service routines should execute CLD before performing any binary addition or subtraction.

HANDLING ARRAYS INCORRECTLY

The following situations are the most common sources of errors:

- If you are counting an index register down to 0, the zero index value may never be used. The solution is to reduce the base address or addresses by 1. For example, if the terminating sequence in a loop is

```
DEX
BNE LOOP
```

the processor will fall through as soon as X is decremented to 0. A typical adjusted loop (clearing NTIMES bytes of memory) is

```
        LDX     #NTIMES
        LDA     #0
CLEAR   STA     BASE-1,X
        DEX
        BNE     CLEAR
```

Note the use of BASE−1 in the indexed store instruction. The program clears addresses BASE through BASE + NTIMES−1.

· Although working backward through an array is often more efficient than working forward, programmers generally find it confusing. Remember that the address BASE+(X) contains the previous entry in a loop like the example shown above. Although the processor can work backward just as easily as it can work forward, programmers usually find themselves conditioned to thinking ahead.

· Be careful not to execute one extra iteration or stop one short. Remember, memory locations BASE through BASE+N contain N+1 entries, not N entries. It is easy to forget the last entry or, as shown above, drop the first one. On the other hand, if you have N entries, they will occupy memory locations BASE through BASE+N-1; now it is easy to find yourself working off the end of the array.

· You cannot extend absolute indexed addressing or zero-page indexed addressing beyond 256 bytes. If an index register contains FF_{16}, incrementing it will produce a result of 00. Similarly, if an index register contains 00, decrementing it will produce a result of FF_{16}. Thus, you must be careful about incrementing or decrementing index registers when you might accidentally exceed the capacity of eight bits. To extend loops beyond 256 bytes, use the indirect indexed (postindexed) addressing mode. Then the following sequence will add 1 to the more significant byte of the indirect address when index register Y is incremented to 0.

```
          INY               ;INCREMENT INDEX REGISTER
          BNE     DONE
          INC     INDIR+1
DONE      NOP
```

Here INDIR and INDIR+1 are the locations on page 0 that contain the indirect address.

Example

1. Let us assume (INDIR) = 80_{16} and (INDIR+1) = $4C_{16}$, so that the initial base address is $4C80_{16}$. If the loop refers to the address (INDIR), Y, the effective address is (INDIR+1) (INDIR) + Y or $4C80_{16}$ + (Y). When Y = FF_{16}, the effective address is

$$4C80_{16} + (Y) = 4C80_{16} + FF_{16} = 4D7F_{16}$$

The sequence shown above for incrementing the index and the indirect address produces the results

$$(Y) = (Y) + 1 = 00$$
$$(INDIR+1) = (INDIR+1) = 1 = 4D_{16}$$

The effective address for the next iteration will be

$$4D80_{16} + (Y) = 4D80_{16} = 00_{16} = 4D80_{16}$$

which is the next higher address in the normal consecutive sequence.

IMPLICIT EFFECTS

Some of the implicit effects you should remember are

· The changing of the Negative and Zero flags by load and transfer instructions, such as LDA, LDX, LDY, PLA, TAX, TAY, TSX, TXA, and TYA.

· The dependence of the results of ADC and SBC instructions on the values of the Carry and Decimal Mode flags.

· The special use of the Negative and Overflow flags by the BIT instruction.

The use of the memory address one larger than the specified one in the indirect, indirect indexed, and indexed indirect addressing modes.

· The changing of the stack pointer by PHA, PHP, PLA, PLP, JSR, RTS, RTI, and BRK. Note that JSR and RTS change the stack pointer by 2, and BRK and RTI change it by 3.

· The saving of the return address minus 1 by JSR and the addition of 1 to the restored address by RTS.

· The inclusion of the Carry in the rotate instructions ROL and ROR. The rotation involves nine bits, not eight bits.

Examples

1. LDX $40

This instruction affects the Negative and Zero flags, so those flags will no longer reflect the value in the accumulator or the result of the most recent operation.

2. ADC #$20

This instruction adds in the Carry flag as well as the immediate data (20_{16}). The result will be binary if the Decimal Mode flag is cleared, but BCD if the Decimal Mode flag is set.

3. BIT $1700

This instruction sets the Overflow flag from the value of bit 6 of memory location 1700_{16}. This is the only instruction that has a completely unexpected effect on that flag.

4. JMP ($1C00)

This instruction transfers control to the address in memory locations $1C00_{16}$ and $1C01_{16}$ (MSB in $1C01_{16}$). Note that $1C01_{16}$ is involved even though it is not specified, since indirect addresses always occupy two bytes of memory.

5. PHA

This instruction not only saves the accumulator in memory, but it also decrements the stack pointer by 1.

6. RTS

This instruction not only loads the program counter from the top two locations in the stack, but it also increments the stack pointer by 2 and the program counter by 1.

7. ROR A

This instruction rotates the accumulator right 1 bit, moving the former contents of bit position 0 into the Carry and the former contents of the Carry into bit position 7.

INITIALIZATION ERRORS

The initialization routines must perform the following tasks, either for the microcomputer system as a whole or for particular routines:

- Load all RAM locations with initial values. This includes indirect addresses and other temporary storage on page 0. You cannot assume that a memory location contains 0 just because you have not used it.
- Load all registers and flags with initial values. Reset initializes only the Interrupt Disable flag (to 1). Note, in particular, the need to initialize the Decimal Mode flag (usually with CLD) and the stack pointer (using the LDX, TXS sequence).
- Load all counters and indirect addresses with initial values. Be particularly careful of addresses on page 0 that are used in either the indirect indexed (postindexed) addressing mode or the indexed indirect (preindexed) mode.

ORGANIZING THE PROGRAM INCORRECTLY

The following problems are the most common:

- Failing to initialize a register, flag, or memory location. You cannot assume that a register, flag, or memory location contains zero just because you have not used it.

- Accidentally reinitializing a register, flag, memory location, index, counter, or indirect address. Be sure that your branches do not cause some or all of the initialization instructions to be repeated.

- Failing to update indexes, counters, or indirect addresses. A problem here may be one path that branches around the updating instructions or changes some of the conditions before executing those instructions.

- Forgetting to save intermediate or final results. It is remarkably easy to calculate a result and then load something else into the accumulator. Errors like this are particularly difficult to locate, since all the instructions that calculate the result work properly and yet the result itself is being lost. A common problem here is for a branch to transfer control to an instruction that writes over the result that was just calculated.

- Forgetting to branch around instructions that should not be executed in a particular path. Remember, the computer will execute instructions consecutively unless told specifically to do otherwise. Thus, it is easy for a program to accidentally fall through to a section that the programmer expects it to reach only via a branch. An awkward feature of the 6502 is its lack of an unconditional relative branch; you must either use JMP with absolute addressing or set a condition and branch on it holding (SEC, BCS, DEST and CLV, BVC DEST).

ERROR RECOGNITION BY ASSEMBLERS

Most assemblers will immediately recognize the following common errors:

- Undefined operation code (usually a misspelling or an omission)
- Undefined name (often a misspelling or an omitted definition)
- Illegal character (for example, a 2 in a binary number or a B in a decimal number)
- Illegal format (for example, an incorrect delimiter or the wrong register or operand)
- Illegal value (usually a number too large for 8 or 16 bits)
- Missing operand
- Double definition (two different values assigned to one name)
- Illegal label (for example, a label attached to a pseudo-operation that does not allow a label)
- Missing label (for example, on an = pseudo-operation that requires one).

These errors are generally easy to correct. Often the only problem is an error, such as omitting the semicolon or other delimiter in front of a comment, that confuses the assembler and results in a series of meaningless error messages.

There are, however, many common errors that assemblers will not recognize. The programmer should be aware that his or her program may contain such errors even if the assembler does not report them. Typical examples are

- Omitted lines. Obviously, the assembler cannot identify a completely omitted line unless that line contains a label or definition that is used later in the program. The easiest lines to omit are repetitions (that is, one or more lines that are the same or sequences that start the same) or instructions that seem to be unnecessary. Typical repetitions are series of shifts, branches, increments, or decrements. Instructions that may appear unnecessary include CLC, SEC, and so forth.
- Omitted designations. The assembler cannot tell if you omitted a designation such as #, H, $, B, or % unless the omission results in an illegal character (such as C in a decimal number). Otherwise, the assembler will assume all addresses to be direct and all numbers to be decimal. Problems occur with numbers that are valid as either decimal or hexadecimal values (such as 44 or 2050) and with binary numbers (such as 00000110).

- Misspellings that are still valid. Typical examples are typing BCC instead of BCS, LDX instead of LDY, and SEC instead of SED. Unless the misspelling is invalid, the assembler has no way of knowing what you meant. Valid misspellings are often a problem if you use similar names or labels such as XXX and XXXX, L121 and L112, or VAR1I and VARII.

- Designating instructions as comments. If you place a semicolon at the start of an instruction line, the assembler will treat the line as a comment. This can be a perplexing error, since the line appears in the listing but is not assembled into object code.

Sometimes you can confuse the assembler by entering invalid instructions. An assembler may accept a totally illogical entry simply because its developer never considered such possibilities. The result can be unpredictable, much like the results of giving someone a completely wrong number (for example, a telephone number instead of a street address or a driver license number instead of a credit card number). Some cases in which a 6502 assembler can go wrong are

- If you designate an impossible register or addressing mode. Some assemblers will accept instructions like INC A, LDA ($40),X, or LDY BASE,Y. They will produce erroneous object code without any warning.

- If you enter an invalid digit, such as Q in a decimal or hexadecimal number or 7 in a binary number. Some assemblers will assign values to such erroneous digits in an aribitrary manner.

- If you enter an invalid operand such as LDA #$HX. Some assemblers will accept this and generate incorrect code.

The assembler will recognize only errors that its developer anticipated. Programmers are often able to make mistakes that the developer never imagined, much as automobile drivers are often capable of performing maneuvers that never occurred in the wildest dreams of a highway designer or traffic planner. Note that only a line-by-line hand checking of the program will find errors that the assembler does not recognize.

IMPLEMENTATION ERRORS

Occasionally, a microprocessor's instructions simply do not work the way the designers or anyone else would expect. The 6502 has one implementation error that is, fortunately, quite rare. The instruction JMP ($XXFF) where the Xs represent any page number, does not work correctly. One would expect this instruction to obtain the destination address from memory locations XXFF and (XX+1)00. Instead, it apparently does not increment the more significant byte of the indirect address; it therefore obtains the destination address from memory locations XXFF and XX00. For example, JMP ($1CFF) will jump to the address stored in memory locations $1CFF_{16}$ (LSB) and $1C00_{16}$ (MSB), surely a curious outcome. Most assemblers expect the programmer to ensure that no indirect jumps ever obtain their destination addresses across page boundaries.

COMMON ERRORS IN I/O DRIVERS

Most errors in I/O drivers involve both hardware and software, so they are often difficult to categorize. Some mistakes you should watch for are

- Confusing input ports and output ports. Many I/O interfaces use the READ/WRITE line for addressing, so that reading and writing the same memory address results in operations on different physical registers. Even when this is not done, it may still be impossible to read back output data unless it is latched and buffered.

- Attempting to perform operations that are physically impossible. Reading data from an output device (such as a display) or sending data to an input device (such as a keyboard) makes no physical sense. However, accidentally using the wrong address will cause no assembly errors; the address, after all, is valid and the assembler has no way of knowing that certain operations cannot be performed on it. Similarly, a program may attempt to save data in a nonexistent address or in a ROM.

· Forgetting implicit hardware effects. Sometimes transferring data to or from a port will change the status lines automatically, particularly if you are using a 6520 or 6522 parallel interface. Even reading or writing a port while debugging a program will change the status lines. Be particularly careful of instructions like comparisons and BIT which read a memory address even though they do not change any registers, and instructions like decrement, increment, and shift which both read and write a memory address (the actual operation, of course, takes place inside the processor).

· Reading or writing without checking status. Many devices can accept or provide data only when a status line indicates they are ready. Transferring data to or from them at other times will have unpredictable effects.

· Ignoring the differences between input and output. Remember that an input device normally starts out in the *not ready* state — it has no data available although the computer is ready to accept data. On the other hand, an output device normally starts out in the *ready* state, that is, it could accept data but the computer usually has none to send it. In many situations, particularly when using 6520, 6522, 6551, or 6850 devices, you may have to disable the outputs initially or send a null character (something that has no effect) to each output port just to change its state from *ready* to *not ready* initially.

· Failing to keep copies of output data. Remember that you may not be able to read the data back from the output port. If you need to repeat it later as part of repeating a transmission that was incorrectly received, change part of it (turn on or off one of several indicator lights attached to the same port), or save it as part of the interrupted status (the data is the current priority level). You must save a copy in memory. The copy must be updated every time the actual data is changed.

· Reading data before it is stable or while it is changing. Be sure that you understand exactly when the input device is guaranteed to produce stable data. In the case of switches that may bounce, you may want to sample them twice (more than a debouncing time apart) before taking any action. In the case of keys that may bounce, you may want to take action only when they are released rather than when they are pressed. The action on release also forces the operator to release the key rather than holding it down. In the case of persistent data (such as in serial I/O), you should center the reception, that is, read the data near the centers of the pulses rather than at the edges where the values may be changing.

· Forgetting to reverse the polarity of data being transferred to or from devices that operate in negative logic. Many simple I/O devices, such as switches and displays, use negative logic. A logic 0 means that a switch is closed or a display is lit. Common ten-position switches or dials also often produce data in negative logic, as do many encoders. The solution is simple — complement the data (using EOR #$FF) after reading it or before sending it.

· Confusing actual I/O ports with registers that are inside I/O devices. Programmable I/O devices, such as the 6520, 6522, 6551, and 6850, have control or command registers which determine how the device operates, and status registers that reflect the current state of the device or the transfer. These registers are inside the I/O devices; they are not connected to peripherals. Transferring data to or from status or control registers is not the same as transferring data to or from actual I/O ports.

· Using bidirectional ports improperly. Many devices, such as the 6520, 6522, 6530, and 6532, have bidirectional I/O ports. The ports (and perhaps even individual lines) can be used either as inputs or outputs. Normally, resetting the computer to avoid initial transients makes these ports inputs, so you must explicitly change them to outputs if necessary. Be cautious when reading bits or ports that are designated as outputs or writing into bits or ports that are designated as inputs. The only way to determine what will happen is to read the documentation for the specific device.

· Forgetting to clear status after performing an I/O operation. Once the processor has read data from an input port, that port should revert to the *not ready* state. Similarly, once the processor has written data into an output port, that port should revert to the *not ready* state. Some I/O devices change the status of their ports automatically after input or output operations, but others either do not or (as in the 6520) change status automatically only after input operations. Leaving the status set can result in an endless loop or highly erratic operation.

COMMON ERRORS IN INTERRUPT SERVICE ROUTINES

Many interrupt-related errors involve both hardware and software, but some of the common mistakes include the following:

· Failing to reenable interrupts during the service routine. The 6502 processor automatically disables interrupts after accepting one. It does reenable interrupts when RTI is executed, since RTI restores the status register from the stack.

· Failing to save and restore registers. The 6502 does not automatically save any registers except the program counter and the status register. So the accumulator, index registers, and scratchpad locations must be saved explicitly in the stack.

· Saving or restoring registers in the wrong order. Registers must be restored in the opposite order from that in which they were saved.

- Enabling interrupts before establishing priorities and other parameters of the interrupt system.

- Forgetting that the response to an interrupt includes saving the status register and the program counter at the top of the stack. The status register is on top and the program counter value is the actual return address, so the situation differs from subroutines in which the return address minus 1 is normally at the top of the stack.

- Not disabling the interrupt during multibyte transfers or instruction sequences that cannot be interrupted. In particular, you must avoid partial updating of data (such as time) that an interrupt service routine may use. In general, interrupts should be disabled when the main program is changing memory locations that it shares with interrupt service routines.

- Failing to reenable the interrupt after a sequence that must run with interrupts disabled. A corollary problem here is that you do not want to enable interrupts if they were not enabled when the sequence was entered. The solution is to save the previous state of the Interrupt Disable flag (using PHP) before executing the sequence and restore the previous state (using PLP) afterward. Note, however, that PLP restores the entire status register.

- Failing to initialize or establish the value of the Decimal Mode flag. An interrupt service routine should not assume a particular value (0) for the D flag. Instead, it should initialize that flag with CLD or SED if it executes ADC or SBC instructions. There is no need to save or restore the old D flag since that is done automatically as part of the saving and restoring of the status register. Initializing the D flag avoids problems if the service routine is entered from a program that runs with the D flag set.

- Failing to clear the signal that caused the interrupt. The service routine must clear the interrupt even if it does not require an immediate response or any input or output operations. Even when the processor has, for example, no data to send to an interrupting output device, it must still either clear the interrrupt or disable it. Otherwise, the processor will get caught in an endless loop. Similarly, a real-time clock interrupt will typically require no servicing other than an updating of time, but the service routine still must clear the clock interrupt. This clearing may involve reading a 6520 or 6522 I/O port or timer.

- Failing to communicate with the main program. The main program will not realize that the interrupt has been serviced unless it is informed explicitly. The usual way to inform the main program is to have the interrupt service routine change a flag that the main program can examine. The main program will then know that the service routine has been executed. The procedure is comparable to the practice of a postal patron raising a flag to indicate that he or she has mail to be picked up. The postman lowers the flag after picking up the mail. Note that this simple procedure means that the main program must examine the flag often enough to avoid missing data or messages. Of course, the programmer can always provide an intermediate storage area (or buffer) that can hold many data items.

· Failing to save and restore priority. The priority of an interrupt is often held in a write-only register or in a memory location. That priority must be saved just like the registers and restored properly at the end of the service routine. If the priority register is write-only, a copy of its contents must be saved in memory.

Introduction to the Program Section

The program section contains sets of assembly language subroutines for the 6502 microprocessor. Each subroutine is documented with an introductory section and comments; each is followed by at least one example of its use. The introductory material contains the following information:

1. Purpose of the routine
2. Procedure followed
3. Registers used
4. Execution time
5. Program size
6. Data memory required
7. Special cases
8. Entry conditions
9. Exit conditions
10. Examples

We have made each routine as general as possible. This is most difficult in the case of the input/output (I/O) and interrupt service routines described in Chapters 10 and 11, since in practice these routines are always computer-dependent. In such cases, we have limited the computer dependence to generalized input and output handlers and interrupt managers. We have drawn specific examples there from the popular Apple II computer, but the general principles are applicable to other 6502-based computers as well.

In all routines, we have used the following parameter passing techniques:

1. A single 8-bit parameter is passed in the accumulator. A second 8-bit parameter is passed in index register Y.

2. A single 16-bit parameter is passed in the accumulator and index register Y with the more significant byte in the accumulator. An accompanying 8-bit parameter is passed in index register X.

3. Larger numbers of parameters are passed in the stack, either directly or indirectly. We assume that subroutines are entered via a JSR instruction that places the return address at the top of the stack, and hence on top of the parameters.

Where there has been a choice between execution time and memory usage, we have chosen the approach that minimizes execution time. For example, in the case of arrays that are more than 256 bytes long, it is faster to handle the full pages, then handle the remaining partial page separately, than to handle the entire array in a single loop. The reason is that the first approach can use an 8-bit counter in an index register, whereas the second approach requires a 16-bit counter in memory.

We have also chosen the approach that minimizes the number of repetitive calculations. For example, in the case of array indexing, the number of bytes between the starting addresses of elements differing only by one in a particular subscript (known as the *size* of that subscript) depends only on the number of bytes per element and the bounds of the array. Thus, the sizes of the various subscripts can be calculated as soon as the bounds of the array are known; the sizes are therefore used as parameters for the indexing routines, so that they need not be calculated each time a particular array is indexed.

As for execution time, we have specified it for most short routines. For longer routines, we have given an approximate execution time. The execution time of programs involving many branches will obviously depend on which path is followed in a particular case. This is further complicated for the 6502 by the fact that branch instructions themselves require different numbers of clock cycles depending on whether the branch is not taken, taken within the current page, or taken across a page boundary. Thus, a precise execution time is often impossible to define. The documentation always contains at least one typical example showing an approximate or maximum execution time.

Our philosophy on error indications and special cases has been the following:

1. Routines should provide an easily tested indicator (such as the Carry flag) of whether any errors or exceptions have occurred.

2. Trivial cases, such as no elements in an array or strings of zero length, should result in immediate exits with minimal effect on the underlying data.

3. Misspecified data (such as a maximum string length of zero or an index beyond the end of an array) should result in immediate exits with minimal effect on the underlying data.

4. The documentation should include a summary of errors and exceptions (under the heading of "Special Cases").

5. Exceptions that may actually be convenient for the user (such as deleting more characters than could possibly be left in a string rather than counting the precise number) should be handled in a reasonable way, but should still be indicated as errors.

Obviously, no method of handling errors or exceptions can ever be completely consistent or well suited to all applications. We have taken the approach that a reasonable set of subroutines must deal with this issue, rather than ignoring it or assuming that the user will always provide data in the proper form.

The subroutines are listed as follows:

Code Conversion

Array Manipulation and Indexing

Arithmetic

Bit Manipulation and Shifts

String Manipulation

Array Operations

Input/Output

Interrupts

Binary to BCD Conversion (BN2BCD) 4A

Converts one byte of binary data to two bytes of BCD data.

Procedure: The program subtracts 100 repeatedly from the original data to determine the hundreds digit, then subtracts ten repeatedly from the remainder to determine the tens digit, and finally shifts the tens digit left four positions and combines it with the ones digit.

Registers Used: All

Execution Time: 133 cycles maximum, depends on the number of subtractions required to determine the tens and hundreds digits.

Program Size: 38 bytes

Data Memory Required: One byte anywhere in RAM (address TEMP).

Entry Conditions

Binary data in the accumulator.

Exit Conditions

Hundreds digit in the accumulator
Tens and ones digits in index register Y.

Examples

1. Data: (A) = $6E_{16}$ (110 decimal)

   Result: (A) = 01_{16} (hundreds digit)
   (Y) = 10_{16} (tens and ones digits)

2. Data: (A) = $B7_{16}$ (183 decimal)

   Result: (A) = 01_{16} (hundreds digit)
   (Y) = 83_{16} (tens and ones digits)

```
;                                                                       ;
;                                                                       ;
;                                                                       ;
;                                                                       ;
;       Title           Binary to BCD conversion                        ;
;       Name:           BN2BCD                                          ;
;                                                                       ;
;                                                                       ;

;                                                                       ;
;       Purpose:        Convert one byte of binary data to two          ;
;                       bytes of BCD data                               ;
;                                                                       ;
;       Entry:          Register A = binary data                        ;
;                                                                       ;
;       Exit:           Register A = high byte of BCD data              ;
;                       Register Y = low  byte of BCD data              ;
;                                                                       ;
```

```
;       Registers used: All                                              ;
;                                                                        ;
;       Time:           133 cycles maximum                               ;
;                                                                        ;
;       Size:           Program 38 bytes                                 ;
;                       Data     1 byte                                  ;
;                                                                        ;
;                                                                        ;


BN2BCD:
        ; CALCULATE 100'S DIGIT
        ;   DIVIDE BY 100
        ; Y = QUOTIENT
        ; A = REMAINDER
        LDY     #0FFH           ;START QUOTIENT AT -1
        SEC                     ;SET CARRY FOR INITIAL SUBTRACTION
D100LP:
        INY                     ;ADD 1 TO QUOTIENT
        SBC     #100            ;SUBTRACT 100
        BCS     D100LP          ;BRANCH IF A IS STILL LARGER THAN 100
        ADC     #100            ;ADD THE LAST 100 BACK
        TAX                     ;SAVE REMAINDER
        TYA
        PHA                     ;SAVE 100'S DIGIT ON THE STACK
        TXA                     ;GET REMAINDER

        ; CALCULATE 10'S AND 1'S DIGITS
        ;  DIVIDE REMAINDER OF THE 100'S DIGIT BY 10
        ; Y = 10'S DIGIT
        ; A = 1'S DIGIT
        LDY     #0FFH           ;START QUOTIENT AT -1
        SEC                     ;SET CARRY FOR INITIAL SUBTRACTION
D10LP:
        INY                     ;ADD 1 TO QUOTIENT
        SBC     #10
        BCS     D10LP           ;BRANCH IF A IS STILL LARGER THAN 10
        ADC     #10             ;ADD THE LAST 10 BACK

        ;COMBINE 1'S AND 10'S DIGITS
        STA     TEMP            ;SAVE 1'S DIGIT
        TYA                     ;GET 10'S DIGIT
        ASL     A
        ASL     A
        ASL     A
        ASL     A               ;MOVE 10'S TO HIGH NIBBLE OF A
        ORA     TEMP            ;OR IN THE 1'S DIGIT

        ;RETURN WITH Y = LOW BYTE A = HIGH BYTE
        TAY                     ;PLACE IN REG Y
        PLA                     ;GET 100'S DIGIT
        RTS

;DATA
TEMP:   .BLOCK  1               ;TEMPORARY USED TO COMBINE 1'S AND 10'S DIGITS
```

```
;                                                                          ;
;                                                                          ;
;       SAMPLE EXECUTION:                                                  ;
;                                                                          ;
;                                                                          ;


SC0401:
        ;CONVERT 0A HEXADECIMAL TO 10 BCD
        LDA     #0AH
        JSR     BN2BCD
        BRK                     ;A=0, Y=10H

        ;CONVERT FF HEXADECIMAL TO 255 BCD
        LDA     #0FFH
        JSR     BN2BCD
        BRK                     ;A=02H, Y=55H

        ;CONVERT 0 HEXADECIMAL TO 0 BCD
        LDA     #0
        JSR     BN2BCD
        BRK                     ;A=0, Y=0

        .END
```

BCD to Binary Conversion (BCD2BN) 4B

Converts one byte of BCD data to one byte of binary data.

Procedure: The program masks off the more significant digit, multiplies it by ten using shifts (10 = 8 + 2, and multiplying by eight or by two is equivalent to three or one left shifts, respectively), and adds the product to the less significant digit.

Registers Used: A, P, Y

Execution Time: 38 cycles

Program Size: 24 bytes

Data Memory Required: One byte anywhere in RAM (Address TEMP).

Entry Conditions

BCD data in the accumulator.

Exit Conditions

Binary data in the accumulator.

Examples

1. Data: (A) = 99_{16}

   Result: (A) = $63_{16} = 99_{10}$

2. Data: (A) = 23_{16}

   Result: (A) = $17_{16} = 23_{10}$

```
;                                                                   ;
;                                                                   ;
;                                                                   ;
;                                                                   ;
;       Title           BCD to binary conversion                    ;
;       Name:           BCD2BN                                      ;
;                                                                   ;
;                                                                   ;

;                                                                   ;
;       Purpose:        Convert one byte of BCD data to one         ;
;                       byte of binary data                         ;
;                                                                   ;
;       Entry:          Register A = BCD data                       ;
;                                                                   ;
;       Exit:           Register A = Binary data                    ;
;                                                                   ;
;       Registers used: A,P,Y                                       ;
;                                                                   ;
;       Time:           38 cycles                                   ;
```

```
;                                                                        ;
;       Size:               Program 24 bytes                             ;
;                           Data     1  byte                             ;
;                                                                        ;
;                                                                        ;


BCD2BN:
        ;MULTIPLY UPPER NIBBLE BY 10 AND SAVE IT
        ; TEMP := UPPER NIBBLE * 10 WHICH EQUALS UPPER NIBBLE * (8 + 2)
        TAY                         ;SAVE ORIGINAL VALUE
        AND     #0F0H               ;GET UPPER NIBBLE
        LSR     A                   ;DIVIDE BY 2 WHICH = UPPER NIBBLE * 8
        STA     TEMP                ;SAVE * 8
        LSR     A                   ;DIVIDE BY 4
        LSR     A                   ;DIVIDE BY 8: A = UPPER NIBBLE * 2
        CLC
        ADC     TEMP
        STA     TEMP                ;REG A = UPPER NIBBLE * 10

        TYA                         ;GET ORIGINAL VALUE
        AND     #0FH                ;GET LOWER NIBBLE
        CLC
        ADC     TEMP                ;ADD TO UPPER NIBBLE

        RTS

;DATA
TEMP:   .BLOCK  1



;                                                                        ;
;                                                                        ;
;       SAMPLE EXECUTION:                                                ;
;                                                                        ;
;                                                                        ;

SC0402:

        ;CONVERT 0 BCD TO 0 HEXADECIMAL
        LDA     #0
        JSR     BCD2BN
        BRK                         ;A=0

        ;CONVERT 99 BCD TO 63 HEXADECIMAL
        LDA     #099H
        JSR     BCD2BN
        BRK                         ;A=63H

        ;CONVERT 23 BCD TO 17 HEXADECIMAL
        LDA     #23H
        JSR     BCD2BN
        BRK                         ;A=17H

        .END
```

Binary to Hexadecimal ASCII Conversion (BN2HEX) 4C

Converts one byte of binary data to two ASCII characters corresponding to the two hexadecimal digits.

Procedure: The program masks off each hexadecimal digit separately and converts it to its ASCII equivalent. This involves a simple addition of 30_{16} if the digit is decimal. If the digit is non-decimal, an additional factor of seven must be added to handle the break between ASCII 9 (39_{16}) and ASCII A (41_{16}).

Registers Used: All

Execution Time: 77 cycles plus three extra cycles for each non-decimal digit.

Program Size: 31 bytes

Data Memory Required: None

Entry Conditions

Binary data in the accumulator.

Exit Conditions

ASCII equivalent of more significant hexadecimal digit in the accumulator
ASCII equivalent of less significant hexadecimal digit in index register Y.

Examples

1. Data: (A) = FB_{16}

   Result: (A) − 46_{16} (ASCII F)
   (Y) = 42_{16} (ASCII B)

2. Data: (A) = 59_{16}

   Result: (A) = 35_{16} (ASCII 5)
   (Y) = 39_{16} (ASCII 9)

```
;                                                              ;
;                                                              ;
;                                                              ;
;                                                              ;
;       Title           Binary to hex ASCII                    ;
;       Name:           BN2HEX                                 ;
;                                                              ;
;                                                              ;

;                                                              ;
;       Purpose:        Convert one byte of binary data to     ;
;                       two ASCII characters                   ;
;                                                              ;
;       Entry:          Register A = Binary data               ;
;                                                              ;
;       Exit:           Register A = First ASCII digit, high order value;
;                       Register Y = Second ASCII digit, low order value;
```

```
;                                                                   ;
;       Registers used: All                                         ;
;                                                                   ;
;       Time:           Approximately 77 cycles                     ;
;                                                                   ;
;       Size:           Program 31 bytes                            ;
;                                                                   ;
;                                                                   ;

BN2HEX:
        ;
        ;CONVERT HIGH NIBBLE
        TAX                             ;SAVE ORIGINAL VALUE
        AND     #0F0H                   ;GET HIGH NIBBLE
        LSR     A
        LSR     A
        LSR     A
        LSR     A                       ;MOVE TO LOWER NIBBLE
        JSR     NASCII                  ;CONVERT TO ASCII
        PHA                             ;SAVE IT ON THE STACK

        ;CONVERT LOW NIBBLE
        TXA
        AND     #0FH                    ;GET LOW NIBBLE
        JSR     NASCII                  ;CONVERT TO ASCII

        TAY                             ;LOW NIBBLE TO REG Y
        PLA                             ;HIGH NIBBLE TO REG A
        RTS

;
;SUBROUTINE NASCII
;PURPOSE:   CONVERT A HEXADECIMAL DIGIT TO ASCII
;ENTRY: A = BINARY DATA IN LOWER NIBBLE
;EXIT:  A = ASCII CHARACTER
;REGISTERS USED: A,P

;

NASCII:
        CMP     #10
        BCC     NAS1                    ;BRANCH IF HIGH NIBBLE < 10
        CLC
        ADC     #7                      ;ELSE ADD 7 SO AFTER ADDING '0' THE
                                        ;  CHARACTER WILL BE IN 'A'..'F'
NAS1:
        ADC     #'0'                    ;MAKE A CHARACTER
        RTS


;                                                                   ;
;                                                                   ;
;       SAMPLE EXECUTION:                                           ;
;                                                                   ;
;                                                                   ;
```

```
SC0403:
        ;CONVERT 0 TO '00'
        LDA     #0
        JSR     BN2HEX
        BRK                         ;A='0'=30H, Y='0'=30H

        ;CONVERT FF HEX TO 'FF'
        LDA     #0FFH
        JSR     BN2HEX
        BRK                         ;A='F'=46H, Y='F'=46H

        ;CONVERT 23 HEX TO '23'
        LDA     #23H
        JSR     BN2HEX
        BRK                         ;A='2'=32H, Y='3'=33H

        .END
```

Hexadecimal ASCII to Binary Conversion (HEX2BN)

4D

Converts two ASCII characters (representing two hexadecimal digits) to one byte of binary data.

Procedure: The program converts each ASCII character separately to a hexadecimal digit. This involves a simple subtraction of 30_{16} (ASCII zero) if the digit is decimal. If the digit is non-decimal, an additional factor of seven must be subtracted to handle the break between ASCII 9 (39_{16}) and ASCII A (41_{16}). The program then shifts the more significant digit left four bits and combines it with the less significant digit. The program does not check the validity of the ASCII characters (i.e., whether they are, in fact, the ASCII representations of hexadecimal digits).

Registers Used: A, P, Y

Execution Time: 74 cycles plus three extra cycles for each non-decimal digit.

Program Size: 30 bytes

Data Memory Required: One byte anywhere in RAM (address TEMP).

Entry Conditions

More significant ASCII digit in the accumulator, less significant ASCII digit in index register Y.

Exit Conditions

Binary data in the accumulator.

Examples:

1. Data: (A) = 44_{16} (ASCII D)
   (Y) = 37_{16} (ASCII 7)

   Result: (A) = $D7_{16}$

2. Data: (A) = 31_{16} (ASCII 1)
   (Y) = 42_{16} (ASCII B)

   Result: (A) = $1B_{16}$

```
;                                                              ;
;                                                              ;
;                                                              ;
;                                                              ;
;       Title           Hex ASCII to binary                    ;
;       Name:           HEX2BN                                 ;
;                                                              ;
;                                                              ;

;                                                              ;
;       Purpose:        Convert two ASCII characters to one    ;
;                       byte of binary data                    ;
;                                                              ;
```

```
;       Entry:          Register A = First ASCII digit, high order value;
;                       Register Y = Second ASCII digit, low order value;
;                                                                       ;
;       Exit:           Register A = Binary data                        ;
;                                                                       ;
;       Registers used: A,P,Y                                           ;
;                                                                       ;
;       Time:           Approximately 74 cycles                         ;
;                                                                       ;
;       Size:           Program 30 bytes                                ;
;                       Data     1 byte                                 ;
;                                                                       ;
;                                                                       ;


HEX2BN:
        PHA                             ;SAVE HIGH CHARACTER
        TYA                             ;GET LOW CHARACTER
        JSR     A2HEX                   ;CONVERT IT
        STA     TEMP                    ;SAVE LOW NIBBLE
        PLA                             ;GET THE HIGH CHARACTER
        JSR     A2HEX                   ;CONVERT IT
        ASL     A
        ASL     A
        ASL     A
        ASL     A                       ;SHIFT HIGH NIBBLE TO THE UPPER 4 BITS
        ORA     TEMP                    ;OR IN THE LOW NIBBLE
        RTS

;
;SUBROUTINE: A2HEX
;PURPOSE: CONVERT ASCII TO A HEX NIBBLE
;ENTRY: A = ASCII CHARACTER
;EXIT:  A = BINARY VALUE OF THE ASCII CHARACTER
;REGISTERS USED: A,P
;

A2HEX:
        SEC                             ;SUBTRACT ASCII OFFSET
        SBC     #'0'
        CMP     #10
        BCC     A2HEX1                  ;BRANCH IF A IS A DECIMAL DIGIT
        SBC     #7                      ;ELSE SUBTRACT OFFSET FOR LETTERS
A2HEX1:
        RTS

;DATA
TEMP:   .BLOCK  1


;                                                                       ;
;                                                                       ;
;       SAMPLE EXECUTION:                                               ;
;                                                                       ;
;                                                                       ;
```

```
SC0404:
        ;CONVERT 'C7' TO C7 HEXADECIMAL
        LDA     #'C'
        LDY     #'7'
        JSR     HEX2BN
        BRK                     ;A=C7H

        ;CONVERT '2F' TO 2F HEXADECIMAL
        LDA     #'2'
        LDY     #'F'
        JSR     HEX2BN          ;A=2FH
        BRK

        ;CONVERT '23' TO 23 HEXADECIMAL
        LDA     #'2'
        LDY     #'3'
        JSR     HEX2BN
        BRK                     ;A=23H

        .END
```

Conversion of a Binary Number to Decimal ASCII (BN2DEC) 4E

Converts a 16-bit signed binary number to an ASCII string, consisting of the length of the number (in bytes), an ASCII minus sign (if necessary), and the ASCII digits.

Procedure: The program takes the absolute value of the number if it is negative and then keeps dividing by ten until it produces a quotient of zero. It converts each digit of the quotient to ASCII (by adding ASCII 0) and concatenates the digits along with an ASCII minus sign (in front) if the original number was negative.

Registers Used: All

Execution Time: Approximately 7,000 cycles

Program Size: 174 bytes

Data Memory Required: Seven bytes anywhere in RAM for the return address (two bytes starting at address RETADR), the sign of the original value (address NGFLAG), temporary storage for the original value (two bytes starting at address VALUE), and temporary storage for the value mod 10 (two bytes starting at address MOD10). Also, two bytes on page 0 for the buffer pointer (address BUFPTR, taken as $00D0_{16}$ and $00D1_{16}$ in the listing). This data memory does not include the output buffer which should be seven bytes long.

Entry Conditions

Order in stack (starting from the top)

Less significant byte of return address
More significant byte of return address

Less significant byte of output buffer address
More significant byte of output buffer address

Less significant byte of value to convert
More significant byte of value to convert

Exit Conditions

Order in buffer

Length of the string in bytes
ASCII − (if original number was negative)
ASCII digits (most significant digit first)

Examples

1. Data: Value to convert = $3EB7_{16}$

   Result (in output buffer):
   05 (number of bytes in buffer)
   31 (ASCII 1)
   36 (ASCII 6)
   30 (ASCII 0)
   35 (ASCII 5)
   35 (ASCII 5)

   That is, $3EB7_{16} = 16055_{10}$.

2. Data: Value to convert = $FFC8_{16}$

   Result (in output buffer):
   03 (number of bytes in buffer)
   2D (ASCII −)
   35 (ASCII 5)
   36 (ASCII 6)

   That is, $FFC8_{16} = -56_{10}$, when considered as a signed two's complement number.

```
;                                                                        ;
;                                                                        ;
;                                                                        ;
;                                                                        ;
;       Title                Binary to decimal ASCII                     ;
;       Name:                BN2DEC                                      ;
;                                                                        ;
;                                                                        ;


;                                                                        ;
;       Purpose:             Convert a 16-bit signed binary number       ;
;                            to ASCII data                               ;
;                                                                        ;
;       Entry:               TOP OF STACK                                ;
;                              Low byte of return address,               ;
;                              High byte of return address,              ;
;                              Low byte of the output buffer address,    ;
;                              High byte of the output buffer address,   ;
;                              Low byte of the value to convert,         ;
;                              High byte of the value to convert         ;
;                                                                        ;
;       Exit:                The first byte of the buffer is the length, ;
;                            followed by the characters.                 ;
;                                                                        ;
;       Registers used: All                                              ;
;                                                                        ;
;       Time:                Approximately 7,000 cycles                  ;
;                                                                        ;
;       Size:                Program 170 bytes                           ;
;                            Data      7 bytes plus                      ;
;                                      2 bytes in page zero              ;
;                                                                        ;
;                                                                        ;


;PAGE ZERO POINTER
BUFPTR: .EQU    0D0H                ;PAGE ZERO BUFFER POINTER

;PROGRAM
BN2DEC:
        ;SAVE PARAMETERS
        PLA
        STA     RETADR              ;SAVE LOW BYTE OF RETURN ADDRESS
        PLA
        STA     RETADR+1            ;SAVE HIGH BYTE
        PLA
        STA     VALUE               ;SAVE LOW BYTE OF VALUE
        PLA
        STA     VALUE+1             ;SAVE HIGH BYTE OF THE VALUE TO CONVERT
        STA     NGFLAG              ;SAVE MSB OF VALUE AS SIGN OF VALUE
        BPL     GETBP               ;BRANCH IF VALUE IS POSITIVE
        LDA     #0                  ;ELSE TAKE ABSOLUTE VALUE (0 - VALUE)
        SEC
        SBC     VALUE
        STA     VALUE
```

```
        LDA     #0
        SBC     VALUE+1
        STA     VALUE+1

GETBP:
        PLA                     ;SAVE STARTING ADDRESS OF OUTPUT BUFFER
        STA     BUFPTR
        PLA
        STA     BUFPTR+1


        ;SET BUFFER TO EMPTY
        LDA     #0
        LDY     #0              ;BUFFER[0] := 0
        STA     (BUFPTR),Y

        ;
        ;CONVERT VALUE TO A STRING
CNVERT:
        ;VALUE := VALUE DIV 10
        ;MOD10 := VALUE MOD 10
        LDA     #0
        STA     MOD10
        STA     MOD10+1

        LDX     #16
        CLC                     ;CLEAR CARRY
DVLOOP:
        ROL     VALUE           ;SHIFT THE CARRY INTO DIVIDEND BIT 0
        ROL     VALUE+1         ;WHICH WILL BE THE QUOTIENT
        ROL     MOD10           ;AND SHIFT DIVIDEND AT THE SAME TIME
        ROL     MOD10+1

        ;
        ;A,Y = DIVIDEND - DIVISOR
        SEC
        LDA     MOD10
        SBC     #10
        TAY                     ;SAVE LOW BYTE IN REG Y
        LDA     MOD10+1
        SBC     #0              ;SUBTRACT CARRY
        BCC     DECCNT          ;BRANCH IF DIVIDEND < DIVISOR
        STY     MOD10           ;ELSE
        STA     MOD10+1         ;  NEXT BIT OF QUOTIENT IS A ONE AND SET
                                ;  DIVIDEND := DIVIDEND - DIVISOR

DECCNT:
        DEX
        BNE     DVLOOP

        ROL     VALUE           ;SHIFT IN THE LAST CARRY FOR THE QUOTIENT
        ROL     VALUE+1

        ;CONCATENATE THE NEXT CHARACTER
```

```
CONCH:
        LDA     MOD10
        CLC
        ADC     #'0'            ;CONVERT 0..9 TO ASCII '0'..'9'
        JSR     CONCAT

        ;IF VALUE <> 0 THEN CONTINUE
        LDA     VALUE
        ORA     VALUE+1
        BNE     CNVERT          ;BRANCH IF VALUE IS NOT ZERO

EXIT:
        LDA     NGFLAG
        BPL     POS             ;BRANCH IF ORIGINAL VALUE WAS POSITIVE
        LDA     #'-'            ;ELSE
        JSR     CONCAT          ; PUT A MINUS SIGN IN FRONT

POS:
        LDA     RETADR+1
        PHA
        LDA     RETADR
        PHA
        RTS                     ;RETURN

;
;SUBROUTINE: CONCAT
;PURPOSE: CONCATENATE THE CHARACTER IN REGISTER A TO THE
;         FRONT OF THE STRING ACCESSED THROUGH BUFPTR
;ENTRY: BUFPTR[0] = LENGTH
;EXIT:  REGISTER A CONCATENATED (PLACED IMMEDIATELY AFTER THE LENGTH BYTE)
;REGISTERS USED: A,P,Y
;

CONCAT:
        PHA                     ;SAVE THE CHARACTER ON THE STACK

        ;MOVE THE BUFFER RIGHT ONE CHARACTER
        LDY     #0
        LDA     (BUFPTR),Y      ;GET CURRENT LENGTH
        TAY
        BEQ     EXITMR          ;BRANCH IF LENGTH = 0
MVELP:
        LDA     (BUFPTR),Y      ;GET NEXT CHARACTER
        INY
        STA     (BUFPTR),Y      ;STORE IT
        DEY
        DEY
        BNE     MVELP           ;CONTINUE UNTIL DONE

EXITMR:
        PLA                     ;GET THE CHARACTER BACK FROM THE STACK
        LDY     #1
        STA     (BUFPTR),Y      ;STORE THE CHARACTER
        LDY     #0
        LDA     (BUFPTR),Y      ;GET LENGTH BYTE
```

```
        CLC
        ADC     #1              ;INCREMENT LENGTH BY 1
        STA     (BUFPTR),Y      ;UPDATE LENGTH

        RTS

;DATA
RETADR: .BLOCK  2               ;SAVE RETURN ADDRESS
NGFLAG: .BLOCK  1               ;SIGN OF ORIGINAL VALUE
VALUE:  .BLOCK  2               ;VALUE TO CONVERT
MOD10:  .BLOCK  2               ;MODULO 10 TEMPORARY


;                                                               ;
;                                                               ;
;       SAMPLE EXECUTION:                                       ;
;                                                               ;
;                                                               ;


SC0405:
        ;CONVERT 0 TO '0'
        LDA     BUFADR+1        ;HIGH BYTE OF BUFFER ADDRESS
        PHA
        LDA     BUFADR          ;LOW BYTE BUFFER ADDRESS
        PHA
        LDA     VALUE1+1        ;HIGH BYTE OF VALUE
        PHA
        LDA     VALUE1          ;LOW BYTE OF VALUE
        PHA
        JSR     BN2DEC          ;CONVERT
        BRK                     ;BUFFER SHOULD = '0'

        ;CONVERT 32767 TO '32767'
        LDA     BUFADR+1        ;HIGH BYTE OF BUFFER ADDRESS
        PHA
        LDA     BUFADR          ;LOW BYTE BUFFER ADDRESS
        PHA
        LDA     VALUE2+1        ;HIGH BYTE OF VALUE
        PHA
        LDA     VALUE2          ;LOW BYTE OF VALUE
        PHA
        JSR     BN2DEC          ;CONVERT
        BRK                     ;BUFFER SHOULD = '32767'

        ;CONVERT -32768 TO '-32768'
        LDA     BUFADR+1        ;HIGH BYTE OF BUFFER ADDRESS
        PHA
        LDA     BUFADR          ;LOW BYTE BUFFER ADDRESS
        PHA
        LDA     VALUE3+1        ;HIGH BYTE OF VALUE
        PHA
        LDA     VALUE3          ;LOW BYTE OF VALUE
        PHA
```

```
        JSR     BN2DEC          ;CONVERT
        BRK                     ;BUFFER SHOULD = '-32768'
        JMP     SC0405

VALUE1: .WORD   0               ;TEST VALUE 1
VALUE2: .WORD   32767           ;TEST VALUE 2
VALUE3: .WORD   -32768          ;TEST VALUE 3
BUFADR: .WORD   BUFFER          ;BUFFER ADDRESS
BUFFER: .BLOCK  7               ;7 BYTE BUFFER

        .END
```

Conversion of ASCII Decimal to Binary (DEC2BN) 4F

Converts an ASCII string consisting of the length of the number (in bytes), a possible ASCII − or + sign, and a series of ASCII digits to two bytes of binary data. Note that the length is an ordinary binary number, not an ASCII number.

Procedure: The program sets a flag if the first ASCII character is a minus sign and skips over a leading plus sign. It then converts each subsequent digit to decimal (by subtracting ASCII zero), multiplies the previous digits by ten (using the fact that 10=8+2, so a multiplication by ten can be reduced to left shifts and additions), and adds the new digit to the product. Finally, the program subtracts the result from zero if the original number was negative. The program exits immediately, setting the Carry flag, if it finds something other than a leading sign or a decimal digit in the string.

Registers Used: All

Execution Time: 670 cycles (approximately)

Program Size: 171 bytes

Data Memory Required: Four bytes anywhere in RAM for an index, a two-byte accumulator (starting address ACCUM), and a flag indicating the sign of the number (address NGLAG), two-bytes on page zero for a pointer to the string (address BUFPTR, taken as $00F0_{16}$ and $00F1_{16}$ in the listing).

Special Cases:

1. If the string contains something other than a leading sign or a decimal digit, the program returns with the Carry flag set to 1. The result in registers A and Y is invalid.

2. If the string contains only a leading sign (ASCII + or ASCII −), the program returns with the Carry flag set to 1 and a result of zero.

Entry Conditions

(A) = More significant byte of string address
(Y) = Less significant byte of string address

Exit Conditions

(A) = More significant byte of binary value
(Y) = Less significant byte of binary value

Carry flag is 0 if the string was valid; Carry flag is 1 if the string contained an invalid character. Note that the result is a signed two's complement 16-bit number.

Examples

1. Data: String consists of
   04 (number of bytes in string)
   31 (ASCII 1)
   32 (ASCII 2)
   33 (ASCII 3)
   34 (ASCII 4)

   That is, the number is $+1{,}234_{10}$.

   Result: (A) = 04_{16} (more significant byte of binary data)
   (Y) = $C2_{16}$ (less significant byte of binary data)

   That is, the number $+1234_{10} = 04C2_{16}$.

2. Data: String consists of
   06 (number of bytes in string)
   2D (ASCII −)
   33 (ASCII 3)
   32 (ASCII 2)
   37 (ASCII 7)
   35 (ASCII 5)
   30 (ASCII 0)

   That is, the number is $-32{,}750_{10}$.

   Result: (A) = 80_{16} (more significant byte of binary data)
   (Y) = 12_{16} (less significant byte of binary data)
   That is, the number $-32{,}750_{10} = 8012_{16}$.

```
;                                                                 ;
;                                                                 ;
;                                                                 ;
;                                                                 ;
;       Title           Decimal ASCII to binary                   ;
;       Name:           DEC2BN                                    ;
;                                                                 ;
;                                                                 ;


;                                                                 ;
;       Purpose:        Convert ASCII characters to two bytes of binary ;
;                       data.                                     ;
;                                                                 ;
;       Entry:          Register A = high byte of string address  ;
;                       Register Y = low byte of string adddress  ;
;                       The first byte of the string is the length of ;
;                       the string.                               ;
;                                                                 ;
;       Exit:           Register A = High byte of the value       ;
;                       Register Y = Low byte of the value        ;
;                       IF NO ERRORS THEN                         ;
;                         CARRY FLAG = 0                          ;
;                       ELSE                                      ;
;                         CARRY FLAG = 1                          ;
;                                                                 ;
;       Registers used: All                                       ;
;                                                                 ;
;       Time:           Approximately 670 cycles                  ;
;                                                                 ;
;       Size:           Program 171 bytes                         ;
;                       Data      4 bytes plus                    ;
;                                 2 bytes in page zero            ;
;                                                                 ;

;PAGE ZERO LOCATION
BUFPTR: .EQU    0F0H            ;PAGE ZERO POINTER TO STRING
;
;PROGRAM
DEC2BN:
        STA     BUFPTR+1
        STY     BUFPTR          ;SAVE THE STRING ADDRESS
```

```
        ;INITIALIZE
        LDY     #0
        LDA     (BUFPTR),Y   ;GET LENGTH
        TAX                  ; TO REGISTER X
        LDA     #1
        STA     INDEX        ;INDEX := 1
        LDA     #0
        STA     ACCUM        ;ACCUM := 0
        STA     ACCUM+1
        STA     NGFLAG       ;SIGN OF NUMBER IS POSITIVE

        ;CHECK THAT THE BUFFER IS NOT ZERO
        TXA
        BNE     INIT1        ;EXIT WITH ACCUM = 0 IF BUFFER IS EMPTY
        JMP     EREXIT       ;ERROR EXIT IF NOTHING IN BUFFER
INIT1:
        LDY     INDEX
        LDA     (BUFPTR),Y   ;GET FIRST CHARACTER
        CMP     #'-'         ;IS IT A MINUS ?
        BNE     PLUS         ;BRANCH IF NOT '-'
        LDA     #0FFH
        STA     NGFLAG       ;ELSE SIGN OF NUMBER IS NEGATIVE
        INC     INDEX        ;SKIP PAST MINUS SIGN
        DEX                  ;DECREMENT COUNT
        BEQ     EREXIT       ;ERROR EXIT IF ONLY '-' IN BUFFER
        JMP     CNVERT       ;START CONVERSION
PLUS:
        CMP     #'+'
        BNE     CHKDIG       ;START CONVERSION IF FIRST CHARACTER IS NOT '+'
        INC     INDEX
        DEX                  ;DECREMENT COUNT, IGNORE PLUS SIGN
        BEQ     EREXIT       ;ERROR EXIT IF ONLY '+' IN BUFFER

CNVERT:
        LDY     INDEX
        LDA     (BUFPTR),Y   ;GET NEXT CHARACTER
CHKDIG: CMP     #'0'
        BMI     EREXIT       ;ERROR IF < '0' (NOT A DIGIT)
        CMP     #'9'+1
        BPL     EREXIT       ;ERROR IF > '9' (NOT A DIGIT)
        PHA                  ;SAVE THE DIGIT ON THE STACK

        ;VALID DECIMAL DIGIT SO
        ;  ACCUM := ACCUM * 10
        ;    = ACCUM * (8 + 2)
        ;    = (ACCUM * 8) + (ACCUM * 2)
        ASL     ACCUM
        ROL     ACCUM+1      ;TIMES 2
        LDA     ACCUM
        LDY     ACCUM+1      ;SAVE ACCUM * 2
        ASL     ACCUM
        ROL     ACCUM+1
        ASL     ACCUM
        ROL     ACCUM+1      ;TIMES 8
        CLC
```

```
        ADC     ACCUM           ;SUM WITH * 2
        STA     ACCUM
        TYA
        ADC     ACCUM+1
        STA     ACCUM+1         ;ACCUM := ACCUM * 10

        ;ADD IN THE NEXT DIGIT
        ; ACCUM := ACCUM + DIGIT
        PLA                     ;GET THE DIGIT BACK
        SEC
        SBC     #'0'            ;CONVERT '0'..'9' TO BINARY 0..9
        CLC
        ADC     ACCUM
        STA     ACCUM
        BCC     D2B1            ;BRANCH IF NO CARRY TO HIGH BYTE
        INC     ACCUM+1         ;ELSE INCREMENT HIGH BYTE
D2B1:
        INC     INDEX           ;INCREMENT TO NEXT CHARACTER
        DEX
        BNE     CNVERT          ;CONTINUE CONVERSION

        LDA     NGFLAG
        BPL     OKEXIT          ;BRANCH IF THE VALUE WAS POSITIVE
        LDA     #0              ;ELSE REPLACE RESULT WITH -RESULT
        SEC
        SBC     ACCUM
        STA     ACCUM
        LDA     #0
        SBC     ACCUM+1
        STA     ACCUM+1

        ;GET THE BINARY VALUE AND RETURN
OKEXIT:
        CLC
        BCC     EXIT

EREXIT:
        SEC

EXIT:
        LDA     ACCUM+1         ;GET HIGH BYTE OF VALUE
        LDY     ACCUM
        RTS

;DATA
INDEX:  .BLOCK  1               ;INDEX INTO THE STRING
ACCUM:  .BLOCK  2               ;ACCUMULATED VALUE (2 BYTES)
NGFLAG: .BLOCK  1               ;SIGN OF NUMBER


;                                                               ;
;                                                               ;
;       SAMPLE EXECUTION:                                       ;
;                                                               ;
;                                                               ;
```

```
SC0406:
        ;CONVERT '1234' TO 04D2 HEX
        LDA     ADRS1+1
        LDY     ADRS1               ;AY = ADDRESS OF S1
        JSR     DEC2BN
        BRK                         ;A = 04, Y = D2 HEX

        ;CONVERT '-32767' TO 7FFF HEX
        LDA     ADRS2+1
        LDY     ADRS2               ;AY = ADDRESS OF S2
        JSR     DEC2BN
        BRK                         ;A = 7F, Y = FF HEX

        ;CONVERT '-32768' TO 8000 HEX
        LDA     ADRS3+1
        LDY     ADRS3               ;AY = ADDRESS OF S3
        JSR     DEC2BN
        BRK                         ;A = 80 HEX, Y = 00 HEX

S1:     .BYTE   4,'1234'
S2:     .BYTE   6,'+32767'
S3:     .BYTE   6,'-32768'

ADRS1:  .WORD   S1                  ;ADDRESS OF S1
ADRS2:  .WORD   S2                  ;ADDRESS OF S2
ADRS3:  .WORD   S3                  ;ADDRESS OF S3

        .END
```

Lower-Case to Upper-Case Translation (LC2UC) 4G

Converts an ASCII lower-case letter to its upper-case equivalent.

Procedure: The program determines from comparisons whether the data is an ASCII lower-case letter. If it is, the program subtracts 20_{16} from it, thus converting it to its upper-case equivalent. If it is not, the program leaves it unchanged.

Registers Used: A, P

Execution Time: 18 cycles if the original character is valid, fewer cycles otherwise.

Program Size: 12 bytes

Data Memory Required: None

Entry Conditions

Character in the accumulator.

Exit Conditions

If the character is an ASCII lower-case letter, the upper-case equivalent is in the accumulator. If the character is not an ASCII lower-case letter, the accumulator is unchanged.

Examples

1. Data: (A) = 62_{16} (ASCII b)

   Result: (A) = 42_{16} (ASCII B)

2. Data: (A) = 74_{16} (ASCII t)

   Result: (A) = 54_{16} (ASCII T)

```
;                                                                    ;
;                                                                    ;
;                                                                    ;
;                                                                    ;
;       Title           Lower case to upper case translation         ;
;       Name:           LC2UC                                        ;
;                                                                    ;
;                                                                    ;

;                                                                    ;
;       Purpose:        Convert one ASCII character to upper case from ;
;                       lower case if necessary.                     ;
;                                                                    ;
;       Entry:          Register A = Lower case ASCII character      ;
;                                                                    ;
```

```
;       Exit:           Register A = Upper case ASCII character if A      ;
;                                    is lower case, else A is unchanged.;
;                                                                        ;
;       Registers used: A,P                                              ;
;                                                                        ;
;       Time:           18 cycles if A is lower case, less otherwise     ;
;                                                                        ;
;       Size:           Program 12 bytes                                 ;
;                       Data     none                                    ;
;                                                                        ;
;                                                                        ;


LC2UC:
        CMP     #'a'
        BCC     $1              ;BRANCH IF < 'a'
        CMP     #'z'+1
        BCS     EXIT            ;BRANCH IF > 'z'
        SEC
        SBC     #20H            ;CHANGE 'a'..'z' into 'A'..'Z'
EXIT:
        RTS


;                                                                        ;
;                                                                        ;
;       SAMPLE EXECUTION:                                                ;
;                                                                        ;
;                                                                        ;


SC0407:
        ;CONVERT LOWER CASE E TO UPPER CASE
        LDA     #'e'
        JSR     LC2UC
        BRK                     ;A='E'=45H

        ;CONVERT LOWER CASE Z TO UPPER CASE
        LDA     #'z'
        JSR     LC2UC
        BRK                     ;A='Z'=5AH

        ;CONVERT UPPER CASE A TO UPPER CASE A
        LDA     #'A'
        JSR     LC2UC
        BRK                     ;A='A'=41H


        .END    ;OF PROGRAM
```

ASCII to EBCDIC Conversion (ASC2EB) 4H

Converts an ASCII character to its EBCDIC equivalent.

Procedure: The program uses a simple table lookup with the data as the index and address EBCDIC as the base. Printable ASCII characters for which there are no EBCDIC equivalents are translated to an EBCDIC space (40_{16}); nonprintable ASCII characters without EBCDIC equivalents are translated to an EBCDIC NUL (00_{16}).

Registers Used: A, P, Y

Execution Time: 14 cycles

Program Size: Seven bytes, plus 128 bytes for the conversion table.

Data Memory Required: None

Entry Conditions

ASCII character in the accumulator.

Exit Conditions

EBCDIC equivalent in the accumulator.

Examples

1. Data: (A) = 35_{16} (ASCII 5)

   Result: (A) = $F5_{16}$ (EBCDIC 5)

2. Data: (A) = 77_{16} (ASCII w)

   Result: (A) = $A6_{16}$ (EBCDIC w)

3. Data: (A) = $2A_{16}$ (ASCII *)

   Result: (A) = $5C_{16}$ (EBCDIC *)

```
;                                                              ;
;                                                              ;
;                                                              ;
;                                                              ;
;       Title           ASCII to EBCDIC conversion             ;
;       Name:           ASC2EB                                 ;
;                                                              ;
;                                                              ;


;                                                              ;
;       Purpose:        Convert an ASCII character to its      ;
;                       corresponding EBCDIC character         ;
;                                                              ;
;       Entry:          Register A = ASCII character           ;
;                                                              ;
;       Exit:           Register A = EBCDIC character          ;
;                                                              ;
```

```
;       Registers used: A,P,Y                                        ;
;                                                                    ;
;       Time:           14 cycles                                    ;
;                                                                    ;
;       Size:           Program 7 bytes                              ;
;                       Data    128 bytes for the table              ;
;                                                                    ;
;                                                                    ;


ASC2EB:
        AND     #7FH            ;BE SURE BIT 7 = 0
        TAY                     ;USE ASCII AS INDEX INTO EBCDIC TABLE
        LDA     EBCDIC,Y        ;GET EBCDIC
        RTS

;ASCII TO EBCDIC TABLE
; PRINTABLE ASCII CHARACTERS FOR WHICH THERE ARE NO EBCDIC EQUIVALENTS
; ARE TRANSLATED TO AN EBCDIC SPACE (040H), NON PRINTABLE ASCII CHARACTERS
; WITH NO EQUIVALENTS ARE TRANSLATED TO A EBCDIC NUL (000H)
EBCDIC:
;               NUL  SOH  STX  ETX  EOT  ENG  ACK  BEL          ;ASCII
        .BYTE   000H,000H,000H,022H,037H,000H,000H,000H         ;EBCDIC
;               BS   HT   LF   VT   FF   CR   SO   SI           ;ASCII
        .BYTE   000H,02BH,025H,000H,000H,02DH,000H,000H         ;EBCDIC
;               DLE  DC1  DC2  DC3  DC4  NAK  SYN  ETB          ;ASCII
        .BYTE   000H,000H,000H,000H,037H,000H,000H,000H         ;EBCDIC
;               CAN  EM   SUB  ESC  FS   GS   RS   VS           ;ASCII
        .BYTE   000H,000H,000H,000H,000H,000H,000H,000H         ;EBCDIC
;               SPACE !   "    #    $    %    &    '            ;ASCII
        .BYTE   040H,05AH,07EH,040H,05BH,06CH,050H,07CH         ;EBCDIC
;                (    )    *    +    ,    -    .    /           ;ASCII
        .BYTE   04DH,05DH,05CH,04EH,06BH,060H,04BH,061H         ;EBCDIC
;                0    1    2    3    4    5    6    7           ;ASCII
        .BYTE   0F0H,0F1H,0F2H,0F3H,0F4H,0F5H,0F6H,0F7H         ;EBCDIC
;                8    9    :    ;    <    =    >    ?           ;ASCII
        .BYTE   0F8H,0F9H,07AH,05EH,04CH,07DH,06EH,06FH         ;EBCDIC
;                @    A    B    C    D    E    F    G           ;ASCII
        .BYTE   07BH,0C1H,0C2H,0C3H,0C4H,0C5H,0C6H,0C7H         ;EBCDIC
;                H    I    J    K    L    M    N    O           ;ASCII
        .BYTE   0C8H,0C9H,0D1H,0D2H,0D3H,0D4H,0D5H,0D6H         ;EBCDIC
;                P    Q    R    S    T    U    V    W           ;ASCII
        .BYTE   0D7H,0D8H,0D9H,0E2H,0E3H,0E4H,0E5H,0E6H         ;EBCDIC
;                X    Y    Z    [    \    ]    ^    <-          ;ASCII
        .BYTE   0E7H,0E8H,0E9H,040H,040H,040H,06AH,040H         ;EBCDIC
;                `    a    b    c    d    e    f    g           ;ASCII
        .BYTE   07CH,081H,082H,083H,084H,085H,086H,087H         ;EBCDIC
;                h    i    j    k    l    m    n    o           ;ASCII
        .BYTE   088H,089H,091H,092H,093H,094H,095H,096H         ;EBCDIC
;                p    q    r    s    t    u    v    w           ;ASCII
        .BYTE   097H,098H,099H,0A2H,0A3H,0A4H,0A5H,0A6H         ;EBCDIC
;                x    y    z    {    |    }    ~    DEL         ;ASCII
        .BYTE   0A7H,0A8H,0A9H,040H,04FH,040H,05FH,007H         ;EBCDIC
```

```
;                                                                    ;
;                                                                    ;
;       SAMPLE EXECUTION:                                            ;
;                                                                    ;
;                                                                    ;


SC0408:
        ;CONVERT ASCII 'A'
        LDA     #'A'                ;ASCII 'A'
        JSR     ASC2EB
        BRK                         ;EBCDIC 'A' = 0C1H

        ;CONVERT ASCII '1'
        LDA     #'1'                ;ASCII '1'
        JSR     ASC2EB
        BRK                         ;EBCDIC '1' = 0F1H

        ;CONVERT ASCII 'a'
        LDA     #'a'                ;ASCII 'a'
        JSR     ASC2EB
        BRK                         ;EBCDIC 'a' = 081H

        .END            ;END PROGRAM
```

EBCDIC to ASCII Conversion (EB2ASC)

Converts an EBCDIC character to its ASCII equivalent.

Procedure: The program uses a simple table lookup with the data as the index and address ASCII as the base. Printable EBCDIC characters for which there are no ASCII equivalents are translated to an ASCII space (20_{16}); nonprintable EBCDIC characters without ASCII equivalents are translated to an ASCII NUL (00_{16}).

Registers Used: A, P, Y

Execution Time: 12 cycles

Program Size: Five bytes, plus 256 bytes for the conversion table.

Data Memory Required: None

Entry Conditions

EBCDIC character in the accumulator.

Exit Conditions

ASCII equivalent in the accumulator.

Examples

1. Data: (A) = 85_{16} (EBCDIC e)

   Result: (A) = 65_{16} (ASCII e)

2. Data: (A) = $4E_{16}$ (EBCDIC +)

   Result: (A) = $2B_{16}$ (ASCII +)

```
;                                                                   ;
;                                                                   ;
;                                                                   ;
;                                                                   ;
;       Title               EBCDIC to ASCII conversion              ;
;       Name:               EB2ASC                                  ;
;                                                                   ;
;                                                                   ;

;                                                                   ;
;       Purpose:            Convert an EBCDIC character to its      ;
;                           corresponding ASCII character           ;
;                                                                   ;
;       Entry:              Register A = EBCDIC character           ;
;                                                                   ;
;       Exit:               Register A = ASCII character            ;
;                                                                   ;
;       Registers used: A,P,Y                                       ;
;                                                                   ;
;       Time:               12 cycles                               ;
;                                                                   ;
```

```
;       Size:               Program 5 bytes                                  ;
;                           Data    256 bytes for the table                  ;
;                                                                            ;
;                                                                            ;


EB2ASC:
        TAY
        LDA     ASCII,Y ;TRANSLATE
        RTS

;EBCDIC TO ASCII TABLE
; PRINTABLE EBCDIC CHARACTERS FOR WHICH THERE ARE NO ASCII EQUIVALENTS
; ARE TRANSLATED TO AN ASCII SPACE (020H), NON PRINTABLE EBCDIC CHARACTERS
; WITH NO EQUIVALENTS ARE TRANSLATED TO A ASCII NUL (000H)
ASCII:
;               NUL                             TAB       DEL           ;EBCDIC
        .BYTE   000H,000H,000H,000H,000H,009H,000H,07FH                 ;ASCII
;                                                                       ;EBCDIC
        .BYTE   000H,000H,000H,000H,000H,000H,000H,000H                 ;ASCII
;                                          NEW LINE                     ;EBCDIC
        .BYTE   000H,000H,000H,000H,000H,00DH,000H,000H                 ;ASCII
;                                                                       ;EBCDIC
        .BYTE   000H,000H,000H,000H,000H,000H,000H,000H                 ;ASCII
;                   ETX                 LF                              ;EBCDIC
        .BYTE   000H,003H,000H,000H,000H,00AH,000H,000H                 ;ASCII
;                             TAB       CR                              ;EBCDIC
        .BYTE   000H,000H,000H,009H,000H,00DH,000H,000H                 ;ASCII
;                                                 EOT                   ;EBCDIC
        .BYTE   000H,000H,000H,000H,000H,000H,000H,004H                 ;ASCII
;                                                                       ;EBCDIC
        .BYTE   000H,000H,000H,000H,000H,000H,000H,000H                 ;ASCII
;               SPACE                                                   ;EBCDIC
        .BYTE   ' ' ,000H,000H,000H,000H,000H,000H,000H                 ;ASCII
;                   BRITISH $   .    <    (    +    |                   ;EBCDIC
        .BYTE   000H,000H,' ' ,'.' ,'<' ,'(' ,'+' ,'|'                  ;ASCII
;                &                                                      ;EBCDIC
        .BYTE   '&' ,000H,000H,000H,000H,000H,000H,000H                 ;ASCII
;                         !    $    *    )    ;    ~                    ;EBCDIC
        .BYTE   000H,000H,'!' ,'$' ,'*' ,')' ,';' ,'~'                  ;ASCII
;                -    /                                                 ;EBCDIC
        .BYTE   '-' ,'/' ,000H,000H,000H,000H,000H,000H                 ;ASCII
;                         ^    ,    %   -.-   >    ?                    ;EBCDIC
        .BYTE   000H,000H,'^' ,',' ,'%' ,040H,'>' ,'?'                  ;ASCII
;                                                                       ;EBCDIC
        .BYTE   000H,000H,000H,000H,000H,000H,000H,000H                 ;ASCII
;                         :    @    '    =    "                         ;EBCDIC
        .BYTE   000H,000H,':' ,'@' ,''' ,'=' ,'"', 000H                 ;ASCII
;                    a    b    c    d    e    f    g                    ;EBCDIC
        .BYTE   000H,'a' ,'b' ,'c' ,'d' ,'e' ,'f' ,'g'                  ;ASCII
;                h    i                                                 ;EBCDIC
        .BYTE   'h' ,'i' ,000H,000H,000H,000H,000H,000H                 ;ASCII
;                    j    k    l    m    n    o    p                    ;EBCDIC
        .BYTE   000H,'j' ,'k' ,'l' ,'m' ,'n' ,'o' ,'p'                  ;ASCII
;                q    r                                                 ;EBCDIC
```

```
        .BYTE   'q' ,'r' ,000H,000H,000H,000H,000H,000H          ;ASCII
;                         s    t    u    v    w    x             ;EBCDIC
        .BYTE   000H,000H,'s' ,'t' ,'u' ,'v' ,'w', 'x'           ;ASCII
;               y    z                                           ;EBCDIC
        .BYTE   'y' ,'z' ,000H,000H,000H,000H,000H,000H          ;ASCII
;                                                                ;EBCDIC
        .BYTE   000H,000H,000H,000H,000H,000H,000H,000H          ;ASCII
;                                                                ;EBCDIC
        .BYTE   000H,000H,000H,000H,000H,000H,000H,000H          ;ASCII
;                    A    B    C    D    E    F    G             ;EBCDIC
        .BYTE   000H,'A' ,'B' ,'C' ,'D' ,'E' ,'F' ,'G'           ;ASCII
;               H    I                                           ;EBCDIC
        .BYTE   'H' ,'I' ,000H,000H,000H,000H,000H,000H          ;ASCII
;                    J    K    L    M    N    O    P             ;EBCDIC
        .BYTE   000H,'J' ,'K' ,'L' ,'M' ,'N' ,'O' ,'P'           ;ASCII
;               Q    R                                           ;EBCDIC
        .BYTE   'Q' ,'R' ,000H,000H,000H,000H,000H,000H          ;ASCII
;                         S    T    U    V    W    X             ;EBCDIC
        .BYTE   000H,000H,'S' ,'T' ,'U' ,'V' ,'W', 'X'           ;ASCII
;               Y    Z                                           ;EBCDIC
        .BYTE   'Y' ,'Z' ,000H,000H,000H,000H,000H,000H          ;ASCII
;               0    1    2    3    4    5    6    7             ;EBCDIC
        .BYTE   '0' ,'1' ,'2' ,'3' ,'4' ,'5' ,'6' ,'7'           ;ASCII
;               9                                                ;EBCDIC
        .BYTE   '9' ,000H,000H,000H,000H,000H,000H,000H          ;ASCII

;                                                                        ;
;                                                                        ;
;       SAMPLE EXECUTION:                                                ;
;                                                                        ;
;                                                                        ;


SC0409:
        ;CONVERT EBCDIC 'A'
        LDA     #0C1H           ;EBCDIC 'A'
        JSR     EB2ASC
        BRK                     ;ASCII 'A' = 041H

        ;CONVERT EBCDIC '1'
        LDA     #0F1H           ;EBCDIC '1'
        JSR     EB2ASC
        BRK                     ;ASCII '1' = 031H

        ;CONVERT EBCDIC 'a'
        LDA     #081H           ;EBCDIC 'a'
        JSR     EB2ASC
        BRK                     ;ASCII 'a' = 061H

        .END            ;END PROGRAM
```

Memory Fill (MFILL)

Places a specified value in each byte of a memory area of known size, starting at a given address.

Procedure: The program fills all the whole pages with the specified value first and then fills the remaining partial page. This approach is faster than dealing with the entire area in one loop, since 8-bit counters can be used instead of a 16-bit counter. The approach does, however, require somewhat more memory than a single loop with a 16-bit counter. A size of 0000_{16} causes an exit with no memory changed.

Registers Used: All

Execution Time: Approximately 11 cycles per byte plus 93 cycles overhead.

Program Size: 68 bytes

Data Memory Required: Five bytes anywhere in RAM for the array size (two bytes starting at address ARYSZ), the value (one byte at address VALUE), and the return address (two bytes starting at address RETADR). Also two bytes on page 0 for an array pointer (taken as addresses $00D0_{16}$ and $00D1_{16}$ in the listing).

Special Cases:

1. A size of zero causes an immediate exit with no memory changed.

2. Filling areas occupied or used by the program itself will cause unpredictable results. Obviously, filling any part of page 0 requires caution, since both this routine and most systems programs use that page.

Entry Conditions

Order in stack (starting from the top)

Less significant byte of return address
More significant byte of return address

Value to be placed in memory

Less significant byte of area size (in bytes)

More significant byte of area size (in bytes)

Less significant byte of starting address
More significant byte of starting address

Exit Conditions

The area from the starting address through the number of bytes given by the area size is filled with the specified value. The area filled thus starts at BASE and continues through BASE + SIZE − 1 (BASE is the starting address and SIZE is the area size).

Examples

1. Data: Value = FF_{16}
   Area size (in bytes) = 0380_{16}
   Starting address = $1AE0_{16}$

   Result: FF_{16} is placed in memory addresses $1AE0_{16}$ through $1E5F_{16}$.

2. Data: Value = EA_{16} (6502 operation code for NOP)
   Area size (in bytes) = $1C65_{16}$
   Starting address = $E34C_{16}$

   Result: EA_{16} is placed in memory addresses $E34C_{16}$ through $FFB0_{16}$

```
;       Title           Memory fill                                  ;
;       Name:           MFILL                                        ;
;                                                                    ;
;                                                                    ;

;                                                                    ;
;       Purpose:        Fill an area of memory with a value          ;
;                                                                    ;
;       Entry:          TOP OF STACK                                 ;
;                         Low byte of return address,                ;
;                         High byte of return address,               ;
;                         Value to be placed in memory,              ;
;                         Low byte of area size in bytes,            ;
;                         High byte of area size in bytes,           ;
;                         Low byte of starting address,              ;
;                         High byte of starting address              ;
;                                                                    ;
;       Exit:           Area filled with value                       ;
;                                                                    ;
;       Registers used: All                                          ;
;                                                                    ;
;       Time:           Approximately 11 cycles per byte plus        ;
;                       93 cycles overhead.                          ;
;                                                                    ;
;       Size:           Program 68 bytes                             ;
;                       Data     5 bytes plus                        ;
;                                2 bytes in page zero                ;
;                                                                    ;
;                                                                    ;

;PAGE ZERO POINTER
ARYPTR: .EQU    0D0H            ;PAGE ZERO POINTER TO THE ARRAY

MFILL:
        ;POP THE PARAMETERS FROM THE STACK
        PLA
```

```
        STA     RETADR
        PLA
        STA     RETADR+1        ;GET THE RETURN ADDRESS

        PLA
        STA     VALUE           ;GET FILL VALUE

        PLA
        STA     ARYSZ
        PLA
        STA     ARYSZ+1         ;GET SIZE OF AREA

        PLA
        STA     ARYPTR
        PLA
        STA     ARYPTR+1        ;GET STARTING ADDRESS OF AREA

        LDA     RETADR+1
        PHA
        LDA     RETADR
        PHA                     ;RESTORE RETURN ADDRESS

        ;
        ;DO THE FULL PAGES FIRST
        LDA     VALUE           ;GET VALUE FOR FILL
        LDX     ARYSZ+1         ;X = NUMBER OF PAGES TO DO
        BEQ     PARTPG          ;BRANCH IF THE HIGH BYTE OF SIZE = 0
        LDY     #0
FULLPG:
        STA     (ARYPTR),Y      ;STORE VALUE
        INY                     ;INCREMENT TO NEXT BYTE
        BNE     FULLPG          ;BRANCH IF NOT DONE WITH THIS PAGE
        INC     ARYPTR+1        ;ADVANCE TO THE NEXT PAGE
        DEX
        BNE     FULLPG          ;BRANCH IF NOT DONE WITH THE FULL PAGES

        ;
        ;DO THE REMAINING PARTIAL PAGE
        ; REGISTER A STILL CONTAINS VALUE
PARTPG:
        LDX     ARYSZ           ;GET THE NUMBER OF BYTES IN THIS FINAL PAGE
        BEQ     EXIT            ;BRANCH IF LOW BYTE OF SIZE = 0
        LDY     #0
PARTLP:
        STA     (ARYPTR),Y      ;STORE VALUE
        INY                     ;INCREMENT INDEX
        DEX                     ;DECREMENT COUNTER
        BNE     PARTLP          ;BRANCH IF PARTIAL PAGE IS NOT DONE

EXIT:
        RTS

;DATA
ARYSZ:  .BLOCK  2               ;NUMBER OF BYTES TO INITIALIZE
VALUE:  .BLOCK  1               ;VALUE TO INITIALIZE ARRAY WITH
```

```
RETADR: .BLOCK   2                 ;TEMPORARY FOR RETURN ADDRESS

;                                                                   ;
;                                                                   ;
;       SAMPLE EXECUTION                                            ;
;                                                                   ;
;                                                                   ;


SC0501:
        ;FILL A SMALL BUFFER WITH 00
        LDA     BF1ADR+1
        PHA
        LDA     BF1ADR
        PHA                        ;PUSH STARTING ADDRESS
        LDA     BF1SZ+1
        PHA
        LDA     BF1SZ
        PHA                        ;PUSH NUMBER OF BYTES
        LDA     #0
        PHA                        ;PUSH VALUE
        JSR     MFILL              ;FILL BUFFER
        BRK

        ;FILL A BIG BUFFER WITH EA HEX (NOP)
        LDA     BF2ADR+1
        PHA
        LDA     BF2ADR
        PHA                        ;PUSH STARTING ADDRESS
        LDA     BF2SZ+1
        PHA
        LDA     BF2SZ
        PHA                        ;PUSH NUMBER OF BYTES
        LDA     #0EAH
        PHA                        ;PUSH VALUE
        JSR     MFILL              ;FILL BUFFER
        BRK
        JMP     SC0501


SIZE1:  .EQU    47H
SIZE2:  .EQU    6000H

BF1ADR: .WORD   BF1
BF2ADR: .WORD   BF2

BF1SZ:  .WORD   SIZE1
BF2SZ:  .WORD   SIZE2

BF1:    .BLOCK  SIZE1
BF2:    .BLOCK  SIZE2

        .END
```

Moves a block of data from a source area to a destination area.

Procedure: The program determines if the starting address of the destination area is within the source area. If it is, then working up from the starting address would overwrite some of the source data. To avoid that problem, the program works down from the highest address (this is sometimes called *move right*). If the starting address of the destination area is not within the source area, the program simply moves the data starting from the lowest address (this is sometimes called a *move left*). In either case, the program moves the data by handling complete pages separately from the remaining partial page. This approach allows the program to use 8-bit counters rather than a 16-bit counter, thus reducing execution time (although increasing memory usage). An area size (number of bytes to move) of 0000_{16} causes an exit with no memory changed.

Important Note: The user should be careful if either the source or the destination area includes the temporary storage used by the program itself. The program provides automatic address wraparound (mod 64K), but the results of any move involving the program's own temporary storage are unpredictable.

Registers Used: All

Execution Time: 128 cycles overhead plus the following:

1. If data can be moved starting from the lowest address (i.e., left):
   20 + 4110 * (more significant byte of number of bytes to move) + 18 * (less significant byte of number of bytes to move).
2. If data must be moved starting from the highest address (i.e., right) because of overlap:
   42 + 4622 * (more significant byte of number of bytes to move) + 18 * (less significant byte of number of bytes to move).

Program Size: 157 bytes

Data Memory Required: Two bytes anywhere in RAM for the length of the move (starting at address MVELEN), four bytes on page 0 for source and destination pointers (starting at addresses MVSRCE and MVDEST taken as addresses $00D0_{16}$ and $00D1_{16}$ – source pointer – and addresses $00D2_{16}$ and $00D3_{16}$ – destination pointer – in the listing).

Special Cases:

1. A size (number of bytes to move) of zero causes an immediate exit with no memory changed.
2. Moving data to or from areas occupied or used by the program itself will produce unpredictable results. Obviously, moving data to or from page 0 requires caution, since both this routine and most systems programs use that page. This routine does provide automatic address wraparound (mod 64K) for consistency, but the user must still approach moves involving page 0 carefully.

Entry Conditions

Order in stack (starting from the top)

Less significant byte of return address
More significant byte of return address

Less significant byte of number of bytes to move
More significant byte of number of bytes to move

Less significant byte of lowest address of destination area
More significant byte of lowest address of destination area

Less significant byte of lowest address of source area
More significant byte of lowest address of source area

Exit Conditions

The block of memory is moved from the source area to the destination area. If the number of bytes to be moved is NBYTES, the lowest address in the destination area is DEST, and the lowest address in the source area is SOURCE, then the area from addresses SOURCE through SOURCE + NBYTES − 1 is moved to addresses DEST through DEST + NBYTES − 1.

Examples

1. Data: Number of bytes to move = 0200_{16}
   Lowest address in destination area = $05D1_{16}$
   Lowest address in source area = $035E_{16}$

   Result: The contents of memory locations $035E_{16}$ through $055D_{16}$ are moved to $05D1_{16}$ through $07D0_{16}$.

2. Data: Number of bytes to move = $1B7A_{16}$
   Lowest address in destination area = $C946_{16}$
   Lowest address in source area = $C300_{16}$

   Result: The contents of memory locations $C300_{16}$ through $DE79_{16}$ are moved to $C946_{16}$ through $E4BF_{16}$

Note that Example 2 presents a more complex problem than Example 1 because the source and destination areas overlap. If, for instance, the program were simply to move data to the destination area starting from the lowest address, it would initially move the contents of $C300_{16}$ to $C946_{16}$. This would destroy the old contents of $C946_{16}$, which are needed later in the move. The solution to this problem is to move the data starting from the highest address if the destination area is above the source area but overlaps it.

```
;       Title               Block Move                                ;
;       Name:               BLKMOV                                    ;
;                                                                     ;
;                                                                     ;

;                                                                     ;
;       Purpose:            Move data from source to destination      ;
;                                                                     ;
;       Entry:              TOP OF STACK                              ;
;                             Low byte of return address,             ;
;                             High byte of return address,            ;
;                             Low byte of number of bytes to move,    ;
;                             High byte of number of bytes to move,   ;
;                             Low byte of lowest address in destination ;
;                               area,                                 ;
;                             High byte of lowest address in destination ;
;                               area,                                 ;
;                             Low byte of lowest address in source area, ;
;                             High byte of lowest address in source area ;
;                                                                     ;
;       Exit:               Data moved from source to destination     ;
;                                                                     ;
;       Registers used: All                                           ;
;                                                                     ;
;       Time:               102 cycles overhead plus move             ;
;                             move left cycles equals                 ;
;                                   20 +                              ;
;                                   (high byte of length * 4110) +    ;
;                                   (low byte of length * 18)         ;
;                                                                     ;
;                             move right cycles equals                ;
;                                   42 +                              ;
;                                   (high byte of length * 4622) +    ;
;                                   (low byte of length * 18)         ;
;                                                                     ;
;       Size:               Program 146 bytes                         ;
;                           Data      2 bytes plus                    ;
;                                     4 bytes in page zero            ;
;                                                                     ;
;                                                                     ;


;PAGE ZERO POINTERS
MVSRCE  .EQU    0D0H            ;SOURCE ADDRESS
MVDEST  .EQU    0D2H            ;DESTINATION ADDRESS

BLKMOV:
        ;GET RETURN ADDRESS
        PLA
        TAY                     ;SAVE LOW BYTE
        PLA
        TAX                     ;SAVE HIGH BYTE

        ;GET NUMBER OF BYTES
        PLA
```

```
        STA     MVELEN          ;STORE LOW BYTE
        PLA
        STA     MVELEN+1        ;STORE HIGH BYTE

        ;GET STARTING DESTINATION ADDRESS
        PLA
        STA     MVDEST          ;STORE LOW BYTE
        PLA
        STA     MVDEST+1        ;STORE HIGH BYTE

        ;GET STARTING SOURCE ADDRESS
        PLA
        STA     MVSRCE          ;STORE LOW BYTE
        PLA
        STA     MVSRCE+1        ;STORE HIGH BYTE

        ;RESTORE RETURN ADDRESS
        TXA
        PHA                     ;RESTORE HIGH BYTE
        TYA
        PHA                     ;RESTORE LOW BYTE


        ;
        ;DETERMINE IF DESTINATION AREA IS ABOVE SOURCE AREA BUT OVERLAPS
        ; IT. REMEMBER, OVERLAP CAN BE MOD 64K. OVERLAP OCCURS IF
        ; STARTING DESTINATION ADDRESS MINUS STARTING SOURCE ADDRESS (MOD 64K)
        ; IS LESS THAN NUMBER OF BYTES TO MOVE
        LDA     MVDEST          ;CALCULATE DESTINATION - SOURCE
        SEC
        SBC     MVSRCE
        TAX
        LDA     MVDEST+1
        SBC     MVSRCE+1        ;MOD 64K IS AUTOMATIC - DISCARD CARRY
        TAY
        TXA                     ;COMPARE WITH NUMBER OF BYTES TO MOVE
        CMP     MVELEN
        TYA
        SBC     MVELEN+1
        BCS     DOLEFT          ;BRANCH IF NO PROBLEM WITH OVERLAP

        ;DESTINATION AREA IS ABOVE SOURCE AREA BUT OVERLAPS IT
        ;MOVE FROM HIGHEST ADDRESS TO AVOID DESTROYING DATA
        JSR     MVERHT
        JMP     EXIT

        ;NO PROBLEM DOING ORDINARY MOVE STARTING AT LOWEST ADDRESS
DOLEFT:
        JSR     MVELFT


EXIT:
        RTS
```

```
;********************************************
;SUBROUTINE: MVELFT
;PURPOSE:  MOVE SOURCE TO DESTINATION STARTING FROM
;       THE LOWEST ADDRESS
;ENTRY: MVSRCE  = 2 BYTE LOWEST ADDRESS OF SOURCE AREA
;       MVDEST  = 2 BYTE LOWEST ADDRESS OF DESTINATION AREA
;       MVELEN  = 2 BYTE NUMBER OF BYTES TO MOVE
;EXIT:  SOURCE MOVED TO DESTINATION
;********************************************

MVELFT:
        LDY     #0              ;ZERO INDEX
        LDX     MVELEN+1        ;X= NUMBER OF FULL PAGES TO MOVE
        BEQ     MLPART          ;IF X = 0 THEN DO PARTIAL PAGE
MLPAGE:
        LDA     (MVSRCE),Y
        STA     (MVDEST),Y      ;MOVE ONE BYTE
        INY                     ;NEXT BYTE
        BNE     MLPAGE          ;CONTINUE UNTIL 256 BYTES ARE MOVED
        INC     MVSRCE+1        ;ADVANCE TO NEXT PAGE OF SOURCE
        INC     MVDEST+1        ; AND DESTINATION
        DEX                     ;DECREMENT PAGE COUNT
        BNE     MLPAGE          ;CONTINUE UNTIL ALL FULL PAGES ARE MOVED

MLPART:
        LDX     MVELEN          ;GET LENGTH OF LAST PAGE
        BEQ     MLEXIT          ;BRANCH IF LENGTH OF LAST PAGE = 0
                                ;REGISTER Y IS 0
MLLAST:
        LDA     (MVSRCE),Y
        STA     (MVDEST),Y      ;MOVE BYTE
        INY                     ;NEXT BYTE
        DEX                     ;DECREMENT COUNTER
        BNE     MLLAST          ;CONTINUE UNTIL LAST PAGE IS DONE

MLEXIT:
        RTS

;********************************************
;SUBROUTINE: MVERHT
;PURPOSE:  MOVE SOURCE TO DESTINATION STARTING FROM
;       THE HIGHEST ADDRESS
;ENTRY: MVSRCE  = 2 BYTE LOWEST ADDRESS OF SOURCE AREA
;       MVDEST  = 2 BYTE LOWEST ADDRESS OF DESTINATION AREA
;       MVELEN  = 2 BYTE NUMBER OF BYTES TO MOVE
;EXIT:  SOURCE MOVED TO DESTINATION
;********************************************

MVERHT:
        ;

        ;MOVE THE PARTIAL PAGE FIRST
        LDA     MVELEN+1
        CLC
        ADC     MVSRCE+1
        STA     MVSRCE+1        ;POINT TO LAST PAGE OF SOURCE
```

```
        LDA     MVELEN+1
        CLC
        ADC     MVDEST+1
        STA     MVDEST+1          ;POINT TO LAST PAGE OF DESTINATION

        ;MOVE THE LAST PARTIAL PAGE FIRST
        LDY     MVELEN            ;GET LENGTH OF LAST PAGE
        BEQ     MRPAGE            ;IF Y = 0 THEN DO THE FULL PAGES

MR0:
        DEY                       ;BACK UP Y TO THE NEXT BYTE
        LDA     (MVSRCE),Y
        STA     (MVDEST),Y        ;MOVE BYTE
        CPY     #0
        BNE     MR0               ;BRANCH IF NOT DONE WITH THE LAST PAGE

MRPAGE:
        LDX     MVELEN+1          ;GET HIGH BYTE OF COUNT AS PAGE COUNTER
        BEQ     MREXIT            ;BRANCH IF HIGH BYTE = 0 (NO FULL PAGES)
MR1:
        DEC     MVSRCE+1          ;BACK UP TO PREVIOUS PAGE OF SOURCE
        DEC     MVDEST+1          ; AND DESTINATION
MR2:
        DEY                       ;BACK UP Y TO THE NEXT BYTE
        LDA     (MVSRCE),Y
        STA     (MVDEST),Y        ;MOVE BYTE
        CPY     #0
        BNE     MR2               ;BRANCH IF NOT DONE WITH THIS PAGE
        DEX                       ;DECREMENT PAGE COUNTER
        BNE     MR1               ;BRANCH IF NOT ALL PAGES ARE MOVED

MREXIT:
        RTS

;
;DATA SECTION
MVELEN  .BLOCK  2                 ;LENGTH OF MOVE

;                                                                       ;
;                                                                       ;
;       SAMPLE EXECUTION: MOVE 0800 THROUGH 097F TO 0900 THROUGH 0A7F   ;
;                                                                       ;
;                                                                       ;


SC0502:
        LDA     SRCE+1
        PHA                       ;PUSH HIGH BYTE OF SOURCE
        LDA     SRCE
        PHA                       ;PUSH LOW BYTE OF SOURCE
        LDA     DEST+1
        PHA                       ;PUSH HIGH BYTE OF DESTINATION
        LDA     DEST
        PHA                       ;PUSH LOW BYTE OF DESTINATION
```

```
        LDA     LEN+1
        PHA                     ;PUSH HIGH BYTE OF LENGTH
        LDA     LEN
        PHA                     ;PUSH LOW BYTE OF LENGTH
        JSR     BLKMOV          ;MOVE DATA FROM SOURCE TO DESTINATION
        BRK                     ; FOR THE DEFAULT VALUES MEMORY FROM 800 HEX
                                ; THROUGH 97F HEX IS MOVED TO 900 HEX THROUGH
                                ; A7F HEX.
        JMP     SC0502

;
;TEST DATA, CHANGE TO TEST OTHER VALUES
SRCE    .WORD   0800H           ;STARTING ADDRESS OF SOURCE AREA
DEST    .WORD   0900H           ;STARTING ADDRESS OF DESTINATION AREA
LEN     .WORD   0180H           ;NUMBER OF BYTES TO MOVE

        .END    ;PROGRAM
```

One-Dimensional Byte Array Index (D1BYTE) 5C

Calculates the address of an element of a byte-length array, given the base address and the subscript (index) of the element.

Procedure: The program simply adds the base address to the subscript. The sum is the address of the element.

Registers Used: All

Execution Time: 74 cycles

Program Size: 37 bytes

Data Memory Required: Four bytes anywhere in RAM to hold the return address (two bytes starting at address RETADR) and the subscript (two bytes starting at address SUBSCR).

Entry Conditions

Order in stack (starting at the top)

Less significant byte of return address
More significant byte of return address

Less significant byte of subscript
More significant byte of subscript

Less significant byte of base address of array
More significant byte of base address of array

Exit Conditions

(A) = More significant byte of address of element

(Y) = Less significant byte of address of element

Examples

1. Data: Base address = $0E00_{16}$
   Subscript = $012C_{16}$

   Result: Address of element = $0E00_{16}$ + $012C_{16}$ = $0F2C_{16}$.

2. Data: Base address = $C4E1_{16}$
   Subscript = $02E4_{16}$

   Result: Address of element = $C4E1_{16}$ + $02E4_{15}$ = $C7C5_{16}$.

```
;       Title               One dimensional byte array indexing          ;
;       Name:               D1BYTE                                        ;
;                                                                         ;
;                                                                         ;

;                                                                         ;
;       Purpose:            Given the base address of a byte array and a  ;
;                           subscript 'I' calculate the address of A[I]   ;
;                                                                         ;
;       Entry:              TOP OF STACK                                  ;
;                             Low byte of return address,                 ;
;                             High byte of return address,                ;
;                             Low byte of subscript,                      ;
;                             High byte of subscript,                     ;
;                             Low byte of base address of array,          ;
;                             High byte of base address of array          ;
;                                                                         ;
;       Exit:               Register A = High byte of address             ;
;                           Register Y = Low byte of address              ;
;                                                                         ;
;       Registers used: All                                               ;
;                                                                         ;
;       Time:               74 cycles                                     ;
;                                                                         ;
;       Size:               Program 37 bytes                              ;
;                           Data     4 bytes                              ;
;                                                                         ;
;                                                                         ;


D1BYTE:
        ;SAVE RETURN ADDRESS
        PLA
        STA     RETADR
        PLA
        STA     RETADR+1

        ;GET SUBSCRIPT
        PLA
        STA     SS
        PLA
        STA     SS+1

        ;ADD BASE ADDRESS TO SUBSCRIPT
        PLA
        CLC
        ADC     SS
        TAY                     ;REGISTER Y = LOW BYTE
        PLA
        ADC     SS+1
        TAX                     ;SAVE HIGH BYTE IN REGISTER X

        ;RESTORE RETURN ADDRESS TO STACK
        LDA     RETADR+1
        PHA
```

```
        LDA     RETADR
        PHA                     ;RESTORE RETURN ADDRESS

        TXA                     ;GET HIGH BYTE BACK TO REGISTER A
        RTS                     ;EXIT


;
;DATA
RETADR: .BLOCK  2               ;TEMPORARY FOR RETURN ADDRESS
SS:     .BLOCK  2               ;SUBSCRIPT INTO THE ARRAY


;                                                                    ;
;                                                                    ;
;       SAMPLE EXECUTION:                                            ;
;                                                                    ;
;                                                                    ;


SC0503:
        ;PUSH ARRAY ADDRESS
        LDA     ARYADR+1        ;HIGH BYTE
        PHA
        LDA     ARYADR          ;LOW BYTE
        PHA

        ;PUSH A SUBSCRIPT
        LDA     SUBSCR+1        ;HIGH BYTE
        PHA
        LDA     SUBSCR          ;LOW BYTE
        PHA
        JSR     D1BYTE          ;CALCULATE ADDRESS
        BRK                     ;AY = ARY+2
                                ;   = ADDRESS OF ARY(2), WHICH CONTAINS 3

        JMP     SC0503

;
;TEST DATA, CHANGE SUBSCR FOR OTHER VALUES
SUBSCR: .WORD   2               ;TEST SUBSCRIPT INTO THE ARRAY
ARYADR: .WORD   ARY             ;BASE ADDRESS OF ARRAY

;THE ARRAY (8 ENTRIES)
ARY:    .BYTE   1,2,3,4,5,6,7,8

        .END    ;PROGRAM
```

One-Dimensional Word Array Index (D1WORD) 5D

Calculates the starting address of an element of a word-length (16-bit) array, given the base address of the array and the subscript (index) of the element. The element occupies the starting address and the address one larger; elements may be organized with either the less significant byte or the more significant byte in the starting address.

Procedure: The program multiplies the subscript by two (using a logical left shift) before adding it to the base address. The sum (BASE + 2*SUBSCRIPT) is then the starting address of the element.

Registers Used: All

Execution Time: 78 cycles

Program Size: 39 bytes

Data Memory Required: Four bytes anywhere in RAM to hold the return address (two bytes starting at address RETADR) and the subscript (two bytes starting at address SUBSCR).

Entry Conditions

Order in stack (starting at the top)

Less significant byte of return address
More significant byte of return address

Less significant byte of subscript
More significant byte of subscript

Less significant byte of base address of array
More significant byte of base address of array

Exit Conditions

(A) = More significant byte of starting address of element

(Y) = Less significant byte of starting address of element

Examples

1. Data: Base address = $A148_{16}$
   Subscript = $01A9_{16}$

   Result: Address of first byte of element
   = $A148_{16} + 2 \times 01A9_{16}$
   = $A148_{16} + 0342_{16} = A49A_{16}$.
   That is, the word-length element occupies addresses $A49A_{16}$ and $A49B_{16}$.

2. Data: Base address = $C4E0_{16}$
   Subscript = $015B_{16}$

   Result: Address of first byte of element
   = $C4E0_{16} + 2 \times 015B_{16}$
   = $C4E0_{16} + 02B6_{16} = C796_{16}$.
   That is, the word-length element occupies addresses $C796_{16}$ and $C797_{16}$.

```
;       Title           One dimensional word array indexing              ;
;       Name:           D1WORD                                           ;
;                                                                        ;
;                                                                        ;


;                                                                        ;
;       Purpose:        Given the base address of a word array and a     ;
;                       subscript 'I' calculate the address of A[I]      ;
;                                                                        ;
;       Entry:          TOP OF STACK                                     ;
;                         Low byte of return address,                    ;
;                         High byte of return address,                   ;
;                         Low byte of subscript,                         ;
;                         High byte of subscript,                        ;
;                         Low byte of base address of array,             ;
;                         High byte of base address of array             ;
;                                                                        ;
;       Exit:           Register A = High byte of address                ;
;                       Register Y = Low byte of address                 ;
;                                                                        ;
;       Registers used: All                                              ;
;                                                                        ;
;       Time:           78 cycles                                        ;
;                                                                        ;
;       Size:           Program 39 bytes                                 ;
;                       Data     4 bytes                                 ;
;                                                                        ;
;                                                                        ;


D1WORD:
        ;SAVE RETURN ADDRESS
        PLA
        STA     RETADR
        PLA
        STA     RETADR+1

        ;GET SUBSCRIPT AND MULTIPLY IT BY 2
        PLA
        ASL     A
        STA     SS
        PLA
        ROL     A
        STA     SS+1

        ;ADD BASE ADDRESS TO DOUBLED SUBSCRIPT
        PLA
        CLC
        ADC     SS
        TAY                     ;REGISTER Y = LOW BYTE
        PLA
        ADC     SS+1
        TAX                     ;SAVE HIGH BYTE IN REGISTER X

        ;RESTORE RETURN ADDRESS TO STACK
```

```
        LDA     RETADR+1
        PHA
        LDA     RETADR
        PHA                             ;RESTORE RETURN ADDRESS

        TXA                             ;GET HIGH BYTE BACK TO REGISTER A
        RTS                             ;EXIT


;
;DATA
RETADR: .BLOCK  2                       ;TEMPORARY FOR RETURN ADDRESS
SS:     .BLOCK  2                       ;SUBSCRIPT INTO THE ARRAY


;                                                                       ;
;                                                                       ;
;       SAMPLE EXECUTION:                                               ;
;                                                                       ;
;                                                                       ;


SC0504:
        ;PUSH ARRAY ADDRESS
        LDA     ARYADR+1
        PHA
        LDA     ARYADR
        PHA

        ;PUSH A SUBSCRIPT OF 3
        LDA     SUBSCR+1
        PHA
        LDA     SUBSCR
        PHA
        JSR     D1WORD                  ;CALCULATE ADDRESS
        BRK                             ;FOR THE INITIAL TEST DATA
                                        ;AY = STARTING ADDRESS OF ARY(3)
                                        ;   = ARY + (3*2)
                                        ;   = ARY + 6
                                        ;   = ARY(3) CONTAINS 240 HEX
        JMP     SC0504

;
;TEST DATA
SUBSCR: .WORD   3                       ;TEST SUBSCRIPT INTO ARY
ARYADR: .WORD   ARY                     ;BASE ADDRESS OF ARRAY

;THE ARRAY (8 ENTRIES)
ARY:    .WORD   0180H,01C0H,0200H,0240H,0280H,02C0H,03E7H,0A34H
        .END    ;PROGRAM
```

Two-Dimensional Byte Array Index (D2BYTE) 5E

Calculates the address of an element of a two-dimensional byte-length array, given the base address of the array, the two subscripts of the element, and the size of a row (that is, the number of columns). The array is assumed to be stored in row major order (that is, by rows) and both subscripts are assumed to begin at zero.

Procedure: The program multiplies the row size (number of columns in a row) times the row subscript (since the elements are stored by rows) and adds the product to the column subscript. It then adds the sum to the base address. The program performs the multiplication using a standard shift-and-add algorithm (see Subroutine 6H).

Registers Used: All

Execution Time: Approximately 1500 cycles, depending mainly on the amount of time required to perform the multiplication.

Program Size: 119 bytes

Data Memory Required: Ten bytes anywhere in memory to hold the return address (two bytes starting at address RETADR), the row subscript (two bytes starting at address SS1), the size (length) of the rows (two bytes starting at address SS1SZ), the column subscript (two bytes starting at address SS2), and the product of row size times row subscript (two bytes starting at address PROD).

Entry Conditions

Order in stack (starting at the top)

Less significant byte of return address
More significant byte of return address

Less significant byte of column subscript
More significant byte of column subscript

Less significant byte of the size of a row
More significant byte of the size of a row

Less significant byte of row subscript
More significant byte of row subscript

Less significant byte of bass address of array
More significant byte of base address of array

Exit Conditions

(A) = More significant byte of address of element

(Y) = Less significant byte of address of element

Examples

1. Data: Base address = $3C00_{16}$
   Column subscript = 0004_{16}
   Size of row (number of columns) = 0018_{16}
   Row subscript = 0003_{16}

   Result: Address of element = $3C00_{16}$ + $0003_{16} \times 0018_{16} + 0004_{16}$ = $3C00_{16} + 0048_{16} + 0004_{16}$ = $3C4C_{16}$.
   Thus the address of ARRAY (3,4) is $3C4C_{16}$.

2. Data: Base address = $6A4A_{16}$
   Column subscript = 0035_{16}
   Size of row (number of columns) = 0050_{16}
   Row subscript = 0002_{16}

   Result: Address of element = $6A4A_{16}$ + $0002_{16} \times 0050_{16}$ + $0035_{16} = 6A4A_{16}$ + $00A0_{16} + 0035_{16} = 6B1F_{16}$.
   Thus the address of ARRAY (2,35) is $6B1F_{16}$.

The general formula is

ADDRESS OF ELEMENT = BASE ADDRESS OF ARRAY + ROW SUBSCRIPT × SIZE OF ROW + COLUMN SUBSCRIPT

Note that we refer to the *size* of the row subscript; the size is the number of consecutive memory addresses for which the subscript has the same value. This is also the number of bytes from the starting address of an element to the starting address of the element with the same column subscript but a row subscript one larger.

```
;       Title              Two dimensional byte array indexing           ;
;       Name:              D2BYTE                                        ;
;                                                                        ;
;                                                                        ;
;                                                                        ;
;       Purpose:           Given the base address of a byte array, two   ;
;                          subscripts 'I','J', and the size of the first ;
;                          subscript in bytes, calculate the address of  ;
;                          A[I,J]. The array is assumed to be stored in  ;
;                          row major order (A[0,0], A[0,1],..., A[K,L]), ;
;                          and both dimensions are assumed to begin at   ;
;                          zero as in the following Pascal declaration:  ;
;                            A:ARRAY[0..2,0..7] OF BYTE;                 ;
;                                                                        ;
;       Entry:             TOP OF STACK                                  ;
;                            Low byte of return address,                 ;
;                            High byte of return address,                ;
;                            Low byte of second subscript,               ;
;                            High byte of second subscript,              ;
;                            Low byte of size of first subscript in bytes, ;
```

```
;                            High byte of size of first subscript in bytes,;
;                            Low byte of first subscript,                  ;
;                            High byte of first subscript,                 ;
;                            Low byte of base address of array,            ;
;                            High byte of base address of array            ;
;                          NOTE:                                           ;
;                            The size of the first subscript is the length ;
;                            of a row                                      ;
;                                                                          ;
;       Exit:              Register A = High byte of address               ;
;                          Register Y = Low byte of address                ;
;                                                                          ;
;       Registers used: All                                                ;
;                                                                          ;
;       Time:              Approximately 1500 cycles                       ;
;                                                                          ;
;       Size:              Program 119 bytes                               ;
;                          Data     10 bytes                               ;
;                                                                          ;
;                                                                          ;


D2BYTE:
        ;SAVE RETURN ADDRESS
        PLA
        STA     RETADR
        PLA
        STA     RETADR+1

        ;GET SECOND SUBSCRIPT
        PLA
        STA     SS2
        PLA
        STA     SS2+1

        ;GET SIZE OF FIRST SUBSCRIPT (LENGTH OF A ROW)
        PLA
        STA     SS1SZ
        PLA
        STA     SS1SZ+1

        ;GET FIRST SUBSCRIPT
        PLA
        STA     SS1
        PLA
        STA     SS1+1


        ;MULTIPLY FIRST SUBSCRIPT * ROW LENGTH USING THE SHIFT AND ADD
        ; ALGORITHM. THE RESULT WILL BE IN SS1
        LDA     #0              ;PARTIAL PRODUCT = ZERO INITIALLY
        STA     PROD
        STA     PROD+1
        LDX     #17             ;NUMBER OF SHIFTS = 17
        CLC
```

```
MULLP:
        ROR     PROD+1          ;SHIFT PARTIAL PRODUCT
        ROR     PROD
        ROR     SS1+1           ;SHIFT MULTIPLIER
        ROR     SS1
        BCC     DECCNT
        CLC                     ;ADD MULTIPLICAND TO PARTIAL PRODUCT
        LDA     SS1SZ           ; IF NEXT BIT OF MULTIPLIER IS 1
        ADC     PROD
        STA     PROD
        LDA     SS1SZ+1
        ADC     PROD+1
        STA     PROD+1

DECCNT:
        DEX
        BNE     MULLP

        ;ADD IN THE SECOND SUBSCRIPT
        LDA     SS1
        CLC
        ADC     SS2
        STA     SS1
        LDA     SS1+1
        ADC     SS2+1
        STA     SS1+1

        ;ADD BASE ADDRESS TO FORM THE FINAL ADDRESS
        PLA
        CLC
        ADC     SS1
        TAY                     ;REGISTER Y = LOW BYTE
        PLA
        ADC     SS1+1
        TAX                     ;SAVE HIGH BYTE IN REGISTER X

        ;RESTORE RETURN ADDRESS TO STACK
        LDA     RETADR+1
        PHA
        LDA     RETADR
        PHA                     ;RESTORE RETURN ADDRESS

        TXA                     ;GET HIGH BYTE BACK TO REGISTER A
        RTS                     ;EXIT

;
;DATA
RETADR: .BLOCK  2               ;TEMPORARY FOR RETURN ADDRESS
SS1:    .BLOCK  2               ;SUBSCRIPT 1
SS1SZ:  .BLOCK  2               ;SIZE OF SUBSCRIPT 1 IN BYTES
SS2:    .BLOCK  2               ;SUBSCRIPT 2
PROD:   .BLOCK  2               ;TEMPORARY FOR THE MULTIPLY
```

```
;                                                                   ;
;                                                                   ;
;       SAMPLE EXECUTION:                                           ;
;                                                                   ;
;                                                                   ;


SC0505:
        ;PUSH ARRAY ADDRESS
        LDA     ARYADR+1
        PHA
        LDA     ARYADR
        PHA

        ;PUSH FIRST SUBSCRIPT
        LDA     SUBS1+1
        PHA
        LDA     SUBS1
        PHA

        ;PUSH SIZE OF FIRST SUBSCRIPT
        LDA     SSUBS1+1
        PHA
        LDA     SSUBS1
        PHA

        ;PUSH SECOND SUBSCRIPT
        LDA     SUBS2+1
        PHA
        LDA     SUBS2
        PHA

        JSR     D2BYTE          ;CALCULATE ADDRESS
        BRK                     ;FOR THE INITIAL TEST DATA
                                ;AY = ADDRESS OF ARY(2,4)
                                ;    = ARY + (2*8) + 4
                                ;    = ARY + 20 (CONTENTS ARE 21)
        JMP     SC0505

;
;DATA
SUBS1:  .WORD   2               ;SUBSCRIPT 1
SSUBS1: .WORD   8               ;SIZE OF SUBSCRIPT 1
SUBS2:  .WORD   4               ;SUBSCRIPT 2
ARYADR: .WORD   ARY             ;ADDRESS OF ARRAY

;THE ARRAY (3 ROWS OF 8 COLUMNS)
ARY:    .BYTE   1 ,2 ,3 ,4 ,5 ,6 ,7 ,8
        .BYTE   9 ,10,11,12,13,14,15,16
        .BYTE   17,18,19,20,21,22,23,24

        .END    ;PROGRAM
```

Two-Dimensional Word Array Index (D2WORD) 5F

Calculates the starting address of an element of a two-dimensional word-length (16-bit) array, given the base address of the array, the two subscripts of the element, and the size of a row in bytes. The array is assumed to be stored in row major order (that is, by rows) and both subscripts are assumed to begin at zero.

Procedure: The program multiplies the row size (in bytes) times the row subscript (since the elements are stored by row), adds the product to the doubled column subscript (doubled because each element occupies two bytes), and adds the sum to the base address. The program uses a standard shift-and-add algorithm (see Subroutine 6H) to multiply.

Registers Used: All

Execution Time: Approximately 1500 cycles, depending mainly on the amount of time required to perform the multiplication of row size in bytes times row subscript.

Program Size: 121 bytes

Data Memory Required: Ten bytes anywhere in memory to hold the return address (two bytes starting at address RETADR), the row subscript (two bytes starting at address SS1), the row size in bytes (two bytes starting at address SS1SZ), the column subscript (two bytes starting at address SS2), and the product of row size times row subscript (two bytes starting at address PROD).

Entry Conditions

Order in stack (starting at the top)

Less significant byte of return address
More significant byte of return address

Less significant byte of column subscript
More significant byte of column subscript

Less significant byte of size of rows (in bytes)
More significant byte of size of rows (in bytes)

Less significant byte of row subscript
More significant byte of row subscript

Less significant byte of base address of array
More significant byte of base address of array

Exit Conditions

(A) = More significant byte of starting address of element

(Y) = Less significant byte of starting address of element

The element occupies the address in AY and the next higher address.

Examples

1. Data: Base address = $5E14_{16}$
   Column subscript = 0008_{16}
   Size of a row (in bytes) = $001C_{16}$ (i.e., each row has 0014_{10} or $000E_{16}$ word-length elements)
   Row subscript = 0005_{16}

   Result: Starting address of element = $5E14_{16} + 0005_{16} \times 001C_{16} + 0008_{16} \times 2 = 5E14_{16} + 008C_{16} + 0010_{16} = 5EB0_{16}$.
   Thus, the starting address of ARRAY (5,8) is $5EB0_{16}$ and the element occupies addresses $5EB0_{16}$ and $5EB1_{16}$.

2. Data: Base address = $B100_{16}$
   Column subscript = 0002_{16}
   Size of a row (in bytes) = 0008_{16} (i.e., each row has 4 word-length elements)
   Row subscript = 0006_{16}

   Result: Starting address of element = $B100_{16} + 0006_{16} \times 0008_{16} + 0002_{16} \times 2 = B100_{16} + 0030_{16} + 0004_{16} = B134_{16}$.
   Thus, the starting address of ARRAY (6,2) is $B134_{16}$ and the element occupies addresses $B134_{16}$ and $B135_{16}$.

The general formula is

STARTING ADDRESS OF ELEMENT
= BASE ADDRESS OF ARRAY
+ ROW SUBSCRIPT × SIZE OF ROW
+ COLUMN SUBSCRIPT × 2

Note that one parameter of this routine is the size of a row in bytes. The size in the case of word-length elements is the number of columns (per row) times two (the size of an element). The reason why we chose this parameter rather than the number of columns or the maximum column index is that this parameter can be calculated once (when the array bounds are determined) and used whenever the array is accessed. The alternative parameters (number of columns or maximum column index) would require extra calculations as part of each indexing operation.

```
;       Title           Two dimensional word array indexing           ;
;       Name:           D2WORD                                        ;
;                                                                     ;
;                                                                     ;

;                                                                     ;
;       Purpose:        Given the base address of a word array, two   ;
;                       subscripts 'I','J', and the size of the first ;
;                       subscript in bytes, calculate the address of  ;
;                       A[I,J]. The array is assumed to be stored in  ;
;                       row major order (A[0,0], A[0,1],..., A[K,L]), ;
```

```
;                       and both dimensions are assumed to begin at   ;
;                       zero as in the following Pascal declaration:  ;
;                         A:ARRAY[0..2,0..7] OF WORD;                 ;
;                                                                     ;
;       Entry:          TOP OF STACK                                  ;
;                         Low byte of return address,                 ;
;                         High byte of return address,                ;
;                         Low byte of second subscript,               ;
;                         High byte of second subscript,              ;
;                         Low byte of size of first subscript in bytes, ;
;                         High byte of size of first subscript in bytes,;
;                         Low byte of first subscript,                ;
;                         High byte of first subscript,               ;
;                         Low byte of base address of array,          ;
;                         High byte of base address of array          ;
;                                                                     ;
;       Exit:           Register A = High byte of address             ;
;                       Register Y = Low byte of address              ;
;                                                                     ;
;       Registers used: ALL                                           ;
;                                                                     ;
;       Time:           Approximately 1500 cycles                     ;
;                                                                     ;
;       Size:           Program 121 bytes                             ;
;                       Data     10 bytes                             ;
;                                                                     ;
;                                                                     ;

D2WORD:
        ;SAVE RETURN ADDRESS
        PLA
        STA     RETADR
        PLA
        STA     RETADR+1

        ;GET SECOND SUBSCRIPT AND MULTIPLY BY 2 FOR WORD-LENGTH ELEMENTS
        PLA
        ASL     A
        STA     SS2
        PLA
        ROL     A
        STA     SS2+1

        ;GET SIZE OF FIRST SUBSCRIPT
        PLA
        STA     SS1SZ
        PLA
        STA     SS1SZ+1

        ;GET FIRST SUBSCRIPT
        PLA
        STA     SS1
        PLA
        STA     SS1+1
```

```
        ;MULTIPLY FIRST SUBSCRIPT * ROW SIZE (IN BYTES) USING THE SHIFT AND ADD
        ;ALGORITHM. THE RESULT WILL BE IN SS1
        LDA     #0              ;PARTIAL PRODUCT = ZERO INITIALLY
        STA     PROD
        STA     PROD+1
        LDX     #17             ;NUMBER OF SHIFTS = 17
        CLC
MULLP:
        ROR     PROD+1          ;SHIFT PARTIAL PRODUCT
        ROR     PROD
        ROR     SS1+1           ;SHIFT MULTIPLIER
        ROR     SS1
        BCC     DECCNT
        CLC                     ;ADD MULTIPLICAND TO PARTIAL PRODUCT
        LDA     SS1SZ           ; IF NEXT BIT OF MULTIPLIER IS 1
        ADC     PROD
        STA     PROD
        LDA     SS1SZ+1
        ADC     PROD+1
        STA     PROD+1

DECCNT:
        DEX
        BNE     MULLP

        ;ADD IN THE SECOND SUBSCRIPT DOUBLED
        LDA     SS1
        CLC
        ADC     SS2
        STA     SS1
        LDA     SS1+1
        ADC     SS2+1
        STA     SS1+1

        ;ADD BASE ADDRESS TO FORM THE FINAL ADDRESS
        PLA
        CLC
        ADC     SS1
        TAY                     ;REGISTER Y = LOW BYTE
        PLA
        ADC     SS1+1
        TAX                     ;SAVE HIGH BYTE IN REGISTER X

        ;RESTORE RETURN ADDRESS TO STACK
        LDA     RETADR+1
        PHA
        LDA     RETADR
        PHA                     ;RESTORE RETURN ADDRESS

        TXA                     ;GET HIGH BYTE BACK TO REGISTER A
        RTS                     ;EXIT


;
;DATA
```

```
RETADR: .BLOCK  2               ;TEMPORARY FOR RETURN ADDRESS
SS1:    .BLOCK  2               ;SUBSCRIPT 1
SS1SZ:  .BLOCK  2               ;SIZE OF SUBSCRIPT 1 IN BYTES
SS2:    .BLOCK  2               ;SUBSCRIPT 2
PROD:   .BLOCK  2               ;TEMPORARY FOR THE MULTIPLY


;                                                                       ;
;                                                                       ;
;       SAMPLE EXECUTION:                                               ;
;                                                                       ;
;                                                                       ;


SC0506:
        ;PUSH ARRAY ADDRESS
        LDA     ARYADR+1
        PHA
        LDA     ARYADR
        PHA

        ;PUSH FIRST SUBSCRIPT
        LDA     SUBS1+1
        PHA
        LDA     SUBS1
        PHA

        ;PUSH SIZE OF FIRST SUBSCRIPT
        LDA     SSUBS1+1
        PHA
        LDA     SSUBS1
        PHA

        ;PUSH SECOND SUBSCRIPT
        LDA     SUBS2+1
        PHA
        LDA     SUBS2
        PHA

        JSR     D2WORD          ;CALCULATE ADDRESS
        BRK                     ;FOR THE INITIAL TEST DATA
                                ;AY = STARTING ADDRESS OF ARY(2,4)
                                ;   = ARY + (2*16) + (4*2)
                                ;   = ARY + 40
                                ;   = ARY(2,4) CONTAINS 2100 HEX
        JMP     SC0506

;
;DATA
SUBS1:  .WORD   2               ;SUBSCRIPT 1
SSUBS1: .WORD   16              ;SIZE OF SUBSCRIPT 1
SUBS2:  .WORD   4               ;SUBSCRIPT 2
ARYADR: .WORD   ARY             ;ADDRESS OF ARRAY

;THE ARRAY (3 ROWS OF 8 COLUMNS)
```

```
ARY:    .WORD   0100H,0200H,0300H,0400H,0500H,0600H,0700H,0800H
        .WORD   0900H,1000H,1100H,1200H,1300H,1400H,1500H,1600H
        .WORD   1700H,1800H,1900H,2000H,2100H,2200H,2300H,2400H

        .END    ;PROGRAM
```

N-Dimensional Array Index (NDIM) 5G

Calculates the starting address of an element of an N-dimensional array given the base address and N pairs of sizes and subscripts. The size of a dimension is the number of bytes from the starting address of an element to the starting address of the element with an index one larger in the dimension but the same in all other dimensions. The array is assumed to be stored in row major order (that is, organized so that subscripts to the right change before subscripts to the left).

Note that the size of the rightmost subscript is simply the size of the elements (in bytes); the size of the next subscript is the size of the elements times the maximum value of the rightmost subscript plus 1, etc. All subscripts are assumed to begin at zero; otherwise, the user must normalize the subscripts (see the second example at the end of the listing).

Procedure: The program loops on each dimension, calculating the offset in that dimension as the subscript times the size. If the size is an easy case (an integral power of 2), the program reduces the multiplication to left shifts. Otherwise, it performs each multiplication using the shift-and-add algorithm of Subroutine 6H. Once the program has calculated the overall offset, it adds that offset to the base address to obtain the starting address of the element.

Registers Used: All

Execution Time: Approximately 1100 cycles per dimension plus 90 cycles overhead. Depends mainly on the time required to perform the multiplications.

Program Size: 192 bytes

Data Memory Required: Eleven bytes anywhere in memory to hold the return address (two bytes starting at address RETADR), the current subscript (two bytes starting at address SS), the current size (two bytes starting at address SIZE), the accumulated offset (two bytes starting at address OFFSET), the number of dimensions (one byte at address NUMDIM), and the product of size times subscript (two bytes starting at address PROD).

Special Case: If the number of dimensions is zero, the program returns with the base address in registers A (more significant byte) and Y (less significant byte).

Entry Conditions

Order in stack (starting at the top)

Less significant byte of return address
More significant byte of return address

Number of dimensions

Less significant byte of size of rightmost dimension
More significant byte of size of rightmost dimension

Less significant byte of rightmost subscript
More significant byte of rightmost subscript

.
.
.

Less significant byte of size of leftmost dimension
More significant byte of size of leftmost dimension

Less significant byte of leftmost subscript
More significant byte of leftmost subscript

Less significant byte of base address of array
More significant byte of base address of array

Exit Conditions

(A) = More significant byte of address of element

(Y) = Less significant byte of address of element

The element occupies memory addresses from the calculated starting address through that address plus the rightmost subscript minus 1. That is, the element occupies memory addresses START through START + SIZE − 1, where START is the calculated address and SIZE is the size of an element in bytes.

Example

Data: Base address = $3C00_{16}$
Number of dimensions = 03_{16}
Rightmost subscript = 0005_{16}
Rightmost size = 0003_{16} (3-byte entries)
Middle subscript = 0003_{16}
Middle size = 0012_{16} (six 3-byte entries)
Leftmost subscript = 0004_{16}
Leftmost size = $007E_{16}$ (seven sets of six 3-byte entries)

Result: Address of entry = $3C00_{16} + 0005_{16} \times 0003_{16} + 0003_{16} \times 0012_{16} + 0004_{16} \times 007E_{16} = 3C00_{16} + 000F_{16} + 0036_{16} + 01F8_{16} = 3E3D_{16}$.
That is, the element is ARRAY (4,3,5); it occupies addresses $3E3D_{16}$ through $3E3F_{16}$. The maximum values of the various subscripts are 6 (leftmost) and 5 (middle). Each element consists of three bytes.

The general formula is

$$\text{STARTING ADDRESS} = \text{BASE ADDRESS} + \sum_{i=0}^{N-1} \text{SUBSCRIPT}_i \times \text{SIZE}_i$$

where:

N is the number of dimensions
SUBSCRIPT_i is the ith subscript
SIZE_i is the size of the ith dimension

Note that we use the sizes of each dimension as parameters to reduce the number of repetitive multiplications and to generalize the procedure. The sizes can be calculated (and saved) as soon as the bounds of the array are known. Those sizes can then be used whenever indexing is performed on that array. Obviously, the sizes do not change if the bounds are fixed and they should not be recalculated as part of each indexing operation. The sizes are also general, since the elements can themselves consist of any number of bytes.

```
;       Title              N dimensional array_indexing                   ;
;       Name:              NDIM                                           ;
;                                                                         ;
;                                                                         ;

;                                                                         ;
;       Purpose:           Calculate the address of an element in a       ;
;                          N dimensional array given the base address,    ;
;                          N pairs of size in bytes and subscript, and the ;
;                          number of dimensions of the array. The array is ;
;                          assumed to be stored in row major order        ;
;                          (A[0,0,0],A[0,0,1],...,A[0,1,0],A[0,1,1],...   ;
;                          Also it is assumed that all dimensions begin   ;
;                          at 0 as in the following Pascal declaration:   ;
;                            A:ARRAY[0..10,0..3,0..5] OF SOMETHING        ;
;                                                                         ;
;       Entry:             TOP OF STACK                                   ;
;                            Low byte of return address,                  ;
;                            High byte of return address,                 ;
;                            Number of dimensions,                        ;
;                            Low byte of size (dim N-1) in bytes,         ;
;                            High byte of size (dim N-1) in bytes,        ;
;                            Low byte of subscript (dim N-1),             ;
;                            High byte of subscript (dim N-1),            ;
```

```
;                                      .                              ;
;                                      .                              ;
;                                      .                              ;
;                      Low byte of size (dim 0) in bytes,             ;
;                      High byte of size (dim 0) in bytes,            ;
;                      Low byte of subscript (dim 0),                 ;
;                      High byte of subscript (dim 0),                ;
;                      Low byte of base address of array,             ;
;                      High byte of base address of array             ;
;                                                                     ;
;       Exit:          Register A = High byte of address              ;
;                      Register Y = Low byte of address               ;
;                                                                     ;
;       Registers used: All                                           ;
;                                                                     ;
;       Time:          Approximately 1100 cycles per dimension        ;
;                      plus 90 cycles overhead.                       ;
;                                                                     ;
;       Size:          Program 192 bytes                              ;
;                      Data     11 bytes                              ;
;                                                                     ;
;                                                                     ;


NDIM:
        ;POP PARAMETERS
        PLA
        STA     RETADR
        PLA
        STA     RETADR+1        ;SAVE RETURN ADDRESS

        PLA
        STA     NUMDIM          ;GET NUMBER OF DIMENSIONS

        ;OFFSET := 0
        LDA     #0
        STA     OFFSET
        STA     OFFSET+1

        ;CHECK FOR ZERO DIMENSIONS JUST IN CASE
        LDA     NUMDIM
        BEQ     ADBASE          ;ASSUME THERE IS A BASE ADDRESS EVEN
                                ; IF THERE ARE NO DIMENSIONS

        ;LOOP ON EACH DIMENSION
        ; DOING OFFSET := OFFSET + (SUBSCRIPT * SIZE)
LOOP:
        PLA                     ;POP SIZE
        STA     SIZE
        PLA
        STA     SIZE+1

        PLA                     ;POP SUBSCRIPT
        STA     SS
        PLA
```

```
        STA     SS+1

        JSR     NXTOFF          ;OFFSET := OFFSET + (SUBSCRIPT * SIZE)

        DEC     NUMDIM          ;DECREMENT NUMBER OF DIMENSIONS
        BNE     LOOP            ;CONTINUE THROUGH ALL DIMENSIONS


ADBASE:
        ;CALCULATE THE STARTING ADDRESS OF THE ELEMENT
        ;OFFSET = BASE + OFFSET
        PLA                     ;GET LOW BYTE OF BASE
        CLC
        ADC     OFFSET          ;ADD LOW BYTE OF OFFSET
        STA     OFFSET
        PLA                     ;GET HIGH BYTE OF BASE
        ADC     OFFSET+1        ;A = HIGH BYTE OF BASE + OFFSET
        STA     OFFSET+1

        ;RESTORE RETURN ADDRESS AND EXIT
        LDA     RETADR+1
        PHA
        LDA     RETADR
        PHA
        LDA     OFFSET+1        ;RETURN THE ADDRESS WHICH IS IN OFFSET
        LDY     OFFSET
        RTS

;
;
;SUBROUTINE NXTOFF
;PURPOSE: OFFSET := OFFSET + (SUBSCRIPT * SIZE);
;ENTRY: OFFSET = CURRENT OFFSET
;       SUBSCRIPT = CURRENT SUBSCRIPT
;       SIZE = CURRENT SIZE OF THIS DIMENSION
;EXIT:  OFFSET = OFFSET + (SUBSCRIPT * SIZE);
;REGISTERS USED: ALL
;

NXTOFF:
        ;
        ;CHECK IF SIZE IS POWER OF 2 OR 8 (EASY MULTIPLICATIONS - SHIFT ONLY)
        LDA     SIZE+1          ;HIGH BYTE = 0 ?
        BNE     BIGSZ           ;BRANCH IF SIZE IS LARGE

        LDA     SIZE
        LDY     #0              ;Y=INDEX INTO EASY ARRAY
        LDX     #SZEASY         ;X=SIZE OF EASY ARRAY
EASYLP:
        CMP     EASYAY,Y
        BEQ     ISEASY          ;BRANCH IF SIZE IS AN EASY ELEMENT
        INY                     ;INCREMENT INDEX
        DEX                     ;DECREMENT COUNT
        BNE     EASYLP          ;BRANCH IF NOT THROUGH ALL EASY ELEMENTS
        BEQ     BIGSZ           ;BRANCH IF SIZE IS NOT EASY
```

```
ISEASY:
        CPY     #0
        BEQ     ADDOFF          ;BRANCH IF SHIFT FACTOR = 0

        ;ELEMENT SIZE * SUBSCRIPT CAN BE PERFORMED WITH A SHIFT LEFT
SHL:
        ASL     SS              ;SHIFT LEFT LOW BYTE
        ROL     SS+1            ;SHIFT LEFT HIGH BYTE
        DEY
        BNE     SHL             ;CONTINUE UNTIL DONE
        BEQ     ADDOFF          ;DONE SO ADD OFFSET + SUBSCRIPT


BIGSZ:
        ;SIZE IS NOT AN EASY MULTIPLICATION SO PERFORM MULTIPLICATION OF
        ; ELEMENT SIZE AND SUBSCRIPT THE HARD WAY
        LDA     #0              ;PARTIAL PRODUCT = ZERO INITIALLY
        STA     PROD
        STA     PROD+1
        LDX     #17             ;NUMBER OF SHIFTS = 17
        CLC
MULLP:
        ROR     PROD+1          ;SHIFT PARTIAL PRODUCT
        ROR     PROD
        ROR     SS+1            ;SHIFT MULTIPLIER
        ROR     SS
        BCC     DECCNT
        CLC                     ;ADD MULTIPLICAND TO PARTIAL PRODUCT
        LDA     SIZE            ; IF NEXT BIT OF MULTIPLIER IS 1
        ADC     PROD
        STA     PROD
        LDA     SIZE+1
        ADC     PROD+1
        STA     PROD+1

DECCNT:
        DEX
        BNE     MULLP


ADDOFF:
        LDA     SS
        CLC
        ADC     OFFSET          ;ADD LOW BYTES
        STA     OFFSET
        LDA     SS+1
        ADC     OFFSET+1        ;ADD HIGH BYTES
        STA     OFFSET+1

        RTS

EASYAY:                 ;SHIFT FACTOR
        .BYTE   1       ;0
        .BYTE   2       ;1
        .BYTE   4       ;2
```

```
                .BYTE   8       ;3
                .BYTE   16.     ;4
                .BYTE   32.     ;5
                .BYTE   64.     ;6
                .BYTE   128.    ;7
SZEASY          .EQU    $-EASYAY

;
;DATA
RETADR:         .BLOCK  2       ;TEMPORARY FOR RETURN ADDRESS
SS:             .BLOCK  2       ;SUBSCRIPT INTO THE ARRAY
SIZE:           .BLOCK  2       ;SIZE OF AN ARRAY ELEMENT
OFFSET:         .BLOCK  2       ;TEMPORARY FOR CALCULATING
NUMDIM:         .BLOCK  1       ;NUMBER OF DIMENSIONS
PROD:           .BLOCK  2       ;TEMPORARY FOR MULTIPLICATION IN NXTOFF

;                                                                     ;
;                                                                     ;
;       SAMPLE EXECUTION:                                             ;
;                                                                     ;
;                                                                     ;


;PROGRAM SECTION
SC0507:
;
;FIND ADDRESS OF AY1[1,3,0]
;  SINCE LOWER BOUNDS OF ARRAY 1 ARE ALL ZERO IT IS NOT
;  NECESSARY TO NORMALIZE THEM

;PUSH BASE ADDRESS OF ARRAY 1
LDA     AY1ADR+1
PHA
LDA     AY1ADR
PHA

;PUSH SUBSCRIPT AND SIZE FOR DIMENSION 1
LDA     #0
PHA
LDA     #1
PHA
LDA     #0
PHA
LDA     #A1SZ1
PHA

;PUSH SUBSCRIPT AND SIZE FOR DIMENSION 2
LDA     #0
PHA
LDA     #3
PHA
LDA     #0
PHA
LDA     #A1SZ2
PHA
```

```
;PUSH SUBSCRIPT AND SIZE FOR DIMENSION 3
LDA     #0
PHA
LDA     #0
PHA
LDA     #0
PHA
LDA     #A1SZ3
PHA

;PUSH NUMBER OF DIMENSIONS
LDA     #A1DIM
PHA

JSR     NDIM              ;CALCULATE ADDRESS
BRK                       ;AY = STARTING ADDRESS OF ARY1(1,3,0)
                          ;    = ARY + (1*126) + (3*21) + (0*3)
                          ;    = ARY + 189

;
;CALCULATE ADDRESS OF AY2[-1,6]
;  SINCE LOWER BOUNDS OF AY 2 DO NOT START AT ZERO THE SUBSCRIPTS
;  MUST BE NORMALIZED
;PUSH BASE ADDRESS OF ARRAY 2
LDA     AY2ADR+1
PHA
LDA     AY2ADR
PHA

;PUSH (SUBSCRIPT - LOWER BOUND) AND SIZE FOR DIMENSION 1
LDA     #-1
SEC
SBC     #A2D1L
TAX                       ;SAVE LOW BYTE
LDA     #0FFH             ;HIGH BYTE OF -1 SUBSCRIPT
SBC     #0FFH             ;HIGH BYTE OF A2D1L
PHA                       ;PUSH HIGH BYTE
TXA
PHA                       ;PUSH LOW BYTE
LDA     #0
PHA
LDA     #A2SZ1
PHA

;PUSH (SUBSCRIPT - LOWER BOUND) AND SIZE FOR DIMENSION 2
LDA     #6
SEC
SBC     #A2D2L
TAX                       ;SAVE LOW BYTE
LDA     #0
SBC     #0
PHA                       ;PUSH HIGH BYTE
TXA
PHA                       ;PUSH LOW BYTE
LDA     #0
```

```
        PHA
        LDA     #A2SZ2
        PHA

        ;PUSH NUMBER OF DIMENSIONS
        LDA     #A2DIM
        PHA

        JSR     NDIM    ;CALCULATE ADDRESS
        BRK             ;AY = STARTING ADDRESS OF ARY1(-1,6)
                        ;    = ARY + (((-1) - (-5))*18) + ((6 - 2)*2)
                        ;    = ARY + 80

        JMP     SC0507

;DATA
AY1ADR: .WORD   AY1     ;ADDRESS OF ARRAY 1
AY2ADR: .WORD   AY2     ;ADDRESS OF ARRAY 2

;
;AY1 : ARRAY[A1D1L..A1D1H,A1D2L..A1D2H,A1D3L..A1D3H] OF THREE BYTE ELEMENTS
;            [ 0  ..  3  , 0  ..  5  ,  0  ..  6 ]
A1DIM:  .EQU    3                       ;NUMBER OF DIMENSIONS OF ARRAY 1
A1D1L:  .EQU    0                       ;LOW BOUND OF ARRAY 1 DIMENSION 1
A1D1H:  .EQU    3                       ;HIGH BOUND OF ARRAY 1 DIMENSION 1
A1D2L:  .EQU    0                       ;LOW BOUND OF ARRAY 1 DIMENSION 2
A1D2H:  .EQU    5                       ;HIGH BOUND OF ARRAY 1 DIMENSION 2
A1D3L:  .EQU    0                       ;LOW BOUND OF ARRAY 1 DIMENSION 3
A1D3H:  .EQU    6                       ;HIGH BOUND OF ARRAY 1 DIMENSION 3
A1SZ3:  .EQU    3                       ;SIZE OF AN ELEMENT IN DIMENSION 3
A1SZ2:  .EQU    ((A1D3H-A1D3L)+1)*A1SZ3 ;SIZE OF AN ELEMENT IN DIMENSION 2
A1SZ1:  .EQU    ((A1D2H-A1D2L)+1)*A1SZ2 ;SIZE OF AN ELEMENT IN DIMENSION 1
AY1:    .BLOCK  ((A1D1H-A1D1L)+1)*A1SZ1 ;THE ARRAY

;AY2 : ARRAY[A1D1L..A1D1H,A1D2L..A1D2H] OF WORD
;            [ -5 ..  -1  ,  2  .. 10 ]
A2DIM:  .EQU    2                       ;NUMBER OF DIMENSIONS OF ARRAY 2
A2D1L:  .EQU    -5                      ;LOW BOUND OF ARRAY 2 DIMENSION 1
A2D1H:  .EQU    -1                      ;HIGH BOUND OF ARRAY 2 DIMENSION 1
A2D2L:  .EQU    2                       ;LOW BOUND OF ARRAY 2 DIMENSION 2
A2D2H:  .EQU    10                      ;HIGH BOUND OF ARRAY 2 DIMENSION 2
A2SZ2:  .EQU    2                       ;SIZE OF AN ELEMENT IN DIMENSION 2
A2SZ1:  .EQU    ((A2D2H-A2D2L)+1)*A2SZ2 ;SIZE OF AN ELEMENT IN DIMENSION 1
AY2:    .BLOCK  ((A2D1H-A2D1L)+1)*A2SZ1 ;THE ARRAY

        .END    ;PROGRAM
```

Adds two 16-bit operands obtained from the stack and places the sum at the top of the stack. All 16-bit numbers are stored in the usual 6502 style with the less significant byte on top of the more significant byte.

Procedure: The program clears the Carry flag initially and adds the operands one byte at a time, starting with the less significant bytes. It sets the Carry flag from the addition of the more significant bytes.

Registers Used: A, P, Y

Execution Time: 80 cycles

Program Size: 38 bytes

Data Memory Required: Four bytes anywhere in memory for the second operand (two bytes starting at address ADEND2) and the return address (two bytes starting at address RETADR).

Entry Conditions

Order in stack (starting from the top)

Less significant byte of return address
More significant byte of return address

Less significant byte of first operand
More significant byte of first operand

Less significant byte of second operand
More significant byte of second operand

Exit Conditions

Order in stack (starting from the top)

Less significant byte of sum
More significant byte of sum

Examples

1. Data: First operand = $03E1_{16}$
   Second operand = $07E4_{16}$

   Result: Sum = $0BC5_{16}$
   Carry = 0

2. Data: First operand = $A45D_{16}$
   Second operand = $97E1_{16}$

   Result: Sum = $3C3E_{16}$
   Carry = 1

```
;       Title             16 bit addition                                    ;
;       Name:             ADD16                                              ;
;                                                                            ;
;                                                                            ;


;                                                                            ;
;       Purpose:          Add 2 16 bit signed or unsigned words and return;
;                         a 16 bit signed or unsigned sum.                   ;
;                                                                            ;
;       Entry:            TOP OF STACK                                       ;
;                           Low byte of return address,                      ;
;                           High byte of return address,                     ;
;                           Low byte of operand 2,                           ;
;                           High byte of operand 2,                          ;
;                           Low byte of operand 1,                           ;
;                           High byte of operand 1                           ;
;                                                                            ;
;       Exit:             Sum = operand 1 + operand 2                        ;
;                         TOP OF STACK                                       ;
;                           Low byte of sum,                                 ;
;                           High byte of sum                                 ;
;                                                                            ;
;       Registers used: A,P,Y                                                ;
;                                                                            ;
;       Time:             80 cycles                                          ;
;                                                                            ;
;       Size:             Program 38 bytes                                   ;
;                         Data     4 bytes                                   ;
;                                                                            ;
;                                                                            ;


ADD16:
        ;SAVE THE RETURN ADDRESS
        PLA
        STA     RETADR
        PLA
        STA     RETADR+1

        ;GET ADDEND 2
        PLA
        STA     ADEND2
        PLA
        STA     ADEND2+1

        ;SUM ADDEND 2 WITH ADDEND 1
        PLA
        CLC
        ADC     ADEND2
        TAY                     ;SAVE LOW BYTE OF SUM
        PLA
        ADC     ADEND2+1

        ;PUSH THE SUM
        PHA                     ;PUSH HIGH BYTE
        TYA
```

```
        PHA                         ;PUSH LOW BYTE

        ;PUSH RETURN ADDRESS AND EXIT
        LDA     RETADR+1
        PHA
        LDA     RETADR
        PHA
        RTS

;DATA
ADEND2: .BLOCK  2                   ;TEMPORARY FOR ADDEND 2
RETADR: .BLOCK  2                   ;TEMPORARY FOR RETURN ADDRESS

;                                                                        ;
;                                                                        ;
;       SAMPLE EXECUTION                                                 ;
;                                                                        ;
;                                                                        ;


SC0601:
        ;SUM OPRND1 + OPRND2
        LDA     OPRND1+1
        PHA
        LDA     OPRND1
        PHA
        LDA     OPRND2+1
        PHA
        LDA     OPRND2
        PHA
        JSR     ADD16
        PLA
        TAY
        PLA
        BRK                         ;A = HIGH BYTE, Y = LOW BYTE
        JMP     SC0601

;TEST DATA, CHANGE FOR DIFFERENT VALUES
OPRND1  .WORD   1023                ;1023 + 123 = 1146 = 047AH
OPRND2  .WORD   123

        .END    ;PROGRAM
```

16-Bit Subtraction (SUB16) 6B

Subtracts two 16-bit operands obtained from the stack and places the difference at the top of the stack. All 16-bit numbers are stored in the usual 6502 style with the less significant byte on top of the more significant byte. The subtrahend (number to be subtracted) is stored on top of the minuend (number from which the subtrahend is subtracted). The Carry flag acts as an inverted borrow, its usual role in the 6502.

Procedure: The program sets the Carry flag (the inverted borrow) initially and subtracts the subtrahend from the minuend one byte at a time, starting with the less significant bytes. It sets the Carry flag from the subtraction of the more significant bytes.

Registers Used: A, P, Y

Execution Time: 80 cycles

Program Size: 38 bytes

Data Memory Required: Four bytes anywhere in memory for the subtrahend (two bytes starting at address SUBTRA) and the return address (two bytes starting at address RETADR).

Entry Conditions

Order in stack (starting from the top)

Less significant byte of return address
More significant byte of return address

Less significant byte of subtrahend
More significant byte of subtrahend

Less significant byte of minuend
More significant byte of minuend

Exit Conditions

Order in stack (starting from the top)

Less significant byte of difference (minuend − subtrahend)

More significant byte of difference (minuend − subtrahend)

Examples

1. Data: Minuend = $A45D_{16}$
   Subtrahend = $97E1_{16}$

   Result: Difference = Minuend − Subtrahend
   = $0C7C_{16}$
   Carry = 1 (no borrow)

2. Data: Minuend = $03E1_{16}$
   Subtrahend = $07E4_{16}$

   Result: Difference = Minuend − Subtrahend
   = $FBFD_{16}$
   Carry = 0 (borrow generated)

```
;       Title             16 bit subtraction                            ;
;       Name:             SUB16                                         ;
;                                                                       ;
;                                                                       ;


;                                                                       ;
;       Purpose:          Subtract 2 16 bit signed or unsigned words and ;
;                         return a 16 bit signed or unsigned difference. ;
;                                                                       ;
;       Entry:            TOP OF STACK                                  ;
;                           Low byte of return address,                 ;
;                           High byte of return address,                ;
;                           Low byte of subtrahend,                     ;
;                           High byte of subtrahend,                    ;
;                           Low byte of minuend,                        ;
;                           High byte of minuend                        ;
;                                                                       ;
;       Exit:             Difference = minuend - subtrahend             ;
;                         TOP OF STACK                                  ;
;                           Low byte of difference,                     ;
;                           High byte of difference                     ;
;                                                                       ;
;       Registers used: A,P,Y                                           ;
;                                                                       ;
;       Time:             80 cycles                                     ;
;                                                                       ;
;       Size:             Program 38 bytes                              ;
;                         Data     4 bytes                              ;
;                                                                       ;
;                                                                       ;

SUB16:
        ;SAVE THE RETURN ADDRESS
        PLA
        STA     RETADR
        PLA
        STA     RETADR+1

        ;GET SUBTRAHEND
        PLA
        STA     SUBTRA
        PLA
        STA     SUBTRA+1

        ;SUBTRACT SUBTRAHEND FROM MINUEND
        PLA
        SEC
        SBC     SUBTRA
        TAY                     ;SAVE LOW BYTE OF THE DIFFERENCE
        PLA
        SBC     SUBTRA+1

        ;PUSH THE DIFFERENCE
        PHA                     ;PUSH HIGH BYTE
        TYA
        PHA                     ;PUSH LOW BYTE
```

```
        ;PUSH RETURN ADDRESS AND EXIT
        LDA     RETADR+1
        PHA
        LDA     RETADR
        PHA
        RTS

;DATA
SUBTRA: .BLOCK  2                       ;TEMPORARY FOR SUBTRAHEND
RETADR: .BLOCK  2                       ;TEMPORARY FOR RETURN ADDRESS

;                                                                       ;
;                                                                       ;
;       SAMPLE EXECUTION                                                ;
;                                                                       ;
;                                                                       ;


SC0602:
        ;SUBTRACT OPRND2 FROM OPRND1
        LDA     OPRND1+1
        PHA
        LDA     OPRND1
        PHA
        LDA     OPRND2+1
        PHA
        LDA     OPRND2
        PHA
        JSR     SUB16
        PLA
        TAY
        PLA
        BRK                             ;A = HIGH BYTE, Y = LOW BYTE
        JMP     SC0602

;TEST DATA - CHANGE TO TEST OTHER VALUES
OPRND1  .WORD   123                     ;123 - 1023 = -900 = 0FC7CH
OPRND2  .WORD   1023

        .END    ;PROGRAM
```

Multiplies two 16-bit operands obtained from the stack and places the less significant word of the product at the top of the stack. All 16-bit numbers are stored in the usual 6502 style with the less significant byte on top of the more significant byte.

Procedure: The program uses an ordinary add-and-shift algorithm, adding the multiplicand to the partial product each time it finds a 1 bit in the multiplier. The partial product and the multiplier are shifted 17 times (the number of bits in the multiplier plus 1) with the extra loop being necessary to move the final Carry into the product. The program maintains a full 32-bit unsigned partial product in memory locations (starting with the most significant byte) HIPROD+1, HIPROD, MLIER+1, and MLIER. The less significant word of the product replaces the multiplier as the multiplier is shifted and examined for 1 bits.

Registers Used: All

Execution Time: Approximately 650 to 1100 cycles, depending largely on the number of 1 bits in the multiplier.

Program Size: 238 bytes

Data Memory Required: Eight bytes anywhere in memory for the multiplicand (two bytes starting at address MCAND), the multiplier and less significant word of the partial product (two bytes starting at address MLIER), the more significant word of the partial product (two bytes starting at address HIPROD), and the return address (two bytes starting at address RETADR).

Entry Conditions

Order in stack (starting from the top)

Less significant byte of return address
More significant byte of return address

Less significant byte of multiplier
More significant byte of multiplier

Less significant byte of multiplicand
More significant byte of multiplicand

Exit Conditions

Order in stack (starting from the top)

Less significant byte of less significant word of product

More significant byte of less significant word of product

Examples

1. Data: Multiplier = 0012_{16} (18_{10})
   Multiplicand = $03D1_{16}$ (977_{10})

   Result: Product = $44B2_{16}$ ($17{,}586_{10}$)

2. Data: Multiplier = $37D1_{16}$ ($14{,}289_{10}$)
   Multiplicand = $A045_{16}$ ($41{,}029_{10}$)

   Result: Product = $AB55_{16}$ ($43{,}861_{10}$). This is actually the less significant 16-bit word of the 32-bit product $22F1AB55_{16}$ ($586{,}264{,}381_{10}$).

Note that MUL16 returns only the less significant word of the product to maintain compatibility with other 16-bit arithmetic operations. The more significant word of the product is available in memory locations HIPROD (less significant byte) and HIPROD+1 (more significant byte), but the user should note that it is correct only if the operands are unsigned. If the operands are signed numbers and either one is negative, the user must determine the sign of the product and replace negative operands with their absolute values (two's complements) before calling MUL16.

```
;       Title           16 bit Multiplication                           ;
;       Name:           MUL16                                           ;
;                                                                       ;
;                                                                       ;

;                                                                       ;
;       Purpose:        Multiply 2 signed or unsigned 16 bit words and  ;
;                       return a 16 bit signed or unsigned product.     ;
;                                                                       ;
;       Entry:          TOP OF STACK                                    ;
;                         Low byte of return address,                   ;
;                         High byte of return address,                  ;
;                         Low byte of multiplier,                       ;
;                         High byte of multiplier,                      ;
;                         Low byte of multiplicand,                     ;
;                         High byte of multiplicand                     ;
;                                                                       ;
;       Exit:           Product = multiplicand * multiplier             ;
;                       TOP OF STACK                                    ;
;                         Low byte of product,                          ;
;                         High byte of product,                         ;
;                                                                       ;
;       Registers used: All                                             ;
;                                                                       ;
;       Time:           Approximately 650 to 1100 cycles                ;
;                                                                       ;
;       Size:           Program 238 bytes                               ;
;                       Data      8 bytes                               ;
;                                                                       ;
;                                                                       ;

;
MUL16:
        ;SAVE RETURN ADDRESS
        PLA
        STA     RETADR
        PLA
        STA     RETADR+1

        ;GET MULTIPLIER
        PLA
        STA     MLIER
        PLA
```

```
        STA     MLIER+1

        ;GET MULTIPLICAND
        PLA
        STA     MCAND
        PLA
        STA     MCAND+1
        ;PERFORM MULTIPLICATION USING THE SHIFT AND ADD ALGORITHM
        ; THIS ALGORITHM PRODUCES A UNSIGNED 32 BIT PRODUCT IN
        ; HIPROD AND MLIER WITH HIPROD BEING THE HIGH WORD.
        LDA     #0
        STA     HIPROD          ;ZERO HIGH WORD OF PRODUCT
        STA     HIPROD+1
        LDX     #17             ;NUMBER OF BITS IN MULTIPLIER PLUS 1, THE
                                ; EXTRA LOOP IS TO MOVE THE LAST CARRY INTO
                                ; THE PRODUCT
        CLC                     ; CLEAR CARRY FOR FIRST TIME THROUGH LOOP
MULLP:
        ;
        ;IF NEXT BIT = 1 THEN
        ;  HIPROD := HIPROD + MULTIPLICAND
        ROR     HIPROD+1
        ROR     HIPROD
        ROR     MLIER+1
        ROR     MLIER
        BCC     DECCNT          ;BRANCH IF NEXT BIT OF MULTIPLIER IS 0

        CLC                     ;NEXT BIT IS 1 SO ADD MULTIPLICAND TO PRODUCT
        LDA     MCAND
        ADC     HIPROD
        STA     HIPROD
        LDA     MCAND+1
        ADC     HIPROD+1
        STA     HIPROD+1        ;CARRY = OVERFLOW FROM ADD

DECCNT:
        DEX
        BNE     MULLP           ;CONTINUE UNTIL DONE


        ;PUSH LOW WORD OF PRODUCT ON TO STACK
        LDA     MLIER+1
        PHA
        LDA     MLIER
        PHA

        ;RESTORE RETURN ADDRESS
        LDA     RETADR+1
        PHA
        LDA     RETADR
        PHA
        RTS


;DATA
MCAND:  .BLOCK  2               ;MULTIPLICAND
```

```
MLIER:   .BLOCK  2                  ;MULTIPLIER AND LOW WORD OF PRODUCT
HIPROD:  .BLOCK  2                  ;HIGH WORD OF PRODUCT
RETADR:  .BLOCK  2                  ;RETURN ADDRESS
;                                                                       ;
;                                                                       ;
;        SAMPLE EXECUTION:                                              ;
;                                                                       ;
;                                                                       ;


SC0603:
         ;MULTIPLY OPRND1 * OPRND2 AND STORE THE PRODUCT AT RESULT
         LDA     OPRND1+1
         PHA
         LDA     OPRND1
         PHA
         LDA     OPRND2+1
         PHA
         LDA     OPRND2
         PHA
         JSR     MUL16              ;MULTIPLY
         PLA
         STA     RESULT
         PLA
         STA     RESULT+1
         BRK                        ;RESULT OF 1023 * -2 = -2046 = 0F802H
                                    ; IN MEMORY RESULT   = 02H
                                    ;           RESULT+1 = F8H
         JMP     SC0603

OPRND1   .WORD   -2
OPRND2   .WORD   1023
RESULT:  .BLOCK  2                  ;2 BYTE RESULT

         .END    ;PROGRAM
```

16-Bit Division
(SDIV16, UDIV16, SREM16, UREM16) 6D

Divides two 16-bit operands obtained from the stack and places either the quotient or the remainder at the top of the stack. There are four entry points: SDIV16 returns a 16-bit signed quotient from dividing two 16-bit signed operands, UDIV16 returns a 16-bit unsigned quotient from dividing two 16-bit unsigned operands, SREM16 returns a 16-bit remainder (a signed number) from dividing two 16-bit signed operands, and UREM16 returns a 16-bit unsigned remainder from dividing two 16-bit unsigned operands. All 16-bit numbers are stored in the usual 6502 style with the less significant byte on top of the more significant byte. The divisor is stored on top of the dividend. If the divisor is zero, the Carry flag is set and a zero result is returned; otherwise, the Carry flag is cleared.

Registers Used: All
Execution Time: Approximately 1000 to 1160 cycles, depending largely on the number of trial subtractions that are successful and thus require the replacement of the previous dividend by the remainder.
Program Size: 293 bytes
Data Memory Required: Eleven bytes anywhere in memory. These are utilized as follows: two bytes for the divisor (starting at address DVSOR); four bytes for the extended dividend (starting at address DVEND) and also for the quotient and remainder; two bytes for the return address (starting at address RETADR); one byte for the sign of the quotient (address SQUOT); one byte for the sign of the remainder (address SREM); and one byte for an index to the result (address RSLTIX).
Special Case: If the divisor is zero, the program returns with the Carry flag set to 1 and a result of zero. Both the quotient and the remainder are zero.

Procedure: If the operands are signed, the program determines the sign of the quotient and takes the absolute values of any negative operands. It also must retain the sign of the dividend, since that determines the sign of the remainder. The program then performs the actual unsigned division by the usual shift-and-subtract algorithm, shifting quotient and dividend and placing a 1 bit in the quotient each time a trial subtraction is successful. If the operands are signed, the program must negate (that is, subtract from zero) any result (quotient or remainder) that is negative. The Carry flag is cleared if the division is proper and set if the divisor is found to be zero. A zero divisor also results in a return with the result (quotient or remainder) set to zero.

Entry Conditions

Order in stack (starting from the top)

Less significant byte of return address
More significant byte of return address

Less significant byte of divisor
More significant byte of divisor

Less significant byte of dividend
More significant byte of dividend

Exit Conditions

Order in stack (starting from the top)

Less significant byte of result
More significant byte of result

If the divisor is non-zero, Carry = 0 and the result is normal. If the divisor is zero, Carry = 1 and the result is 0000_{16}.

Examples

1. Data: Dividend = $03E0_{16} = 992_{10}$
   Divisor = $00B6_{16} = 182_{10}$

   Result: Quotient (from UDIV16) = 0005_{16}
   Remainder (from UREM16) = 0052_{16} = 0082_{10}
   Carry = 0 (no divide-by-zero error)

2. Data: Dividend = $D73A_{16} = -10{,}438_{10}$
   Divisor = $02F1_{16} = 753_{10}$

   Result: Quotient (from SDIV16) = $FFF3_{16}$ = -13_{10}
   Remainder (from SREM16) = $FD77_{16}$ = -649_{10}
   Carry = 0 (no divide-by-zero error)

Note that we have taken the view that the remainder of a signed division may be either positive or negative. In our procedure, the remainder always takes the sign of the dividend. The user can easily examine the quotient and change the form to obtain a remainder that is always positive. In that case, the final result of Example 2 would be

Quotient = $FFF2_{16} = -14_{10}$

Remainder (always positive) = 0068_{16} = 104_{10}

Regardless of the entry point used, the program always calculates both the quotient and the remainder. Upon return, the quotient is available in addresses DVEND and DVEND+1 (more significant byte in DVEND+1) and the remainder in addresses DVEND+2 and DVEND+3 (more significant byte in DVEND+3). Thus, the user can always obtain the result that is not returned in the stack.

```
;       Title               16 bit division                              ;
;       Name:               SDIV16, UDIV16, SREM16, UREM16               ;
;                                                                        ;
;                                                                        ;

;                                                                        ;
;       Purpose:            SDIV16                                       ;
;                             Divide 2 signed 16 bit words and return a  ;
;                             16 bit signed quotient.                    ;
;                                                                        ;
;                           UDIV16                                       ;
;                             Divide 2 unsigned 16 bit words and return a ;
;                             16 bit unsigned quotient.                  ;
;                                                                        ;
;                           SREM16                                       ;
;                             Divide 2 signed 16 bit words and return a  ;
;                             16 bit signed remainder.                   ;
;                                                                        ;
;                           UREM16                                       ;
;                             Divide 2 unsigned 16 bit words and return a ;
;                             16 bit unsigned remainder.                 ;
;                                                                        ;
;       Entry:              TOP OF STACK                                 ;
```

```
;                           Low byte of return address,          ;
;                           High byte of return address,         ;
;                           Low byte of divisor,                 ;
;                           High byte of divisor,                ;
;                           Low byte of dividend,                ;
;                           High byte of dividend                ;
;                                                                ;
;       Exit:             TOP OF STACK                           ;
;                           Low byte of result,                  ;
;                           High byte of result,                 ;
;                                                                ;
;                         If no errors then                      ;
;                           carry := 0                           ;
;                         else                                   ;
;                           divide by zero error                 ;
;                           carry := 1                           ;
;                           quotient := 0                        ;
;                           remainder := 0                       ;
;                                                                ;
;       Registers used: All                                      ;
;                                                                ;
;       Time:             Approximately 1000 to 1160 cycles      ;
;                                                                ;
;       Size:             Program 293 bytes                      ;
;                         Data     13 bytes                      ;
;                                                                ;
;                                                                ;
;UNSIGNED DIVISION
UDIV16:
        LDA     #0              ;RESULT IS QUOTIENT (INDEX=0)
        BEQ     UDIVMD

;UNSIGNED REMAINDER
UREM16:
        LDA     #2              ;RESULT IS REMAINDER (INDEX=2)

UDIVMD:
        STA     RSLTIX          ;RESULT INDEX (0 FOR QUOTIENT,
                                ;              2 FOR REMAINDER)

        ;SAVE RETURN ADDRESS
        PLA
        STA     RETADR
        PLA
        STA     RETADR+1

        ;GET DIVISOR
        PLA
        STA     DVSOR
        PLA
        STA     DVSOR+1

        ;GET DIVIDEND
        PLA
        STA     DVEND
        PLA
```

```
        STA     DVEND+1

        ;PERFORM DIVISION
        JSR     UDIV
        BCC     DIVOK           ;BRANCH IF NO ERRORS
DIVER:  JMP     EREXIT
DIVOK:  JMP     OKEXIT

;
;SIGNED DIVISION
SDIV16:
        LDA     #0              ;RESULT IS QUOTIENT (INDEX=0)
        BEQ     SDIVMD

;SIGNED REMAINDER
SREM16:
        LDA     #2              ;RESULT IS REMAINDER (INDEX=2)
        BNE     SDIVMD

SDIVMD:
        STA     RSLTIX          ;RESULT INDEX (0 FOR QUOTIENT,
                                ;               2 FOR REMAINDER)

        ;SAVE RETURN ADDRESS
        PLA
        STA     RETADR
        PLA
        STA     RETADR+1

        ;GET DIVISOR
        PLA
        STA     DVSOR
        PLA
        STA     DVSOR+1

        ;GET DIVIDEND
        PLA
        STA     DVEND
        PLA
        STA     DVEND+1

        ;DETERMINE SIGN OF QUOTIENT BY PERFORMING AN EXCLUSIVE OR OF THE
        ; HIGH BYTES. IF THE SIGNS ARE THE SAME THEN BIT 7 WILL BE 0 AND THE
        ; QUOTIENT IS POSITIVE. IF THE SIGNS ARE DIFFERENT THEN THE QUOTIENT
        ; IS NEGATIVE.
        LDA     DVEND+1
        EOR     DVSOR+1
        STA     SQUOT

        ;SIGN OF REMAINDER IS THE SIGN OF THE DIVIDEND
        LDA     DVEND+1
        STA     SREM

        ;TAKE THE ABSOLUTE VALUE OF THE DIVISOR
        LDA     DVSOR+1
        BPL     CHKDE           ;BRANCH IF ALREADY POSITIVE
```

```
        LDA     #0              ;SUBTRACT DIVISOR FROM ZERO
        SEC
        SBC     DVSOR
        STA     DVSOR
        LDA     #0
        SBC     DVSOR+1
        STA     DVSOR+1

        ;TAKE THE ABSOLUTE VALUE OF THE DIVIDEND
CHKDE:
        LDA     DVEND+1
        BPL     DODIV           ;BRANCH IF DIVIDEND IS POSITIVE
        LDA     #0              ;SUBTRACT DIVIDEND FROM ZERO
        SEC
        SBC     DVEND
        STA     DVEND
        LDA     #0
        SBC     DVEND+1
        STA     DVEND+1

        ;DIVIDE ABSOLUTE VALUES
DODIV:  JSR     UDIV
        BCS     EREXIT          ;EXIT IF DIVIDE BY ZERO

        ;NEGATE QUOTIENT IF IT IS NEGATIVE
        LDA     SQUOT
        BPL     DOREM           ;BRANCH IF QUOTIENT IS POSITIVE
        LDA     #0              ;SUBTRACT QUOTIENT FROM ZERO
        SEC
        SBC     DVEND
        STA     DVEND
        LDA     #0
        SBC     DVEND+1
        STA     DVEND+1

DOREM:
        ;NEGATE REMAINDER IF IT IS NEGATIVE
        LDA     SREM
        BPL     OKEXIT          ;BRANCH IF REMAINDER IS POSITIVE
        LDA     #0
        SEC
        SBC     DVEND+2
        STA     DVEND+2
        LDA     #0
        SBC     DVEND+3
        STA     DVEND+3
        JMP     OKEXIT

        ;ERROR EXIT (CARRY = 1, RESULTS ARE ZERO)
EREXIT:
        LDA     #0
        STA     DVEND
        STA     DVEND+1         ;QUOTIENT := 0
        STA     DVEND+2
        STA     DVEND+3         ;REMAINDER := 0
        SEC                     ;CARRY = 1 IF ERROR
```

```
        BCS     DVEXIT

        ;GOOD EXIT (CARRY = 0)
OKEXIT:
        CLC                         ;CARRY = 0, NO ERRORS

DVEXIT:
        ;PUSH RESULT
        LDX     RSLTIX              ;GET INDEX TO RESULT (0=QUOTIENT, 2=REMAINDER)
        LDA     DVEND+1,X
        PHA
        LDA     DVEND,X
        PHA

        ;RESTORE RETURN ADDRESS
        LDA     RETADR+1
        PHA
        LDA     RETADR
        PHA
        RTS

;***************************************
;ROUTINE: UDIV
;PURPOSE: DIVIDE A 16 BIT DIVIDEND BY A 16 BIT DIVISOR
;ENTRY: DVEND = DIVIDEND
;       DVSOR = DIVISOR
;EXIT:  DVEND = QUOTIENT
;       DVEND+2 = REMAINDER
;REGISTERS USED: ALL
;***************************************

UDIV:
        ;ZERO UPPER WORD OF DIVIDEND THIS WILL BE CALLED DIVIDEND[1] BELOW
        LDA     #0
        STA     DVEND+2
        STA     DVEND+3

        ;FIRST CHECK FOR DIVISION BY ZERO
        LDA     DVSOR
        ORA     DVSOR+1
        BNE     OKUDIV              ;BRANCH IF DIVISOR IS NOT ZERO
        SEC                         ;ELSE ERROR EXIT
        RTS

        ;PERFORM THE DIVISION BY TRIAL SUBTRACTIONS
OKUDIV:
        LDX     #16                 ;LOOP THROUGH 16 BITS
DIVLP:
        ROL     DVEND               ;SHIFT THE CARRY INTO BIT 0 OF DIVIDEND
        ROL     DVEND+1             ;WHICH WILL BE THE QUOTIENT
        ROL     DVEND+2             ;AND SHIFT DIVIDEND AT THE SAME TIME
        ROL     DVEND+3

        ;
        ;CHECK IF DIVIDEND[1] IS LESS THAN DIVISOR
```

```
CHKLT:
        SEC
        LDA     DVEND+2
        SBC     DVSOR
        TAY                     ;SAVE LOW BYTE IN REG Y
        LDA     DVEND+3
        SBC     DVSOR+1         ;SUBTRACT HIGH BYTES WITH RESULT IN REG A
        BCC     DECCNT          ;BRANCH IF DIVIDEND < DIVISOR AND CARRY
        STY     DVEND+2         ;ELSE
        STA     DVEND+3         ;  DIVIDEND[1] := DIVIDEND[1] - DIVISOR

DECCNT:
        DEX
        BNE     DIVLP

        ROL     DVEND           ;SHIFT IN THE LAST CARRY FOR THE QUOTIENT
        ROL     DVEND+1
        CLC                     ;NO ERRORS, CLEAR CARRY
        RTS

;DATA
DVSOR:  .BLOCK  2               ;DIVISOR
DVEND:  .BLOCK  2               ;DIVIDEND[0] AND QUOTIENT
        .BLOCK  2               ;DIVIDEND[1] AND REMAINDER
RETADR: .BLOCK  2               ;RETURN ADDRESS
SQUOT:  .BLOCK  1               ;SIGN OF QUOTIENT
SREM:   .BLOCK  1               ;SIGN OF REMAINDER
RSLTIX: .BLOCK  1               ;INDEX TO THE RESULT 0 IS QUOTIENT,
                                ; 2 IS REMAINDER

;                                                                   ;
;                                                                   ;
;       SAMPLE EXECUTION:                                           ;
;                                                                   ;
;                                                                   ;


;PROGRAM SECTION
SC0604:
        ;SIGNED DIVIDE, OPRND1 / OPRND2, STORE THE QUOTIENT AT QUOT
        LDA     OPRND1+1
        PHA
        LDA     OPRND1
        PHA
        LDA     OPRND2+1
        PHA
        LDA     OPRND2
        PHA
        JSR     SDIV16          ;SIGNED DIVIDE
        PLA
        STA     QUOT
        PLA
        STA     QUOT+1
        BRK                     ;RESULT OF -1023 / 123 = -8
                                ; IN MEMORY QUOT   = F8 HEX
                                ;           QUOT+1 = FF HEX
```

```
;UNSIGNED DIVIDE, OPRND1 / OPRND2, STORE THE QUOTIENT AT QUOT
LDA     OPRND1+1
PHA
LDA     OPRND1
PHA
LDA     OPRND2+1
PHA
LDA     OPRND2
PHA
JSR     UDIV16          ;UNSIGNED DIVIDE
PLA
STA     QUOT
PLA
STA     QUOT+1
BRK                     ;RESULT OF 64513 / 123 = 524
                        ; IN MEMORY QUOT   = 0C HEX
                        ;           QUOT+1 = 02 HEX

;SIGNED REMAINDER, OPRND1 / OPRND2, STORE THE REMAINDER AT REM
LDA     OPRND1+1
PHA
LDA     OPRND1
PHA
LDA     OPRND2+1
PHA
LDA     OPRND2
PHA
JSR     SREM16          ;REMAINDER
PLA
STA     REM
PLA
STA     REM+1
BRK                     ;THE REMAINDER OF -1023 / 123 = -39
                        ; IN MEMORY REM   = D9 HEX
                        ;           REM+1 = FF HEX

;UNSIGNED REMAINDER, OPRND1 / OPRND2, STORE THE REMAINDER AT REM
LDA     OPRND1+1
PHA
LDA     OPRND1
PHA
LDA     OPRND2+1
PHA
LDA     OPRND2
PHA
JSR     UREM16          ;REMAINDER
PLA
STA     REM
PLA
STA     REM+1
PLA
BRK                     ;THE REMAINDER OF 64513 / 123 = 61
                        ; IN MEMORY REM    = 3D HEX
                        ;           REM+1  = 00
```

```
        JMP     SC0604

;DATA
OPRND1  .WORD   -1023           ;DIVIDEND (64513 UNSIGNED)
OPRND2  .WORD   123             ;DIVISOR
QUOT:   .BLOCK  2               ;QUOTIENT
REM:    .BLOCK  2               ;REMAINDER

        .END    ;PROGRAM
```

Compares two 16-bit operands obtained from the stack and sets the flags accordingly. All 16-bit numbers are stored in the usual 6502 style with the less significant byte on top of the more significant byte. The comparison is performed by subtracting the top operand (or subtrahend) from the bottom operand (or minuend). The Zero flag always indicates whether the numbers are equal. If the numbers are unsigned, the Carry flag indicates which one is larger (Carry = 0 if top operand or subtrahend is larger and 1 otherwise). If the numbers are signed, the Negative flag indicates which one is larger (Negative = 1 if top operand or subtrahend is larger and 0 otherwise); two's complement overflow is considered and the Negative flag is inverted if it occurs.

Procedure: The program first compares the less significant bytes of the subtrahend and the minuend. It then subtracts the more significant byte of the subtrahend from the more significant byte of the minuend, thus setting the flags. If the less significant bytes of the operands are not equal, the program clears the Zero flag by logically ORing the accumulator with 01_{16}. If the subtraction results in two's complement overflow, the program complements the Negative flag by logically Exclusive ORing the accumulator with 80_{16} (10000000_2); it also clears the Zero flag by the method described earlier.

Registers Used: A, P

Execution Time: Approximately 90 cycles

Program Size: 65 bytes

Data Memory Required: Six bytes anywhere in memory for the minuend or WORD1 (2 bytes starting at address MINEND), the subtrahend or WORD2 (2 bytes starting at address SUBTRA), and the return address (2 bytes starting at address RETADR).

Entry Conditions

Order in stack (starting from the top)

Less significant byte of return address
More significant byte of return address

Less significant byte of subtrahend (top operand or WORD2)
More significant byte of subtrahend (top operand or WORD2)

Less significant byte of minuend (bottom operand or WORD1)
More significant byte of minuend (bottom operand or WORD1)

Exit Conditions

Flags set as if subtrahend had been subtracted from minuend, with a correction if two's complement overflow occurred.

Zero flag = 1 if subtrahend and minuend are equal, 0 if they are not equal.

Carry flag = 0 if subtrahend is larger than minuend in the unsigned sense, 1 if it is less than or equal to the minuend.

Negative flag = 1 if subtrahend is larger than minuend in the signed sense, 0 if it is less than or equal to the minuend. This flag is corrected if two's complement overflow occurs.

Examples

1. Data: Minuend (bottom operand) = $03E1_{16}$
   Subtrahend (top operand) = $07E4_{16}$

   Result: Carry = 0, indicating subtrahend is larger in unsigned sense.
   Zero = 0, indicating operands not equal
   Negative = 1, indicating subtrahend is larger in signed sense

2. Data: Minuend (bottom operand) = $C51A_{16}$
   Subtrahend (top operand) = $C51A_{16}$

   Result: Carry = 1, indicating subtrahend is not larger in unsigned sense
   Zero = 1, indicating operands are equal
   Negative = 0, indicating subtrahend is not larger in signed sense

3. Data: Minuend (bottom operand) = $A45D_{16}$
   Subtrahend (top operand) = $77E1_{16}$

   Result: Carry = 1, indicating subtrahend is not larger in unsigned sense
   Zero = 0, indicating operands are not equal
   Negative = 1, indicating subtrahend is larger in signed sense

In Example 3, the bottom operand is a negative two's complement number, whereas the top operand is a positive two's complement number.

```
;       Title           16 bit compare                              ;
;       Name:           CMP16                                       ;
;                                                                   ;
;                                                                   ;
;                                                                   ;
;       Purpose:        Compare 2 16 bit signed or unsigned words and ;
;                       return the C,Z,N flags set or cleared.      ;
;                                                                   ;
;       Entry:          TOP OF STACK                                ;
;                         Low byte of return address,               ;
;                         High byte of return address,              ;
;                         Low byte of word 2 (subtrahend),          ;
;                         High byte of word 2 (subtrahend),         ;
;                         Low byte of word 1 (minuend),             ;
;                         High byte of word 1 (minuend)             ;
;                                                                   ;
;       Exit:           Flags returned based on word 1 - word 2     ;
;                       IF WORD1 AND WORD2 ARE 2'S COMPLEMENT NUMBERS ;
;                       THEN                                        ;
;                        IF WORD1 = WORD2 THEN                      ;
;                          Z=1,N=0                                  ;
```

```
;                         IF WORD1 > WORD2 THEN                              ;
;                           Z=0,N=0                                          ;
;                         IF WORD1 < WORD2 THEN                              ;
;                           Z=0,N=1                                          ;
;                       ELSE                                                 ;
;                         IF WORD1 = WORD2 THEN                              ;
;                           Z=1,C=1                                          ;
;                         IF WORD1 > WORD2 THEN                              ;
;                           Z=0,C=1                                          ;
;                         IF WORD1 < WORD2 THEN                              ;
;                           Z=0,C=0                                          ;
;                                                                            ;
;       Registers used: A,P                                                  ;
;                                                                            ;
;       Time:           Approximately 90 cycles                              ;
;                                                                            ;
;       Size:           Program 65 bytes                                     ;
;                       Data     6 bytes                                     ;
;                                                                            ;
;                                                                            ;

CMP16:
        ;SAVE THE RETURN ADDRESS
        PLA
        STA     RETADR
        PLA
        STA     RETADR+1

        ;GET SUBTRAHEND
        PLA
        STA     SUBTRA
        PLA
        STA     SUBTRA+1

        ;GET MINUEND
        PLA
        STA     MINEND
        PLA
        STA     MINEND+1

        ;RESTORE RETURN ADDRESS
        LDA     RETADR+1
        PHA
        LDA     RETADR
        PHA

        LDA     MINEND
        CMP     SUBTRA          ;COMPARE LOW BYTES
        BEQ     EQUAL           ;BRANCH IF THEY ARE EQUAL

        ;LOW BYTES ARE NOT EQUAL - COMPARE HIGH BYTES
        LDA     MINEND+1
        SBC     SUBTRA+1        ;COMPARE HIGH BYTES
        ORA     #1              ;MAKE Z = 0, SINCE LOW BYTES ARE NOT EQUAL
        BVS     OVFLOW          ;MUST HANDLE OVERFLOW FOR SIGNED ARITHMATIC
        RTS                     ;EXIT
```

```
        ;LOW BYTES ARE EQUAL   - COMPARE HIGH BYTES
EQUAL:
        LDA     MINEND+1
        SBC     SUBTRA+1        ;UPPER BYTES
        BVS     OVFLOW          ;MUST HANDLE OVERFLOW FOR SIGNED ARITHMETIC
        RTS                     ;RETURN WITH FLAGS SET

        ;OVERFLOW WITH SIGNED ARITHMETIC SO COMPLEMENT THE NEGATIVE FLAG
        ; DO NOT CHANGE THE CARRY FLAG AND MAKE THE ZERO FLAG EQUAL 0.
        ; COMPLEMENT NEGATIVE FLAG BY EXCLUSIVE-ORING 80H AND ACCUMULATOR.
OVFLOW:
        EOR     #80H            ;COMPLEMENT NEGATIVE FLAG
        ORA     #1              ;IF OVERFLOW THEN THE WORDS ARE NOT EQUAL Z=0
                                ;CARRY UNCHANGED
        RTS


;DATA
MINEND: .BLOCK  2               ;TEMPORARY FOR THE MINUEND
SUBTRA: .BLOCK  2               ;TEMPORARY FOR THE SUBTRAHEND
RETADR: .BLOCK  2               ;TEMPORARY FOR THE RETURN ADDRESS

;                                                                       ;
;                                                                       ;
;       SAMPLE EXECUTION                                                ;
;                                                                       ;
;                                                                       ;


SC0605:
        ;COMPARE OPRND1 AND OPRND2
        LDA     OPRND1+1
        PHA
        LDA     OPRND1
        PHA
        LDA     OPRND2+1
        PHA
        LDA     OPRND2
        PHA
        JSR     CMP16
        BRK                     ;LOOK AT THE FLAGS
                                ;  FOR 123 AND 1023
                                ;    C = 0, Z = 0, N = 1
        JMP     SC0605

OPRND1  .WORD   123             ;MINUEND
OPRND2  .WORD   1023            ;SUBTRAHEND

        .END    ;PROGRAM
```

Multiple-Precision Binary Addition (MPBADD) 6F

Adds two multi-byte unsigned binary numbers. Both numbers are stored with their least significant bytes first (at the lowest address). The sum replaces one of the numbers (the one with the starting address lower in the stack). The length of the numbers (in bytes) is 255 or less.

Procedure: The program clears the Carry flag initially and adds the operands one byte at a time, starting with the least significant bytes. The final Carry flag reflects the addition of the most significant bytes. The sum replaces the operand with the starting address lower in the stack (array 1 in the listing). A length of 00 causes an immediate exit with no addition operations.

Registers Used: All

Execution Time: 23 cycles per byte plus 82 cycles overhead. For example, adding two 6-byte operands takes $23 \times 6 + 82$ or 220 cycles

Program Size: 48 bytes

Data Memory Required: Two bytes anywhere in RAM plus four bytes on page 0. The two bytes anywhere in RAM are temporary storage for the return address (starting at address RETADR). The four bytes on page 0 hold pointers to the two numbers (starting at addresses AY1PTR and AY2PTR, respectively). In the listing, AY1PTR is taken as address $00D0_{16}$ and AY2PTR as address $00D2_{16}$.

Special Case: A length of zero causes an immediate exit with the sum equal to the bottom operand (i.e., array 1 is unchanged). The Carry flag is set to 1.

Entry Conditions

Order in stack (starting from the top)

Less significant byte of return address
More significant byte of return address

Length of the operands in bytes

Less significant byte of starting address of second operand (address containing the least significant byte of array 2)
More significant byte of starting address of second operand (address containing the least significant byte of array 2)

Less significant byte of starting address of first operand and result (address containing the least significant byte of array 1)
More significant byte of starting address of first operand and result (address containing the least significant byte of array 1)

Exit Conditions

First operand (array 1) replaced by first operand (array 1) plus second operand (array 2).

Example

Data: Length of operands (in bytes) = 6
Top operand (array 2) = $19D028A193EA_{16}$
Bottom operand (array 1) = $293EABF059C7_{16}$

Result: Bottom operand (array 1) = Bottom operand (array 1) + Top operand (array 2) = $430ED491EDB1_{16}$
Carry = 0

```
;       Title               Multiple-Precision Binary Addition           ;
;       Name:               MPBADD                                       ;
;                                                                        ;
;                                                                        ;

;                                                                        ;
;       Purpose:            Add 2 arrays of binary bytes                 ;
;                           Array1 := Array1 + Array2                    ;
;                                                                        ;
;       Entry:              TOP OF STACK                                 ;
;                             Low byte of return address,                ;
;                             High byte of return address,               ;
;                             Length of the arrays in bytes,             ;
;                             Low byte of array 2 address,               ;
;                             High byte of array 2 address,              ;
;                             Low byte of array 1 address,               ;
;                             High byte of array 1 address               ;
;                                                                        ;
;                             The arrays are unsigned binary numbers with a ;
;                             maximum length of 255 bytes, ARRAY[0] is the  ;
;                             least significant byte, and ARRAY[LENGTH-1]   ;
;                             the most significant byte.                 ;
;                                                                        ;
;       Exit:               Array1 := Array1 + Array2                    ;
;                                                                        ;
;       Registers used: All                                              ;
;                                                                        ;
;       Time:               23 cycles per byte plus 82 cycles            ;
;                           overhead.                                    ;
;                                                                        ;
;       Size:               Program 48 bytes                             ;
;                           Data     2 bytes plus                        ;
;                                    4 bytes in page zero                ;
;                                                                        ;
;                                                                        ;

;EQUATES
AY1PTR: .EQU    0D0H            ;PAGE ZERO FOR ARRAY 1 POINTER
AY2PTR: .EQU    0D2H            ;PAGE ZERO FOR ARRAY 2 POINTER

MPBADD:
        ;SAVE RETURN ADDRESS
```

```
        PLA
        STA     RETADR
        PLA
        STA     RETADR+1

        ;GET LENGTH OF ARRAYS
        PLA
        TAX

        ;GET STARTING ADDRESS OF ARRAY 2
        PLA
        STA     AY2PTR
        PLA
        STA     AY2PTR+1

        ;GET STARTING ADDRESS OF ARRAY 1
        PLA
        STA     AY1PTR
        PLA
        STA     AY1PTR+1

        ;RESTORE RETURN ADDRESS
        LDA     RETADR+1
        PHA
        LDA     RETADR
        PHA

        ;INITIALIZE
        LDY     #0
        CPX     #0              ;IS LENGTH OF ARRAYS = 0 ?
        BEQ     EXIT            ;YES, EXIT
        CLC                     ;CLEAR CARRY
LOOP:
        LDA     (AY1PTR),Y      ;GET NEXT BYTE
        ADC     (AY2PTR),Y      ;ADD BYTES
        STA     (AY1PTR),Y      ;STORE SUM
        INY                     ;INCREMENT ARRAY INDEX
        DEX                     ;DECREMENT COUNTER
        BNE     LOOP            ;CONTINUE UNTIL COUNTER = 0
EXIT:
        RTS

;
;DATA
RETADR  .BLOCK  2               ;TEMPORARY FOR RETURN ADDRESS

;                                                               ;
;                                                               ;
;       SAMPLE EXECUTION:                                       ;
;                                                               ;
;                                                               ;

SC0606:
```

```
        LDA     AY1ADR+1
        PHA
        LDA     AY1ADR
        PHA                     ;PUSH AY1 ADDRESS

        LDA     AY2ADR+1
        PHA
        LDA     AY2ADR
        PHA                     ;PUSH AY2 ADDRESS

        LDA     #SZAYS
        PHA                     ;PUSH SIZE OF ARRAYS
        JSR     MPBADD          ;MULTIPLE-PRECISION BINARY ADDITION
        BRK                     ;RESULT OF 1234567H + 1234567H = 2468ACEH
                                ; IN MEMORY AY1     = CEH
                                ;           AY1+1   = 8AH
                                ;           AY1+2   = 46H
                                ;           AY1+3   = 02H
                                ;           AY1+4   = 00H
                                ;           AY1+5   = 00H
                                ;           AY1+6   = 00H
        JMP     SC0606

SZAYS:  .EQU    7       ;SIZE OF ARRAYS

AY1ADR: .WORD   AY1     ;ADDRESS OF ARRAY 1
AY2ADR: .WORD   AY2     ;ADDRESS OF ARRAY 2

AY1:
        .BYTE   067H
        .BYTE   045H
        .BYTE   023H
        .BYTE   001H
        .BYTE   0
        .BYTE   0
        .BYTE   0

AY2:
        .BYTE   067H
        .BYTE   045H
        .BYTE   023H
        .BYTE   001H
        .BYTE   0
        .BYTE   0
        .BYTE   0

        .END    ;PROGRAM
```

Multiple-Precision Binary Subtraction (MPBSUB) 6G

Subtracts two multi-byte unsigned binary numbers. Both numbers are stored with their least significant byte at the lowest address. The starting address of the subtrahend (number to be subtracted) is stored on top of the starting address of the minuend (number from which the subtrahend is subtracted). The difference replaces the minuend in memory. The length of the numbers (in bytes) is 255 or less.

Procedure: The program sets the Carry flag (the inverted borrow) initially and subtracts the subtrahend from the minuend one byte at a time, starting with the least significant bytes. The final Carry flag reflects the subtraction of the most significant bytes. The difference replaces the minuend (the operand with the starting address lower in the stack, array 1 in the listing). A length of 00 causes an immediate exit with no subtraction operations.

Registers Used: All

Execution Time: 23 cycles per byte plus 82 cycles overhead. For example, subtracting two 6-byte operands takes $23 \times 6 + 82$ or 220 cycles.

Program Size: 48 bytes

Data Memory Required: Two bytes anywhere in RAM plus four bytes on page 0. The two bytes anywhere in RAM are temporary storage for the return address (starting at address RETADR). The four bytes on page 0 hold pointers to the two numbers (starting at addresses MINPTR and SUBPTR, respectively). In the listing, MINPTR is taken as address $00D0_{16}$ and SUBPTR as address $00D2_{16}$.

Special Case: A length of zero causes an immediate exit with the minuend unchanged (that is, the difference is equal to the bottom operand). The Carry flag is set to 1.

Entry Conditions

Order in stack (starting from the top)

Less significant byte of return address
More significant byte of return address

Length of the operands in bytes

Less significant byte of starting address of subtrahend (address containing the least significant byte of array 2)
More significant byte of starting address of subtrahend (address containing the least significant byte of array 2)

Less significant byte of starting address of minuend (address containing the least significant byte of array 1)
More significant byte of starting address of minuend (address containing the least significant byte of array 1)

Exit Conditions

Minuend replaced by minuend minus subtrahend.

Example

Data: Length of operands (in bytes) = 4
Minuend = $2F5BA7C3_{16}$
Subtrahend = $14DF35B8_{16}$

Result: Difference = $1A7C720B_{16}$.
This number replaces the original minuend in memory. The Carry flag is set to 1 in accordance with its usual role (in 6502 programming) as an inverted borrow.

```
;       Title               Multiple-Precision Binary Subtraction          ;
;       Name:               MPBSUB                                         ;
;                                                                          ;
;                                                                          ;

;                                                                          ;
;       Purpose:            Subtract 2 arrays of binary bytes              ;
;                           Minuend := Minuend - Subtrahend                ;
;                                                                          ;
;       Entry:              TOP OF STACK                                   ;
;                             Low byte of return address,                  ;
;                             High byte of return address,                 ;
;                             Length of the arrays in bytes,               ;
;                             Low byte of subtrahend address,              ;
;                             High byte of subtrahend address,             ;
;                             Low byte of minuend address,                 ;
;                             High byte of minuend address                 ;
;                                                                          ;
;                             The arrays are unsigned binary numbers with a ;
;                             maximum length of 255 bytes, ARRAY[0] is the  ;
;                             least significant byte, and ARRAY[LENGTH-1]   ;
;                             the most significant byte.                    ;
;                                                                          ;
;       Exit:               Minuend := Minuend - Subtrahend                ;
;                                                                          ;
;       Registers used: All                                                ;
;                                                                          ;
;       Time:               23 cycles per byte plus 82 cycles              ;
;                           overhead.                                      ;
;                                                                          ;
;       Size:               Program 48 bytes                               ;
;                           Data     2 bytes plus                          ;
;                                    4 bytes in page zero                  ;
;                                                                          ;
;                                                                          ;

;EQUATES
MINPTR: .EQU    0D0H            ;PAGE ZERO FOR MINUEND POINTER
SUBPTR: .EQU    0D2H            ;PAGE ZERO FOR SUBTRAHEND POINTER
```

```
MPBSUB:
        ;SAVE RETURN ADDRESS
        PLA
        STA     RETADR
        PLA
        STA     RETADR+1

        ;GET LENGTH OF ARRAYS
        PLA
        TAX

        ;GET STARTING ADDRESS OF SUBTRAHEND
        PLA
        STA     SUBPTR
        PLA
        STA     SUBPTR+1

        ;GET STARTING ADDRESS OF MINUEND
        PLA
        STA     MINPTR
        PLA
        STA     MINPTR+1

        ;RESTORE RETURN ADDRESS
        LDA     RETADR+1
        PHA
        LDA     RETADR
        PHA

        ;INITIALIZE
        LDY     #0
        CPX     #0              ;IS LENGTH OF ARRAYS = 0 ?
        BEQ     EXIT            ;YES, EXIT
        SEC                     ;SET CARRY
LOOP:
        LDA     (MINPTR),Y      ;GET NEXT BYTE
        SBC     (SUBPTR),Y      ;SUBTRACT BYTES
        STA     (MINPTR),Y      ;STORE DIFFERENCE
        INY                     ;INCREMENT ARRAY INDEX
        DEX                     ;DECREMENT COUNTER
        BNE     LOOP            ;CONTINUE UNTIL COUNTER = 0

EXIT:
        RTS

;
;DATA
RETADR  .BLOCK  2               ;TEMPORARY FOR RETURN ADDRESS

;                                                                       ;
;                                                                       ;
;       SAMPLE EXECUTION:                                               ;
;                                                                       ;
;                                                                       ;
```

```
SC0607:
        LDA     AY1ADR+1
        PHA
        LDA     AY1ADR
        PHA                         ;PUSH AY1 ADDRESS

        LDA     AY2ADR+1
        PHA
        LDA     AY2ADR
        PHA                         ;PUSH AY2 ADDRESS

        LDA     #SZAYS
        PHA                         ;PUSH SIZE OF ARRAYS
        JSR     MPBSUB              ;MULTIPLE-PRECISION BINARY SUBTRACTION
        BRK                         ;RESULT OF 7654321H - 1234567H = 641FDBAH
                                    ; IN MEMORY AY1      = 0BAH
                                    ;           AY1+1    = 0FDH
                                    ;           AY1+2    = 41H
                                    ;           AY1+3    = 06H
                                    ;           AY1+4    = 00H
                                    ;           AY1+5    = 00H
                                    ;           AY1+6    = 00H
        JMP     SC0607

SZAYS:  .EQU    7       ;SIZE OF ARRAYS

AY1ADR: .WORD   AY1     ;ADDRESS OF ARRAY 1 (MINUEND)
AY2ADR: .WORD   AY2     ;ADDRESS OF ARRAY 2 (SUBTRAHEND)

AY1:
        .BYTE   021H
        .BYTE   043H
        .BYTE   065H
        .BYTE   007H
        .BYTE   0
        .BYTE   0
        .BYTE   0

AY2:
        .BYTE   067H
        .BYTE   045H
        .BYTE   023H
        .BYTE   001H
        .BYTE   0
        .BYTE   0
        .BYTE   0

        .END    ;PROGRAM
```

Multiple-Precision Binary Multiplication (MPBMUL)

Multiplies two multi-byte unsigned binary numbers. Both numbers are stored with their least significant byte at the lowest address. The product replaces one of the numbers (the one with the starting address lower in the stack). The length of the numbers (in bytes) is 255 or less. Only the least significant bytes of the product are returned to retain compatibility with other multiple-precision binary operations.

Procedure: The program uses an ordinary add-and-shift algorithm, adding the multiplicand (array 2) to the partial product each time it finds a 1 bit in the multiplier (array 1). The partial product and the multiplier are shifted through the bit length plus 1 with the extra loop being necessary to move the final carry into the product. The program maintains a full double-length unsigned partial product in memory locations starting at HIPROD (more significant bytes) and in array 1 (less significant bytes). The less significant bytes of the product replace the multiplier as the multiplier is shifted and examined for 1 bits. A length of 00 causes an exit with no multiplication.

Registers Used: All

Execution Time: Depends on the length of the operands and on the number of 1 bits in the multiplier (requiring actual additions). If the average number of 1 bits in the multiplier is four per byte, the execution time is approximately

$$316 \times \text{LENGTH}^2 + 223 \times \text{LENGTH} + 150$$

cycles where LENGTH is the number of bytes in the operands. If, for example, LENGTH = 4, the approximate execution time is

$$316 \times 4^2 + 223 \times 4 + 150 = 316 \times 16 + 892 + 150 = 5056 + 1042 = 6{,}098 \text{ cycles.}$$

Program Size: 145 bytes

Data Memory Required: 260 bytes anywhere in RAM plus four bytes on page 0. The 260 bytes anywhere in RAM are temporary storage for the more significant bytes of the product (255 bytes starting at address HIPROD), the return address (two bytes starting at address RETADR), the loop counter (two bytes starting at address COUNT), and the length of the operands in bytes (one byte at address LENGTH). The four bytes on page 0 hold pointers to the two operands (the pointers start at addresses AY1PTR and AY2PTR, respectively). In the listing, AY1PTR is taken as address $00D0_{16}$ and AY2PTR as address $00D2_{16}$.

Special Case: A length of zero causes an immediate exit with the product equal to the original multiplier (that is, array 1 is unchanged) and the more significant bytes of the product (starting at address HIPROD) undefined.

Entry Conditions

Order in stack (starting from the top)

Less significant byte of return address
More significant byte of return address

Length of the operands in bytes

Less significant byte of starting address of multiplicand (address containing the least significant byte of array 2)
More significant byte of starting address of multiplicand (address containing the least significant byte of array 2)

Less significant byte of starting address of multiplier (address containing the least significant byte of array 1)
More significant byte of starting address of multiplier (address containing the least significant byte of array 1)

Exit Conditions

Multiplier (array 1) replaced by multiplier (array 1) times multiplicand (array 2).

Example

Data: Length of operands (in bytes) = 04

Top operand (array 2 or multiplicand) = $0005D1F7_{16} = 381{,}431_{10}$

Bottom operand (array 1 or multiplier) = $00000AB1_{16} = 2{,}737_{10}$

Result: Bottom operand (array 1) = Bottom operand (array 1)* Top operand (array 2) = $3E39D1C7_{16}$ = $1{,}043{,}976{,}647_{10}$

Note that MPBMUL returns only the less significant bytes (that is, the number of bytes in the multiplicand and multiplier) of the product to maintain compatibility with other multiple-precision binary arithmetic operations. The more significant bytes of the product are available starting with their least significant byte at address HIPROD. The user may need to check those bytes for a possible overflow or extend the operands with additional zeros.

```
;       Title             Multiple-Precision Binary Multiplication   ;
;       Name:             MPBMUL                                     ;
;                                                                    ;
;                                                                    ;

;                                                                    ;
;       Purpose:          Multiply 2 arrays of binary bytes          ;
;                         Arrayl := Arrayl * Array2                  ;
;                                                                    ;
;       Entry:            TOP OF STACK                               ;
;                           Low byte of return address,              ;
;                           High byte of return address,             ;
;                           Length of the arrays in bytes,           ;
;                           Low byte of array 2 (multiplicand) address, ;
;                           High byte of array 2 (multiplicand) address, ;
;                           Low byte of array 1 (multiplier) address, ;
;                           High byte of array 1 (multiplier) address ;
;                                                                    ;
;                           The arrays are unsigned binary numbers with a ;
;                           maximum length of 255 bytes, ARRAY[0] is the ;
;                           least significant byte, and ARRAY[LENGTH-1] ;
;                           the most significant byte.               ;
;                                                                    ;
;       Exit:             Arrayl := Arrayl * Array2                  ;
;                                                                    ;
;       Registers used: All                                          ;
;                                                                    ;
;       Time:             Assuming the average number of 1 bits in array 1;
;                         is 4 * length then the time is approximately ;
;                          (316 * length^2) + (223 * length) + 150 cycles ;
;                                                                    ;
;       Size:             Program 145 bytes                          ;
;                         Data    260 bytes plus                     ;
;                                   4 bytes in page zero             ;
;                                                                    ;
;                                                                    ;

;EQUATES
AY1PTR: .EQU    0D0H            ;PAGE ZERO FOR ARRAY 1 POINTER
AY2PTR: .EQU    0D2H            ;PAGE ZERO FOR ARRAY 2 POINTER

MPBMUL:
        ;SAVE RETURN ADDRESS
        PLA
        STA     RETADR
        PLA
        STA     RETADR+1        ;SAVE RETURN ADDRESS

        ;GET LENGTH OF ARRAYS
        PLA
        STA     LENGTH

        ;GET ADDRESS OF ARRAY 2 AND SUBTRACT 1 SO THAT THE ARRAYS MAY
        ; BE INDEXED FROM 1 TO LENGTH RATHER THAN 0 TO LENGTH-1
        PLA
        SEC
```

```
        SBC     #1              ;SUBTRACT 1 FROM LOW BYTE
        STA     AY2PTR
        PLA
        SBC     #0              ;SUBTRACT BORROW IF ANY
        STA     AY2PTR+1

        ;GET ADDRESS OF ARRAY 1 AND SUBTRACT 1
        PLA
        SEC
        SBC     #1              ;SUBTRACT 1 FROM LOW BYTE
        STA     AY1PTR
        PLA
        SBC     #0              ;SUBTRACT BORROW IF ANY
        STA     AY1PTR+1

        ;RESTORE RETURN ADDRESS
        LDA     RETADR+1
        PHA
        LDA     RETADR
        PHA

        ;EXIT IF LENGTH IS ZERO
        LDA     LENGTH          ;IS LENGTH OF ARRAYS = 0 ?
        BEQ     EXIT            ;YES, EXIT

        ;SET COUNT TO NUMBER OF BITS IN ARRAY PLUS 1
        ; COUNT := (LENGTH * 8) + 1
        STA     COUNT           ;INITIALIZE COUNTER TO LENGTH
        LDA     #0
        ASL     COUNT           ;COUNT * 2
        ROL     A               ;A WILL BE UPPER BYTE
        ASL     COUNT           ;COUNT * 4
        ROL     A
        ASL     COUNT           ;COUNT * 8
        ROL     A
        STA     COUNT+1         ;STORE UPPER BYTE OF COUNT
        INC     COUNT           ;INCREMENT LOW BYTE OF COUNT
        BNE     ZEROPD
        INC     COUNT+1         ;INCREMENT HIGH BYTE IF LOW BYTE BECOMES 0

        ;ZERO HIGH PRODUCT ARRAY
ZEROPD:
        LDX     LENGTH
        LDA     #0
ZEROLP:
        STA     HIPROD-1,X      ;THE MINUS 1 FOR INDEXING FROM 1 TO LENGTH
        DEX
        BNE     ZEROLP

        ;MULTIPLY USING THE SHIFT AND ADD ALGORITHM
        ; ARRAY 1 WILL BE THE MULTIPLIER AND ARRAY 2 THE MULTIPLICAND
        CLC                     ;CLEAR CARRY FIRST TIME THROUGH
LOOP:
        ;SHIFT CARRY INTO THE UPPER PRODUCT ARRAY AND THE LEAST SIGNIFICANT
        ; BIT OF THE UPPER PRODUCT ARRAY TO CARRY
        LDX     LENGTH
```

```
SRPLP:
        ROR     HIPROD-1,X        ;MINUS 1 FOR INDEXING FROM 1 TO LENGTH
        DEX
        BNE     SRPLP             ;CONTINUE UNTIL INDEX = 0

        ;SHIFT CARRY WHICH IS THE NEXT BIT OF LOWER PRODUCT INTO THE MOST
        ; SIGNIFICANT BIT OF ARRAY 1. THIS IS THE NEXT BIT OF THE PRODUCT.
        ; THIS ALSO SHIFTS THE NEXT BIT OF MULTIPLIER TO CARRY.
        LDY     LENGTH
SRA1LP:
        LDA     (AY1PTR),Y
        ROR     A                 ;ROTATE NEXT BYTE
        STA     (AY1PTR),Y
        DEY
        BNE     SRA1LP            ;CONTINUE UNTIL INDEX = 0

        ;IF NEXT BIT OF THE MULTIPLIER IS 1 THEN
        ;  ADD ARRAY 2 AND UPPER ARRAY OF PRODUCT
        BCC     DECCNT            ;BRANCH IF NEXT BIT IS ZERO

        ;ADD ARRAY 2 AND HIPROD
        LDY     #1
        LDX     LENGTH
        CLC
ADDLP:
        LDA     (AY2PTR),Y
        ADC     HIPROD-1,Y        ;ADD BYTES
        STA     HIPROD-1,Y
        INY                       ;INCREMENT INDEX
        DEX                       ;DECREMENT COUNTER
        BNE     ADDLP             ;CONTINUE UNTIL COUNT = 0

        ;DECREMENT BIT COUNTER AND EXIT IF DONE
        ;DOES NOT CHANGE CARRY !
DECCNT:
        DEC     COUNT             ;DECREMENT LOW BYTE OF COUNT
        BNE     LOOP              ;BRANCH IF IT IS NOT ZERO
        LDX     COUNT+1           ;GET HIGH BYTE
        BEQ     EXIT              ;EXIT IF COUNT IS ZERO
        DEX                       ;ELSE DECREMENT HIGH BYTE OF COUNT
        STX     COUNT+1
        JMP     LOOP

EXIT:
        RTS

;
;DATA
RETADR: .BLOCK  2                 ;TEMPORARY FOR RETURN ADDRESS
COUNT:  .BLOCK  2                 ;TEMPORARY FOR LOOP COUNTER
LENGTH: .BLOCK  1                 ;LENGTH OF ARRAYS
HIPROD: .BLOCK  255               ;HIGH PRODUCT BUFFER

;                                                                    ;
;                                                                    ;
```

```
;       SAMPLE EXECUTION:                                                ;
;                                                                        ;
;                                                                        ;


SC0608:
        LDA     AY1ADR+1
        PHA
        LDA     AY1ADR
        PHA                     ;PUSH AY1 ADDRESS

        LDA     AY2ADR+1
        PHA
        LDA     AY2ADR
        PHA                     ;PUSH AY2 ADDRESS

        LDA     #SZAYS
        PHA                     ;PUSH SIZE OF ARRAYS
        JSR     MPBMUL          ;MULTIPLE-PRECISION BINARY MULTIPLY
        BRK                     ;RESULT OF 12345H * 1234H = 14B60404H
                                ; IN MEMORY AY1      = 04H
                                ;           AY1+1    = 04H
                                ;           AY1+2    = B6H
                                ;           AY1+3    = 14H
                                ;           AY1+4    = 00H
                                ;           AY1+5    = 00H
                                ;           AY1+6    = 00H
        JMP     SC0608

SZAYS:  .EQU    7               ;SIZE OF ARRAYS

AY1ADR: .WORD   AY1             ;ADDRESS OF ARRAY 1
AY2ADR: .WORD   AY2             ;ADDRESS OF ARRAY 2

AY1:
        .BYTE   045H
        .BYTE   023H
        .BYTE   001H
        .BYTE   0
        .BYTE   0
        .BYTE   0
        .BYTE   0

AY2:
        .BYTE   034H
        .BYTE   012H
        .BYTE   0
        .BYTE   0
        .BYTE   0
        .BYTE   0
        .BYTE   0

        .END    ;PROGRAM
```

Divides two multi-byte unsigned binary numbers. Both numbers are stored with their least significant byte at the lowest address. The quotient replaces the dividend (the operand with the starting address lower in the stack). The length of the numbers (in bytes) is 255 or less. The remainder is not returned, but its starting address (least significant byte) is available in memory locations HDEPTR and HDEPTR+1. The Carry flag is cleared if no errors occur; if a divide by zero is attempted, the Carry flag is set to 1, the dividend is left unchanged, and the remainder is set to zero.

Procedure: The program performs division by the usual shift-and-subtract algorithm, shifting quotient and dividend and placing a 1 bit in the quotient each time a trial subtraction is successful. An extra buffer is used to hold the result of the trial subtraction and that buffer is simply switched with the buffer holding the dividend if the trial subtraction is successful. The program exits immediately, setting the Carry flag, if it finds the divisor to be zero. The Carry flag is cleared otherwise.

Registers Used: All

Execution Time: Depends on the length of the operands and on the number of 1 bits in the quotient (requiring a buffer switch). If the average number of 1 bits in the quotient is four per byte, the execution time is approximately

$$480 \times \text{LENGTH}^2 + 438 \times \text{LENGTH} + 208$$

cycles where LENGTH is the number of bytes in the operands. If, for example, LENGTH = 4 (32-bit division), the approximate execution time is

$$480 \times 4^2 + 438 \times 4 + 208 =$$
$$480 \times 16 + 1752 + 208 =$$
$$7680 + 1960 = 9{,}640 \text{ cycles}$$

Program Size: 206 bytes

Data Memory Required: 519 bytes anywhere in RAM plus eight bytes on page 0. The 519 bytes anywhere in RAM are temporary storage for the high dividend (255 bytes starting at address HIDE1), the result of the trial subtraction (255 bytes starting at address HIDE2), the return address (two bytes starting at address RETADR), the loop counter (two bytes starting at address COUNT), the length of the operands (one byte at address LENGTH), and the addresses of the high dividend buffers (two bytes starting at address AHIDE1 and two bytes starting at address AHIDE2). The eight bytes on page 0 hold pointers to the two operands and to the two temporary buffers for the high dividend. The pointers start at addresses AY1PTR ($00D0_{16}$ in the listing), AY2PTR ($00D2_{16}$ in the listing), HDEPTR ($00D4_{16}$ in the listing), and ODEPTR ($00D6_{16}$ in the listing). HDEPTR contains the address of the least significant byte of the remainder at the conclusion of the program.

Special Cases:

1. A length of zero causes an immediate exit with the Carry flag cleared, the quotient equal to the original dividend, and the remainder undefined.

2. A divisor of zero causes an exit with the Carry flag set to 1, the quotient equal to the original dividend, and the remainder equal to zero.

Entry Conditions

Order in stack (starting from the top)

Less significant byte of return address
More significant byte of return address

Length of the operands in bytes

Less significant byte of starting address of divisor (address containing the least significant byte of array 2)
More significant byte of starting address of divisor (address containing the least significant byte of array 2)

Less significant byte of starting address of dividend (address containing the least significant byte of array 1)
More significant byte of starting address of dividend (address containing the least significant byte of array 1)

Exit Conditions

Dividend (array 1) replaced by dividend (array 1) divided by divisor (array 2).

If the divisor is non-zero, Carry = 0 and the result is normal.

If the divisor is zero, Carry = 1, the dividend is unchanged and the remainder is zero.

The remainder is available with its least significant byte stored at the address in HDEPTR and HDEPTR+1

Example

Data: Length of operands (in bytes) = 03
Top operand (array 2 or divisor) = $000F45_{16} = 3{,}909_{10}$
Bottom operand (array 1 or dividend) = $35A2F7_{16} = 3{,}515{,}127_{10}$

Result: Bottom operand (array 1) = Bottom operand (array 1) / Top operand (array 2) $= 000383_{16} = 899_{10}$
Remainder (starting at address in HDEPTR and HDEPTR+1) = $0003A8_{16} = 936_{10}$
Carry flag is 0 to indicate no divide by zero error

```
;       Title            Multiple-Precision Binary Division          ;
;       Name:            MPBDIV                                      ;
;                                                                    ;
;                                                                    ;

;                                                                    ;
;       Purpose:         Divide 2 arrays of binary bytes             ;
;                        Arrayl := Arrayl / Array2                   ;
;                                                                    ;
;       Entry:           TOP OF STACK                                ;
;                          Low byte of return address,               ;
;                          High byte of return address,              ;
;                          Length of the arrays in bytes,            ;
;                          Low byte of array 2 (divisor) address,    ;
;                          High byte of array 2 (divisor) address,   ;
;                          Low byte of array 1 (dividend) address,   ;
;                          High byte of array 1 (dividend) address   ;
;                                                                    ;
;                          The arrays are unsigned binary numbers with a ;
;                          maximum length of 255 bytes, ARRAY[0] is the  ;
;                          least significant byte, and ARRAY[LENGTH-1]   ;
;                          the most significant byte.                ;
;                                                                    ;
;       Exit:            Arrayl := Arrayl / Array2                   ;
;                        If no errors then                           ;
;                          carry := 0                                ;
;                        ELSE                                        ;
;                          divide by 0 error                         ;
;                          carry := 1                                ;
;                          quotient := array 1 unchanged             ;
;                          remainder := 0                            ;
;                                                                    ;
;       Registers used: All                                          ;
;                                                                    ;
;       Time:            Assuming there are length/2 1 bits in the   ;
;                        quotient then the time is approximately     ;
;                         (480 * length^2) + (438 * length) + 208 cycles ;
;                                                                    ;
;       Size:            Program 206 bytes                           ;
;                        Data    519 bytes plus                      ;
;                                  8 bytes in page zero              ;
;                                                                    ;
;                                                                    ;

;EQUATES
AY1PTR: .EQU    0D0H            ;PAGE ZERO FOR ARRAY 1 POINTER
AY2PTR: .EQU    0D2H            ;PAGE ZERO FOR ARRAY 2 POINTER
HDEPTR: .EQU    0D4H            ;PAGE ZERO FOR HIGH DIVIDEND POINTER
ODEPTR: .EQU    0D6H            ;PAGE ZERO FOR OTHER HIGH DIVIDEND POINTER
MPBDIV:
        ;SAVE RETURN ADDRESS
        PLA
        STA     RETADR
        PLA
        STA     RETADR+1
```

```
        ;GET LENGTH OF ARRAYS
        PLA
        STA     LENGTH

        ;GET STARTING ADDRESS OF DIVISOR
        PLA
        STA     AY2PTR
        PLA
        STA     AY2PTR+1

        ;GET STARTING ADDRESS OF DIVIDEND
        PLA
        STA     AY1PTR
        PLA
        STA     AY1PTR+1

        ;RESTORE RETURN ADDRESS
        LDA     RETADR+1
        PHA
        LDA     RETADR
        PHA

        ;INITIALIZE
        LDA     LENGTH          ;IS LENGTH OF ARRAYS = 0 ?
        BNE     INIT
        JMP     OKEXIT          ;YES, EXIT

        ;SET COUNT TO NUMBER OF BITS IN THE ARRAYS
        ; COUNT := (LENGTH * 8) + 1
INIT:
        STA     COUNT           ;INITIALIZE COUNTER TO LENGTH
        LDA     #0
        ASL     COUNT           ;COUNT * 2
        ROL     A               ;A WILL BE UPPER BYTE
        ASL     COUNT           ;COUNT * 4
        ROL     A
        ASL     COUNT           ;COUNT * 8
        ROL     A
        STA     COUNT+1         ;STORE UPPER BYTE OF COUNT
        INC     COUNT           ;INCREMENT COUNT
        BNE     ZEROPD
        INC     COUNT+1

        ;ZERO BOTH HIGH DIVIDEND ARRAYS
ZEROPD:
        LDX     LENGTH
        LDA     #0
ZEROLP:
        STA     HIDE1-1,X       ;THE MINUS 1 FOR INDEXING FROM 1 TO LENGTH
        STA     HIDE2-1,X
        DEX
        BNE     ZEROLP

        ;SET HIGH DIVIDEND POINTER TO HIDE1
        LDA     AHIDE1
```

```
        STA     HDEPTR
        LDA     AHIDE1+1
        STA     HDEPTR+1

        ;SET OTHER HIGH DIVIDEND POINTER TO HIDE2
        LDA     AHIDE2
        STA     ODEPTR
        LDA     AHIDE2+1
        STA     ODEPTR+1

        ;CHECK IF DIVISOR IS ZERO
        LDX     LENGTH              ;LOGICALLY OR ALL BYTES OF DIVISOR
        LDY     #0
        TYA
CHK0LP:
        ORA     (AY2PTR),Y
        INY                         ;INCREMENT INDEX
        DEX
        BNE     CHK0LP              ;CONTINUE UNTIL REGISTER X = 0
        CMP     #0
        BNE     DIV                 ;BRANCH IF DIVISOR IS NOT ZERO
        JMP     EREXIT              ; ELSE EXIT INDICATING ERROR

        ;DIVIDE USING THE TRIAL SUBTRACTION ALGORITHM
DIV:
        CLC                         ;CLEAR CARRY FOR THE FIRST TIME THROUGH
LOOP:
        ;SHIFT CARRY INTO LOWER DIVIDEND ARRAY AS THE NEXT BIT OF QUOTIENT
        ; AND THE MOST SIGNIFICANT BIT OF THE LOWER DIVIDEND TO CARRY.
        LDX     LENGTH
        LDY     #0
SLLP1:
        LDA     (AY1PTR),Y
        ROL     A                   ;ROTATE NEXT BYTE
        STA     (AY1PTR),Y
        INY                         ;INCREMENT THE INDEX
        DEX
        BNE     SLLP1               ;CONTINUE UNTIL REGISTER X = 0

        ;DECREMENT BIT COUNTER AND EXIT IF DONE
        ;CARRY IS NOT CHANGED !!
DECCNT:
        DEC     COUNT               ;DECREMENT LOW BYTE OF COUNT
        BNE     SLUPR               ;BRANCH IF IT IS NOT ZERO
        LDX     COUNT+1             ;GET HIGH BYTE
        BEQ     OKEXIT              ;EXIT IF COUNT IS ZERO
        DEX                         ;ELSE DECREMENT HIGH BYTE OF COUNT
        STX     COUNT+1

        ;SHIFT THE CARRY INTO THE LEAST SIGNIFICANT BIT OF THE UPPER DIVIDEND
SLUPR:
        LDX     LENGTH
        LDY     #0
SLLP2:
        LDA     (HDEPTR),Y
        ROL     A
```

```
        STA     (HDEPTR),Y
        INY                     ;INCREMENT INDEX
        DEX
        BNE     SLLP2           ;CONTINUE UNTIL REGISTER X = 0

        ;SUBTRACT ARRAY 2 FROM HIGH DIVIDEND PLACING THE DIFFERENCE INTO
        ; OTHER HIGH DIVIDEND ARRAY
        LDY     #0
        LDX     LENGTH
        SEC
SUBLP:
        LDA     (HDEPTR),Y
        SBC     (AY2PTR),Y      ;SUBTRACT THE BYTES
        STA     (ODEPTR),Y      ;STORE THE DIFFERENCE
        INY                     ;INCREMENT INDEX
        DEX
        BNE     SUBLP           ;CONTINUE UNTIL REGISTER X = 0

        ;IF NO CARRY IS GENERATED FROM THE SUBTRACTION THEN THE HIGH DIVIDEND
        ; IS LESS THAN ARRAY 2 SO THE NEXT BIT OF THE QUOTIENT IS 0.
        ; IF THE CARRY IS SET THEN THE NEXT BIT OF THE QUOTIENT IS 1
        ; AND WE REPLACE DIVIDEND WITH REMAINDER BY SWITCHING POINTERS.
        BCC     LOOP            ;WAS TRIAL SUBTRACTION SUCCESSFUL ?
        LDY     HDEPTR          ;YES, EXCHANGE POINTERS THUS REPLACING
        LDX     HDEPTR+1        ;     DIVIDEND WITH REMAINDER
        LDA     ODEPTR
        STA     HDEPTR
        LDA     ODEPTR+1
        STA     HDEPTR+1
        STY     ODEPTR
        STX     ODEPTR+1

        ;CONTINUE WITH NEXT BIT A 1 (CARRY = 1)
        JMP     LOOP


        ;CLEAR CARRY TO INDICATE NO ERRORS
OKEXIT:
        CLC
        BCC     EXIT

        ;SET CARRY TO INDICATE A DIVIDE BY ZERO ERROR
EREXIT:
        SEC

EXIT:
        ;ARRAY 1 IS THE QUOTIENT
        ;HDEPTR CONTAINS THE ADDRESS OF THE REMAINDER
        RTS

;
;DATA
RETADR: .BLOCK  2               ;TEMPORARY FOR RETURN ADDRESS
COUNT:  .BLOCK  2               ;TEMPORARY FOR LOOP COUNTER
LENGTH: .BLOCK  1               ;LENGTH OF ARRAYS
```

```
AHIDE1: .WORD   HIDE1           ;ADDRESS OF HIGH DIVIDEND BUFFER 1
AHIDE2: .WORD   HIDE2           ;ADDRESS OF HIGH DIVIDEND BUFFER 2
HIDE1:  .BLOCK  255             ;HIGH DIVIDEND BUFFER 1
HIDE2:  .BLOCK  255             ;HIGH DIVIDEND BUFFER 2


;                                                                   ;
;                                                                   ;
;       SAMPLE EXECUTION:                                           ;
;                                                                   ;
;                                                                   ;


SC0609:
        LDA     AY1ADR+1
        PHA
        LDA     AY1ADR
        PHA                     ;PUSH AY1 ADDRESS

        LDA     AY2ADR+1
        PHA
        LDA     AY2ADR
        PHA                     ;PUSH AY2 ADDRESS

        LDA     #SZAYS
        PHA                     ;PUSH SIZE OF ARRAYS
        JSR     MPBDIV          ;MULTIPLE-PRECISION BINARY DIVIDE
        BRK                     ;RESULT OF 14B60404H / 1234H = 12345H
                                ; IN MEMORY AY1      = 45H
                                ;           AY1+1    = 23H
                                ;           AY1+2    = 01H
                                ;           AY1+3    = 00H
                                ;           AY1+4    = 00H
                                ;           AY1+5    = 00H
                                ;           AY1+6    = 00H
        JMP     SC0609

SZAYS:  .EQU    7               ;SIZE OF ARRAYS

AY1ADR: .WORD   AY1             ;ADDRESS OF ARRAY 1 (DIVIDEND)
AY2ADR: .WORD   AY2             ;ADDRESS OF ARRAY 2 (DIVISOR)

AY1:
        .BYTE   004H
        .BYTE   004H
        .BYTE   0B6H
        .BYTE   014H
        .BYTE   0
        .BYTE   0
        .BYTE   0

AY2:
        .BYTE   034H
        .BYTE   012H
        .BYTE   0
        .BYTE   0
```

```
        .BYTE   0
        .BYTE   0
        .BYTE   0

        .END    ;PROGRAM
```

Multiple-Precision Binary Comparison (MPBCMP)

6J

Compares two multi-byte unsigned binary numbers and sets the Carry and Zero flags appropriately. The Zero flag is set to 1 if the operands are equal and to 0 if they are not equal. The Carry flag is set to 0 if the operand with the address higher in the stack (the subtrahend) is larger than the other operand (the minuend); the Carry flag is set to 1 otherwise. Thus, the flags are set as if the subtrahend had been subtracted from the minuend.

Procedure: The program compares the operands one byte at a time, starting with the most significant bytes and continuing until it finds corresponding bytes that are not equal. If all the bytes are equal, it exits with the Zero flag set to 1. Note that the comparison works through the operands starting with the most significant bytes, whereas the subtraction (Subroutine 6G) starts with the least significant bytes.

Registers Used: All

Execution Time: 17 cycles per byte that must be compared plus 90 cycles overhead. That is, the program continues until it finds corresponding bytes that are not equal; each pair of bytes it must examine requires 17 cycles.

Examples:

1. Comparing two 6-byte numbers that are equal
   $17 \times 6 + 90 = 192$ cycles
2. Comparing two 8-byte numbers that differ in the next to most significant bytes
   $17 \times 2 + 90 = 124$ cycles

Program Size: 54 bytes

Data Memory Required: Two bytes anywhere in RAM and four bytes on page 0. The two bytes anywhere in RAM are temporary storage for the return address (starting at address RETADR). The four bytes on page 0 hold pointers to the two numbers; the pointers start at addresses MINPTR ($00D0_{16}$ in the listing) and SUBPTR ($00D2_{16}$ in the listing).

Special Case: A length of zero causes an immediate exit with the Carry flag and the Zero flag both set to 1.

Entry Conditions

Order in stack (starting from top)

Less significant byte of return address
More significant byte of return address

Length of the operands in bytes

Less significant byte of starting address of subtrahend (address containing the least significant byte)

More significant byte of starting address of subtrahend (address containing the least significant byte)

Less significant byte of starting address of minuend (address containing the least sig-

Exit Conditions

Flags set as if subtrahend had been subtracted from minuend

Zero flag = 1 if subtrahend and minuend are equal, 0 if they are not equal

Carry flag = 0 if subtrahend is larger than minuend in the unsigned sense, 1 if it is less than or equal to the minuend.

nificant byte)
More significant byte of starting address of minuend (address containing the least significant byte)

Examples

1. Data: Length of operands (in bytes) = 6
   Top operand (subtrahend) = $19D028A193EA_{16}$
   Bottom operand (minuend) = $4E67BC15A266_{16}$

   Result: Zero flag = 0 (operands are not equal)
   Carry flag = 1 (subtrahend is not larger than minuend)

2. Data: Length of operands (in bytes) = 6
   Top operand (subtrahend) = $19D028A193EA_{16}$
   Bottom operand (minuend) = $19D028A193EA_{16}$

   Result: Zero flag = 1 (operands are equal)
   Carry flag = 1 (subtrahend is not larger than minuend)

3. Data: Length of operands (in bytes) = 6
   Top operand (subtrahend) = $19D028A193EA_{16}$
   Bottom operand (minuend) = $0F37E5991D7C_{16}$

   Result: Zero flag = 0 (operands are not equal)
   Carry flag = 0 (subtrahend is larger than minuend)

```
;       Title           Multiple-Precision Binary Comparision          ;
;       Name:           MPBCMP                                          ;
;                                                                       ;
;                                                                       ;


;                                                                       ;
;       Purpose:        Compare 2 arrays of binary bytes and return     ;
;                       the CARRY and ZERO flags set or cleared         ;
;                                                                       ;
;       Entry:          TOP OF STACK                                    ;
;                         Low byte of return address,                   ;
;                         High byte of return address,                  ;
;                         Length of the arrays in bytes,                ;
;                         Low byte of array 2 (subtrahend) address,     ;
;                         High byte of array 2 (subtrahend) address,    ;
;                         Low byte of array 1 (minuend) address,        ;
;                         High byte of array 1 (minuend) address        ;
;                                                                       ;
```

```
;                             The arrays are unsigned binary numbers with a ;
;                             maximum length of 255 bytes, ARRAY[0] is the  ;
;                             least significant byte, and ARRAY[LENGTH-1]   ;
;                             the most significant byte.                    ;
;                                                                           ;
;       Exit:                IF ARRAY 1 = ARRAY 2 THEN                      ;
;                              C=1,Z=1                                      ;
;                            IF ARRAY 1 > ARRAY 2 THEN                      ;
;                              C=1,Z=0                                      ;
;                            IF ARRAY 1 < ARRAY 2 THEN                      ;
;                              C=0,Z=0                                      ;
;                                                                           ;
;       Registers used: All                                                 ;
;                                                                           ;
;       Time:                17 cycles per byte that must be examined       ;
;                            plus 90 cycles overhead.                       ;
;                                                                           ;
;       Size:                Program 54 bytes                               ;
;                            Data     2 bytes plus                          ;
;                                     4 bytes in page zero                  ;
;                                                                           ;
;                                                                           ;

;EQUATES
MINPTR: .EQU    0D0H            ;PAGE ZERO FOR ARRAY 1 POINTER
SUBPTR: .EQU    0D2H            ;PAGE ZERO FOR ARRAY 2 POINTER

MPBCMP:
        ;SAVE RETURN ADDRESS
        PLA
        STA     RETADR
        PLA
        STA     RETADR+1        ;SAVE RETURN ADDRESS

        ;GET LENGTH OF ARRAYS
        PLA
        TAY

        ;GET ADDRESS OF SUBTRAHEND AND SUBTRACT 1 TO SIMPLIFY INDEXING
        PLA
        SEC
        SBC     #1              ;SUBTRACT 1 FROM LOW BYTE
        STA     SUBPTR
        PLA
        SBC     #0              ;SUBTRACT ANY BORROW FROM HIGH BYTE
        STA     SUBPTR+1

        ;GET ADDRESS OF MINUEND AND ALSO SUBTRACT 1
        PLA
        SEC
        SBC     #1              ;SUBTRACT 1 FROM LOW BYTE
        STA     MINPTR
        PLA
        SBC     #0              ;SUBTRACT ANY BORROW FROM HIGH BYTE
        STA     MINPTR+1
```

```
        ;RESTORE RETURN ADDRESS
        LDA     RETADR+1
        PHA
        LDA     RETADR
        PHA

        ;INITIALIZE
        CPY     #0                  ;IS LENGTH OF ARRAYS = 0 ?
        BEQ     EXIT                ;YES, EXIT WITH C=1,Z=1

LOOP:
        LDA     (MINPTR),Y          ;GET NEXT BYTE
        CMP     (SUBPTR),Y          ;COMPARE BYTES
        BNE     EXIT                ;EXIT IF THEY ARE NOT EQUAL, THE FLAGS ARE SET
        DEY                         ;DECREMENT INDEX
        BNE     LOOP                ;CONTINUE UNTIL COUNTER = 0
                                    ; IF WE FALL THROUGH THEN THE ARRAYS ARE EQUAL
                                    ; AND THE FLAGS ARE SET PROPERLY
EXIT:
        RTS

;
;DATA
RETADR  .BLOCK  2                   ;TEMPORARY FOR RETURN ADDRESS

;                                                                       ;
;                                                                       ;
;       SAMPLE EXECUTION:                                               ;
;                                                                       ;
;                                                                       ;

SC0610:
        LDA     AY1ADR+1
        PHA
        LDA     AY1ADR
        PHA                         ;PUSH AY1 ADDRESS

        LDA     AY2ADR+1
        PHA
        LDA     AY2ADR
        PHA                         ;PUSH AY2 ADDRESS

        LDA     #SZAYS
        PHA                         ;PUSH SIZE OF ARRAYS
        JSR     MPBCMP              ;MULTIPLE-PRECISION BINARY COMPARISON
        BRK                         ;RESULT OF COMPARE(7654321H,1234567H) IS
                                    ;  C=1,Z=0
        JMP     SC0610

SZAYS:  .EQU    7       ;SIZE OF ARRAYS

AY1ADR: .WORD   AY1     ;ADDRESS OF ARRAY 1 (MINUEND)
AY2ADR: .WORD   AY2     ;ADDRESS OF ARRAY 2 (SUBTRAHEND)

AY1:
```

```
        .BYTE   021H
        .BYTE   043H
        .BYTE   065H
        .BYTE   007H
        .BYTE   0
        .BYTE   0
        .BYTE   0

AY2:
        .BYTE   067H
        .BYTE   045H
        .BYTE   023H
        .BYTE   001H
        .BYTE   0
        .BYTE   0
        .BYTE   0

        .END    ;PROGRAM
```

Multiple-Precision Decimal Addition (MPDADD)

6K

Adds two multi-byte unsigned decimal numbers. Both numbers are stored with their least significant digits at the lowest address. The sum replaces one of the numbers (the one with the starting address lower in the stack). The length of the numbers (in bytes) is 255 or less. The program returns with the Decimal Mode (D) flag cleared (binary mode).

Procedure: The program first enters the decimal mode by setting the D flag. It then clears the Carry flag initially and adds the operands one byte (two digits) at a time, starting with the least significant digits. The sum replaces the operand with the starting address lower in the stack (array 1 in the listing). A length of 00 causes an immediate exit with no addition operations. The program clears the D flag (thus placing the processor in the binary mode) before exiting. The final Carry flag reflects the addition of the most significant digits.

Registers Used: All

Execution Time: 23 cycles per byte plus 82 cycles overhead. For example, adding two 8-byte (16-digit) operands takes 23 × 8 + 86 or 270 cycles.

Program Size: 50 bytes

Data Memory Required: Two bytes anywhere in RAM and four bytes on page 0. The two bytes anywhere in RAM are temporary storage for the return address (starting at address RETADR). The four bytes on page 0 hold pointers to the two operands; the pointers start at addresses AY1PTR ($00D0_{16}$ in the listing) and AY2PTR ($00D2_{16}$ in the listing).

Special Case: A length of zero causes an immediate exit with array 1 unchanged (that is, the sum is equal to bottom operand). The Decimal Mode flag is cleared (binary mode) and the Carry flag is set to 1.

Entry Conditions

Order in stack (starting from top)

Less significant byte of return address
More significant byte of return address

Length of the operands in bytes

Less significant byte of starting address of second operand (address containing the least significant byte of array 2)
More significant byte of starting address of second operand (address containing the least significant byte of array 2)

Less significant byte of starting address of first operand and result (address containing the least significant byte of array 1)

Exit Conditions

First operand (array 1) replaced by first operand (array 1) plus second operand (array 2).

D flag set to zero (binary mode).

More significant byte of starting address of first operand and result (address containing the least significant byte of array 1)

Example

Data: Length of operands (in bytes) = 6
Top operand (array 2) = 196028819315_{16}
Bottom operand (array 1) = 293471605987_{16}

Result: Bottom operand (array 1) = Bottom operand (array 1) + Top operand (array 2) = 489500425302_{16}
Carry = 0, Decimal Mode flag = 0 (binary mode)

```
;       Title               Multiple-Precision Decimal Addition          ;
;       Name:               MPDADD                                       ;
;                                                                        ;
;                                                                        ;

;                                                                        ;
;       Purpose:            Add 2 arrays of BCD bytes                    ;
;                           Array1 := Array1 + Array2                    ;
;                                                                        ;
;       Entry:              TOP OF STACK                                 ;
;                             Low byte of return address,                ;
;                             High byte of return address,               ;
;                             Length of the arrays in bytes,             ;
;                             Low byte of array 2 address,               ;
;                             High byte of array 2 address,              ;
;                             Low byte of array 1 address,               ;
;                             High byte of array 1 address               ;
;                                                                        ;
;                             The arrays are unsigned BCD numbers with a ;
;                             maximum length of 255 bytes, ARRAY[0] is the ;
;                             least significant byte, and ARRAY[LENGTH-1] ;
;                             the most significant byte.                 ;
;                                                                        ;
;       Exit:               Array1 := Array1 + Array2                    ;
;                                                                        ;
;       Registers used: All                                              ;
;                                                                        ;
;       Time:               23 cycles per byte plus 86 cycles            ;
;                           overhead.                                    ;
;                                                                        ;
```

```
;       Size:            Program 50 bytes                              ;
;                        Data     2 bytes plus                         ;
;                                 4 bytes in page zero                 ;
;                                                                      ;
;                                                                      ;

;EQUATES
AY1PTR: .EQU    0D0H            ;PAGE ZERO FOR ARRAY 1 POINTER
AY2PTR: .EQU    0D2H            ;PAGE ZERO FOR ARRAY 2 POINTER

MPDADD:
        ;SAVE RETURN ADDRESS
        PLA
        STA     RETADR
        PLA
        STA     RETADR+1

        ;GET LENGTH OF ARRAYS
        PLA
        TAX

        ;GET STARTING ADDRESS OF ARRAY 2
        PLA
        STA     AY2PTR
        PLA
        STA     AY2PTR+1

        ;GET STARTING ADDRESS OF ARRAY 1
        PLA
        STA     AY1PTR
        PLA
        STA     AY1PTR+1

        ;RESTORE RETURN ADDRESS
        LDA     RETADR+1
        PHA
        LDA     RETADR
        PHA

        ;INITIALIZE SUM AND DECIMAL MODE, EXIT IF LENGTH = 0
        LDY     #0
        CPX     #0              ;IS LENGTH OF ARRAYS = 0 ?
        BEQ     EXIT            ;BRANCH IF LENGTH IS 0
        SED                     ;SET DECIMAL MODE
        CLC                     ;CLEAR CARRY

LOOP:
        LDA     (AY1PTR),Y      ;GET NEXT BYTE
        ADC     (AY2PTR),Y      ;ADD BYTES
        STA     (AY1PTR),Y      ;STORE SUM
        INY                     ;INCREMENT ARRAY INDEX
        DEX                     ;DECREMENT COUNTER
        BNE     LOOP            ;CONTINUE UNTIL COUNTER = 0

EXIT:
        CLD                     ;RETURN IN BINARY MODE
```

```
        RTS

;
;DATA
RETADR  .BLOCK  2               ;TEMPORARY FOR RETURN ADDRESS

;                                                               ;
;                                                               ;
;       SAMPLE EXECUTION:                                       ;
;                                                               ;
;                                                               ;

SC0611:
        LDA     AY1ADR+1
        PHA
        LDA     AY1ADR
        PHA                     ;PUSH AY1 ADDRESS

        LDA     AY2ADR+1
        PHA
        LDA     AY2ADR
        PHA                     ;PUSH AY2 ADDRESS

        LDA     #SZAYS
        PHA                     ;PUSH SIZE OF ARRAYS
        JSR     MPDADD          ;MULTIPLE-PRECISION BCD ADDITION
        BRK                     ;RESULT OF 1234567 + 1234567 = 2469134
                                ; IN MEMORY AY1     = 34H
                                ;           AY1+1   = 91H
                                ;           AY1+2   = 46H
                                ;           AY1+3   = 02H
                                ;           AY1+4   = 00H
                                ;           AY1+5   = 00H
                                ;           AY1+6   = 00H
        JMP     SC0611

SZAYS:  .EQU    7               ;SIZE OF ARRAYS

AY1ADR: .WORD   AY1             ;ADDRESS OF ARRAY 1
AY2ADR: .WORD   AY2             ;ADDRESS OF ARRAY 2

AY1:
        .BYTE   067H
        .BYTE   045H
        .BYTE   023H
        .BYTE   001H
        .BYTE   0
        .BYTE   0
        .BYTE   0

AY2:
        .BYTE   067H
        .BYTE   045H
        .BYTE   023H
```

```
        .BYTE   001H
        .BYTE   0
        .BYTE   0
        .BYTE   0

        .END    ;PROGRAM
```

Multiple-Precision Decimal Subtraction (MPDSUB)

6L

Subtracts two multi-byte unsigned decimal numbers. Both numbers are stored with their least significant digits at the lowest address. The starting address of the subtrahend (number to be subtracted) is stored on top of the starting address of the minuend (number from which the subtrahend is subtracted). The difference replaces the minuend in memory. The length of the numbers (in bytes) is 255 or less. The program returns with the Decimal Mode (D) flag cleared (binary mode).

Procedure: The program first enters the decimal mode by setting the D flag. It then sets the Carry flag (the inverted borrow) initially and subtracts the subtrahend from the minuend one byte (two digits) at a time, starting with the least significant digits. The final Carry flag reflects the subtraction of the most significant digits. The difference replaces the minuend (the operand with the starting address lower in the stack, array 1 in the listing). A length of 00 causes an immediate exit with no subtraction operations. The program clears the D flag (thus placing the processor in the binary mode) before exiting.

Registers Used: All

Execution Time: 23 cycles per byte plus 86 cycles overhead. For example, subtracting two 8-byte (16-digit) operands takes 23 × 8 + 86 or 270 cycles.

Program Size: 50 bytes

Data Memory Required: Two bytes anywhere in RAM and four bytes on page 0. The two bytes anywhere in RAM are temporary storage for the return address (starting at address RETADR). The four bytes on page 0 hold pointers to the two operands; the pointers start at addresses AY1PTR ($00D0_{16}$ in the listing) and AY2PTR ($00D2_{16}$ in the listing).

Special Case: A length of zero causes an immediate exit with the difference equal to the original minuend, the Decimal Mode flag cleared (binary mode), and the Carry flag set to 1.

Entry Conditions

Order in stack (starting from the top)

Less significant byte of return address
More significant byte of return address

Length of the operands in bytes

Less significant byte of starting address of subtrahend (address containing the least significant byte of array 2)

More significant byte of starting address of subtrahend (address containing the least significant byte of array 2)

Less significant byte of starting address of

Exit Conditions

Minuend (array 1) replaced by minuend (array 1) minus subtrahend (array 2).

D flag set to zero (binary mode).

minuend (address containing the least significant byte of array 1)

More significant byte of starting address of minuend (address containing the least significant byte of array 1)

Example

Data: Length of operands (in bytes) = 6
Minuend (array 1) = 293471605987_{16}
Subtrahend (array 2) = 196028819315_{16}

Result: Difference (array 1) = 097442786672_{16}.
This number replaces the original minuend in memory. The Carry flag is set to 1 in accordance with its usual role (in 6502 programming) as an inverted borrow.
Decimal Mode flag = 0 (binary mode)

```
;       Title            Multiple-Precision Decimal Subtraction     ;
;       Name:            MPDSUB                                     ;
;                                                                   ;
;                                                                   ;

;                                                                   ;
;       Purpose:         Subtract 2 arrays of BCD bytes             ;
;                        Minuend := Minuend - Subtrahend            ;
;                                                                   ;
;       Entry:           TOP OF STACK                               ;
;                          Low byte of return address,              ;
;                          High byte of return address,             ;
;                          Length of the arrays in bytes,           ;
;                          Low byte of subtrahend address,          ;
;                          High byte of subtrahend address,         ;
;                          Low byte of minuend address,             ;
;                          High byte of minuend address             ;
;                                                                   ;
;                          The arrays are unsigned BCD numbers with a ;
;                          maximum length of 255 bytes, ARRAY[0] is the ;
;                          least significant byte, and ARRAY[LENGTH-1] ;
;                          the most significant byte.               ;
;                                                                   ;
;       Exit:            Array1 := Array1 - Array2                  ;
;                                                                   ;
;       Registers used: All                                         ;
```

```
;                                                                  ;
;       Time:               23 cycles per byte plus 86 cycles     ;
;                           overhead.                             ;
;                                                                  ;
;       Size:               Program 50 bytes                      ;
;                           Data     2 bytes plus                 ;
;                                    4 bytes in page zero         ;
;                                                                  ;
;                                                                  ;

;EQUATES
MINPTR: .EQU    0D0H            ;PAGE ZERO FOR MINUEND POINTER
SUBPTR: .EQU    0D2H            ;PAGE ZERO FOR SUBTRAHEND POINTER

MPDSUB:
        ;SAVE RETURN ADDRESS
        PLA
        STA     RETADR
        PLA
        STA     RETADR+1

        ;GET LENGTH OF ARRAYS
        PLA
        TAX

        ;GET STARTING ADDRESS OF SUBTRAHEND
        PLA
        STA     SUBPTR
        PLA
        STA     SUBPTR+1

        ;GET STARTING ADDRESS OF MINUEND
        PLA
        STA     MINPTR
        PLA
        STA     MINPTR+1

        ;RESTORE RETURN ADDRESS
        LDA     RETADR+1
        PHA
        LDA     RETADR
        PHA

        ;INITIALIZE
        LDY     #0
        CPX     #0              ;IS LENGTH OF ARRAYS = 0 ?
        BEQ     EXIT            ;YES, EXIT
        SED                     ;SET DECIMAL MODE
        SEC                     ;SET CARRY

LOOP:
        LDA     (MINPTR),Y      ;GET NEXT BYTE
        SBC     (SUBPTR),Y      ;SUBTRACT BYTES
        STA     (MINPTR),Y      ;STORE DIFFERENCE
        INY                     ;INCREMENT ARRAY INDEX
        DEX                     ;DECREMENT COUNTER
        BNE     LOOP            ;CONTINUE UNTIL COUNTER = 0
```

```
EXIT:
        CLD                             ;RETURN IN BINARY MODE
        RTS

;
;DATA
RETADR  .BLOCK  2                       ;TEMPORARY FOR RETURN ADDRESS

;                                                                       ;
;                                                                       ;
;       SAMPLE EXECUTION:                                               ;
;                                                                       ;
;                                                                       ;


SC0612:
        LDA     AY1ADR+1
        PHA
        LDA     AY1ADR
        PHA                             ;PUSH AY1 ADDRESS
        LDA     AY2ADR+1
        PHA
        LDA     AY2ADR
        PHA                             ;PUSH AY2 ADDRESS

        LDA     #SZAYS
        PHA                             ;PUSH SIZE OF ARRAYS
        JSR     MPDSUB                  ;MULTIPLE-PRECISION BCD SUBTRACTION
        BRK                             ;RESULT OF 2469134 - 1234567 = 1234567
                                        ; IN MEMORY AY1      = 67H
                                        ;           AY1+1    = 45H
                                        ;           AY1+2    = 23H
                                        ;           AY1+3    = 01H
                                        ;           AY1+4    = 00H
                                        ;           AY1+5    = 00H
                                        ;           AY1+6    = 00H
        JMP     SC0612

SZAYS:  .EQU    7                       ;SIZE OF ARRAYS

AY1ADR: .WORD   AY1                     ;ADDRESS OF ARRAY 1 (MINUEND)
AY2ADR: .WORD   AY2                     ;ADDRESS OF ARRAY 2 (SUBTRAHEND)

AY1:
        .BYTE   034H
        .BYTE   091H
        .BYTE   046H
        .BYTE   002H
        .BYTE   0
        .BYTE   0
        .BYTE   0
```

```
AY2:
        .BYTE   067H
        .BYTE   045H
        .BYTE   023H
        .BYTE   001H
        .BYTE   0
        .BYTE   0
        .BYTE   0

        .END    ;PROGRAM
```

Multiple-Precision Decimal Multiplication (MPDMUL) 6M

Multiplies two multi-byte unsigned decimal numbers. Both numbers are stored with their least significant digits at the lowest address. The product replaces one of the numbers (the one with the starting address lower in the stack). The length of the numbers (in bytes) is 255 or less. Only the least significant bytes of the product are returned to retain compatibility with other multiple-precision decimal operations. The program returns with the Decimal Mode (D) flag cleared (binary mode).

Procedure: The program handles each digit of the multiplicand (array 1) separately. It masks that digit off, shifts it (if it is in the upper nibble of a byte), and then uses it as a counter to determine how many times to add the multiplier to the partial product. The least significant digit of the partial product is saved as the next digit of the full product and the partial product is shifted right four bits. The program uses a flag to determine whether it is currently working with the upper or lower digit of a byte. A length of 00 causes an exit with no multiplication.

Registers Used: All

Execution Time: Depends on the length of the operands and on the size of the digits in the multiplicand (since those digits determine how many times the multiplier is added to the partial product).

If the average digit in the multiplicand has a value of 5, then the execution time is approximately

$$322 \times \text{LENGTH}^2 + 390 \times \text{LENGTH} + 100$$

cycles where LENGTH is the number of bytes in the operand. If, for example, LENGTH = 6 (12 digits), the approximate execution time is

$$322 \times 6^2 + 390 \times 6 + 100 = 322 \times 36 + 2340 + 100 = 11{,}592 + 2440 = 14{,}032 \text{ cycles.}$$

Program Size: 203 bytes

Data Memory Required: 517 bytes anywhere in RAM plus four bytes on page 0. The 517 bytes anywhere in RAM are temporary storage for the partial product (255 bytes starting at address PROD), the multiplicand (255 bytes starting at address MCAND), the return address (two bytes starting at address RETADR), the length of the operands in bytes (one byte at address LENGTH), the next digit in the operand (one byte at address NDIGIT), the digit counter (one byte at address DCNT), the byte index into the operands (one byte at address IDX), and the overflow byte (1 byte at address OVERFLW). The four bytes on page 0 hold pointers to the two operands; the pointers start at addresses AY1PTR ($00D0_{16}$ in the listing) and AY2PTR ($00D2_{16}$ in the listing).

Special Case: A length of zero causes an immediate exit with the product equal to the original multiplicand (array 1 is unchanged), the Decimal Mode flag cleared (binary mode), and the more significant bytes of the product (starting at address PROD) undefined.

Entry Conditions

Order in stack (starting from the top)

Less significant byte of return address
More significant byte of return address

Length of the operands in bytes

Exit Conditions

Multiplicand (array 1) replaced by multiplicand (array 1) times multiplier (array 2).

D flag set to zero (binary mode).

Less significant byte of starting address of multiplier (address containing the least significant byte of array 2)
More significant byte of starting address of multiplier (address containing the least significant byte of array 2)

Less significant byte of starting address of multiplicand (address containing the least significant byte of array 1)
More significant byte of starting address of multiplicand (address containing the least significant byte of array 1)

Example

Data: Length of operands (in bytes) = 04

Top operand (array 2 or multiplier) = 00003518_{16}

Bottom operand (array 1 or multiplicand) = 00006294_{16}

Result: Bottom operand (array 1) = Bottom operand (array 1) * Top operand (array 2) = 22142292_{16}.

Decimal Mode flag = 0 (binary mode)

Note that MPDMUL returns only the less significant bytes of the product (that is, the number of bytes in the multiplicand and multiplier) to maintain compatibility with other multiple-precision decimal arithmetic operations. The more significant bytes of the product are available starting with their least significant digits at address PROD. The user may need to check those bytes for a possible overflow or extend the operands with additional zeros.

```
;       Title             Multiple-Precision Decimal Multiplication      ;
;       Name:             MPDMUL                                         ;
;                                                                        ;
;       Purpose:          Multiply 2 arrays of BCD bytes                 ;
;                         Arrayl := Arrayl * Array2                      ;
;                                                                        ;
;       Entry:            TOP OF STACK                                   ;
;                           Low byte of return address,                  ;
;                           High byte of return address,                 ;
;                           Length of the arrays in bytes,               ;
;                           Low byte of array 2 (mulitplicand) address,  ;
;                           High byte of array 2 (multiplicand) address, ;
;                           Low byte of array 1 (multiplier) address,    ;
;                           High byte of array 1 (multiplier) address    ;
;                                                                        ;
;                           The arrays are unsigned BCD numbers with a   ;
;                           maximum length of 255 bytes, ARRAY[0] is the ;
;                           least significant byte, and ARRAY[LENGTH-1]  ;
;                           the most significant byte.                   ;
;                                                                        ;
;       Exit:             Arrayl := Arrayl * Array2                      ;
```

```
;
;       Registers used: All                                          ;
;                                                                    ;
;       Time:          Assuming the average digit value of ARRAY 1 is ;
;                      5 then the time is approximately              ;
;                       (322 * length^2) + (390 * length) + 100 cycles ;
;                                                                    ;
;       Size:          Program 203 bytes                             ;
;                      Data    517 bytes plus                        ;
;                                4 bytes in page zero                ;
;                                                                    ;
;                                                                    ;

;EQUATES
AY1PTR: .EQU    0D0H            ;PAGE ZERO FOR ARRAY 1 POINTER
AY2PTR: .EQU    0D2H            ;PAGE ZERO FOR ARRAY 2 POINTER

MPDMUL:
        ;SAVE RETURN ADDRESS
        PLA
        STA     RETADR
        PLA
        STA     RETADR+1

        ;GET LENGTH OF ARRAYS
        PLA
        STA     LENGTH

        ;GET STARTING ADDRESS OF ARRAY 2
        PLA
        STA     AY2PTR
        PLA
        STA     AY2PTR+1

        ;GET STARTING ADDRESS OF ARRAY 1
        PLA
        STA     AY1PTR
        PLA
        STA     AY1PTR+1

        ;RESTORE RETURN ADDRESS
        LDA     RETADR+1
        PHA
        LDA     RETADR
        PHA

        ;INITIALIZE
        SED                     ;PUT PROCESSOR IN DECIMAL MODE
        LDY     #0
        LDX     LENGTH          ;IS LENGTH ZERO ?
        BNE     INITLP
        JMP     EXIT            ;YES, EXIT

        ;MOVE ARRAY 1 TO MULTIPLICAND ARRAY, ZERO ARRAY 1, AND
        ; ZERO PRODUCT ARRAY.
INITLP:
        LDA     (AY1PTR),Y
        STA     MCAND,Y         ;MOVE ARY1[Y] TO MCAND[Y]
```

```
        LDA     #0
        STA     (AY1PTR),Y      ;ZERO ARY1[Y]
        STA     PROD,Y          ;ZERO PROD
        INY
        DEX                     ;DECREMENT LOOP COUNTER
        BNE     INITLP          ;CONTINUE UNTIL DONE

        ;INITIALIZE CURRENT INDEX TO ZERO
        LDA     #0
        STA     IDX

        ;
        ;LOOP THROUGH ALL THE BYTES OF THE MULTIPLICAND
LOOP:
        LDA     #0
        STA     DCNT            ;START WITH LOW DIGIT

        ;LOOP THROUGH 2 DIGITS PER BYTE
        ; DURING THE FIRST DIGIT DCNT = 0
        ; DURING THE SECOND DIGIT DCNT = FF HEX (-1)
DLOOP:
        LDA     #0
        STA     OVRFLW          ;ZERO OVERFLOW
        LDY     IDX
        LDA     MCAND,Y         ;GET NEXT BYTE
        LDX     DCNT
        BPL     DLOOP1          ;BRANCH IF FIRST DIGIT
        LSR     A               ;SHIFT RIGHT 4 BITS
        LSR     A
        LSR     A
        LSR     A
DLOOP1:
        AND     #0FH            ;AND OFF UPPER DIGIT
        BEQ     SDIGIT          ;BRANCH IF NEXT DIGIT IS ZERO
        STA     NDIGIT          ;SAVE

        ;ADD MULTIPLIER TO PRODUCT NDIGIT TIMES
ADDLP:
        LDY     #0              ;Y = INDEX INTO ARRAYS
        LDX     LENGTH          ;X = LENGTH IN BYTES
        CLC                     ;CLEAR CARRY INITIALY
INNER:
        LDA     (AY2PTR),Y      ;GET NEXT BYTE
        ADC     PROD,Y          ;ADD TO PRODUCT
        STA     PROD,Y          ;STORE
        INY                     ;INCREMENT ARRAY INDEX
        DEX                     ;DECREMENT LOOP COUNTER
        BNE     INNER           ;CONTINUE UNTIL LOOP COUNTER = 0
        BCC     DECND           ;BRANCH IF NO OVERFLOW FROM ADDITION
        INC     OVRFLW          ;ELSE INCREMENT OVERFLOW BYTE

DECND:
        DEC     NDIGIT
        BNE     ADDLP           ;CONTINUE UNTIL NDIGIT = 0
```

```
        ;STORE THE LEAST SIGNIFICANT DIGIT OF PRODUCT
        ; AS THE NEXT DIGIT OF ARRAY 1
SDIGIT:
        LDA     PROD
        AND     #0FH            ;CLEAR UPPER DIGIT
        LDX     DCNT
        BPL     SD1             ;BRANCH IF FIRST DIGIT
        ASL     A               ;ELSE SHIFT LEFT 4 BITS TO PLACE
        ASL     A               ; IN THE UPPER DIGIT
        ASL     A
        ASL     A
SD1:
        LDY     IDX             ;GET CURRENT BYTE INDEX
        ORA     (AY1PTR),Y      ;OR IN NEXT DIGIT
        STA     (AY1PTR),Y      ;STORE NEW VALUE

        ;SHIFT RIGHT PRODUCT 1 DIGIT (4 BITS)
        LDY     LENGTH          ;SHIFT RIGHT FROM THE FAR END

SHFTLP:
        DEY                     ;DECREMENT Y SO IT POINTS AT THE NEXT BYTE
        LDA     PROD,Y
        PHA                     ;SAVE LOW DIGIT OF PROD,Y
        AND     #0F0H           ;CLEAR LOW DIGIT

        ;MAKE LOW DIGIT OF OVERFLOW = HIGH DIGIT OF PROD,Y
        ;MAKE HIGH DIGIT OF PROD,Y = LOW DIGIT OF PROD,Y
        LSR     OVRFLW          ;SHIFT OVERFLOW RIGHT
        ORA     OVRFLW          ;BIT 0..2 AND CARRY = OVERFLOW
                                ;BITS 4..7 = PROD
        ROR     A
        ROR     A
        ROR     A
        ROR     A               ;NOW PROD IN BITS 0..3 AND OVERFLOW IN 4..7
        STA     PROD,Y          ;STORE NEW PRODUCT
        PLA                     ;GET OLD PROD,Y
        AND     #0FH            ;CLEAR UPPER DIGIT
        STA     OVRFLW          ;STORE IN OVERFLOW
        TYA                     ;CHECK FOR Y = 0
        BNE     SHFTLP          ;BRANCH IF NOT DONE

        ;CHECK IF WE ARE DONE WITH BOTH DIGITS OF THIS BYTE
        DEC     DCNT            ;MAKE 0 GOTO FF HEX TO INDICATE SECOND DIGIT
        LDA     DCNT
        CMP     #0FFH           ;HAVE WE ALREADY DONE BOTH DIGITS ?
        BEQ     DLOOP           ;BRANCH IF NOT

        ;INCREMENT TO NEXT BYTE AND SEE IF WE ARE DONE
        INC     IDX
        LDA     IDX
        CMP     LENGTH
        BCS     EXIT            ;BRANCH IF BYTE INDEX >= LENGTH
        JMP     LOOP            ;ELSE CONTINUE

EXIT:
```

```
        CLD                         ;RETURN IN BINARY MODE
        RTS


;
;DATA
RETADR:         .BLOCK  2           ;TEMPORARY FOR RETURN ADDRESS
LENGTH:         .BLOCK  1           ;LENGTH OF ARRAYS
NDIGIT:         .BLOCK  1           ;NEXT DIGIT IN ARRAY
DCNT:           .BLOCK  1           ;DIGIT COUNTER FOR BYTES IN ARRAYS
IDX:            .BLOCK  1           ;BYTE INDEX INTO ARRAYS
OVRFLW:         .BLOCK  1           ;OVERFLOW BYTE
PROD:           .BLOCK  255         ;PRODUCT BUFFER
MCAND:          .BLOCK  255         ;MULTIPLICAND BUFFER

;                                                                     ;
;                                                                     ;
;       SAMPLE EXECUTION:                                             ;
;                                                                     ;
;                                                                     ;

SC0613:
        LDA     AY1ADR+1
        PHA
        LDA     AY1ADR
        PHA                         ;PUSH AY1 ADDRESS

        LDA     AY2ADR+1
        PHA
        LDA     AY2ADR
        PHA                         ;PUSH AY2 ADDRESS

        LDA     #SZAYS
        PHA                         ;PUSH LENGTH OF ARRAYS
        JSR     MPDMUL              ;MULTIPLE-PRECISION BCD MULTIPLICATION
        BRK                         ;RESULT OF 1234 * 1234 = 1522756
                                    ; IN MEMORY AY1      = 56H
                                    ;           AY1+1    = 27H
                                    ;           AY1+2    = 52H
                                    ;           AY1+3    = 01H
                                    ;           AY1+4    = 00H
                                    ;           AY1+5    = 00H
                                    ;           AY1+6    = 00H
        JMP     SC0613

SZAYS:  .EQU    7                   ;LENGTH OF ARRAYS

AY1ADR: .WORD   AY1                 ;ADDRESS OF ARRAY 1
AY2ADR: .WORD   AY2                 ;ADDRESS OF ARRAY 2

AY1:
        .BYTE   034H
        .BYTE   012H
        .BYTE   0
        .BYTE   0
```

```
        .BYTE   0
        .BYTE   0
        .BYTE   0

AY2:
        .BYTE   034H
        .BYTE   012H
        .BYTE   0
        .BYTE   0
        .BYTE   0
        .BYTE   0
        .BYTE   0

        .END    ;PROGRAM
```

Multiple-Precision Decimal Division (MPDDIV) 6N

Divides two multi-byte unsigned decimal numbers. Both numbers are stored with their least significant byte at the lowest address. The quotient replaces the dividend (the operand with the starting address lower in the stack). The length of the numbers (in bytes) is 255 or less. The remainder is not returned but the address of its least significant byte is available starting at memory location HDEPTR. The Carry flag is cleared if no errors occur; if a divide by zero is attempted, the Carry flag is set to 1, the dividend is left unchanged, and the remainder is set to zero. The program returns with the Decimal Mode (D) flag cleared (binary mode).

Procedure: The program performs division by trial subtractions, a digit at a time. It determines how many times the divisor can be subtracted from the dividend and then saves that number in the quotient and makes the remainder into the new dividend. It then rotates the dividend and the quotient left one digit. The program exits immediately, setting the Carry flag, if it finds the divisor to be zero. The Carry flag is cleared otherwise.

Registers Used: All

Execution Time: Depends on the length of the operands and on the size of the digits in the quotient (determining how many trial subtractions must be performed). If the average digit in the quotient has a value of 5, then the execution time is approximately

$$440 \times \text{LENGTH}^2 + 765 \times \text{LENGTH} + 228$$

cycles where LENGTH is the number of bytes in the operands. If, for example, LENGTH = 6 (12 digits), the approximate execution time is

$$440 \times 6^2 + 765 \times 6 + 228 = 440 \times 36 + 4590 + 228 = 15{,}840 + 4818 = 20{,}658 \text{ cycles.}$$

Program Size: 246 bytes

Data Memory Required: 522 bytes anywhere in RAM plus eight bytes on page 0. The 522 bytes anywhere in RAM are temporary storage for the high dividend (255 bytes starting at address HIDE1), the result of the trial subtraction (255 bytes starting at address HIDE2), the return address (two bytes starting at address RETADR), a pointer to the dividend (two bytes starting at address AY1PTR), the length of the operands (one byte at address LENGTH), the next digit in the array (one byte at address NDIGIT), the divide loop counter (one byte at address COUNT), and the addresses of the high dividend buffers (two bytes each, starting at addresses AHIDE1 and AHIDE2). The eight bytes on page 0 hold pointers to the divisor (address AY2PTR, $00D0_{16}$ in the listing), the current high dividend and remainder (address HDEPTR, $00D2_{16}$ in the listing), the other high dividend (address ODEPTR, $00D4_{16}$ in the listing), and the temporary array used in the left rotation (address RLPTR, $00D6_{16}$ in the listing).

Special Cases:

1. A length of zero causes an immediate exit with the Carry flag cleared, the quotient equal to the original dividend (array 1 unchanged), the remainder undefined, and the Decimal Mode flag cleared (binary mode).

2. A divisor of zero causes an exit with the Carry flag set to 1, the quotient equal to the original dividend (array 1 unchanged), the remainder equal to zero, and the Decimal Mode flag cleared (binary mode).

Entry Conditions

Order in stack (starting from the top)

Less significant byte of return address
More significant byte of return address

Length of the operands in bytes

Less significant byte of starting address of divisor (address containing the least significant byte of array 2)
More significant byte of starting address of divisor (address containing the least significant byte of array 2)

Less significant byte of starting address of dividend (address containing the least significant byte of array 1)
More significant byte of starting address of dividend (address containing the least significant byte of array 1)

Exit Conditions

Dividend (array 1) replaced by dividend (array 1) divided by divisor (array 2)

If the divisor is non-zero, Carry = 0 and the result is normal.

If the divisor is zero, Carry = 1, the dividend is unchanged, and the remainder is zero.

The remainder is available with its least significant digits stored at the address in HDEPTR and HDEPTR+1

D flag set to zero (binary mode).

Example

Data: Length of operands (in bytes) = 04
Top operand (array 2 or divisor) = 00006294_{16}
Bottom operand (array 1 or dividend) = 22142298_{16}

Result: Bottom operand (array 1) = Bottom operand (array 1)/Top operand (array 2) = 00003518_{16}
Remainder (starting at address in HDEPTR and HDEPTR+1) = $00000006_{16} = 6_{10}$
Decimal Mode flag = 0 (binary mode)
Carry flag is 0 to indicate no divide by zero error.

```
;       Title           Multiple-Precision Decimal Division           ;
;       Name:           MPDDIV                                        ;
;                                                                     ;
;                                                                     ;

;                                                                     ;
;       Purpose:        Divide 2 arrays of BCD bytes                  ;
;                       Array1 := Array1 / Array2                     ;
;                                                                     ;
;       Entry:          TOP OF STACK                                  ;
;                         Low byte of return address,                 ;
;                         High byte of return address,                ;
;                         Length of the arrays in bytes,              ;
;                         Low byte of array 2 (divisor) address,      ;
;                         High byte of array 2 (divisor) address,     ;
;                         Low byte of array 1 (dividend) address,     ;
;                         High byte of array 1 (dividend)  address    ;
;                                                                     ;
;                         The arrays are unsigned BCD numbers with a  ;
;                         maximum length of 255 bytes, ARRAY[0] is the ;
;                         least significant byte, and ARRAY[LENGTH-1] ;
;                         the most significant byte.                  ;
;                                                                     ;
;       Exit:           Array1 := Array1 / Array2                     ;
;                       Dvbuf := remainder                            ;
;                       If no errors then                             ;
;                         carry := 0                                  ;
;                       ELSE                                          ;
;                         divide by 0 error                           ;
;                         carry := 1                                  ;
;                         ARRAY 1 := unchanged                        ;
;                         remainder := 0                              ;
;                                                                     ;
;       Registers used: All                                           ;
;                                                                     ;
;       Time:           Assuming the average digit value in the       ;
;                       quotient is 5 then the time is approximately  ;
;                        (440 * length^2) + (765 * length) + 228 cycles ;
;                                                                     ;
;       Size:           Program 246 bytes                             ;
;                       Data    522 bytes plus                        ;
;                                 8 bytes in page zero                ;
;                                                                     ;
;                                                                     ;


;EQUATES
AY2PTR: .EQU    0D0H            ;PAGE ZERO FOR ARRAY 2 (DIVISOR) POINTER
HDEPTR: .EQU    0D2H            ;PAGE ZERO WHICH POINTS TO THE CURRENT
                                ; HIGH DIVIDEND POINTER
ODEPTR: .EQU    0D4H            ;PAGE ZERO WHICH POINTS TO THE OTHER
                                ; HIGH DIVIDEND POINTER
RLPTR:  .EQU    0D6H            ;PAGE ZERO FOR ROTATE LEFT ARRAY

MPDDIV:
```

```
        ;GET RETURN ADDRESS
        PLA
        STA     RETADR
        PLA
        STA     RETADR+1

        ;GET LENGTH OF ARRAYS
        PLA
        STA     LENGTH

        ;GET STARTING ADDRESS OF DIVISOR
        PLA
        STA     AY2PTR
        PLA
        STA     AY2PTR+1

        ;GET STARTING ADDRESS OF DIVIDEND
        PLA
        STA     AY1PTR
        PLA
        STA     AY1PTR+1

        ;RESTORE RETURN ADDRESS
        LDA     RETADR+1
        PHA
        LDA     RETADR
        PHA

        ;INITIALIZE
        CLD                     ;PUT PROCESSOR INTO BINARY MODE

        ;CHECK FOR ZERO LENGTH ARRAYS
        LDA     LENGTH
        BNE     INIT            ;BRANCH IF NOT ZERO
        JMP     OKEXIT          ;ELSE EXIT

        ;ZERO BOTH DIVIDEND BUFFERS
INIT:
        LDA     #0              ;A = 0
        LDY     LENGTH          ;X = LENGTH
INITLP:
        STA     HIDE1-1,Y
        STA     HIDE2-1,Y
        DEY
        BNE     INITLP

        ;SET UP THE HIGH DIVIDEND POINTERS
        LDA     AHIDE1
        STA     HDEPTR
        LDA     AHIDE1+1
        STA     HDEPTR+1
        LDA     AHIDE2
        STA     ODEPTR
        LDA     AHIDE2+1
        STA     ODEPTR+1
```

```
        ;NDIGIT := 0
        LDA     #0
        STA     NDIGIT

        ;SET COUNT TO NUMBER OF DIGITS PLUS 1
        ; COUNT := (LENGTH * 2) + 1
        LDA     LENGTH
        ASL     A               ;LENGTH * 2
        STA     COUNT
        LDA     #0
        ROL     A               ;MOVE OVERFLOW FROM * 2 INTO A
        STA     COUNT+1         ;STORE HIGH BYTE OF COUNT
        INC     COUNT
        BNE     CHKDV0          ;BRANCH IF NO OVERFLOW
        INC     COUNT+1

        ;CHECK FOR DIVIDE BY ZERO
CHKDV0:
        LDX     LENGTH
        LDY     #0
        TYA
DV01:
        ORA     (AY2PTR),Y
        INY
        DEX
        BNE     DV01            ;CONTINUE ORING ALL THE BYTES

        CMP     #0
        BNE     DVLOOP          ;BRANCH IF DIVISOR IS NOT 0
        JMP     EREXIT          ;ERROR EXIT

        ;PERFORM DIVISION BY TRIAL SUBTRACTIONS
DVLOOP:
        ;ROTATE LEFT THE LOWER DIVIDEND AND THE QUOTIENT (ARRAY 1)
        ; THE HIGH DIGIT OF NDIGIT BECOMES THE LEAST SIGNIFICANT DIGIT
        ; OF THE QUOTIENT (ARRAY 1) AND THE MOST SIGNIFICANT DIGIT
        ; OF ARRAY 1 (DIVIDEND) GOES TO THE HIGH DIGIT OF NDIGIT
        LDA     AY1PTR+1
        LDY     AY1PTR
        JSR     RLARY           ;ROTATE ARRAY 1

        ;IF COUNT = 0 THEN WE ARE DONE
        DEC     COUNT
        BNE     ROLDVB          ;BRANCH IF LOWER BYTE IS NOT 0
        LDA     COUNT+1         ;ELSE GET HIGH BYTE
        BEQ     OKEXIT          ;CONTINUE UNTIL COUNT = 0
        DEC     COUNT+1         ;DECREMENT UPPER BYTE OF COUNT

        ;

        ;ROTATE LEFT THE HIGH DIVIDEND WHERE THE LEAST SIGNIFICANT DIGIT
        ; OF HIGH DIVIDEND BECOMES THE HIGH DIGIT OF NDIGIT
ROLDVB:
        LDA     HDEPTR+1
        LDY     HDEPTR
        JSR     RLARY
```

```
        ;
        ;SEE HOW MANY TIMES THE DIVISOR WILL GO INTO THE HIGH DIVIDEND
        ; WHEN WE EXIT FROM THIS LOOP THE HIGH DIGIT OF NDIGIT IS THE NEXT
        ; QUOTIENT DIGIT AND HIGH DIVIDEND IS THE REMAINDER
        LDA     #0
        STA     NDIGIT              ;NDIGIT := 0
        SED                         ;ENTER DECIMAL MODE
SUBLP:
        LDY     #0                  ;Y = INDEX INTO ARRAYS
        LDX     LENGTH              ;X = LENGTH
        SEC                         ;SET INVERTED BORROW

INNER:
        LDA     (HDEPTR),Y          ;GET NEXT BYTE OF DIVIDEND
        SBC     (AY2PTR),Y          ;SUBTRACT BYTE OF DIVISOR
        STA     (ODEPTR),Y          ;SAVE DIFFERENCE FOR NEXT SUBTRACTION
        INY                         ;INCREMENT ARRAY INDEX
        DEX                         ;DECREMENT LOOP COUNTER
        BNE     INNER               ;CONTINUE THROUGH ALL THE BYTES
        BCC     DVLOOP              ;BRANCH WHEN BORROW OCCURS AT WHICH TIME
                                    ; NDIGIT IS THE NUMBER OF TIMES THE DIVISOR
                                    ; GOES INTO THE ORIGINAL HIGH DIVIDEND AND
                                    ; HIGH DIVIDEND CONTAINS THE REMAINDER.

        ;INCREMENT NEXT DIGIT WHICH IS IN THE HIGH DIGIT OF NDIGIT
        LDA     NDIGIT
        CLC
        ADC     #10H
        STA     NDIGIT

        ;EXCHANGE POINTERS, THUS MAKING REMAINDER THE NEW DIVIDEND
        LDX     HDEPTR
        LDY     HDEPTR+1
        LDA     ODEPTR
        STA     HDEPTR
        LDA     ODEPTR+1
        STA     HDEPTR+1
        STX     ODEPTR
        STY     ODEPTR+1

        JMP     SUBLP               ;CONTINUE UNTIL DIFFERENCE GOES NEGATIVE

        ;NO ERRORS, CLEAR CARRY
OKEXIT:
        CLC
        BCC     EXIT

        ;DIVIDE BY ZERO ERROR, SET CARRY

EREXIT:
        SEC

EXIT:
        ;HDEPTR CONTAINS THE ADDRESS OF THE REMAINDER
        CLD                         ;RETURN IN BINARY MODE
        RTS
```

```
;
;***********************************
;SUBROUTINE: RLARY
;PURPOSE:    ROTATE LEFT AN ARRAY ONE DIGIT (4 BITS)
;ENTRY: A = HIGH BYTE OF ARRAY ADDRESS
;       Y = LOW BYTE OF ARRAY ADDRESS
;       THE HIGH DIGIT OF NDIGIT IS THE DIGIT TO ROTATE THROUGH
;EXIT:  ARRAY ROTATED LEFT THROUGH THE HIGH DIGIT OF NDIGIT
;REGISTERS USED: ALL
;***********************************

RLARY:
        ;STORE ARRAY ADDRESS
        STA     RLPTR+1
        STY     RLPTR

        ;SHIFT NDIGIT INTO LOW DIGIT OF ARRAY AND
        ; SHIFT ARRAY LEFT
        LDX     LENGTH
        LDY     #0              ;START AT ARY1[0]

SHIFT:
        LDA     (RLPTR),Y       ;GET NEXT BYTE
        PHA                     ;SAVE HIGH DIGIT
        AND     #0FH            ;CLEAR HIGH DIGIT

        ASL     NDIGIT
        ORA     NDIGIT          ;BITS 0..3 = LOW DIGIT OF ARRAY
                                ;BITS 5..7 AND CARRY = NEXT DIGIT
        ROL     A
        ROL     A
        ROL     A
        ROL     A               ;NOW NDIGIT IN BITS 0..3 AND
                                ; LOW DIGIT IN HIGH DIGIT
        STA     (RLPTR),Y       ;STORE IT
        PLA                     ;GET OLD HIGH DIGIT
        AND     #0F0H           ;CLEAR LOWER DIGIT
        STA     NDIGIT          ;STORE IN NDIGIT
        INY                     ;INCREMENT TO NEXT BYTE
        DEX                     ;DECREMENT COUNT
        BNE     SHIFT           ;BRANCH IF NOT DONE

        RTS


;
;DATA
RETADR:         .BLOCK  2       ;TEMPORARY FOR RETURN ADDRESS
AY1PTR:         .BLOCK  2       ;ARRAY 1 ADDRESS
LENGTH:         .BLOCK  1       ;LENGTH OF ARRAYS
NDIGIT:         .BLOCK  1       ;NEXT DIGIT IN ARRAY
COUNT:          .BLOCK  2       ;DIVIDE LOOP COUNTER
AHIDE1:         .WORD   HIDE1   ;ADDRESS OF HIGH DIVIDEND BUFFER 1
AHIDE2:         .WORD   HIDE2   ;ADDRESS OF HIGH DIVIDEND BUFFER 2
HIDE1:          .BLOCK  255.    ;HIGH DIVIDEND BUFFER 1
HIDE2:          .BLOCK  255.    ;HIGH DIVIDEND BUFFER 2
```

```
;                                                               ;
;                                                               ;
;       SAMPLE EXECUTION:                                       ;
;                                                               ;
;                                                               ;

SC0614:
        LDA     AY1ADR+1
        PHA
        LDA     AY1ADR
        PHA                     ;PUSH AY1 ADDRESS

        LDA     AY2ADR+1
        PHA
        LDA     AY2ADR
        PHA                     ;PUSH AY2 ADDRESS

        LDA     #SZAYS
        PHA                     ;PUSH LENGTH OF ARRAYS
        JSR     MPDDIV          ;MULTIPLE-PRECISION BCD DIVISION
        BRK                     ;RESULT OF 1522756 / 1234 = 1234
                                ; IN MEMORY AY1     = 34H
                                ;           AY1+1   = 12H
                                ;           AY1+2   = 00H
                                ;           AY1+3   = 00H
                                ;           AY1+4   = 00H
                                ;           AY1+5   = 00H
                                ;           AY1+6   = 00H
        JMP     SC0614

SZAYS:  .EQU    7               ;LENGTH OF ARRAYS

AY1ADR: .WORD   AY1             ;ADDRESS OF ARRAY 1 (DIVIDEND)
AY2ADR: .WORD   AY2             ;ADDRESS OF ARRAY 2 (DIVISOR)

AY1:
        .BYTE   056H
        .BYTE   027H
        .BYTE   052H
        .BYTE   01H
        .BYTE   0
        .BYTE   0
        .BYTE   0

AY2:
        .BYTE   034H
        .BYTE   012H
        .BYTE   0
        .BYTE   0
        .BYTE   0
        .BYTE   0
        .BYTE   0

        .END    ;PROGRAM
```

Multiple-Precision Decimal Comparison 6O

Compares two multi-byte unsigned decimal (BCD) numbers and sets the Carry and Zero flags appropriately. The Zero flag is set to 1 if the operands are equal and to 0 if they are not equal. The Carry flag is set to 0 if the operand with the address higher in the stack (the subtrahend) is larger then the other operand (the minuend); the Carry flag is set to 1 otherwise. Thus the flags are set as if the subtrahend had been subtracted from the minuend.

Note: This program is exactly the same as Subroutine 6J, the multiple-precision binary comparison, since the CMP instruction operates the same in the decimal mode as in the binary mode. Hence, see Subroutine 6J for a listing and other details.

Examples

1. Data: Length of operands (in bytes) = 6
   Top operand (subtrahend) = 196528719340_{16}
   Bottom operand (minuend) = 456780153266_{16}

   Result: Zero flag = 0 (operands are not equal)
   Carry flag = 1 (subtrahend is not larger than minuend)

2. Data: Length of operands (in bytes) = 6
   Top operand (subtrahend) = 196528719340_{16}
   Bottom operand (minuend) = 196528719340_{16}

   Result: Zero flag = 1 (operands are equal)
   Carry flag = 1 (subtrahend is not larger than minuend)

3. Data: Length of operands (in bytes) = 6
   Top operand (subtrahend) = 196528719340_{16}
   Bottom operand (minuend) = 073785991074_{16}

   Result: Zero flag = 0 (operands are not equal)
   Carry flag = 0 (subtrahend is larger than minuend)

Bit Set (BITSET)

Sets a specified bit in a 16-bit word to 1.

Procedure: The program uses bits 0 through 2 of register X to determine which bit position to set and bit 3 to select a particular byte of the original word-length data. It then logically ORs the selected byte with a mask containing a 1 in the chosen bit position and 0s elsewhere. The masks with one 1 bit are available in a table.

Registers Used: All

Execution Time: 57 cycles

Program Size: 42 bytes

Data Memory Required: Two bytes anywhere in RAM (starting at address VALUE).

Special Case: Bit positions above 15 will be interpreted mod 16. That is, for example, bit position 16 is equivalent to bit position 0.

Entry Conditions

More significant byte of data in accumulator

Less significant byte of data in register Y

Bit number to set in register X

Exit Conditions

More significant byte of result in accumulator

Less significant byte of result in register Y

Examples

1. Data: (A) = $6E_{16}$ = 01101110_2 (more significant byte)
   (Y) = 39_{16} = 00111001_2 (less significant byte)
   (X) = $0C_{16}$ = 12_{10} (bit position to set)

   Result: (A) = $7E_{16}$ = 01111110_2 (more significant byte, bit 12 set to 1)
   (Y) = 39_{16} = 00111001_2 (less significant byte)

2. Data: (A) = $6E_{16}$ = 01101110_2 (more significant byte)
   (Y) = 39_{16} = 00111001_2 (less significant byte)
   (X) = 02_{16} = 2_{10} (bit position to set)

   Result: (A) = $6E_{16}$ = 01101110_2 (more significant byte)
   (Y) = $3D_{16}$ = 00111101_2 (less significant byte, bit 2 set to 1)

```
;       Title           Bit set                                       ;
;       Name:           BITSET                                        ;
;                                                                     ;
;                                                                     ;

;                                                                     ;
;       Purpose:        Set a bit in a 16 bit word.                   ;
;                                                                     ;
;       Entry:          Register A = High byte of word                ;
;                       Register Y = Low byte of word                 ;
;                       Register X = Bit number to set                ;
;                                                                     ;
;       Exit:           Register A = High byte of word with bit set   ;
;                       Register Y = Low byte of word with bit set    ;
;                                                                     ;
;       Registers used: All                                           ;
;                                                                     ;
;       Time:           57 cycles                                     ;
;                                                                     ;
;       Size:           Program 42 bytes                              ;
;                       Data     2 bytes                              ;
;                                                                     ;
;                                                                     ;

BITSET:
        ;SAVE THE DATA WORD
        STA     VALUE+1
        STY     VALUE

        ;BE SURE THAT THE BIT NUMBER IS BETWEEN 0 AND 15
        TXA
        AND     #0FH

        ;DETERMINE WHICH BYTE AND WHICH BIT IN THAT BYTE
        TAX                     ;SAVE BIT NUMBER IN X
        AND     #07H            ;THE LOWER 3 BITS OF THE BIT NUMBER
        TAY                     ; IS THE BIT IN THE BYTE, SAVE IN Y
        TXA                     ;RESTORE BIT NUMBER
        LSR     A               ;DIVIDE BY 8 TO DETERMINE BYTE
        LSR     A
        LSR     A
        TAX                     ;SAVE BYTE NUMBER (0 OR 1) IN X

        ;SET THE BIT
        LDA     VALUE,X         ;GET THE BYTE
        ORA     BITMSK,Y        ;SET THE BIT
        STA     VALUE,X

        ;RETURN THE RESULT IN REGISTERS A AND Y

        LDA     VALUE+1
        LDY     VALUE
        RTS
```

```
BITMSK: .BYTE    00000001B          ;BIT 0 = 1
        .BYTE    00000010B          ;BIT 1 = 1
        .BYTE    00000100B          ;BIT 2 = 1
        .BYTE    00001000B          ;BIT 3 = 1
        .BYTE    00010000B          ;BIT 4 = 1
        .BYTE    00100000B          ;BIT 5 = 1
        .BYTE    01000000B          ;BIT 6 = 1
        .BYTE    10000000B          ;BIT 7 = 1


;DATA
VALUE:  .BLOCK  2                   ;TEMPORARY FOR THE DATA WORD


;                                                                  ;
;                                                                  ;
;       SAMPLE EXECUTION                                           ;
;                                                                  ;
;                                                                  ;


SC0701:
        LDA      VAL+1              ;LOAD DATA WORD INTO A,Y
        LDY      VAL
        LDX      BITN               ;GET BIT NUMBER IN X
        JSR      BITSET             ;SET THE BIT
        BRK                         ;RESULT OF VAL = 5555H AND BITN = 0F
                                    ; REGISTER A = D5H, REGISTER Y = 55H
        JMP      SC0701

;TEST DATA, CHANGE FOR DIFFERENT VALUES
VAL:    .WORD    5555H
BITN:   .BYTE    0FH

        .END     ;PROGRAM
```

Bit Clear (BITCLR) 7B

Clears a specified bit in a 16-bit word.

Procedure: the program uses bits 0 through 2 of register X to determine which bit position to clear and bit 3 to select a particular byte of the original word-length data. It then logically ANDs the selected byte with a mask containing a 0 in the chosen bit position and 1s elsewhere. The masks with one 0 bit are available in a table.

Registers Used: All

Execution Time: 57 cycles

Program Size: 42 bytes

Data Memory Required: Two bytes anywhere in RAM (starting at address VALUE).

Special Case: Bit positions above 15 will be interpreted mod 16. That is, for example, bit position 16 is equivalent to bit position 0.

Entry Conditions

More significant byte of data in accumulator

Less significant byte of data in register Y

Bit number to clear in register X

Exit Conditions

More significant byte of result in accumulator

Less significant byte of result in register Y

Examples

1. Data: (A) = $6E_{16}$ = 01101110_2 (more significant byte)
   (Y) = 39_{16} = 00111001_{16} (less significant byte)
   (X) = $0E_{16}$ = 14_{10} (bit position to clear)

   Result: (A) = $2E_{16}$ = 01101110_2 (more significant byte, bit 14 cleared)
   (Y) = 39_{16} = 00111001_2 (less significant byte)

2. Data: (A) = $6E_{16}$ = 01101110_{16} (more significant byte)
   (Y) = 39_{16} = 00111001_2 (less significant byte)
   (X) = 04_{16} = 4_{10} (bit position to clear)

   Result: (A) = $6E_{16}$ = 01101110_2 (more significant byte)
   (Y) = 29_{16} = 00101001_2 (less significant byte, bit 4 cleared)

```
;       Title              Bit clear                                ;
;       Name:              BITCLR                                   ;
;                                                                   ;
;                                                                   ;

;                                                                   ;
;       Purpose:           Clear a bit in a 16 bit word.            ;
;                                                                   ;
;       Entry:             Register A = High byte of word           ;
;                          Register Y = Low byte of word            ;
;                          Register X = Bit number to clear         ;
;                                                                   ;
;       Exit:              Register A = High byte of word with bit cleared ;
;                          Register Y = Low byte of word with bit cleared  ;
;                                                                   ;
;       Registers used: All                                         ;
;                                                                   ;
;       Time:              57 cycles                                ;
;                                                                   ;
;       Size:              Program 42 bytes                         ;
;                          Data     2 bytes                         ;
;                                                                   ;
;                                                                   ;


BITCLR:
        ;SAVE THE DATA WORD
        STA     VALUE+1
        STY     VALUE

        ;BE SURE THAT THE BIT NUMBER IS BETWEEN 0 AND 15
        TXA
        AND     #0FH

        ;DETERMINE WHICH BYTE AND WHICH BIT IN THAT BYTE
        TAX                     ;SAVE BIT NUMBER IN X
        AND     #07H            ;THE LOWER 3 BITS OF THE BIT NUMBER
        TAY                     ; IS THE BIT IN THE BYTE, SAVE IN Y
        TXA                     ;RESTORE BIT NUMBER
        LSR     A               ;DIVIDE BY 8 TO DETERMINE BYTE
        LSR     A
        LSR     A
        TAX                     ;SAVE BYTE NUMBER (0 OR 1) IN X

        ;CLEAR THE BIT
        LDA     VALUE,X         ;GET THE BYTE
        AND     BITMSK,Y        ;CLEAR THE BIT
        STA     VALUE,X

        ;RETURN THE RESULT IN REGISTERS A AND Y

        LDA     VALUE+1
        LDY     VALUE
        RTS
```

```
BITMSK: .BYTE    11111110B        ;BIT 0 = 0
        .BYTE    11111101B        ;BIT 1 = 0
        .BYTE    11111011B        ;BIT 2 = 0
        .BYTE    11110111B        ;BIT 3 = 0
        .BYTE    11101111B        ;BIT 4 = 0
        .BYTE    11011111B        ;BIT 5 = 0
        .BYTE    10111111B        ;BIT 6 = 0
        .BYTE    01111111B        ;BIT 7 = 0


;DATA
VALUE:  .BLOCK   2                ;TEMPORARY FOR THE DATA WORD

;                                                                  ;
;                                                                  ;
;       SAMPLE EXECUTION                                           ;
;                                                                  ;
;                                                                  ;


SC0702:
        LDA      VAL+1            ;LOAD DATA WORD INTO A,Y
        LDY      VAL
        LDX      BITN             ;GET BIT NUMBER IN X
        JSR      BITCLR           ;CLEAR THE BIT
        BRK                       ;RESULT OF VAL = 5555H AND BITN = 00H IS
                                  ; REGISTER A = 55H, REGISTER Y = 54H
        JMP      SC0702

;TEST DATA, CHANGE FOR DIFFERENT VALUES
VAL:    .WORD    5555H
BITN:   .BYTE    0

        .END     ;PROGRAM
```

Sets the Carry flag to the value of a specified bit in a 16-bit word.

Procedure: The program uses bits 0 through 2 of register X to determine which bit position to test and bit 3 to select a particular byte of the original word-length data. It then logically ANDs the selected byte with a mask containing a 1 in the chosen bit position and 0s elsewhere. Since the result is zero if the tested bit is 0 and non-zero if the tested bit is 1, the Zero flag is set to the complement of the tested bit. Finally, the program sets the Carry flag to the complement of the Zero flag, thus making it the same as the tested bit through a double inversion.

Registers Used: All

Execution Time: Approximately 50 cycles

Program Size: 37 bytes

Data Memory Required: Two bytes anywhere in RAM (starting at address VALUE).

Special Case: Bit positions above 15 will be interpreted mod 16. That is, for example, bit position 16 is equivalent to bit position 0.

Entry Conditions

More significant byte of data in accumulator

Less significant byte of data in register Y

Bit position to test in register X

Exit Conditions

Carry set to value of specified bit position in data.

Examples

1. Data: $(A) = 6E_{16} = 01101110_2$ (more significant byte)
   $(Y) = 39_{16} = 00111001_2$ (less significant byte)
   $(X) = 0B_{16} = 11_{10}$ (bit position to test)

   Result: Carry = 1 (value of bit 11)

2. Data: $(A) = 6E_{16} = 01101110_2$ (more significant byte)
   $(Y) = 39_{16} = 00111001_2$ (less significant byte)
   $(X) = 06_{16} = 6_{10}$ (bit position to test)

   Result: Carry = 0 (value of bit 6)

```
;       Title               Bit test                                        ;
;       Name:               BITTST                                          ;
;                                                                           ;
;                                                                           ;

;                                                                           ;
;       Purpose:            Test a bit in a 16 bit word.                    ;
;                                                                           ;
;       Entry:              Register A = High byte of word                  ;
;                           Register Y = Low byte of word                   ;
;                           Register X = Bit number to test                 ;
;                                                                           ;
;       Exit:               CARRY = value of the tested bit                 ;
;                                                                           ;
;       Registers used: All                                                 ;
;                                                                           ;
;       Time:               Approximately 50 cycles                         ;
;                                                                           ;
;       Size:               Program 37 bytes                                ;
;                           Data     2 bytes                                ;
;                                                                           ;
;                                                                           ;


BITTST:
        ;SAVE THE DATA WORD
        STA     VALUE+1
        STY     VALUE

        ;BE SURE THAT THE BIT NUMBER IS BETWEEN 0 AND 15
        TXA
        AND     #0FH

        ;DETERMINE WHICH BYTE AND WHICH BIT IN THAT BYTE
        TAX                     ;SAVE BIT NUMBER IN X
        AND     #07H            ;THE LOWER 3 BITS OF THE BIT NUMBER
        TAY                     ; IS THE BIT IN THE BYTE, SAVE IN Y
        TXA                     ;RESTORE BIT NUMBER
        LSR     A               ;DIVIDE BY 8 TO DETERMINE BYTE
        LSR     A
        LSR     A
        TAX                     ;SAVE BYTE NUMBER (0 OR 1) IN X

        ;SET THE ZERO FLAG TO THE COMPLEMENT OF THE BIT
        LDA     VALUE,X         ;GET THE BYTE
        AND     BITMSK,Y        ;GET THE BIT
                                ;IF THE BIT IS 0 REGISTER A IS 0 AND Z IS 1
                                ;ELSE REGISTER A IS NOT 0 AND Z IS 0

        ;SET THE CARRY FLAG TO THE COMPLEMENT OF THE ZERO FLAG

        CLC                     ;ASSUME THE BIT IS 0
        BNE     EXIT            ;BRANCH IF THE BIT IS 0
        SEC                     ;ELSE THE BIT WAS 1
EXIT:
        RTS
```

```
BITMSK: .BYTE    00000001B         ;BIT 0 = 1
        .BYTE    00000010B         ;BIT 1 = 1
        .BYTE    00000100B         ;BIT 2 = 1
        .BYTE    00001000B         ;BIT 3 = 1
        .BYTE    00010000B         ;BIT 4 = 1
        .BYTE    00100000B         ;BIT 5 = 1
        .BYTE    01000000B         ;BIT 6 = 1
        .BYTE    10000000B         ;BIT 7 = 1

;DATA
VALUE:  .BLOCK   2                 ;TEMPORARY FOR THE DATA WORD

;                                                                        ;
;                                                                        ;
;       SAMPLE EXECUTION                                                 ;
;                                                                        ;
;                                                                        ;

SC0703:
        LDA      VAL+1             ;LOAD DATA WORD INTO A,Y
        LDY      VAL
        LDX      BITN              ;GET BIT NUMBER IN X
        JSR      BITTST            ;TEST THE BIT
        BRK                        ;RESULT OF VAL = 5555H AND BITN = 01 IS
                                   ;CARRY = 0
        JMP      SC0703

;TEST DATA, CHANGE FOR DIFFERENT VALUES
VAL:    .WORD    5555H
BITN:   .BYTE    01H

        .END     ;PROGRAM
```

Extracts a field of bits from a word and returns the field in the least significant bit positions. The width of the field and its starting bit position are specified.

Procedure: The program obtains a mask with the specified number of 1 bits from a table, shifts the mask left to align it with the specified starting bit position, and obtains the field by logically ANDing the mask and the data. It then normalizes the bit field by shifting it right so that it starts in bit 0.

Registers Used: All

Execution Time: 34 * STARTING BIT POSITION plus 138 cycles overhead. The starting bit position determines the number of times the mask must be shifted left and the bit field right. For example, if the field starts in bit 6, the execution time is

34 * 6 + 138 = 204 + 138 = 342 cycles

Program Size: 134 bytes

Data Memory Required: Six bytes anywhere in RAM for the index (one byte at address INDEX), the width of the field (one byte at address WIDTH), the data value (two bytes starting at address VALUE), and the mask (two bytes starting at address MASK).

Special Cases:

1. Requesting a field that would extend beyond the end of the word causes the program to return with only the bits through bit 15. That is, no wraparound is provided. If, for example, the user asks for a 10-bit field starting at bit 8, the program will return only 8 bits (bits 8 through 15).

2. Both the starting bit position and the number of bits in the field are interpreted mod 16. That is, for example, bit position 17 is equivalent to bit position 1 and a field of 20 bits is equivalent to a field of 4 bits.

Entry Conditions

Order in stack (starting from the top)

Less significant byte of return address
More significant byte of return address

Starting (lowest) bit position of field

Number of bits in the field

Less significant byte of data value
More significant byte of data value

Exit Conditions

More significant byte of bit field in accumulator

Less significant byte of bit field in register Y

Examples

1. Data: Value = $F67C_{16}$ = 1111011001111100_2
Starting bit position = 4
Number of bits in the field = 8

Result: Bit field = 0067_{16} = 0000000001100111_2
We have extracted 8 bits from the original data, starting with bit 4 (that is, bits 4 through 11).

2. Data: Value = $A2D4_{16} = 1010001011010100_2$
Starting bit position = 6
Number of bits in the field = 5

Result: Bit field = $000B_{16} = 0000000000001011_2$
We have extracted 5 bits from the original data, starting with bit 6 (that is, bits 6 through 10).

```
;       Title               Bit Field Extraction                           ;
;       Name:               BFE                                            ;
;                                                                          ;
;                                                                          ;
;                                                                          ;
;       Purpose:            Extract a field of bits from a 16 bit word and ;
;                           return the field normalized to bit 0.          ;
;                           NOTE: IF THE REQUESTED FIELD IS TOO LONG, THEN ;
;                                 ONLY THE BITS THROUGH BIT 15 WILL BE     ;
;                                 RETURNED. FOR EXAMPLE IF A 4 BIT FIELD IS ;
;                                 REQUESTED STARTING AT BIT 15 THEN ONLY 1 ;
;                                 BIT (BIT 15) WILL BE RETURNED.           ;
;                                                                          ;
;       Entry:              TOP OF STACK                                   ;
;                             Low byte of return address,                  ;
;                             High byte of return address,                 ;
;                             Starting (lowest) bit position in the field  ;
;                               (0..15),                                   ;
;                             Number of bits in the field (1..16),         ;
;                             Low byte of data word,                       ;
;                             High byte of data word,                      ;
;                                                                          ;
;       Exit:               Register A = High byte of field                ;
;                           Register Y = Low byte of field                 ;
;                                                                          ;
;       Registers used: All                                                ;
;                                                                          ;
;       Time:               138 cycles overhead plus                       ;
;                             (34 * starting bit position) cycles          ;
;                                                                          ;
;       Size:               Program 134 bytes                              ;
;                           Data      6 bytes                              ;
;                                                                          ;
;                                                                          ;

BFE:

        ;SAVE RETURN ADDRESS IN Y,X
        PLA
        TAY
        PLA
        TAX
```

```
        ;GET THE STARTING BIT POSITION OF THE FIELD
        PLA
        AND     #0FH            ;MAKE SURE INDEX IS A VALUE BETWEEN 0 AND 15
        STA     INDEX           ;SAVE INDEX

        ;GET THE NUMBER OF BITS IN THE FIELD (MAP FROM 1..WIDTH TO 0..WIDTH-1)
        PLA
        SEC
        SBC     #1              ;SUBTRACT 1
        AND     #0FH            ;MAKE SURE IT IS 0 TO 15
        STA     WIDTH           ;SAVE WIDTH

        ;GET THE DATA WORD
        PLA
        STA     VALUE
        PLA
        STA     VALUE+1

        ;RESTORE THE RETURN ADDRESS
        TXA
        PHA
        TYA
        PHA

        ;CONSTRUCT THE MASK
        ; INDEX INTO THE MASK ARRAY USING THE WIDTH PARAMETER
        LDA     WIDTH
        ASL     A               ;MULTIPLY BY 2 SINCE MASKS ARE WORD-LENGTH
        TAY
        LDA     MSKARY,Y
        STA     MASK
        INY
        LDA     MSKARY,Y
        STA     MASK+1

        ;SHIFT MASK LEFT INDEX TIMES TO ALIGN IT WITH THE BEGINNING
        ; OF THE FIELD
        LDY     INDEX
        BEQ     GETFLD          ;BRANCH IF INDEX = 0
SHFTLP:
        ASL     MASK            ;SHIFT LOW BYTE, CARRY := BIT 7
        ROL     MASK+1          ;ROTATE HIGH BYTE, BIT 0 := CARRY
        DEY
        BNE     SHFTLP          ;CONTINUE UNTIL INDEX = 0

        ;GET THE FIELD BY ANDING THE MASK AND THE VALUE
GETFLD:
        LDA     VALUE
        AND     MASK            ;AND LOW BYTE OF VALUE WITH MASK
        STA     VALUE           ;STORE IN VALUE
        LDA     VALUE+1
        AND     MASK+1          ;AND HIGH BYTE OF VALUE WITH MASK
        STA     VALUE+1         ;STORE IT
```

```
        ;NORMALIZE THE FIELD TO BIT 0 BY SHIFTING RIGHT INDEX TIMES
        LDY     INDEX
        BEQ     EXIT            ;BRANCH IF INDEX = 0
NORMLP:
        LSR     VALUE+1         ;SHIFT HIGH BYTE RIGHT, CARRY := BIT 0
        ROR     VALUE           ;ROTATE LOW BYTE RIGHT, BIT 7 := CARRY
        DEY
        BNE     NORMLP          ;CONTINUE UNTIL DONE

EXIT:
        LDY     VALUE
        LDA     VALUE+1
        RTS

        ;
        ;MASK ARRAY WHICH IS USED TO CREATE THE MASK
MSKARY:
        .WORD   0000000000000001B
        .WORD   0000000000000011B
        .WORD   0000000000000111B
        .WORD   0000000000001111B
        .WORD   0000000000011111B
        .WORD   0000000000111111B
        .WORD   0000000001111111B
        .WORD   0000000011111111B
        .WORD   0000000111111111B
        .WORD   0000001111111111B
        .WORD   0000011111111111B
        .WORD   0000111111111111B
        .WORD   0001111111111111B
        .WORD   0011111111111111B
        .WORD   0111111111111111B
        .WORD   1111111111111111B

INDEX:  .BLOCK  1               ;INDEX INTO WORD
WIDTH:  .BLOCK  1               ;WIDTH OF FIELD (NUMBER OF BITS)
VALUE:  .BLOCK  2               ;DATA WORD TO EXTRACT THE FIELD FROM
MASK:   .BLOCK  2               ;TEMPORARY FOR CREATING THE MASK


;                                                                   ;
;                                                                   ;
;       SAMPLE EXECUTION:                                           ;
;                                                                   ;
;                                                                   ;


SC0704:
        LDA     VAL+1
        PHA
        LDA     VAL
        PHA                     ;PUSH THE DATA WORD
        LDA     NBITS
        PHA                     ;PUSH FIELD WIDTH (NUMBER OF BITS)
        LDA     POS
```

```
        PHA                          ;PUSH INDEX TO FIRST BIT OF THE FIELD
        JSR     BFE                  ;EXTRACT
        BRK                          ;RESULT FOR VAL = 1234H, NBITS = 4, POS = 4 IS
                                     ;  REGISTER A = 0, REGISTER Y = 3
        JMP     SC0704

;TEST DATA, CHANGE FOR OTHER VALUES

        VAL:    .WORD   01234H
        NBITS:  .BYTE   4
        POS:    .BYTE   4

                .END    ;PROGRAM
```

Bit Field Insertion (BFI) 7E

Inserts a field of bits into a word. The width of the field and its starting (lowest) bit position are specified.

Procedure: The program obtains a mask with the specified number of 0 bits from a table. It then shifts the mask and the bit field left to align them with the specified starting bit position. It logically ANDs the mask and the original data word, thus clearing the required bit positions, and then logically ORs the result with the shifted bit field.

Registers Used: All

Execution Time: 31 * STARTING BIT POSITION plus 142 cycles overhead. The starting bit position of the field determines how many times the mask and the field must be shifted left. For example, if the field is inserted starting in bit 10, the execution time is

$$31 * 10 + 142 = 310 + 142 = 452 \text{ cycles.}$$

Program Size: 130 bytes

Data Memory Required: Eight bytes anywhere in RAM for the index (one byte at address INDEX), the width of the field (one byte at address WIDTH), the value to be inserted (two bytes starting at address INSVAL), the data value (two bytes starting at address VALUE), and the mask (two bytes starting at address MASK).

Special Cases:

1. Attempting to insert a field that would extend beyond the end of the word causes the program to insert only the bits through bit 15. That is, no wraparound is provided. If, for example, the user attempts to insert a 6-bit field starting at bit 14, only 2 bits (bits 14 and 15) are actually replaced.

2. Both the starting bit position and the length of the bit field are interpreted mod 16. That is, for example, bit position 17 is the same as bit position 1 and a 20-bit field is the same as a 4-bit field.

Entry Conditions

Order in stack (starting from the top)

Less significant byte of return address
More significant byte of return address

Lowest bit position (starting position) of field

Number of bits in the field

Less significant byte of bit field (value to insert)
More significant byte of bit field (value to insert)

Less significant byte of original data value
More significant byte of original data value

Exit Conditions

More significant byte of result in accumulator

Less significant byte of result in register Y

The result is the original data value with the bit field inserted, starting at the specified bit position.

Examples

1. Data: Value = $F67C_{16}$ = 1111011001111100_2
   Starting bit position = 4
   Number of bits in the field = 8
   Bit field = $008B_{16}$ = 0000000010001011_2

   Result: Value with bit field inserted = $F8BC_{16}$ = 1111100010111100_2
   The 8-bit field has been inserted into the original value starting at bit 4 (that is, into bits 4 through 11).

2. Data: Value = $A2D4_{16}$ = 1010001011010100_2
   Starting bit position = 6
   Number of bits in the field = 5
   Bit field = 0015_{16} = 0000000000010101_2

   Result: Value with bit field inserted = $A554_{16}$ = 1010010101010100_2
   The 5-bit field has been inserted into the original value starting at bit 6 (that is, into bits 6 through 10). Those five bits were 01011_2 ($0B_{16}$) and are now 10101_2 (15_{16}).

```
;       Title               Bit Field Insertion                        ;
;       Name:               BFI                                        ;
;                                                                      ;
;                                                                      ;

;                                                                      ;
;       Purpose:            Insert a field of bits which is normalized to ;
;                           bit 0 into a 16 bit word.                  ;
;                           NOTE: IF THE REQUESTED FIELD IS TOO LONG, THEN ;
;                                 ONLY THE BITS THROUGH BIT 15 WILL BE ;
;                                 INSERTED. FOR EXAMPLE IF A 4 BIT FIELD IS ;
;                                 TO BE INSERTED STARTING AT BIT 15 THEN ;
;                                 ONLY THE FIRST BIT WILL BE INSERTED AT ;
;                                 BIT 15.                              ;
;                                                                      ;
;       Entry:              TOP OF STACK                               ;
;                             Low byte of return address,              ;
;                             High byte of return address,             ;
;                             Bit position at which inserted field will ;
;                              start (0..15),                          ;
;                             Number of bits in the field (1..16),     ;
;                             Low byte of value to insert,             ;
;                             High byte of value to insert,            ;
;                             Low byte of value,                       ;
;                             High byte of value                       ;
;                                                                      ;
;       Exit:               Register A = High byte of value with field ;
;                                        inserted                      ;
;                           Register Y = Low byte of value with field  ;
;                                        inserted                      ;
;                                                                      ;
;       Registers used: All                                            ;
```

```
;                                                                      ;
;       Time:           142 cycles overhead plus                       ;
;                        (31 * starting bit position) cycles           ;
;                                                                      ;
;       Size:           Program 130 bytes                              ;
;                       Data      8 bytes                              ;
;                                                                      ;
;                                                                      ;

BFI:
        ;SAVE RETURN ADDRESS IN Y,X
        PLA
        TAY
        PLA
        TAX

        ;GET THE LOWEST BIT NUMBER OF THE FIELD
        PLA
        AND     #0FH            ;MAKE SURE INDEX IS A VALUE BETWEEN 0 AND 15
        STA     INDEX           ;SAVE INDEX

        ;GET THE NUMBER OF BITS IN THE FIELD (MAP FROM 1..WIDTH TO 0..WIDTH-1)
        PLA
        SEC
        SBC     #1              ;SUBTRACT 1
        AND     #0FH            ;MAKE SURE IT IS 0 TO 15
        STA     WIDTH           ;SAVE WIDTH

        ;GET THE VALUE TO BE INSERTED (BIT FIELD)
        PLA
        STA     INSVAL
        PLA
        STA     INSVAL+1

        ;GET THE DATA WORD
        PLA
        STA     VALUE
        PLA
        STA     VALUE+1

        ;RESTORE THE RETURN ADDRESS
        TXA
        PHA
        TYA
        PHA

        ;CONSTRUCT THE MASK
        ; INDEX INTO THE MASK ARRAY USING THE WIDTH PARAMETER
        LDA     WIDTH
        ASL     A               ;MULTIPLY BY 2 SINCE MASKS ARE WORD-LENGTH
        TAY
        LDA     MSKARY,Y
        STA     MASK
        INY
        LDA     MSKARY,Y
        STA     MASK+1
```

```
        ;SHIFT MASK AND BIT FIELD LEFT INDEX TIMES TO ALIGN THEM
        ; WITH THE BEGINING OF THE FIELD
        LDY     INDEX
        BEQ     INSERT          ;BRANCH IF INDEX = 0
SHFTLP:
        SEC                     ;FILL THE MASK WITH ONES
        ROL     MASK            ;ROTATE LOW BYTE SHIFTING A 1 TO BIT 0 AND
                                ; BIT 7 TO CARRY
        ROL     MASK+1          ;ROTATE HIGH BYTE, BIT 0 := CARRY
        ASL     INSVAL          ;SHIFT THE INSERT VALUE SHIFTING IN ZEROS
        ROL     INSVAL+1
        DEY
        BNE     SHFTLP          ;CONTINUE UNTIL INDEX = 0

        ;USE THE MASK TO ZERO THE FIELD AND THEN OR IN THE INSERT VALUE
INSERT:

        LDA     VALUE
        AND     MASK            ;AND LOW BYTE OF VALUE WITH MASK
        ORA     INSVAL
        TAY                     ;REGISTER Y = LOW BYTE OF THE NEW VALUE
        LDA     VALUE+1
        AND     MASK+1          ;AND HIGH BYTE OF VALUE WITH MASK
        ORA     INSVAL+1        ;REGISTER A = HIGH BYTE OF THE NEW VALUE

        ;RETURN
        RTS

        ;MASK ARRAY WHICH IS USED TO CREATE THE MASK
MSKARY:
        .WORD   1111111111111110B
        .WORD   1111111111111100B
        .WORD   1111111111111000B
        .WORD   1111111111110000B
        .WORD   1111111111100000B
        .WORD   1111111111000000B
        .WORD   1111111110000000B
        .WORD   1111111100000000B
        .WORD   1111111000000000B
        .WORD   1111110000000000B
        .WORD   1111100000000000B
        .WORD   1111000000000000B
        .WORD   1110000000000000B
        .WORD   1100000000000000B
        .WORD   1000000000000000B
        .WORD   0000000000000000B

INDEX:  .BLOCK  1               ;INDEX INTO WORD
WIDTH:  .BLOCK  1               ;WIDTH OF FIELD
INSVAL: .BLOCK  2               ;VALUE TO INSERT
VALUE:  .BLOCK  2               ;DATA WORD
MASK:   .BLOCK  2               ;TEMPORARY FOR CREATING THE MASK
```

```
;                                                                          ;
;                                                                          ;
;       SAMPLE EXECUTION:                                                  ;
;                                                                          ;
;                                                                          ;


SC0705:
        LDA     VAL+1           ;PUSH THE DATA WORD
        PHA
        LDA     VAL
        PHA
        LDA     VALINS+1        ;PUSH THE VALUE TO INSERT
        PHA
        LDA     VALINS
        PHA
        LDA     NBITS           ;PUSH THE FIELD WIDTH
        PHA
        LDA     POS             ;PUSH THE STARTING POSITION OF THE FIELD
        PHA
        JSR     BFI             ;INSERT
        BRK                     ;RESULT FOR VAL = 1234H, VALINS = 0EH,
                                ;           NBITS = 4, POS = 0CH IS
                                ;  REGISTER A = E2H, REGISTER Y = 34H
        JMP     SC0705

;TEST DATA, CHANGE FOR OTHER VALUES
VAL:    .WORD   01234H
VALINS: .WORD   0EH
NBITS:  .BYTE   04H
POS:    .BYTE   0CH

        .END    ;PROGRAM
```

Multiple-Precision Arithmetic Shift Right (MPASR) 7F

Shifts a multi-byte operand right arithmetically by a specified number of bit positions. The length of the number (in bytes) is 255 or less. The Carry flag is set to the value of the last bit shifted out of the rightmost bit position. The operand is stored with its least significant byte at the lowest address.

Procedure: The program obtains the sign bit from the most significant byte, shifts that bit to the Carry, and then rotates the entire operand right one bit, starting with the most significant byte. It repeats the operation for the specified number of shifts.

Registers Used: All

Execution Time: NUMBER OF SHIFTS * (18 + 18 * LENGTH OF OPERAND IN BYTES) + 85 cycles.

If, for example, NUMBER OF SHIFTS = 6 and LENGTH OF OPERAND IN BYTES = 8, the execution time is

6 * (18 + 18 * 8) + 85 = 6 * 162 + 85 = 1057 cycles

Program Size: 69 bytes

Data Memory Required: Three bytes anywhere in RAM plus two bytes on page 0. The three bytes anywhere in RAM are temporary storage for the number of shifts (one byte at address NBITS) and the length of the operand (one byte at address LENGTH) and the most significant byte of the operand (one byte at address MSB). The two bytes on page 0 hold a pointer to the operand (starting at address PTR, $00D0_{16}$ in the listing).

Special Cases:

1. If the length of the operand is zero, the program exits immediately with the operand unchanged and the Carry flag cleared.
2. If the number of shifts is zero, the program exits immediately with the operand unchanged and the Carry flag cleared.

Entry Conditions

Order in stack (starting from the top)

Less significant byte of return address
More significant byte of return address

Number of shifts (bit positions)

Length of the operand in bytes

Less significant byte of starting address of operand (address of its least significant byte)
More significant byte of starting address of operand (address of its least significant byte)

Exit Conditions

Operand shifted right arithmetically by the specified number of bit positions. The original sign bit is extended to the right. The Carry flag is set according to the last bit shifted from the rightmost bit position (or cleared if either the number of shifts or the length of the operand is zero).

Examples

1. Data: Length of operand (in bytes) = 08
   Operand = $85A4C719FE06741E_{16}$
   Number of shifts = 04

   Result: Shifted operand = $F85A4C719FE06741_{16}$.
   This is the original operand shifted right four bits arithmetically (the four most significant bits thus all take on the value of the original sign bit, which was 1).
   Carry = 1, since the last bit shifted from the rightmost bit position was 1.

2. Data: Length of operand (in bytes) = 04
   Operand = $3F6A42D3_{16}$
   Number of shifts = 03

   Result: Shifted operand = $07ED485A_{16}$.
   This is the original operand shifted right three bits arithmetically (the three most significant bits thus all take on the value of the original sign bit, which was 0).
   Carry = 0, since the last bit shifted from the rightmost bit position was 0.

```
;       Title               Multiple-precision arithmetic shift right     ;
;       Name:               MPASR                                         ;
;                                                                         ;
;                                                                         ;

;                                                                         ;
;       Purpose:            Arithmetic shift right a multi-byte operand   ;
;                           N bits.                                       ;
;                                                                         ;
;       Entry:              TOP OF STACK                                  ;
;                             Low byte of return address,                 ;
;                             High byte of return address,                ;
;                             Number of bits to shift,                    ;
;                             Length of the operand in bytes,             ;
;                             Low byte of address of the operand,         ;
;                             High byte of address of the operand         ;
;                                                                         ;
;                             The operand is stored with ARRAY[0] as its  ;
;                             least significant byte and ARRAY[LENGTH-1]  ;
;                             its most significant byte.                  ;
;                                                                         ;
;       Exit:               Operand shifted right with the most significant ;
;                           bit propagated.                               ;
;                           CARRY := Last bit shifted from least          ;
;                                    significant position.                ;
;                                                                         ;
;       Registers used: All                                               ;
;                                                                         ;
;       Time:               85 cycles overhead plus                       ;
;                            ((18 * length) + 18) cycles per shift        ;
;                                                                         ;
;       Size:               Program 69 bytes                              ;
;                           Data     3 bytes plus                         ;
;                                    2 bytes in page zero                 ;
;                                                                         ;
;                                                                         ;
```

```
        ;EQUATES
        PTR: .EQU       0D0H            ;PAGE ZERO FOR POINTER TO OPERAND

MPASR:
        ;SAVE RETURN ADDRESS
        PLA
        TAY
        PLA
        TAX

        ;GET NUMBER OF BITS
        PLA
        STA     NBITS
        ;GET LENGTH OF OPERAND
        PLA
        STA     LENGTH

        ;GET STARTING ADDRESS OF THE OPERAND
        PLA
        STA     PTR
        PLA
        STA     PTR+1

        ;RESTORE THE RETURN ADDRESS
        TXA
        PHA
        TYA
        PHA                     ;RESTORE RETURN ADDRESS

        ;INITIALIZE
        CLC                     ;CLEAR CARRY
        LDA     LENGTH
        BEQ     EXIT            ;EXIT IF LENGTH OF OPERAND IS 0
        LDA     NBITS
        BEQ     EXIT            ;EXIT IF NUMBER OF BITS TO SHIFT IS 0
                                ; WITH CARRY CLEAR

        ;DECREMENT POINTER SO THAT THE LENGTH BYTE MAY BE USED BOTH
        ; AS A COUNTER AND THE INDEX
        LDA     PTR
        BNE     MPASR1
        DEC     PTR+1           ;DECREMENT HIGH BYTE IF A BORROW IS NEEDED
MPASR1: DEC     PTR             ;ALWAYS DECREMENT LOW BYTE

        ;LOOP ON THE NUMBER OF SHIFTS TO PERFORM
        LDY     LENGTH
        LDA     (PTR),Y         ;GET THE MOST SIGNIFICANT BYTE
        STA     MSB             ;SAVE IT FOR THE SIGN

ASRLP:
        LDA     MSB             ;GET THE MOST SIGNIFICANT BYTE
        ASL     A               ;SHIFT BIT 7 TO CARRY FOR SIGN EXTENSION
        LDY     LENGTH          ;Y = INDEX TO LAST BYTE AND THE COUNTER

        ;SHIFT RIGHT ONE BIT
```

```
LOOP:
        LDA     (PTR),Y         ;GET NEXT BYTE
        ROR     A               ;ROTATE BIT 7 := CARRY, CARRY := BIT 0
        STA     (PTR),Y         ;STORE NEW VALUE
        DEY                     ;DECREMENT COUNTER
        BNE     LOOP            ;CONTINUE THROUGH ALL THE BYTES

        ;DECREMENT NUMBER OF SHIFTS
        DEC     NBITS           ;DECREMENT SHIFT COUNTER
        BNE     ASRLP           ;CONTINUE UNTIL DONE

EXIT:
        RTS

;DATA SECTION
NBITS:  .BLOCK  1               ;NUMBER OF BITS TO SHIFT
LENGTH: .BLOCK  1               ;LENGTH OF OPERAND IN BYTES
MSB:    .BLOCK  1               ;MOST SIGNIFICANT BYTE

;                                                                       ;
;                                                                       ;
;       SAMPLE EXECUTION:                                               ;
;                                                                       ;
;                                                                       ;


SC0706:
        LDA     AYADR+1 ;PUSH STARTING ADDRESS OF OPERAND
        PHA
        LDA     AYADR
        PHA

        LDA     #SZAY   ;PUSH LENGTH OF OPERAND
        PHA

        LDA     SHIFTS  ;PUSH NUMBER OF SHIFTS
        PHA
        JSR     MPASR   ;SHIFT
        BRK             ;RESULT OF SHIFTING AY = EDCBA987654321H, 4 BITS IS
                        ;                   AY = FEDCBA98765432H, C=0
                        ;  IN MEMORY AY   = 032H
                        ;            AY+1 = 054H
                        ;            AY+2 = 076H
                        ;            AY+3 = 098H
                        ;            AY+4 = 0BAH
                        ;            AY+5 = 0DCH
                        ;            AY+6 = 0FEH

        JMP     SC0706

;
;DATA SECTION
SZAY:   .EQU    7       ;LENGTH OF OPERAND
SHIFTS: .BYTE   4       ;NUMBER OF SHIFTS
AYADR:  .WORD   AY      ;STARTING ADDRESS OF OPERAND
AY:     .BYTE   21H,43H,65H,87H,0A9H,0CBH,0EDH

        .END    ;PROGRAM
```

Multiple-Precision Logical Shift Left (MPLSL) 7G

Shifts a multi-byte operand left logically by a specified number of bit positions. The length of the operand (in bytes) is 255 or less. The Carry flag is set to the value of the last bit shifted out of the leftmost bit position. The operand is stored with its least significant byte at the lowest address.

Procedure: The program clears the Carry initially (to fill with a 0 bit) and then rotates the entire operand left one bit, starting with the least significant byte. It repeats the operation for the specified number of shifts.

Registers Used: All

Execution Time: NUMBER OF SHIFTS * (16 + 20 * LENGTH OF OPERAND IN BYTES) + 73 cycles.

If, for example, NUMBER OF SHIFTS = 4 and LENGTH OF OPERAND IN BYTES = 6 (i.e., a 4-bit shift of a byte operand) the execution time is

4 * (6 + 20 * 6) + 73 = 4 * (136) + 73 = 617 cycles.

Data Memory Required: Two bytes anywhere in RAM plus two bytes on page 0. The two bytes anywhere in RAM are temporary storage for the number of shifts (one byte at address NBITS) and the length of the operand in bytes (one byte at address LENGTH). The two bytes on page 0 hold a pointer to the operand (starting at address PTR, $00D0_{16}$ in the listing).

Special Cases:

1. If the length of the operand is zero, the program exits immediately with the operand unchanged and the Carry flag cleared.
2. If the number of shifts is zero, the program exits immediately with the operand unchanged and the Carry flag cleared.

Entry Conditions

Order in stack (starting from the top)

Less significant byte of return address
More significant byte of return address

Number of shifts (bit positions)

Length of the operand in bytes

Less significant byte of starting address of operand (address of its least significant byte)

More significant byte of starting address of operand (address of its least significant byte)

Exit Conditions

Operand shifted left logically by the specified number of bit positions (the least significant bit positions are filled with zeros). The Carry flag is set according to the last bit shifted from the leftmost bit position (or cleared if either the number of shifts or the length of the operand is zero).

Examples

1. Data: Length of operand (in bytes) = 08
   Operand = $85A4C719FE06741E_{16}$
   Number of shifts = 04

   Result: Shifted operand = $5A4C719FE06741E0_{16}$. This is the original operand shifted left four bits logically; the four least significant bits are all cleared.

   Carry = 0, since the last bit shifted from the leftmost bit position was 0.

2. Data: Length of operand (in bytes) = 04
   Operand = $3F6A42D3_{16}$
   Number of shifts = 03

   Result: Shifted operand = $FB521698_{16}$. This is the original operand shifted left three bits logically; the three least significant bits are all cleared.

   Carry = 1, since the last bit shifted from the leftmost bit position was 1.

```
;       Title               Multiple-precision logical shift left      ;
;       Name:               MPLSL                                      ;
;                                                                      ;
;                                                                      ;
;                                                                      ;
;       Purpose:            Logical shift left a multi-byte operand N bits ;
;                                                                      ;
;       Entry:              TOP OF STACK                               ;
;                             Low byte of return address,              ;
;                             High byte of return address,             ;
;                             Number of bits to shift,                 ;
;                             Length of the operand in bytes,          ;
;                             Low byte of address of the operand,      ;
;                             High byte of address of the operand      ;
;                                                                      ;
;                             The operand is stored with ARRAY[0] as its ;
;                             least significant byte and ARRAY[LENGTH-1] ;
;                             its most significant byte.               ;
;                                                                      ;
;       Exit:               Operand shifted left filling the least     ;
;                           significant bits with zeros.               ;
;                           CARRY := Last most significant bit         ;
;                                                                      ;
;       Registers used: All                                            ;
;                                                                      ;
;       Time:               73 cycles overhead plus                    ;
;                             ((20 * length) + 16) cycles per shift    ;
;                                                                      ;
;       Size:               Program 54 bytes                           ;
;                           Data     2 bytes plus                      ;
;                                    2 bytes in page zero              ;
;                                                                      ;
```

```
        ;EQUATES
        PTR: .EQU       0D0H              ;PAGE ZERO FOR POINTER TO OPERAND

MPLSL:
        ;SAVE RETURN ADDRESS
        PLA
        TAY
        PLA
        TAX

        ;GET NUMBER OF BITS
        PLA
        STA     NBITS

        ;GET LENGTH OF OPERAND
        PLA
        STA     LENGTH

        ;GET STARTING ADDRESS OF THE OPERAND
        PLA
        STA     PTR
        PLA
        STA     PTR+1

        ;RESTORE THE RETURN ADDRESS
        TXA
        PHA
        TYA
        PHA                       ;RESTORE RETURN ADDRESS

        ;INITIALIZE
        CLC                       ;CLEAR CARRY
        LDA     LENGTH
        BEQ     EXIT              ;EXIT IF LENGTH OF THE OPERAND IS 0
        LDA     NBITS
        BEQ     EXIT              ;EXIT IF NUMBER OF BITS TO SHIFT IS 0
                                  ; WITH CARRY CLEAR

        ;LOOP ON THE NUMBER OF SHIFTS TO PERFORM
LSLLP:
        LDY     #0                ;Y = INDEX TO LOW BYTE OF THE OPERAND
        LDX     LENGTH            ;X = NUMBER OF BYTES
        CLC                       ;CLEAR CARRY TO FILL WITH ZEROS

        ;SHIFT LEFT ONE BIT
LOOP:
        LDA     (PTR),Y           ;GET NEXT BYTE
        ROL     A                 ;ROTATE BIT 0 := CARRY, CARRY := BIT 7
        STA     (PTR),Y           ;STORE NEW VALUE
        INY                       ;INCREMENT TO NEXT BYTE
        DEX                       ;DECREMENT COUNTER
        BNE     LOOP              ;CONTINUE THROUGH ALL THE BYTES

        ;DECREMENT NUMBER OF SHIFTS
        DEC     NBITS             ;DECREMENT SHIFT COUNTER
        BNE     LSLLP             ;CONTINUE UNTIL DONE
```

```
EXIT:
        RTS

;DATA SECTION
NBITS:  .BLOCK  1               ;NUMBER OF BITS TO SHIFT
LENGTH: .BLOCK  1               ;LENGTH OF OPERAND


;                                                                       ;
;                                                                       ;
;       SAMPLE EXECUTION:                                               ;
;                                                                       ;
;                                                                       ;


SC0707:
        LDA     AYADR+1 ;PUSH STARTING ADDRESS OF OPERAND
        PHA
        LDA     AYADR
        PHA

        LDA     #SZAY   ;PUSH LENGTH OF OPERAND
        PHA

        LDA     SHIFTS  ;PUSH NUMBER OF SHIFTS
        PHA
        JSR     MPLSL   ;SHIFT
        BRK             ;RESULT OF SHIFTING AY = EDCBA987654321H, 4 BITS IS
                        ;                    AY = DCBA9876543210H, C=0
                        ;  IN MEMORY AY   = 010H
                        ;            AY+1 = 032H
                        ;            AY+2 = 054H
                        ;            AY+3 = 076H
                        ;            AY+4 = 098H
                        ;            AY+5 = 0BAH
                        ;            AY+6 = 0DCH
        JMP     SC0707

;
;DATA SECTION
SZAY:   .EQU    7       ;LENGTH OF OPERAND
SHIFTS: .BYTE   4       ;NUMBER OF SHIFTS
AYADR:  .WORD   AY      ;STARTING ADDRESS OF OPERAND
AY:     .BYTE   21H,43H,65H,87H,0A9H,0CBH,0EDH

        .END    ;PROGRAM
```

Multiple-Precision Logical Shift Right (MPLSR) 7H

Shifts a multi-byte number right logically by a specified number of bit positions. The length of the operand (in bytes) is 255 or less. The Carry flag is set to the value of the last bit shifted out of the rightmost bit position. The operand is stored with its least significant byte at the lowest address.

Procedure: The program clears the Carry initially (to fill with a 0 bit) and then rotates the entire operand right one bit, starting with the most significant byte. It repeats the operation for the specified number of shifts.

Registers Used: All

Execution Time: NUMBER OF SHIFTS * (14 + 18 * LENGTH OF OPERAND IN BYTES) + 80 cycles.

If, for example, NUMBER OF SHIFTS = 4 and LENGTH OF OPERAND IN BYTES = 8 (i.e., a 4-bit shift of an 8-byte operand), the execution time is

4 * (14 + 18 * 8) + 80 = 4 * (158) + 80 = 712 cycles.

Program Size: 59 bytes

Data Memory Required: Two bytes anywhere in RAM plus two bytes on page 0. The two bytes anywhere in RAM are temporary storage for the number of shifts (one byte at address NBITS) and the length of the operand in bytes (one byte at address LENGTH). The two bytes on page 0 hold a pointer to the operand (starting at address PTR, $00D0_{16}$ in the listing).

Special Cases:

1. If the length of the operand is zero, the program exits immediately with the operand unchanged and the Carry flag cleared.

2. If the number of shifts is zero, the program exits immediately with the operand unchanged and the Carry flag cleared.

Entry Conditions

Order in stack (starting from the top)

Less significant byte of return address
More significant byte of return address

Number of shifts (bit positions)

Length of the operand in bytes

Less significant byte of starting address of operand (address of its least significant byte)

More significant byte of starting address of operand (address of its least significant byte)

Exit Conditions

Operand shifted right logically by the specified number of bit positions (the most significant bit positions are filled with zeros). The Carry flag is set according to the last bit shifted from the rightmost bit position (or cleared if either the the number of shifts or the length of the operand is zero).

Examples

1. Data: Length of operand (in bytes) = 08
   Operand = $85A4C719FE06741E_{16}$
   Number of shifts = 04

   Result: Shifted operand = $085A4C719FE06741_{16}$.
   This is the original operand shifted right four bits logically; the four most significant bits are all cleared.
   Carry = 1, since the last bit shifted from the rightmost position was 1.

2. Data: Length of operand (in bytes) = 04
   Operand = $3F6A42D3_{16}$
   Number of shifts = 03

   Result: Shifted operand = $07ED485A_{16}$.
   This is the original operand shifted right three bits logically; the three least significant bits are all cleared.
   Carry = 0, since the last bit shifted from the rightmost bit position was 0.

```
;                                                                    ;
;       Title           Multiple-Precision logical shift right      ;
;       Name:           MPLSR                                        ;
;                                                                    ;
;                                                                    ;

;                                                                    ;
;       Purpose:        Logical shift right a multi-byte operand N bits ;
;                                                                    ;
;       Entry:          TOP OF STACK                                 ;
;                         Low byte of return address,                ;
;                         High byte of return address,               ;
;                         Number of bits to shift,                   ;
;                         Length of the operand in bytes,            ;
;                         Low byte of address of the operand,        ;
;                         High byte of address of the operand        ;
;                                                                    ;
;                         The operand is stored with ARRAY[0] as its ;
;                         least significant byte and ARRAY[LENGTH-1] ;
;                         its most significant byte.                 ;
;                                                                    ;
;       Exit:           Operand shifted right filling the most       ;
;                       significant bits with zeros                  ;
;                       CARRY := Last bit shifted from the least     ;
;                                significant position                ;
;                                                                    ;
;       Registers used: All                                          ;
;                                                                    ;
;       Time:           85 cycles overhead plus                      ;
;                        ((18 * length) + 14) cycles per shift       ;
;                                                                    ;
;       Size:           Program 59 bytes                             ;
;                       Data     2 bytes plus                        ;
;                                2 bytes in page zero                ;
;                                                                    ;
;                                                                    ;
```

```
        ;EQUATES
        PTR: .EQU       0D0H              ;PAGE ZERO FOR POINTER TO OPERAND

MPLSR:
        ;SAVE RETURN ADDRESS
        PLA
        TAY
        PLA
        TAX

        ;GET NUMBER OF BITS
        PLA
        STA     NBITS

        ;GET LENGTH OF OPERAND
        PLA
        STA     LENGTH

        ;GET STARTING ADDRESS OF THE OPERAND
        PLA
        STA     PTR
        PLA
        STA     PTR+1

        ;RESTORE THE RETURN ADDRESS
        TXA
        PHA
        TYA
        PHA                     ;RESTORE RETURN ADDRESS

        ;INITIALIZE
        CLC                     ;CLEAR CARRY
        LDA     LENGTH
        BEQ     EXIT            ;EXIT IF LENGTH OF OPERAND IS 0
        LDA     NBITS
        BEQ     EXIT            ;EXIT IF NUMBER OF BITS TO SHIFT IS 0
                                ; WITH CARRY CLEAR

        ;DECREMENT POINTER SO THAT THE LENGTH BYTE MAY BE USED BOTH
        ; AS A COUNTER AND THE INDEX
        LDA     PTR
        BNE     MPLSR1
        DEC     PTR+1           ;DECREMENT HIGH BYTE IF A BORROW IS NEEDED
MPLSR1: DEC     PTR             ;ALWAY DECREMENT HIGH BYTE

        ;LOOP ON THE NUMBER OF SHIFTS TO PERFORM
LSRLP:
        LDY     LENGTH          ;Y = INDEX TO MSB AND COUNTER
        CLC                     ;CLEAR CARRY TO FILL WITH ZEROS

        ;SHIFT RIGHT ONE BIT
LOOP:
        LDA     (PTR),Y         ;GET NEXT BYTE
        ROR     A               ;ROTATE BIT 7 := CARRY, CARRY := BIT 0
        STA     (PTR),Y         ;STORE NEW VALUE
```

```
        DEY                          ;DECREMENT COUNTER
        BNE     LOOP                 ;CONTINUE THROUGH ALL THE BYTES

        ;DECREMENT NUMBER OF SHIFTS
        DEC     NBITS                ;DECREMENT SHIFT COUNTER
        BNE     LSRLP                ;CONTINUE UNTIL DONE

EXIT:
        RTS

;DATA SECTION
NBITS:  .BLOCK  1                    ;NUMBER OF BITS TO SHIFT
LENGTH: .BLOCK  1                    ;LENGTH OF OPERAND

;                                                                   ;
;                                                                   ;
;       SAMPLE EXECUTION:                                           ;
;                                                                   ;
;                                                                   ;


SC0708:
        LDA     AYADR+1 ;PUSH STARTING ADDRESS OF OPERAND
        PHA
        LDA     AYADR
        PHA

        LDA     #SZAY   ;PUSH LENGTH OF OPERAND
        PHA

        LDA     SHIFTS  ;PUSH NUMBER OF SHIFTS
        PHA
        JSR     MPLSR   ;SHIFT
        BRK             ;RESULT OF SHIFTING AY = EDCBA987654321H, 4 BITS IS
                        ;                   AY = 0EDCBA98765432H, C=0
                        ;  IN MEMORY AY   = 032H
                        ;            AY+1 = 054H
                        ;            AY+2 = 076H
                        ;            AY+3 = 098H
                        ;            AY+4 = 0BAH
                        ;            AY+5 = 0DCH
                        ;            AY+6 = 00EH

        JMP     SC0708

;
;DATA SECTION
SZAY:   .EQU    7       ;LENGTH OF OPERAND
SHIFTS: .BYTE   4       ;NUMBER OF SHIFTS
AYADR:  .WORD   AY      ;STARTING ADDRESS OF OPERAND
AY:     .BYTE   21H,43H,65H,87H,0A9H,0CBH,0EDH

        .END    ;PROGRAM
```

Multiple-Precision Rotate Right (MPRR) 7I

Rotates a multi-byte operand right by a specified number of bit positions (as if the most significant bit and least significant bit were connected directly). The length of the operand in bytes is 255 or less. The Carry flag is set to the value of the last bit shifted out of the rightmost bit position. The operand is stored with its least significant byte at the lowest address.

Procedure: The program shifts bit 0 of the least significant byte of the operand to the Carry flag and then rotates the entire operand right one bit, starting with the most significant byte. It repeats the operation for the specified number of shifts.

Registers used: All

Execution Time: NUMBER OF SHIFTS * (21 + 18 * LENGTH OF OPERAND IN BYTES) + 85 cycles.

If for example, NUMBER OF SHIFTS = 6 and LENGTH OF OPERAND IN BYTES = 4 (i.e. a 6-bit shift of a 4-byte operand), the execution time is

6 * (21 + 18 * 4) + 85 = 6 * (93) + 85 + 643 cycles.

Program Size: 63 bytes

Data Memory Required: Two bytes anywhere in RAM plus two bytes on page 0. The two bytes anywhere in RAM are temporary storage for the number of shifts (one byte at address NBITS) and the length of the operand in bytes (one byte at address LENGTH). The two bytes on page 0 hold a pointer to the operand (starting at address PTR, $00D0_{16}$ in the listing).

Special Cases:

1. If the length of the operand is zero, the program exits immediately with the operand unchanged and the Carry flag cleared.

2. If the number of shifts is zero, the program exits immediately with the operand unchanged and the Carry flag cleared.

Entry Conditions

Order in stack (starting from the top)

Less significant byte of return address
More significant byte of return address

Number of shifts (bit positions)

Length of the operand in bytes

Less significant byte of starting address of operand (address of its least significant byte)

More significant byte of starting address of operand (address of its least significant byte)

Exit Conditions

Operand rotated right by the specified number of bit positions (the most significant bit positions are filled from the least significant bit positions). The Carry flag is set according to the last bit shifted from the rightmost bit position (or cleared if either the number of shifts or the length of the operand is zero).

Examples

1. Data: Length of operand (in bytes) = 08
   Operand = $85A4C719FE06741E_{16}$
   Number of shifts = 04

   Result: Shifted operand = $E85A4C719F306741_{16}$. This is the original operand rotated right four bits: the four most significant bits are equivalent to the original four least significant bits.

   Carry = 1, since the last bit shifted from the rightmost bit position was 1.

2. Data: Length of operand (in bytes) = 04
   Operand = $3F6A42D3_{16}$
   Number of shifts = 03

   Result: Shifted operand = $67ED485A_{16}$. This is the original operand rotated right 3 bits; the three most significant bits (011) are equivalent to the original three least significant bits.

   Carry = 0, since the last bit shifted from the rightmost bit position was 0.

```
;       Title              Multiple-precision rotate right           ;
;       Name:              MPRR                                      ;
;                                                                    ;
;                                                                    ;

;                                                                    ;
;       Purpose:           Rotate right a multi-byte operand N bits  ;
;                                                                    ;
;       Entry:             TOP OF STACK                              ;
;                            Low byte of return address,             ;
;                            High byte of return address,            ;
;                            Number of bits to shift,                ;
;                            Length of the operand in bytes,         ;
;                            Low byte of address of the operand,     ;
;                            High byte of address of the operand     ;
;                                                                    ;
;                            The operand is stored with ARRAY[0] as its ;
;                            least significant byte and ARRAY[LENGTH-1] ;
;                            its most significant byte.              ;
;                                                                    ;
;       Exit:              Operand rotated right                     ;
;                          CARRY := Last bit shifted from the least  ;
;                                   significant position             ;
;                                                                    ;
;       Registers used: All                                          ;
;                                                                    ;
;       Time:              85 cycles overhead plus                   ;
;                           ((18 * length) + 21) cycles per shift    ;
;                                                                    ;
;       Size:              Program 63 bytes                          ;
;                          Data     2 bytes plus                     ;
;                                   2 bytes in page zero             ;
;                                                                    ;
;                                                                    ;

;EQUATES
PTR:  .EQU         0D0H                ;PAGE ZERO FOR POINTER TO OPERAND
```

```
MPRR:
        ;SAVE RETURN ADDRESS
        PLA
        TAY
        PLA
        TAX

        ;GET NUMBER OF BITS
        PLA
        STA     NBITS

        ;GET LENGTH OF OPERAND


        PLA
        STA     LENGTH

        ;GET STARTING ADDRESS OF THE OPERAND
        PLA
        STA     PTR
        PLA
        STA     PTR+1

        ;RESTORE THE RETURN ADDRESS
        TXA
        PHA
        TYA
        PHA                         ;RESTORE RETURN ADDRESS

        ;INITIALIZE
        CLC                         ;CLEAR CARRY
        LDA     LENGTH
        BEQ     EXIT                ;EXIT IF LENGTH OF THE OPERAND IS 0
        LDA     NBITS
        BEQ     EXIT                ;EXIT IF NUMBER OF BITS TO SHIFT IS 0
                                    ; WITH CARRY CLEAR

        ;DECREMENT POINTER SO THAT THE LENGTH BYTE MAY BE USED BOTH
        ; AS A COUNTER AND THE INDEX
        LDA     PTR
        BNE     MPRR1
        DEC     PTR+1               ;DECREMENT HIGH BYTE IF A BORROW IS NEEDED
MPRR1:  DEC     PTR                 ;ALWAYS DECREMENT LOW BYTE

        ;LOOP ON THE NUMBER OF SHIFTS TO PERFORM
RRLP:
        LDY     #1
        LDA     (PTR),Y             ;GET LOW BYTE OF THE OPERAND
        LSR     A                   ;CARRY := BIT 0 OF LOW BYTE
        LDY     LENGTH              ;Y = INDEX TO HIGH BYTE AND COUNTER

        ;ROTATE RIGHT ONE BIT
LOOP:
        LDA     (PTR),Y             ;GET NEXT BYTE
        ROR     A                   ;ROTATE BIT 7 := CARRY, CARRY := BIT 0
```

```
        STA     (PTR),Y           ;STORE NEW VALUE
        DEY                       ;DECREMENT COUNTER
        BNE     LOOP              ;CONTINUE THROUGH ALL THE BYTES

        ;DECREMENT NUMBER OF SHIFTS
        DEC     NBITS             ;DECREMENT SHIFT COUNTER
        BNE     RRLP              ;CONTINUE UNTIL DONE

EXIT:
        RTS

;DATA SECTION
NBITS:  .BLOCK  1                 ;NUMBER OF BITS TO SHIFT
LENGTH: .BLOCK  1                 ;LENGTH OF OPERAND


;                                                                       ;
;                                                                       ;
;       SAMPLE EXECUTION:                                               ;
;                                                                       ;
;                                                                       ;


SC0709:
        LDA     AYADR+1 ;PUSH STARTING ADDRESS OF OPERAND
        PHA
        LDA     AYADR
        PHA

        LDA     #SZAY   ;PUSH LENGTH OF OPERAND
        PHA

        LDA     SHIFTS  ;PUSH NUMBER OF SHIFTS
        PHA
        JSR     MPRR    ;ROTATE
        BRK             ;RESULT OF ROTATING AY = EDCBA987654321H 4 BITS IS
                        ;                   AY = 1EDCBA98765432H C=0
                        ;  IN MEMORY AY   = 032H
                        ;            AY+1 = 054H
                        ;            AY+2 = 076H
                        ;            AY+3 = 098H
                        ;            AY+4 = 0BAH
                        ;            AY+5 = 0DCH
                        ;            AY+6 = 01EH
        JMP     SC0709

;
;DATA SECTION
SZAY:   .EQU    7       ;LENGTH OF OPERAND IN BYTES
SHIFTS: .BYTE   4       ;NUMBER OF SHIFTS
AYADR:  .WORD   AY      ;STARTING ADDRESS OF OPERAND
AY:     .BYTE   21H,43H,65H,87H,0A9H,0CBH,0EDH

        .END    ;PROGRAM
```

Multiple-Precision Rotate Left (MPRL) 7J

Rotates a multi-byte operand left by a specified number of bit positions (i.e., as if the most significant bit and least significant bit were connected directly). The length of the operand in bytes is 255 or less. The Carry flag is set to the value of the last bit shifted out of the leftmost bit position. The operand is stored with its least significant byte at the lowest address.

Procedure: The program shifts bit 7 of the most significant byte of the operand to the Carry flag. It then rotates the entire operand left one bit, starting with the least significant byte. It repeats the operation for the specified number of shifts.

Registers Used: All

Execution Time: NUMBER OF SHIFTS * (27 + 20 * LENGTH OF OPERAND IN BYTES) + 73 cycles.

If, for example, NUMBER OF SHIFTS = 4 and LENGTH OF OPERAND IN BYTES = 8 (i.e., a 4-bit shift of an 8-byte operand), the execution time is

4 * (27 + 20 * 8) + 73 = 4 * (187) + 73 = 821 cycles.

Program Size: 60 bytes

Data Memory Required: Two bytes anywhere in RAM plus two bytes on page 0. The two bytes anywhere in RAM are temporary storage for the number of shifts (one byte at address NBITS) and the length of the operand in bytes (one byte at address LENGTH). The two bytes on page 0 hold a pointer to the operand (starting at address PTR, $00D0_{16}$ in the listing).

Special Cases:

1. If the length of the operand is zero, the program exits immediately with the operand unchanged and the Carry flag cleared.
2. If the number of shifts is zero, the program exits immediately with the operand unchanged and the Carry flag cleared.

Entry Conditions

Order in stack (starting from the top)

Less significant byte of return address
More significant byte of return address

Number of shifts (bit positions)

Length of the operand in bytes

Less significant byte of starting address of operand (address of its least significant byte)

More significant byte of starting address of operand (address of its least significant byte)

Exit Conditions

Operand rotated left by the specified number of bit positions (the least significant bit positions are filled from the most significant bit positions). The Carry flag is set according to the last bit shifted from the leftmost bit position (or cleared if either the number of shifts or the length of the operand is zero).

Examples

1. Data: Length of operand (in bytes) = 08
   Operand = $85A4C719FE06741E_{16}$
   Number of shifts = 04

   Result: Shifted operand = $5A4C719FE06741E8_{16}$. This is the original operand rotated left four bits; the four least significant bits are equivalent to the original four most significant bits.

   Carry = 0, since the last bit shifted from the leftmost bit position was 0.

2. Data: Length of operand (in bytes) = 04
   Operand = $3F6A42D3_{16}$
   Number of shifts = 03

   Result: Shifted operand = $FB521699_{16}$. This is the original operand rotated left three bits; the three least significant bits (001) are equivalent to the original three most significant bits.

   Carry = 1, since the last bit shifted from the leftmost bit position was 1.

```
;       Title              Multiple-precision rotate left              ;
;       Name:              MPRL                                        ;
;                                                                      ;
;                                                                      ;
;                                                                      ;
;       Purpose:           Rotate left a multi-byte operand N bits     ;
;                                                                      ;
;       Entry:             TOP OF STACK                                ;
;                            Low byte of return address,               ;
;                            High byte of return address,              ;
;                            Number of bits to shift,                  ;
;                            Length of the operand in bytes,           ;
;                            Low byte of address of the operand,       ;
;                            High byte of address of the operand       ;
;                                                                      ;
;                            The operand is stored with ARRAY[0] as its ;
;                            least significant byte and ARRAY[LENGTH-1] ;
;                            its most significant byte.                ;
;                                                                      ;
;       Exit:              Number rotated left                         ;
;                          CARRY := Last bit shifted from the most     ;
;                                   significant position               ;
;                                                                      ;
;       Registers used: All                                            ;
;                                                                      ;
;       Time:              73 cycles overhead plus                     ;
;                           ((20 * length) + 27) cycles per shift      ;
;                                                                      ;
;       Size:              Program 60 bytes                            ;
;                          Data     2 bytes plus                       ;
;                                   2 bytes in page zero               ;
;                                                                      ;
;                                                                      ;

;EQUATES
PTR:  .EQU      0D0H            ;PAGE ZERO FOR POINTER TO OPERAND
```

```
MPRL:
        ;SAVE RETURN ADDRESS
        PLA
        TAY
        PLA
        TAX

        ;GET NUMBER OF BITS
        PLA
        STA     NBITS

        ;GET LENGTH OF OPERAND

        PLA
        STA     LENGTH

        ;GET STARTING ADDRESS OF THE OPERAND
        PLA
        STA     PTR
        PLA
        STA     PTR+1

        ;RESTORE THE RETURN ADDRESS
        TXA
        PHA
        TYA
        PHA                         ;RESTORE RETURN ADDRESS

        ;INITIALIZE
        CLC                         ;CLEAR CARRY
        LDA     LENGTH
        BEQ     EXIT                ;EXIT IF THE LENGTH OF THE OPERAND IS 0
        LDA     NBITS
        BEQ     EXIT                ;EXIT IF NUMBER OF BITS TO SHIFT IS 0
                                    ; WITH CARRY CLEAR

        ;LOOP ON THE NUMBER OF SHIFTS TO PERFORM
RLLP:
        LDY     LENGTH
        DEY
        LDA     (PTR),Y             ;GET HIGH BYTE OF THE OPERAND
        ASL     A                   ;CARRY := BIT 7 OF HIGH BYTE
        LDY     #0                  ;Y = INDEX TO LEAST SIGNIFICANT BYTE
        LDX     LENGTH              ;X = NUMBER OF BYTES

        ;ROTATE LEFT ONE BIT
LOOP:
        LDA     (PTR),Y             ;GET NEXT BYTE
        ROL     A                   ;ROTATE BIT 7 := CARRY, CARRY := BIT 0
        STA     (PTR),Y             ;STORE NEW VALUE
        INY                         ;INCREMENT TO NEXT BYTE
        DEX                         ;DECREMENT COUNTER
        BNE     LOOP                ;CONTINUE THROUGH ALL THE BYTES

        ;DECREMENT NUMBER OF SHIFTS
        DEC     NBITS               ;DECREMENT SHIFT COUNTER
        BNE     RLLP                ;CONTINUE UNTIL DONE
```

```
EXIT:
        RTS

;DATA SECTION
NBITS:  .BLOCK  1               ;NUMBER OF BITS TO SHIFT
LENGTH: .BLOCK  1               ;LENGTH OF OPERAND

;                                                              ;
;                                                              ;
;       SAMPLE EXECUTION:                                      ;
;                                                              ;
;                                                              ;


SC0710:
        LDA     AYADR+1 ;PUSH STARTING ADDRESS OF OPERAND
        PHA
        LDA     AYADR
        PHA

        LDA     #SZAY   ;PUSH LENGTH OF OPERAND
        PHA

        LDA     SHIFTS  ;PUSH NUMBER OF SHIFTS
        PHA
        JSR     MPRL    ;ROTATE
        BRK             ;RESULT OF ROTATING AY = EDCBA987654321H, 4 BITS IS
                        ;                   AY = DCBA987654321EH, C=0
                        ;  IN MEMORY AY   = 01EH
                        ;            AY+1 = 032H
                        ;            AY+2 = 054H
                        ;            AY+3 = 076H
                        ;            AY+4 = 098H
                        ;            AY+5 = 0BAH
                        ;            AY+6 = 0DCH
        JMP     SC0710

;
;DATA SECTION
SZAY:   .EQU    7       ;LENGTH OF OPERAND IN BYTES
SHIFTS: .BYTE   4       ;NUMBER OF SHIFTS
AYADR:  .WORD   AY      ;ADDRESS OF OPERAND
AY:     .BYTE   21H,43H,65H,87H,0A9H,0CBH,0EDH

        .END    ;PROGRAM
```

String Compare (STRCMP)

Compares two strings and sets the Carry and Zero flags appropriately. The Zero flag is set to 1 if the strings are identical and to 0 otherwise. The Carry flag is set to 0 if the string with the address higher in the stack (string 2) is larger than the other string (string 1); the Carry flag is set to 1 otherwise. The strings are a maximum of 255 bytes long and the actual characters are preceded by a byte containing the length. If the two strings are identical through the length of the shorter, then the longer string is considered to be larger.

Procedure: The program first determines which string is shorter from the lengths which precede the actual characters. It then compares the strings one byte at a time through the length of the shorter. If the program finds corresponding bytes that are not the same through the length of the shorter, the program sets the flags by comparing the lengths.

Registers Used: All

Execution Time:

1. If the strings are not identical through the length of the shorter, the approximate execution time is

81 + 19 * NUMBER OF CHARACTERS COMPARED.

If, for example, the routine compares five characters before finding a difference, the execution time is

81 + 19 * 5 = 81 + 95 = 176 cycles.

2. If the strings are identical through the length of the shorter, the approximate execution time is

93 + 19 * LENGTH OF SHORTER STRING.

If, for example, the shorter string is eight bytes long, the execution time is

93 + 19 * 8 = 93 + 152 = 245 cycles.

Program Size: 52 bytes

Data Memory Required: Four bytes on page 0, two bytes starting at address S1ADR ($00D0_{16}$ in the listing) for a pointer to string 1 and two bytes starting at address S2ADR ($00D2_{16}$ in the listing) for a pointer to string 2.

Entry Conditions

Order in stack (starting from the top)

Less significant byte of return address
More significant byte of return address

Less significant byte of starting address of string 2

More significant byte of starting address of string 2

Less significant byte of starting address of string 1

More significant byte of starting address of string 1

Exit Conditions

Flags set as if string 2 had been subtracted from string 1 or, if the strings are equal through the length of the shorter, as if the length of string 2 had been subtracted from the length of string 1.

Zero flag = 1 if the strings are identical, 0 if they are not identical.

Carry flag = 0 if string 2 is larger than string 1, 1 if they are identical or string 1 is larger. If the strings are the same through the length of the shorter, the longer one is considered to be larger.

Examples

1. Data: String 1 = 05'PRINT' (05 is the length of the string)
   String 2 = 03'END' (03 is the length of the string)

   Result: Zero flag = 0 (strings are not identical)
   Carry flag = 1 (string 2 is not larger than string 1)

2. Data: String 1 = 05'PRINT' (05 is the length of the string)
   String 2 = 02'PR' (02 is the length of the string)

   Result: Zero flag = 0 (strings are not identical)
   Carry flag = 1 (string 2 is not larger than string 1)

The longer string (string 1) is considered to be larger. If you want to determine whether string 2 is an abbreviation of string 1, you could use Subroutine 8C (FIND THE POSITION OF A SUBSTRING) and determine whether string 2 was part of string 1 and started at the first character.

3. Data: String 1 = 05'PRINT' (05 is the length of the string)
   String 2 = 06'SYSTEM' (06 is the length of the string)

   Result: Zero flag = 0 (strings are not identical)
   Carry flag = 0 (string 2 is larger than string 1)

We are assuming here that the strings consist of ASCII characters. Note that the byte preceding the actual characters contains a hexadecimal number (the length of the string), not a character. We have represented this byte as two hexadecimal digits in front of the string; the string itself is surrounded by single quotation marks.

Note also that this particular routine treats spaces like any other characters. If for example, the strings are ASCII, the routine will find that SPRINGMAID is larger than SPRING MAID, since an ASCII M ($4D_{16}$) is larger than an ASCII space (20_{16}).

```
;       Title           String compare                                  ;
;       Name:           STRCMP                                          ;
;                                                                       ;
;                                                                       ;

;                                                                       ;
;       Purpose:        Compare 2 strings and return C and Z flags set ;
;                       or cleared.                                     ;
;                                                                       ;
;       Entry:          TOP OF STACK                                    ;
;                         Low byte of return address,                   ;
;                         High byte of return address,                  ;
;                         Low byte of string 2 address,                 ;
;                         High byte of string 2 address,                ;
;                         Low byte of string 1 address,                 ;
;                         High byte of string 1 address                 ;
;                                                                       ;
;                         A string is a maximum of 255 bytes long plus ;
;                         a length byte which precedes it.              ;
;                                                                       ;
;       Exit:           IF string 1 = string 2 THEN                     ;
;                         Z=1,C=1                                       ;
```

```
;                         IF string 1 > string 2 THEN                  ;
;                           Z=0,C=1                                    ;
;                         IF string 1 < string 2 THEN                  ;
;                           Z=0,C=0                                    ;
;                                                                      ;
;       Registers used: All                                            ;
;                                                                      ;
;       Time:             Worst case timing for strings which are equal. ;
;                           93 cycles maximum overhead plus (19 * length) ;
;                                                                      ;
;       Size:             Program 52 bytes                             ;
;                         Data     4 bytes in page zero                ;
;                                                                      ;
;                                                                      ;

;EQUATES
S1ADR   .EQU    0D0H            ;PAGE ZERO POINTER TO STRING 1
S2ADR   .EQU    0D2H            ;PAGE ZERO POINTER TO STRING 2


STRCMP:
        ;GET RETURN ADDRESS
        PLA
        TAY
        PLA
        TAX

        ;GET THE STARTING ADDRESS OF STRING 2
        PLA
        STA     S2ADR
        PLA
        STA     S2ADR+1

        ;GET THE STARTING ADDRESS OF STRING 1
        PLA
        STA     S1ADR
        PLA
        STA     S1ADR+1

        ;RESTORE RETURN ADDRESS
        TXA
        PHA
        TYA
        PHA

        ;
        ;DETERMINE WHICH STRING IS SHORTER
        LDY     #0
        LDA     (S1ADR),Y       ;GET LENGTH OF STRING #1
        CMP     (S2ADR),Y
        BCC     BEGCMP          ;IF STRING #2 IS SHORTER THEN
        LDA     (S2ADR),Y       ; USE ITS LENGTH INSTEAD

        ;
        ;COMPARE THE STRINGS THROUGH THE LENGTH OF THE SHORTER STRING
```

```
BEGCMP:
        TAX                     ;X IS THE LENGTH OF THE SHORTER STRING
        BEQ     TSTLEN          ;BRANCH IF LENGTH IS ZERO

        LDY     #1              ;POINT AT FIRST CHARACTER OF STRINGS
CMPLP:
        LDA     (S1ADR),Y
        CMP     (S2ADR),Y
        BNE     EXIT            ;BRANCH IF CHARACTERS ARE NOT EQUAL
                                ;  Z,C WILL BE PROPERLY SET OR CLEARED
                                ;ELSE
        INY                     ; NEXT CHARACTER
        DEX                     ; DECREMENT COUNTER
        BNE     CMPLP           ; CONTINUE UNTIL ALL BYTES ARE COMPARED

        ;
        ;THE 2 STRINGS ARE EQUAL TO THE LENGTH OF THE SHORTER
        ;SO USE THE LENGTHS AS THE BASIS FOR SETTING THE FLAGS
TSTLEN:
        LDY     #0              ;COMPARE LENGTHS
        LDA     (S1ADR),Y
        CMP     (S2ADR),Y       ;SET OR CLEAR THE FLAGS

        ;
        ;EXIT FROM STRING COMPARE
EXIT:
        RTS
;                                                                       ;
;                                                                       ;
;       SAMPLE EXECUTION:                                               ;
;                                                                       ;
;                                                                       ;

SC0801:
        LDA     SADR1+1         ;PUSH STARTING ADDRESS OF STRING 1
        PHA
        LDA     SADR1
        PHA
        LDA     SADR2+1         ;PUSH STARTING ADDRESS OF STRING 2
        PHA
        LDA     SADR2
        PHA
        JSR     STRCMP          ;COMPARE
        BRK                     ;RESULT OF COMPARING "STRING 1" AND "STRING 2"
                                ;IS STRING 1 LESS THAN STRING 2 SO
                                ;  Z=0,C=0
        JMP     SC0801          ;LOOP FOR ANOTHER TEST

;
;TEST DATA, CHANGE TO TEST OTHER VALUES
SADR1   .WORD   S1
SADR2   .WORD   S2
S1      .BYTE   20H,"STRING 1                        "
S2      .BYTE   20H,"STRING 2                        "

        .END    ;PROGRAM
```

String Concatenation (CONCAT) 8B

Combines (concatenates) two strings, placing the second immediately after the first in memory. If the concatenation would produce a string longer than a specified maximum, the program concatenates only enough of string 2 to give the combined string its maximum length. The Carry flag is cleared if all of string 2 can be concatenated and set to 1 if part of string 2 must be dropped. Both strings are a maximum of 255 bytes long and the actual characters are preceded by a byte containing the length.

Procedure: The program uses the length of string 1 to determine where to start adding characters and the length of string 2 to determine how many characters to add. If the sum of the lengths exceeds the maximum, the program indicates an overflow and reduces the number of characters it must add (the number is the maximum length minus the length of string 1). It then moves the appropriate number of characters from string 2 to the end of string 1, updates the length of string 1, and sets the Carry flag to indicate whether any characters had to be discarded.

Registers Used: All

Execution Time: Approximately 40 * NUMBER OF CHARACTERS CONCATENATED plus 164 cycles overhead. The NUMBER OF CHARACTERS CONCATENATED is normally the length of string 2, but will be the maximum length of string 1 minus its current length if the combined string would be longer than the maximum. If, for example, NUMBER OF CHARACTERS CONCATENATED is 14_{16} (20_{10}), the execution time is

$$40 * 20 + 161 = 800 + 164 = 964 \text{ cycles.}$$

Program Size: 141 bytes

Data Memory Required: Seven bytes anywhere in RAM plus four bytes on page 0. The seven bytes anywhere in RAM are temporary storage for the maximum length of string 1 (1 byte at address MAXLEN), the length of string 1 (1 byte at address S1LEN), the length of string 2 (1 byte at address S2LEN), a running index for string 1 (1 byte at address S1IDX), a running index for string 2 (1 byte at address S2IDX), a concatenation counter (1 byte at address COUNT), and a flag that indicates whether the combined strings overflowed (1 byte at address STRGOV). The four bytes on page 0 hold pointers to string 1 (two bytes starting at address S1ADR, address $00D0_{16}$ in the listing) and to string 2 (two bytes starting at address S1ADR, address $00D0_{16}$ in the listing).

Special Cases:

1. If the concatenation would result in a string longer than the specified maximum length, the program concatenates only enough of string 2 to reach the maximum. If any of string 2 must be truncated, the Carry flag is set to 1.
2. If string 2 has a length of zero, the program exits with the Carry flag cleared (no errors) and string 1 unchanged. That is, a length of zero for either string is interpreted as zero, not 256.
3. If the original length of string 1 exceeds the specified maximum length, the program exits with the Carry flag set to 1 (indicating an error) and string 1 unchanged.

Entry Conditions

Order in stack (starting from the top)

Less significant byte of return address
More significant byte of return address

Maximum length of string 1

Less significant byte of starting address of string 2
More significant byte of starting address of string 2

Less significant byte of starting address of string 1
More significant byte of starting address of string 1

Exit Conditions

String 2 concatenated at the end of string 1 and the length of string 1 increased appropriately. If the resulting string would exceed the maximum length, only the part of string 2 that would give string 1 its maximum length is concatenated. If any part of string 2 must be dropped, the Carry flag is set to 1. Otherwise, the Carry flag is cleared.

Examples

1. Data: Maximum length of string 1 = $0E_{16} = 14_{10}$
   String 1 = 07'JOHNSON' (07 is the length of the string)
   String 2 = 05', DON' (05 is the length of the string)

   Result: String 1 = 0C'JOHNSON, DON' ($0C_{16} = 12_{10}$ is the length of the combined string with string 2 placed after string 1).
   Carry = 0, since the concatenation did not produce a string exceeding the maximum length.

2. Data: Maximum length of string 1 = $0E_{16} = 14_{10}$
   String 1 = 07'JOHNSON' (07 is the length of the string)
   String 2 = 09', RICHARD' (09 is the length of the string)

   Result: String 1 = 0E'JOHNSON, RICHA' ($0E_{16} = 14_{10}$ is the maximum length allowed, so the last two characters of string 2 have been dropped.)
   Carry = 1, since the concatenation produced a string longer than the maximum length.

Note that we are representing the initial byte (containing the length of the string) as two hexadecimal digits in both examples.

```
;       Title               String Concatenation                        ;
;       Name:               CONCAT                                      ;
;                                                                       ;
;                                                                       ;

;                                                                       ;
;       Purpose:            Concatenate 2 strings into one string.      ;
;                                                                       ;
;       Entry:              TOP OF STACK                                ;
;                             Low byte of return address,               ;
;                             High byte of return address,              ;
;                             Maximum length of string 1,               ;
;                             Low byte of string 2 address,             ;
;                             High byte of string 2 address,            ;
;                             Low byte of string 1 address,             ;
;                             High byte of string 1 address             ;
;                                                                       ;
;                             A string is a maximum of 255 bytes long plus ;
;                             a length byte which precedes it.          ;
;                                                                       ;
;       Exit:               string 1 := string 1 concatenated with string 2 ;
;                           If no errors then                           ;
;                             CARRY := 0                                ;
;                           else                                        ;
;                             begin                                     ;
;                               CARRY := 1                              ;
;                               if the concatenation makes string 1 too ;
;                               long concatenate only the part of string 2 ;
;                               which will result in string 1 having its ;
;                               maximum length                          ;
;                               if length(string1) > maximum length then ;
;                                 no concatenation is done              ;
;                             end;                                      ;
;                                                                       ;
;       Registers used: All                                             ;
;                                                                       ;
;       Time:               Approximately 40 * (length of string 2) cycles ;
;                           plus 161 cycles overhead                    ;
;                                                                       ;
;       Size:               Program 141 bytes                           ;
;                           Data      7 bytes plus                      ;
;                                     4 bytes in page zero              ;
;                                                                       ;
;                                                                       ;

;EQUATES
S1ADR   .EQU    0D0H            ;PAGE ZERO POINTER TO STRING 1
S2ADR   .EQU    0D2H            ;PAGE ZERO POINTER TO STRING 2

CONCAT:

        ;GET RETURN ADDRESS
        PLA
        TAY                     ;SAVE LOW BYTE
        PLA
        TAX                     ;SAVE HIGH BYTE
```

```
        ;GET MAXIMUM LENGTH OF STRING 1
        PLA
        STA     MAXLEN

        ;GET THE STARTING ADDRESS OF STRING 2
        PLA
        STA     S2ADR
        PLA
        STA     S2ADR+1

        ;GET THE STARTING ADDRESS OF STRING 1
        PLA
        STA     S1ADR
        PLA
        STA     S1ADR+1

        ;RESTORE RETURN ADDRESS
        TXA
        PHA                     ;RESTORE HIGH BYTE
        TYA
        PHA                     ;RESTORE LOW BYTE

        ;DETERMINE WHERE TO START CONCATENATING
        LDY     #0
        LDA     (S1ADR),Y       ;GET CURRENT LENGTH OF STRING 1
        STA     S1LEN
        STA     S1IDX
        INC     S1IDX           ;START CONCATENATING AT THE END OF STRING 1
        LDA     (S2ADR),Y       ;GET LENGTH OF STRING 2
        STA     S2LEN
        LDA     #1
        STA     S2IDX           ;START CONCATENATION AT BEGINNING OF STRING 2

        ;
        ;DETERMINE THE NUMBER OF CHARACTERS TO CONCATENATE
        LDA     S2LEN           ;GET LENGTH OF STRING 2
        CLC
        ADC     S1LEN           ;ADD TO CURRENT LENGTH OF STRING 1
        BCS     TOOLNG          ;BRANCH IF LENGTH WILL EXCEED 255 BYTES
        CMP     MAXLEN          ;CHECK AGAINST MAXIMUM LENGTH
        BEQ     LENOK           ;BRANCH IF LENGTH DOES NOT EXCEED MAXIMUM
        BCC     LENOK

        ;
        ;RESULTING STRING WILL BE TOO LONG SO
        ; INDICATE A STRING OVERFLOW, STRGOV := 0FFH
        ; SET NUMBER OF CHARACTERS TO CONCATENATE =  MAXLEN - S1LEN
        ; SET LENGTH OF STRING 1 TO MAXIMUM LENGTH
TOOLNG:
        LDA     #0FFH
        STA     STRGOV          ;INDICATE OVERFLOW
        LDA     MAXLEN
        SEC
        SBC     S1LEN
        BCC     EXIT            ;EXIT IF MAXIMUM LENGTH < STRING 1 LENGTH
```

```
                                        ; (THE ORIGINAL STRING WAS TOO LONG !!)
        STA     COUNT                   ;SET COUNT TO S1LEN - MAXLEN
        LDA     MAXLEN
        STA     S1LEN                   ;SET LENGTH OF STRING 1 TO MAXIMUM
        JMP     DOCAT                   ;PERFORM CONCATENATION


        ;RESULTING LENGTH DOES NOT EXCEED MAXIMUM
        ; LENGTH OF STRING 1 = S1LEN + S2LEN
        ; INDICATE NO OVERFLOW, STRGOV := 0
        ; SET NUMBER OF CHARACTERS TO CONCATENATE TO LENGTH OF STRING 2
LENOK:
        STA     S1LEN                   ;SAVE THE SUM OF THE 2 LENGTHS
        LDA     #0
        STA     STRGOV                  ;INDICATE NO OVERFLOW
        LDA     S2LEN
        STA     COUNT                   ;COUNT := LENGTH OF STRING 2

        ;
        ;CONCATENATE THE STRINGS
DOCAT:
        LDA     COUNT
        BEQ     EXIT                    ;EXIT IF NO BYTES TO CONCATENATE

CATLP:
        LDY     S2IDX
        LDA     (S2ADR),Y               ;GET NEXT BYTE FROM STRING 2
        LDY     S1IDX
        STA     (S1ADR),Y               ;MOVE IT TO END OF STRING 1
        INC     S1IDX                   ;INCREMENT STRING 1 INDEX
        INC     S2IDX                   ;INCREMENT STRING 2 INDEX
        DEC     COUNT                   ;DECREMENT COUNTER
        BNE     CATLP                   ;CONTINUE UNTIL COUNT = 0

EXIT:
        LDA     S1LEN                   ;UPDATE LENGTH OF STRING 1
        LDY     #0
        STA     (S1ADR),Y
        LDA     STRGOV                  ;GET OVERFLOW INDICATOR
        ROR     A                       ;CARRY = 1 IF OVERLOW, 0 IF NOT
        RTS

;
;DATA
MAXLEN: .BLOCK  1                       ;MAXIMUM LENGTH OF S1
S1LEN:  .BLOCK  1                       ;LENGTH OF S1
S2LEN:  .BLOCK  1                       ;LENGTH OF S2
S1IDX:  .BLOCK  1                       ;RUNNING INDEX INTO S1
S2IDX:  .BLOCK  1                       ;RUNNING INDEX INTO S2
COUNT:  .BLOCK  1                       ;CONCATENATION COUNTER
STRGOV: .BLOCK  1                       ;STRING OVERFLOW FLAG

;                                                                       ;
;                                                                       ;
;       SAMPLE EXECUTION:                                               ;
;                                                                       ;
```

```
;                                                             ;

SC0802:
        LDA     SADR1+1 ;PUSH ADDRESS OF STRING 1
        PHA
        LDA     SADR1
        PHA
        LDA     SADR2+1 ;PUSH ADDRESS OF STRING 2
        PHA
        LDA     SADR2
        PHA
        LDA     #20H    ;PUSH MAXIMUM LENGTH OF STRING 1
        PHA
        JSR     CONCAT  ;CONCATENATE
        BRK             ;RESULT OF CONCATENATING "LASTNAME" AND ", FIRSTNAME"
                        ; IS S1 = 13H,"LASTNAME, FIRSTNAME"
        JMP     SC0802  ;LOOP FOR ANOTHER TEST

;
;TEST DATA, CHANGE FOR OTHER VALUES
SADR1   .WORD   S1              ;STARTING ADDRESS OF STRING 1
SADR2   .WORD   S2              ;STARTING ADDRESS OF STRING 2
S1      .BYTE   8H              ;LENGTH OF S1
        .BYTE   "LASTNAME                         " ;32 BYTE MAX LENGTH
S2      .BYTE   0BH             ;LENGTH OF S2
        .BYTE   ", FIRSTNAME                      " ;32 BYTE MAX LENGTH

        .END    ;PROGRAM
```

Find the Position of a Substring (POS) 8C

Searches for the first occurrence of a substring within a string. Returns the index at which the substring starts if it is found and 0 if it is not found. The string and the substring are both a maximum of 255 bytes long and the actual characters are preceded by a byte containing the length. Thus, if the substring is found, its starting index cannot be less than 1 or more than 255.

Procedure: The program moves through the string searching for the substring until it either finds a match or the remaining part of the string is shorter than the substring and hence cannot possibly contain it. If the substring does not appear in the string, the program clears the accumulator; otherwise, the program places the starting index of the substring in the accumulator.

Registers Used: All

Execution Time: Data-dependent, but the overhead is 135 cycles, each successful match of one character takes 47 cycles, and each unsuccessful match of one character takes 50 cycles. The worst case occurs when the string and substring always match except for the last character in the substring, such as

String = 'AAAAAAAAB'
Substring = 'AAB'

The execution time in that case is

(STRING LENGTH − SUBSTRING LENGTH + 1) * (47 * (SUBSTRING LENGTH − 1) + 50) + 135

If, for example, STRING LENGTH = 9 and SUBSTRING LENGTH = 3, the execution time is

$(9 - 3 + 1) * (47 * (3 - 1) + 50) + 135 = 7 * 144 + 135 = 1008 + 135 = 1143$ cycles.

Program Size: 124 bytes

Data Memory Required: Six bytes anywhere in RAM plus four bytes on page 0. The six bytes anywhere in RAM are temporary storage for the length of the string (one byte at address SLEN), the length of the substring (one byte at address SUBLEN), a running index into the string (one byte at address SIDX), a running index into the substring (one byte at address SUBIDX), a search counter (one byte at address COUNT), and an index into the string (one byte at address INDEX). The four bytes on page 0 hold pointers to the substring (two bytes starting at address SUBSTG, $00D0_{16}$ in the listing) and to the string (two bytes starting at address STRING, $00D2_{16}$ in the listing).

Special Cases:

1. If either the string or the substring has a length of zero, the program exits with zero in the accumulator, indicating that it did not find the substring.
2. If the substring is longer than the string, the program exits with zero in the accumulator, indicating that it did not find the substring.
3. If the program returns an index of 1, the substring may be regarded as an abbreviation of the string. That is, the substring occurs in the string, starting at the first character. A typical example would be a string PRINT and a substring PR.
4. If the substring occurs more than once in the string, the program will return only the index to the first occurrence (the occurrence with the lowest starting index).

Entry Conditions

Order in stack (starting from the top)

Less significant byte of return address
More significant byte of return address

Less significant byte of starting address of substring
More significant byte of starting address of substring

Less significant byte of starting address of string
More significant byte of starting address of string

Exit Conditions

Accumulator contains index at which first occurrence of substring starts if it is found; accumulator contains zero if substring is not found.

Examples

1. Data: String = 1D' ENTER SPEED IN MILES PER HOUR' ($1D_{16} = 29_{10}$ is the length of the string).
   Substring = 05'MILES' (05 is the length of the substring)

   Result: Accumulator contains 10_{16} (16_{10}), the index at which the substring 'MILES' starts.

2. Data: String = 1B'SALES FIGURES FOR JUNE 1981' ($1B_{16} = 27_{10}$ is the length of the string)
   Substring = 04'JUNE' (04 is the length of the substring)

   Result: Accumulator contains 13_{16} (19_{10}), the index at which the substring 'JUNE' starts.

3. Data: String = 10'LET Y1 = X1 + R7' ($10_{16} = 16_{10}$ is the length of the string)
   Substring = 02'R4' (02 is the length of the substring)

   Result: Accumulator contains 00, since the substring 'R4' does not appear in the string LET Y1 = X1 + R7.

4. Data: String =07'RESTORE' (07 is the length of the string)
   Substring = 03'RES' (03 is the length of the substring)

   Result: Accumulator contains 01, the index at which the substring "RES" starts. An index of 01 indicates that the substring could be an abbreviation of the string; such abbreviations are, for example, often used in interactive programs (such as BASIC interpreters) to save on typing and storage.

```
;       Title           Find the position of a substring in a string    ;
;       Name:           POS                                             ;
;                                                                       ;
;                                                                       ;
;                                                                       ;
;       Purpose:        Search for the first occurrence of a substring  ;
;                       within a string and return its starting index.  ;
;                       If the substring is not found a 0 is returned.  ;
;                                                                       ;
;       Entry:          TOP OF STACK                                    ;
;                         Low byte of return address,                   ;
;                         High byte of return address,                  ;
;                         Low byte of substring address,                ;
;                         High byte of substring address,               ;
;                         Low byte of string address,                   ;
;                         High byte of string address                   ;
;                                                                       ;
;                         A string is a maximum of 255 bytes long plus  ;
;                         a length byte which precedes it.              ;
;                                                                       ;
;       Exit:           If the substring is found then                  ;
;                         Register A = its starting index               ;
;                       else                                            ;
;                         Register A = 0                                ;
;                                                                       ;
;       Registers used: All                                             ;
;                                                                       ;
;                                                                       ;
;       Time:           Since the algorithm is so data dependent        ;
;                       a simple formula is impossible but the          ;
;                       following statements are true and a             ;
;                       worst case is given below:                      ;
;                                                                       ;
;                       135 cycles overhead.                            ;
;                       Each match of 1 character takes 47 cycles       ;
;                       A mismatch takes 50 cycles.                     ;
;                                                                       ;
;                       Worst case timing will be when the              ;
;                       string and substring always match               ;
;                       except for the last character of the            ;
;                       substring, Such as:                             ;
;                           string = 'AAAAAAAAAB'                       ;
;                           substring = 'AAB'                           ;
;                       135 cycles overhead plus                        ;
;                    (length(string) - length(substring) + 1) *         ;
;                           (((length(substring)-1) * 47) + 50)         ;
;                                                                       ;
;       Size:           Program 124 bytes                               ;
;                       Data      6 bytes plus                          ;
;                                 4 bytes in page zero                  ;
;                                                                       ;
;                                                                       ;


;EQUATES
```

```
SUBSTG  .EQU    0D0H            ;PAGE ZERO POINTER TO SUBSTRING
STRING  .EQU    0D2H            ;PAGE ZERO POINTER TO STRING

POS:
        ;GET RETURN ADDRESS
        PLA
        TAY                     ;SAVE LOW BYTE
        PLA
        TAX                     ;SAVE HIGH BYTE

        ;GET THE STARTING ADDRESS OF SUBSTRING
        PLA
        STA     SUBSTG
        PLA
        STA     SUBSTG+1

        ;GET THE STARTING ADDRESS OF STRING
        PLA
        STA     STRING
        PLA
        STA     STRING+1

        ;RESTORE RETURN ADDRESS
        TXA
        PHA                     ;RESTORE HIGH BYTE
        TYA
        PHA                     ;RESTORE LOW BYTE

        ;SET UP TEMPORARY LENGTH AND INDEX BYTES
        LDY     #0
        LDA     (STRING),Y      ;GET LENGTH OF STRING
        BEQ     NOTFND          ;EXIT IF LENGTH OF STRING = 0
        STA     SLEN
        LDA     (SUBSTG),Y      ;GET LENGTH OF SUBSTRING
        BEQ     NOTFND          ;EXIT IF LENGTH OF SUBSTRING = 0
        STA     SUBLEN

        ;IF THE SUBSTRING IS LONGER THAN THE STRING DECLARE THE
        ; SUBSTRING NOT FOUND
        LDA     SUBLEN
        CMP     SLEN
        BEQ     LENOK
        BCS     NOTFND          ;CANNOT FIND SUBSTRING IF IT IS LONGER THAN
                                ; STRING
        ;START SEARCH, CONTINUE  UNTIL REMAINING STRING SHORTER THAN SUBSTRING
LENOK:
        LDA     #1
        STA     INDEX           ;START LOOKING AT FIRST CHARACTER OF STRING
        LDA     SLEN            ;CONTINUE UNTIL REMAINING STRING TOO SHORT
        SEC                     ; COUNT=STRING LENGTH - SUBSTRING LENGTH + 1
        SBC     SUBLEN
        STA     COUNT
        INC     COUNT

        ;SEARCH FOR SUBSTRING IN STRING
SLP1:
```

```
        LDA     INDEX
        STA     SIDX            ;START STRING INDEX AT INDEX
        LDA     #1
        STA     SUBIDX          ;START SUBSTRING INDEX AT 1

        ;LOOK FOR SUBSTRING BEGINNING AT INDEX
CMPLP:
        LDY     SIDX
        LDA     (STRING),Y      ;GET NEXT CHARACTER FROM STRING
        LDY     SUBIDX
        CMP     (SUBSTG),Y      ;COMPARE TO NEXT CHARACTER IN SUBSTRING
        BNE     SLP2            ;BRANCH IF SUBSTRING IS NOT HERE
        LDY     SUBIDX
        CPY     SUBLEN          ;TEST IF WE ARE DONE
        BEQ     FOUND           ;BRANCH IF ALL CHARACTERS WERE EQUAL
        INY                     ;ELSE INCREMENT TO NEXT CHARACTER
        STY     SUBIDX
        INC     SIDX            ;INCREMENT STRING INDEX
        JMP     CMPLP           ;CONTINUE

        ;ARRIVE HERE IF THE SUBSTRING IS NOT YET FOUND
SLP2:
        INC     INDEX           ;INCREMENT INDEX
        DEC     COUNT           ;DECREMENT COUNT
        BNE     SLP1            ;BRANCH IF NOT DONE
        BEQ     NOTFND          ;ELSE EXIT NOT FOUND

FOUND:
        LDA     INDEX           ;SUBSTRING FOUND, A = STARTING INDEX
        JMP     EXIT

NOTFND:
        LDA     #0              ;SUBSTRING NOT FOUND, A = 0

EXIT
        RTS

;
;DATA
SLEN:   .BLOCK  1               ;LENGTH OF STRING
SUBLEN: .BLOCK  1               ;LENGTH OF SUBSTRING
SIDX:   .BLOCK  1               ;RUNNING INDEX INTO STRING
SUBIDX: .BLOCK  1               ;RUNNING INDEX INTO SUBSTRING
COUNT:  .BLOCK  1               ;SEARCH COUNTER
INDEX:  .BLOCK  1               ;CURRENT INDEX INTO STRING

;                                                               ;
;                                                               ;
;       SAMPLE EXECUTION:                                       ;
;                                                               ;
;                                                               ;


SC0803:
        LDA     SADR+1          ;PUSH ADDRESS OF THE STRING
```

```
        PHA
        LDA     SADR
        PHA
        LDA     SUBADR+1        ;PUSH ADDRESS OF THE SUBSTRING
        PHA
        LDA     SUBADR
        PHA
        JSR     POS             ;FIND POSITION OF SUBSTRING
        BRK                     ;RESULT OF SEARCHING "AAAAAAAAAB" FOR "AAB" IS
                                ; REGISTER A=8
        JMP     SC0803          ;LOOP FOR ANOTHER TEST

;
;TEST DATA, CHANGE FOR OTHER VALUES
SADR    .WORD   STG
SUBADR  .WORD   SSTG
STG     .BYTE   0AH             ;LENGTH OF STRING
        .BYTE   "AAAAAAAAAB                     " ;32 BYTE MAX LENGTH
SSTG    .BYTE   3H              ;LENGTH OF SUBSTRING
        .BYTE   "AAB                            " ;32 BYTE MAX LENGTH

        .END    ;PROGRAM
```

Copy a Substring from a String (COPY) 8D

Copies a substring from a string, given a starting index and the number of bytes to copy. The strings are a maximum of 255 bytes long and the actual characters are preceded by a byte containing the length. If the starting index of the substring is zero (i.e., the substring would start in the length byte) or is beyond the end of the string, the substring is given a length of zero and the Carry flag is set to 1. If the substring would exceed its maximum length or would extend beyond the end of the string, then only the maximum number or the available number of characters (up to the end of the string) are placed in the substring, and the Carry flag is set to 1. If the substring can be formed as specified, the Carry flag is cleared.

Procedure: The program exits immediately if the number of bytes to copy, the maximum length of the substring, or the starting index is zero. It also exits immediately if the starting index exceeds the length of the string. If none of these conditions holds, the program checks if the number of bytes to copy exceeds either the maximum length of the substring or the number of characters available in the string. If either one is exceeded, the program reduces the number of bytes to copy appropriately. It then copies the proper number of bytes from the string to the substring. The program clears the Carry flag if the substring can be formed as specified and sets the Carry flag if it cannot.

Registers Used: All

Execution Time: Approximately 36 * NUMBER OF BYTES COPIES plus 200 cycles overhead. NUMBER OF BYTES COPIED is the number specified (if no problems occur) or the number available or the maximum length of the substring if the copying would go beyond the end of either the string or the substring. If, for example, NUMBER OF BYTES COPIED = 12_{10} ($0C_{16}$), the execution time is

36 * 12 + 200 = 432 +200 = 632 cycles.

Program Size: 173 bytes.

Data Memory Required: Six bytes anywhere in RAM plus four bytes on page 0. The six bytes anywhere in RAM hold the length of the string (one byte at address SLEN), the length of the substring (one byte at address DLEN), the maximum length of the substring (one byte at address MAXLEN), the search counter (one byte at address COUNT), the current index into the string (one byte at address INDEX), and an error flag (one byte at address CPYERR). The four bytes on page 0 hold pointers to the string (two bytes starting at address DSTRG, $00D0_{16}$ in the listing) and to the substring (two bytes starting at address SSTRG, $00D2_{16}$ in the listing).

Special Cases:

1. If the number of bytes to copy is zero, the program assigns the substring a length of zero and clears the Carry flag, indicating no error.
2. If the maximum length of the substring is zero, the program assigns the substring a length of zero and sets the Carry flag to 1, indicating an error.
3. If the starting index of the substring is zero, the program assigns the substring a length of zero and sets the Carry flag to 1, indicating an error.
4. If the source string does not even reach the specified starting index, the program assigns the substring a length of zero and sets the Carry flag to 1, indicating an error.
5. If the substring would extend beyond the end of the source string, the program places all the available characters in the substring and sets the Carry flag to 1, indicating an error. The available characters are the ones from the starting index to the end of the string.
6. If the substring would exceed its specified maximum length, the program places only the specified maximum number of characters in the substring. It sets the Carry flag to 1, indicating an error.

Entry Conditions

Order in stack (starting from the top)

Less significant byte of return address
More significant byte of return address

Maximum length of substring (destination string)

Less significant byte of starting address of substring (destination string)
More significant byte of starting address of substring (destination string)

Number of bytes to copy

Starting index to copy from

Less significant byte of starting address of string (source string)
More significant byte of starting address of string (source string)

Exit Conditions

Substring contains characters copied from string. If the starting index is zero, the maximum length of the substring is zero, or the starting index is beyond the length of the string, the substring will have a length of zero and the Carry flag will be set to 1. If the substring would extend beyond the end of the string or would exceed its specified maximum length, only the available characters from the string (up to the maximum length of the substring) are copied into the substring; the Carry flag is set in this case also. If no problems occur in forming the substring, the Carry flag is cleared.

Examples

1. Data: String = 10'LET Y1 = R7 + X4' ($10_{16} = 16_{10}$ is the length of the string)
   Maximum length of substring = 2
   Number of bytes to copy = 2
   Starting index = 5

   Result: Substring = 02'Y1' (2 is the length of the substring)
   Carry = 0, since no problems occur in forming the substring

2. Data: String = 0E'8657 POWELL ST' ($0E_{16} = 14_{10}$ is the length of the string)
   Maximum length of substring = $10_{16} = 16_{10}$
   Number of bytes to copy = $0D_{16} = 13_{10}$
   Starting index = 06

   Result: Substring = 09'POWELL ST' (09 is the length of the substring)
   Carry = 1, since there were not enough characters available in the string to provide the specified number of bytes to copy.

3. Data: String = 16'9414 HEGENBERGER DRIVE' ($16_{16} = 22_{10}$ is the length of the string)
   Maximum length of substring = $10_{16} = 16_{10}$
   Number of bytes to copy = $11_{16} = 17_{10}$
   Starting index = 06

   Result: Substring = 10'HEGENBERGER DRIV' ($10_{16} = 16_{10}$ is the length of the substring)
   Carry = 1, since the number of bytes to copy exceeded the maximum length of the substring

```
;       Title               Copy a substring from a string              ;
;       Name:               Copy                                        ;
;                                                                       ;
;                                                                       ;
;                                                                       ;
;       Purpose:            Copy a substring from a string given a starting ;
;                           index and the number of bytes.              ;
;                                                                       ;
;       Entry:              TOP OF STACK                                ;
;                             Low byte of return address,               ;
;                             High byte of return address,              ;
;                             Maximum length of destination string,     ;
;                             Low byte of destination string address,   ;
;                             High byte of destination string address,  ;
;                             Number of bytes to copy,                  ;
;                             Starting index to copy from,              ;
;                             Low byte of source string address,        ;
;                             High byte of source string address        ;
;                                                                       ;
;                             A string is a maximum of 255 bytes long plus ;
;                             a length byte which precedes it.          ;
;                                                                       ;
;       Exit:               Destination string := The substring from the ;
;                           string.                                     ;
;                           if no errors then                           ;
;                             CARRY := 0                                ;
;                           else                                        ;
;                             begin                                     ;
;                               the following conditions cause an       ;
;                               error and the CARRY flag = 1.           ;
;                               if (index = 0) or (maxlen = 0) or       ;
;                                   (index > length(sstrg) then         ;
;                                 the destination string will have a zero ;
;                                 length.                               ;
;                               if (index + count) > length(sstrg)) then ;
;                                 the destination string becomes everything ;
;                                 from index to the end of source string. ;
;                             END;                                      ;
;                                                                       ;
;       Registers used: All                                             ;
;                                                                       ;
;                                                                       ;
;       Time:               Approximately (36 * count) cycles plus 200  ;
;                           cycles overhead.                            ;
;                                                                       ;
;       Size:               Program 173 bytes                           ;
;                           Data      6 bytes plus                      ;
;                                     4 bytes in page zero              ;
;                                                                       ;
;                                                                       ;


;EQUATES
DSTRG   .EQU    0D0H            ;PAGE ZERO POINTER TO DESTINATION STRING
SSTRG   .EQU    0D2H            ;PAGE ZERO POINTER TO SOURCE STRING
```

```
COPY:
        ;GET RETURN ADDRESS
        PLA
        TAY                         ;SAVE LOW BYTE
        PLA
        TAX                         ;SAVE HIGH BYTE

        ;GET MAXIMUM LENGTH OF DESTINATION STRING
        PLA
        STA     MAXLEN

        ;GET STARTING ADDRESS OF DESTINATION STRING
        PLA
        STA     DSTRG               ;SAVE LOW BYTE
        PLA
        STA     DSTRG+1             ;SAVE HIGH BYTE

        ;GET NUMBER OF BYTES TO COPY
        PLA
        STA     COUNT

        ;GET STARTING INDEX OF SUBSTRING
        PLA
        STA     INDEX

        ;GET STARTING ADDRESS OF SOURCE STRING
        PLA
        STA     SSTRG               ;SAVE LOW BYTE  (NOTE SSTRG=SOURCE STRING)
        PLA
        STA     SSTRG+1             ;SAVE HIGH BYTE

        ;RESTORE RETURN ADDRESS
        TXA
        PHA                         ;RESTORE HIGH BYTE
        TYA
        PHA                         ;RESTORE LOW BYTE

        ;INITIALIZE LENGTH OF DESTINATION STRING AND THE ERROR FLAG TO 0
        LDA     #0
        STA     DLEN                ;LENGTH OF DESTINATION STRING IS ZERO
        STA     CPYERR              ;ASSUME NO ERRORS

        ;CHECK FOR ZERO BYTES TO COPY OR ZERO MAXIMUM SUBSTRING LENGTH
        LDA     COUNT
        BEQ     OKEXIT              ;BRANCH IF ZERO BYTES TO COPY, NO ERROR
                                    ; DSTRG WILL JUST HAVE ZERO LENGTH
        LDA     MAXLEN
        BEQ     EREXIT              ;ERROR EXIT IF SUBSTRING HAS ZERO
                                    ;  MAXIMUM LENGTH.

        LDA     INDEX
        BEQ     EREXIT              ;ERROR EXIT IF STARTING INDEX IS ZERO

        ;CHECK IF THE SOURCE STRING REACHES THE STARTING INDEX
        ;IF NOT, EXIT
        LDY     #0
```

```
        LDA     (SSTRG),Y       ;GET LENGTH OF SOURCE STRING
        STA     SLEN            ;SAVE SOURCE LENGTH
        CMP     INDEX           ;COMPARE TO STARTING INDEX
        BCC     EREXIT          ;ERROR EXIT IF INDEX IS TOO LARGE

        ;CHECK THAT WE DO NOT COPY BEYOND THE END OF THE SOURCE STRING
        ;IF INDEX + COUNT - 1 > LENGTH(SSTRG) THEN
        ; COUNT := LENGTH(SSTRG) - INDEX + 1;
        LDA     INDEX
        CLC
        ADC     COUNT
        BCS     RECALC          ;BRANCH IF INDEX + COUNT > 255
        TAX
        DEX
        CPX     SLEN
        BCC     CNT1OK          ;BRANCH IF INDEX + COUNT - 1 < LENGTH(SSTRG)
        BEQ     CNT1OK          ;BRANCH IF EQUAL

        ;THE CALLER ASKED FOR TOO MANY CHARACTERS JUST RETURN EVERYTHING
        ; BETWEEN INDEX AND THE END OF THE SOURCE STRING.
        ; SO SET COUNT := LENGTH(SSTRG) - INDEX + 1;
RECALC:
        LDA     SLEN            ;RECALCULATE COUNT
        SEC
        SBC     INDEX
        STA     COUNT
        INC     COUNT           ;COUNT := LENGTH(SSTRG) - INDEX + 1
        LDA     #0FFH
        STA     CPYERR          ;INDICATE A TRUNCATION OF THE COUNT

        ;CHECK IF THE COUNT IS LESS THAN OR EQUAL TO THE MAXIMUM LENGTH OF THE
        ; DESTINATION STRING. IF NOT, THEN SET COUNT TO THE MAXIMUM LENGTH
        ;  IF COUNT > MAXLEN THEN
        ;     COUNT := MAXLEN
CNT1OK:
        LDA     COUNT           ;IS COUNT > MAXIMUM SUBSTRING LENGTH ?
        CMP     MAXLEN
        BCC     CNT2OK          ;BRANCH IF COUNT < MAX LENGTH
        BEQ     CNT2OK          ;BRANCH IF COUNT = MAX LENGTH
        LDA     MAXLEN
        STA     COUNT           ;ELSE COUNT := MAXLEN
        LDA     #0FFH
        STA     CPYERR          ;INDICATE DESTINATION STRING OVERFLOW

        ;EVERYTHING IS SET UP SO MOVE THE SUBSTRING TO DESTINATION STRING
CNT2OK:
        LDX     COUNT           ;REGISTER X WILL BE THE COUNTER
        BEQ     EREXIT          ;ERROR EXIT IF COUNT IS ZERO
        LDA     #1              ;START WITH FIRST CHARACTER OF DESTINATION
        STA     DLEN            ;DLEN IS RUNNING INDEX FOR DESTINATION
                                ;INDEX IS RUNNING INDEX FOR SOURCE
MVLP:
        LDY     INDEX
        LDA     (SSTRG),Y       ;GET NEXT SOURCE CHARACTER
        LDY     DLEN
        STA     (DSTRG),Y       ;MOVE NEXT CHARACTER TO DESTINATION
```

```
        INC     INDEX           ;INCREMENT SOURCE INDEX
        INC     DLEN            ;INCREMENT DESTINATION INDEX
        DEX                     ;DECREMENT COUNTER
        BNE     MVLP            ;CONTINUE UNTIL COUNTER = 0
        DEC     DLEN            ;SUBSTRING LENGTH=FINAL DESTINATION INDEX - 1
        LDA     CPYERR          ;CHECK FOR ANY ERRORS
        BNE     EREXIT          ;BRANCH IF A TRUNCATION OR STRING OVERFLOW

        ;GOOD EXIT
OKEXIT:
        CLC
        BCC     EXIT

        ;ERROR EXIT
EREXIT:
        SEC

        ;STORE LENGTH BYTE IN FRONT OF SUBSTRING
EXIT:
        LDA     DLEN
        LDY     #0
        STA     (DSTRG),Y       ;SET LENGTH OF DESTINATION STRING
        RTS

;
;DATA SECTION
SLEN:   .BLOCK  1               ;LENGTH OF SOURCE STRING
DLEN:   .BLOCK  1               ;LENGTH OF DESTINATION STRING
MAXLEN: .BLOCK  1               ;MAXIMUM LENGTH OF DESTINATION STRING
COUNT:  .BLOCK  1               ;SEARCH COUNTER
INDEX:  .BLOCK  1               ;CURRENT INDEX INTO STRING
CPYERR: .BLOCK  1               ;COPY ERROR FLAG

;                                                                       ;
;                                                                       ;
;       SAMPLE EXECUTION:                                               ;
;                                                                       ;
;                                                                       ;


SC0804:
        LDA     SADR+1  ;PUSH ADDRESS OF SOURCE STRING
        PHA
        LDA     SADR
        PHA
        LDA     IDX     ;PUSH STARTING INDEX FOR COPYING
        PHA
        LDA     CNT     ;PUSH NUMBER OF CHARACTERS TO COPY
        PHA
        LDA     DADR+1  ;PUSH ADDRESS OF DESTINATION STRING
        PHA
        LDA     DADR
        PHA
        LDA     MXLEN   ;PUSH MAXIMUM LENGTH OF DESTINATION STRING
        PHA
        JSR     COPY    ;COPY
```

```
        BRK             ;RESULT OF COPYING 3 CHARACTERS STARTING AT INDEX 4
                        ;FROM THE STRING "12.345E+10" IS 3,"345"
        JMP     SC0804  ;LOOP FOR MORE TESTING

;
;DATA SECTION
IDX     .BYTE   4                   ;STARTING INDEX FOR COPYING
CNT     .BYTE   3                   ;NUMBER OF CHARACTERS TO COPY
MXLEN   .BYTE   20H                 ;MAXIMUM LENGTH OF DESTINATION STRING
SADR    .WORD   SSTG
DADR    .WORD   DSTG
SSTG    .BYTE   0AH                 ;LENGTH OF STRING
        .BYTE   "12.345E+10                             " ;32 BYTE MAX LENGTH
DSTG    .BYTE   0                   ;LENGTH OF SUBSTRING
        .BYTE   "                                       " ;32 BYTE MAX LENGTH

        .END    ;PROGRAM
```

Delete a Substring from a String (DELETE) 8E

Deletes a substring from a string, given a starting index and a length. The string is a maximum of 255 bytes long and the actual characters are preceded by a byte containing the length. The Carry flag is cleared if the deletion can be performed as specified. The Carry flag is set if the starting index is zero or beyond the length of the string; the string is left unchanged in either case. If the deletion extends beyond the end of the string, the Carry flag is set (to 1) and only the characters from the starting index to the end of the string are deleted.

Procedure: The program exits immediately if the starting index or the number of bytes to delete is zero. It also exits if the starting index is beyond the length of the string. If none of these conditions holds, the program checks to see if the string extends beyond the area to be deleted. If it does not, the program simply truncates the string by setting the new length to the starting index minus 1. If it does, the program compacts the resulting string by moving the bytes above the deleted area down. The program then determines the new string's length and exits with the Carry cleared if the specified number of bytes were deleted and set to 1 if any errors occurred.

Registers Used: All

Execution Time: Approximately

36 * NUMBER OF BYTES MOVED DOWN + 165

where NUMBER OF BYTES MOVED DOWN is zero if the string can be truncated and is STRING LENGTH – STARTING INDEX – NUMBER OF BYTES TO DELETE + 1 if the string must be compacted.

Examples

1. STRING LENGTH = 20_{16} (32_{10})
   STARTING INDEX = 19_{16} (25_{10})
   NUMBER OF BYTES TO DELETE = 08

Since there are exactly eight bytes left in the string starting at index 19_{16}, all the routine must do is truncate the string. This takes

36 * 0 + 165 = 165 cycles.

2. STRING LENGTH = 40_{16} (64_{10})
   STARTING LENGTH = 19_{16} (25_{10})
   NUMBER OF BYTES TO DELETE = 08

Since there are 20_{16} (32_{16}) bytes above the truncated area, the routine must move them down eight positions. The execution time is

36 * 32 + 165 = 1152 + 165 = 1317 cycles.

Program Size: 139 bytes

Data Memory Required: Five bytes anywhere in RAM plus two bytes on page 0. The five bytes anywhere in RAM hold the length of the string (one byte at address SLEN), the search counter (one byte at address COUNT), an index into the string (one byte at address INDEX), the source index for use during the move (one byte at address SIDX), and an error flag (one byte at address DELERR). The two bytes on page 0 hold a pointer to the string (starting at address STRG, $00D0_{16}$ in the listing).

Special Cases:

1. If the number of bytes to delete is zero, the program exits with the Carry flag cleared (no errors) and the string unchanged.

2. If the string does not even extend to the specified starting index, the program exits with the Carry flag set to 1 (error indicated) and the string unchanged.

3. If the number of bytes to delete exceeds the number available, the program deletes all bytes from the starting index to the end of the string and exits with the Carry flag set to 1 (error indicated).

Entry Conditions

Order in stack (starting from the top)

Less significant byte of return address
More significant byte of return address

Number of bytes to delete

Starting index to delete from

Less significant byte of starting address of string

More significant byte of starting address of string

Exit Conditions

Substring deleted from string. If no errors occur, the Carry flag is cleared. If the starting index is zero or beyond the length of the string, the Carry flag is set and the string is unchanged. If the number of bytes to delete would go beyond the end of the string, the Carry flag is set and the characters from the starting index to the end of the string are deleted.

Examples

1. Data: String = 1E'SALES FOR MARCH AND APRIL 1980' ($1E_{16} = 30_{10}$ is the length of the string)

   Number of bytes to delete = $0A_{16} = 10_{10}$

   Starting index to delete from = $10_{16} = 16_{10}$

   Result: String = 14'SALES FOR MARCH 1980' ($14_{16} = 20_{10}$ is the length of the string with ten bytes deleted starting with the 16th character — the deleted material is 'AND APRIL ').

   Carry = 0, since no problems occurred in the deletion.

2. Data: String = 28'THE PRICE IS $3.00 ($2.00 BEFORE JUNE 1)' ($28_{16} = 40_{10}$ is the length of the string).

   Number of bytes to delete = $30_{16} = 48_{10}$

   Starting index to delete from = $13_{16} = 19_{10}$

   Result: String = 12'THE PRICE IS $3.00' ($12_{16} = 18_{10}$ is the length of the string with all remaining bytes deleted).

   Carry = 1, since there were not as many bytes left in the string as were supposed to be deleted.

```
;       Title           Delete a substring from a string            ;
;       Name:           Delete                                      ;
;                                                                   ;
;                                                                   ;

;                                                                   ;
;       Purpose:        Delete a substring from a string given a    ;
;                       starting index and a length.                ;
;                                                                   ;
;       Entry:          TOP OF STACK                                ;
;                         Low byte of return address,               ;
;                         High byte of return address,              ;
;                         Number of bytes to delete (count),        ;
;                         Starting index to delete from (index),    ;
;                         Low byte of string address,               ;
;                         High byte of string address               ;
```

```
;                                                                        ;
;                         A string is a maximum of 255 bytes long plus  ;
;                         a length byte which precedes it.               ;
;                                                                        ;
;       Exit:            Substring deleted.                              ;
;                        if no errors then                               ;
;                          CARRY := 0                                    ;
;                        else                                            ;
;                          begin                                         ;
;                            the following conditions cause an           ;
;                            error with the CARRY flag = 1.              ;
;                            if (index = 0) or (index > length(string))  ;
;                              then do not change the string             ;
;                            if count is too large then                  ;
;                              delete only the characters from           ;
;                              index to the end of the string            ;
;                          end;                                          ;
;                                                                        ;
;       Registers used: All                                              ;
;                                                                        ;
;       Time:            Approximately 36 * (LENGTH(STRG)-INDEX-COUNT+1) ;
;                        plus 165 cycles overhead.                       ;
;                                                                        ;
;       Size:            Program 139 bytes                               ;
;                        Data      5 bytes plus                          ;
;                                  2 bytes in page zero                  ;
;                                                                        ;
;                                                                        ;


;EQUATES
STRG    .EQU    0D0H            ;PAGE ZERO POINTER TO SOURCE STRING

DELETE:
        ;GET RETURN ADDRESS
        PLA
        TAY                     ;SAVE LOW BYTE
        PLA
        TAX                     ;SAVE HIGH BYTE

;GET NUMBER OF BYTES TO DELETE
PLA
STA     COUNT

;GET STARTING INDEX DELETION
PLA
STA     INDEX

;GET STARTING ADDRESS OF STRING
PLA
STA     STRG            ;SAVE LOW BYTE
PLA
STA     STRG+1          ;SAVE HIGH BYTE

;RESTORE RETURN ADDRESS
TXA
```

```
        PHA                         ;RESTORE HIGH BYTE
        TYA
        PHA                         ;RESTORE LOW BYTE

        ;INITIALIZE ERROR INDICATOR (DELERR) TO 0
        ;GET STRING LENGTH
        LDY     #0
        STY     DELERR
        LDA     (STRG),Y            ;GET LENGTH OF STRING
        STA     SLEN                ;SAVE STRING LENGTH

        ;CHECK FOR A NON ZERO COUNT AND INDEX
        LDA     COUNT
        BEQ     OKEXIT              ;GOOD EXIT IF NOTHING TO DELETE

        LDA     INDEX
        BEQ     EREXIT              ;ERROR EXIT IF STARTING INDEX = 0

        ;CHECK FOR STARTING INDEX WITHIN THE STRING
        ; EXIT IF IT IS NOT
        LDA     SLEN                ;IS INDEX WITHIN THE STRING ?
        CMP     INDEX
        BCC     EREXIT              ;NO, TAKE ERROR EXIT

        ;BE SURE THE NUMBER OF CHARACTERS REQUESTED TO BE DELETED ARE PRESENT
        ; IF NOT THEN ONLY DELETE FROM THE INDEX TO THE END OF THE STRING
        LDA     INDEX
        CLC
        ADC     COUNT
        BCS     TRUNC               ;TRUNCATE IF INDEX + COUNT > 255
        STA     SIDX                ;SAVE INDEX + COUNT AS THE SOURCE INDEX
        TAX                         ;X = INDEX + COUNT
        DEX
        CPX     SLEN
        BCC     CNTOK               ;BRANCH IF INDEX + COUNT - 1 < LENGTH(SSTRG)
                                    ;ELSE JUST TRUNCATE THE STRING
        BEQ     TRUNC               ;TRUNCATE BUT NO ERROR (EXACTLY ENOUGH
                                    ; CHARACTERS)
        LDA     #0FFH
        STA     DELERR              ;INDICATE ERROR - NOT ENOUGH CHARACTERS TO
                                    ; DELETE

        ;TRUNCATE THE STRING - NO COMPACTING NECESSARY
TRUNC:
        LDX     INDEX               ;STRING LENGTH = STARTING INDEX - 1
        DEX
        STX     SLEN
        LDA     DELERR
        BEQ     OKEXIT              ;GOOD EXIT
        BNE     EREXIT              ;ERROR EXIT


        ;DELETE THE SUBSTRING BY COMPACTING
        ; MOVE ALL CHARACTERS ABOVE THE DELETED AREA DOWN
CNTOK:
        ;CALCULATE NUMBER OF CHARACTERS TO MOVE (SLEN - SIDX + 1)
```

```
        LDA     SLEN            ;GET STRING LENGTH
        SEC
        SBC     SIDX            ;SUBTRACT STARTING INDEX
        TAX
        INX                     ;ADD 1 TO INCLUDE LAST CHARACTER
        BEQ     OKEXIT          ;BRANCH IF COUNT = 0

MVLP:
        LDY     SIDX
        LDA     (STRG),Y        ;GET NEXT CHARACTER
        LDY     INDEX
        STA     (STRG),Y        ;MOVE IT DOWN
        INC     INDEX           ;INCREMENT DESTINATION INDEX
        INC     SIDX            ;INCREMENT SOURCE INDEX
        DEX                     ;DECREMENT COUNTER
        BNE     MVLP            ;CONTINUE UNTIL COUNTER = 0
        LDX     INDEX
        DEX                     ;STRING LENGTH = FINAL DESTINATION INDEX - 1
        STX     SLEN

        ;GOOD EXIT
OKEXIT:
        CLC
        BCC     EXIT

        ;ERROR EXIT
EREXIT:
        SEC

EXIT:
        LDA     SLEN
        LDY     #0
        STA     (STRG),Y        ;SET LENGTH OF STRING
        RTS

;
;DATA
SLEN:   .BLOCK  1               ;LENGTH OF SOURCE STRING
COUNT:  .BLOCK  1               ;SEARCH COUNTER
INDEX:  .BLOCK  1               ;CURRENT INDEX INTO STRING
SIDX:   .BLOCK  1               ;SOURCE INDEX DURING MOVE
DELERR: .BLOCK  1               ;DELETE ERROR FLAG

;                                                                       ;
;                                                                       ;
;       SAMPLE EXECUTION:                                               ;
;                                                                       ;
;                                                                       ;


SC0805:
        LDA     SADR+1  ;PUSH STRING ADDRESS
        PHA
        LDA     SADR
        PHA
        LDA     IDX     ;PUSH STARTING INDEX FOR DELETION
```

```
        PHA
        LDA     CNT     ;PUSH NUMBER OF CHARACTERS TO DELETE
        PHA
        JSR     DELETE  ;DELETE
        BRK             ;RESULT OF DELETING 4 CHARACTERS STARTING AT INDEX 1
                        ; FROM "JOE HANDOVER" IS "HANDOVER"
        JMP     SC0805  ;LOOP FOR ANOTHER TEST

;
;DATA SECTION
IDX     .BYTE   1                       ;INDEX TO START OF DELETION
CNT     .BYTE   4                       ;NUMBER OF CHARACTERS TO DELETE
SADR    .WORD   SSTG
SSTG    .BYTE   12                      ;LENGTH OF STRING
        .BYTE   "JOE HANDOVER"

        .END    ;PROGRAM
```

Insert a Substring into a String (INSERT)

Inserts a substring into a string, given a starting index. The string and substring are both a maximum of 255 bytes long and the actual characters are preceded by a byte containing the length. The Carry flag is cleared if the insertion can be accomplished with no problems. The Carry flag is set if the starting index is zero or beyond the length of the string. In the second case, the substring is concatenated to the end of the string. The Carry flag is also set if the string with the insertion would exceed a specified maximum length; in that case, the program inserts only enough of the substring to give the string its maximum length.

Procedure: The program exits immediately if the starting index is zero or if the length of the substring is zero. If neither of these conditions holds, the program checks to see if the insertion would produce a string longer than the maximum. If it would, the program truncates the substring. The program then checks to see if the starting index is within the string. If it is not, the program simply concatenates the substring by moving it to the memory locations immediately after the end of the string. If the starting index is within the string, the program must first open a space for the insertion by moving the remaining characters up in memory. This move must start at the highest address to avoid writing over any data. Finally, the program can move the substring into the open area. The program then determines the new string length and exits with the Carry flag set appropriately (to 0 if no problems occurred and to 1 if the starting index was zero, the substring had to be truncated, or the starting index was beyond the length of the string).

Registers Used: All

Execution Time: Approximately 36 * NUMBER OF BYTES MOVED + 36 * NUMBER OF BYTES INSERTED + 207

NUMBER OF BYTES MOVED is the number of bytes that must be moved to open up space for the insertion. If the starting index is beyond the end of the string, this is zero since the substring is simply concatenated to the string. Otherwise, this is STRING LENGTH − STARTING INDEX + 1, since the bytes at or above the starting index must be moved.

NUMBER OF BYTES INSERTED is the length of the substring if no truncation occurs. It is the maximum length of the string minus its current length if inserting the substring would produce a string longer than the maximum.

Examples

1. STRING LENGTH = 20_{16} (32_{10})
   STARTING INDEX = 19_{16} (25_{10})
   MAXIMUM LENGTH = 30_{16} (48_{10})
   SUBSTRING LENGTH = 06

   That is, we want to insert a substring six bytes long, starting at the 25th character. Since there are eight bytes that must be moved up (20_{16} − 19_{16} + 1 = NUMBER OF BYTES MOVED) and six bytes that must be inserted, the execution time is approximately

   36 * 8 + 36 * 6 + 207 = 288 + 216 + 207
   = 711 cycles.

2. STRING LENGTH = 20_{16} (32_{10})
   STARTING INDEX = 19_{16} (25_{10})
   MAXIMUM LENGTH = 24_{16} (36_{10})
   SUBSTRING LENGTH = 06

As opposed to Example 1, here only four bytes of the substring can be inserted without exceeding the maximum length of the string. Thus NUMBER OF BYTES MOVED = 8 and NUMBER OF BYTES INSERTED = 4. The execution time is approximately

$$36 * 8 + 36 * 4 + 207 = 288 + 144 + 207 = 639 \text{ cycles.}$$

Program Size: 212 bytes

Data Memory Required: Seven bytes anywhere in RAM plus four bytes on page 0. The seven bytes anywhere in RAM hold the length of the string (one byte at address SLEN), the length of the substring (one byte at address SUBLEN), the maximum length of the string (one byte at address MAXLEN), the current index into the string (one byte at address INDEX), running indexes for use during the move (one byte at address SIDX and one byte at address DIDX), and an error flag (one byte at address INSERR). The four bytes on page 0 hold pointers to the substring (two bytes starting at address SUBSTG, $00D0_{16}$ in the listing) and the string (two bytes starting at address STRG, $00D2_{16}$ in the listing).

Special Cases:

1. If the length of the substring (the insertion) is zero, the program exits with the Carry flag cleared (no error) and the string unchanged.

2. If the starting index for the insertion is zero (i.e., the insertion begins in the length byte), the program exits with the Carry flag set to 1 (indicating an error) and the string unchanged.

3. If the string with the substring inserted exceeds the specified maximum length, the program inserts only enough characters to reach the maximum length. The Carry flag is set to 1 to indicate that the insertion has been truncated.

4. If the starting index of the insertion is beyond the end of the string, the program concatenates the insertion at the end of the string and indicates an error by setting the Carry flag to 1.

5. If the original length of the string exceeds its specified maximum length, the program exits with the Carry flag set to 1 (indicating an error) and the string unchanged.

Entry Conditions

Order in stack (starting from the top)

Less significant byte of return address
More significant byte of return address

Less significant byte of starting address of substring

More significant byte of starting address of substring

Maximum length of string

Starting index at which to insert the substring

Less significant byte of starting address of string

More significant byte of starting address of string

Exit Conditions

Substring inserted into string. If no errors occur, the Carry flag is cleared. If the starting index is zero or the length of the substring is zero, the Carry flag is set and the string is not changed. If the starting index is beyond the length of the string, the Carry flag is set and the substring is concatenated to the end of the string. If the string with the substring inserted would exceed the specified maximum length, the Carry flag is set and only those characters from the substring which bring the string to maximum length are inserted.

Examples

1. Data: String = 0A'JOHN SMITH' ($0A_{16} = 10_{10}$ is the length of the string)
   Substring = 08'WILLIAM ' (08 is the length of the substring)
   Maximum length of string = $14_{16} = 20_{10}$
   Starting index = 06

   Result: String = 12'JOHN WILLIAM SMITH' ($12_{16} = 18_{16}$ is the length of the string with the substring inserted).
   Carry = 0, since no problems occurred in the insertion.

2. Data: String = 0A'JOHN SMITH' ($0A_{16} = 10_{10}$ is the length of the string)
   Substring = 0C'ROCKEFELLER ' ($0C_{16} = 12_{10}$ is the length of the substring)
   Maximum length of string = $14_{16} = 20_{10}$
   Starting index = 06

   Result: String = 14'JOHN ROCKEFELLESMITH' ($14_{16} = 20_{10}$ is the length of the string with as much of the substring inserted as the maximum length would allow)
   Carry = 1, since some of the substring could not be inserted without exceeding the maximum length of the string.

```
;       Title               Insert a substring into a string          ;
;       Name:               Insert                                    ;
;                                                                     ;
;                                                                     ;

;                                                                     ;
;       Purpose:            Insert a substring into a string given a  ;
;                           starting index.                           ;
;                                                                     ;
;       Entry:              TOP OF STACK                              ;
;                             Low byte of return address,             ;
;                             High byte of return address,            ;
;                             Low byte of substring address,          ;
;                             High byte of substring address,         ;
;                             Maximum length of (source) string,      ;
;                             Starting index to insert the substring, ;
;                             Low byte of (source) string address,    ;
;                             High byte of (source) string address    ;
;                                                                     ;
;                             A string is a maximum of 255 bytes long plus ;
;                             a length byte which precedes it.        ;
;                                                                     ;
;       Exit:               Substring inserted into string.           ;
;                           if no errors then                         ;
;                             CARRY = 0                               ;
;                           else                                      ;
;                             begin                                   ;
;                               the following conditions cause the    ;
;                               CARRY flag to be set.                 ;
;                               if index = 0 then                     ;
;                                 do not insert the substring         ;
;                               if length(strg) > maximum length then ;
;                                 do not insert the substring         ;
```

```
;                               if index > length(strg) then             ;
;                                 concatenate substg onto the end of the  ;
;                                 source string                           ;
;                               if length(strg)+length(substring) > maxlen ;
;                                 then insert only enough of the substring ;
;                                 to reach maximum length                  ;
;                             end;                                         ;
;                                                                          ;
;       Registers used: All                                                ;
;                                                                          ;
;       Time:           Approximately                                      ;
;                        36 * (LENGTH(STRG) - INDEX + 1) +                 ;
;                        36 * (LENGTH(SUBSTG)) +                           ;
;                        207 cycles overhead.                              ;
;                                                                          ;
;       Size:           Program 214 bytes                                  ;
;                       Data      7 bytes plus                             ;
;                                 4 bytes in page zero                     ;
;                                                                          ;
;                                                                          ;

;EQUATES
SUBSTG  .EQU    0D0H            ;PAGE ZERO POINTER TO SUBSTRING
STRG    .EQU    0D2H            ;PAGE ZERO POINTER TO STRING

INSERT:
        ;GET RETURN ADDRESS
        PLA
        TAY                     ;SAVE LOW BYTE
        PLA
        TAX                     ;SAVE HIGH BYTE

        ;GET STARTING ADDRESS OF SUBSTRING
        PLA
        STA     SUBSTG          ;SAVE LOW BYTE
        PLA
        STA     SUBSTG+1        ;SAVE HIGH BYTE

        ;GET MAXIMUM LENGTH OF STRING
        PLA
        STA     MAXLEN

        ;GET STARTING INDEX for insertion
        PLA
        STA     INDEX

        ;GET STARTING ADDRESS OF SOURCE STRING
        PLA
        STA     STRG            ;SAVE LOW BYTE
        PLA
        STA     STRG+1          ;SAVE HIGH BYTE

        ;RESTORE RETURN ADDRESS
        TXA
        PHA                     ;RESTORE HIGH BYTE
        TYA
```

```
        PHA                             ;RESTORE LOW BYTE

        ;ASSUME NO ERRORS
        LDA     #0
        STA     INSERR                  ;ASSUME NO ERRORS WILL BE FOUND

        ;GET SUBSTRING AND STRING LENGTHS
        ; IF LENGTH(SUBSTG) = 0 THEN EXIT BUT NO ERROR
        LDY     #0
        LDA     (STRG),Y
        STA     SLEN                    ;GET LENGTH OF STRING
        LDA     (SUBSTG),Y
        STA     SUBLEN                  ;GET LENGTH OF SUBSTRING
        BNE     IDX0
        JMP     OKEXIT                  ;EXIT IF NOTHING TO INSERT (NO ERROR)
        ;IF STARTING INDEX IS ZERO THEN ERROR EXIT
IDX0:
        LDA     INDEX
        BNE     CHKLEN                  ;BRANCH IF INDEX NOT EQUAL 0
        JMP     EREXIT                  ;ELSE ERROR EXIT

        ;CHECK THAT THE RESULTING STRING AFTER THE INSERTION FITS IN THE
        ; SOURCE STRING. IF NOT THEN TRUNCATE THE SUBSTRING AND SET THE
        ; TRUNCATION FLAG.
CHKLEN:
        LDA     SUBLEN                  ;GET SUBSTRING LENGTH
        CLC
        ADC     SLEN
        BCS     TRUNC                   ;TRUNCATE SUBSTRING IF NEW LENGTH > 255
        CMP     MAXLEN
        BCC     IDXLEN                  ;BRANCH IF NEW LENGTH < MAX LENGTH
        BEQ     IDXLEN                  ;BRANCH IF NEW LENGTH = MAX LENGTH

        ;SUBSTRING DOES NOT FIT, SO TRUNCATE IT
TRUNC:
        LDA     MAXLEN                  ;SUBSTRING LENGTH = MAXIMUM LENGTH - STRING
                                        ; LENGTH
        SEC
        SBC     SLEN
        BCC     EREXIT                  ;ERROR EXIT IF MAXIMUM LENGTH < STRING LENGTH
        BEQ     EREXIT                  ;ERROR EXIT IF SUBSTRING LENGTH IS ZERO
                                        ; (THE ORIGINAL STRING WAS TOO LONG !!)
        STA     SUBLEN
        LDA     #0FFH
        STA     INSERR                  ;INDICATE SUBSTRING WAS TRUNCATED

        ;CHECK THAT INDEX IS WITHIN THE STRING. IF NOT CONCATENATE THE
        ; SUBSTRING ONTO THE END OF THE STRING.
IDXLEN:
        LDA     SLEN                    ;GET STRING LENGTH
        CMP     INDEX                   ;COMPARE TO INDEX
        BCS     LENOK                   ;BRANCH IF STARTING INDEX IS WITHIN STRING
        LDX     SLEN                    ;ELSE JUST CONCATENATE (PLACE SUBSTRING AT
                                        ; END OF STRING)
        INX
```

```
        STX     INDEX           ;START RIGHT AFTER END OF STRING
        LDA     #0FFH
        STA     INSERR          ;INDICATE ERROR IN INSERT
        LDA     SLEN            ;ADD SUBSTRING LENGTH TO STRING LENGTH
        CLC
        ADC     SUBLEN
        STA     SLEN
        JMP     MVESUB          ;JUST PERFORM MOVE, NOTHING TO OPEN UP

        ;OPEN UP A SPACE IN SOURCE STRING FOR THE SUBSTRING BY MOVING THE
        ; CHARACTERS FROM THE END OF THE SOURCE STRING DOWN TO INDEX, UP BY
        ; THE SIZE OF THE SUBSTRING.
LENOK:
        ;CALCULATE NUMBER OF CHARACTERS TO MOVE
        ; COUNT := STRING LENGTH - STARTING INDEX + 1
        LDA     SLEN
        SEC
        SBC     INDEX
        TAX
        INX                     ;X = NUMBER OF CHARACTERS TO MOVE

        ;SET THE SOURCE INDEX AND CALCULATE THE DESTINATION INDEX
        LDA     SLEN
        STA     SIDX            ;SOURCE ENDS AT END OF ORIGINAL STRING
        CLC
        ADC     SUBLEN
        STA     DIDX            ;DESTINATION ENDS FURTHER BY SUBSTRING LENGTH
        STA     SLEN            ;SET THE NEW LENGTH TO THIS VALUE ALSO

OPNLP:
        LDY     SIDX
        LDA     (STRG),Y        ;GET NEXT CHARACTER
        LDY     DIDX
        STA     (STRG),Y        ;MOVE IT UP IN MEMORY
        DEC     SIDX            ;DECREMENT SOURCE INDEX
        DEC     DIDX            ;DECREMENT DESTINATION INDEX
        DEX                     ;DECREMENT COUNTER
        BNE     OPNLP           ;CONTINUE UNTIL COUNTER = 0

        ;MOVE THE SUBSTRING INTO THE OPEN AREA
MVESUB:
        LDA     #1
        STA     SIDX            ;START AT ONE IN THE SUBSTRING
                                ;START AT INDEX IN THE STRING
        LDX     SUBLEN          ;X = NUMBER OF CHARACTERS TO MOVE

MVELP:
        LDY     SIDX
        LDA     (SUBSTG),Y      ;GET NEXT CHARACTER
        LDY     INDEX
        STA     (STRG),Y        ;STORE CHARACTER
        INC     SIDX            ;INCREMENT SUBSTRING INDEX
        INC     INDEX           ;INCREMENT STRING INDEX
        DEX                     ;DECREMENT COUNT
        BNE     MVELP           ;CONTINUE UNTIL COUNTER = 0
        LDA     INSERR          ;GET ERROR FLAG
```

```
        BNE     EREXIT          ;BRANCH IF SUBSTRING WAS TRUNCATED

OKEXIT:
        CLC                     ;NO ERROR
        BCC     EXIT

EREXIT:
        SEC                     ;ERROR EXIT

EXIT:
        LDA     SLEN
        LDY     #0
        STA     (STRG),Y        ;SET NEW LENGTH OF STRING
        RTS
;
;DATA SECTION
SLEN:   .BLOCK  1               ;LENGTH OF STRING
SUBLEN: .BLOCK  1               ;LENGTH OF SUBSTRING
MAXLEN: .BLOCK  1               ;MAXIMUM LENGTH OF STRING
INDEX:  .BLOCK  1               ;CURRENT INDEX INTO STRING
SIDX:   .BLOCK  1               ;A RUNNING INDEX
DIDX:   .BLOCK  1               ;A RUNNING INDEX
INSERR: .BLOCK  1               ;FLAG USED TO INDICATE IF AN ERROR

;                                                                ;
;                                                                ;
;       SAMPLE EXECUTION:                                        ;
;                                                                ;
;                                                                ;


SC0806:
        LDA     SADR+1  ;PUSH ADDRESS OF SOURCE STRING
        PHA
        LDA     SADR
        PHA
        LDA     IDX     ;PUSH STARTING INDEX FOR INSERTION
        PHA
        LDA     MXLEN   ;PUSH MAXIMUM LENGTH OF SOURCE STRING
        PHA
        LDA     SUBADR+1 ;PUSH ADDRESS OF THE SUBSTRING
        PHA
        LDA     SUBADR
        PHA
        JSR     INSERT  ;INSERT
        BRK             ;RESULT OF INSERTING "-" INTO "123456" AT
                        ; INDEX 1 IS "-123456"
        JMP     SC0806  ;LOOP FOR ANOTHER TEST

;
;DATA SECTION
IDX     .BYTE   1               ;INDEX TO START INSERTION
MXLEN   .BYTE   20H             ;MAXIMUM LENGTH OF DESTINATION
SADR    .WORD   STG             ;STARTING ADDRESS OF STRING
SUBADR  .WORD   SSTG            ;STARTING ADDRESS OF SUBSTRING
STG     .BYTE   06H             ;LENGTH OF STRING
```

```
        .BYTE   "123456                          " ;32 BYTE MAX LENGTH
SSTG    .BYTE   1                   ;LENGTH OF SUBSTRING
        .BYTE   "-                               " ;32 BYTE MAX LENGTH

        .END    ;PROGRAM
```

Adds the elements of a byte-length array, producing a 16-bit sum. The size of the array is specified and is a maximum of 255 bytes.

Procedure: The program clears both bytes of the sum initially. It then adds the elements successively to the less significant byte of the sum, starting with the element at the highest address. Whenever an addition produces a carry, the program increments the more significant byte of the sum.

Registers Used: All

Execution Time: Approximately 16 cycles per byte plus 39 cycles overhead. If, for example, (X) = $1A_{16}$ = 26_{10}, the execution time is approximately

$16 * 26 + 39 = 416 + 39 = 455$ cycles.

Program Size: 30 bytes

Data Memory Required: Two bytes on page 0 to hold a pointer to the array (starting at address ARYADR, $00D0_{16}$ in the listing).

Special Case: An array size of zero causes an immediate exit with the sum equal to zero.

Entry Conditions

(A) = More significant byte of starting address of array

(Y) = Less significant byte of starting address of array

(X) = Size of array in bytes

Exit Conditions

(A) = More significant byte of sum

(Y) = Less significant byte of sum

Example

Data: Size of array (in bytes) = (X) = 08

Array elements

$F7_{16} = 247_{10}$
$23_{16} = 35_{10}$
$31_{16} = 49_{10}$
$70_{16} = 112_{10}$
$5A_{16} = 90_{10}$
$16_{16} = 22_{10}$
$CB_{16} = 203_{10}$
$E1_{16} = 225_{10}$

Result: Sum = $03D7_{16} = 983_{10}$

(A) = more significant byte of sum = 03_{16}

(Y) = less significant byte of sum = $D7_{16}$

```
;       Title               8 BIT ARRAY SUMMATION                         ;
;       Name:               ASUM8                                         ;
;                                                                         ;
;                                                                         ;

;                                                                         ;
;       Purpose:            SUM the data of an array, yielding a 16 bit   ;
;                           result. Maximum size is 255.                  ;
;                                                                         ;
;       Entry:              Register A = High byte of starting array address;
;                           Register Y = Low byte of starting array address ;
;                           Register X = Size of array in bytes           ;
;                                                                         ;
;       Exit:               Register A = High byte of sum                 ;
;                           Register Y = Low byte of sum                  ;
;                                                                         ;
;       Registers used: All                                               ;
;                                                                         ;
;       Time:               Approximately 16 cycles per byte plus         ;
;                           39 cycles overhead.                           ;
;                                                                         ;
;       Size:               Program 30 bytes                              ;
;                           Data     2 bytes in page zero                 ;
;                                                                         ;
;                                                                         ;

;
;EQUATES SECTION
ARYADR: .EQU    0D0H            ;PAGE ZERO POINTER TO ARRAY

ASUM8:
        ;
        ;STORE STARTING ADDRESS
        STY     ARYADR
        STA     ARYADR+1

        ;DECREMENT STARTING ADDRESS BY 1 FOR EFFICIENT PROCESSING
        TYA                     ;GET LOW BYTE OF STARTING ADDRESS
        BNE     ASUM81          ;IS LOW BYTE ZERO ?
        DEC     ARYADR+1        ;YES, BORROW FROM HIGH BYTE
ASUM81: DEC     ARYADR          ;ALWAYS DECREMENT LOW BYTE

        ;EXIT IF LENGTH OF ARRAY IS ZERO
        TXA
        TAY
        BEQ     EXIT            ;EXIT IF LENGTH IS ZERO

        ;INITIALIZATION
        LDA     #0              ;INITIALIZE SUM TO 0
        TAX

        ;SUMMATION LOOP
SUMLP:
        CLC
        ADC     (ARYADR),Y      ;ADD NEXT BYTE TO LSB OF SUM
        BCC     DECCNT
        INX                     ;INCREMENT MSB OF SUM IF A CARRY OCCURS
```

```
DECCNT:
        DEY                     ;DECREMENT COUNT
        BNE     SUMLP           ;CONTINUE UNTIL REGISTER Y EQUALS 0

EXIT:
        TAY                     ;REGISTER Y = LOW BYTE OF SUM
        TXA                     ;REGISTER A = HIGH BYTE OF SUM
        RTS


;                                                                   ;
;                                                                   ;
;       SAMPLE EXECUTION                                            ;
;                                                                   ;
;                                                                   ;


;
SC0901:
        LDY     BUFADR          ;Y IS LOW BYTE OF BUFFER ADDRESS
        LDA     BUFADR+1        ;A IS HIGH BYTE OF BUFFER ADDRESS
        LDX     BUFSZ           ;X IS SIZE OF BUFFER
        JSR     ASUM8
        BRK                     ;SUM OF THE INITIAL TEST DATA IS 07F8 HEX,
                                ; REGISTER A = 07, REGISTER Y = F8H
        JMP     SC0901

;TEST DATA, CHANGE FOR OTHER VALUES
SIZE    .EQU    010H            ;SIZE OF BUFFER
BUFADR: .WORD   BUF             ;STARTING ADDRESS OF BUFFER

BUFSZ:  .BYTE   SIZE            ;SIZE OF BUFFER

BUF:    .BYTE   00H             ;BUFFER
        .BYTE   11H             ;DECIMAL ELEMENTS ARE 0,17,34,51,68
        .BYTE   22H             ; 85,102,119,136,153,170,187,204
        .BYTE   33H             ; 221,238,255
        .BYTE   44H
        .BYTE   55H
        .BYTE   66H
        .BYTE   77H
        .BYTE   88H
        .BYTE   99H
        .BYTE   0AAH
        .BYTE   0BBH
        .BYTE   0CCH
        .BYTE   0DDH
        .BYTE   0EEH
        .BYTE   0FFH            ;SUM = 07F8 (2040 DECIMAL)

        .END                    ;PROGRAM
```

16-Bit Array Summation (ASUM16) 9B

Adds the elements of a word-length array, producing a 24-bit sum. The size of the array is specified and is a maximum of 255 16-bit words. The 16-bit elements are stored in the usual 6502 style with the less significant byte first.

Procedure: The program clears a 24-bit accumulator in three bytes of memory and then adds the elements to the memory accumulator, starting at the lowest address. The most significant byte of the memory accumulator is incremented each time the addition of the more significant byte of an element and the middle byte of the sum produces a carry. If the array occupies more than one page of memory, the program must increment the more significant byte of the array pointer before proceeding to the second page.

Registers Used: All

Execution Time: Approximately 43 cycles per byte plus 46 cycles overhead. If, for example, (X) = 12_{16} = 18_{10}, the execution time is approximately

$$43 * 18 + 46 = 774 + 46 = 820 \text{ cycles.}$$

Program Size: 60 bytes

Data Memory Required: Three bytes anywhere in RAM plus two bytes on page 0. The three bytes anywhere in RAM hold the memory accumulator (starting at address SUM); the two bytes on page 0 hold a pointer to the array (starting at address ARYADR, $00D0_{16}$ in the listing).

Special Case: An array size of 0 causes an immediate exit with the sum equal to zero.

Entry Conditions

(A) = More significant byte of starting address of array

(Y) = Less significant byte of starting address of array

(X) = Size of array in 16-bit words

Exit Conditions

(X) = Most significant byte of sum

(A) = Middle byte of sum

(Y) = Least significant byte of sum

Example

Data: Size of array (in 16-bit words) = (X) = 08

Array elements

$F7A1_{16} = 63{,}393_{10}$

$239B_{16} = 9{,}115_{10}$

$31D5_{16} = 12{,}757_{10}$

$70F2_{16} = 28{,}914_{10}$

$5A36_{16} = 23{,}094_{10}$

$166C_{16} = 5{,}740_{10}$

$CBF5_{16} = 52{,}213_{10}$

$E107_{16} = 57{,}607_{10}$

Result: Sum = $03DBA1_{16} = 252{,}833_{10}$

(X) = most significant byte of sum = 03_{16}

(A) = middle byte of sum = DB_{16}

(Y) = least significant byte of sum = $A1_{16}$

```
;       Title           16 BIT ARRAY SUMMATION                       ;
;       Name:           ASUM16                                       ;
;                                                                    ;
;                                                                    ;

;                                                                    ;
;       Purpose:        Sum the data of an array, yielding a 24 bit  ;
;                       result. Maximum size is 255 16 bit elements. ;
;                                                                    ;
;       Entry:          Register A = High byte of starting array address;
;                       Register Y = Low byte of starting array address ;
;                       Register X = size of array in 16 bit elements   ;
;                                                                    ;
;       Exit:           Register X = High byte of sum                ;
;                       Register A = Middle byte of sum              ;
;                       Register Y = Low byte of sum                 ;
;                                                                    ;
;       Registers used: All                                          ;
;                                                                    ;
;       Time:           Approximately 43 cycles per byte plus        ;
;                       46 cycles overhead.                          ;
;                                                                    ;
;       Size:           Program 60 bytes                             ;
;                       Data     3 bytes plus                        ;
;                                2 bytes in page zero                ;
;                                                                    ;
;                                                                    ;

;
;EQUATES SECTION
ARYADR: .EQU    0D0H            ;PAGE ZERO POINTER TO ARRAY

ASUM16:
        ;
        ;STORE STARTING ADDRESS
        STY     ARYADR
        STA     ARYADR+1

        ;ZERO SUM AND INITIALIZE INDEX
        LDA     #0
        STA     SUM             ;SUM = 0
        STA     SUM+1
        STA     SUM+2
        TAY                     ;INDEX = 0

        ;EXIT IF THE ARRAY LENGTH IS ZERO
        TXA
        BEQ     EXIT

        ;SUMMATION LOOP
SUMLP:
        LDA     SUM
        CLC
        ADC     (ARYADR),Y      ;ADD LOW BYTE OF ELEMENT TO SUM
        STA     SUM
```

```
        LDA     SUM+1
        INY                         ;INCREMENT INDEX TO HIGH BYTE OF ELEMENT
        ADC     (ARYADR),Y          ;ADD HIGH BYTE WITH CARRY TO SUM
        STA     SUM+1               ;STORE IN MIDDLE BYTE OF SUM
        BCC     NXTELM
        INC     SUM+2               ;INCREMENT HIGH BYTE OF SUM IF A CARRY
NXTELM:
        INY                         ;INCREMENT INDEX TO NEXT ARRAY ELEMENT
        BNE     DECCNT
        INC     ARYADR+1            ;MOVE POINTER TO SECOND PAGE OF ARRAY
DECCNT:
        DEX                         ;DECREMENT COUNT
        BNE     SUMLP               ;CONTINUE UNTIL REGISTER X EQUALS 0

EXIT:
        LDY     SUM                 ;Y=LOW BYTE
        LDA     SUM+1               ;A=MIDDLE BYTE
        LDX     SUM+2               ;X=HIGH BYTE
        RTS

;DATA SECTION
SUM:    .BLOCK  3                   ;TEMPORARY 24 BIT ACCUMULATOR IN MEMORY

;                                                                          ;
;                                                                          ;
;       SAMPLE EXECUTION                                                   ;
;                                                                          ;
;                                                                          ;


;
SC0902:
        LDY     BUFADR              ;A,Y = STARTING ADDRES OF BUFFER
        LDA     BUFADR+1
        LDX     BUFSZ               ;X = BUFFER SIZE IN WORDS
        JSR     ASUM16              ;RESULT OF THE INITIAL TEST DATA IS 12570
        BRK                         ; REGISTER X = 0, REGISTER A = 31H,
                                    ; REGISTER Y = 1AH
        JMP     SC0902              ;LOOP FOR MORE TESTING

;
SIZE    .EQU    010H                ;SIZE OF BUFFER IN WORDS
BUFADR: .WORD   BUF                 ;STARTING ADDRESS OF BUFFER
BUFSZ:  .BYTE   SIZE                ;SIZE OF BUFFER IN WORDS
BUF:    .WORD   0                   ;BUFFER
        .WORD   111
        .WORD   222
        .WORD   333
        .WORD   444
        .WORD   555
        .WORD   666
        .WORD   777
        .WORD   888
        .WORD   999
        .WORD   1010
        .WORD   1111
        .WORD   1212
```

```
        .WORD   1313
        .WORD   1414
        .WORD   1515                    ;SUM = 12570 = 311AH

        .END    ;PROGRAM
```

Find Maximum Byte-Length Element (MAXELM) 9C

Finds the maximum element in an array of unsigned byte-length elements. The size of the array is specified and is a maximum of 255 bytes.

Procedure: The program exits immediately (setting Carry to 1) if the array size is zero. If the size is non-zero, the program assumes that the last byte of the array is the largest and then proceeds backward through the array, comparing the supposedly largest element to the current element and retaining the larger value and its index. Finally, the program clears the Carry to indicate a valid result.

Registers Used: All

Execution Time: Approximately 15 to 23 cycles per byte plus 52 cycles overhead. The extra eight cycles are used whenever the supposed maximum and its index must be replaced by the current element and its index. If, on the average, that replacement occurs half the time, the execution time is approximately

38 * ARRAY SIZE/2 + 52 cycles.

If, for example, ARRAY SIZE = 18_{16} = 24_{10}, the approximate execution time is

38 * 12 + 52 = 456 + 52 = 508 cycles.

Program Size: 45 bytes

Data Memory Required: One byte anywhere in RAM plus two bytes on page 0. The one byte anywhere in RAM holds the index of the largest element (at address INDEX). The two bytes on page 0 hold a pointer to the array (starting at address ARYADR, $00D0_{16}$ in the listing).

Special Cases:

1. An array size of 0 causes an immediate exit with the Carry flag set to 1 to indicate an invalid result.

2. If more than one element has the largest unsigned value, the program returns with the smallest possible index. That is, the index designates the occurrence of the maximum value closest to the starting address.

Entry Conditions

(A) = More significant byte of starting address of array

(Y) = Less significant byte of starting address of array

(X) = Size of array in bytes

Exit Conditions

(A) = Largest unsigned element

(Y) = Index to largest unsigned element

Carry = 0 if result is valid, 1 if size of array is 0 and result is meaningless.

Example

Data: Size of array (in bytes) = (X) = 08

Array elements

$35_{16} = 53_{10}$	$44_{16} = 68_{10}$
$A6_{16} = 166_{10}$	$59_{16} = 89_{10}$
$D2_{16} = 210_{10}$	$7A_{16} = 122_{10}$
$1B_{16} = 27_{10}$	$CF_{16} = 207_{10}$

Result: The largest unsigned element is element #2 ($D2_{16} = 210_{10}$)

(A) = largest element ($D2_{16}$)

(Y) = index to largest element (02)

Carry flag = 0, indicating that array size is non-zero and the result is valid

```
;       Title           Find the maximum element in an array of unsigned;
;                       bytes.                                          ;
;       Name:           MAXELM                                          ;
;                                                                       ;
;                                                                       ;


;                                                                       ;
;       Purpose:        Given the starting address of an array and      ;
;                       the size of the array, find the largest element ;
;                                                                       ;
;       Entry:          Register A = High byte of starting  address     ;
;                       Register Y = Low byte of starting address       ;
;                       Register X = Size of array in bytes             ;
;                                                                       ;
;       Exit:           If size of the array is not zero then           ;
;                         CARRY FLAG = 0                                ;
;                         Register A = Largest element                  ;
;                         Register Y = Index to that element            ;
;                          if there are duplicate values of the largest ;
;                          element, register Y will have the index      ;
;                          nearest to the first array element           ;
;                       else                                            ;
;                         CARRY flag = 1                                ;
;                                                                       ;
;       Registers used: All                                             ;
;                                                                       ;
;       Time:           Approximately 15 to 23 cycles per byte          ;
;                       plus 52 cycles overhead.                        ;
;                                                                       ;
;       Size:           Program 45 bytes                                ;
;                       Data     1 byte plus                            ;
;                                2 bytes in page zero                   ;
;                                                                       ;
;                                                                       ;

;EQUATES
ARYADR: .EQU    0D0H            ;PAGE ZERO FOR ARRAY POINTER

MAXELM:
        ;STORE STARTING ARRAY ADDRESS
        STA     ARYADR+1
        STY     ARYADR

        ;SUBTRACT 1 FROM STARTING ADDRESS TO INDEX FROM 1 TO SIZE
        TYA
        BNE     MAX1
        DEC     ARYADR+1        ;BORROW FROM HIGH BYTE IF LOW BYTE = 0
MAX1:   DEC     ARYADR          ;ALWAYS DECREMENT THE LOW BYTE

        ;TEST FOR SIZE EQUAL TO ZERO AND INITIALIZE TEMPORARIES

        TXA
        BEQ     EREXIT          ;ERROR EXIT IF SIZE IS ZERO
        TAY                     ;REGISTER Y = SIZE AND INDEX
        LDA     (ARYADR),Y      ;GET LAST BYTE OF ARRAY
        STY     INDEX           ;SAVE ITS INDEX
```

```
        DEY
        BEQ     OKEXIT          ;EXIT IF ONLY ONE ELEMENT

        ;WORK FROM THE END OF THE ARRAY TOWARDS THE BEGINNING COMPARING
        ; AGAINST THE CURRENT MAXIMUM WHICH IS IN REGISTER A
MAXLP:
        CMP     (ARYADR),Y
        BEQ     NEWIDX          ;REPLACE INDEX ONLY IF ELEMENT = MAXIMUM
        BCS     NXTBYT          ;BRANCH IF CURRENT MAXIMUM > ARY[Y]
                                ;ELSE ARY[Y] >= CURRENT MAXIMUM SO
        LDA     (ARYADR),Y      ; NEW CURRENT MAXIMUM AND
NEWIDX: STY     INDEX           ; NEW INDEX
NXTBYT:
        DEY                     ;DECREMENT TO NEXT ELEMENT
        BNE     MAXLP           ;CONTINUE

        ;
        ;EXIT
OKEXIT:
        LDY     INDEX           ;GET INDEX OF THE MAXIMUM ELEMENT
        DEY                     ;NORMALIZE INDEX TO (0,SIZE-1)
        CLC                     ;NO ERRORS
        RTS

EREXIT:
        SEC                     ;ERROR, NO ELEMENTS IN THE ARRAY
        RTS

;DATA SECTION
INDEX:  .BLOCK  1               ;INDEX OF LARGEST ELEMENT

;                                                                       ;
;                                                                       ;
;       SAMPLE EXECUTION:                                               ;
;                                                                       ;
;                                                                       ;


SC0903:
        LDA     AADR+1          ;A,Y = STARTING ADDRESS OF ARRAY
        LDY     AADR
        LDX     #SZARY          ;X = SIZE OF ARRAY
        JSR     MAXELM
        BRK                     ;RESULT FOR THE INITIAL TEST DATA IS
                                ; A = FF HEX (MAXIMUM), Y=08 (INDEX TO MAXIMUM)
        JMP     SC0903          ;LOOP FOR MORE TESTING


SZARY:  .EQU    10H             ;SIZE OF ARRAY
AADR:   .WORD   ARY             ;STARTING ADDRESS OF ARRAY

ARY:    .BYTE   8
        .BYTE   7
        .BYTE   6
        .BYTE   5
```

```
        .BYTE   4
        .BYTE   3
        .BYTE   2
        .BYTE   1
        .BYTE   0FFH
        .BYTE   0FEH
        .BYTE   0FDH
        .BYTE   0FCH
        .BYTE   0FBH
        .BYTE   0FAH
        .BYTE   0F9H
        .BYTE   0F8H

        .END    ;PROGRAM
```

Finds the minimum element in an array of unsigned byte-length elements. The size of the array is specified and is a maximum of 255 bytes.

Procedure: The program exits immediately, setting Carry to 1, if the array size is zero. If the size is non-zero, the program assumes that the last byte of the array is the smallest and then proceeds backward through the array, comparing the supposedly smallest element to the current element and retaining the smaller value and its index. Finally, the program clears the Carry flag to indicate a valid result.

Registers Used: All

Execution Time: Approximately 15 to 23 cycles per byte plus 52 cycles overhead. The extra eight cycles are used whenever the supposed minimum and its index must be replaced by the current element and its index. If, on the average, that replacement occurs half the time, the execution time is approximately

38 * ARRAY SIZE/2 + 52 cycles.

If, for example, ARRAY SIZE = $14_{16} = 20_{10}$, the approximate execution time is

38 * 10 + 52 = 380 + 52 = 432 cycles.

Program Size: 45 bytes

Data Memory Required: One byte anywhere in RAM plus two bytes on page 0. The one byte anywhere in RAM holds the index of the smallest element (at address INDEX). The two bytes on page 0 hold a pointer to the array (starting at address ARYADR, $00D0_{16}$ in the listing).

Special Cases:

1. An array size of 0 causes an immediate exit with the Carry flag set to 1 to indicate an invalid result.

2. If more than one element has the smallest unsigned value, the program returns with the smallest possible index. That is, the index designates the occurrence of the minimum value closest to the starting address.

Entry Conditions

(A) = More significant byte of starting address of array

(Y) = Less significant byte of starting address of array

(X) = Size of array in bytes

Exit Conditions

(A) = Smallest unsigned element

(Y) = Index to smallest unsigned element

Carry = 0 if result is valid, 1 if size of array is zero and result is meaningless.

Example

Data: Size of array (in bytes) = (X) = 08

Array elements

$35_{16} = 53_{10}$	$44_{16} = 68_{10}$
$A6_{16} = 166_{10}$	$59_{16} = 89_{10}$
$D2_{16} = 210_{10}$	$7A_{16} = 122_{10}$
$1B_{16} = 27_{10}$	$CF_{16} = 207_{10}$

Result: The smallest unsigned element is element #3 ($1B_{16} = 27_{10}$)

(A) = smallest element ($1B_{16}$)

(Y) = index to smallest element (03)

Carry flag = 0, indicating that array size is non-zero and the result is valid.

```
;       Title               Find the minimum element in an array of unsigned;
;                           bytes.                                          ;
;       Name:               MINELM                                          ;
;                                                                           ;
;                                                                           ;

                                                                            ;
;       Purpose:            Given the STARTING ADDRESS and the size of an   ;
;                           array, find the smallest element.               ;
;                                                                           ;
;       Entry:              Register A = High byte of starting  address     ;
;                           Register Y = Low byte of starting address       ;
;                           Register X = Size of array in bytes             ;
;                                                                           ;
;       Exit:               If size of the array is not zero then           ;
;                             CARRY FLAG = 0                                ;
;                             Register A = Smallest element                 ;
;                             Register Y = Index to that element            ;
;                              if there are duplicate values of the smallest;
;                              element Register Y will have the index       ;
;                              nearest to the first array element           ;
;                           else                                            ;
;                             CARRY flag = 1                                ;
;                                                                           ;
;       Registers used: All                                                 ;
;                                                                           ;
;       Time:               Approximately 15 to 23 cycles per byte          ;
;                           plus 52 cycles overhead.                        ;
;                                                                           ;
;       Size:               Program 45 bytes                                ;
;                           Data     1 bytes plus                           ;
;                                    2 bytes in page zero                   ;
;                                                                           ;
;                                                                           ;

;EQUATES
ARYADR: .EQU    0D0H            ;PAGE ZERO POINTER TO ARRAY

MINELM:
        ;STORE STARTING ARRAY ADDRESS
        STA     ARYADR+1
        STY     ARYADR

        ;DECREMENT ARRAY ADDRESS BY 1 TO INDEX FROM 1 TO SIZE
        TYA
        BNE     MIN1
        DEC     ARYADR+1        ;BORROW FROM HIGH BYTE IF LOW BYTE = 0
MIN1:   DEC     ARYADR          ;ALWAYS DECREMENT THE LOW BYTE

        ;TEST FOR SIZE EQUAL TO ZERO AND INITIALIZE TEMPORARIES

        TXA
        BEQ     EREXIT          ;ERROR EXIT IF SIZE IS ZERO
        TAY                     ;REGISTER Y = SIZE AND INDEX
        LDA     (ARYADR),Y      ;GET LAST BYTE OF ARRAY
        STY     INDEX           ;SAVE ITS INDEX
```

```
        DEY
        BEQ     OKEXIT          ;EXIT IF ONLY ONE ELEMENT

        ;WORK FROM THE END OF THE ARRAY TOWARDS THE BEGINNING COMPARING
        ; AGAINST THE CURRENT MINIMUM WHICH IS IN REGISTER A
MINLP:
        CMP     (ARYADR),Y
        BEQ     NEWIDX          ;REPLACE INDEX IF MINIMUM = ELEMENT
        BCC     NXTBYT          ;BRANCH IF CURRENT MINIMUM < ELEMENT
                                ;ELSE ELEMENT <= CURRENT MINIMUM
        LDA     (ARYADR),Y      ; NEW CURRENT MINIMUM AND
NEWIDX: STY     INDEX           ; NEW INDEX
NXTBYT:
        DEY                     ;DECREMENT TO NEXT BYTE
        BNE     MINLP

        ;
        ;EXIT
OKEXIT:
        LDY     INDEX           ;GET INDEX OF THE MINIMUM ELEMENT
        DEY                     ;NORMALIZE INDEX TO (0,SIZE-1)
        CLC                     ;NO ERRORS
        RTS

EREXIT:
        SEC                     ;ERROR, NO ELEMENTS IN THE ARRAY
        RTS

;DATA SECTION
INDEX:  .BLOCK  1               ;INDEX OF SMALLEST ELEMENT

;                                                                   ;
;                                                                   ;
;       SAMPLE EXECUTION:                                           ;
;                                                                   ;
;                                                                   ;


SC0904:
        LDA     AADR+1          ;A,Y = STARTING ADDRESS OF ARRAY
        LDY     AADR
        LDX     #SZARY          ;X = SIZE OF ARRAY
        JSR     MINELM
        BRK                     ;RESULT FOR THE INITIAL TEST DATA IS
                                ; A = 01H (MINIMUM), Y=07 (INDEX TO MINIMUM)
        JMP     SC0904          ;LOOP FOR MORE TESTING


SZARY:  .EQU    10H             ;SIZE OF ARRAY
AADR:   .WORD   ARY             ;STARTING ADDRESS OF ARRAY
ARY:    .BYTE   8
        .BYTE   7
        .BYTE   6
        .BYTE   5
        .BYTE   4
```

```
.BYTE    3
.BYTE    2
.BYTE    1
.BYTE    0FFH
.BYTE    0FEH
.BYTE    0FDH
.BYTE    0FCH
.BYTE    0FBH
.BYTE    0FAH
.BYTE    0F9H
.BYTE    0F8H

.END     ;PROGRAM
```

Searches an array of unsigned byte-length elements for a particular value. The array is assumed to be ordered with the smallest element at the starting (lowest) address. Returns the index to the value and the Carry flag cleared if it finds the value; returns the Carry flag set to 1 if it does not find the value. The size of the array is specified and is a maximum of 255 bytes. The approach used is a binary search in which the value is compared with the middle element in the remaining part of the array; if the two are not equal, the part of the array that cannot possibly contain the value (because of the ordering) is discarded and the process is repeated.

Procedure: The program retains upper and lower bounds (indexes) that specify the part of the array still being searched. In each iteration, the new trial index is the average of the upper and lower bounds. The program compares the value and the element with the trial index; if the two are not equal, the program discards the part of the array that could not possibly contain the element. That is, if the value is larger than the element with the trial index, the part at or below the trial index is discarded. If the value is smaller than the element with the trial index, the part at or above the trial index is discarded. The program exits if it finds a match or if there are no elements left to be searched (that is, if the part of the array being searched no longer contains anything). The program sets the Carry flag to 1 if it finds the value and to 0 if it does not.

In the case of Example 1 shown later (the value is $0D_{16}$), the procedure works as follows:

In the first iteration, the lower bound is zero and the upper bound is the length of the array minus 1 (since we have started our indexing at zero). So we have

LOWER BOUND = 0
UPPER BOUND = LENGTH − 1 = $0F_{16}$ = 15_{10}
GUESS = (UPPER BOUND + LOWER BOUND)/2 = 07 (the result is truncated)

ARRAY(GUESS) = ARRAY (7) = 10_{16} = 16_{10}

Since our value ($0D_{16}$) is less than ARRAY(7), there is no use looking at the elements with indexes of 7 or more, so we have

LOWER BOUND = 0
UPPER BOUND = GUESS − 1 = 06

Registers Used: All

Execution Time: Approximately 52 cycles per iteration plus 80 cycles overhead. A binary search will require on the order of $\log_2 N$ iterations, where N is the size of the array (number of elements).

If, for example, N = 32, the binary search will require approximately $\log_2 32$ iterations or 5 iterations. The execution time will then be approximately

$52 * 5 + 80 = 260 + 80 = 340$ cycles.

Program Size: 89 bytes

Data Memory Required: Three bytes anywhere in RAM plus two bytes on page 0. The three bytes anywhere in RAM hold the value being searched for (one byte at address VALUE), the lower bound of the area being searched (one byte at address LBND), and the upper bound of the area being searched (one byte at address UBND). The two bytes on page 0 hold a pointer to the array (starting at address ARYADR, $00D0_{16}$ in the listing).

Special Case: A size or length of zero causes an immediate exit with the Carry flag set to 1. That is, the length is assumed to be zero and the value surely cannot be found.

GUESS = (UPPER BOUND + LOWER BOUND)/2 = 03
ARRAY(GUESS) = ARRAY(3) = 07

Since our value ($0D_{16}$) is greater than ARRAY (3), there is no use looking at the elements with indexes of 3 or less, so we have

LOWER BOUND = GUESS + 1 = 04
UPPER BOUND = 06
GUESS = (UPPER BOUND + LOWER BOUND)/2 = 05
ARRAY (GUESS) = ARRAY(5) = 09

Since our value ($0D_{16}$) is greater than ARRAY(5), there is no use looking at the elements with indexes of 5 or less, so we have

LOWER BOUND = GUESS + 1 = 06
UPPER BOUND = 06
GUESS = (UPPER BOUND + LOWER BOUND)/2 = 06
ARRAY(GUESS) = ARRAY(6) = $0D_{16}$

Since our value ($0D_{16}$) is equal to ARRAY(6), we have found the element. If, on the other hand, our value were $0E_{16}$, the new lower bound would be 07 and there would no longer be any elements in the part of the array left to be searched.

Entry Conditions

Order in stack (starting from the top)

Less significant byte of return address
More significant byte of return address

Value to find

Size of the array (in bytes)

Less significant byte of starting address of array (address of smallest unsigned element)
More significant byte of starting address of array (address of smallest unsigned element)

Exit Conditions

Carry = 0 if the value is found, Carry = 1 if it is not found. If the value is found, (A) = index to the value in the array.

Examples

Length of array = 10_{16} = 16_{10}
Elements of array are 01_{16}, 02_{16}, 05_{16}, 07_{16}, 09_{16}, 09_{16}, $0D_{16}$, 10_{16}, $2E_{16}$, 37_{16}, $5D_{16}$, $7E_{16}$, $A1_{16}$, $B4_{16}$, $D7_{16}$, $E0_{16}$

1. Data: Value to find = $0D_{16}$
   Result: Carry = 0, indicating value found
   (A) = 06, the index of the value in the array

2. Data: Value to find = $9B_{16}$
   Result: Carry = 1, indicating value not found

```
;       Title               Binary Search                                ;
;       Name:               BINSCH                                       ;
;                                                                        ;
;                                                                        ;

;                                                                        ;
;       Purpose:            Search an ordered array of unsigned bytes,   ;
;                           with a maximum size of 255 elements.         ;
;                                                                        ;
;       Entry:              TOP OF STACK                                 ;
;                             Low byte of return address,                ;
;                             High byte of return address,               ;
;                             Value to find,                             ;
;                             Length (size) of array,                    ;
;                             Low byte of starting array address,        ;
;                             High byte of starting array address        ;
;                                                                        ;
;       Exit:               If the value is found then                   ;
;                             CARRY flag = 0                             ;
;                             Register A = index to the value in the array ;
;                           ELSE                                         ;
;                             CARRY flag = 1                             ;
;                                                                        ;
;       Registers used: All                                              ;
;                                                                        ;
;       Time:               Approximately 52 cycles for each time through ;
;                           the search loop plus 80 cycles overhead.     ;
;                           A binary search will take on the order of log ;
;                           base 2 of N searches, where N is the number of ;
;                           elements in the array.                       ;
;                                                                        ;
;       Size:               Program 89 bytes                             ;
;                           Data     3 bytes plus                        ;
;                                    2 bytes in page zero                ;
;                                                                        ;
;                                                                        ;


;
;EQUATES SECTION
ARYADR: .EQU    0D0H    ;PAGE ZERO POINTER TO ARRAY

;
BINSCH:
        ;GET RETURN ADDRESS
        PLA
        TAY
        PLA
        TAX

        ;GET THE VALUE TO SEARCH FOR
        PLA
        STA     VALUE

        ;GET THE LENGTH OF THE ARRAY
        PLA
        STA     UBND
```

```
        ;GET THE STARTING ADDRESS OF ARRAY
        PLA
        STA     ARYADR
        PLA
        STA     ARYADR+1

        ;RESTORE THE RETURN ADDRESS
        TXA
        PHA
        TYA
        PHA

        ;
        ;CHECK THAT LENGTH IS NOT ZERO
        LDX     UBND            ;GET LENGTH
        BEQ     NOTFND          ;EXIT NOT FOUND IF LENGTH EQUALS ZERO

        ;SET UPPER AND LOWER SEARCH BOUNDS
        DEX
        STX     UBND            ;UPPER BOUND EQUALS LENGTH MINUS 1
        LDA     #0
        STA     LBND            ;LOWER BOUND EQUALS 0

        ;SEARCH LOOP
        ;  COMPUTE NEXT INDEX TO BE HALF WAY BETWEEN UPPER BOUND AND
        ;  LOWER BOUND
NXTBYT:
        LDA     UBND
        CLC
        ADC     LBND            ;ADD LOWER AND UPPER BOUNDS
        ROR     A               ;DIVIDE BY 2, TRUNCATING FRACTION
        TAY                     ;REGISTER Y BECOMES INDEX

        ;IF INDEX IS GREATER THAN UPPER BOUND THEN THE ELEMENT IS NOT HERE
        CPY     UBND
        BEQ     TSTLB           ;BRANCH IF INDEX EQUALS UPPER BOUND
        BCS     NOTFND          ;BRANCH IF INDEX IS GREATER THAN UPPER BOUND

        ;IF INDEX IS LESS THAN LOWER BOUND THEN THE ELEMENT IS NOT HERE
TSTLB:
        CPY     LBND
        BCC     NOTFND          ;BRANCH IF INDEX IS LESS THAN LOWER BOUND

        ;TEST IF WE HAVE FOUND THE ELEMENT
        LDA     VALUE
        CMP     (ARYADR),Y
        BCC     SMALL           ;BRANCH IF VALUE IS SMALLER THAN ARYADR[Y]
        BEQ     FND             ;BRANCH IF FOUND

        ;VALUE IS LARGER THAN ARYADR[Y] SO SET LOWER BOUND TO BE
        ; Y + 1 (VALUE CAN ONLY BE FURTHER UP)
        INY
        STY     LBND
        BNE     NXTBYT          ;CONTINUE SEARCHING IF LOWER BOUND DOES NOT
                                ; OVERFLOW
        BEQ     NOTFND          ;BRANCH IF LOWER BOUND OVERFLOWED FROM 0FFH
                                ; TO 0
```

```
        ;VALUE IS SMALLER THAN ARYADR[Y] SO SET UPPER BOUND TO BE
        ; Y - 1 (VALUE CAN ONLY BE FURTHER DOWN)
SMALL:
        DEY
        STY     UBND
        CPY     #0FFH
        BNE     NXTBYT          ;CONTINUE SEARCHING IF UPPER BOUND DOES NOT
                                ; UNDERFLOW
        BEQ     NOTFND          ;BRANCH IF INDEX UNDERFLOWED

        ;FOUND THE VALUE
FND:
        CLC                     ;INDICATE VALUE FOUND
        TYA                     ;GET INDEX OF VALUE TO REGISTER A
        RTS

        ;DID NOT FIND THE VALUE
NOTFND:
        SEC                     ;INDICATE VALUE NOT FOUND
        RTS

;DATA SECTION
VALUE   .BLOCK  1               ;VALUE TO FIND
LBND    .BLOCK  1               ;INDEX OF LOWER BOUND
UBND    .BLOCK  1               ;INDEX OF UPPER BOUND


;                                                                       ;
;                                                                       ;
;       SAMPLE EXECUTION                                                ;
;                                                                       ;
;                                                                       ;

;
SC0905:
        ;SEARCH FOR A VALUE WHICH IS IN THE ARRAY
        LDA     BFADR+1
        PHA                     ;PUSH HIGH BYTE OF STARTING ADDRESS
        LDA     BFADR
        PHA                     ;PUSH LOW BYTE OF STARTING ADDRESS
        LDA     BFSZ
        PHA                     ;PUSH LENGTH (SIZE OF ARRAY)
        LDA     #7
        PHA                     ;PUSH VALUE TO FIND
        JSR     BINSCH          ;SEARCH
        BRK                     ;CARRY FLAG SHOULD BE 0 AND REGISTER A = 4

        ;SEARCH FOR A VALUE WHICH IS NOT IN THE ARRAY
        LDA     BFADR+1
        PHA                     ;PUSH HIGH BYTE OF STARTING ADDRESS
        LDA     BFADR
        PHA                     ;PUSH LOW BYTE OF STARTING ADDRESS
        LDA     BFSZ
        PHA                     ;PUSH LENGTH (SIZE OF ARRAY)
        LDA     #0
        PHA                     ;PUSH VALUE TO FIND
```

```
        JSR     BINSCH          ;SEARCH
        BRK                     ;CARRY FLAG SHOULD BE 1

        JMP     SC0905          ;LOOP FOR MORE TESTS
;
;DATA
SIZE    .EQU    010H            ;SIZE OF BUFFER
BFADR:  .WORD   BF              ;STARTING ADDRESS OF BUFFER
BFSZ:   .BYTE   SIZE            ;SIZE OF BUFFER
BF:                             ;BUFFER
        .BYTE   1
        .BYTE   2
        .BYTE   4
        .BYTE   5
        .BYTE   7
        .BYTE   9
        .BYTE   10
        .BYTE   11
        .BYTE   23
        .BYTE   50
        .BYTE   81
        .BYTE   123
        .BYTE   191
        .BYTE   199
        .BYTE   250
        .BYTE   255

        .END    ;PROGRAM
```

Bubble Sort (BUBSRT) 9F

Arranges an array of unsigned byte-length elements into ascending order using a bubble sort algorithm. An iteration of this algorithm moves the largest remaining element to the top by comparisons with all other elements, performing interchanges if necessary along the way. The algorithm continues until it has either worked its way through all elements or has completed an iteration without interchanging anything. The size of the array is specified and is a maximum of 255 bytes.

Procedure: The program starts by considering the entire array. It examines pairs of elements, interchanging them if they are out of order and setting a flag to indicate that the interchange occurred. At the end of an iteration, the program checks the interchange flag to see if the array is already in order. If it is not, the program performs another iteration, reducing the number of elements examined by one since the largest remaining element has been bubbled to the top. The program exits immediately if the length of the array is less than two, since no ordering is then necessary. Note that the number of pairs is always one less than the number of elements being considered, since the last element has no successor.

Registers Used: All

Execution Time: Approximately

$34 * N * N + 25 * N + 70$

cycles, where N is the size (length) of the array in bytes. If, for example, N is 20_{16} (32_{10}), the execution time is approximately

$34 * 32 * 32 + 25 * 32 + 70 = 34 * 1024 + 870$
$= 34{,}816 + 870 = 35{,}686$ cycles.

Program Size: 79 bytes

Data Memory Required: Two bytes anywhere in RAM plus four bytes on page 0. The two bytes anywhere in RAM hold the length of the array (one byte at address LEN) and the interchange flag (one byte at address XCHGFG). The four bytes on page 0 hold pointers to the first and second elements of the array (two bytes starting at address A1ADR, $00D0_{16}$ in the listing, and two bytes starting at address A2ADR, $00D2_{16}$ in the listing).

Special Case: A size (or length) of 00 or 01 causes an immediate exit with no sorting.

Entry Conditions

Order in stack (starting from the top)

Less significant byte of return address
More significant byte of return address

Length (size) of array in bytes

Less significant byte of starting address of array

More significant byte of starting address of array

Exit Conditions

Array sorted into ascending order, considered the elements as unsigned bytes. Thus, the smallest unsigned byte is now in the starting address.

Example

Data: Length (size) of array = 06

Elements = 35_{16}, $6A_{16}$, $2B_{16}$, $3E_{16}$, $D4_{16}$, $4F_{16}$

Result: After the first iteration, we have

35_{16}, $2B_{16}$, $3E_{16}$, $6A_{16}$, $4F_{16}$, $D4_{16}$.

The largest element is now at the end of the array and need not be considered further.

After the second iteration, we have

$2B_{16}$, 35_{16}, $3E_{16}$, $4F_{16}$, $6A_{16}$, $D4_{16}$.

The next to largest element is now in the correct position and need not be considered further.

The third iteration leaves the array unchanged, since the elements are already in ascending order.

```
;       Title               Bubble sort                                     ;
;       Name:               BUBSRT                                          ;
;                                                                           ;
;                                                                           ;

;                                                                           ;
;       Purpose:            Arrange an array of unsigned bytes into         ;
;                           ascending order using a bubble sort, with a     ;
;                           maximum size of 255 bytes.                      ;
;                                                                           ;
;       Entry:              TOP OF STACK                                    ;
;                             Low byte of return address,                   ;
;                             High byte of return address,                  ;
;                             Length (size) of array,                       ;
;                             Low byte of starting array address,           ;
;                             High byte of starting array address           ;
;                                                                           ;
;       Exit:               The array is sorted into ascending order.       ;
;                                                                           ;
;       Registers used: All                                                 ;
;                                                                           ;
;       Time:               Approximately (34 * N * N) + (25 * N) cycles    ;
;                           plus 70 cycles overhead, where N is the size of ;
;                           the array.                                      ;
;                                                                           ;
;       Size:               Program 79 bytes                                ;
;                           Data     2 bytes plus                           ;
;                                    4 bytes in page zero                   ;
;                                                                           ;
;                                                                           ;

;
;EQUATES SECTION
A1ADR:  .EQU    0D0H            ;ADDRESS OF FIRST ELEMENT
A2ADR:  .EQU    0D2H            ;ADDRESS OF SECOND ELEMENT

;
BUBSRT:
        ;GET THE PARAMETERS FROM THE STACK
        PLA
        TAY                     ;SAVE LOW BYTE OF RETURN ADDRESS
```

```
        PLA
        TAX                             ;SAVE HIGH BYTE OF RETURN ADDRESS

        PLA
        STA     LEN                     ;SAVE THE LENGTH (SIZE)
        PLA
        STA     A1ADR                   ;SAVE THE LOW BYTE OF THE ARRAY ADDRESS
        CLC
        ADC     #1
        STA     A2ADR                   ;SET LOW BYTE OF A2ADR TO A1ADR + 1
        PLA
        STA     A1ADR+1                 ;SAVE THE HIGH BYTE OF THE ARRAY ADDRESS
        ADC     #0
        STA     A2ADR+1                 ;SET HIGH BYTE OF A2ADR
        TXA
        PHA                             ;RESTORE HIGH BYTE OF RETURN ADDRESS
        TYA
        PHA                             ;RESTORE LOW BYTE OF RETURN ADDRESS

        ;BE SURE THE LENGTH IS GREATER THAN 1
        LDA     LEN
        CMP     #2
        BCC     DONE                    ;EXIT IF THE LENGTH OF THE ARRAY IS
                                        ; LESS THAN 2

        ;REDUCE LENGTH BY 1 SINCE THE LAST ELEMENT HAS NO SUCCESSOR
        DEC     LEN

        ;BUBBLE SORT LOOP
SRTLP:
        LDX     LEN                     ;X BECOMES NUMBER OF TIMES THROUGH INNER LOOP
        LDY     #0                      ;Y BECOMES BEGINNING INDEX
        STY     XCHGFG                  ;INITIALIZE EXCHANGE FLAG TO 0
INLOOP:
        LDA     (A2ADR),Y
        CMP     (A1ADR),Y               ;COMPARE 2 ELEMENTS
        BCS     AFTSWP                  ;BRANCH IF SECOND ELEMENT >= FIRST ELEMENT
        PHA                             ;SECOND ELEMENT LESS, SO EXHANGE ELEMENTS
        LDA     (A1ADR),Y               ;GET SECOND ELEMENT
        STA     (A2ADR),Y               ;STORE IT INTO THE FIRST ELEMENT
        PLA
        STA     (A1ADR),Y               ;STORE FIRST ELEMENT INTO SECOND
        LDA     #1
        STA     XCHGFG                  ;SET EXCHANGE FLAG SINCE AN EXCHANGE OCCURRED

AFTSWP:
        INY                             ;INCREMENT TO NEXT ELEMENT
        DEX
        BNE     INLOOP                  ;BRANCH NOT DONE WITH INNER LOOP

        ;INNER LOOP IS COMPLETE IF THERE WERE NO EXCHANGES THEN EXIT
        LDA     XCHGFG                  ;GET EXCHANGE FLAG
        BEQ     DONE                    ;EXIT IF NO EXCHANGE WAS PERFORMED
        DEC     LEN
        BNE     SRTLP                   ;CONTINUE IF LENGTH IS NOT ZERO
```

```
DONE:
        RTS

;DATA SECTION
LEN:    .BLOCK  1                   ;LENGTH OF THE ARRAY
XCHGFG: .BLOCK  1                   ;EXCHANGE FLAG (1=EXCHANGE, 0=NO EXCHANGE)

;                                                               ;
;                                                               ;
;       SAMPLE EXECUTION                                        ;
;                                                               ;
;                                                               ;


;
;PROGRAM SECTION
SC0906:
        ;SORT AN ARRAY
        LDA     BFADR+1
        PHA                         ;PUSH HIGH BYTE OF STARTING ADDRESS
        LDA     BFADR
        PHA                         ;PUSH LOW BYTE OF STARTING ADDRESS
        LDA     BFSZ
        PHA                         ;PUSH LENGTH (SIZE OF ARRAY)
        JSR     BUBSRT              ;SORT
        BRK                         ;THE RESULT FOR THE INITIAL TEST DATA IS
                                    ; 0,1,2,3, ... ,14,15
        JMP     SC0906              ;LOOP FOR MORE TESTS

;
;DATA SECTION
SIZE    .EQU    010H                ;SIZE OF BUFFER
BFADR:  .WORD   BF                  ;STARTING ADDRESS OF BUFFER
BFSZ:   .BYTE   SIZE                ;SIZE OF BUFFER
BF:                                 ;BUFFER
        .BYTE   15
        .BYTE   14
        .BYTE   13
        .BYTE   12
        .BYTE   11
        .BYTE   10
        .BYTE   9
        .BYTE   8
        .BYTE   7
        .BYTE   6
        .BYTE   5
        .BYTE   4
        .BYTE   3
        .BYTE   2
        .BYTE   1
        .BYTE   0

        .END    ;PROGRAM
```

RAM Test (RAMTST)

Performs a test of an area of RAM memory specified by a starting address and a length in bytes. Writes the values 00, FF_{16}, AA_{16} (10101010_2), and 55_{16} (01010101_2) into each byte and checks to see if they can be read back correctly. Places a single 1 bit in each position of each byte and sees if that can be read back correctly. Clears the Carry flag if all tests can be performed; if it finds an error it immediately exits, setting the Carry flag and returning the address in which the error occurred and the value that was being used in the test.

Procedure: The program performs the single value checks (with 00, FF_{16}, AA_{16}, and 55_{16}) by first filling the memory area and then comparing each byte with the specified value. Filling the entire area first should provide enough delay between writing and reading to detect a failure to retain data (perhaps caused by improperly designed refresh circuitry). The program then performs the walking bit test, starting with bit 7; here it writes the data into memory and immediately attempts to read it back for a comparison. In all the tests, the program handles complete pages first and then handles the remaining partial page; the program can thus use 8-bit counters rather than a 16-bit counter. This approach reduces execution time but increases memory usage as compared to handling the entire area with one loop. Note that the program exits immediately if it finds an error, setting the Carry flag to 1 and returning the location and the value being used in the test. If all the tests can be performed correctly, the program clears the Carry flag before exiting.

Registers Used: All

Execution Time: Approximately 245 cycles per byte tested plus 650 cycles overhead. Thus, for example, to test an area of size $0400_{16} = 1024_{10}$ would take

$$245 * 1024 + 650 = 250{,}880 + 650 = 251{,}530 \text{ cycles.}$$

Program Size: 229 bytes

Data Memory Required: Six bytes anywhere in RAM plus two bytes on page 0. The six bytes anywhere in RAM hold the address of the first element (two bytes starting at address ADDR), the length of the tested area (two bytes starting at address LEN), and the temporary length (two bytes starting at address TLEN). The two bytes on page 0 hold a pointer to the tested area (starting at address TADDR, $00D0_{16}$ in the listing).

Special Cases:

1. An area size of 0000_{16} causes an immediate exit with no memory tested. The Carry flag is cleared to indicate no errors.

2. Since the routine changes all bytes in the tested area, using it to test an area that includes its own temporary storage will produce unpredictable results.

Note that Case 1 means you cannot ask this routine to test the entire memory, but such a request would be meaningless anyway since it would require the routine to test its own temporary storage.

3. Attempting to test a ROM area will cause a return with an error indication as soon as the program attempts to store a value in a ROM location that is not already there.

Entry Conditions

Order in stack (starting from the top)

Less significant byte of return address
More significant byte of return address
Less significant byte of size (length) of area in bytes
More significant byte of size (length) of area in bytes
Less significant byte of starting address of test area
More significant byte of starting address of test area

Exit Conditions

1. If an error is found,
   Carry = 1
   (A) = More significant byte of address containing error
   (Y) = Less significant byte of address containing error
   (X) = Expected value (value being used in test)
2. If no error is found,
   Carry = 0
   All bytes in test area contain 00.

Example

Data: Starting address = 0380_{16}
Length (size) of area = 0200_{16}

Result: Area tested is the 0200_{16} bytes, starting at addresses 0380_{16}. That is, address 0380_{16} through $057F_{16}$. The order of the tests is:

1. Write and read 00
2. Write and read FF_{16}
3. Write and read AA_{16} (10101010_2)
4. Write and read 55_{16} (01010101_2)
5. Walking bit test, starting with bit 7 and moving right. That is, starting with 80_{16} (1000000_2) and moving the 1 bit one position right in each subsequent test of a single byte.

```
;       Title           RAM test                                   ;
;       Name:           RAMTST                                     ;
;                                                                  ;
;                                                                  ;

;                                                                  ;
;       Purpose:        Perform a test of RAM memory               ;
;                         1) Write all 00 hex and test             ;
;                         2) Write all FF hex and test             ;
;                         3) Write all AA hex and test             ;
;                         4) Write all 55 hex and test             ;
;                         5) Shift a single 1 bit thourgh all of memory ;
;                                                                  ;
;                         If the program finds an error, it exits  ;
;                         immediately with the CARRY flag set and  ;
;                         indicates where the error occurred and   ;
;                         what value it used in the test.          ;
;                                                                  ;
```

```
;       Entry:          TOP OF STACK                                  ;
;                         Low byte of return address,                 ;
;                         High byte of return address,                ;
;                         Low byte of length in bytes,                ;
;                         High byte of length in bytes,               ;
;                         Low byte of starting address of test area,  ;
;                         High byte of starting address of test area  ;
;                                                                     ;
;       Exit:           If there are no errors then                   ;
;                         CARRY flag equals 0                         ;
;                         test area contains 00 in all bytes          ;
;                       else                                          ;
;                         CARRY flag equals 1                         ;
;                         Register A = High byte of the address       ;
;                                      containing the error           ;
;                         Register Y = Low byte of the address        ;
;                                      containing the error           ;
;                         Register X = Expected value                 ;
;                                                                     ;
;       Registers used: All                                           ;
;                                                                     ;
;       Time:           Approximately 245 cycles per byte plus        ;
;                       650 cycles overhead.                          ;
;                                                                     ;
;       Size:           Program 228 bytes                             ;
;                       Data      6 bytes plus                        ;
;                                 2 bytes in page zero                ;
;                                                                     ;
;                                                                     ;

;
;EQUATES SECTION

TADDR:  .EQU    0D0H            ;PAGE ZERO POINTER TO TEST AREA

;
RAMTST:
        ;GET THE RETURN ADDRESS
        PLA
        TAY
        PLA
        TAX

        ;GET THE LENGTH OF THE TEST AREA
        PLA
        STA     LEN
        PLA
        STA     LEN+1

        ;GET THE STARTING ADDRESS OF THE TEST AREA
        PLA
        STA     ADDR
        PLA
        STA     ADDR+1
```

```
        ;RESTORE THE RETURN ADDRESS
        TXA
        PHA
        TYA
        PHA

        ;BE SURE THE LENGTH IS NOT ZERO
        LDA     LEN
        ORA     LEN+1
        BEQ     EXITOK          ;EXIT WITH NO ERRORS IF LENGTH IS ZERO

        ;FILL MEMORY WITH FF HEX (ALL 1'S) AND COMPARE
        LDA     #0FFH
        JSR     FILCMP
        BCS     EXITER          ;EXIT IF AN ERROR

        ;FILL MEMORY WITH AA HEX (ALTERNATING 1'S AND 0'S) AND COMPARE
        LDA     #0AAH
        JSR     FILCMP
        BCS     EXITER          ;EXIT IF AN ERROR

        ;FILL MEMORY WITH 55 HEX (ALTERNATING 0'S AND 1'S) AND COMPARE
        LDA     #55H
        JSR     FILCMP
        BCS     EXITER          ;EXIT IF AN ERROR

        ;FILL MEMORY WITH 0 AND COMPARE
        LDA     #0
        JSR     FILCMP
        BCS     EXITER

        ;PERFORM WALKING BIT TEST
        JSR     ITEMPS          ;INITIALIZE TEMPORARIES

        ;WALK THROUGH THE 256 BYTE PAGES
        LDX     TLEN+1          ;CHECK IF ANY FULL PAGES TO DO
        BEQ     WLKPRT          ;BRANCH IF NONE
        LDY     #0              ;REGISTER Y IS INDEX

WLKLP:
        LDA     #80H            ;SET BIT 7 TO 1, ALL OTHER BITS TO ZERO
WLKLP1:
        STA     (TADDR),Y       ;STORE TEST PATTERN IN MEMORY
        CMP     (TADDR),Y       ;COMPARE VALUE WITH WHAT IS READ BACK
        BNE     EXITER          ;EXIT INDICATING ERROR IF NOT THE SAME
        LSR     A               ;SHIFT TEST PATTERN RIGHT ONE BIT
        BNE     WLKLP1          ;BRANCH IF NOT DONE WITH BYTE
        STA     (TADDR),Y       ;STORE A ZERO BACK INTO THE LAST BYTE
        INY                     ;INCREMENT TO NEXT BYTE IN PAGE
        BNE     WLKLP           ;BRANCH IF NOT DONE WITH PAGE
        INC     TADDR+1         ;INCREMENT TO NEXT PAGE
        DEX                     ;DECREMENT PAGE COUNTER
        BNE     WLKLP           ;BRANCH IF NOT DONE WITH ALL OF THE PAGES

        ;WALK THROUGH LAST PARTIAL PAGE
```

```
WLKPRT:
        LDX     TLEN            ;GET NUMBER OF BYTES IN LAST PAGE
        BEQ     EXITOK          ;EXIT IF NONE
        LDY     #0              ;INITIALIZE INDEX TO ZERO

WLKLP2:
        LDA     #80H            ;START WITH BIT 7 EQUAL TO 1
WLKLP3:
        STA     (TADDR),Y       ;STORE TEST PATTERN IN MEMORY
        CMP     (TADDR),Y       ;COMPARE VALUE WITH WHAT IS READ BACK
        BNE     EXITER          ;EXIT INDICATING ERROR IF NOT THE SAME
        LSR     A               ;SHIFT TEST PATTERN RIGHT
        BNE     WLKLP3          ;BRANCH IF NOT DONE
        STA     (TADDR),Y       ;STORE A ZERO BACK INTO THE LAST BYTE
        INY                     ;INCREMENT TO NEXT BYTE
        DEX                     ;DECREMENT BYTE COUNTER
        BNE     WLKLP2          ;BRANCH IF NOT DONE

EXITOK:
        CLC                     ;RETURN WITH NO ERROR
        RTS

EXITER:
        JSR     ERROR           ;RETURN WITH AN ERROR
        RTS

;************************************
;ROUTINE: FILCMP
;PURPOSE: FILL MEMORY WITH A VALUE AND TEST
;         THAT MEMORY CONTAINS THAT VALUE
;ENTRY: REGISTER A = VALUE
;       ADDR = STARTING ADDRESS
;       LEN = LENGTH
;EXIT:  IF NO ERRORS THEN
;         CARRY FLAG EQUALS 0
;       ELSE
;         CARRY FLAG EQUALS 1
;         REGISTER A = HIGH BYTE OF ERROR LOCATION
;         REGISTER Y = LOW BYTE OF ERROR LOCATION
;         REGISTER X = EXPECTED VALUE
;REGISTERS USED: ALL
;************************************

FILCMP:
        JSR     ITEMPS          ;INITIALIZE TEMPORARIES

        ;FILL MEMORY WITH THE VALUE IN REGISTER A
        ;FILL FULL PAGES
        LDX     TLEN+1
        BEQ     FILPRT
        LDY     #0              ;START AT INDEX 0
FILLP:
        STA     (TADDR),Y       ;STORE THE VALUE
        INY                     ;INCREMENT TO NEXT LOCATION
        BNE     FILLP           ;BRANCH IF NOT DONE WITH THIS PAGE
```

```
        INC     TADDR+1             ;INCREMENT HIGH BYTE OF TEMPORARY ADDRESS
        DEX                         ;DECREMENT PAGE COUNT
        BNE     FILLP               ;BRANCH IF NOT DONE WITH FILL

FILPRT:
        ;FILL PARTIAL PAGE
        LDX     TLEN                ;REGISTER Y IS SET TO SIZE OF LAST PAGE
        LDY     #0
FILLP1:
        STA     (TADDR),Y
        INY
        DEX
        BNE     FILLP1              ;CONTINUE


        ;COMPARE MEMORY AGAINST THE VALUE IN REGISTER A
CMPARE:
        JSR     ITEMPS              ;INITIALIZE TEMPORARIES

        ;COMPARE MEMORY WITH THE VALUE IN REGISTER A
        ; COMPARE FULL PAGES FIRST
        LDX     TLEN+1
        BEQ     CMPPRT
        LDY     #0                  ;START AT INDEX 0
CMPLP:
        CMP     (TADDR),Y           ;CAN THE STORED VALUE BE READ BACK ?
        BNE     CMPER               ;NO, EXIT INDICATING ERROR
        INY                         ;INCREMENT TO NEXT LOCATION
        BNE     CMPLP               ;BRANCH IF NOT DONE WITH THIS PAGE
        INC     TADDR+1             ;INCREMENT HIGH BYTE OF TEMPORARY ADDRESS
        DEX                         ;DECREMENT PAGE COUNT
        BNE     CMPLP               ;BRANCH IF NOT DONE WITH FILL

CMPPRT:
        ;COMPARE THE LAST PARTIAL PAGE
        LDX     TLEN                ;REGISTER Y = SIZE OF PARTIAL PAGE
        LDY     #0
CMPLP1:
        CMP     (TADDR),Y           ;CAN THE STORED VALUE BE READ BACK ?
        BNE     CMPER               ;NO, EXIT INDICATING ERROR
        INY
        DEX
        BNE     CMPLP1              ;CONTINUE


CMPOK:
        CLC                         ;INDICATE NO ERROR
        RTS

CMPER:
        JSR     ERROR
        RTS

;************************************
;ROUTINE: ITEMPS
;PURPOSE: INITIALIZE TEMPORARIES
```

```
;ENTRY: ADDR IS BEGINNING ADDRESS
;       LEN IS NUMBER OF BYTES
;EXIT:  TADDR IS SET TO ADDR
;       TLEN IS SET TO LEN
;REGISTERS USED: Y,P
;***********************************

ITEMPS:
        LDY     ADDR
        STY     TADDR
        LDY     ADDR+1
        STY     TADDR+1

        LDY     LEN
        STY     TLEN
        LDY     LEN+1
        STY     TLEN+1
        RTS


;****************************************
;ROUTINE: ERROR
;PURPOSE: SET UP THE REGISTERS FOR AN ERROR EXIT
;ENTRY: REGISTER A IS EXPECTED BYTE
;       TADDR IS BASE ADDRESS
;       REGISTER Y IS INDEX
;EXIT   REGISTER X IS SET TO EXPECTED BYTE
;       REGISTER A IS SET TO HIGH BYTE OF THE ADDRESS CONTAINING THE ERROR
;       REGISTER Y IS SET TO LOW BYTE OF THE ADDRESS CONTAINING THE ERROR
;       CARRY FLAG IS SET TO 1
;REGISTERS USED: ALL
;****************************************

ERROR:
        TAX                     ;REGISTER X = EXPECTED BYTE
        TYA                     ;GET INDEX
        CLC                     ;ADDRESS OF ERROR = BASE + INDEX
        ADC     TADDR
        TAY                     ;REGISTER Y = LOW BYTE OF ERROR LOCATION
        LDA     TADDR+1
        ADC     #0              ;REGISTER A = HIGH BYTE OF ERROR LOCATION
        SEC                     ;INDICATE AN ERROR BY SETTING CARRY TO 1
        RTS


;DATA SECTION
ADDR:   .BLOCK  2               ;ADDRESS OF FIRST ELEMENT
LEN:    .BLOCK  2               ;LENGTH
TLEN:   .BLOCK  2               ;TEMPORARY LENGTH

;                                                                       ;
;                                                                       ;
;       SAMPLE EXECUTION                                                ;
;                                                                       ;
;                                                                       ;
```

```
SC0907:
        ;TEST MEMORY
        LDA     ADR+1
        PHA                     ;PUSH HIGH BYTE OF STARTING ADDRESS
        LDA     ADR
        PHA                     ;PUSH LOW BYTE OF STARTING ADDRESS
        LDA     SZ+1
        PHA                     ;PUSH HIGH BYTE OF LENGTH
        LDA     SZ
        PHA                     ;PUSH LOW BYTE OF LENGTH
        JSR     RAMTST          ;TEST
        BRK                     ;CARRY FLAG SHOULD BE 0
        JMP     SC0907          ;LOOP FOR MORE TESTING

ADR     .WORD   2000H
SZ      .WORD   1010H

        .END    ;PROGRAM
```

Jump Table (JTAB) 9H

Transfers control to an address selected from a table according to an index. The addresses are stored in the usual 6502 style (less significant byte first), starting at address TABLE. The size of the table (number of addresses) is a constant LENSUB, which must be less than or equal to 128. If the index is greater than or equal to LENSUB, the program returns control immediately with the Carry flag set to 1.

Procedure: The program first checks if the index is greater than or equal to the size of the table (LENSUB). If it is, the program returns control with the Carry flag set. If it is not, the program obtains the starting address of the appropriate subroutine from the table, stores it in memory, and jumps to it indirectly.

Registers Used: A, P

Execution Time: 31 cycles overhead, besides the time required to execute the subroutine.

Program Size: 23 bytes plus 2*LENSUB bytes for the table of starting addresses, where LENSUB is the number of subroutines.

Data Memory Required: Two bytes anywhere in RAM (starting at address TMP) to hold the indirect address obtained from the table.

Special Case: Entry with (A) greater than or equal to LENSUB causes an immediate exit with Carry flag set to 1.

Entry Conditions

(A) = index

Exit Conditions

If (A) is greater than LENSUB, an immediate return with Carry = 1. Otherwise, control transferred to appropriate subroutine as if an indexed call had been performed. The return address remains at the top of the stack.

Example

Data:	LENSUB (size of subroutine table) = 03.
	Table consists of addresses SUB0, SUB1, and SUB2.
	Index = (A) = 02
Result:	Control transferred to address SUB2 (PC = SUB2).

```
;       Title           Jump table                                      ;
;       Name:           JTAB                                            ;
;                                                                       ;
;                                                                       ;


;                                                                       ;
;       Purpose:        Given an index, jump to the subroutine with     ;
;                       that index in a table                           ;
;                                                                       ;
;       Entry:          Register A is the subroutine number 0 to        ;
;                            LENSUB-1, the number of subroutines,       ;
;                            LENSUB must be less than or equal to       ;
;                            128.                                       ;
;                                                                       ;
;       Exit:           If the routine number is valid then             ;
;                         execute the routine                           ;
;                       else                                            ;
;                         CARRY flag equals 1                           ;
;                                                                       ;
;       Registers used: A,P                                             ;
;                                                                       ;
;       Time:           31 cycles plus execution time of subroutine     ;
;                                                                       ;
;       Size:           Program 23 bytes plus size of table (2*LENSUB)  ;
;                       Data     2 bytes                                ;
;                                                                       ;
;                                                                       ;


;
JTAB:
        CMP     #LENSUB
        BCS     JTABER          ;BRANCH IF REGISTER A IS TOO LARGE
        ASL     A               ;MULTIPLY VALUE BY 2 FOR WORD-LENGTH INDEX
        TAY
        LDA     TABLE,Y         ;MOVE STARTING ADDRESS TO TEMPORARY STORAGE
        STA     TMP
        LDA     TABLE+1,Y
        STA     TMP+1
        JMP     (TMP)           ;JUMP INDIRECTLY TO SUBROUTINE

JTABER:
        SEC                     ;INDICATE A BAD ROUTINE NUMBER
        RTS

LENSUB  .EQU    3
TABLE:
        .WORD   SUB1            ;ROUTINE 0
        .WORD   SUB2            ;ROUTINE 1
        .WORD   SUB3            ;ROUTINE 2

TMP:    .BLOCK  2               ;TEMPORARY ADDRESS TO JUMP INDIRECT THROUGH
```

```
;THREE SUBROUTINES WHICH ARE IN THE JUMP TABLE
SUB1:
        LDA     #1
        RTS

SUB2:
        LDA     #2
        RTS

SUB3:
        LDA     #3
        RTS

;                                                                           ;
;                                                                           ;
;       SAMPLE EXECUTION                                                    ;
;                                                                           ;
;                                                                           ;

;
;PROGRAM SECTION
SC0908:
        LDA     #0
        JSR     JTAB
        BRK                     ;EXECUTE ROUTINE 0, REGISTER A EQUALS 1
        LDA     #1
        JSR     JTAB
        BRK                     ;EXECUTE ROUTINE 1, REGISTER A EQUALS 2
        LDA     #2
        JSR     JTAB
        BRK                     ;EXECUTE ROUTINE 2, REGISTER A EQUALS 3
        LDA     #3
        JSR     JTAB
        BRK                     ;ERROR CARRY FLAG EQUALS 1
        JMP     SC0908          ;LOOP FOR MORE TESTS

        .END    ;PROGRAM
```

Read a Line of Characters from a Terminal (RDLINE) 10A

Reads ASCII characters from a terminal and saves them in a buffer until it encounters a carriage return character. Defines the control characters Control H (08 hex), which deletes the character most recently entered into the buffer, and Control X (18 hex), which deletes all characters in the buffer. Sends a bell character (07 hex) to the terminal if the buffer becomes full. Echoes to the terminal each character placed in the buffer. Sends a new line sequence (typically carriage return, line feed) to the terminal before exiting.

RDLINE assumes the existence of the following system-dependent subroutines:

1. RDCHAR reads a single character from the terminal and places it in the accumulator.
2. WRCHAR sends the character in the accumulator to the terminal.
3. WRNEWL sends a new line sequence (typically consisting of carriage return and line feed characters) to the terminal.

These subroutines are assumed to change the contents of all the user registers.

RDLINE is intended as an example of a typical terminal input handler. The specific control characters and I/O subroutines in a real system will, of course, be computer-dependent. A specific example in the listing describes an Apple II computer with the following features:

1. The entry point for the routine that reads a character from the keyboard is $FD0C_{16}$. This routine returns with bit 7 set, so that bit must be cleared for normal ASCII operations.
2. The entry point for the routine that sends a character to the monitor is $FDED_{16}$. This routine requires bit 7 of the character (in the accumulator) to be set.
3. The entry point for the routine that issues the appropriate new line character (a carriage return) is $FD8E_{16}$.
4. An 08_{16} character moves the cursor left one position.

A standard reference describing the Apple II computer is L. Poole et al., *Apple II User's Guide,* Berkeley: Osborne/McGraw-Hill, 1981.

Registers Used: All

Execution Time: Approximately 67 cycles to place an ordinary character in the buffer, not considering the execution time of either RDCHAR or WRCHAR.

Program Size: 138 bytes

Data Memory Required: Four bytes anywhere in RAM plus two bytes on page 0. The four bytes anywhere in RAM hold the buffer index (one byte at address BUFIDX), the buffer length (one byte at address BUFLEN), the count for the backspace routine (one byte at address COUNT), and the index for the backspace routine (one byte at address INDEX). The two bytes on page 0 hold a pointer to the input buffer (starting at address BUFADR, $00D0_{16}$ in the listing).

Special Cases:

1. Typing Control H (delete one character) or Control X (delete the entire line) when there is nothing in the buffer has no effect on the buffer and does not cause anything to be sent to the terminal.
2. If the program receives an ordinary character when the buffer is full, it sends a Bell character to the terminal (ringing the bell), discards the received character, and continues its normal operations.

Procedure: The program first reads a character using the RDCHAR routine and exits if the character is a carriage return. If the character is not a carriage return, the program checks for the special characters Control H and Control X. In response to Control H, the program decrements the buffer index and sends a backspace string (consisting of cursor left, space, cursor left) to the terminal if there is anything in the buffer. In response to Control X, the program repeats the response to Control H until it empties the buffer. If the character is not special, the program checks to see if the buffer is full. If the buffer is full, the program sends a bell character to the terminal and continues. If the buffer is not full, the program stores the character in the buffer, echoes it to the terminal, and adds one to the buffer index. Before exiting, the program sends a new line sequence to the terminal using the WRNEWL routine.

Entry Conditions

(A) = More significant byte of starting address of buffer

(Y) = Less significant byte of starting address of buffer

(X) = Length (size) of the buffer in bytes.

Exit Conditions

(X) = Number of characters in the buffer.

Examples

1. Data: Line (from keyboard is 'ENTERcr'

 Result: Buffer index = 5 (length of line)

 Buffer contains 'ENTER'

 'ENTER' echoed to terminal, followed by the new line sequence (typically either carriage return, line feed or just carriage return)

 Note that the 'cr' (carriage return) character does not appear in the buffer.

2. Data: Line (from keyboard) is 'DMcontrolHN controlXENTETcontrolHRcr'.

 Result: Buffer index = 5 (length of actual line)

 Buffer contains 'ENTER'

 'ENTER' echoed to terminal, followed by the new line sequence (typically either carriage return, line feed or just carriage return)

The sequence of operations is as follows:

Character Typed	Initial Buffer	Final Buffer
D	empty	'D'
M	'D'	'DM'
control H	'DM'	'D'
N	'D'	'DN'
control X	'DN'	empty
E	empty	'E'
N	'E'	'EN'
T	'EN'	'ENT'
E	'ENT'	'ENTE'
T	'ENTE'	'ENTET'
control H	'ENTET'	'ENTE'
R	'ENTE'	'ENTER'
cr	'ENTER'	'ENTER'

What has happened is the following:

a. The operator types 'D', 'M'

b. The operator recognizes that 'M' is incorrect (should be 'N'), types control H to delete it, and types 'N'.

c. The operator then recognizes that the initial 'D' is incorrect also (should be 'E'). Since the character to be deleted is not the latest one, the operator types control X to delete the entire line, and then types 'ENTET'.

d. The operator recognizes that the second 'T' is incorrect (should be 'R'), types control H to delete it, and types 'R'.

e. The operator types a carriage return to conclude the line.

```
;       Title               Read line                                       ;
;       Name:               RDLINE                                          ;
;                                                                           ;
;                                                                           ;

;                                                                           ;
;       Purpose:            Read characters from the input device until     ;
;                           a carriage return is found. RDLINE defines the  ;
;                           following control characters:                   ;
;                             Control H -- Delete the previous character.   ;
;                             Control X -- Delete all characters.           ;
;                                                                           ;
;       Entry:              Register A = High byte of buffer address        ;
;                           Register Y = Low byte of buffer address         ;
;                           Register X = Length of the buffer               ;
;                                                                           ;
;       Exit:               Register X = Number of characters in the buffer ;
;                                                                           ;
;       Registers used: All                                                 ;
;                                                                           ;
;       Time:               Not applicable.                                 ;
;                                                                           ;
;       Size:               Program 138 bytes                               ;
;                           Data      4 bytes plus                          ;
;                                     2 bytes in page zero                  ;
;                                                                           ;
;                                                                           ;


;PAGE ZERO POINTER
BUFADR  .EQU    0D0H    ;INPUT BUFFER ADDRESS

;EQUATES
DELKEY  .EQU    018H    ;DELETE LINE KEYBOARD CHARACTER
BSKEY   .EQU    08H     ;BACKSPACE KEYBOARD CHARACTER
```

```
CRKEY   .EQU    0DH         ;CARRIAGE RETURN KEYBOARD CHARACTER
SPACE   .EQU    020H        ;SPACE CHARACTER
BELL    .EQU    07H         ;BELL CHARACTER TO RING THE BELL ON THE TERMINAL


RDLINE:
        ;SAVE PARAMETERS
        STA     BUFADR+1            ;SAVE HIGH BYTE OF INPUT BUFFER ADDRESS
        STY     BUFADR              ;SAVE LOW BYTE OF INPUT BUFFER ADDRESS
        STX     BUFLEN              ;SAVE MAXIMUM LENGTH

        ;INITIALIZE BUFFER INDEX TO ZERO
INIT:
        LDA     #0
        STA     BUFIDX

        ;READ LOOP
        ;READ CHARACTERS UNTIL A CARRIAGE RETURN OCCURS
RDLOOP:
        JSR     RDCHAR              ;READ A CHARACTER FROM THE KEYBOARD
                                    ;DOES NOT ECHO

        ;CHECK FOR CARRIAGE RETURN AND EXIT IF FOUND
        CMP     #CRKEY
        BEQ     EXITRD

        ;CHECK FOR BACKSPACE AND BACK UP IF FOUND
        CMP     #BSKEY
        BNE     RDLP1               ;BRANCH IF NOT BACKSPACE CHARACTER
        JSR     BACKSP              ;IF BACKSPACE, BACK UP ONE CHARACTER
        JMP     RDLOOP              ; THEN START READ LOOP AGAIN

        ;CHECK FOR DELETE LINE CHARACTER AND DELETE LINE IF FOUND
RDLP1:
        CMP     #DELKEY
        BNE     RDLP2               ;BRANCH IF NOT DELETE LINE CHARACTER
DEL1:
        JSR     BACKSP              ;DELETE A CHARACTER
        LDA     BUFIDX              ;CONTINUE DELETING UNTIL BUFFER IS EMPTY
        BNE     DEL1
        BEQ     RDLOOP              ;THEN GO READ THE NEXT CHARACTER

        ;NOT A SPECIAL CHARACTER
        ; CHECK IF BUFFER IS FULL
        ; IF NOT FULL STORE CHARACTER AND ECHO
RDLP2:
        LDY     BUFIDX              ;IS BUFFER FULL?
        CPY     BUFLEN
        BCC     STRCH               ;BRANCH IF NOT
        LDA     #BELL               ;YES IT IS FULL, RING THE TERMINAL'S BELL
        JSR     WRCHAR
        JMP     RDLOOP              ;THEN CONTINUE THE READ LOOP

STRCH:
        STA     (BUFADR),Y          ;STORE THE CHARACTER
        JSR     WRCHAR              ;ECHO CHARACTER TO TERMINAL
```

```
        INC     BUFIDX              ;INCREMENT BUFFER INDEX
        JMP     RDLOOP              ;THEN CONTINUE THE READ LOOP

        ;EXIT SEQUENCE
        ;ECHO NEW LINE SEQUENCE (USUALLY CR,LF)
        ;GET LENGTH OF BUFFER
EXITRD:
        JSR     WRNEWL              ;ECHO THE NEW LINE SEQUENCE
        LDX     BUFIDX              ;RETURN THE LENGTH IN X
        RTS                         ;RETURN


;**********************************************
;
; THE FOLLOWING SUBROUTINES ARE SYSTEM SPECIFIC,
; THE APPLE II WAS USED IN THESE EXAMPLES.
;
;**********************************************

;*********************************************
;ROUTINE: RDCHAR
;PURPOSE: READ A CHARACTER BUT DO NOT ECHO TO OUTPUT DEVICE
;ENTRY: NONE
;EXIT:  REGISTER A = CHARACTER
;REGISTERS USED: ALL
;****************************************

RDCHAR:
        JSR     0FD0CH              ;APPLE MONITOR READ KEYBOARD
        AND     #01111111B          ;ZERO BIT 7
        RTS

;****************************************
;ROUTINE: WRCHAR
;PURPOSE: WRITE A CHARACTER TO THE OUTPUT DEVICE
;ENTRY: REGISTER A = CHARACTER
;EXIT:  NONE
;REGISTERS USED: ALL
;****************************************

WRCHAR:
        ORA     #10000000B          ;SET BIT 7
        JSR     0FDEDH              ;APPLE MONITOR CHARACTER OUTPUT ROUTINE
        RTS

;*****************************************
;ROUTINE: WRNEWL
;PURPOSE: ISSUE THE APPROPRIATE NEW LINE CHARACTER OR
;         CHARACTERS. NORMALLY, THIS IS A CARRIAGE RETURN
;         AND LINE FEED, BUT SOME COMPUTERS (SUCH AS APPLE II)
;         REQUIRE ONLY A CARRIAGE RETURN.
;ENTRY: NONE
;EXIT:  NONE
;REGISTERS USED: ALL
;******************************************
```

```
WRNEWL:
        JSR     0FD8EH          ;ECHO CARRIAGE RETURN AND LINE FEED
        RTS

;****************************************
;ROUTINE: BACKSP
;PURPOSE: PERFORM A DESTRUCTIVE BACKSPACE
;ENTRY: BUFIDX = INDEX TO NEXT AVAILABLE LOCATION IN BUFFER
;EXIT:  CHARACTER REMOVED FROM BUFFER
;REGISTERS USED: ALL
;****************************************

BACKSP:

        ;CHECK FOR EMPTY BUFFER
        LDA     BUFIDX
        BEQ     EXITBS          ;EXIT IF NO CHARACTERS IN BUFFER

        ;BUFFER IS NOT EMPTY SO DECREMENT BUFFER INDEX
        DEC     BUFIDX          ;DECREMENT BUFFER INDEX

        ;OUTPUT BACKSPACE STRING
        LDA     #LENBSS
        STA     COUNT           ;COUNT = LENGTH OF BACKSPACE STRING
        LDA     #0
        STA     INDEX           ;INDEX = INDEX TO FIRST CHARACTER
BSLOOP:
        LDA     COUNT
        BEQ     EXITBS          ;EXIT IF ALL CHARACTERS HAVE BEEN SENT
        LDY     INDEX
        LDA     BSSTRG,Y        ;GET NEXT CHARACTER
        JSR     WRCHAR          ;OUTPUT CHARACTER
        INC     INDEX
        DEC     COUNT
        JMP     BSLOOP

EXITBS:
        RTS

CSRLFT  .EQU    08H     ;CHARACTER WHICH MOVES CURSOR LEFT ONE LOCATION
LENBSS: .EQU    3       ;LENGTH OF BACKSPACE STRING
BSSTRG: .BYTE   CSRLFT,SPACE,CSRLFT


;DATA
BUFIDX: .BLOCK  1               ;INDEX TO NEXT AVAILABLE CHARACTER IN BUFFER
BUFLEN: .BLOCK  1               ;BUFFER LENGTH
COUNT:  .BLOCK  1               ;COUNT FOR BACKSPACE AND RETYPE
INDEX:  .BLOCK  1               ;INDEX FOR BACKSPACE AND RETYPE


;                                                                       ;
;                                                                       ;
;       SAMPLE EXECUTION:                                               ;
;                                                                       ;
;                                                                       ;
```

```
SC1001:
        ;READ LINE
        LDA     #"?"
        JSR     WRCHAR          ;OUTPUT PROMPT (QUESTION MARK)
        LDA     ADRBUF+1        ;GET THE BUFFER ADDRESS
        LDY     ADRBUF
        LDX     #LINBUF         ;GET THE BUFFER LENGTH
        JSR     RDLINE          ;READ A LINE

        ;ECHO LINE
        STX     CNT             ;STORE NUMBER OF CHARACTERS IN THE BUFFER
        LDA     #0
        STA     IDX
TLOOP:
        LDA     CNT
        BNE     TLOOP1          ;BRANCH IF THERE ARE MORE CHARACTERS TO SEND
        JSR     WRNEWL          ;IF NOT ISSUE NEW LINE (CR,LF)
        JMP     SC1001          ;AND START OVER

TLOOP1:
        LDY     IDX
        LDA     INBUFF,Y        ;GET THE NEXT CHARACTER
        JSR     WRCHAR          ;OUTPUT IT
        INC     IDX
        DEC     CNT             ;DECREMENT LOOP COUNTER
        JMP     TLOOP


;DATA SECTION
IDX:    .BLOCK  1               ;INDEX
CNT:    .BLOCK  1               ;COUNTER
ADRBUF: .WORD   INBUFF          ;ADDRESS OF INPUT BUFFER
LINBUF: .EQU    10H             ;LENGTH OF INPUT BUFFER
INBUFF: .BLOCK  LINBUF          ;DEFINE THE INPUT BUFFER


        .END    ;PROGRAM
```

Write a Line of Characters to an Output Device
(WRLINE) 10B

Writes characters to an output device using the computer-dependent subroutine WRCHAR, which writes the character in the accumulator on the output device. Continues until it empties a buffer with given length and starting address. This subroutine is intended as an example of a typical output driver. The specific I/O subroutines will, of course, be computer-dependent. The specific example described is the Apple II computer with the following features:

1. The entry point for the routine that sends a character to the monitor is $FDED_{16}$.

2. The character to be written must be placed in the accumulator with bit 7 set to 1.

Procedure: The program exits immediately if the buffer length is zero. Otherwise, the program sends characters to the output device one at a time until the buffer is emptied. The program saves all its temporary data in memory rather than in registers to avoid dependence on the WRCHAR routine.

Registers Used: All

Execution Time: 24 cycles overhead plus 25 cycles per byte (besides the execution time of subroutine WRCHAR).

Program Size: 37 bytes

Data Memory Required: Two bytes anywhere in RAM plus two bytes on page 0. The two bytes anywhere in RAM hold the buffer index (one byte at address BUFIDX) and the buffer length (one byte at address BUFLEN). The two bytes on page 0 hold a pointer to the output buffer (starting at address BUFADR, $00D0_{16}$ in the listing).

Special Case:

A buffer length of zero causes an immediate exit with no characters sent to the output device.

Entry Conditions

(A) = More significant byte of starting address of buffer

(Y) = Less significant byte of starting address of buffer

(X) = Length (size) of the buffer in bytes.

Exit Conditions

None

Example

Data: Buffer length = 5
Buffer contains 'ENTER'

Result: 'ENTER' sent to the output device.

```
;       Title           Write line                                      ;
;       Name:           WRLINE                                          ;
;                                                                       ;
;                                                                       ;


;                                                                       ;
;       Purpose:        Write characters to the output device           ;
;                                                                       ;
;       Entry:          Register A = High byte of buffer address        ;
;                       Register Y = Low byte of buffer address         ;
;                       Register X = Length of the buffer in bytes      ;
;                                                                       ;
;       Exit:           None                                            ;
;                                                                       ;
;       Registers used: All                                             ;
;                                                                       ;
;       Time:           24 cycles overhead plus                         ;
;                       (25 + execution time of WRCHAR) cycles per byte ;
;                                                                       ;
;       Size:           Program 37 bytes                                ;
;                       Data     2 bytes plus                           ;
;                                2 bytes in page zero                   ;
;                                                                       ;
;                                                                       ;


;PAGE ZERO POINTER
BUFADR  .EQU    0D0H            ;OUTPUT BUFFER ADDRESS

WRLINE:
        ;SAVE PARAMETERS
        STA     BUFADR+1        ;SAVE HIGH BYTE OF OUTPUT BUFFER ADDRESS
        STY     BUFADR          ;SAVE LOW BYTE OF OUTPUT BUFFER ADDRESS
        STX     BUFLEN          ;SAVE LENGTH
        BEQ     EXIT            ;EXIT IF LENGTH = 0

        ;INITIALIZE BUFFER INDEX TO ZERO
        LDA     #0
        STA     BUFIDX
WRLOOP:
        LDY     BUFIDX
        LDA     (BUFADR),Y      ;GET NEXT CHARACTER
        JSR     WRCHAR          ;OUTPUT CHARACTER
        INC     BUFIDX          ;INCREMENT BUFFER INDEX
        DEC     BUFLEN          ;DECREMENT BUFFER LENGTH
        BNE     WRLOOP          ;BRANCH IF NOT DONE

EXIT:
        RTS

;***********************************************
;
; THE FOLLOWING SUBROUTINES ARE SYSTEM SPECIFIC,
; THE APPLE II WAS USED IN THIS EXAMPLE.
;
;***********************************************
```

```
;****************************************
;ROUTINE: WRCHAR
;PURPOSE: WRITE A CHARACTER TO THE OUTPUT DEVICE
;ENTRY: REGISTER A = CHARACTER
;EXIT:  NONE
;REGISTERS USED: ALL
;****************************************

WRCHAR:
        ORA     #10000000B          ;SET BIT 7
        JSR     0FDEDH              ;APPLE MONITOR CHARACTER OUTPUT ROUTINE
        RTS

;******************************
;
; DATA SECTION
BUFIDX: .BLOCK  1                   ;INDEX TO NEXT AVAILABLE CHARACTER IN BUFFER
BUFLEN: .BLOCK  1                   ;BUFFER LENGTH


;                                                                               ;
;                                                                               ;
;       SAMPLE EXECUTION:                                                       ;
;                                                                               ;
;                                                                               ;


SC1002:
        ;READ LINE USING THE APPLE MONITOR GETLN ROUTINE AT 0FD6AH
        ; 33H = ADDRESS CONTAINING APPLE PROMPT CHARACTER
        ; 200H = BUFFER ADDRESS
        LDA     #"?" OR 80H         ;USE ? FOR PROMPT WITH BIT 7 SET
        STA     033H                ;SET UP APPLE PROMPT CHARACTER
        JSR     0FD6AH              ;CALL APPLE MONITOR GETLN ROUTINE
        STX     LENGTH              ;RETURN LENGTH IN REGISTER X

        ;WRITE THE LINE
        LDA     #02H                ;A = HIGH BYTE OF BUFFER ADDRESS
        LDY     #0                  ;Y = LOW BYTE OF BUFFER ADDRESS
        LDX     LENGTH              ;X = LENGTH OF BUFFER
        JSR     WRLINE              ;OUTPUT THE BUFFER
        JSR     0FD8EH              ;OUTPUT CARRIAGE RETURN VIA APPLE MONITOR

        JMP     SC1002              ;CONTINUE

;DATA SECTION
LENGTH: .BLOCK  1



        .END    ;PROGRAM
```

Generate Even Parity (GEPRTY) 10C

Generates even parity for a seven-bit character and places it in bit 7. Even parity for a seven-bit character is a bit that makes the total number of 1 bits in the byte even.

Procedure: The program generates even parity by counting the number of 1 bits in the seven least significant bits of the accumulator. The counting is accomplished by shifting the data left logically and incrementing the count by one if the bit shifted into the Carry is 1. The least significant bit of the count is an even parity bit; the program concludes by shifting that bit to the Carry and then to bit 7 of the original data.

Registers Used: A, F

Execution Time: 114 cycles maximum. Depends on the number of 1 bits in the data and how rapidly the series of logical shifts makes the data zero. The program exits as soon as the remaining bits of data are all zeros, so the execution time is shorter if the less significant bits are all zeros.

Program Size: 39 bytes

Data Memory Required: One byte anywhere in RAM (at address VALUE) for the data.

Entry Conditions

Data in the accumulator (bit 7 is not used).

Exit Conditions

Data with even parity in bit 7 in the accumulator.

Examples

1. Data: (A) = 42_{16} = 01000010_2 (ASCII B)

   Result: (A) = 42_{16} = 01000010_2 (ASCII B with bit 7 cleared)
   Even parity is 0, since 01000010_2 has an even number (2) of 1 bits.

2. Data: (A) = 43_{16} = 01000011_2 (ASCII C)

   Result: (A) = $C3_{16}$ = 11000011_2 (ASCII C with bit 7 set)

```
;       Title               Generate even parity                        ;
;       Name:               GEPRTY                                      ;
;                                                                       ;
;                                                                       ;

;                                                                       ;
;       Purpose:            Generate even parity in bit 7 for a 7-bit   ;
;                           character.                                  ;
;                                                                       ;
;       Entry:              Register A = Character                      ;
```

```
;       Exit:             Register A = Character with even parity    ;
;                                                                     ;
;       Registers used: A,F                                           ;
;                                                                     ;
;       Time:             114 cycles maximum                          ;
;                                                                     ;
;       Size:             Program 39 bytes                            ;
;                         Data     1 byte                             ;
;                                                                     ;
;                                                                     ;


GEPRTY:
        ;SAVE THE DATA
        STA     VALUE

        ;SAVE X AND Y REGISTERS
        PHA
        TXA
        PHA
        TYA

        ;COUNT THE NUMBER OF 1 BITS IN BITS 0 THROUGH 6 OF THE DATA
        LDY     #0        ;INITIALIZE NUMBER OF 1 BITS TO ZERO
        LDA     VALUE     ;GET DATA
        ASL     A         ;DROP BIT 7 OF THE DATA, NEXT BIT TO BIT 7
        STA     VALUE
GELOOP: BPL     SHFT      ;BRANCH IF NEXT BIT (BIT 7) IS 0
        INY               ;ELSE INCREMENT NUMBER OF 1 BITS
SHFT:   ASL     A
        BNE     GELOOP    ;BRANCH IF THERE ARE MORE 1 BITS IN THE BYTE

        TYA               ;BIT 0 OF NUMBER OF 1 BITS IS EVEN PARITY
        LSR     A         ;MOVE PARITY TO CARRY
        LDA     VALUE
        ROR     A         ;ROTATE ONCE TO FORM BYTE WITH PARITY IN BIT 7
        STA     VALUE

        ;RESTORE X AND Y AND EXIT

        PLA
        TAY
        PLA
        TAX
        LDA     VALUE     ;GET VALUE WITH PARITY
        RTS               ;RETURN

;DATA SECTION
VALUE:  .BLOCK  1         ;TEMPORARY DATA STORAGE

;                                                                     ;
;                                                                     ;
;       SAMPLE EXECUTION:                                             ;
;                                                                     ;
;                                                                     ;
```

```
;GENERATE PARITY FOR VALUES FROM 0..127 AND STORE THEM IN BUFFER
SC1003:
        LDX     #0
SC1LP:
        TXA
        JSR     GEPRTY          ;GENERATE EVEN PARITY
        STA     BUFFER,X        ;STORE THE VALUE WITH EVEN PARITY
        INX
        CPX     #80H
        BNE     SC1LP           ;BRANCH IF NOT DONE
        BRK

BUFFER  .BLOCK  128


        .END    ;PROGRAM
```

Check Parity (CKPRTY) 10D

Sets the Carry flag to 0 if a data byte has even parity and to 1 if it has odd parity. A byte has even parity if it has an even number of 1 bits and odd parity if it has an odd number of 1 bits.

Procedure: The program counts the number of 1 bits in the data by shifting the data left logically and incrementing a count if the bit shifted into the Carry is 1. The program quits as soon as the shifted data becomes zero (since zero obviously does not contain any 1 bits). The least significant bit of the count is 0 if the data byte contains an even number of 1 bits and 1 if the data byte contains an odd number of 1 bits. The program concludes by shifting the least significant bit of the count to the Carry flag.

Registers Used: A, F

Execution Time: 111 cycles maximum. Depends on the number of 1 bits in the data and how rapidly the series of logical shifts makes the data zero. The program exits as soon as the remaining bits of data are all zeros, so the execution time is shorter if the less significant bits are all zeros.

Program Size: 25 bytes

Data Memory Required: One byte anywhere in RAM (at address VALUE) for the data.

Entry Conditions

Data byte in the accumulator (bit 7 is included in the parity generation).

Exit Conditions

Carry = 0 if the parity of the data byte is even, 1 if the parity is odd.

Examples

1. Data: (A) = 42_{16} = 01000010_2 (ASCII B)

   Result: Carry = 0, since 42_{16} (01000010_2) has an even number (2) of 1 bits.

2. Data: A) = 43_{16} = 01000011_2 (ASCII C)

   Result: Carry = 1, since 43_{16} (01000011_2) has an odd number (3) of 1 bits.

```
;       Title           Check parity                                 ;
;       Name:           CKPRTY                                       ;
;                                                                    ;
;                                                                    ;

;                                                                    ;
;       Purpose:        Check parity of a byte                       ;
;                                                                    ;
;       Entry:          Register A = Byte with parity in bit 7       ;
;                                                                    ;
;       Exit:           Carry = 0 if parity is even.                 ;
;                       Carry = 1 if parity is odd.                  ;
;                                                                    ;
;       Registers used: A,F                                          ;
;                                                                    ;
;       Time:           111 cycles maximum                           ;
;                                                                    ;
;       Size:           Program 25 bytes                             ;
;                       Data     1 byte                              ;
;                                                                    ;
;                                                                    ;


CKPRTY:
        ;SAVE DATA VALUE
        STA     VALUE

        ;SAVE REGISTERS X AND Y
        TXA
        PHA
        TYA
        PHA

        ;COUNT THE NUMBER OF 1 BITS IN THE VALUE
        LDY     #0      ;NUMBER OF 1 BITS = 0
        LDA     VALUE
CKLOOP: BPL     SHFT    ;BRANCH IF NEXT BIT = 0 (BIT 7)
        INY             ;ELSE INCREMENT NUMBER OF 1 BITS
SHFT:   ASL     A       ;SHIFT NEXT BIT TO BIT 7
        BNE     CKLOOP  ;CONTINUE UNTIL ALL BITS ARE 0

        TYA
        LSR     A       ;CARRY FLAG = LSB OF NUMBER OF 1 BITS

        ;RESTORE REGISTERS X AND Y AND EXIT
        PLA
        TAY
        PLA
        TAX
        RTS
```

```
VALUE   .BLOCK  1          ;DATA BYTE

;                                                                   ;
;                                                                   ;
;       SAMPLE EXECUTION:                                           ;
;                                                                   ;
;                                                                   ;


;CHECK PARITY FOR VALUES FROM 0..255 AND STORE THEM IN BUFFER
;BUFFER[VALUE] = 0 FOR EVEN PARITY
;BUFFER[VALUE] = 1 FOR ODD PARITY
SC1004:
        LDX     #0
SCLP:
        TXA
        JSR     CKPRTY          ;CHECK PARITY
        LDA     #0
        ROL     A               ;GET PARITY TO BIT 0
        STA     BUFFER,X        ;STORE THE PARITY
        INX                     ;INCREMENT VALUE
        BNE     SCLP            ;CONTINUE THROUGH ALL THE VALUES
        BRK
        JMP     SC1004

BUFFER  .BLOCK  256

        .END    ;PROGRAM
```

CRC-16 Checking and Generation (ICRC16,CRC16) 10E

Generates a 16-bit cyclic redundancy check (CRC) based on the IBM Binary Synchronous Communications (BSC or Bisync) protocol. Uses the polynomial $X^{16} + X^{15} + X^2 + 1$ to generate the CRC. The entry point ICRC16 initializes the CRC to 0 and the polynomial to the appropriate bit pattern. The entry point CRC16 combines the previous CRC with the CRC generated from the next byte of data. The entry point GCRC16 returns the CRC.

Procedure: Subroutine ICRC16 initializes the CRC to zero and the polynomial to the appropriate value (one in each bit position corresponding to a power of X present in the polynomial). Subroutine CRC16 updates the CRC according to a specific byte of data. It updates the CRC by shifting the data and the CRC left one bit and exclusive-ORing the CRC with the polynomial whenever the exclusive-OR of the data bit and the most significant bit of the CRC is 1. Subroutine CRC16 leaves the CRC in memory locations CRC (less significant byte) and CRC+1 (more significant byte). Subroutine GCRC16 loads the CRC into the accumulator (more significant byte) and index register Y (less significant byte).

Registers Used:

1. By ICRC16: A, F
2. By CRC16: None
3. By GCRC16: A, F, Y

Execution Time:

1. For ICRC16: 28 cycles
2. For CRC16: 302 cycles minimum if no 1 bits are generated and the polynomial and the CRC never have to be EXCLUSIVE-ORed. 19 extra cycles for each time the polynomial and the CRC must be EXCLUSIVE-ORed. Thus, the maximum execution time is 302 + 19*8 = 454 cycles.
3. For GCRC16: 14 cycles

Program Size:

1. For ICRC16: 19 bytes
2. For CRC16: 53 bytes
3. For GCRC16: 7 bytes

Data Memory Required: Five bytes anywhere in RAM for the CRC (two bytes starting at address CRC), the polynomial (two bytes starting at address PLY), and the data byte (one byte at address VALUE).

Entry Conditions

1. For ICRC16: none

2. For CRC16: data byte in the accumulator, previous CRC in memory locations CRC (less significant byte) and CRC+1 (more significant byte), CRC polynomial in memory locations PLY (less significant byte) and PLY+1 (more significant byte)

3. For GCRC16: CRC in memory locations CRC (less significant byte), and CRC+1 (more significant byte).

Exit Conditions

1. For ICRC16: zero (initial CRC value) in memory locations CRC (less significant byte) and CRC+1 (more significant byte)

CRC polynomial in memory locations PLY (less significant byte) and PLY+1 (more significant byte)

2. For CRC16: CRC with current data byte included in memory locations CRC (less significant byte) and CRC+1 (more significant byte)

3. For GCRC16: CRC in the accumulator (more significant byte) and index register Y (less significant byte).

Examples

1. Generating a CRC.

Call ICRC16 to initialize the polynomial and start the CRC at zero.

Call CRC16 to update the CRC for each byte of data for which the CRC is to be generated.

Call GCRC16 to obtain the resulting CRC (more significant byte in A, less significant byte in Y).

2. Checking a CRC.

Call ICRC16 to initialize the polynomial and start the CRC at zero.

Call CRC16 to update the CRC for each byte of data (including the stored CRC) for checking.

Call GCRC16 to obtain the resulting CRC (more significant byte in A, less significant byte in Y). If there were no errors, both bytes should be zero.

Note that only subroutine ICRC16 depends on the particular CRC polynomial being used. To change the polynomial requires only a change of the data that ICRC16 loads into memory locations PLY (less significant byte) and PLY+1 (more significant byte).

Reference

J.E. McNamara, *Technical Aspects of Data Communications,* Digital Equipment Corp., Maynard, Mass., 1977. This book contains explanations of CRC and the various communications protocols.

```
;       Title           Generate CRC-16                                   ;
;       Name:           CRC16                                             ;
;                                                                         ;
;                                                                         ;

;                                                                         ;
;       Purpose:        Generate a 16 bit CRC based on the IBM binary     ;
;                       synchronous communications protocol. The CRC is   ;
;                       based on the following polynomial:                ;
;                         (^ indicates "to the power")                    ;
;                               X^16 + X^15 + X^2 +1                      ;
;                                                                         ;
;                       To generate a CRC:                                ;
;                           1)  Call ICRC16 to initialize the CRC to 0    ;
;                               and the CRC polynomial.                   ;
;                           2)  Call CRC16 for each byte of data for      ;
;                               which the CRC is to be generated.         ;
;                           3)  Call GCRC16 to get the resulting CRC.     ;
;                               It should then be appended to the data,   ;
;                               high byte first.                          ;
;                                                                         ;
;                       To check a CRC:                                   ;
;                           1)  Call ICRC16 to initialize the CRC.        ;
;                           2)  Call CRC16 for each byte of data and      ;
;                               the 2 bytes of CRC previously generated.;
;                           3)  Call GCRC16 to obtain the CRC. It will    ;
;                               be zero if no errors have occurred.       ;
;                                                                         ;
;       Entry:          Register A = Data byte                            ;
;                                                                         ;
;       Exit:           CRCLO and CRCHI updated                           ;
;                       Register A = Data byte                            ;
;                                                                         ;
;       Registers used: None                                              ;
;                                                                         ;
;       Time:           302 cycles minimum if no 1 bits are generated.    ;
;                       454 cycles maximum if all 1 bits are generated.   ;
;                                                                         ;
;       Size:           Program 53 bytes                                  ;
;                       Data    5 bytes                                   ;
;                                                                         ;
;                                                                         ;


CRC16:
        ;SAVE THE DATA BYTE
        STA     VALUE

        ;SAVE ALL REGISTERS
        PHP
        PHA
        TYA
        PHA
        TXA
        PHA
```

```
        ;LOOP THROUGH EACH BIT GENERATING THE CRC
        LDX     #8                  ;8 BITS PER BYTE
CRCLP:
        ASL     VALUE               ;MOVE BIT 7 TO CARRY
        ROR     A                   ;MOVE CARRY TO BIT 7
        AND     #10000000B          ;MASK OFF ALL OTHER BITS
        EOR     CRC+1               ;EXCLUSIVE OR BIT 7 WITH BIT 16 OF THE CRC
        ASL     CRC                 ;SHIFT CRC LEFT 1 BIT (FIRST THE LOW BYTE,
        ROL     A                   ; THEN THE HIGH BYTE)
        BCC     CRCLP1              ;BRANCH IF THE MSB OF THE CRC IS 1

        ;BIT 7 IS 1 SO EXCLUSIVE-OR THE CRC WITH THE POLYNOMIAL
        TAY                         ;SAVE CRC HIGH IN Y
        LDA     CRC
        EOR     PLY                 ;EXCLUSIVE OR LOW BYTE WITH THE POLYNOMIAL
        STA     CRC
        TYA
        EOR     PLY+1               ;DO HIGH BYTE ALSO

CRCLP1:
        STA     CRC+1               ;STORE THE HIGH BYTE OF THE CRC
        DEX
        BNE     CRCLP               ;BRANCH IF NOT DONE WITH ALL 8 BITS

        ;RESTORE THE REGISTERS AND EXIT
        PLA
        TAX
        PLA
        TAY
        PLA
        PLP
        RTS

;****************************************
;ROUTINE: ICRC16
;PURPOSE: INITIALIZE CRCHI, CRCLO, PLYHI, PLYLO
;ENTRY: NONE
;EXIT:  CRC AND POLYNOMIAL INITIALIZED
;REGISTERS USED: A,F
;****************************************

ICRC16:
        LDA     #0
        STA     CRC                 ;CRC = 0
        STA     CRC+1
        LDA     #5
        STA     PLY                 ;PLY = 8005H
                                    ;8005H IS FOR X^16+X^15+X^2+1
                                    ; (1 IN EACH POSITION FOR WHICH A POWER
                                    ;  APPEARS IN THE FORMULA)
        LDA     #80H
        STA     PLY+1
        RTS
```

```
;*****************************************
;ROUTINE: GCRC16
;PURPOSE: GET THE CRC16 VALUE
;ENTRY: NONE
;EXIT:   REGISTER A = CRC16 HIGH BYTE
;        REGISTER Y = CRC16 LOW BYTE
;REGISTERS USED: A,F,Y
;*****************************************

GCRC16:
        LDA     CRC+1               ;A = HIGH BYTE
        LDY     CRC                 ;Y = LOW BYTE
        RTS

VALUE:  .BLOCK  1                   ;DATA BYTE
CRC:    .BLOCK  2                   ;CRC VALUE
PLY:    .BLOCK  2                   ;POLYNOMIAL VALUE USED TO GENERATE THE CRC


;                                                                       ;
;                                                                       ;
;       SAMPLE EXECUTION:                                               ;
;                                                                       ;
;                                                                       ;


        ;GENERATE A CRC FOR A VALUE OF 1 AND CHECK IT
SC1005:
        JSR     ICRC16
        LDA     #1
        JSR     CRC16               ;GENERATE CRC
        JSR     GCRC16
        TAX                         ;SAVE CRC HIGH BYTE IN REGISTER X
        JSR     ICRC16              ;INITIALIZE AGAIN
        LDA     #1
        JSR     CRC16               ;CHECK CRC BY GENERATING IT FOR DATA
        TXA
        JSR     CRC16               ; AND THE STORED CRC ALSO
        TYA
        JSR     CRC16
        JSR     GCRC16
        BRK                         ;THE CRC SHOULD BE ZERO IN REGISTERS A AND Y

        ;GENERATE A CRC FOR THE VALUES FROM 0..255 AND CHECK IT
        JSR     ICRC16
        LDX     #0
GENLP:
        TXA                         ;GET NEXT BYTE
        JSR     CRC16               ;UPDATE CRC
        INX
        BNE     GENLP               ;BRANCH IF NOT DONE

        JSR     GCRC16              ;GET RESULTING CRC
        STA     CRCVAL+1            ;AND SAVE IT
        STY     CRCVAL
```

```
        ;CHECK THE CRC BY GENERATING IT AGAIN
        JSR     ICRC16
        LDX     #0
CHKLP:
        TXA
        JSR     CRC16
        INX
        BNE     CHKLP

        ;ALSO INCLUDE STORED CRC IN CHECK
        LDA     CRCVAL+1
        JSR     CRC16           ;HIGH BYTE OF CRC FIRST
        LDA     CRCVAL
        JSR     CRC16           ;THEN LOW BYTE OF CRC

        JSR     GCRC16          ;GET RESULTING CRC
        BRK                     ;IT SHOULD BE 0
        JMP     SC1005

CRCVAL: BLOCK   2

        .END
```

I/O Device Table Handler (IOHDLR) 10F

Registers Used
1. By IOHDRL: All
2. By INITL: A, F
3. By ADDDL: All

Execution Time
1. For IOHDLR: 93 cycles overhead plus 59 cycles for each unsuccessful match of a device number
2. For INITL: 14 cycles
3. For ADDDL: 48 cycles

Program Size
1. For IOHDLR: 101 bytes
2. For INITL: 9 bytes
3. For ADDDL: 21 bytes

Data Memory Required: Three bytes anywhere in RAM plus six bytes on page 0. The three bytes anywhere in RAM hold an indirect address used to vector to an I/O subroutine (two bytes starting at address OPADR) and the X register (one byte at address SVXREG). The six bytes on page 0 hold the starting address of the I/O control block (two bytes starting at address IOCB), the head of the list of devices (two bytes starting at address DVLST), and the starting address of the current device table entry (two bytes starting at address CURDEV).

Performs input and output in a device-independent manner using I/O control blocks and an I/O device table. The I/O device table consists of a linked list; each entry contains a link to the next entry, the device number, and starting addresses for routines that initialize the device, determine its input status, read data from it, determine its output status, and write data to it. An I/O control block is an array containing the device number, the operation number, device status, the starting address of the device's buffer, and the length of the device's buffer. The user must provide IOHDLR with the address of an appropriate I/O control block and the data if only one byte is to be written. IOHDLR will return a copy of the status byte and the data if only one byte is read.

This subroutine is intended as an example of how to handle input and output in a device-independent manner. The I/O device table must be constructed using subroutines INITIO, which initializes the device list to empty, and ADDDL, which adds a device to the list. A specific example for the Apple II sets up the Apple II console as device 1 and the printer as device 2; a test routine reads a line from the console and echoes it to the console and the printer.

A general purpose program will perform input or output by obtaining or constructing an I/O control block and then calling IOHDLR. Subroutine IOHDLR will then determine which device to use and how to transfer control to its I/O driver by using the I/O device table.

Procedure: The program first initializes the status byte to zero, indicating no errors. It then searches the device table, looking for the device number in the I/O control block. If it does not find a match in the table, it exits with an appropriate error number in the status byte. If the program finds a device with the proper device number, it checks for a valid operation and transfers control to the appropriate routine from the entry in the device table. That routine must then transfer control back to the original calling routine. If the operation is invalid (the operation number is too large or the starting address for the routine is zero), the program returns with an error indication in the status byte.

Subroutine INITDL initializes the device list, setting the initial link to zero.

Subroutine ADDDL adds an entry to the device list, making its address the head of the list and setting its link field to the old head of the list.

Entry Conditions

1. For IOHDLR:

(A) = More significant byte of starting address of input/output control block

(Y) = Less significant byte of starting address of input/output control block

(X) = Byte of data if the operation is to write one byte.

2. For INITL: None

3. For ADDDL:

(A) = More significant byte of starting address of a device table entry

(Y) = Less significant byte of starting address of a device table entry.

Exit Conditions

1. For IOHDLR:

(A) = I/O control block status byte if an error is found; otherwise, the routine exits to the appropriate I/O driver.

(X) = Byte of data if the operation is to read one byte.

2. For INITL:

Device list header (addresses DVLST and DVLST+1) cleared to indicate empty list.

3. For ADDDL:

Device table entry added to list.

Example

In the example provided, we have the following structure:

INPUT/OUTPUT OPERATIONS

Operation Number	Operation
0	Initialize device
1	Determine input status
2	Read 1 byte from input device
3	Read N bytes from input device (normally one line)
4	Determine output status
5	Write one byte to output device
6	Write N bytes to output device (normally one line)

INPUT/OUTPUT CONTROL BLOCK

Index	Contents
0	Device number
1	Operation number
2	Status
3	Less significant byte of starting address of buffer
4	More significant byte of starting address of buffer
5	Less significant byte of buffer length
6	More significant byte of buffer length

DEVICE TABLE ENTRY

Index	Contents
0	Less significant byte of link field (starting address of next element)
1	More significant byte of link field (starting address of next element)
2	Device number
3	Less significant byte of starting address of device initialization routine
4	More significant byte of starting address of device initialization routine
5	Less significant byte of starting address of input status determination routine
6	More significant byte of starting address of input status determination routine
7	Less significant byte of starting address of input driver routine (read 1 byte only)
8	More significant byte of starting address of input driver routine (read 1 byte only)
9	Less significant byte of starting address of input driver routine (N bytes or 1 line)
10	More significant byte of starting address of input driver routine (N bytes or 1 line)
11	Less significant byte of starting address of output status determination routine
12	More significant byte of starting address of output status determination routine
13	Less significant byte of starting address of output driver routine (write 1 byte only)
14	More significant byte of starting address of output driver routine (write 1 byte only)
15	Less significant byte of starting address of output driver routine (N bytes or l line)
16	More significant byte of starting address of output driver routine (N bytes or 1 line)

If an operation is irrelevant or undefined for a particular device (e.g., output status determination for a keyboard or an input driver routine for a printer), the corresponding starting address in the device table must be set to zero (i.e., 0000_{16}).

STATUS VALUES

Value	Description
0	No errors
1	Bad device number (no such device)
2	Data available from input device, no such operation for I/O
3	Output device ready

```
;        Title            I/O Device table handler                    ;
;        Name:            IOHDLR                                      ;
;                                                                     ;
;                                                                     ;

;                                                                     ;
;        Purpose:         Perform I/O in a device independent manner. ;
;                         This can only be implemented by accessing all ;
;                         devices  in the same way using a I/O Control ;
;                         Block (IOCB) and a device table. The routines ;
;                         here will allow the following operations:   ;
;                                                                     ;
```

```
;                     Operation number  Description                ;
;                          0            Initialize device          ;
;                          1            Input status               ;
;                          2            Read 1 byte                ;
;                          3            Read N bytes               ;
;                          4            Output status              ;
;                          5            Write 1 byte               ;
;                          6            Write N bytes              ;
;                                                                  ;
;                     Other operations that could be included are  ;
;                     Open, Close, Delete, Rename, and Append which ;
;                     would support devices such as floppy disks.  ;
;                                                                  ;
;                     A IOCB will be an array of the following form: ;
;                                                                  ;
;                     IOCB + 0 = Device number                     ;
;                     IOCB + 1 = Operation number                  ;
;                     IOCB + 2 = Status                            ;
;                     IOCB + 3 = Low byte buffer address           ;
;                     IOCB + 4 = High byte of buffer address       ;
;                     IOCB + 5 = Low byte of buffer length         ;
;                     IOCB + 6 = High byte of buffer length        ;
;                                                                  ;
;                     The device table is implemented as a linked  ;
;                     list. Two routines maintain the list: INITIO, ;
;                     which initializes the device list to empty, and ;
;                     ADDDL, which adds a device to the list.      ;
;                     A device table entry has the following form: ;
;                                                                  ;
;                     DVTBL + 0 = Low byte of link field           ;
;                     DVTBL + 1 = High byte of link field          ;
;                     DVTBL + 2 = Device number                    ;
;                     DVTBL + 3 = Low byte of initialize device    ;
;                     DVTBL + 4 = High byte of initialize device   ;
;                     DVTBL + 5 = Low byte of input status routine ;
;                     DVTBL + 6 = High byte of input status routine ;
;                     DVTBL + 7 = Low byte of input 1 byte routine ;
;                     DVTBL + 8 = High byte of input 1 byte routine ;
;                     DVTBL + 9 = Low byte of input N bytes routine ;
;                     DVTBL + 10= High byte of input N bytes routine ;
;                     DVTBL + 11= Low byte of output status routine ;
;                     DVTBL + 12= High byte of output status routine ;
;                     DVTBL + 13= Low byte of output 1 byte routine ;
;                     DVTBL + 14= High byte of output 1 byte routine ;
;                     DVTBL + 15= Low byte of output N bytes routine ;
;                     DVTBL + 16= High byte of output N bytes routine ;
;                                                                  ;
;       Entry:        Register A = High byte of IOCB               ;
;                     Register Y = Low byte of IOCB                ;
;                     Register X = For write 1 byte contains the byte ;
;                                  to write, a buffer is not used. ;
;                                                                  ;
;       Exit:         Register A = a copy of the IOCB status byte  ;
;                     Register X = For read 1 byte contains the byte ;
;                                  read, a buffer is not used.     ;
;                     Status byte of IOCB is 0 if the operation was ;
```

```
;                       completed successfully; otherwise it contains   ;
;                       the error number.                               ;
;                                                                       ;
;                       Status value    Description                     ;
;                           0           No errors                       ;
;                           1           Bad device number               ;
;                           2           Input data available, no such   ;
;                                       operation                       ;
;                           3           Output ready                    ;
;                                                                       ;
;                                                                       ;
;       Registers used: All                                             ;
;                                                                       ;
;       Time:           93 cycles minimum plus 59 cycles for each       ;
;                       device in the list which is not the requested   ;
;                       device.                                         ;
;                                                                       ;
;       Size:           Program 131 bytes                               ;
;                       Data     3 bytes plus                           ;
;                                6 bytes in page zero                   ;
;                                                                       ;
;                                                                       ;


;IOCB AND DEVICE TABLE EQUATES
IOCBDN: .EQU    0       ;IOCB DEVICE NUMBER
IOCBOP: .EQU    1       ;IOCB OPERATION NUMBER
IOCBST: .EQU    2       ;IOCB STATUS
IOCBBA: .EQU    3       ;IOCB BUFFER ADDRESS
IOCBBL: .EQU    5       ;IOCB BUFFER LENGTH
DTLNK:  .EQU    0       ;DEVICE TABLE LINK FIELD
DTDN:   .EQU    2       ;DEVICE TABLE DEVICE NUMBER
DTSR:   .EQU    3       ;BEGINNING OF DEVICE TABLE SUBROUTINES

;OPERATION NUMBERS
NUMOP:  .EQU    7       ;NUMBER OF OPERATIONS
INIT:   .EQU    0       ;INITIALIZATION
ISTAT:  .EQU    1       ;INPUT STATUS
R1BYTE: .EQU    2       ;READ 1 BYTE
RNBYTE: .EQU    3       ;READ N BYTES
OSTAT:  .EQU    4       ;OUTPUT STATUS
W1BYTE: .EQU    5       ;WRITE 1 BYTE
WNBYTE: .EQU    6       ;WRITE N BYTES

;PAGE ZERO DEFINITIONS
IOCBA:  .EQU    0D0H    ;ADDRESS OF THE IOCB
DVLST:  .EQU    0D2H    ;ADDRESS OF A LIST OF DEVICES
CURDEV: .EQU    0D4H    ;STARTING ADDRESS OF THE CURRENT DEVICE TABLE ENTRY

IOHDLR:
        ;SAVE IOCB ADDRESS AND X REGISTER
        STA     IOCBA+1
        STY     IOCBA
        STX     SVXREG
```

```
        ;INITIALIZE STATUS BYTE TO ZERO (NO ERRORS)
        LDY     #IOCBST
        LDA     #0
        STA     (IOCBA),Y       ;STATUS := 0

        ;SEARCH DEVICE LIST FOR THIS DEVICE
        LDA     DVLST           ;START AT THE BEGINNING OF THE DEVICE LIST
        STA     CURDEV
        LDA     DVLST+1
        STA     CURDEV+1

        ;GET DEVICE NUMBER FROM IOCB TO REGISTER X
        LDY     #IOCBDN
        LDA     (IOCBA),Y
        TAX

SRCHLP:
        ;CHECK IF AT END OF DEVICE TABLE LIST (LINK FIELD = 0000)
        LDA     CURDEV
        ORA     CURDEV+1
        BEQ     BADDN           ;BRANCH IF NO MORE DEVICES

        ;CHECK IF THIS IS THE CORRECT DEVICE
        TXA
        LDY     #DTDN
        CMP     (CURDEV),Y      ;COMPARE THIS DEVICE NUMBER WITH THE REQUESTED
                                ; NUMBER
        BEQ     FOUND           ;BRANCH IF THE DEVICE IS FOUND

        ;ADVANCE TO THE NEXT DEVICE TABLE ENTRY THROUGH THE LINK FIELD
        ; MAKE CURRENT DEVICE = LINK
        LDY     #DTLNK
        LDA     (CURDEV),Y      ;GET LOW BYTE OF LINK FIELD
        PHA                     ; SAVE ON STACK
        INY
        LDA     (CURDEV),Y      ;GET HIGH BYTE OF LINK FIELD
        STA     CURDEV+1
        PLA                     ;RECOVER LOW BYTE OF LINK FIELD
        STA     CURDEV
        JMP     SRCHLP          ;CONTINUE SEARCHING


        ;FOUND THE DEVICE SO VECTOR TO THE APPROPRIATE ROUTINE IF ANY
FOUND:
        ;CHECK THAT THE OPERATION IS VALID
        LDY     #IOCBOP
        LDA     (IOCBA),Y       ;GET OPERATION NUMBER
        CMP     #NUMOP
        BCS     BADOP           ;BRANCH IF OPERATION NUMBER IS TOO LARGE

        ;GET OPERATION ADDRESS (ZERO INDICATES INVALID OPERATION)
        ASL     A               ;MULTIPLY OPERATION NUMBER BY 2 TO INDEX
        CLC                     ; ADDRESSES
        ADC     #DTSR           ;ADD TO OFFSET FOR DEVICE TABLE SUBROUTINES
        TAY                     ;USE AS INDEX INTO DEVICE TABLE
```

```
        LDA     (CURDEV),Y
        STA     OPADR           ;STORE LOW BYTE
        INY
        LDA     (CURDEV),Y
        STA     OPADR+1         ;STORE HIGH BYTE
        ORA     OPADR           ;CHECK FOR NON-ZERO OPERATION ADDRESS
        BEQ     BADOP           ;BRANCH IF OPERATION IS INVALID (ADDRESS = 0)

        LDX     SVXREG          ;RESTORE X REGISTER
        JMP     (OPADR)         ;GOTO ROUTINE

BADDN:
        LDA     #1              ;ERROR CODE 1 -- NO SUCH DEVICE
        BNE     EREXIT

BADOP:
        LDA     #2              ;ERROR CODE 2 -- NO SUCH OPERATION

EREXIT:
        LDY     #IOCBST
        STA     (IOCBA),Y       ;STORE ERROR STATUS
        RTS


;****************************************
;ROUTINE: INITDL
;PURPOSE: INITIALIZE THE DEVICE LIST TO EMPTY
;ENTRY: NONE
;EXIT:  THE DEVICE LIST SET TO NO ITEMS
;REGISTERS USED: A,F
;****************************************

INITDL:
        ;INITIALIZE DEVICE LIST TO 0 TO INDICATE NO DEVICES
        LDA     #0
        STA     DVLST
        STA     DVLST+1
        RTS


;******************************************
;ROUTINE: ADDDL
;PURPOSE: ADD A DEVICE TO THE DEVICE LIST
;ENTRY: REGISTER A = HIGH BYTE OF A DEVICE TABLE ENTRY
;       REGISTER Y = LOW BYTE OF A DEVICE TABLE ENTRY
;EXIT:  THE DEVICE TABLE ADDED TO THE DEVICE LIST
;REGISTERS USED: ALL
;******************************************

ADDDL:
        ;X,Y = NEW DEVICE TABLE ENTRY
        TAX

        ;PUSH CURRENT HEAD OF DEVICE LIST ON TO STACK
        LDA     DVLST+1
```

```
        PHA                             ;PUSH HIGH BYTE OF CURRENT HEAD OF DEVICE LIST
        LDA     DVLST
        PHA                             ;PUSH LOW BYTE ALSO

        ;MAKE NEW DEVICE TABLE ENTRY THE HEAD OF THE DEVICE LIST
        STY     DVLST
        STX     DVLST+1

        ;SET LINK FIELD OF THE NEW DEVICE TO THE OLD HEAD OF THE DEVICE LIST
        PLA
        LDY     #0
        STA     (DVLST),Y               ;STORE THE LOW BYTE
        PLA
        INY
        STA     (DVLST),Y               ;STORE THE HIGH BYTE

        RTS

;
;DATA SECTION
OPADR:  .BLOCK  2                       ;OPERATION ADDRESS USED TO VECTOR TO
                                        ; SUBROUTINE
SVXREG: .BLOCK  1                       ;TEMPORARY STORAGE FOR X REGISTER



;                                                                         ;
;                                                                         ;
;       SAMPLE EXECUTION:                                                 ;
;                                                                         ;
;         This test routine will set up the APPLE II console as           ;
;       device 1 and an APPLE II printer which is assumed to be           ;
;       in slot 1 as device 2. The test routine will then read            ;
;       a line from the console and echo it to the console and            ;
;       the printer.                                                      ;
;                                                                         ;
;                                                                         ;

;EQUATE
CR      .EQU    08DH                    ;APPLE II CARRIAGE RETURN CHARACTER
CBUF    .EQU    0D6H                    ;STARTING ADDRESS OF I/O BUFFER

SC1006:
        ;INITIALIZE DEVICE LIST
        JSR     INITDL

        ;SET UP APPLE CONSOLE AS DEVICE 1
        LDA     CONDVA+1
        LDY     CONDVA
        JSR     ADDDL                   ;ADD CONSOLE DEVICE TO DEVICE LIST
        LDA     #INIT                   ;INITIALIZE OPERATION
        STA     IOCB+IOCBOP
        LDA     #1
        STA     IOCB+IOCBDN             ;DEVICE NUMBER = 1
        LDA     AIOCB+1
        LDY     AIOCB
        JSR     IOHDLR                  ;PERFORM INITIALIZATION
```

```
        ;SET UP APPLE PRINTER AS DEVICE 2
        LDA     PRTDVA+1
        LDY     PRTDVA
        JSR     ADDDL           ;ADD PRINTER DEVICE TO DEVICE LIST
        LDA     #INIT           ;INITIALIZE OPERATION
        STA     IOCB+IOCBOP
        LDA     #2
        STA     IOCB+IOCBDN     ;DEVICE NUMBER = 2
        LDA     AIOCB+1
        LDY     AIOCB
        JSR     IOHDLR          ;INITIALIZE PRINTER DEVICE

        ;LOOP READING LINES FROM CONSOLE, AND ECHOING THEM TO
        ; THE CONSOLE AND PRINTER UNTIL A BLANK LINE IS ENTERED
TSTLP:
        LDA     #1              ;SET DEVICE TO NUMBER 1 (CONSOLE)
        STA     IOCB+IOCBDN
        LDA     #RNBYTE         ;SET OPERATION TO READ N BYTES
        STA     IOCB+IOCBOP
        LDA     #LENBUF         ;SET BUFFER LENGTH TO LENBUF
        STA     IOCB+IOCBBL
        LDA     #0              ;THE HIGH BYTE OF LENBUF IS 0 IN OUR EXAMPLE
        STA     IOCB+IOCBBL+1
        LDA     AIOCB+1         ;SET REGISTERS A,Y TO THE IOCB ADDRESS
        LDY     AIOCB
        JSR     IOHDLR          ;READ A LINE

        ;ECHO THE LINE TO THE CONSOLE
        ;DEVICE IS STILL CONSOLE FROM THE READ LINE ABOVE
        LDA     #WNBYTE         ;SET OPERATION TO WRITE N BYTES
        STA     IOCB+IOCBOP
        LDA     AIOCB+1         ;SET REGISTERS A,Y TO THE IOCB ADDRESS
        LDY     AIOCB
        JSR     IOHDLR          ;WRITE N BYTES

        ;OUTPUT A CARRIAGE RETURN TO CONSOLE
        LDX     #CR             ;SET REGISTER X TO CARRIAGE RETURN CHARACTER
        LDA     #W1BYTE         ;SET OPERATION TO WRITE 1 BYTE
        STA     IOCB+IOCBOP
        LDA     AIOCB+1         ;SET REGISTERS A,Y TO THE IOCB ADDRESS
        LDY     AIOCB
        JSR     IOHDLR          ;WRITE 1 BYTE

        ;ECHO THE LINE TO THE PRINTER ALSO
        LDA     #2              ;SET DEVICE TO NUMBER 2 (PRINTER)
        STA     IOCB+IOCBDN
        LDA     #WNBYTE         ;SET OPERATION TO WRITE N BYTES
        STA     IOCB+IOCBOP
        LDA     AIOCB+1         ;SET REGISTERS A,Y TO THE IOCB ADDRESS
        LDY     AIOCB
        JSR     IOHDLR          ;WRITE N BYTES

        ;WRITE A CARRIAGE RETURN TO THE PRINTER
        LDX     #8DH            ;SET REGISTER X TO CARRIAGE RETURN CHARACTER
        LDA     #W1BYTE         ;SET OPERATION TO WRITE 1 BYTE
```

```
        STA     IOCB+IOCBOP
        LDA     AIOCB+1         ;SET REGISTERS A,Y TO THE IOCB ADDRESS
        LDY     AIOCB
        JSR     IOHDLR          ;WRITE 1 BYTE

        LDA     IOCB+IOCBBL     ;GET LOW BYTE
        LDY     #1
        ORA     IOCB+IOCBBL,Y   ;OR WITH HIGH BYTE
        BNE     TSTLP           ;BRANCH IF BUFFER LENGTH IS NOT ZERO

        BRK
        JMP     SC1006


;IOCB FOR PREFORMING THE IO
AIOCB:  .WORD   IOCB            ;ADDRESS OF THE IOCB
IOCB    .BLOCK  1               ;DEVICE NUMBER
        .BLOCK  1               ;OPERATION NUMBER
        .BLOCK  1               ;STATUS
        .WORD   BUFFER          ;BUFFER ADDRESS
        .WORD   LENBUF          ;BUFFER LENGTH

;BUFFER
LENBUF  .EQU    127
BUFFER  .BLOCK  LENBUF


;DEVICE TABLE ENTRIES
CONDVA: .WORD   CONDV           ;CONSOLE DEVICE ADDRESS
CONDV:  .WORD   0               ;LINK FIELD
        .BYTE   1               ;DEVICE 1
        .WORD   CINIT           ;CONSOLE INITIALIZE
        .WORD   CISTAT          ;CONSOLE INPUT STATUS
        .WORD   CIN             ;CONSOLE INPUT 1 BYTE
        .WORD   CINN            ;CONSOLE INPUT N BYTES
        .WORD   COSTAT          ;CONSOLE OUTPUT STATUS
        .WORD   COUT            ;CONSOLE OUTPUT 1 BYTE
        .WORD   COUTN           ;CONSOLE OUTPUT N BYTES

PRTDVA: .WORD   PRTDV           ;PRINTER DEVICE ADDRESS
PRTDV:  .WORD   0               ;LINK FIELD
        .BYTE   2               ;DEVICE 2
        .WORD   PINIT           ;PRINTER INITIALIZE
        .WORD   0               ;NO PRINTER INPUT STATUS
        .WORD   0               ;NO PRINTER INPUT 1 BYTE
        .WORD   0               ;NO PRINTER INPUT N BYTES
        .WORD   POSTAT          ;PRINTER OUTPUT STATUS
        .WORD   POUT            ;PRINTER OUTPUT 1 BYTE
        .WORD   POUTN           ;PRINTER OUTPUT N BYTES

;***********************************
;CONSOLE I/O ROUTINES
;***********************************
```

```
;CONSOLE INITIALIZE
CINIT:
        LDA     #0                  ;A = STATUS NO ERRORS
        RTS                         ;NO INITIALIZATION NECESSARY

;CONSOLE INPUT STATUS (READY IS BIT 7 OF ADDRESS 0C000H)
CISTAT:
        LDA     0C000H              ;GET KEYBOARD STATUS BYTE
        BPL     CNONE               ;BRANCH IF CHARACTER IS NOT READY
        LDA     #2                  ;INDICATE CHARACTER IS READY
        BNE     CIS1                ;BRANCH ALWAYS TAKEN

CNONE:
        LDA     #0                  ;NOT READY
CIS1
        LDY     #IOCBST
        STA     (IOCBA),Y           ;STORE STATUS AND LEAVE IT IN REGISTER A
        RTS


;CONSOLE READ 1 BYTE
CIN:
        LDA     C000H
        BPL     CIN                 ;WAIT FOR CHARACTER TO BECOME READY
        TXA                         ;MOVE CHARACTER TO REGISTER X
        LDA     #0                  ;STATUS = NO ERRORS
        RTS

;CONSOLE READ N BYTES
CINN:
        ;READ LINE USING THE APPLE MONITOR GETLN ROUTINE AT 0FD6AH
        ; 33H = PROMPT LOCATION
        ; 200H = BUFFER ADDRESS
        LDA     #"?" OR 80H         ;SET BIT 7
        STA     033H                ;SET UP APPLE PROMPT CHARACTER
        JSR     0FD6AH              ;CALL APPLE MONITOR GETLN ROUTINE

        ;VERIFY THAT THE NUMBER OF BYTES READ WILL FIT INTO THE CALLERS BUFFER
        LDY     #IOCBBL+1
        LDA     (IOCBA),Y           ;GET HIGH BYTE
        BNE     CINN1               ;BRANCH IF HIGH BYTE IS NOT ZERO
        DEY
        TXA
        CMP     (IOCBA),Y
        BCC     CINN1               ;BRANCH IF THE NUMBER OF CHARACTERS READ IS
                                    ; LESS THAN THE BUFFER LENGTH
        BEQ     CINN1               ;BRANCH IF THE LENGTHS ARE EQUAL

        LDA     (IOCBA),Y
        TAX                         ;OTHERWISE TRUNCATE THE NUMBER OF CHARACTERS
                                    ; READ TO THE BUFFER LENGTH
CINN1:
        TXA
        STA     (IOCBA),Y           ;SET BUFFER LENGTH TO NUMBER OF CHARACTERS READ
        LDA     #0
        INY
        STA     (IOCBA),Y           ;ZERO UPPER BYTE OF BUFFER LENGTH
```

```
        ;MOVE THE DATA FROM APPLE BUFFER AT 200H TO CALLER'S BUFFER
        LDY     #IOCBBA         ;GET POINTER TO CALLER'S BUFFER FROM IOCB
        LDA     (IOCBA),Y
        STA     CBUF            ;SAVE POINTER ON PAGE ZERO
        INY
        LDA     (IOCBA),Y       ;SET UP MSB OF POINTER ALSO
        STA     CBUF+1
        TXA
        BEQ     CINN3           ;EXIT IF NO BYTES TO MOVE
        LDY     #0

        ;NOW MOVE THE DATA TO CALLER'S BUFFER
CINN2:
        LDA     200H,Y          ;GET A BYTE FROM APPLE BUFFER
        STA     (CBUF),Y        ;MOVE BYTE TO CALLER'S BUFFER
        INY
        DEX
        BNE     CINN2           ;COUNT BYTES

        ;GOOD STATUS (0) - NO ERRORS
CINN3:
        LDA     #0              ;NO ERRORS
        RTS


;CONSOLE OUTPUT STATUS
COSTAT:
        LDA     #3              ;STATUS IS ALWAYS READY TO OUTPUT
        RTS


;CONSOLE OUTPUT 1 BYTE
COUT:
        TXA
COUT1:
        JSR     0FDEDH          ;APPLE CHARACTER OUTPUT ROUTINE
        LDA     #0              ;STATUS = NO ERRORS
        RTS

COUT1A: .WORD   COUT1           ;ADDRESS OF OUTPUT ROUTINE TO BE PLACED IN A,Y


;CONSOLE OUTPUT N BYTES
COUTN:
        LDA     COUT1A+1
        LDY     COUT1A          ;A,Y = ADDRESS OF OUTPUT ROUTINE
        JSR     OUTN            ;CALL OUTPUT N CHARACTERS
        LDA     #0              ;STATUS = NO ERRORS
        RTS


;****************************************
;PRINTER ROUTINES
; ASSUME PRINTER CARD IS IN SLOT 1
;****************************************
```

```
;PRINTER INITIALIZE
PINIT:
        LDA     #0                  ;NOTHING TO DO, RETURN NO ERRORS
        RTS

;PRINTER OUTPUT STATUS
POSTAT:
        LDA     #0                  ;ASSUME IT IS ALWAYS READY
        RTS

;PRINTER OUTPUT 1 BYTE
POUT:
        TXA
POUT1:
        JSR     0C107H              ;CHARACTER OUTPUT ROUTINE
        LDA     #0
        RTS

POUT1A: .WORD   POUT1               ;ADDRESS OF CHARACTER OUTPUT ROUTINE TO BE
                                    ; PLACED IN A,Y

;PRINTER OUTPUT N BYTES
POUTN:
        LDA     POUT1A+1
        LDY     POUT1A              ;A,Y = ADDRESS OF OUTPUT ROUTINE
        JSR     OUTN                ;CALL OUTPUT N CHARACTERS
        LDA     #0                  ;NO ERRORS
        RTS


;****************************************
;ROUTINE: OUTN
;PURPOSE: OUTPUT N CHARACTERS
;ENTRY: REGISTER A = HIGH BYTE OF CHARACTER OUTPUT SUBROUTINE ADDRESS
;       REGISTER Y = LOW BYTE OF CHARACTER OUTPUT SUBROUTINE ADDRESS
;       IOCBA = STARTING ADDRESS OF AN IOCB
;EXIT:  DATA OUTPUT
;REGISTERS USED: ALL
;****************************************

OUTN:
        ;STORE ADDRESS OF THE CHARACTER OUTPUT SUBROUTINE
        STA     COSR+1
        STY     COSR

        ;GET OUTPUT BUFFER ADDRESS FROM IOCB, SAVE ON PAGE ZERO
        LDY     #IOCBBA
        LDA     (IOCBA),Y
        STA     CBUF
        INY
        LDA     (IOCBA),Y
        STA     CBUF+1
```

```
        ;GET BUFFER LENGTH FROM IOCB, EXIT IF IT IS ZERO
        LDY     #IOCBBL
        LDA     (IOCBA),Y
        STA     BUFLEN
        INY
        LDA     (IOCBA),Y
        STA     BUFLEN+1
        ORA     BUFLEN
        BEQ     OUT3                ;BRANCH IF BUFFER LENGTH IS ZERO

        ;START AT BEGINNING OF BUFFER
        LDA     #0
        STA     IDX
OUTLP:
        LDY     IDX
        LDA     (CBUF),Y            ;GET NEXT CHARACTER FROM BUFFER
        JSR     LP0                 ;WRITE CHARACTER TO OUTPUT DEVICE
        JMP     LP1

LP0:    JMP     (COSR)              ;OUTPUT THE CHARACTER VIA THE CURRENT
                                    ; OUTPUT SUBROUTINE

LP1:
        ;INCREMENT TO THE NEXT CHARACTER IN THE BUFFER
        INC     IDX
        BNE     LP2
        INC     CBUF+1              ;INCREMENT THE HIGH BYTE IS NECESSARY

        ;DECREMENT BUFFER LENGTH, CONTINUE LOOPING IF IT IS NOT ZERO
LP2:
        LDA     BUFLEN
        BNE     DECLS
        DEC     BUFLEN+1            ;BORROW FROM HIGH BYTE IF NECESSARY
DECLS:  DEC     BUFLEN              ;ALWAYS DECREMENT LOW BYTE
        BNE     OUTLP
        LDA     BUFLEN+1
        BNE     OUTLP               ;CONTINUE UNLESS ALL CHARACTERS SENT

OUT3:
        RTS

COSR:   .WORD   0                   ;ADDRESS OF THE CHARACTER OUTPUT SUBROUTINE
BUFLEN: .WORD   0                   ;TEMPORARY BUFFER LENGTH
IDX:    .BYTE   0                   ;TEMPORARY INDEX

        .END
```

Initialize I/O Ports (IOPORTS)

Initializes a set of I/O ports from an array of port addresses and initial values. Examples are given of initializing programmable I/O devices such as the 6520 Peripheral Interface Device (Adapter), the 6522 Versatile Interface Adapter, the 6530 Multifunction Device, the 6532 Multifunction Device, the 6551 Asychronous Communications Device Adapter, and the 6850 Asynchronous Communications Device Adapter.

This subroutine is intended as a generalized method for initializing I/O sections. The initialization may involve data ports, data direction registers that determine whether bits are inputs or outputs, control or command registers that determine the operating modes of programmable devices, counters (in timers), priority registers, and other external registers or storage locations.

Some of the tasks the user may perform with this routine are:

1. Assign bidirectional I/O lines as inputs or outputs.

2. Initialize output ports to known starting values.

3. Enable or disable interrupts from peripheral chips.

4. Determine operating modes, such as whether inputs are latched, whether strobes are produced, how priorities are assigned, whether timers operate continuously or only on demand, etc.

5. Load initial counts into timers.

6. Select bit rates for communications.

7. Clear or reset devices that are not tied to the overall system reset line.

8. Initialize priority registers or assign initial priorities to interrupts or other operations.

9. Initialize vectors used in servicing interrupts, DMA requests, and other inputs.

Procedure: The program loops through the specified number of ports, obtaining the port address and the initial value from the array and storing the initial value in the port address. This procedure does not depend on the type of devices used in the I/O section or on the number of devices. Additions and deletions can be made by means of appropriate changes in the array and in the parameters of the routine, without changing the routine itself.

Registers Used: All

Execution Time: 16 cycles overhead plus 52 cycles per port entry. If, for example, NUMBER OF PORT ENTRIES = 10, execution time is

$$52 * 10 + 16 = 520 + 16 = 536 \text{ cycles.}$$

Program Size: 40 bytes plus the size of the table (three bytes per entry)

Data Memory Required: Four bytes on page 0, two for a pointer to the array (starting at address ARYADR, $00D0_{16}$ in the listing) and two for a pointer to the port (starting at address PRTADR, $00D2_{16}$ in the listing).

Entry Conditions

(A) = More significant byte of starting address of array of ports and initial values

(Y) = Less significant byte of starting address of array of ports and initial values

(X) = Number of entries in array (number of ports to initialize).

Exit Conditions

All ports initialized.

Example

Data: Number of ports to initialize = 3

Array elements are:

- High byte of port 1 address
- Low byte of port 1 address
- Initial value for port 1
- High byte of port 2 address
- Low byte of port 2 address
- Initial value for port 2
- High byte of port 3 address
- Low byte of port 3 address
- Initial value for port 3

Result: Initial value for port 1 stored in port 1 address

Initial value for port 2 stored in port 2 address

Initial value for port 3 stored in port 3 address.

Note that each element in the array consists of 3 bytes containing:

Less significant byte of port address

More significant byte of port address

Initial value for port

```
;                                                                       ;
;                                                                       ;
;                                                                       ;
;                                                                       ;
;       Title           Initialize I/O ports                            ;
;       Name:           IPORTS                                          ;
;                                                                       ;
;                                                                       ;

;                                                                       ;
;       Purpose:        Initialize I/O ports from an array of port      ;
;                       addresses and values.                           ;
;                                                                       ;
;       Entry:          Register A = High byte of array address         ;
```

```
;                         Register Y = Low byte of array address          ;
;                         Register X = Number of ports to initialize      ;
;                                                                         ;
;                         The array consists of 3 byte elements.          ;
;                            array+0 = High byte of port 1 address        ;
;                            array+1 = Low byte of port 1 address         ;
;                            array+2 = Value to store in port 1 address   ;
;                            array+3 = High byte of port 2 address        ;
;                            array+4 = Low byte of port 2 address         ;
;                            array+5 = Value to store in port 2 address   ;
;                                       .                                 ;
;                                       .                                 ;
;                                       .                                 ;
;                                                                         ;
;        Exit:            None                                            ;
;                                                                         ;
;        Registers used: All                                              ;
;                                                                         ;
;        Time:            16 cycles overhead plus                         ;
;                         52 cycles per port to initialize                ;
;                                                                         ;
;        Size:            Program 40 bytes                                ;
;                         Data     2 bytes in page zero                   ;
;                                                                         ;
;                                                                         ;


;PAGE ZERO POINTERS
ARYADR  .EQU    0D0H            ;ARRAY ADDRESS
PRTADR  .EQU    0D2H            ;PORT ADDRESS

IPORTS:
        ;SAVE STARTING ADDRESS OF INITIALIZATION ARRAY
        STA     ARYADR+1
        STY     ARYADR

        ;EXIT IF THE NUMBER OF PORTS IS ZERO
        TXA                     ;SET FLAGS
        BEQ     EXITIP          ;EXIT IF NUMBER OF PORTS = 0
        ;LOOP PICKING UP THE PORT ADDRESS AND
        ; SENDING THE VALUE UNTIL ALL PORTS ARE INITIALIZED
LOOP:
        ;GET PORT ADDRESS FROM ARRAY AND SAVE IT
        LDY     #0
        LDA     (ARYADR),Y      ;GET LOW BYTE OF PORT ADDRESS
        STA     PRTADR
        INY
        LDA     (ARYADR),Y      ;GET HIGH BYTE OF PORT ADDRESS
        STA     PRTADR+1

        ;GET THE INITIAL VALUE AND SEND IT TO THE PORT
        INY
        LDA     (ARYADR),Y      ;GET INITIAL VALUE
        LDY     #0
        STA     (PRTADR),Y      ;OUTPUT TO PORT
```

```
        ;POINT TO THE NEXT ARRAY ELEMENT
        LDA     ARYADR
        CLC
        ADC     #3              ;ADD 3 TO LOW BYTE OF THE ADDRESS
        STA     ARYADR
        BCC     LOOP1
        INC     ARYADR+1        ;INCREMENT HIGH BYTE IF A CARRY
LOOP1:

        ;DECREMENT NUMBER OF PORTS TO DO,EXIT WHEN ALL PORTS ARE INITIALIZED
        DEX
        BNE     LOOP

EXITIP:
        RTS


;                                                                       ;
;                                                                       ;
;       SAMPLE EXECUTION:                                               ;
;                                                                       ;
;                                                                       ;


;
;INITIALIZE
;   6520 PIA
;   6522 VIA
;   6530 ROM/RAM/IO/TIMER
;   6532 RAM/IO/TIMER
;   6850 SERIAL INTERFACE(ACIA)
;   6551 SERIAL INTERFACE(ACIA)
SC1007:
        LDA     ADRARY+1
        LDY     ADRARY
        LDX     SZARY
        JSR     IPORTS          ;INITIALIZE THE PORTS
        BRK

ARRAY:
        ;INITIALIZE 6520, ASSUME BASE ADDRESS FOR REGISTERS AT 2000H
        ;  PORT A = INPUT
        ;  CA1 = DATA AVAILABLE, SET ON LOW TO HIGH TRANSITION, NO INTERRUPTS
        ;  CA2 = DATA ACKNOWLEDGE HANDSHAKE
        .WORD   2001H           ;6520 CONTROL REGISTER A ADDRESS
        .BYTE   00000000B       ;INDICATE NEXT ACCESS TO DATA DIRECTION
                                ; REGISTER (SAME ADDRESS AS DATA REGISTER)
        .WORD   2000H           ;6520 DATA REGISTER A ADDRESS
        .BYTE   00000000B       ;ALL BITS = INPUT
        .WORD   2001H           ;6520 CONTROL REGISTER A ADDRESS
        .BYTE   00100110B       ;SET UP CA1,CA2 AND SET BIT 2 TO DATA REGISTER

        ;  PORT B = OUTPUT
        ;  CB1 = DATA ACKNOWLEDGE,SET ON HIGH TO LOW TRANSITION, NO INTERRUPTS
        ;  CB2 = DATA AVAILABLE, CLEARED BY WRITING DATA REGISTER B
        ;                        SET TO 1 BY HIGH TO LOW TRANSITION ON CB1
```

```
.WORD   2003H           ;6520 CONTROL REGISTER B ADDRESS
.BYTE   00000000B       ;INDICATE NEXT ACCESS TO DATA DIRECTION
                        ; REGISTER
.WORD   2002H           ;6520 DATA REGISTER B ADDRESS
.BYTE   11111111B       ;ALL BITS = OUTPUT
.WORD   2003H           ;6520 CONTROL REGISTER B ADDRESS
.BYTE   00100100B       ;SET UP CB1,CB2 AND SET BIT 2 TO DATA REGISTER


;INITIALIZE 6522, ASSUME BASE ADDRESS FOR REGISTERS AT 2010H
; PORT A = BITS 0..3 = OUTPUT, BITS 4..7 = INPUT
; CA1, CA2 ARE NOT USED.
; PORT B = LATCHED INPUT
;  CB1 = DATA AVAILABLE, SET ON LOW TO HIGH TRANSITION
;  CB2 = DATA ACKNOWLEDGE HANDSHAKE
.WORD   2013H           ;6522 DATA DIRECTION REGISTER A
.BYTE   00001111B       ;BITS 0..3 = OUTPUT, 4..7 = INPUT
.WORD   2012H           ;6522 DATA DIRECTION REGISTER B
.BYTE   00000000B       ;ALL BITS = INPUT
.WORD   201CH           ;6522 PERIPHERAL CONTROL REGISTER
.BYTE   10010000B       ;SET UP CB1, CB2
.WORD   201BH           ;6522 AUXILIARY CONTROL REGISTER
.BYTE   00000010B       ;MAKE PORT B LATCH THE INPUT DATA

;INITIALIZE 6530, ASSUME BASE ADDRESS FOR REGISTERS AT 2020H
; PORT A = OUTPUT
; PORT B = INPUT
.WORD   2021H           ;6530 DATA DIRECTION REGISTER A
.BYTE   11111111B       ;ALL BITS = OUTPUT
.WORD   2023H           ;6530 DATA DIRECTION REGISTER B
.BYTE   00000000B       ;ALL BITS = INPUT

;INITIALIZE 6532, ASSUME BASE ADDRESS FOR REGISTERS AT 2030H
; PORT A = BITS 0..6 = OUTPUT
;          BIT 7 = INPUT FOR PORT B DATA AVAILABLE.
; PORT B = INPUT
.WORD   2031H           ;6532 DATA DIRECTION REGISTER A
.BYTE   01111111B       ;BITS 0..6 = OUTPUT, BIT 7 = INPUT
.WORD   2033H           ;6532 DATA DIRECTION REGISTER B
.BYTE   00000000B       ;ALL BITS = INPUT

;INITIALIZE 6551, ASSUME BASE ADDRESS FOR REGISTERS AT 2040H
; 8 BIT DATA, NO PARITY
; 1 STOP BIT
; 9600 BAUD FROM ON BOARD BAUD RATE GENERATOR
; NO INTERRUPTS
.WORD   2041H           ;WRITE TO 6551 STATUS REGISTER TO RESET
.BYTE   0               ;THIS VALUE COULD BE ANYTHING
.WORD   2042H           ;6551 CONTROL REGISTER
.BYTE   10011110B       ;1 STOP, 8 BIT DATA, INTERNAL 9600 BAUD
.WORD   2043H           ;6551 COMMAND REGISTER
.BYTE   00000011B       ;NO PARITY, NO ECHO, NO RECEIVER INTERRUPT,
                        ;DTR LOW

;INITIALIZE 6850, ASSUME BASE ADDRESS FOR REGISTERS AT 2050H
; 8 BIT DATA, NO PARITY
```

```
        ; 1 STOP BIT
        ; DIVIDE MASTER CLOCK BY 1
        ; NO INTERRUPTS
        .WORD   2050H           ;WRITE TO 6850 CONTROL REGISTER
        .BYTE   00000011B       ;PERFORM A MASTER RESET
        .WORD   2050H           ;6850 CONTROL REGISTER
        .BYTE   00010101B       ;NO INTERRUPTS, RTS LOW,
                                ;8 BITS, 1 STOP, DIVIDE BY 1

ENDARY:                                 ;END OF ARRAY
ADRARY: .WORD   ARRAY                   ;ADDRESS OF ARRAY
SZARY:  .BYTE   (ENDARY - ARRAY) / 3    ;NUMBER OF PORTS TO INITIALIZE

        .END    ;PROGRAM
```

Delay Milliseconds (DELAY)

Provides a delay of between 1 and 255 milliseconds, depending on the parameter supplied. The user must calculate the value MSCNT to fit a particular computer.

MSCENT = (100/CYCLETIME − 10)/5
= 200/CYCLETIME − 2

CYCLETIME is the number of microseconds per clock period for a particular computer (1 for KIM-1, SYM-1, and AIM-65, 0.9799269 for APPLE II™).

Procedure: The program simply counts down the index registers for the appropriate amount of time as determined by the user-supplied constant. A few extra NOPs take account of the call instruction, the return instruction, and the routine overhead.

Registers Used: X, Y, P

Execution Time: 1 millisecond * (Y). If (Y) = 0, the minimum time is 17 cycles including a JSR instruction.

Program Size: 156 bytes

Data Memory Required: None

Special Case: (Y) = 0 causes an exit with a minimum execution time of 17 cycles including a JSR instruction. (Y) = 0 and (X) is unchanged.

Entry Conditions

(Y) = Number of milliseconds to delay (1 to 255).

Exit Conditions

Returns after the specified number of milliseconds with (X) = (Y) = 0.

Example

Data: (Y) = number of milliseconds = $2A_{16} = 42_{10}$

Result: Software delay of $2A_{16}$ (42_{10}) milliseconds, assuming that user supplies the proper value of MSCNT.

```
;                                                               ;
;                                                               ;
;                                                               ;
;                                                               ;
;       Title           Delay milliseconds                      ;
;       Name:           Delay                                   ;
;                                                               ;
;                                                               ;


;                                                               ;
;       Purpose:        Delay from 1 to 255 milliseconds        ;
```

```
;                                                                       ;
;       Entry:            Register Y = number of milliseconds to delay. ;
;                                                                       ;
;       Exit:             Returns to calling routine after the          ;
;                         specified delay.                              ;
;                                                                       ;
;       Registers used: X,Y,P                                           ;
;                                                                       ;
;       Time:             1 millisecond * Register Y.                   ;
;                         If Y = 0 then the minimum time is 17          ;
;                         cycles including the JSR overhead.            ;
;                                                                       ;
;                                                                       ;
;       Size:             Program 29 bytes                              ;
;                         Data       NONE                               ;
;                                                                       ;
;                                                                       ;


; HERE IS THE FORMULA FOR COMPUTING THE DELAY COUNTS MSCNT1 AND MSCNT2
;
; MSCNT = 200/CYCLETIME - 2 WHERE CYCLE TIME IS THE LENGTH
;         OF A PARTICULAR COMPUTER'S CLOCK PERIOD IN MICROSECONDS
;
; EXAMPLES: KIM, SYM, AIM HAVE 1 MHz CLOCKS, SO MSCNT = 198,
;           APPLE HAS A 1.023 MHz CLOCK, SO MSCNT = 202.
;
; IN THE LAST ITERATION, WE REDUCE THE COUNT BY 3 (MSCNT)
;  TO DELAY 1 MILLISECOND LESS THE OVERHEAD WHERE THE
;  OVERHEAD IS:
;                6 CYCLES ==> JSR DELAY
;                2 CYCLES ==> CPY #0
;                2 CYCLES ==> BEQ EXIT (ASSUMED NOT TAKEN)
;                2 CYCLES ==> NOP
;                2 CYCLES ==> CPY #1
;                3 CYCLES ==> BNE DELAYA (ASSUMED TAKEN)
;                2 CYCLES ==> DEY
;               -1 CYCLE  ==> THE LAST BNE DELAY1 NOT TAKEN
;                2 CYCLES ==> LDX #MSCNT2
;               -1 CYCLE  ==> THE LAST BNE DELAY2 NOT TAKEN
;                6 CYCLES ==> RTS
;              ------
;               25 CYCLES OVERHEAD
;
;EQUATES
;       1 MHZ CLOCK
;MSCNT  .EQU    0C6H    ;198 TIMES THROUGH DELAY1
;
;       APPLE (1.023 MHZ)
MSCNT   .EQU    0CAH    ;202 TIMES THROUGH DELAY1

DELAY:
        CPY     #0      ; 2 CYCLES
        BEQ     EXIT    ; 2 CYCLES (EXIT IF DELAY = 0)
        NOP             ; 2 CYCLES (TO MAKE OVERHEAD = 25 CYCLES)
```

```
        ;IF DELAY IS TO BE 1 MILLISECOND THEN GOTO LAST1
        ; THIS LOGIC IS DESIGNED TO BE 5 CYCLES THROUGH EITHER PATH
        CPY     #1      ; 2 CYCLES
        BNE     DELAYA  ; 3 CYCLES (IF TAKEN ELSE 2 CYCLES)
        JMP     LAST1   ; 3 CYCLES

        ;DELAY 1 MILLISECOND TIMES(Y-1)
DELAYA:
        DEY             ; 2 CYCLES (PREDECREMENT Y)
DELAY0:
        LDX     #MSCNT  ; 2 CYCLES
DELAY1:
        DEX             ; 2 CYCLES
        BNE     DELAY1  ; 3 CYCLES
        NOP             ; 2 CYCLES
        NOP             ; 2 CYCLES
        DEY             ; 2 CYCLES
        BNE     DELAY0  ; 3 CYCLES

LAST1:
        ;DELAY THE LAST TIME 25 CYCLES LESS TO TAKE THE
        ; CALL, RETURN, AND ROUTINE OVERHEAD INTO ACCOUNT
        LDX     #MSCNT-3 ; 2 CYCLES
DELAY2:
        DEX             ; 2 CYCLES
        BNE     DELAY2  ; 3 CYCLES

EXIT:
        RTS             ; 6 CYCLES


;                                                                       ;
;                                                                       ;
;       SAMPLE EXECUTION:                                               ;
;                                                                       ;
;                                                                       ;


SC1008:
        ;
        ;DELAY 10 SECONDS
        ;  CALL DELAY 40 TIMES AT 250 MILLISECONDS EACH
        LDA     #40     ;40 TIMES (28 HEX)
        STA     COUNT

        ;DELAY 1/4 SECOND
QTRSCD:
        LDY     #250    ;250 MILLISECONDS (FA HEX)
        JSR     DELAY
        DEC     COUNT
        BNE     QTRSCD

        BRK             ;STOP AFTER 10 SECONDS
        JMP     SC1008
```

```
;DATA SECTION
COUNT    .BYTE    0


         .END     ;PROGRAM
```

Unbuffered Interrupt-Driven Input/Output Using a 6850 ACIA (SINTIO) 11A

Performs interrupt-driven input and output using a 6850 ACIA and single-character input and output buffers. Consists of the following subroutines:

1. INCH reads a character from the input buffer.

2. INST determines whether there is a character available in the input buffer.

3. OUTCH writes a character into the output buffer.

4. OUTST determines whether the output buffer is full.

5. INIT initializes the 6850 ACIA, the interrupt vectors, and the software flags (used to transfer data between the main program and the interrupt service routine).

6. IOSRVC determines which interrupt occurred and provides the proper input or output service. In response to the input interrupt, it reads a character from the ACIA into the input buffer. In response to the output interrupt, it writes a character from the output buffer into the ACIA.

Examples describe a 6850 ACIA on an Apple II serial I/O board in slot 1.

Procedures:

1. INCH waits for a character to become available, clears the Data Ready flag (RECDF), and loads the character into the accumulator.

2. INST sets the Carry flag from the Data Ready flag (memory location RECDF).

3. OUTCH waits for the character buffer to empty, places the character in the buffer, and sets the Character Available flag (TRNDF).

4. OUTST sets the Carry flag from the Character Available flag (memory location TRNDF).

5. INIT clears the software flags, sets up the interrupt vector, resets the ACIA (a master reset, since the ACIA has no reset input), and initializes the ACIA by placing the appropriate value in its control register (input interrupts enabled, output interrupts disabled).

6. IOSRVC determines whether the interrupt was an input interrupt (bit 0 of the ACIA status register = 1), an output interrupt (bit

Registers Used:

1. INCH A, F, Y
2. INST A, F
3. OUTCH A, F, Y
4. OUTST A, F
5. INIT A, F

Execution Time:

1. INCH 33 cycles if a character is available
2. INST 12 cycles
3. OUTCH 92 cycles if the output buffer is empty and the ACIA is ready to send data
4. OUTST 12 cycles
5. INIT 73 cycles
6. IOSRVC 39 cycles to service an input interrupt, 59 cycles to service an output interrupt, 24 cycles to determine interrupt is from another device

Program Size: 168 bytes

Data Memory Required: Six bytes anywhere in RAM. One byte for the received data (at address RECDAT), one byte for the receive data flag (at address RECDF), one byte for the transmit data (at address TRNDAT), one byte for the transmit data flag (at address TRNDF), and two bytes for the address of the next interrupt service routine (starting at address NEXTSR).

1 of the ACIA status register = 1), or the product of some other device. If the input interrupt occurred, the program reads the data, saves it in memory, and sets the Data Ready flag (RECDF). If the output interrupt occurred, the program determines whether data is available. If not, the program simply disables the output interrupt. If data is available, the program sends it to the ACIA, clears the Character Available flag (TRNDF), and enables both the input and the output interrupts.

The only special problem in using these routines is that an output interrupt may occur when no data is available. We cannot ignore the interrupt or it will assert itself indefinitely, creating an endless loop. The solution is to disable output interrupts. But now we create a new problem when data is ready to be sent. That is, if we have disabled output interrupts, the system cannot learn from an interrupt that the ACIA is ready to transmit. The solution to this is to create an additional, non-interrupt-driven entry to the routine that sends a character to the ACIA. Since this entry is not caused by an interrupt, we must check the ACIA to see that its output register is actually empty before sending it a character.

The special sequence of operations is the following:

1. Output interrupt occurs before new data is available (that is, the ACIA becomes ready for data). The response is to disable the output interrupt, since there is no data to be sent. Note that this sequence will not occur initially, since INIT disables the output interrupt. Otherwise, the output interrupt would occur immediately, since the ACIA surely starts out empty and therefore ready to transmit data.

2. Output data becomes available. That is, the system now has data to transmit. But there is no use sitting back and waiting for the output interrupt, since it has been disabled.

3. The main program calls the routine (OUTDAT) that sends data to the ACIA. Checking the ACIA's status shows that it is, in fact, ready to transmit a character (it told us it was when the output interrupt occurred). The routine then sends the character and reenables the interrupts.

The basic problem here is that output devices may request service before the computer is ready for them. That is, the devices can accept data but the computer has nothing to send. In particular, we have an initialization problem caused by output interrupts asserting themselves and expecting service. Input devices, on the other hand, request service only when they have data. They start out in the not ready state; that is, an input device has no data to send initially, while the computer is ready to accept data. Thus output devices cause more initialization and sequencing problems in interrupt-driven systems than do input devices.

Our solution may, however, result in an odd situation. Let us assume that the system has some data ready for output but the ACIA is not yet ready for it. Then the system must wait with interrupts disabled for the ACIA to become ready; that is, an interrupt-driven system must disable its interrupts and wait idly, polling the output device. We could eliminate this drawback by keeping a software flag that would be changed when the output interrupt occurred at a time when there was no data. Then the system could check the software flag and determine whether the output interrupt had already occurred. (See Subroutine 11C.)

Entry Conditions

1. INCH: none
2. INST: none
3. OUTCH: character to transmit in accumulator
4. OUTST: none
5. INIT: none

Exit Conditions

1. INCH: character in accumulator
2. INST: Carry flag = 0 if no character is available, 1 is a character is available
3. OUTCH: none
4. OUTST: Carry flag = 0 if output buffer is empty, 1 if it is full.

```
;       Title               Simple interrupt input and output using a 6850  ;
;                           ACIA and a single character buffer.             ;
;       Name:               SINTIO                                          ;
;                                                                           ;
;                                                                           ;


;                                                                           ;
;       Purpose:            This program consists of 5 subroutines which    ;
;                           perform interrupt driven input and output using ;
;                           a 6850 ACIA.                                    ;
;                                                                           ;
;                           INCH                                            ;
;                             Read a character.                             ;
;                           INST                                            ;
;                             Determine input status (whether the input     ;
;                             buffer is empty).                             ;
;                           OUTCH                                           ;
;                             Write a character.                            ;
;                           OUTST                                           ;
;                             Determine output status (whether the output   ;
;                             buffer is full).                              ;
;                           INIT                                            ;
;                             Initialize.                                   ;
;                                                                           ;
;       Entry:              INCH                                            ;
;                             No parameters.                                ;
;                           INST                                            ;
;                             No parameters.                                ;
;                           OUTCH                                           ;
;                             Register A = character to transmit            ;
;                           OUTST                                           ;
;                             No parameters.                                ;
;                           INIT                                            ;
;                             No parameters.                                ;
;                                                                           ;
;       Exit:               INCH                                            ;
;                             Register A = character.                       ;
;                           INST                                            ;
;                             Carry flag equals 0 if input buffer is empty, ;
;                             1 if character is available.                  ;
```

```
;                       OUTCH                                        ;
;                         No parameters                              ;
;                       OUTST                                        ;
;                         Carry flag equals 0 if output buffer is    ;
;                         empty, 1 if it is full.                    ;
;                       INIT                                         ;
;                         No parameters.                             ;
;                                                                    ;
;       Registers used: INCH                                         ;
;                         A,F,Y                                      ;
;                       INST                                         ;
;                         A,F                                        ;
;                       OUTCH                                        ;
;                         A,F,Y                                      ;
;                       OUTST                                        ;
;                         A,F                                        ;
;                       INIT                                         ;
;                         A,F                                        ;
;                                                                    ;
;       Time:           INCH                                         ;
;                         33 cycles if a character is available      ;
;                       INST                                         ;
;                         12 cycles                                  ;
;                       OUTCH                                        ;
;                         92 cycles if the output buffer is empty and ;
;                            the ACIA is ready to transmit           ;
;                       OUTST                                        ;
;                         12 cycles                                  ;
;                       INIT                                         ;
;                         73 cycles                                  ;
;                       IOSRVC                                       ;
;                         24 cycles minimum if the interrupt is not ours;
;                         39 cycles to service a input interrupt     ;
;                         59 cycles to service a output interrupt    ;
;                                                                    ;
;       Size:           Program 168 bytes                            ;
;                       Data      6 bytes                            ;
;                                                                    ;
;                                                                    ;

;EXAMPLE 6850 ACIA PORT DEFINITIONS FOR AN APPLE SERIAL BOARD IN SLOT 1
ACIASR  .EQU    0C094H          ;ACIA STATUS REGISTER
ACIADR  .EQU    0C095H          ;ACIA DATA REGISTER
ACIACR  .EQU    0C094H          ;ACIA CONTROL REGISTER
IRQVEC  .EQU    03FEH           ;APPLE IRQ VECTOR ADDRESS

;READ A CHARACTER
INCH:
        JSR     INST            ;GET INPUT STATUS
        BCC     INCH            ;WAIT IF CHARACTER IS NOT AVAILABLE
        PHP                     ;SAVE CURRENT STATE OF INTERRUPT SYSTEM
        SEI                     ;DISABLE INTERRUPTS
        LDA     #0
        STA     RECDF           ;INDICATE BUFFER IS NOW EMPTY
        LDA     RECDAT          ;GET THE CHARACTER FROM THE BUFFER
        PLP                     ;RESTORE FLAGS
```

```
        RTS

;RETURN INPUT STATUS (CARRY = 1 IF DATA IS AVAILABLE)
INST:
        LDA     RECDF           ;GET THE DATA READY FLAG
        LSR     A               ;SET CARRY FROM FLAG
                                ; CARRY = 1 IF CHARACTER IS AVAILABLE
        RTS
;WRITE A CHARACTER
OUTCH:
        PHP                     ;SAVE STATE OF INTERRUPT FLAG
        PHA                     ;SAVE CHARACTER TO OUTPUT

        ;WAIT FOR THE CHARACTER BUFFER TO EMPTY, THEN STORE THE NEXT CHARACTER
WAITOC:
        JSR     OUTST           ;GET THE OUTPUT STATUS
        BCS     WAITOC          ;WAIT IF THE OUTPUT BUFFER IS FULL
        SEI                     ;DISABLE INTERRUPTS WHILE LOOKING AT THE
                                ; SOFTWARE FLAGS
        PLA                     ;GET THE CHARACTER
        STA     TRNDAT          ;STORE THE CHARACTER
        LDA     #0FFH           ;INDICATE CHARACTER AVAILABLE (BUFFER FULL)
        STA     TRNDF
        JSR     OUTDAT          ;SEND THE DATA TO THE PORT
        PLP                     ;RESTORE FLAGS
        RTS

;OUTPUT STATUS (CARRY = 1 IF BUFFER IS FULL)
OUTST:
        LDA     TRNDF           ;CARRY = 1 IF CHARACTER IS IN THE BUFFER
        LSR     A
        RTS

;INITIALIZE
INIT:
        PHP                     ;SAVE CURRENT STATE OF FLAGS
        SEI                     ;DISABLE INTERRUPTS DURING INITIALIZATION

        ;INITIALIZE THE SOFTWARE FLAGS
        LDA     #0
        STA     RECDF           ;NO INPUT DATA AVAILABLE
        STA     TRNDF           ;OUTPUT BUFFER EMPTY

        ;SAVE THE CURRENT IRQ VECTOR IN NEXTSR
        LDA     IRQVEC
        STA     NEXTSR
        LDA     IRQVEC+1
        STA     NEXTSR+1

        ;SET THE IRQ VECTOR TO OUR INPUT SERVICE ROUTINE
        LDA     AIOS
        STA     IRQVEC
        LDA     AIOS+1
        STA     IRQVEC+1

        ;INITIALIZE THE 6850
        LDA     #011B
        STA     ACIACR          ;MASTER RESET ACIA
        LDA     #10010001B
        STA     ACIACR          ;INITIALIZE ACIA MODE TO
```

```
                                ;  DIVIDE BY 16
                                ;  8 DATA BITS
                                ;  2 STOP BITS
                                ;  OUTPUT INTERRUPTS DISABLED (NOTE THIS)
                                ;  INPUT INTERRUPTS ENABLED

        PLP                     ;RESTORE CURRENT STATE OF THE FLAGS
        RTS

AIOS:   .WORD   IOSRVC          ;ADDRESS OF INPUT OUTPUT SERVICE ROUTINE

;INPUT OUTPUT INTERRUPT SERVICE ROUTINE
IOSRVC:
        PHA                     ;SAVE REGISTER A
        CLD                     ;BE SURE PROCESSOR IS IN BINARY MODE

        ;GET THE ACIA STATUS: BIT 0 = 1 IF AN INPUT INTERRUPT
        ;BIT 1 = 1 IF AN OUTPUT INTERRUPT
        LDA     ACIASR
        LSR     A               ;BIT 0 TO CARRY
        BCS     IINT            ;BRANCH IF AN INPUT INTERRUPT
        LSR     A               ;BIT 1 TO CARRY
        BCS     OINT            ;BRANCH IF AN OUTPUT INTERRUPT

        ;THE INTERRUPT WAS NOT CAUSED BY THIS ACIA
        PLA
        JMP     (NEXTSR)        ;GOTO THE NEXT SERVICE ROUTINE

;SERVICE INPUT INTERRUPTS
IINT:
        LDA     ACIADR          ;READ THE DATA
        STA     RECDAT          ;STORE IT AWAY
        LDA     #0FFH
        STA     RECDF           ;INDICATE WE HAVE A CHARACTER IN RECDAT
        JMP     EXIT            ;EXIT IOSRVC

;SERVICE OUTPUT INTERRUPTS
OINT:
        LDA     TRNDF           ;GET DATA AVAILABLE FLAG
        BEQ     NODATA          ;BRANCH IF NO DATA TO SEND
        JSR     OUTDT1          ; ELSE OUTPUT THE DATA,
                                ;  (WE DO NOT NEED TO TEST THE STATUS)
        JMP     EXIT

;IF AN OUTPUT INTERRUPT OCCURS WHEN NO DATA IS AVAILABLE,
; WE MUST DISABLE THE INTERRUPT TO AVOID AN ENDLESS LOOP.
; LATER WHEN A CHARACTER BECOMES AVAILABLE, WE CALL THE
; OUTPUT  ROUTINE, OUTDAT, WHICH MUST TEST ACIA STATUS BEFORE
; SENDING THE DATA. THE OUTPUT ROUTINE MUST ALSO REENABLE THE OUTPUT
; INTERRUPT AFTER SENDING THE DATA. THIS PROCEDURE OVERCOMES THE
; PROBLEMS OF AN UNSERVICED OUTPUT INTERRUPT ASSERTING ITSELF
; REPEATEDLY, WHILE STILL ENSURING THAT OUTPUT INTERRUPTS ARE
; RECOGNIZED AND THAT DATA IS NEVER SENT TO AN ACIA THAT IS
; NOT READY FOR IT. THE BASIC PROBLEM HERE IS THAT AN OUTPUT
; DEVICE MAY REQUEST SERVICE BEFORE THE COMPUTER HAS
; ANYTHING TO SEND (WHEREAS AN INPUT DEVICE HAS DATA WHEN IT
```

```
; REQUESTS SERVICE)

NODATA:
        LDA     #10010001B      ;DISABLE OUTPUT INTERRUPTS, ENABLE INPUT
                                ; INTERRUPTS, 8 DATA BITS, 2 STOP BITS, DIVIDE
                                ; BY 16 CLOCK
        STA     ACIACR          ;TURN OFF OUTPUT INTERRUPTS

EXIT:
        PLA                     ;RESTORE REGISTER A
        RTI                     ;RETURN FROM INTERRUPT

;*************************************
;ROUTINE: OUTDAT, OUTDT1 (OUTDAT IS NON-INTERRUPT DRIVEN ENTRY POINT)
;PURPOSE: SEND A CHARACTER TO THE ACIA
;ENTRY: TRNDAT = CHARACTER TO SEND
;EXIT:  NONE
;REGISTERS USED: A,F
;***************************************

;NON-INTERRUPT ENTRY. MUST CHECK IF ACIA IS READY OR WAIT FOR IT
OUTDAT:
        LDA     ACIASR          ;CAME HERE WITH INTERRUPTS DISABLED
        AND     #00000010B      ;TEST THE ACIA OUTPUT REGISTER FOR EMPTY
        BEQ     OUTDAT          ;BRANCH IF IT IS NOT EMPTY

OUTDT1: LDA     TRNDAT          ;GET THE CHARACTER
        STA     ACIADR          ;OUTPUT DATA
        LDA     #0
        STA     TRNDF           ;INDICATE BUFFER EMPTY
        LDA     #10110001B
        STA     ACIACR          ;ENABLE 6850 OUTPUT AND INPUT INTERRUPTS,
                                ; 8 DATA BITS, 2 STOP BITS, DIVIDE BY 16 CLOCK
        RTS


;DATA SECTION
RECDAT  .BLOCK  1               ;RECEIVE DATA
RECDF   .BLOCK  1               ;RECEIVE DATA FLAG (0 = NO DATA, FF = DATA)
TRNDAT  .BLOCK  1               ;TRANSMIT DATA
TRNDF   .BLOCK  1               ;TRANSMIT DATA FLAG (0 = BUFFER EMPTY,
                                ;                   FF = BUFFER FULL)
NEXTSR  .BLOCK  2               ;ADDRESS OF THE NEXT INTERRUPT SERVICE ROUTINE


;                                                                      ;
;                                                                      ;
;       SAMPLE EXECUTION:                                              ;
;                                                                      ;
;                                                                      ;


SC1101:
        JSR     INIT            ;INITIALIZE
        CLI                     ;ENABLE INTERRUPTS
```

```
        ;SIMPLE EXAMPLE
LOOP:
        JSR     INCH            ;READ A CHARACTER
        PHA
        JSR     OUTCH           ;ECHO IT
        PLA
        CMP     #1BH            ;IS IT AN ESCAPE CHARACTER ?
        BNE     LOOP            ;STAY IN LOOP IF NOT
        BRK

        ;AN ASYNCHRONOUS EXAMPLE
        ; OUTPUT "A" TO THE CONSOLE CONTINUOUSLY BUT ALSO LOOK AT THE
        ; INPUT SIDE, READING AND ECHOING ANY INPUT CHARACTERS.
ASYNLP:
        ;OUTPUT AN "A" IF OUTPUT IS NOT BUSY
        JSR     OUTST           ;IS OUTPUT BUSY ?
        BCS     ASYNLP          ;BRANCH IF IT IS
        LDA     #"A"
        JSR     OUTCH           ;OUTPUT THE CHARACTER

        ;GET A CHARACTER FROM THE INPUT PORT IF ANY
        JSR     INST            ;IS INPUT DATA AVAILABLE ?
        BCC     ASYNLP          ;BRANCH IF NOT (SEND ANOTHER "A")
        JSR     INCH            ;GET THE CHARACTER
        CMP     #1BH            ;IS IT AN ESCAPE CHARACTER ?
        BEQ     DONE            ;BRANCH IF IT IS
        JSR     OUTCH           ;ELSE ECHO IT
        JMP     ASYNLP          ;AND CONTINUE

DONE:
        BRK
        JMP     SC1101

        .END    ;PROGRAM
```

Unbuffered Interrupt-Driven Input/Output Using a 6522 VIA (PINTIO) 11B

Performs interrupt-driven input and output using a 6522 VIA and single-character input and output buffers. Consists of the following subroutines:

1. INCH reads a character from the input buffer.

2. INST determines whether there is a character available in the input buffer.

3. OUTCH writes a character into the output buffer.

4. OUTST determines whether the output buffer is full.

5. INIT initializes the 6522 VIA, the interrupt vectors, and the software flags.

6. IOSRVC determines which interrupt occurred and provides the proper input or output service (i.e., it reads a character from the VIA into the input buffer in response to the input interrupt and it writes a character from the output buffer into the VIA in response to the output interrupt).

Examples describe a 6522 VIA attached to an Apple II computer.

Registers Used:

1. INCH: A, F, Y
2. INST: A, F
3. OUTCH: A, F, Y
4. INIT A, F

Execution Time:

1. INCH: 33 cycles if a character is available
2. INST: 12 cycles
3. OUTCH: 83 cycles if the output buffer is empty and the VIA is ready for data
4. OUTST: 12 cycles
5. INIT: 93 cycles
6. IOSRVC: 43 cycles to service an input interrupt, 81 cycles to service an output interrupt, 24 cycles to determine that interrupt is from another device

Program Size: 194 bytes

Data Memory Required: Seven bytes anywhere in RAM. One byte for the received data (at address RECDAT), one byte for the Receive Data flag (at address RECDF), one byte for the transmit data (at address TRNDAT), one byte for the Transmit Data flag (at address TRNDF), one byte for the Output Interrupt flag (at address OIE), and two bytes for the address of the next interrupt service routine (starting at address NEXTSR).

Procedure:

1. INCH waits for a character to be available in the input buffer, clears the Data Ready flag (RECDF), and loads the character from the buffer into the accumulator.

2. INST sets the Carry flag from the Data Ready flag (memory location RECDF).

3. OUTCH waits for the output buffer to be emptied, places the character (from the accumulator) in the buffer, and sets the character available (buffer full) flag (TRNDF). If an unserviced output interrupt has occurred (i.e., the output device has requested service when no data was available), OUTCH actually sends the data to the VIA.

4. OUTST sets the Carry flag from the Character Available flag (memory location TRNDF).

5. INIT clears the software flags, sets up the interrupt vector, and initializes the 6522 VIA. It makes port A an input port, port B an output port, control lines CA1 and CB1 active low-to-high, control line CA2 a brief

output pulse indicating input acknowledge (active-low after the CPU reads the data), and control line CB2 a write strobe (active-low after the CPU writes the data and lasting until the peripheral becomes ready again). INIT also enables the input interrupt on CA1 and the output interrupt on CB1.

6. IOSRVC determines whether the interrupt was an input interrupt (bit 1 of the VIA interrupt flag register = 1), an output interrupt (bit 4 of the VIA interrupt flag register = 1), or the product of some other device. If the input interrupt occurred, the program reads the data, saves it in the input buffer, and sets the Data Ready flag (RECDF). If the output interrupt occurred, the program determines whether any data is available. If not, the program simply clears the interrupt and clears the flag (OIE) that indicates the output device is actually ready (that is, an output interrupt has occurred at a time when no data was available). If data is available, the program sends it from the output buffer to the VIA, clears the Character Available flag (TRNDF), sets the Output Interrupt flag (OIE), and enables both the input and the output interrupts.

The only special problem in using these routines is that an output interrupt may occur when no data is available to send. We cannot ignore the interrupt or it will assert itself indefinitely, creating an endless loop. The solution is to simply clear the interrupt by reading the data register in port B. But now we create a new problem when the main program has data ready to be sent. The interrupt indicating that the output device is ready has already occurred (and been cleared), so there is no use waiting for it. The solution is to establish an extra flag that indicates (with a 0) that the output interrupt has occurred without being serviced. We call this flag OIE, the Output Interrupt flag. The initialization routine sets it initially (since the output device has not requested service), and the output service routine clears it when an output interrupt occurs that cannot be serviced (no data is available) and sets it after sending data to the VIA (in case it might have been cleared). Now the output routine OUTCH can check OIE to determine whether the output interrupt has already occurred (a 0 value indicates it has, FF hex that it has not).

Note that we can clear a VIA interrupt without actually sending any data. We cannot do this with a 6850 ACIA (see Subroutines 11A and 11C), so the procedures there are somewhat different. This problem of unserviced interrupts occurs only with output devices, since input devices request service only when they have data ready to transfer.

Entry Conditions

1. INCH: none
2. INST: none
3. OUTCH: character to transmit in accumulator
4. OUTST: none
5. INIT: none

Exit Conditions

1. INCH: character in accumulator
2. INST: Carry flag = 0 if no character is available, 1 if a character is available
3. OUTCH: none
4. OUTST: Carry flag = 0 if output buffer is empty, 1 if it is full.
5. INIT: none

```
;       Title           Simple interrupt input and output using a 6522  ;
;                       VIA and a single character buffer.               ;
;       Name:           PINTIO                                           ;
;                                                                        ;
;                                                                        ;

;                                                                        ;
;       Purpose:        This program consists of 5 subroutines which    ;
;                       perform interrupt driven input and output using ;
;                       a 6522 VIA.                                      ;
;                                                                        ;
;                       INCH                                             ;
;                         Read a character.                              ;
;                       INST                                             ;
;                         Determine input status (whether the input     ;
;                         buffer is empty).                              ;
;                       OUTCH                                            ;
;                         Write a character.                             ;
;                       OUTST                                            ;
;                         Determine output status (whether the output   ;
;                         buffer is full).                               ;
;                       INIT                                             ;
;                         Initialize.                                    ;
;                                                                        ;
;       Entry:          INCH                                             ;
;                         No parameters.                                 ;
;                       INST                                             ;
;                         No parameters.                                 ;
;                       OUTCH                                            ;
;                         Register A = character to transmit             ;
;                       OUTST                                            ;
;                         No parameters.                                 ;
;                       INIT                                             ;
;                         No parameters.                                 ;
;                                                                        ;
;       Exit:           INCH                                             ;
;                         Register A = character.                        ;
;                       INST                                             ;
```

```
;                          Carry flag equals 0 if input buffer is empty, ;
;                          1 if character is available.                  ;
;                        OUTCH                                           ;
;                          No parameters                                 ;
;                        OUTST                                           ;
;                          Carry flag equals 0 if output buffer is       ;
;                          empty, 1 if it is full.                       ;
;                        INIT                                            ;
;                          No parameters.                                ;
;                                                                        ;
;       Registers used:  INCH                                            ;
;                          A,F,Y                                         ;
;                        INST                                            ;
;                          A,F                                           ;
;                        OUTCH                                           ;
;                          A,F,Y                                         ;
;                        OUTST                                           ;
;                          A,F                                           ;
;                        INIT                                            ;
;                          A,F                                           ;
;                                                                        ;
;       Time:            INCH                                            ;
;                          33 cycles if a character is available         ;
;                        INST                                            ;
;                          12 cycles                                     ;
;                        OUTCH                                           ;
;                          83 cycles if the output buffer is empty and   ;
;                             the VIA is ready to transmit               ;
;                        OUTST                                           ;
;                          12 cycles                                     ;
;                        INIT                                            ;
;                          93 cycles                                     ;
;                        IOSRVC                                          ;
;                          24 cycles minimum if the interrupt is not ours;
;                          43 cycles to service a input interrupt        ;
;                          81 cycles to service a output interrupt       ;
;                                                                        ;
;       Size:            Program 194 bytes                               ;
;                        Data      7 bytes                               ;
;                                                                        ;
;                                                                        ;

;EXAMPLE 6522 VIA PORT DEFINITIONS
VIA     .EQU    0C090H          ;VIA BASE ADDRESS
VIABDR  .EQU    VIA             ;VIA PORT B DATA REGISTER
VIAADR  .EQU    VIA+1           ;VIA PORT A DATA REGISTER, WITH HANDSHAKING
VIABDD  .EQU    VIA+2           ;VIA PORT B DATA DIRECTION REGISTER
VIAADD  .EQU    VIA+3           ;VIA PORT A DATA DIRECTION REGISTER
VIAACR  .EQU    VIA+11          ;VIA AUXILIARY CONTROL REGISTER
VIAPCR  .EQU    VIA+12          ;VIA PERIPHERAL CONTROL REGISTER
VIAIFR  .EQU    VIA+13          ;VIA INTERRUPT FLAG REGISTER
VIAIER  .EQU    VIA+14          ;VIA INTERRUPT ENABLE REGISTER

IRQVEC  .EQU    03FEH           ;APPLE IRQ VECTOR ADDRESS

;READ A CHARACTER
```

```
INCH:
        JSR     INST            ;GET INPUT STATUS
        BCC     INCH            ;WAIT IF CHARACTER IS NOT AVAILABLE
        PHP                     ;SAVE CURRENT STATE OF INTERRUPT SYSTEM
        SEI                     ;DISABLE INTERRUPTS
        LDA     RECDAT          ;GET THE CHARACTER FROM THE BUFFER
        LDA     #0
        STA     RECDF           ;INDICATE BUFFER IS NOW EMPTY
        LDA     RECDAT          ;GET THE CHARACTER FROM THE BUFFER
        PLP                     ;RESTORE FLAGS
        RTS

;RETURN INPUT STATUS (CARRY = 1 IF DATA IS AVAILABLE)
INST:
        LDA     RECDF           ;GET THE DATA READY FLAG
        LSR     A               ;SET CARRY FROM FLAG
                                ; CARRY = 1 IF CHARACTER IS AVAILABLE
        RTS

;WRITE A CHARACTER
OUTCH:
        PHP                     ;SAVE STATE OF INTERRUPT FLAG
        PHA                     ;SAVE CHARACTER TO OUTPUT

        ;WAIT FOR THE CHARACTER BUFFER TO EMPTY, THEN STORE THE NEXT CHARACTER
WAITOC:
        JSR     OUTST           ;GET THE OUTPUT STATUS
        BCS     WAITOC          ;WAIT IF THE OUTPUT BUFFER IS FULL
        SEI                     ;DISABLE INTERRUPTS WHILE LOOKING AT THE
                                ; SOFTWARE FLAGS
        PLA                     ;GET THE CHARACTER
        STA     TRNDAT          ;STORE THE CHARACTER
        LDA     #0FFH           ;INDICATE CHARACTER AVAILABLE (BUFFER FULL)
        STA     TRNDF
        LDA     OIE             ;HAS THE OUTPUT DEVICE ALREADY REQUESTED
                                ; SERVICE?
        BNE     OUTCH1          ; NO, BRANCH AND WAIT FOR AN INTERRUPT
        JSR     OUTDAT          ; YES, SEND THE DATA TO THE PORT NOW
OUTCH1: PLP                     ;RESTORE FLAGS
        RTS

;OUTPUT STATUS (CARRY = 1 IF BUFFER IS FULL)
OUTST:
        LDA     TRNDF           ;CARRY = 1 IF CHARACTER IS IN THE BUFFER
        LSR     A
        RTS

;INITIALIZE
INIT:
        PHP                     ;SAVE CURRENT STATE OF FLAGS
        SEI                     ;DISABLE INTERRUPTS

        ;INITIALIZE THE SOFTWARE FLAGS
```

```
        LDA     #0
        STA     RECDF              ;NO INPUT DATA AVAILABLE
        STA     TRNDF              ;OUTPUT BUFFER EMPTY
        LDA     #0FFH              ;OUTPUT DEVICE HAS NOT REQUESTED SERVICE
        STA     OIE

        ;SAVE THE CURRENT IRQ VECTOR IN NEXTSR
        LDA     IRQVEC
        STA     NEXTSR
        LDA     IRQVEC+1
        STA     NEXTSR+1

        ;SET THE IRQ VECTOR TO OUR INPUT SERVICE ROUTINE
        LDA     AIOS
        STA     IRQVEC
        LDA     AIOS+1
        STA     IRQVEC+1

        ;INITIALIZE THE 6522 VIA
        LDA     #00000000B
        STA     VIAADD             ;SET PORT A TO INPUT
        LDA     #11111111B
        STA     VIABDD             ;SET PORT B TO OUTPUT
        LDA     #10001010B
        STA     VIAPCR             ;SET PORT A TO
                                   ; INTERRUPT ON A LOW TO HIGH OF CA1 (BIT 0 = 1)
                                   ; OUTPUT A LOW PULSE ON CA2 (BITS 1..3 = 101)
                                   ;SET PORT B TO
                                   ; INTERRUPT ON A LOW TO HIGH OF CB1 (BIT 4 = 1)
                                   ; HANDSHAKE OUTPUT MODE (BITS 5..7 = 001)
        LDA     #00000001B
        STA     VIAACR             ;SET AUXILIARY CONTROL TO ENABLE INPUT LATCHING
                                   ; FOR PORT A
        LDA     #00010010B         ;SET INTERRUPT ENABLE REGISTER TO ALLOW
                                   ; INTERRUPTS ON CA1 (BIT 1) AND CB1 (BIT 4)
                                   ;
        STA     VIAIER
        PLP                        ;RESTORE CURRENT STATE OF THE FLAGS
        RTS

AIOS:   .WORD   IOSRVC             ;ADDRESS OF INPUT OUTPUT SERVICE ROUTINE

;INPUT OUTPUT INTERRUPT SERVICE ROUTINE
IOSRVC:
        PHA                        ;SAVE REGISTER A
        CLD                        ;BE SURE PROCESSOR IS IN BINARY MODE

        ;GET THE VIA STATUS: BIT 1 = 1 IF AN INPUT INTERRUPT
        ;BIT 4 = 1 IF AN OUTPUT INTERRUPT
        LDA     VIAIFR
        AND     #10B               ;TEST BIT 1
        BNE     IINT               ;GOTO INPUT INTERRUPT IF BIT 1 = 1
        LDA     VIAIFR
        AND     #1000B             ;TEST BIT 4
        BNE     OINT               ;GOTO OUTPUT INTERRUPT IF BIT 4 = 1
```

```
        ;THE INTERRUPT WAS NOT CAUSED BY THIS VIA
        PLA
        JMP     (NEXTSR)        ;GOTO THE NEXT SERVICE ROUTINE

;SERVICE INPUT INTERRUPTS
IINT:
        LDA     VIAADR          ;READ THE DATA
                                ; (WHICH PULSES CA2 FOR THE HANDSHAKE AND
                                ;  CLEARS THE INTERRUPT FLAG)
        STA     RECDAT          ;STORE DATA
        LDA     #0FFH
        STA     RECDF           ;INDICATE WE HAVE A CHARACTER IN RECDAT
        JMP     EXIT            ;EXIT IOSRVC

;SERVICE OUTPUT INTERRUPTS
;NOTE THAT WE CAN CLEAR A 6522 INTERRUPT BY READING THE DATA
; REGISTER. THUS WE CAN CLEAR AN OUTPUT INTERRUPT WITHOUT
; SERVICING IT OR DISABLING IT. HOWEVER, IF WE DO THIS, WE
; MUST HAVE A FLAG (OIE) THAT INDICATES THE OUTPUT INTERRUPT
; HAS OCCURRED BUT HAS NOT BEEN SERVICED. OUTCH CAN THEN USE
; THE OIE FLAG TO DETERMINE WHETHER TO SEND THE DATA IMMEDIATELY
; OR WAIT FOR AN OUTPUT INTERRUPT TO SEND IT.
OINT:
        LDA     TRNDF           ;GET DATA AVAILABLE FLAG
        BNE     NODATA          ;BRANCH IF THERE IS NO DATA TO SEND
        JSR     OUTDAT          ; ELSE OUTPUT THE DATA
        JMP     EXIT

NODATA:
        LDA     VIABDR          ;READ THE PORT B DATA REGISTER TO CLEAR THE
                                ; INTERRUPT.
        LDA     #0              ;INDICATE OUTPUT INTERRUPT HAS OCCURRED
        STA     OIE             ; BUT HAS NOT BEEN SERVICED

EXIT:
        PLA                     ;RESTORE REGISTER A
        RTI                     ;RETURN FROM INTERRUPT

;****************************************
;ROUTINE: OUTDAT
;PURPOSE: SEND A CHARACTER TO THE VIA
;ENTRY: TRNDAT = CHARACTER TO SEND
;EXIT:  NONE
;REGISTERS USED: A,F
;****************************************

OUTDAT:
        LDA     TRNDAT          ;GET THE CHARACTER
        STA     VIABDR          ;OUTPUT DATA TO PORT B
        LDA     #0
        STA     TRNDF           ;INDICATE BUFFER EMPTY
        LDA     #0FFH
        STA     OIE             ;INDICATE NO UNSERVICED OUTPUT INTERRUPT
        RTS
```

```
;DATA SECTION
RECDAT  .BLOCK  1               ;RECEIVE DATA
RECDF   .BLOCK  1               ;RECEIVE DATA FLAG (0 = NO DATA, FF = DATA)
TRNDAT  .BLOCK  1               ;TRANSMIT DATA
TRNDF   .BLOCK  1               ;TRANSMIT DATA FLAG (0 = BUFFER EMPTY
                                ;                    FF = BUFFER FULL)
OIE     .BLOCK  1               ;OUTPUT INTERRUPT FLAG
                                ; (0  = INTERRUPT OCCURRED WITHOUT SERVICE
                                ;  FF = INTERRUPT SERVICED)
NEXTSR  .BLOCK  2               ;ADDRESS OF THE NEXT INTERRUPT SERVICE ROUTINE


;                                                                       ;
;                                                                       ;
;       SAMPLE EXECUTION:                                               ;
;                                                                       ;
;                                                                       ;


SC1102:
        JSR     INIT            ;INITIALIZE
        CLI                     ;ENABLE INTERRUPTS

        ;SIMPLE EXAMPLE
LOOP:
        JSR     INCH            ;READ A CHARACTER
        PHA
        JSR     OUTCH           ;ECHO IT
        PLA
        CMP     #1BH            ;IS IT AN ESCAPE CHARACTER ?
        BNE     LOOP            ;STAY IN LOOP IF NOT
        BRK

        ;AN ASYNCHRONOUS EXAMPLE
        ; OUTPUT "A" TO THE CONSOLE CONTINUOUSLY BUT ALSO LOOK AT THE
        ; INPUT SIDE, READING AND ECHOING ANY INPUT CHARACTERS.
ASYNLP:
        ;OUTPUT AN "A" IF OUTPUT IS NOT BUSY
        JSR     OUTST           ;IS OUTPUT BUSY ?
        BCS     ASYNLP          ;BRANCH IF IT IS
        LDA     #"A"
        JSR     OUTCH           ;OUTPUT THE CHARACTER

        ;GET A CHARACTER FROM THE INPUT PORT IF ANY
        JSR     INST            ;IS INPUT DATA AVAILABLE ?
        BCC     ASYNLP          ;BRANCH IF NOT (SEND ANOTHER "A")
        JSR     INCH            ;GET THE CHARACTER
        CMP     #1BH            ;IS IT AN ESCAPE CHARACTER ?
        BEQ     DONE            ;BRANCH IF IT IS
        JSR     OUTCH           ;ELSE ECHO IT
        JMP     ASYNLP          ;AND CONTINUE

DONE:
        BRK
        JMP     SC1102

        .END    ;PROGRAM
```

Buffered Interrupt-Driven Input/Output Using a 6850 ACIA (SINTB) 11C

Performs interrupt-driven input and output using a 6850 ACIA and multiple-character buffers. Consists of the following subroutines:

1. INCH reads a character from the input buffer.

2. INST determines whether there are any characters in the input buffer.

3. OUTCH writes a character into the output buffer.

4. OUTST determines whether the output buffer is full.

5. INIT initializes the buffers and the 6850 device.

6. IOSRVC determines which interrupt occurred and provides the proper input or output service.

Procedures:

1. INCH waits for a character to become available, gets the character from the head of the input buffer, moves the head of the buffer up one position, and decreases the input buffer counter by 1.

2. INST sets the Carry to 0 if the input buffer counter is zero and to 1 if the counter is non-zero.

3. OUTCH waits until there is empty space in the output buffer (that is, until the output buffer is not full), stores the character at the tail of the output buffer, moves the tail of the buffer up one position, and increases the output buffer counter by 1.

4. OUTST sets the Carry flag to 1 if the output buffer counter is equal to the buffer's length and to 0 if it is not.

Registers Used:

1. INCH: A, F, Y
2. INST: A, F
3. OUTCHA, F, Y
4. OUTST:A, F
5. INIT: A, F

Execution Time:

1. INCH: 70 cycles if a character is available
2. INST: 18 cycles
3. OUTCH: 75 cycles minimum, 105 cycles maximum if the output buffer is not full and the ACIA is ready to transmit
4. OUTST: 12 cycles
5. INIT: 89 cycles
6. IOSRVC: 73 cycles to service an input interrupt, 102 cycles to service an output interrupt, 27 cycles to determine the interrupt is from another device.

Program Size: 258 bytes

Data Memory Required: Seven bytes anywhere in RAM plus the input and output buffers. The seven bytes anywhere in RAM hold the input buffer counter (one byte at address ICNT), the index to the head of the input buffer (one byte at address IHEAD), the index to the tail of the input buffer (one byte at address ITAIL), the output buffer counter (one byte at address OCNT), the index to the head of the output buffer (one byte at address OHEAD), the index to the tail of the output buffer (one byte at address OIE), and an Output Interrupt Enable flag (one byte at address OIE). The input buffer starts at address IBUF and its size is IBSZ; the output buffer starts at address OBUF and its size is OBSZ.

5. INIT clears the buffer counters, sets both the heads and the tails of the buffers to zero, sets up the interrupt vector, resets the ACIA by performing a master reset on its control register (the ACIA has no reset input), and places the ACIA in its required operating mode by storing the appropriate

value in its control register. INIT enables the input interrupt and disables the output interrupt. It does, however, clear the output interrupt enable flag, thus indicating that the ACIA is ready to transmit data, although it cannot cause an output interrupt.

6. IOSRVC determines whether the interrupt was an input interrupt (bit 0 of the ACIA status register = 1), an output interrupt (bit 1 of the ACIA status register = 1), or the product of some other device. If the input interrupt occurred, the program reads the data and determines if there is room for it in the buffer. If there is room, the processor stores the character at the tail of the input buffer, moves the tail of the buffer up one position, and increases the input buffer counter by 1. If the output interrupt occurred, the program determines whether there is any data in the output buffer. If there is none, the program disables the output interrupt (so it will not interrupt repeatedly) and clears an Output Interrupt flag that indicates the ACIA is actually ready. The flag lets the main program know that the ACIA is ready even through it cannot declare its readiness by forcing an interrupt. If there is data in the output buffer, the program obtains a character from the head of the buffer, sends it to the ACIA, moves the head of the buffer up one position, and decreases the output buffer counter by 1. It then enables both input and output interrupts and sets the Output Interrupt flag (in case that flag had been cleared earlier).

The new problem that occurs in using multiple-character buffers is the management of queues. The main program must read the data in the same order in which the input interrupt service routine receives it. Similarly, the output interrupt service routine must send the data in the same order that the main program stores it. Thus we have the following requirements for handling input:

1. The main program must know whether there is anything in the input buffer.

2. If the input buffer is not empty, the main program must know where the oldest character is (that is, the one that was received first).

3. The input interrupt service routine must know whether the input buffer is full.

4. If the input buffer is not full, the input interrupt service routine must know where the next empty place is (that is, it must know where it should store the new character).

The output interrupt service routine and the main program have a similar set of requirements for the output buffer, although the roles of sender and receiver are reversed.

We meet requirements 1 and 3 by maintaining a counter ICNT. INIT initializes ICNT to zero, the interrupt service routine adds 1 to it whenever it receives a character (assuming the buffer is not full), and the main program subtracts 1 from it whenever it removes a character from the buffer (assuming the buffer is not empty). Thus the main program can determine whether the input buffer is empty by checking if ICNT is zero. Similarly, the interrupt service routine can determine whether the input buffer is full by checking if ICNT is equal to the size of the buffer.

We meet requirements 2 and 4 by maintaining two indexes, IHEAD and ITAIL, defined as follows:

1. ITAIL is the index of the next empty location in the buffer.

2. IHEAD is the index of the oldest character in the buffer.

INIT initializes IHEAD and ITAIL to zero. Whenever the interrupt service routine receives a character, it places it in the buffer at index ITAIL and increments ITAIL by 1 (assuming that the buffer is not full). Whenever the main program reads a character, it removes it from the buffer at index IHEAD and increments IHEAD by 1 (assuming that the buffer is not empty). Thus IHEAD "chases" ITAIL across the buffer with the service routine entering characters at one end (the tail) while the main program removes them from the other end (the head). The occupied part of the buffer thus could start and end anywhere. If either IHEAD or ITAIL reaches the physical end of the buffer, we simply set it back to zero. Thus we allow wraparound on the buffer; that is, the occupied part of the buffer could start near the end (say, at byte #195 of a 200-byte buffer) and continue back to the beginning (say, to byte #10). Thus IHEAD would be 195, ITAIL would be 10, and the buffer would contain 15 characters occupying bytes #195 through 199 and 0 through 9.

Entry Conditions

1. INCH: none
2. INST: none
3. OUTCH: character to transmit in accumulator
4. OUTST: none
5. INIT: none

Exit Conditions

1. INCH: character in accumulator
2. INST: Carry flag = 0 if no characters are available, 1 if a character is available
3. OUTCH: none
4. OUTST: Carry flag = 0 if output buffer is not full, 1 if it is full
5. INIT: none

```
;       Title           Interrupt input and output using a 6850       ;
;                       ACIA and a multiple character buffer.         ;
;       Name:           SINTB                                         ;
;                                                                     ;
;                                                                     ;


;                                                                     ;
;       Purpose:        This program consists of 5 subroutines which  ;
;                       perform interrupt driven input and output using ;
;                       a 6850 ACIA.                                  ;
;                                                                     ;
;                       INCH                                          ;
;                         Read a character.                           ;
```

```
;                       INST                                    ;
;                         Determine input status (whether a character ;
;                         is available).                        ;
;                       OUTCH                                   ;
;                         Write a character.                    ;
;                       OUTST                                   ;
;                         Determine output status (whether the output ;
;                         buffer is full).                      ;
;                       INIT                                    ;
;                         Initialize.                           ;
;                                                               ;
;       Entry:          INCH                                    ;
;                         No parameters.                        ;
;                       INST                                    ;
;                         No parameters.                        ;
;                       OUTCH                                   ;
;                         Register A = character to transmit    ;
;                       OUTST                                   ;
;                         No parameters.                        ;
;                       INIT                                    ;
;                         No parameters.                        ;
;                                                               ;
;       Exit:           INCH                                    ;
;                         Register A = character.               ;
;                       INST                                    ;
;                         Carry flag equals 0 if no characters are ;
;                         available, 1 if character is available. ;
;                       OUTCH                                   ;
;                         No parameters                         ;
;                       OUTST                                   ;
;                         Carry flag equals 0 if output buffer is ;
;                         empty, 1 if it is full.               ;
;                       INIT                                    ;
;                         No parameters.                        ;
;                                                               ;
;       Registers used: INCH                                    ;
;                         A,F,Y                                 ;
;                       INST                                    ;
;                         A,F                                   ;
;                       OUTCH                                   ;
;                         A,F,Y                                 ;
;                       OUTST                                   ;
;                         A,F                                   ;
;                       INIT                                    ;
;                         A,F                                   ;
;                                                               ;
;                                                               ;
;       Registers used: INCH                                    ;
;                         A,F,Y                                 ;
;                       INST                                    ;
;                         A,F                                   ;
;                       OUTCH                                   ;
;                         A,F,Y                                 ;
;                       OUTST                                   ;
;                         A,F                                   ;
;                       INIT                                    ;
```

```
;                         A,F                                       ;
;                                                                   ;
;       Time:            INCH                                       ;
;                          70 cycles if a character is available    ;
;                        INST                                       ;
;                          18 cycles                                ;
;                        OUTCH                                      ;
;                          75 cycles minimum, if the output buffer is ;
;                             not full and the ACIA is ready to transmit ;
;                        OUTST                                      ;
;                          12 cycles                                ;
;                        INIT                                       ;
;                          89 cycles                                ;
;                        IOSRVC                                     ;
;                          27 cycles minimum if the interrupt is not ours;
;                          73 cycles to service a input interrupt   ;
;                          102 cycles to service a output interrupt ;
;                                                                   ;
;       Size:            Program 258 bytes                          ;
;                        Data      7 bytes plus size of buffers     ;
;                                                                   ;
;       Buffers:                                                    ;
;                        The routines assume two buffers starting at ;
;                        addresses IBUF and OBUF. The lengths of the ;
;                        buffers in bytes are IBSZ and OBSZ. For the ;
;                        input buffer, IHEAD is the index of the oldest ;
;                        character (the next one the main program should ;
;                        read), ITAIL is the index of the next empty ;
;                        element (the next one the service routine  ;
;                        should fill), and ICNT is the number of bytes ;
;                        currently filled with characters. For the  ;
;                        output buffer, OHEAD is the index of the oldest ;
;                        character (the next one the service routine ;
;                        should send), OTAIL is the index of the next ;
;                        empty element (the next one the main program ;
;                        should fill), and OCNT is the number of bytes ;
;                        currently filled with characters.          ;
;                                                                   ;
;       Note:            Wraparound is provided on both buffers, so that ;
;                        the currently filled area may start anywhere ;
;                        and extend through the end of the buffer and ;
;                        back to the beginning. For example, if the ;
;                        output buffer is 40 hex bytes long, the section ;
;                        filled with characters could exetend from  ;
;                        OBUF+32H (OHEAD=32H) to OBUF+10H (OTAIL=11H). ;
;                        That is, there are 19H filled bytes occupying ;
;                        addresses OBUF+32H through OBUF+39H and    ;
;                        continuing to OBUF through OBUF+10H. The buffer ;
;                        thus looks like a television picture with the ;
;                        vertical hold skewed, so that the frame starts ;
;                        above the bottom of the screen, leaves off at ;
;                        the top, and continues at the bottom.      ;
;                                                                   ;
;                                                                   ;

;EXAMPLE 6850 ACIA PORT DEFINITIONS FOR AN APPLE SERIAL BOARD IN SLOT 1
```

```
ACIASR  .EQU    0C094H          ;ACIA STATUS REGISTER
ACIADR  .EQU    0C095H          ;ACIA DATA REGISTER
ACIACR  .EQU    0C094H          ;ACIA CONTROL REGISTER
IRQVEC  .EQU    03FEH           ;APPLE IRQ VECTOR ADDRESS

;READ A CHARACTER
INCH:
        JSR     INST            ;IS A CHARACTER AVAILABLE ?
        BCC     INCH            ;BRANCH IF NOT
        PHP                     ;SAVE CURRENT STATE OF INTERRUPTS
        SEI                     ;DISABLE INTERRUPTS
        LDY     IHEAD
        LDA     IBUF,Y          ;GET CHARACTER AT HEAD OF BUFFER
        INY
        CPY     #IBSZ           ;DO WE NEED WRAPAROUND IN BUFFER ?
        BCC     INCH1           ;BRANCH IF NOT
        LDY     #0              ;ELSE SET HEAD BACK TO ZERO
INCH1:
        STY     IHEAD
        DEC     ICNT            ;DECREMENT CHARACTER COUNT
        PLP                     ;RESTORE FLAGS
        RTS

;RETURN INPUT STATUS (CARRY = 1 IF CHARACTERS ARE AVAILABLE, 0 IF NOT)
INST:
        CLC                     ;CLEAR CARRY (ASSUME NO CHARACTERS AVAILABLE)
        LDA     ICNT
        BEQ     INST1           ;BRANCH IF THERE ARE NONE
        SEC                     ;CARRY = 1 (CHARACTERS ARE AVAILABLE)
INST1:
        RTS

;WRITE A CHARACTER
OUTCH:
        PHP                     ;SAVE STATE OF INTERRUPT FLAG
        PHA                     ;SAVE CHARACTER TO OUTPUT

        ;WAIT UNTIL THERE IS EMPTY SPACE IN THE OUTPUT BUFFER
WAITOC:
        JSR     OUTST           ;IS THE OUTPUT BUFFER FULL ?
        BCS     WAITOC          ;BRANCH IF IT IS FULL
        SEI                     ;DISABLE INTERRUPTS WHILE LOOKING AT THE
                                ; SOFTWARE FLAGS
        PLA                     ;GET THE CHARACTER
        LDY     OTAIL
        STA     OBUF,Y          ;STORE CHARACTER IN THE BUFFER
        INY
        CPY     #OBSZ           ;DO WE NEED WRAPAROUND ON THE BUFFER ?
        BCC     OUTCH1          ;BRANCH IF NOT
        LDY     #0              ;ELSE SET TAIL BACK TO ZERO
OUTCH1:
        STY     OTAIL
        INC     OCNT            ;INCREMENT BUFFER COUNTER
        LDA     OIE             ;ARE INTERRUPTS DISABLED BUT THE ACIA IS
                                ; ACTUALLY READY ?
        BNE     OUTCH2          ;EXIT IF ACIA INTERRUPTS NOT READY AND ENABLED
```

```
        JSR     OUTDAT              ;ELSE SEND THE DATA TO THE PORT AND ENABLE
                                    ; INTERRUPTS
OUTCH2:
        PLP                         ;RESTORE FLAGS
        RTS



;OUTPUT STATUS
OUTST:
        LDA     OCNT
        CMP     #OBSZ               ;IS OUTPUT BUFFER FULL ?
                                    ; IF OCNT >= OBSZ THEN
                                    ;   CARRY = 1 INDICATING THAT THE OUTPUT
                                    ;             BUFFER IS FULL
                                    ; ELSE
                                    ;   CARRY = 0 INDICATING THAT THE CHARACTER
                                    ;             CAN BE PLACED IN THE BUFFER
        RTS


;INITIALIZE
INIT:
        PHP                         ;SAVE CURRENT STATE OF FLAGS
        SEI                         ;DISABLE INTERRUPTS

        ;INITIALIZE THE SOFTWARE FLAGS
        LDA     #0
        STA     ICNT                ;NO INPUT DATA
        STA     IHEAD
        STA     ITAIL
        STA     OCNT                ;NO OUTPUT DATA
        STA     OHEAD
        STA     OTAIL
        STA     OIE                 ;ACIA IS READY TO TRANSMIT (NOTE THIS !!)

        ;SAVE THE CURRENT IRQ VECTOR IN NEXTSR
        LDA     IRQVEC
        STA     NEXTSR
        LDA     IRQVEC+1
        STA     NEXTSR+1

        ;SET THE IRQ VECTOR TO OUR INPUT SERVICE ROUTINE
        LDA     AIOS
        STA     IRQVEC
        LDA     AIOS+1
        STA     IRQVEC+1

        ;INITIALIZE THE 6850 ACIA
        LDA     #011B
        STA     ACIACR              ;MASTER RESET ACIA
        LDA     #10010001B
        STA     ACIACR              ;INITIALIZE ACIA MODE TO
                                    ;  DIVIDE BY 16
                                    ;  8 DATA BITS
                                    ;  2 STOP BITS
```

```
                                ;   OUTPUT INTERRUPTS DISABLED (NOTE THIS !!)
                                ;   INPUT INTERRUPTS ENABLED

        PLP                     ;RESTORE CURRENT STATE OF THE FLAGS
        RTS

AIOS:   .WORD   IOSRVC          ;ADDRESS OF INPUT OUTPUT SERVICE ROUTINE

;INPUT OUTPUT INTERRUPT SERVICE ROUTINE
IOSRVC:
        PHA                     ;SAVE REGISTER A
        CLD                     ;BE SURE PROCESSOR IS IN BINARY MODE

        ;GET THE ACIA STATUS: BIT 0 = 1 IF AN INPUT INTERRUPT
        ;BIT 1 = 1 IF AN OUTPUT INTERRUPT
        LDA     ACIASR
        LSR     A               ;BIT 0 TO CARRY
        BCS     IINT            ;BRANCH IF AN INPUT INTERRUPT
        LSR     A               ;BIT 1 TO CARRY
        BCS     OINT            ;BRANCH IF AN OUTPUT INTERRUPT

        ;THE INTERRUPT WAS NOT OURS
        PLA
        JMP     (NEXTSR)        ;GOTO THE NEXT SERVICE ROUTINE

;SERVICE INPUT INTERRUPTS
IINT:
        TYA
        PHA                     ;SAVE REGISTER Y

        ;GET THE DATA AND STORE IT IN THE BUFFER IF THERE IS ROOM
        LDA     ACIADR          ;READ THE DATA
        LDY     ICNT            ;IS THERE ROOM IN THE BUFFER ?
        CPY     #IBSZ
        BCS     EXIT            ;EXIT, NO ROOM IN THE BUFFER
        LDY     ITAIL           ;ELSE STORE THE DATA IN THE BUFFER
        STA     IBUF,Y
        INY                     ;INCREMENT TAIL INDEX
        CPY     #IBSZ           ;DO WE NEED WRAPAROUND ON THE BUFFER ?
        BCC     IINT1           ;BRANCH IF NOT
        LDY     #0              ;ELSE SET TAIL BACK TO ZERO
IINT1:
        STY     ITAIL           ;STORE NEW TAIL INDEX
        INC     ICNT            ;INCREMENT INPUT BUFFER COUNTER
        JMP     EXIT            ;EXIT IOSRVC

;SERVICE OUTPUT INTERRUPTS
OINT:
        TYA
        PHA                     ;SAVE REGISTER Y

        LDA     OCNT            ;IS THERE ANY DATA IN THE OUTPUT BUFFER ?
        BEQ     NODATA          ;BRANCH IF NOT (DISABLE THE INTERRUPTS)
        JSR     OUTDAT          ;ELSE SEND A CHARACTER
        JMP     EXIT
```

```
NODATA:
        LDA     #10010001B      ;DISABLE OUTPUT INTERRUPTS, ENABLE INPUT
                                ; INTERRUPTS, 8 DATA BITS, 2 STOP BITS, DIVIDE
                                ; BY 16 CLOCK
        STA     ACIACR          ;TURN OFF INTERRUPTS
        LDA     #0
        STA     OIE             ;INDICATE OUTPUT INTERRUPTS ARE DISABLED
                                ; BUT ACIA IS ACTUALLY READY
EXIT:
        PLA
        TAY                     ;RESTORE REGISTER Y
        PLA                     ;RESTORE REGISTER A
        RTI                     ;RETURN FROM INTERRUPT

;*************************************
;ROUTINE: OUTDAT
;PURPOSE: SEND A CHARACTER TO THE ACIA FROM THE OUTPUT BUFFER
;ENTRY: OHEAD IS THE INDEX INTO OBUF OF THE CHARACTER TO SEND
;EXIT:  NONE
;REGISTERS USED: A,F
;*************************************

OUTDAT:
        LDA     ACIASR
        AND     #00000010B      ;IS ACIA OUTPUT REGISTER EMPTY ?
        BEQ     OUTDAT          ;BRANCH IF NOT EMPTY (BIT 1 = 0)
        LDY     OHEAD
        LDA     OBUF,Y          ;GET THE CHARACTER FROM THE BUFFER
        STA     ACIADR          ;SEND THE DATA
        INY
        CPY     #OBSZ           ;DO WE NEED WRAPAROUND ON THE BUFFER ?
        BCC     OUTD1           ;BRANCH IF NOT
        LDY     #0              ;ELSE SET HEAD BACK TO ZERO
OUTD1:
        STY     OHEAD           ;SAVE NEW HEAD INDEX
        DEC     OCNT            ;DECREMENT OUTPUT BUFFER COUNTER
        LDA     #10110001B
        STA     ACIACR          ;ENABLE 6850 OUTPUT AND INPUT INTERRUPTS,
                                ; 8 DATA BITS, 2 STOP BITS, DIVIDE BY 16 CLOCK
        LDA     #0FFH
        STA     OIE             ;INDICATE THE OUTPUT INTERRUPTS ARE ENABLED

        RTS


;DATA SECTION
ICNT    .BLOCK  1               ;INPUT BUFFER COUNTER
IHEAD   .BLOCK  1               ;INDEX TO HEAD OF INPUT BUFFER
ITAIL   .BLOCK  1               ;INDEX TO TAIL OF INPUT BUFFER
OCNT    .BLOCK  1               ;OUTPUT BUFFER COUNTER
OHEAD   .BLOCK  1               ;INDEX TO HEAD OF OUTPUT BUFFER
OTAIL   .BLOCK  1               ;INDEX TO TAIL OF OUTPUT BUFFER
OIE     .BLOCK  1               ;OUTPUT INTERRUPT ENABLE FLAG

IBSZ    .EQU    80              ;INPUT BUFFER SIZE
IBUF    .BLOCK  IBSZ            ;INPUT BUFFER
```

```
OBSZ     .EQU     80                  ;OUTPUT BUFFER SIZE
OBUF     .BLOCK   OBSZ                ;OUTPUT BUFFER
NEXTSR   .BLOCK   2                   ;ADDRESS OF THE NEXT INTERRUPT SERVICE ROUTINE


;                                                                                   ;
;                                                                                   ;
;        SAMPLE EXECUTION:                                                          ;
;                                                                                   ;
;                                                                                   ;


SC1103:
         JSR      INIT                ;INITIALIZE
         CLI                          ;ENABLE INTERRUPTS

         ;SIMPLE EXAMPLE
LOOP:
         JSR      INCH                ;READ A CHARACTER
         PHA
         JSR      OUTCH               ;ECHO IT
         PLA
         CMP      #1BH                ;IS CHARACTER AN ESCAPE ?
         BNE      LOOP                ;BRANCH IF NOT, CONTINUE LOOPING
         BRK

         ;AN ASYNCHRONOUS EXAMPLE
         ; OUTPUT "A" TO THE CONSOLE CONTINUOUSLY BUT ALSO LOOK AT THE
         ; INPUT SIDE, READING AND ECHOING ANY INPUT CHARACTERS.
ASYNLP:
         ;OUTPUT AN "A" IF OUTPUT IS NOT BUSY

         JSR      OUTST               ;IS OUTPUT BUSY ?
         BCS      ASYNLP              ;BRANCH IF IT IS
         LDA      #"A"
         JSR      OUTCH               ;OUTPUT THE CHARACTER

         ;GET A CHARACTER FROM THE INPUT PORT IF ANY
         JSR      INST                ;IS INPUT AVAILABLE ?
         BCC      ASYNLP              ;BRANCH IF NOT (SEND ANOTHER "A")
         JSR      INCH                ;GET THE CHARACTER
         CMP      #1BH                ;IS CHARACTER AN ESCAPE ?
         BEQ      DONE                ;BRANCH IF IT IS
         JSR      OUTCH               ;ELSE ECHO IT
         JMP      ASYNLP              ; AND CONTINUE

DONE:
         BRK

         .END     ;PROGRAM
```

Maintains a time-of-day 24-hour clock and a calendar based on a real-time clock interrupt. Consists of the following subroutines:

1. CLOCK returns the starting address of the clock variables.

2. ICLK initializes the clock interrupt and initializes the clock variables to their default values.

3. CLKINT updates the clock after each interrupt (assumed to be spaced one tick apart).

A long example in the listing describes a time display routine for the Apple II computer. The routine prompts the operator for an initial date and time. It then continuously displays the date and time in the center of the monitor screen. The routine assumes an interrupt board in slot 2.

Procedure:

1. CLOCK loads the starting address of the clock variables into the accumulator (more significant byte) and index register Y (less significant byte). The clock variables are stored in the following order (lowest address first): ticks, seconds, minutes, hours, days, months, less significant byte of year, more significant byte of year.

2. ICLK loads the clock variables with their default values (8 bytes starting at address DFLTS) and initializes the clock interrupt (this would be mostly system-dependent).

3. CLKINT decrements the remaining tick count by one and updates the rest of the clock if necessary. Of course, the number of seconds and minutes must be less than 60 and the number of hours must be less than 24. The day of the month must be less than or equal to the last day for the current month; an array of the last days of each month begins at address LASTDY. If the month is February (that is, month 2), the program must check to see if the current year is a leap year. This requires a determination of whether the two least significant bits of memory location YEAR are both zeros. If the current year is a leap year, the last day of February is the 29th, not the 28th. The month number may not exceed 12 (December) or a carry to the year number is necessary. The program must reinitialize the variables properly when carries occur; that is, TICK to DTICK; seconds, minutes, and hours to zero; day and month to 1 (meaning the first day and January, respectively).

Registers Used:

1. CLOCK:	A, F, Y
2. ICLK:	A, Y
3. CLKINT:	none

Execution Time:

1. CLOCK: 14 cycles
2. ICLK: 166 cycles
3. CLKINT: 33 cycles if only TICK must be decremented, 184 maximum if changing to a new year.

Program Size:

1. CLOCK:	7 bytes
2. ICLK:	39 bytes
3. CLKINT:	145 bytes

Data Memory Required: 18 bytes anywhere in RAM. These include eight bytes for the clock variables (starting at address ACVAR), eight bytes for the defaults (starting at address DFLTS), and two bytes for the address of the next service routine (starting at address NEXTSR).

Entry Conditions

1. CLOCK: none
2. ICLK: none
3. CLKINT: none

Exit Conditions

1. CLOCK: more significant byte of starting address of clock variables in accumulator, less significant byte in register Y
2. ICLK: none
3. CLKINT: none

Examples

These examples assume that the tick rate is DTICK Hz (less than 256 Hz — typical values would be 60 Hz or 100 Hz) and that the clock and calendar are saved in memory locations

TICK	number of ticks remaining before a carry occurs, counted down from DTICK
SEC	seconds (0 to 59)
MIN	minutes (0 to 59)
HOUR	hour of day (0 to 23)
DAY	day of month (1 to 28, 30, or 31, depending on month)
MONTH	month of year (1 through 12 for January through December)
YEAR & YEAR+1	current year

1. Starting values are March 7, 1982. 11:59.59 and 1 tick left.

That is,

(TICK) = 1
(SEC) = 59
(MIN) = 59
(HOUR) = 23
(DAY) = 07
(MONTH) = 03
(YEAR) = 1982

Result (after the tick): March 8, 1982 12:00.00 and DTICK ticks

That is,

(TICK) = DTICK
(SEC) = 0
(MIN) = 0
(HOUR) = 0
(DAY) = 08
(MONTH) = 03
(YEAR) = 1982

2. Starting values are Dec. 31, 1982. 11:59.59 p.m. and 1 tick left

That is,

(TICK) = 1
(SEC) = 59
(MIN) = 59
(HOUR) = 23
(DAY) = 31
(MONTH) = 12
(YEAR) = 1982

Result (after the tick): Jan. 1, 1983. 12:00.00 a.m. and DTICK ticks

That is,

(TICK) = DTICK
(SEC) = 0
(MIN) = 0
(HOUR) = 0
(DAY) = 1
(MONTH) = 1
(YEAR) = 1983

```
;       Title           Real time clock and calendar                ;
;       Name:           CLOCK                                       ;
;                                                                   ;
;                                                                   ;
;                                                                   ;
;       Purpose:        This program maintains a time of day 24 hour ;
;                       clock and a calendar based on a real time clock ;
;                       interrupt.                                  ;
;                                                                   ;
;                       CLOCK                                       ;
;                         Returns the address of the clock variables ;
;                       ICLK                                        ;
;                         Initialize the clock interrupt            ;
;                                                                   ;
;       Entry:          CLOCK                                       ;
;                         None                                      ;
;                       ICLK                                        ;
;                         None                                      ;
;                                                                   ;
;       Exit:           CLOCK                                       ;
;                         Register A = High byte of the address of the ;
;                                      time variables.              ;
;                         Register Y = Low byte of the address of the ;
;                                      time variables.              ;
;                       ICLK                                        ;
;                         None                                      ;
;                                                                   ;
;       Registers used: All                                         ;
;                                                                   ;
;       Time:           CLOCK                                       ;
;                         14 cycles                                 ;
;                       ICLCK                                       ;
;                         166 cycles                                ;
;                       CLKINT                                      ;
;                         22 cycles minimum if the interrupt is not ours;
;                         33 cycles normally if decrementing tick   ;
;                        184 cycles maximum if changing to a new year ;
;                                                                   ;
;       Size:           Program 191 bytes                           ;
;                       Data     18 bytes                           ;
;                                                                   ;
;                                                                   ;

IRQVEC: .EQU    03FEH           ;APPLE IRQ VECTOR
CLKPRT: .EQU    0C0A0H          ;SLOT 2 IO LOCATION OF AN INTERRUPT BOARD
CLKIM:  .EQU    01H             ;BIT 0 = INTERRUPT REQUEST BIT
TRUE:   .EQU    0FFH            ;NOT ZERO = TRUE
FALSE:  .EQU    0               ;ZERO = FALSE

;RETURN ADDRESS OF THE CLOCK VARIABLES
CLOCK:
        LDA     ACVAR+1
        LDY     ACVAR           ;GET ADDRESS OF CLOCK VARIABLES
        RTS
```

```
;INITIALIZE CLOCK INTERRUPT
ICLK:
        PHP                         ;SAVE FLAGS
        SEI                         ;DISABLE INTERRUPTS

        ;INITIALIZE CLOCK VARIABLES TO THE DEFAULT VALUEs
        LDY     #8
ICLK1:
        LDA     DFLTS-1,Y
        STA     CLKVAR-1,Y
        DEY
        BNE     ICLK1

        ;SAVE CURRENT IRQ VECTOR
        LDA     IRQVEC
        STA     NEXTSR
        LDA     IRQVEC+1
        STA     NEXTSR

        ;SET IRQ VECTOR TO CLKINT
        LDA     ACINT
        STA     IRQVEC
        LDA     ACINT+1
        STA     IRQVEC+1

        ;HERE SHOULD BE CODE TO INITIALIZE INTERRUPT HARDWARE

        ;EXIT
        PLP                         ;RESTORE FLAGS
        RTS

;HANDLE THE CLOCK INTERRUPT
CLKINT:
        PHA                         ;SAVE REGISTER A
        CLD                         ;BE SURE PROCESSOR IS IN BINARY MODE

        ;CHECK IF THIS IS OUR INTERRUPT
        ;  THIS IS AN EXAMPLE ONLY
        LDA     CLKPRT
        AND     #CLKIM              ;LOOK AT THE INTERRUPT REQUEST BIT
        BNE     OURINT              ;BRANCH IF IS OUR INTERRUPT
        PLA                         ;RESTORE REGISTER A
        JMP     (NEXTSR)            ;WAS NOT OUR INTERRUPT,
                                    ; TRY NEXT SERVICE ROUTINE

        ;PROCESS OUR INTERRUPT
OURINT:
        DEC     TICK
        BNE     EXIT1               ;BRANCH IF TICK DOES NOT EQUAL ZERO YET
                                    ; EXIT1 RESTORES ONLY REGISTER A
        LDA     DTICK
        STA     TICK                ;RESET TICK TO DEFAULT VALUE

        ;SAVE X AND Y NOW ALSO
        TYA
        PHA
```

```
        TXA
        PHA

        ;INCREMENT SECONDS
        INC     SEC
        LDA     SEC
        CMP     #60             ;SECONDS = 60 ?
        BCC     EXIT            ;EXIT IF LESS THAN 60 SECONDS
        LDY     #0              ;ELSE
        STY     SEC             ; ZERO SECONDS, GO TO NEXT MINUTE

        ;INCREMENT MINUTES
        INC     MIN
        LDA     MIN
        CMP     #60             ;MINUTES = 60 ?
        BCC     EXIT            ;EXIT IF LESS THAN 60 MINUTES
        STY     MIN             ;ELSE
                                ; ZERO MINUTES, GO TO NEXT HOUR

        ;INCREMENT HOURS
        INC     HOUR
        LDA     HOUR
        CMP     #24             ;HOURS = 24 ?
        BCC     EXIT            ;EXIT IF LESS THAN 24 HOURS
        STY     HOUR            ;ELSE
                                ; ZERO HOURS, GO TO NEXT DAY

        ;INCREMENT DAYS
        INC     DAY
        LDA     DAY
        LDX     MONTH           ;GET CURRENT MONTH
        CMP     LASTDY-1,X      ;DAY = LAST DAY OF THE MONTH ?
        BCC     EXIT            ;EXIT IF LESS THAN LAST DAY

        ;INCREMENT MONTH (HANDLE 29TH OF FEBRUARY)
        CPX     #2              ;IS THIS FEBRUARY ?
        BNE     INCMTH          ;BRANCH IF NOT FEBRUARY
        LDA     YEAR            ;IS IT A LEAP YEAR?
        AND     #00000011B
        BNE     INCMTH          ;BRANCH IF YEAR IS NOT LEAP YEAR

        ;THIS IS A FEBRUARY AND A LEAP YEAR SO 29 DAYS NOT 28 DAYS
        LDA     DAY
        CMP     #29
        BEQ     EXIT            ;EXIT IF NOT 29TH OF FEBRUARY

INCMTH:
        LDY     #1
        STY     DAY             ;CHANGE DAY TO 1, INCREMENT MONTH
        INC     MONTH
        LDA     MONTH
        CMP     #13             ;DONE WITH DECEMBER ?
        BCC     EXIT            ;EXIT IF NOT
        STY     MONTH           ;ELSE
                                ; CHANGE MONTH TO 1 (JANUARY)
```

```
        ;INCREMENT YEAR
        INC     YEAR                ;INCREMENT LOW BYTE
        BNE     EXIT
        INC     YEAR+1              ;INCREMENT HIGH BYTE

EXIT:
        ;RESTORE REGISTERS
        PLA
        TAX
        PLA
        TAY
EXIT1:
        PLA
        RTI                         ;RETURN FROM INTERRUPT


;ARRAY OF THE LAST DAYS OF EACH MONTH
LASTDY:
        .BYTE   31                  ;JANUARY
        .BYTE   28                  ;FEBRUARY (EXCEPT LEAP YEARS)
        .BYTE   31                  ;MARCH
        .BYTE   30                  ;APRIL
        .BYTE   31                  ;MAY
        .BYTE   30                  ;JUNE
        .BYTE   31                  ;JULY
        .BYTE   31                  ;AUGUST
        .BYTE   30                  ;SEPTEMBER
        .BYTE   31                  ;OCTOBER
        .BYTE   30                  ;NOVEMBER
        .BYTE   31                  ;DECEMBER

;CLOCK VARIABLES
ACVAR:  .WORD   CLKVAR              ;BASE ADDRESS OF CLOCK VARIABLES
CLKVAR:
TICK:   .BLOCK  1                   ;TICKS LEFT IN CURRENT SECOND
SEC:    .BLOCK  1                   ;SECONDS
MIN:    .BLOCK  1                   ;MINUTES
HOUR:   .BLOCK  1                   ;HOURS
DAY:    .BLOCK  1                   ;DAY = 1 THROUGH NUMBER OF DAYS IN A MONTH
MONTH:  .BLOCK  1                   ;MONTH 1=JANUARY .. 12=DECEMBER
YEAR:   .WORD   0                   ;YEAR

;DEFAULTS
DFLTS:
DTICK:  .BYTE   60                  ;DEFAULT TICK (60HZ INTERRUPT)
DSEC:   .BYTE   0                   ;DEFAULT SECONDS
DMIN:   .BYTE   0                   ;DEFAULT MINUTES
DHR:    .BYTE   0                   ;DEFAULT HOURS
DDAY:   .BYTE   1                   ;DEFAULT DAY
DMTH:   .BYTE   1                   ;DEFAULT MONTH
DYEAR:  .WORD   1981                ;DEFAULT YEAR

NEXTSR: .BLOCK  2                   ;ADDRESS OF THE NEXT INTERRUPT SERVICE ROUTINE
ACINT:  .WORD   CLKINT              ;ADDRESS OF THE CLOCK INTERRUPT ROUTINE
```

```
;                                                                        ;
;                                                                        ;
;         SAMPLE EXECUTION:                                              ;
;                                                                        ;
;       This routine prompts the operator for an initial date and time,  ;
;       it then continuously displays the date and time in the center of ;
;       the screen.                                                      ;
;                                                                        ;
;       The operator may use the escape key to abort the routine. Any    ;
;       other key will reprompt for another initial date and time.       ;
;                                                                        ;
;                                                                        ;


;CLK VARIABLE OFFSETS
OTICK:  .EQU    0               ;OFFSET TO TICK
OSEC:   .EQU    1               ;OFFSET TO SECONDS
OMIN:   .EQU    2               ;OFFSET TO MINUTES
OHR:    .EQU    3               ;OFFSET TO HOURS
ODAY:   .EQU    4               ;OFFSET TO DAY
OMTH:   .EQU    5               ;OFFSET TO MONTH
OYEAR:  .EQU    6               ;OFFSET TO YEAR

;PAGE ZERO TEMPORARY
CVARS:  .EQU    0D0H            ;PAGE ZERO TEMPORARY FOR THE CLOCK VARIABLES
                                ; ADDRESS

;APPLE EQUATES FOR THE EXAMPLE
ESC:    .EQU    1BH             ;ESCAPE CHARACTER
CH      .EQU    24H             ;APPLE MONITOR CURSOR HORIZONTAL POSITION
CV      .EQU    25H             ;APPLE MONITOR CURSOR VERTICAL POSITION
HOME:   .EQU    0FC58H          ;APPLE MONITOR HOME ROUTINE
VTAB:   .EQU    0FC22H          ;APPLE MONITOR VTAB ROUTINE
RCHAR:  .EQU    0FD0CH          ;APPLE MONITOR CHARACTER INPUT ROUTINE
COUT:   .EQU    0FDEDH          ;APPLE MONITOR CHARACTER OUTPUT ROUTINE
GETLN1: .EQU    0FD6FH          ;APPLE MONITOR GET LINE WITH OUR PROMPT ROUTINE


SC1104:
        JSR     ICLK            ;INITIALIZE

        ;GET TODAYS DATE AND TIME MM/DD/YY HR:MIN:SEC
        ; PRINT PROMPT
PROMPT:
        JSR     HOME            ;HOME AND CLEAR SCREEN
        LDA     #0
        STA     MSGIDX
PMTLP:
        LDY     MSGIDX
        LDA     MSG,Y
        BEQ     RDTIME          ;BRANCH IF END OF MESSAGE
        INC     MSGIDX          ;INCREMENT TO NEXT CHARACTER
        JSR     WRCHAR          ;OUTPUT CHARACTER THROUGH APPLE MONITOR
        JMP     PMTLP           ;CONTINUE

        ;READ THE TIME STRING
```

```
RDTIME:
        JSR     RDLINE          ;READ A LINE INTO THE APPLE LINE BUFFER AT
                                ; 200H. RETURNS WITH LENGTH IN X

        ;GET THE ADDRESS OF THE CLOCK VARIABLES
        JSR     CLOCK           ;GET CLOCK VARIABLES
        STA     CVARS+1
        STY     CVARS           ;STORE ADDRESS

        ;INITIALIZE VARIABLES FOR READING NUMBERS
        STX     LLEN            ;SAVE LENGTH OF LINE
        LDA     #0
        STA     LIDX            ;INITIALIZE LINE INDEX TO ZERO

        ;GET MONTH
        JSR     NXTNUM          ;GET NEXT NUMBER FROM INPUT LINE
        LDY     #OMTH
        STA     (CVARS),Y       ;SET MONTH

        ;GET DAY
        JSR     NXTNUM
        LDY     #ODAY
        STA     (CVARS),Y

        ;GET YEAR
        JSR     NXTNUM
        LDY     #OYEAR
        STA     (CVARS),Y
        CLC
        ADC     CEN20           ;ADD 1900 TO ENTRY
        STA     (CVARS),Y       ;SET LOW BYTE OF YEAR
        LDA     CEN20+1
        ADC     #0
        INY
        STA     (CVARS),Y       ;SET HIGH BYTE OF YEAR

        ;GET HOUR
        JSR     NXTNUM
        LDY     #OHR
        STA     (CVARS),Y

        ;GET MINUTES
        JSR     NXTNUM
        LDY     #OMIN
        STA     (CVARS),Y

        ;GET SECONDS
        JSR     NXTNUM
        LDY     #OSEC
        STA     (CVARS),Y

        ;ENABLE INTERRUPTS
        CLI                     ;ENABLE INTERRUPTS

        ;HOME AND CLEAR THE SCREEN
```

```
        JSR     HOME

        ;LOOP PRINTING THE TIME EVERY SECOND
        ;MOVE CURSOR TO LINE 12 CHARACTER 12
LOOP:
        LDA     #11
        STA     CV              ;SET CURSOR VERTICAL POSITION
        STA     CH              ;SET CURSOR HORIZONTAL POSITION
        JSR     VTAB            ;POSITION CURSOR

        ;PRINT MONTH
        LDY     #OMTH
        LDA     (CVARS),Y
        JSR     PRTNUM          ;PRINT THE NUMBER
        LDA     #"/"
        JSR     WRCHAR          ;PRINT A SLASH

        ;PRINT DAY
        LDY     #ODAY
        LDA     (CVARS),Y
        JSR     PRTNUM          ;PRINT THE NUMBER
        LDA     #"/"
        JSR     WRCHAR          ;PRINT A SLASH

        ;PRINT YEAR
        LDY     #OYEAR
        LDA     (CVARS),Y
        SEC
        SBC     CEN20           ;NORMALIZE YEAR TO 20TH CENTURY
        JSR     PRTNUM          ;PRINT THE NUMBER

        ;PRINT SPACE AS DELIMITER
        LDA     #" "
        JSR     WRCHAR          ;PRINT A SPACE BETWEEN DATE AND TIME

        ;PRINT HOURS
        LDY     #OHR
        LDA     (CVARS),Y
        JSR     PRTNUM          ;PRINT THE NUMBER
        LDA     #":"
        JSR     WRCHAR          ;PRINT A COLON

        ;PRINT MINUTES
        LDY     #OMIN
        LDA     (CVARS),Y
        JSR     PRTNUM          ;PRINT THE NUMBER
        LDA     #":"
        JSR     WRCHAR          ;PRINT A COLON

        ;PRINT SECONDS
        LDY     #OSEC
        LDA     (CVARS),Y
        JSR     PRTNUM          ;PRINT THE NUMBER

        ;WAIT UNTIL SECONDS CHANGE THEN PRINT AGAIN
        ;EXIT IF OPERATOR PRESSES A KEY
```

```
        LDY     #OSEC
        LDA     (CVARS),Y
        STA     CURSEC          ;SAVE IN CURRENT SECOND
WAIT:
        ;CHECK KEYBOARD
        JSR     KEYPRS
        BCS     RDKEY           ;BRANCH IF OPERATOR PRESSES A KEY
        LDA     (CVARS),Y       ;GET SECONDS
        CMP     CURSEC
        BEQ     WAIT            ;WAIT UNTIL SECONDS CHANGE
        JMP     LOOP            ;CONTINUE

        ;OPERATOR PRESSED A KEY - DONE IF ESCAPE, PROMPT OTHERWISE
RDKEY:
        JSR     RDCHAR          ;GET CHARACTER
        CMP     #ESC            ;IS IT AN ESCAPE?
        BEQ     DONE            ;BRANCH IF IT IS, ROUTINE IS FINISHED
        JMP     PROMPT          ;ELSE PROMPT OPERATOR FOR NEW STARTING TIME

DONE:
        LDA     #0
        STA     CH              ;CURSOR TO HORIZONTAL POSITION 0
        LDA     #12
        STA     CV
        JSR     VTAB            ;MOVE CURSOR TO LINE 13 BELOW DISPLAY
        BRK
        JMP     SC1104          ;CONTINUE AGAIN

;********************************
;ROUTINE: KEYPRS
;PURPOSE: DETERMINE IF OPERATOR HAS PRESSED A KEY
;ENTRY: NONE
;EXIT:  IF OPERATOR HAS PRESSED A KEY THEN
;         CARRY = 1
;       ELSE
;         CARRY = 0
;REGISTERS USED: P
;********************************

KEYPRS:
        PHA
        LDA     0C000H          ;READ APPLE KEYBOARD PORT
        ASL     A               ;MOVE BIT 7 TO CARRY
                                ; CARRY = 1 IF CHARACTER IS READY ELSE 0
        PLA
        RTS


;********************************
;ROUTINE: RDCHAR
;PURPOSE: READ A CHARACTER
;ENTRY: NONE
;EXIT:  REGISTER A = CHARACTER
;REGISTERS USED: A,P
;********************************
```

```
RDCHAR:
        PHA                         ;SAVE A,X,Y
        TYA
        PHA
        TXA
        PHA

        JSR     RCHAR               ;APPLE MONITOR RDCHAR
        TSX
        AND     #01111111B          ;ZERO BIT 7
        STA     103H,X              ;STORE CHARACTER IN STACK SO IT WILL BE
                                    ; RESTORED TO REGISTER A
        PLA                         ;RESTORE A,X,Y
        TAX
        PLA
        TAY
        PLA
        RTS

;********************************
;ROUTINE: WRCHAR
;PURPOSE: WRITE A CHARACTER
;ENTRY: REGISTER A = CHARACTER
;EXIT:  NONE
;REGISTERS USED: P
;********************************

WRCHAR:
        PHA                         ;SAVE A,X,Y
        TYA
        PHA
        TXA
        PHA

        TSX
        LDA     103H,X              ;GET REGISTER A BACK FROM STACK
        ORA     #10000000B          ;SET BIT 7
        JSR     COUT                ;OUTPUT VIA APPLE MONITOR

        PLA                         ;RESTORE A,X,Y
        TAX
        PLA
        TAY
        PLA
        RTS

;********************************
;ROUTINE: RDLINE
;PURPOSE: READ A LINE TO 200H USING THE APPLE MONITOR
;ENTRY: NONE
;EXIT:  REGISTER X = LENGTH OF LINE
;REGISTERS USED: ALL
;********************************
```

```
RDLINE:
        JSR     GETLN1          ;CALL THE APPLE MONITOR GETLN1
        RTS

;********************************
;ROUTINE: NXTNUM
;PURPOSE: GET A NUMBER FROM THE INPUT LINE IF ANY
;        IF NONE RETURN A 0
;ENTRY: LLEN = LENGTH OF THE LINE
;        LIDX = INDEX INTO THE LINE OF NEXT CHARACTER
;EXIT:   REGISTER A = LOW BYTE OF NUMBER
;        REGISTER Y = HIGH BYTE OF NUMBER
;        LIDX = INDEX OF THE FIRST NON NUMERICAL CHARACTER
;REGISTERS USED: ALL
;********************************

NXTNUM:
        LDA     #0
        STA     NUM
        STA     NUM+1           ;INITIALIZE NUMBER TO 0

        ;WAIT UNTIL A DECIMAL DIGIT IS FOUND (A CHARACTER BETWEEN 30H AND 39H)
        JSR     GETCHR          ;GET NEXT CHARACTER
        BCS     EXITNN          ;EXIT IF END OF LINE
        CMP     #"0"
        BCC     NXTNUM          ;WAIT IF LESS THAN "0"
        CMP     #"9"+1
        BCS     NXTNUM          ;WAIT IF GREATER THAN "9"

        ;FOUND A NUMBER
GETNUM:
        PHA                     ;SAVE CHARACTER ON STACK

        ;MULTIPLY NUM BY TEN
        LDA     NUM
        ASL     A
        ROL     NUM+1
        STA     NUM             ;NUM = LOW BYTE OF NUM * 2
        LDX     NUM+1           ;REGISTER X = HIGH BYTE OF NUM * 2
        ASL     A
        ROL     NUM+1
        ASL     A               ;REGISTER A = LOW BYTE OF NUM * 8
        ROL     NUM+1           ;NUM + 1 = HIGH BYTE OF NUM * 8
        CLC                     ;(NUM * 8) + (NUM * 2) = NUM * 10
        ADC     NUM
        STA     NUM
        TXA
        ADC     NUM+1
        STA     NUM+1

        ;ADD THE CHARACTER TO NUM
        PLA                     ;GET NEXT CHARACTER
        AND     #00001111B      ;NORMALIZE THE CHARACTER TO 0..9
        CLC
        ADC     NUM
        STA     NUM
```

```
        BCC     GETNM1
        INC     NUM+1
GETNM1:

        ;GET THE NEXT CHARACTER
        JSR     GETCHR
        BCS     EXITNN          ;EXIT IF END OF LINE
        CMP     #"0"
        BCC     EXITNN          ;EXIT IF LESS THAN "0"
        CMP     #"9"+1
        BCC     GETNUM          ;STAY IN LOOP IF DIGIT (BETWEEN "0" AND "9")

EXITNN:
        LDA     NUM             ;RETURN THE NUMBER
        LDY     NUM+1
        RTS


;*********************************
;ROUTINE: GETCHR
;PURPOSE: GET A CHARACTER FOR THE LINE
;ENTRY: LIDX = NEXT CHARACTER TO GET
;       LLEN = LENGTH OF LINE
;EXIT:  IF NO MORE CHARACTERS THEN
;         CARRY = 1
;       ELSE
;         CARRY = 0
;         REGISTER A = CHARACTER
;REGISTERS USED: ALL
;********************************

GETCHR:
        LDA     LIDX
        CMP     LLEN
        BCS     EXITGC          ;EXIT CHARACTER GET WITH CARRY = 1 TO
                                ; INDICATE END OF LINE (LIDX >= LLEN)
                                ; OTHERWISE, CARRY IS CLEARED
        TAY
        LDA     200H,Y          ;GET CHARACTER
        AND     #01111111B      ;CLEAR BIT 7
        INY                     ;INCREMENT TO NEXT CHARACTER
        STY     LIDX
                                ; CARRY IS STILL CLEARED
EXITGC:
        RTS

;*******************************
;ROUTINE: PRTNUM
;PURPOSE: PRINT A NUMBER BETWEEN 0..99
;ENTRY: A = NUMBER TO PRINT
;EXIT:  NONE
;REGISTERS USED: ALL
;******************************
```

```
PRTNUM:
        LDY     #"0"-1          ;INITIALIZE Y TO "0" - 1
        SEC                     ;  Y WILL BE THE 10'S PLACE
DIV10:
        INY                     ;INCREMENT 10'S
        SBC     #10
        BCS     DIV10
        ADC     #10+"0"         ;MAKE REGISTER A AN ASCII DIGIT

        ;REG A = 1'S PLACE
        ;REG Y = 10'S PLACE
        TAX                     ;SAVE 1'S
        TYA
        JSR     WRCHAR          ;OUTPUT 10'S PLACE
        TXA
        JSR     WRCHAR          ;OUTPUT 1'S PLACE
        RTS

;DATA SECTION
CR      .EQU    0DH             ;ASCII CARRIAGE RETURN
MSG     .BYTE   "ENTER DATE AND TIME ",CR,"(MM/DD/YR HR:MN:SC)? ",0
MSGIDX  .BLOCK  1               ;INDEX INTO MESSAGE
NUM:    .BLOCK  2               ;NUMBER
LLEN:   .BLOCK  1               ;LENGTH OF INPUT LINE
LIDX:   .BLOCK  1               ;INDEX OF INPUT LINE
CEN20:  .WORD   1900            ;20TH CENTURY
CURSEC: .BLOCK  1               ;CURRENT SECOND

        .END    ;PROGRAM
```

Appendix A 6502 Instruction Set Summary

Table A-1. 6502 Instructions in Alphabetical Order

INSTRUCTIONS		IMMEDIATE			ABSOLUTE			ZERO PAGE			ACCUM			IMPLIED			(IND, X)			(IND), Y			Z, PAGE, X			ABS, X			ABS, Y			RELATIVE			INDIRECT			Z, PAGE, Y			CONDITION CODES					
MNEMONIC	OPERATION	OP	N	#	OP	N	#	OP	N	#	OP	N	#	OP	N	#	OP	N	#	OP	N	#	OP	N	#	OP	N	#	OP	N	#	OP	N	#	OP	N	#	OP	N	#	N	Z	C	I	D	V
ADC	A + M + C → A (4) (1)	69	2	2	6D	4	3	65	3	2							61	6	2	71	5	2	75	4	2	7D	4	3	79	4	3										✓	✓	✓	—	—	✓
AND	A ∧ M → A (1)	29	2	2	2D	4	3	25	3	2							21	6	2	31	5	2	35	4	2	3D	4	3	39	4	3										✓	✓	—	—	—	—
ASL	C ← [7 0] ← Ø				ØE	6	3	Ø6	5	2	ØA	2	1										16	6	2	1E	7	3													✓	✓	✓	—	—	—
BCC	BRANCH ON C=Ø (2)																															9Ø	2	2							—	—	—	—	—	—
BCS	BRANCH ON C=1 (2)																															BØ	2	2							—	—	—	—	—	—
BEQ	BRANCH ON Z=1 (2)																															FØ	2	2							—	—	—	—	—	—
BIT	A ∧ M				2C	4	3	24	3	2																															M_7	✓	—	—	—	M_6
BMI	BRANCH ON N=1 (2)																															3Ø	2	2							—	—	—	—	—	—
BNE	BRANCH ON Z=Ø (2)																															DØ	2	2							—	—	—	—	—	—
BPL	BRANCH ON N=Ø (2)																															1Ø	2	2							—	—	—	—	—	—
BRK	(See Fig. A-1)													ØØ	7	1																									—	—	—	—	—	—
BVC	BRANCH ON V=Ø (2)																															5Ø	2	2							—	—	—	—	—	—
BVS	BRANCH ON V=1 (2)																															7Ø	2	2							—	—	—	—	—	—
CLC	Ø → C													18	2	1																									—	—	Ø	—	—	—
CLD	Ø → D													D8	2	1																									—	—	—	—	Ø	—
CLI	Ø → 1													58	2	1																									—	—	—	Ø	—	—
CLV	Ø → V													B8	2	1																									—	—	—	—	—	Ø
CMP	A-M (1)	C9	2	2	CD	4	3	C5	3	2							C1	6	2	D1	5	2	D5	4	2	DD	4	3	D9	4	3										✓	✓	✓	—	—	—
CPX	X-M	EØ	2	2	EC	4	3	E4	3	2																															✓	✓	✓	—	—	—
CPY	Y-M	CØ	2	2	CC	4	3	C4	3	2																															✓	✓	✓	—	—	—
DEC	M-1 → M				CE	6	3	C6	5	2													D6	6	2	DE	7	3													✓	✓	—	—	—	—
DEX	X-1 → X													CA	2	1																									✓	✓	—	—	—	—
DEY	Y-1 → Y													88	2	1																									✓	✓	—	—	—	—
EOR	A ⊻ M → A (1)	49	2	2	4D	4	3	45	3	2							41	6	2	51	5	2	55	4	2	5D	4	3	59	4	3										✓	✓	—	—	—	—
INC	M + 1 → M				EE	6	3	E6	5	2													F6	6	2	FE	7	3													✓	✓	—	—	—	—
INX	X + 1 → X													E8	2	1																									✓	✓	—	—	—	—
INY	Y + 1 → Y													C8	2	1																									✓	✓	—	—	—	—
JMP	JUMP TO NEW LOC				4C	3	3																												6C	5	3				—	—	—	—	—	—
JSR	(See Fig. A-2) JUMP SUB				2Ø	6	3																																		—	—	—	—	—	—
LDA	M → A (1)	A9	2	2	AD	4	3	A5	3	2							A1	6	2	B1	5	2	B5	4	2	BD	4	3	B9	4	3										✓	✓	—	—	—	—

Table A-1. 6502 Instructions in Alphabetical Order (Continued)

MNEMONIC	OPERATION	IMMEDIATE			ABSOLUTE			ZERO PAGE			ACCUM.			IMPLIED			(IND, X)			(IND), Y			Z, PAGE, X			ABS, X			ABS, Y			RELATIVE			INDIRECT			Z, PAGE, Y			CONDITION CODES					
		OP	N	#	OP	N	#	OP	N	#	OP	N	#	OP	N	#	OP	N	#	OP	N	#	OP	N	#	OP	N	#	OP	N	#	OP	N	#	OP	N	#	OP	N	#	N	Z	C	I	D	V
LDX	M → X (1)	A2	2	2	AE	4	3	A6	3	2																			BE	4	3							B6	4	2	√	√	—	—	—	—
LDY	M → Y (1)	A0	2	2	AC	4	3	A4	3	2													B4	4	2	BC	4	3													√	√	—	—	—	—
LSR	0 → [7 … 0] → C				4E	6	3	46	5	2	4A	2	1										56	6	2	5E	7	3													0	√	√	—	—	—
NOP	NO OPERATION													EA	2	1																									—	—	—	—	—	—
ORA	A V M → A	09	2	2	0D	4	3	05	3	2							01	6	2	11	5	2	15	4	2	1D	4	3	19	4	3										√	√	—	—	—	—
PHA	A → Ms S−1 → S													48	3	1																									—	—	—	—	—	—
PHP	P → Ms S−1 → S													08	3	1																									—	—	—	—	—	—
PLA	S + 1 → S Ms → A													68	4	1																									√	√	—	—	—	—
PLP	S + 1 → S Ms → P													28	4	1																									(RESTORED)					
ROL	←[7 … 0]←[C]←				2E	6	3	26	5	2	2A	2	1										36	6	2	3E	7	3													√	√	√	—	—	—
ROR	→[C]→[7 … 0]→				6E	6	3	66	5	2	6A	2	1										76	6	2	7E	7	3													√	√	√	—	—	—
RTI	(See Fig. A-1) RTRN INT.													40	6	1																									RESTORED)					
RTS	(See Fig. A-2) RTRN SUB													60	6	1																									—	—	—	—	—	—
SBC	A−M−$\overline{C}$ → A (1)	E9	2	2	ED	4	3	E5	3	2							E1	6	2	F1	5	2	F5	4	2	FD	4	3	F9	4	3										√	√	(3)	—	—	√
SEC	1 → C													38	2	1																									—	—	1	—	—	—
SED	1 → D													F8	2	1																									—	—	—	—	1	—
SEI	1 → I													78	2	1																									—	—	—	1	—	—
STA	A → M				8D	4	3	85	3	2							81	6	2	91	6	2	95	4	2	9D	5	3	99	5	3										—	—	—			
STX	X → M				8E	4	3	86	3	2																												96	4	2	—	—	—	—	—	—
STY	Y → M				8C	4	3	84	3	2													94	4	2																—	—	—	—	—	
TAX	A → X													AA	2	1																									√	√	—	—	—	—
TAY	A → Y													A8	2	1																									√	√	—	—	—	—
TSX	S → X													BA	2	1																									√	√	—	—	—	—
TXA	X → A													8A	2	1																									√	√	—	—	—	—
TXS	X → S													9A	2	1																									—	—	—	—	—	—
TYA	Y → A													98	2	1																									√	√	—	—	—	—

(1) ADD 1 TO "N" IF PAGE BOUNDARY IS CROSSED
(2) ADD 1 TO "N" IF BRANCH OCCURS TO SAME PAGE
ADD 2 TO "N" IF BRANCH OCCURS TO DIFFERENT PAGE
(3) CARRY NOT = BORROW
(4) IF IN DECIMAL MODE Z FLAG IS INVALID
ACCUMULATOR MUST BE CHECKED FOR ZERO RESULT

X INDEX X
Y INDEX Y
A ACCUMULATOR
M MEMORY PER EFFECTIVE ADDRESS
Ms MEMORY PER STACK POINTER

+ ADD
— SUBTRACT
∧ AND
V OR
⊻ EXCLUSIVE OR
√ MODIFIED

- NOT MODIFIED
M_7 MEMORY BIT 7
M_6 MEMORY BIT 6
N NUMBER OF CLOCK CYCLES
\# NUMBER OF BYTES

Table A-2. 6502 Operation Codes in Numerical Order

MSD \ LSD	0	1	2	3	4	5	6	7	8	9	A	B	C	D	E	F	LSD / MSD
0	BRK	ORA-IND, X		–		ORA-Z, Page	ASL-Z, PAGE		PHP	ORA-IMM	ASL-A			ORA-ABS	ASL-ABS		0
1	BPL	ORA-IND, Y				ORA-Z, Page, X	ASL-Z, Page, X		CLC	ORA-ABS, Y				ORA-ABS, X	ASL-ABS, X		1
2	JSR	AND-IND, X			BIT-Z, Page	AND-Z, Page	ROL-Z, Page		PLP	AND-IMM	ROL-A		BIT-ABS	AND-ABS	ROL-ABS		2
3	BMI	AND-IND, Y				AND-Z, Page, X	ROL-Z, Page, X		SEC	AND-ABS, Y				AND-ABS, X	ROL-ABS, X		3
4	RTI	EOR-IND, X				EOR-Z, Page	LSR-Z, Page		PHA	EOR-IMM	LSR-A		JMP-ABS	EOR-ABS	LSR-ABS		4
5	BVC	EOR-IND, Y				EOR-Z, Page, X	LSR-Z, Page, X		CLI	EOR-ABS, Y				EOR-ABS, X	LSR-ABS, X		5
6	RTS	ADC-IND, X				ADC-Z, Page	ROR-Z, Page		PLA	ADC-IMM	ROR-A		JMP-IND	ADC-ABS	ROR-ABS		6
7	BVS	ADC-IND, Y				ADC-Z, Page, X			SEI	ADC-ABS, Y				ADC-ABS, X			7
8		STA-IND, X			STY-Z, Page	STA-Z, Page	STX-Z, Page		DEY		TXA		STY-ABS	STA-ABS	STX-ABS		8
9	BCC	STA-IND, Y			STY-Z, Page, X	STA-Z, Page, X	STX-Z, Page, Y		TYA	STA-ABS, Y	TXS			STA-ABS, X			9
A	LDY-IMM	LDA-IND, X	LDX-IMM		LDY-Z, Page	LDA-Z, Page	LDX-Z, Page		TAY	LDA-IMM	TAX		LDY-ABS	LDA-ABS	LDX-ABS		A
B	BCS	LDA-IND, Y			LDY-Z, Page, X	LDA-Z, Page, X	LDX-Z, Page, Y		CLV	LDA-ABS, Y	TSK		LDY-ABS, X	LDA-ABS, X	LDX-ABS, Y		B
C	CPY-IMM	CMP-IND, X			CPY-Z, Page	CMP-Z, Page	DEC-Z, Page		INV	CMP-IMM	DEX		CPY-ABS	CMP-ABS	DEC-ABS		C
D	BNE	CMP-IND, Y				CMP-Z, Page, X	DEC-Z, Page, X		CLD	CMP-ABS, Y				CMP-ABS, X	DEC-ABS, X		D
E	CPX-IMM	SBC-IND, X			CPX-Z, Page	SBC-Z, Page	INC-Z, Page		INX	SBC-IMM	NOP		CPX-ABS	SBC-ABS	INC-ABS		E
F	BEQ	SBC-IND, Y				SBC-Z, Page, X	INC-Z, Page, X		SED	SBC-ABS, Y				SBC-ABS, X	INC-ABS, X		F

Table A-3. Summary of 6502 Addressing Modes

IMM · IMMEDIATE ADDRESSING – THE OPERAND IS CONTAINED IN THE SECOND BYTE OF THE INSTRUCTION.

ABS · ABSOLUTE ADDRESSING – THE SECOND BYTE OF THE INSTRUCTION CONTAINS THE 8 LOW ORDER BITS OF THE EFFECTIVE ADDRESS. THE THIRD BYTE CONTAINS THE 8 HIGH ORDER BITS OF THE EFFECTIVE ADDRESS.

Z, PAGE · ZERO PAGE ADDRESSING – SECOND BYTE CONTAINS THE 8 LOW ORDER BITS OF THE EFFECTIVE ADDRESS. THE 8 HIGH ORDER BITS ARE ZERO.

A, · ACCUMULATOR – ONE BYTE INSTRUCTION OPERATING ON THE ACCUMULATOR.

Z, PAGE, X · Z PAGE, Y · ZERO PAGE INDEXED – THE SECOND BYTE OF THE INSTRUCTION IS ADDED TO THE INDEX (CARRY IS DROPPED) TO FORM THE LOW ORDER BYTE OF THE EA. THE HIGH ORDER BYTE OF THE EA IS ZERO

ABS, X ABS, Y ABSOLUTE INDEXED – THE EFFECTIVE ADDRESS IS FORMED BY ADDING THE INDEX TO THE SECOND AND THIRD BYTE OF THE INSTRUCTION.

(IND, X) · INDEXED INDIRECT – THE SECOND BYTE OF THE INSTRUCTION IS ADDED TO THE X INDEX, DISCARDING THE CARRY, THE RESULTS POINTS TO A LOCATION ON PAGE ZERO WHICH CONTAINS THE 8 LOW ORDER BITS OF THE EA. THE NEXT BYTE CONTAINS THE 8 HIGH ORDER BITS.

(IND), Y · INDIRECT INDEXED – THE SECOND BYTE OF THE INSTRUCTION POINTS TO A LOCATION IN PAGE ZERO. THE CONTENTS OF THIS MEMORY LOCATION IS ADDED TO THE Y INDEX, THE RESULT BEING THE LOW ORDER EIGHT BITS OF THE EA. THE CARRY FROM THIS OPERATION IS ADDED TO THE CONTENTS OF THE NEXT PAGE ZERO LOCATION, THE RESULTS BEING THE 8 HIGH ORDER BITS OF THE EA.

Table A-4. 6502 Assembler Directives, Labels, and Special Characters

ASSEMBLER DIRECTIVES

- OPT – SPECIFIES OPTIONS FOR ASSEMBLY
  OPTIONS ARE: (OPTIONS LISTED FIRST ARE THE DEFAULT VALUES).
  NOC (COU OR CNT) – DO NOT LIST ALL INSTRUCTIONS AND THEIR USAGE.
  NOG (GEN) – DO NOT GENERATE MORE THAN ONE LINE OF CODE FOR ASCII STRINGS.
  XRE (NOX) – PRODUCE A CROSS-REFERENCE LIST IN THE SYMBOL TABLE.
  ERR (NOE) – CREATE AN ERROR FILE.
  MEM (NOM) – CREATE AN ASSEMBLER OBJECT OUTPUT FILE.
  LIS (NOL) – PRODUCE A FULL ASSEMBLY LISTING.
- BYTE – PRODUCES A SINGLE BYTE IN MEMORY EQUAL TO EACH OPERAND SPECIFIED.
- WORD – PRODUCES AN ADDRESS (2 BYTES) IN MEMORY EQUAL TO EACH OPERAND SPECIFIED.
- DBYTE – PRODUCES TWO BYTES IN MEMORY EQUAL TO EACH OPERAND SPECIFIED.
- SKIP – GENERATE THE NUMBER OF BLANK LINES SPECIFIED BY THE OPERAND.
- PAGE – ADVANCE THE LISTING TO THE TOP OF A NEW PAGE AND CHANGE TITLE.
- END – DEFINES THE END OF A SOURCE PROGRAM.
- * = – DEFINES THE BEGINNING OF A NEW PROGRAM COUNTER SEQUENCE.

LABELS

LABELS ARE THE FIRST FIELD AND MUST BE FOLLOWED BY AT LEAST ONE SPACE OR A COLON (:)
LABELS CAN BE UP TO 6 ALPHANUMERIC CHARACTERS LONG AND MUST BEGIN WITH AN ALPHA CHARACTER.
A,X,Y,S,P AND THE 56 OPCODES ARE RESERVED AND CANNOT BE USED AS LABELS.
LABEL = EXPRESSION CAN BE USED TO EQUATE LABELS TO VALUES.
LABEL *=* +N CAN BE USED TO RESERVE AREAS IN MEMORY.

CHARACTERS USED AS SPECIAL PREFIXES:

. INDICATES AN ASSEMBLER DIRECTIVE
SPECIFIES THE IMMEDIATE MODE OF ADDRESSING
$ SPECIFIES A HEXADECIMAL NUMBER
@ SPECIFIES AN OCTAL NUMBER
% SPECIFIES A BINARY NUMBER
' SPECIFIES AN ASCII LITERAL CHARACTER
( ) INDICATES INDIRECT ADDRESSING
; INDICATES FOLLOWING TEXT ARE COMMENTS
< SPECIFIES LOWER HALF OF A 16 BIT VALUE
> SPECIFIES UPPER HALF OF A 16 BIT VALUE

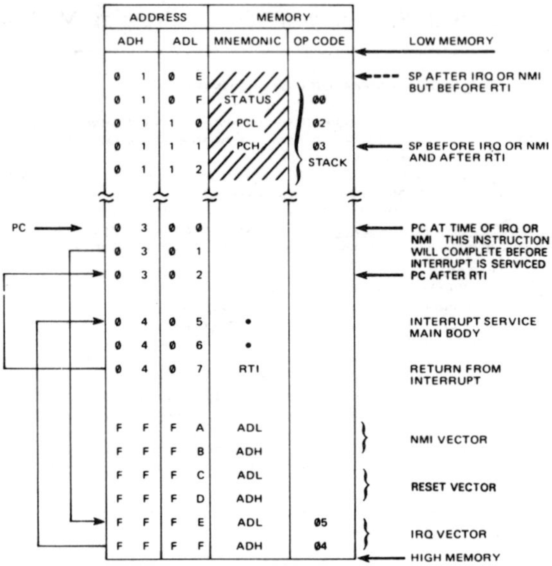

Figure A-1. Response to $\overline{\text{IRQ}}$ and $\overline{\text{NMI}}$ Inputs and Operation of the RTI and BRK Instructions

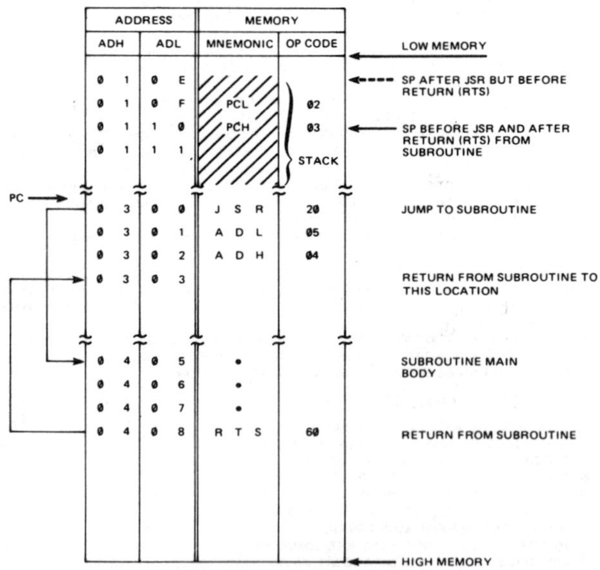

Figure A-2. Operation of the JSR and RTS Instructions

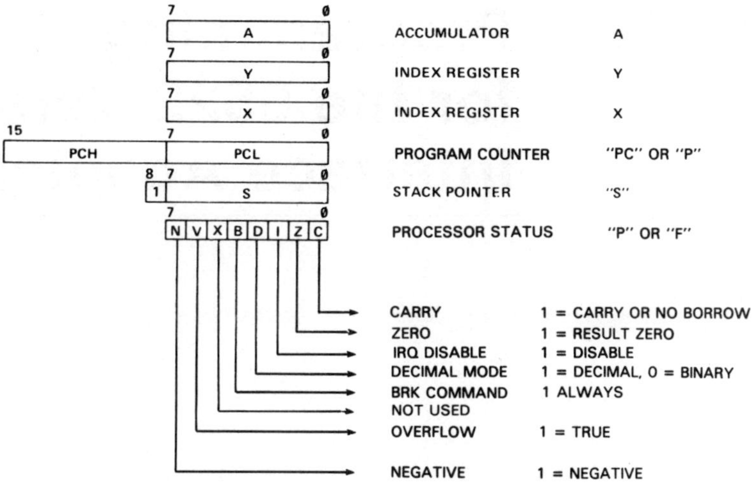

Figure A-3. Programming Model of the 6502 Microprocessor

Appendix B **Programming Reference for the 6522 Versatile Interface Adapter (VIA)**

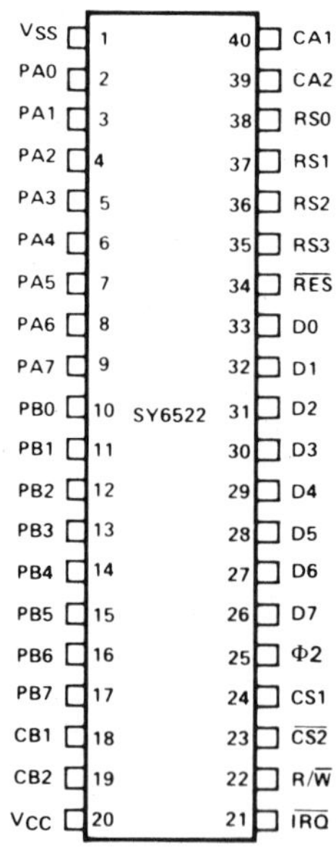

Figure B-1. 6522 Pin Assignments

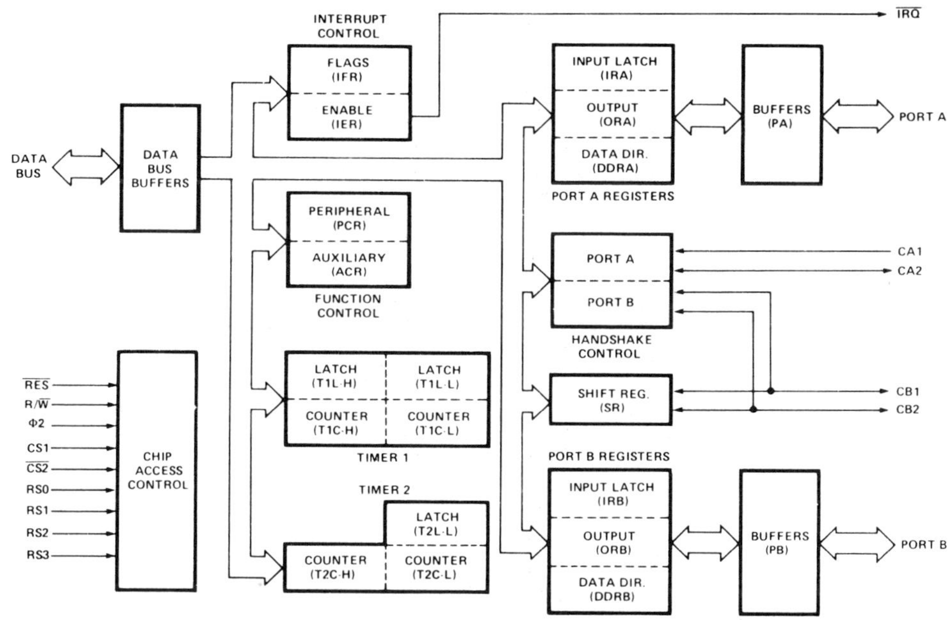

Figure B-2. Block Diagram of the 6522 Versatile Interface Adapter (VIA)

Table B-1. 6522 Internal Registers

Register Number	RS Coding				Register Desig.	Description	
	RS3	RS2	RS1	RS0		Write	Read
0	0	0	0	0	ORB/IRB	Output Register "B"	Input Register "B"
1	0	0	0	1	ORA/IRA	Output Register "A"	Input Register "A"
2	0	0	1	0	DDRB	Data Direction Register "B"	
3	0	0	1	1	DDRA	Data Direction Register "A"	
4	0	1	0	0	T1C-L	T1 Low-Order Latches	T1 Low-Order Counter
5	0	1	0	1	T1C-H	T1 High-Order Counter	
6	0	1	1	0	T1L-L	T1 Low-Order Latches	
7	0	1	1	1	T1L-H	T1 High-Order Latches	
8	1	0	0	0	T2C-L	T2 Low-Order Latches	T2 Low-Order Counter
9	1	0	0	1	T2C-H	T2 High-Order Counter	
10	1	0	1	0	SR	Shift Register	
11	1	0	1	1	ACR	Auxiliary Control Register	
12	1	1	0	0	PCR	Peripheral Control Register	
13	1	1	0	1	IFR	Interrupt Flag Register	
14	1	1	1	0	IER	Interrupt Enable Register	
15	1	1	1	1	ORA/IRA	Same as Reg 1 Except No "Handshake"	

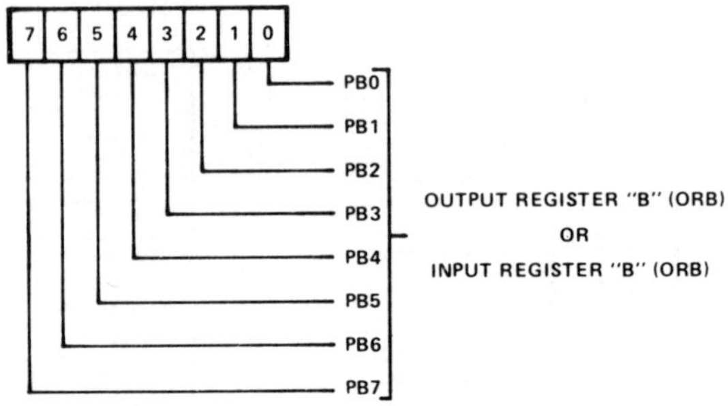

Pin Data Direction Selection	WRITE	READ
DDRB = "1" (OUTPUT)	MPU writes Output Level (ORB)	MPU reads output register bit in ORB. Pin level has no affect.
DDRB = "0" (INPUT) (Input latching disabled)	MPU writes into ORB, but no effect on pin level, until DDRB changed.	MPU reads input level on PB pin.
DDRB = "0" (INPUT) (Input latching enabled)		MPU reads IRB bit, which is the level of the PB pin at the time of the last CB1 active transition.

Figure B-3. Output Register B and Input Register B (Register 0)

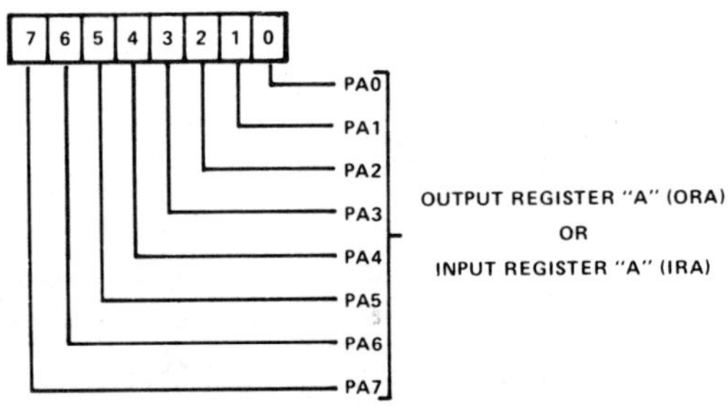

Pin Data Direction Selection	WRITE	READ
DDRA = "1" (OUTPUT) (Input latching disabled)	MPU writes Output Level (ORA).	MPU reads level on PA pin.
DDRA = "1" (OUTPUT) (Input latching enabled)		MPU reads IRA bit which is the level of the PA pin at the time of the last CA1 active transition.
DDRA = "0" (INPUT) (Input latching disabled)	MPU writes into ORA, but no effect on pin level, until DDRA changed.	MPU reads level on PA pin.
DDRA = "0" (INPUT) (Input latching enabled)		MPU reads IRA bit which is the level of the PA pin at the time of the last CA1 active transition.

Figure B-4. Output Register A and Input Register A (Register 1)

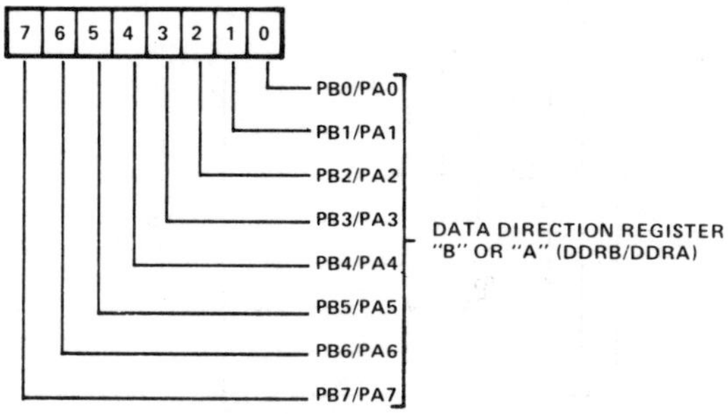

"0" ASSOCIATED PB/PA PIN IS AN INPUT (HIGH-IMPEDANCE)

"1" ASSOCIATED PB/PA PIN IS AN OUTPUT, WHOSE LEVEL IS DETERMINED BY ORB/ORA REGISTER BIT.

Figure B-5. Data Direction Registers B (Register 2) and A (Register 3)

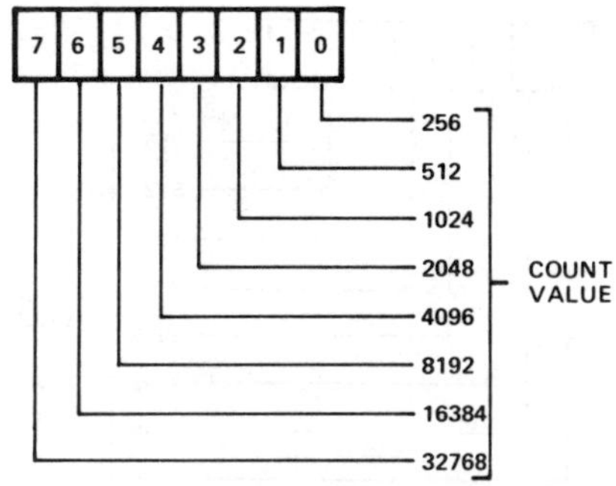

WRITE – 8 BITS LOADED INTO T1 HIGH-ORDER LATCHES. ALSO, AT THIS TIME BOTH HIGH AND LOW-ORDER LATCHES TRANSFERRED INTO T1 COUNTER. T1 INTERRUPT FLAG ALSO IS RESET.

READ – 8 BITS FROM T1 HIGH-ORDER COUNTER TRANSFERRED TO MPU.

Figure B-7. Timer 1 High-Order Counter (Register 5)

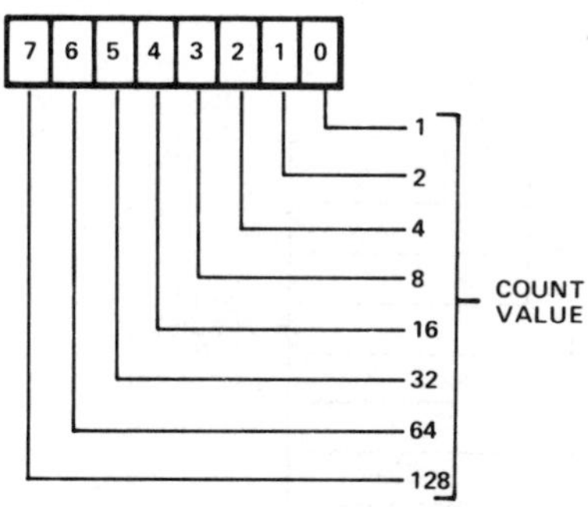

WRITE – 8 BITS LOADED INTO T1 LOW-ORDER LATCHES. LATCH CONTENTS ARE TRANSFERRED INTO LOW-ORDER COUNTER AT THE TIME THE HIGH-ORDER COUNTER IS LOADED (REG 5).

READ – 8 BITS FROM T1 LOW-ORDER COUNTER TRANSFERRED TO MPU. IN ADDITION, T1 INTERRUPT FLAG IS RESET (BIT 6 IN INTERRUPT FLAG REGISTER).

Figure B-6. Timer 1 Low-Order Counter (Register 4)

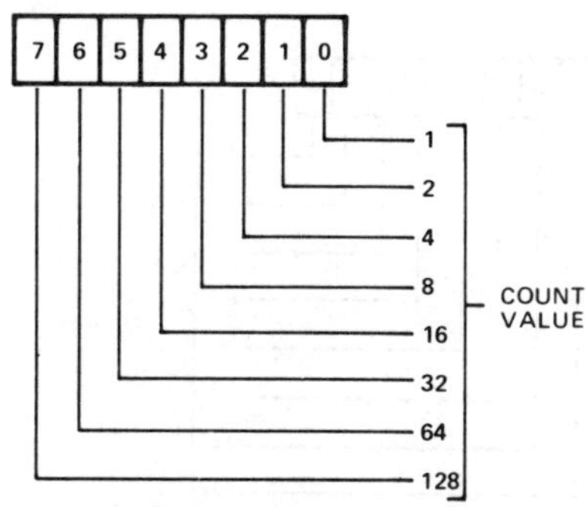

WRITE – 8 BITS LOADED INTO T1 LOW-ORDER LATCHES. THIS OPERATION IS THE SAME AS WRITING INTO REGISTER 4.

READ – 8 BITS FROM T1 LOW-ORDER LATCHES TRANSFERRED TO MPU. UNLIKE REG 4 OPERATION, THIS DOES NOT CAUSE RESET OF T1 INTERRUPT FLAG.

Figure B-8. Timer 1 Low-Order Latches (Register 6)

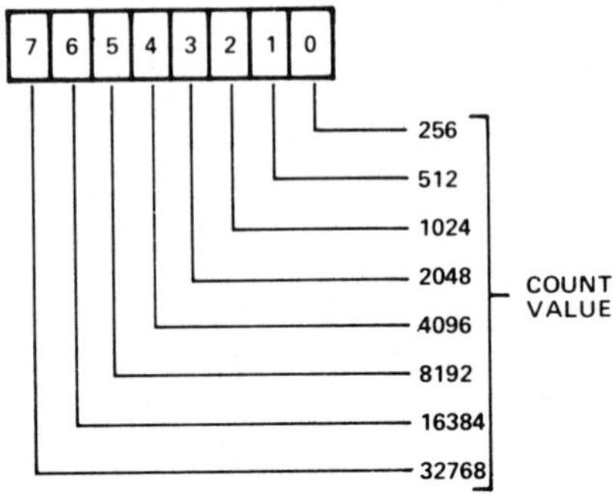

WRITE – 8 BITS LOADED INTO T1 HIGH-ORDER LATCHES. UNLIKE REG 4 OPERATION NO LATCH-TO-COUNTER TRANSFERS TAKE PLACE.

READ – 8 BITS FROM T1 HIGH-ORDER LATCHES TRANSFERRED TO MPU.

Figure B-9. Timer 1 High-Order Latches (Register 7)

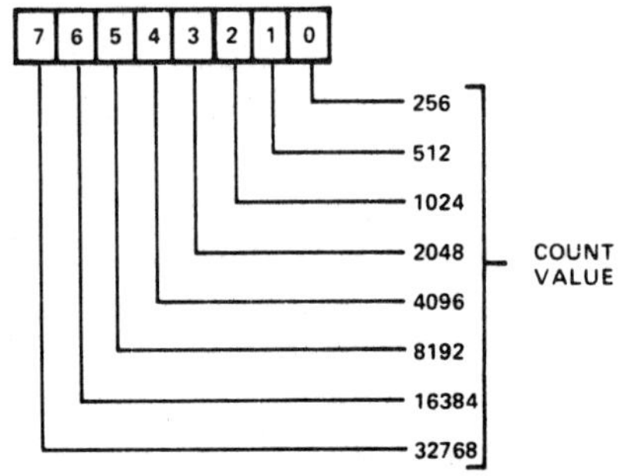

WRITE – 8 BITS LOADED INTO T2 HIGH-ORDER COUNTER. ALSO, LOW-ORDER LATCHES TRANSFERRED TO LOW-ORDER COUNTER. IN ADDITION, T2 INTERRUPT FLAG IS RESET.

READ – 8 BITS FROM T2 HIGH-ORDER COUNTER TRANSFERRED TO MPU.

Figure B-11. Timer 2 High-Order Counter (Register 9)

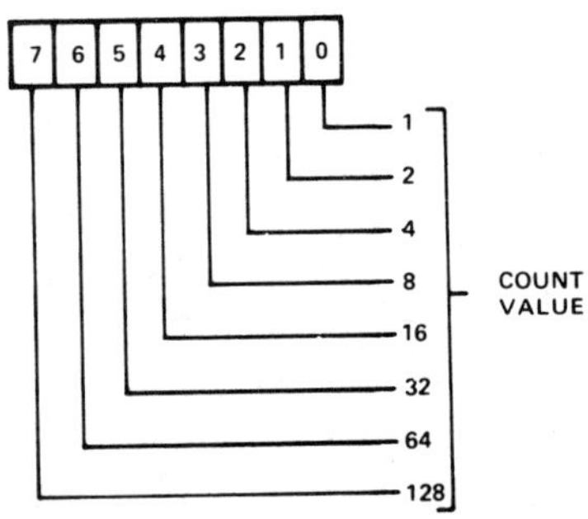

WRITE – 8 BITS LOADED INTO T2 LOW-ORDER LATCHES.

READ – 8 BITS FROM T2 LOW-ORDER COUNTER TRANSFERRED TO MPU. T2 INTERRUPT FLAG IS RESET.

Figure B-10. Timer 2 Low-Order Counter (Register 8)

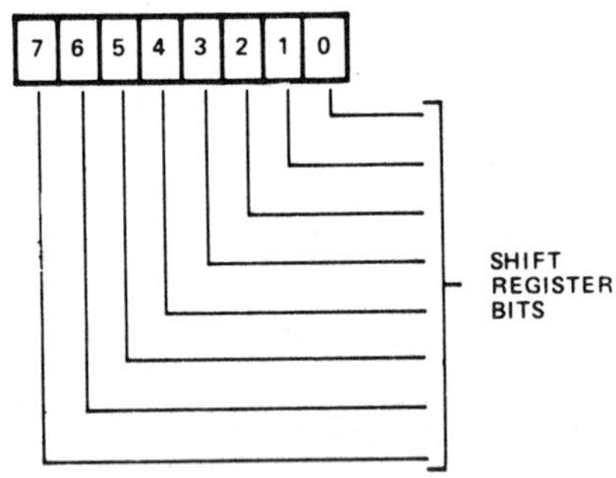

NOTES:
1. WHEN SHIFTING OUT, BIT 7 IS THE FIRST BIT OUT AND SIMULTANEOUSLY IS ROTATED BACK INTO BIT 0.
2. WHEN SHIFTING IN, BITS INITIALLY ENTER BIT 0 AND ARE SHIFTED TOWARDS BIT 7.

Figure B-12. Shift Register (Register 10)

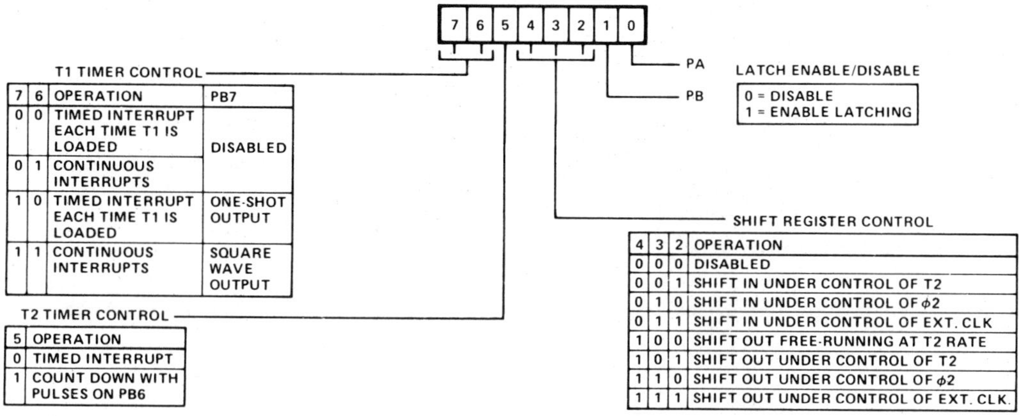

Figure B-13. Auxiliary Control Register (Register 11)

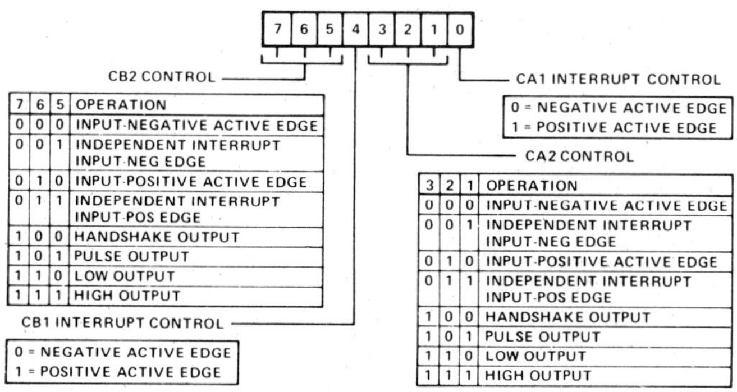

Figure B-14. Peripheral Control Register (Register 12)

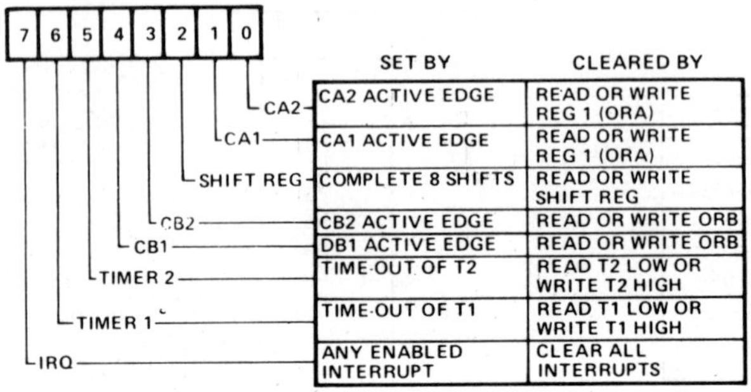

Figure B-15. Interrupt Flag Register (Register 13)

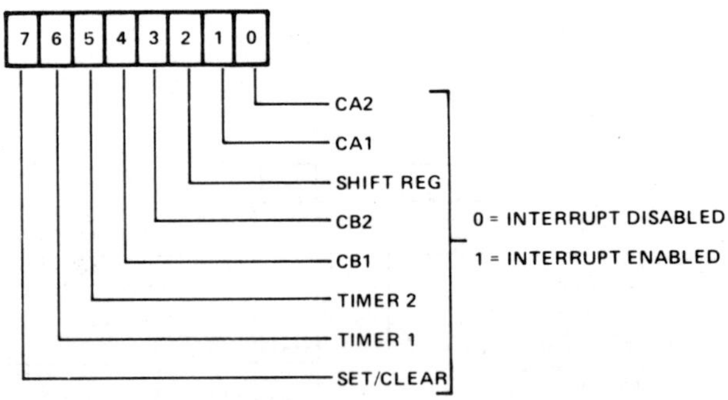

NOTES:
1. IF BIT 7 IS A "0", THEN EACH "1" IN BITS 0 - 6 DISABLES THE CORRESPONDING INTERRUPT.
2. IF BIT 7 IS A "1", THEN EACH "1" IN BITS 0 - 6 ENABLES THE CORRESPONDING INTERRUPT.
3. IF A READ OF THIS REGISTER IS DONE, BIT 7 WILL BE "1" AND ALL OTHER BITS WILL REFLECT THEIR ENABLE/DISABLE STATE.

Figure B-16. Interrupt Enable Register (Register 14)

Appendix C **ASCII Character Set**

LSD	MSD	0 000	1 001	2 010	3 011	4 100	5 101	6 110	7 111
0	0000	NUL	DLE	SP	0	@	P	`	p
1	0001	SOH	DC1	!	1	A	Q	a	q
2	0010	STX	DC2	"	2	B	R	b	r
3	0011	ETX	DC3	#	3	C	S	c	s
4	0100	EOT	DC4	$	4	D	T	d	t
5	0101	ENG	NAK	%	5	E	U	e	u
6	0110	ACK	SYN	&	6	F	V	f	v
7	0111	BEL	ETB	'	7	G	W	g	w
8	1000	BS	CAN	(	8	H	X	h	x
9	1001	HT	EM	)	9	I	Y	i	y
A	1010	LF	SUB	*	:	J	Z	j	z
B	1011	VT	ESC	+	;	K	[	k	}
C	1100	FF	FS	,	<	L	\	l	|
D	1101	CR	GS	—	=	M	]	m	{
E	1110	SO	RS	•	>	N	^	n	~
F	1111	SI	VS	/	?	O	—	o	DEL

Glossary

A

Absolute address. An address that identifies a storage location or a device without the use of a base, offset, or other factor. *See also* Effective address, Relative offset.

Absolute addressing. An addressing mode in which the instruction contains the actual address required for its execution. In 6502 terminology, absolute addressing refers to a type of direct addressing in which the instruction contains a full 16-bit address as opposed to zero page addressing in which the instruction contains only an 8-bit address on page 0.

Absolute indexed addressing. A form of indexed addressing in which the instruction contains a full 16-bit base address.

Accumulator. A register that is the implied source of one operand and the destination of the result for most arithmetic and logic operations.

ACIA (Asynchronous Communications Interface Adapter). A serial interface device. Common ACIAs in 6502-based computers are the 6551 and 6850 devices. *See also* UART.

Active transition (in a PIA or VIA). The edge on the control line that sets an Interrupt flag. The alternatives are a negative edge (1 to 0 transition) or a positive edge (0 to 1 transition).

Address. The identification code that distinguishes one memory location or input/output port from another and that can be used to select a specific one.

Addressing modes. The methods for specifying the addresses to be used in executing an instruction. Common addressing modes are direct, immediate, indexed, indirect, and relative.

Address register. A register that contains a memory address.

Address space. The total range of addresses to which a particular computer may refer.

ALU. See Arithmetic-logic unit.

Arithmetic-logic unit (ALU). A device that can perform any of a variety of arithmetic or logical functions; function inputs select which function is performed during a particular cycle.

Arithmetic shift. A shift operation that preserves the value of the sign bit (most significant bit). In a right shift, this results in the sign bit being copied into the succeeding bit positions (called *sign extension*).

Arm. See Enable, but most often applied to interrupts.

Array. A collection of related data items, usually stored in consecutive memory addresses.

ASCII (American Standard Code for Information Interchange). A 7-bit character code widely used in computers and communications.

Assembler. A computer program that converts assembly language programs into a form (machine language) that the computer can execute directly. The assembler translates mnemonic operation codes and names into their numerical equivalents and assigns locations in memory to data and instructions.

Assembly language. A computer language in which the programmer can use mnemonic operation codes, labels, and names to refer to their numerical equivalents.

Asynchronous. Operating without reference to an overall timing source, that is, at irregular intervals.

Autodecrementing. The automatic decrementing of an address register as part of the execution of an instruction that uses it.

Autoincrementing. The automatic incrementing of an address register as part of the execution of an instruction that uses it.

Automatic mode (of a peripheral chip). An operating mode in which the peripheral chip produces control signals automatically without specific program intervention.

B

Base address. The address in memory at which an array or table starts. Also called *starting address* or *base.*

Baud. A measure of the rate at which serial data is transmitted, bits per second, but including both data bits and bits used for synchronization, error checking, and other purposes. Common baud rates are 110, 300, 1200, 2400, 4800, and 9600.

Baud rate generator. A device that generates the proper time intervals between bits for serial data transmission.

BCD (Binary-Coded Decimal). A representation of decimal numbers in which each decimal digit is coded separately into a binary number.

Bidirectional. Capable of transporting signals in either direction.

Binary-coded decimal. See BCD.

Binary search. A search in which the set of items to be searched is divided into two equal (or nearly equal) parts during each iteration. The part containing the item being sought is then determined and used as the set in the next iteration. A binary search thus halves the size of the set being searched with each iteration. This method obviously assumes the set of items is ordered.

Bit test. An operation that determines whether a bit is 0 or 1. Usually refers to a logical AND operation with an appropriate mask.

Block. An entire group or section, such as a set of registers or a section of memory.

Block comparison (or block compare). A search that extends through a block of memory until either the item being sought is found or the entire block is examined.

Block move. Moving an entire set of data from one area of memory to another.

Boolean variable. A variable that has only two possible values, which may be represented as true and false or as 1 and 0. *See also* Flag.

Borrow. A bit which is set to 1 if a subtraction produces a negative result and to 0 if it produces a positive or zero result. The borrow is used commonly to subtract numbers that are too long to be handled in a single operation.

Bounce. To move back and forth between states before reaching a final state.

Branch instruction. See Jump instruction.

Break instruction. See Trap.

Breakpoint. A condition specified by the user under which program execution is to end temporarily. Breakpoints are used as an aid in debugging. The specification of the conditions under which execution will end is referred to as *setting breakpoints* and the deactivation of those conditions is referred to as *clearing breakpoints.*

BSC (Binary Synchronous Communications or BISYNC). An older line protocol often used by IBM computers and terminals.

Bubble sort. A sorting technique which goes through an array exchanging each pair of elements that are out of order.

Buffer. Temporary storage area generally used to hold data before it is transferred to its final destination.

Buffer empty. A signal that is active when any data entered into a buffer or register has been transferred to its final destination.

Buffer full. A signal that is active when a buffer or register is completely occupied with data that has not been transferred to its final destination.

Buffer index. The index of the next available address in a buffer.

Buffer pointer. A storage location that contains the next available address in a buffer.

Bug. An error or flaw.

Byte. A unit of eight bits. May be described as consisting of a high nibble or digit (the four most significant bits) and a low nibble or digit (the four least significant bits).

Byte-length. A length of eight bits per item.

C

Call (a subroutine). Transfers control to the subroutine while retaining the information required to resume the current program. A call differs from a jump or branch in that a call retains information concerning its origin, whereas a jump or branch does not.

Carry. A bit that is 1 if an addition overflows into the succeeding digit position.

Carry flag. A flag that is 1 if the last operation generated a carry from the most significant bit and 0 if it did not.

CASE statement. A statement in a high-level computer language that directs the computer to perform one of several subprograms, depending on the value of a variable. That is, the computer performs the first subprogram if the variable has the first value specified, etc. The computed GO TO statement serves a similar function in FORTRAN.

Central processing unit (CPU). The control section of the computer which controls its operations, fetches and executes instructions, and performs arithmetic and logical functions.

Checksum. A logical sum that is included in a block of data to guard against recording or transmission errors. Also referred to as *longitudinal parity* or *longitudinal redundancy check* (LRC).

Circular shift. See Rotate.

Cleaning the stack. Removing unwanted items from the stack, usually by adjusting the stack pointer.

Clear. Set to zero.

Clock. A regular timing signal that governs transitions in a system.

Close (a file). To make a file inactive. The final contents of the file are the last information the user stored in it. The user must generally close a file after working with it.

Coding. Writing instructions in a computer language.

Combo chip. See Multifunction device.

Command register. See Control register.

Comment. A section of a program that has no function other than documentation. Comments are neither translated nor executed, but are simply copied into the program listing.

Complement. Invert; *see also* one's complement, two's complement.

Concatenation. Linking together, chaining, or uniting in a series. In string operations, placing of one string after another.

Condition code. See Flag.

Control (command) register. A register whose contents determine the state of a transfer or the operating mode of a device.

Control signal. A signal that directs an I/O transfer or changes the operating mode of a peripheral.

Cyclic redundancy check (CRC). An error-detecting code generated from a polynomial that can be added to a block of data or a storage area.

D

Data accepted. A signal that is active when the most recent data has been transferred successfully.

Data direction register. A register that determines whether bidirectional I/O lines are being used as inputs or outputs. Abbreviated as DDR in some diagrams.

Data-link control. A set of conventions governing the format and timing of data exchange between communicating systems. Also called a *protocol.*

Data ready. A signal that is active when new data is available to the receiver. Same as *valid data.*

Data register. In a PIA or VIA, the actual input/output port. Also called an *output register* or a *peripheral register.*

DDCMP (Digital Data Communications Message Protocol). A widely used protocol that supports any method of physical data transfer (synchronous or asynchronous, serial or parallel).

Debounce. Convert the output from a contact with bounce into a single, clean transition between states. Debouncing is most commonly applied to outputs from mechanical keys or switches which bounce back and forth before settling into their final positions.

Debounce time. The amount of time required to debounce a change of state.

Debugger. A program that helps in locating and correcting errors in a user program. Some versions are referred to as dynamic debugging tools or DDT after the famous insecticide.

Debugging. The process of locating and correcting errors in a program.

Device address. The address of a port associated with an input or output device.

Diagnostic. A program that checks the operation of a device and reports its findings.

Digit shift. A shift of one BCD digit position or four bit positions.

Direct addressing. An addressing mode in which the instruction contains the address required for its execution. The 6502 microprocessor has two types of direct addressing: zero page addressing (requiring only an 8-bit address on page 0) and absolute addressing (requiring a full 16-bit address in two bytes of memory).

Disarm. *See* Disable, but most often applied to interrupts.

Disable (or disarm). Prohibit an activity from proceeding or a signal (such as an interrupt) from being recognized.

Double word. A unit of 32 bits.

Driver. See I/O driver.

Dump. A facility that displays the contents of an entire section of memory or group of registers on an output device.

Dynamic allocation (of memory). The allocation of memory for a subprogram from whatever is available when the subprogram is called. This is as opposed to the *static allocation* of a fixed area of storage to each subprogram. Dynamic allocation often reduces memory usage because subprograms can share areas; it does, however, generally require additional execution time and overhead spent in memory management.

E

EBCDIC (Expanded Binary-Coded Decimal Interchange Code). An 8-bit character code often used in large computers.

Echo. Reflects transmitted information back to the transmitter; sends back to a terminal the information received from it.

Editor. A program that manipulates text material and allows the user to make corrections, additions, deletions, and other changes.

Effective address. The actual address used by an instruction to fetch or store data.

EIA RS-232. See RS-232.

Enable (or arm). Allows an activity to proceed or a signal (such as an interrupt) to be recognized.

Endless loop or *jump-to-self instruction.* An instruction that transfers control to itself, thus executing indefinitely (or until a hardware signal interrupts it).

Error-correcting code. A code that the receiver can use to correct errors in messages; the code itself does not contain any additional message.

Error-detecting code. A code that the receiver can use to detect errors in messages; the code itself does not contain any additional message.

Even parity. A 1-bit error-detecting code that makes the total number of 1 bits in a unit of data (including the parity bit) even.

EXCLUSIVE OR function. A logical function that is true if either of its inputs is true but not both. It is thus true if its inputs are not equal (that is, if one of them is a logic 1 and the other is a logic 0).

External reference. The use in a program of a name that is defined in another program.

F

F (flag) register. See Processor status register.

File. A collection of related information that is treated as a unit for purposes of storage or retrieval.

Fill. Placing values in storage areas not previously in use, initializing memory or storage.

Flag (or condition code or status bit). A single bit that indicates a condition within the computer, often used to choose between alternative instruction sequences.

Flag (software). An indicator that is either on (1) or off (0) and can be used to select between two alternative courses of action. *Boolean variable* and *semaphore* are other terms with the same meaning.

Flag register. See Processor status register.

Free-running mode. An operating mode for a timer in which it indicates the end of a time interval and then starts another of the same length. Also referred to as a *continuous mode.*

Function key. A key that causes a system to perform a function (such as clearing the screen of a video terminal) or execute a procedure.

G

Global. This is a universal variable. Defined in more than one section of a computer program, rather than used only locally.

H

Handshake. An asynchronous transfer in which sender and receiver exchange predetermined signals to establish synchronization and to indicate the status of the data transfer. Typically, the sender indicates that new data is available and the receiver reads the data and indicates that it is ready for more.

Hardware stack. A stack that the computer automatically manages when executing instructions that use it.

Head (of a queue). The location of the item most recently entered into the queue.

Header, queue. See Queue header.

Hexadecimal (or hex). Number system with base 16. The digits are the decimal numbers 0 through 9, followed by the letters A through F.

Hex code. See Object code.

High-level language. A programming language that is aimed toward the solution of problems, rather than being designed for convenient conversion into computer instructions.A compiler or interpreter translates a program written in a high-level language into a form that the computer can execute. Common high-level languages include BASIC, COBOL, FORTRAN, and Pascal.

I

Immediate addressing. An addressing mode in which the data required by an instruction is part of the instruction. The data immediately follows the operation code in memory.

Independent mode (of a parallel interface). An operating mode in which the status and control signals associated with a parallel I/O port can be used independently of data transfers through the port.

Index. A data item used to identify a particular element of an array or table.

Indexed addressing. An addressing mode in which the address is modified by the contents of an index register to determine the effective address (the actual address used).

Indexed indirect addressing. An addressing mode in which the effective address is determined by indexing from the base address and then using the indexed address indirectly. This is also known as *preindexing,* since the indexing is performed before the indirection. Of course, the array starting at the given base address must consist of addresses that can be used indirectly.

Index register. A register that can be used to modify memory addresses.

Indirect addressing. An addressing mode in which the effective address is the contents of the address included in the instruction, rather than the address itself.

Indirect indexed addressing. An addressing mode in which the effective address is determined by first obtaining the base address indirectly and then indexing from that base address. Also known as *postindexing,* since the indexing is performed after the indirection.

Indirect jump. A jump instruction that transfers control to the address stored in a register or memory location, rather than to a fixed address.

Input/output control block (IOCB). A group of storage locations that contain the information required to control the operation of an I/O device. Typically included in the information are the addresses of routines that perform operations such as transferring a single unit of data or determining device status.

Input/output control system (IOCS). A set of computer routines that control the performance of I/O operations.

Instruction. A group of bits that defines a computer operation and is part of the instruction set.

Instruction cycle. The process of fetching, decoding, and executing an instruction.

Instruction execution time. The time required to fetch, decode, and execute an instruction.

Instruction fetch. The process of addressing memory and reading an instruction into the CPU for decoding and execution.

Instruction length. The amount of memory needed to store a complete instruction.

Instruction set. The set of general-purpose instructions available on a given computer. The set of inputs to which the CPU will produce a known response when they are fetched, decoded, and executed.

Interpolation. Estimating values of a function at points between those at which the values are already known.

Interrupt. A signal that temporarily suspends the computer's normal sequence of operations and transfers control to a special routine.

Interrupt-driven. Dependent on interrupts for its operation, may idle until it receives an interrupt.

Interrupt flag. A bit in the input/output section that is set when an event occurs that requires servicing by the CPU. Typical events include an active transition on a control line and the exhaustion of a count by a timer.

Interrupt mask (or interrupt enable). A bit that determines whether interrupts will be recognized. A mask or disable bit must be cleared to allow interrupts, whereas an enable bit must be set.

Interrupt request. A signal that is active when a peripheral is requesting service, often used to cause a CPU interrupt. *See also* Interrupt flag.

Interrupt service routine. A program that performs the actions required to respond to an interrupt.

Inverted borrow. A bit which is set to 0 if a subtraction produces a negative result and to 1 if it produces a positive or 0 result. An inverted borrow can be used like a true borrow, except that the complement of its value (i.e., 1 minus its value) must be used in the extension to longer numbers.

IOCB. See Input/output control block.

IOCS. See Input/output control system.

I/O device table. A table that establishes the correspondence between the logical devices to which programs refer and the physical devices that are actually used in data transfers. An I/O device table must be placed in memory in order to run a program that refers to logical devices on a computer with a particular set of actual (physical) devices. The I/O device table may, for example, contain the starting addresses of the I/O drivers that handle the various devices.

I/O driver. A computer program that transfers data to or from an I/O device, also called a *driver* or *I/O utility*. The driver must perform initialization functions and handle status and control, as well as physically transfer the actual data.

J

Jump instruction (or Branch instruction). An instruction that places a new value in the program counter, thus departing from the normal one-step incrementing. Jump instructions may be conditional; that is, the new value may be placed in the program counter only if a condition holds.

Jump table. A table consisting of the starting addresses of executable routines, used to transfer control to one of them.

L

Label. A name attached to an instruction or statement in a program that identifies the location in memory of the machine language code or assignment produced from that instruction or statement.

Latch. A device that retains its contents until new data is specifically entered into it.

Leading edge (of a binary pulse). The edge that marks the beginning of a pulse.

Least significant bit. The rightmost bit in a group of bits, that is, bit 0 of a byte or a 16-bit word.

Library program. A program that is part of a collection of programs and is written and documented according to a standard format.

LIFO (last-in, first-out) memory. A memory that is organized according to the order in which elements are entered and from which elements can be retrieved only in the order opposite from that in which they were entered. *See also* Stack.

Linearization. The mathematical approximation of a function by a straight line between two points at which its values are known.

Linked list. A list in which each item contains a pointer (or *link*) to the next item. Also called a *chain* or *chained list.*

List. An ordered set of items.

Logical device. The input or output device to which a program refers. The actual or physical device is determined by looking up the logical device in an I/O device table — a table containing actual I/O addresses (or starting addresses for I/O drivers) corresponding to the logical device numbers.

Logical shift. A shift operation that moves zeros in at the end as the original data is shifted.

Longitudinal parity. See Checksum.

Logical sum. A binary sum with no carries between bit positions. *See also* Checksum, EXCLUSIVE OR function.

Longitudinal redundancy check (LRC). *See* Checksum.

Lookup table. An array of data organized so that the answer to a problem may be determined merely by selecting the correct entry (without any calculations).

Low-level language. A computer language in which each statement is translated directly into a single machine language instruction.

M

Machine language. The programming language that the computer can execute directly with no translation other than numeric conversions.

Maintenance (of programs). Updating and correcting computer programs that are in use.

Majority logic. A combinational logic function that is true when more than half the inputs are true.

Manual mode (of a peripheral chip). An operating mode in which the chip produces control signals only when specifically directed to do so by a program.

Mark. The 1 state on a serial data communications line.

Mask. A bit pattern that isolates one or more bits from a group of bits.

Maskable interrupt. An interrupt that the system can disable.

Memory capacity. The total number of different memory addresses (usually specified in terms of bytes) that can be attached to a particular computer.

Microcomputer. A computer that has a microprocessor as its central processing unit.

Microprocessor. A complete central processing unit for a computer constructed from one or a few integrated circuits.

Mnemonic. A memory jogger, a name that suggests the actual meaning or purpose of the object to which it refers.

Modem (Modulator/demodulator). A device that adds or removes a carrier frequency, thereby allowing data to be transmitted on a high-frequency channel or received from such a channel.

Modular programming. A programming method whereby the overall program is divided into logically separate sections or *modules.*

Module. A part or section of a program.

Monitor. A program that allows the computer user to enter programs and data, run programs, examine the contents of the computer's memory and registers, and utilize the computer's peripherals. *See also* Operating system.

Most significant bit. The leftmost bit in a group of bits, that is, bit 7 of a byte or bit 15 of a 16-bit word.

Multifunction device. A device that performs more than one function in a computer system; the term commonly refers to devices containing memory, input/output ports, timers, etc., such as the 6530, 6531, and 6532 devices.

Multitasking. Used to execute many tasks during a single period of time, usually by working on each one for a specified part of the period and suspending tasks that must wait for input, output, the completion of other tasks, or external events.

Murphy's Law. The famous maxim that "whatever can go wrong, will."

N

Negate. Finds the two's complement (negative) of a number.

Negative edge (of a binary pulse). A 1-to-0 transition.

Negative flag. See Sign flag.

Negative logic. Circuitry in which a logic zero is the active or ON state.

Nesting. Constructing programs in a hierarchical manner with one level contained within another, and so forth. The nesting level is the number of transfers of control required to reach a particular part of a program without ever returning to a higher level.

Nibble (or nybble). A unit of four bits. A byte (eight bits) may be described as consisting of a high nibble (four most significant bits) and a low nibble (four least significant bits).

Nine's complement. The result of subtracting a decimal number from a number having nines in each digit position.

Nonmaskable interrupt. An interrupt that cannot be disabled within the CPU.

Nonvolatile memory. A memory that retains its contents when power is removed.

No-op (or no operation). An instruction that does nothing other than increment the program counter.

Normalization (of numbers). Adjusting a number into a regular or standard format. A typical example is the scaling of a binary fraction so that its most significant bit is 1.

O

Object code (or object program). The program that is the output of a translator program, such as an assembler. Usually it is a machine language program ready for execution.

Odd parity. A 1-bit error-detecting code that makes the total number of 1 bits in a unit of data (including the parity bit) odd.

Offset. Distance from a starting point or base address.

One's complement. A bit-by-bit logical complement of a number, obtained by replacing each 0 bit with a 1 and each 1 bit with a 0.

One-shot. A device that produces a pulse output of known duration in response to a pulse input. A timer operates in a *one-shot mode* when it indicates the end of a single interval of known duration.

Open (a file). Make a file ready for use. The user generally must open a file before working with it.

Operating system (OS). A computer program that controls the overall operations of a computer and performs such functions as assigning places in memory to programs and data, scheduling the execution of programs, processing interrupts, and controlling the overall input/output system. Also known as a monitor, executive, or master-control program, although the term *monitor* is usually reserved for a simple operating system with limited functions.

Operation code (op code). The part of an instruction that specifies the operation to be performed.

OS. See Operating system.

Output register. In a PIA or VIA, the actual input/output port. Also called a *data register* or a *peripheral register.*

Overflow (of a stack). Exceeding the amount of memory allocated to a stack.

Overflow, two's complement. See Two's complement overflow.

P

P register. See Processor status register, Program counter. Most 6502 reference material abbreviates program counter as PC and processor status register as P, but some refer to the program counter as P and the processor status (flag) register as F.

Packed decimal. A binary-coded decimal format in which each 8-bit byte contains two decimal digits.

Page. A subdivision of the memory. In 6502 terminology, a page is a 256-byte section of memory in which all addresses have the same eight most significant bits (or page number). For example, page C6 consists of memory addresses C600 through C6FF.

Paged address. The identifier that characterizes a particular memory address on a known page. In 6502 terminology, this is the eight least significant bits of a memory address.

Page number. The identifier that characterizes a particular page of memory. In 6502 terminology, this is the eight most significant bits of a memory address.

Page 0. In 6502 terminology, the lowest 256 addresses in memory (addresses 0000 through 00FF).

Parallel interface. An interface between a CPU and input or output devices that handle data in parallel (more than one bit at a time).

Parameter. An item that must be provided to a subroutine or program in order for it to be executed.

Parity. A 1-bit error-detecting code that makes the total number of 1 bits in a unit of data, including the parity bit, odd (odd parity) or even (even parity). Also called *vertical parity* or *vertical redundancy check* (VRC).

Passing parameters. Making the required parameters available to a subroutine.

Peripheral Interface. One of the 6500 family versions of a parallel interface; examples are the 6520, 6522, 6530, and 6532 devices.

Peripheral ready. A signal that is active when a peripheral can accept more data.

Peripheral register. In a PIA or VIA, the actual input or output port. Also called a *data register* or an *output* register.

Physical device. An actual input or output device, as opposed to a logical device.

PIA. (Peripheral Interface Adapter). The common name for the 6520 or 6820 device which consists of two bidirectional 8-bit I/O ports, two status lines, and two bidirectional status or control lines. The 6821 is a similar device.

Pointer. A storage place that contains the address of a data item rather than the item itself. A pointer tells where the item is located.

Polling. Determining which I/O devices are ready by examining the status of one device at a time.

Polling interrupt system. An interrupt system in which a program determines the source of a particular interrupt by examining the status of potential sources one at a time.

Pop. Removes an operand from a stack.

Port. The basic addressable unit of the computer's input/output section.

Positive edge (of a binary pulse). A 0-to-1 transition.

Postdecrementing. Decrementing an address register after using it.

Postincrementing. Incrementing an address register after using it.

Postindexing. See Indirect indexed addressing.

Power fail interrupt. An interrupt that informs the CPU of an impending loss of power.

Predecrementing. Decrements an address register before using it.

Preincrementing. Increments an address register before using it.

Preindexing. See Indexed indirect addressing.

Priority interrupt system. An interrupt system in which some interrupts have precedence over others, that is, they will be serviced first or can interrupt the others' service routines.

Processor status (P or F) *register.* A register that defines the current state of a computer, often containing various bits indicating internal conditions. Other names for this register include condition code register, flag (F) register, status register, and status word.

Program counter (PC or P register). A register that contains the address of the next instruction to be fetched from memory.

Programmable I/O device. An I/O device that can have its mode of operation determined by loading registers under program control.

Programmable peripheral chip. A chip that can operate in a variety of modes; its current operating mode is determined by loading control registers under program control.

Programmable timer. A device that can handle a variety of timing tasks, including the generation of delays, under program control.

Program relative addressing. A form of relative addressing in which the base address is the program counter. Use of this form of addressing makes it easy to move programs from one place in memory to another.

Programmed input/output. Input or output performed under program control without using interrupts or other special hardware techniques.

Protocol. See Data-link control.

Pseudo-operation (or pseudo-op or pseudo-instruction). An assembly language operation code that directs the assembler to perform some action but does not result in the generation of a machine language instruction.

Pull. Removes an operand from a stack, same as *pop.*

Push. Stores an operand in a stack.

Q

Queue. A set of tasks, storage addresses, or other items that are used in a first-in, first-out manner; that is, the first item entered in the queue is the first to be removed.

Queue header. A set of storage locations describing the current location and status of a queue.

R

RAM. See Random-access memory.

Random-access memory (RAM). A memory that can be both read and altered (written) in normal operation.

Read-only memory (ROM). A memory that can be read but not altered in normal operation.

Ready for data. A signal that is active when the receiver can accept more data.

Real-time. In synchronization with the actual occurrence of events.

Real-time clock. A device that interrupts a CPU at regular time intervals.

Real-time operating system. An operating system that can act as a supervisor for programs that have real-time requirements. May also be referred to as a *real-time executive* or *real-time monitor.*

Reentrant. A program or routine that can be executed concurrently while the same routine is being interrupted or otherwise held in abeyance.

Register. A storage location inside the CPU.

Relative addressing. An addressing mode in which the address specified in the instruction is the offset from a base address.

Relative offset. The difference between the actual address to be used in an instruction and the current value of the program counter.

Relocatable. Can be placed anywhere in memory without changes; that is, a program that can occupy any set of consecutive memory addresses.

Return (from a subroutine). Transfers control back to the program that originally called the subroutine and resumes its execution.

RIOT. (ROM/I/O/timer or RAM/I/O/timer). A device containing memory (ROM or RAM), I/O ports, and timers.

ROM. See Read-only memory.

Rotate. A shift operation that treats the data as if it were arranged in a circle, that is, as if the most significant and least significant bits were connected either directly or through a Carry bit.

Row major order. Storing elements of a multidimensional array in a linear memory by changing the indexes starting with the rightmost first. That is, if the elements are A(I,J,K) and begin with A(0,0,0), the order is A(0,0,0), A(0,0,1), ...,A(0,1,0), A(0,1,1),... The opposite technique (change leftmost index first) is called *column major order.*

RRIOT. ROM/RAM/I/O/timer, a device containing read-only memory, read/write memory, I/O ports, and timers.

RS-232 (or EIA RS-232). A standard interface for the transmission of serial digital data, sponsored by the Electronic Industries Association of Washington, D.C. It has been partially superseded by RS-449.

S

Scheduler. A program that determines when other programs should be started and terminated.

Scratchpad. An area of memory that is especially easy and quick to use for storing variable data or intermediate results. Page 0 is generally used as a scratchpad in 6502-based computers.

SDLC (Synchronous Data Link Control). The successor protocol to BSC for IBM computers and terminals.

Semaphore. See Flag.

Serial. One bit at a time.

Serial interface. An interface between a CPU and input or output devices that handle data serially. Serial interfaces commonly used in 6502-based computers are the 6551 and 6850 devices. *See also* UART.

Shift instruction. An instruction that moves all the bits of the data by a certain number of bit positions, just as in a shift register.

Signed number. A number in which one or more bits represent whether the number is positive or negative. A common format is for the most significant bit to represent the sign (0 = positive, 1 = negative).

Sign extension. The process of copying the sign (most significant) bit to the right as in an arithmetic shift. Sign extension preserves the sign when two's complement numbers are being divided or normalized.

Sign flag. A flag that contains the most significant bit of the result of the previous operation. It is sometimes called a *negative flag,* since a value of 1 indicates a negative signed number.

Sign function. A function that is 0 if its parameter is positive and 1 if its parameter is negative.

Software delay. A program that has no function other than to waste time.

Software interrupt. See Trap.

Software stack. A stack that is managed by means of specific instructions, as opposed to a hardware stack which the computer manages automatically.

Source code (or source program). A computer program written in assembly language or in a high-level language.

Space. The zero state on a serial data communications line.

Stack. A section of memory that can be accessed only in a last-in, first-out manner. That is, data can be added to or removed from the stack only through its top; new data is placed above the old data and the removal of a data item makes the item below it the new top.

Stack pointer. A register that contains the address of the top of a stack.The 6502's stack pointer contains the address on page 1 of the next available (empty) stack location.

Standard (or 8,4,2,1) *BCD.* A BCD representation in which the bit positions have the same weights as in ordinary binary numbers.

Standard teletypewriter. A teletypewriter that operates asynchronously at a rate of ten characters per second.

Start bit. A 1-bit signal that indicates the start of data transmission by an asynchronous device.

Static allocation (of memory). Assignment of fixed storage areas for data and programs, as opposed to *dynamic allocation* in which storage areas are assigned at the time when they are needed.

Status register. A register whose contents indicate the current state or operating mode of a device. *See also* Processor status register.

Status signal. A signal that describes the current state of a transfer or the operating mode of a device.

Stop bit. A 1-bit signal that indicates the end of data transmission by an asynchronous device.

String. An array (set of data) consisting of characters.

String functions. Procedures that allow the programmer to operate on data consisting of characters rather than numbers. Typical functions are insertion, deletion, concatenation, search, and replacement.

Strobe. A signal that identifies or describes another set of signals and that can be used to control a buffer, latch, or register.

Subroutine. A subprogram that can be executed (called) from more than one place in a main program.

Subroutine call. The process whereby a computer transfers control from its current program to a subroutine while retaining the information required to resume the current program.

Subroutine linkage. The mechanism whereby a computer retains the information required to resume its current program after it completes the execution of a subroutine.

Suspend (a task). Halts execution and preserves the status of the task until some future time.

Synchronization (or sync) character. A character that is used only to synchronize the transmitter and the receiver.

Synchronous. Operating according to an overall timing source or clock, that is, at regular intervals.

Systems software. Programs that perform administrative functions or aid in the development of other programs but do not actually perform any of the computer's ultimate workload.

T

Tail (of a queue). The location of the oldest item in the queue, that is, the earliest entry.

Task. A self-contained program that can serve as part of an overall system under the control of a supervisor.

Task status. The set of parameters that specify the current state of a task. A task can be suspended and resumed as long as its status is saved and restored.

Teletypewriter. A device containing a keyboard and a serial printer that is often used in communications and with computers. Also referred to as a Teletype (a registered trademark of Teletype Corporation of Skokie, Illinois) or TTY.

Ten's complement. The result of subtracting a decimal number from zero (ignoring the negative sign), the nine's complement plus one.

Terminator. A data item that has no function other than to signify the end of an array.

Threaded code. A program consisting of subroutines, each of which automatically transfers control to the next one upon its completion.

Timeout. A period during which no activity is allowed to proceed, an inactive period.

Top of the stack. The address containing the item most recently entered into the stack.

Trace. A debugging aid that provides information about a program while the program is being executed. The trace usually prints all or some of the intermediate results.

Trailing edge (of a binary pulse). The edge that masks the end of a pulse.

Translate instruction. An instruction that converts its operand into the corresponding entry in a table.

Transparent routine. A routine that operates without interfering with the operations of other routines.

Trap (or software interrupt). An instruction that forces a jump to a specific (CPU-dependent) address, often used to produce breakpoints or to indicate hardware or software errors.

True borrow. See Borrow.

Two's complement. A binary number that, when added to the original number in a binary adder, produces a zero result. The two's complement of a number may be obtained by subtracting the number from zero or by adding 1 to the one's complement.

Two's complement overflow. A situation in which a signed arithmetic operation produces a result that cannot be represented correctly — that is, the magnitude overflows into the sign bit.

U

UART (Universal Asynchronous Receiver/Transmitter). An LSI device that acts as an interface between systems that handle data in parallel and devices that handle data in asynchronous serial form.

Underflow (of a stack). Attempting to remove more data from a stack than has been entered into it.

Unsigned number. A number in which all the bits are used to represent magnitude.

Utility. A general-purpose program, usually supplied by the computer manufacturer or part of an operating system, that executes a standard or common operation such as sorting, converting data from one format to another, or copying a file.

V

Valid data. A signal that is active when new data is available to the receiver.

Vectored interrupt. An interrupt that produces an identification code (or *vector*) that the CPU can use to transfer control to the appropriate service routine. The process whereby control is transferred to the service routine is called *vectoring.*

Versatile Interface Adapter (VIA). The name commonly given to the 6522 parallel interface device; it consists of two 8-bit bidirectional I/O ports, four status and control lines, two 16-bit timers, and a shift register.

VIA. See Versatile Interface Adapter.

Volatile memory. A memory that loses its contents when power is removed.

W

Walking bit test. A procedure whereby a single 1 bit is moved through each bit position in an area of memory and a check is made as to whether it can be read back correctly.

Word. The basic grouping of bits that a computer can process at one time. In dealing with microprocessors, the term often refers to a 16-bit unit of data.

Word boundary. A boundary between 16-bit storage units containing two bytes of information. If information is being stored in word-length units, only pairs of bytes conforming to (aligned with) word boundaries contain valid information. Misaligned pairs of bytes contain one byte from one word and one byte from another.

Word-length. A length of 16 bits per item.

Wraparound. Organization in a circular manner as if the ends were connected. A storage area exhibits wraparound if operations on it act as if the boundary locations were contiguous.

Write-only register. A register that the CPU can change but cannot read. If a program must determine the contents of such a register, it must save a copy of the data placed there.

Z

Zero flag. A flag that is 1 if the last operation produced a result of zero and 0 if it did not.

Zero page. In 6502 terminology, the lowest 256 memory addresses (addresses 0000 through 00FF).

Zero page addressing. In 6502 terminology, a form of direct addressing in which the instruction contains only an 8-bit address on page 0. That is, zero is implied as the more significant byte of the direct address and need not be included specifically in the instruction.

Zero-page indexed addressing. A form of indexed addressing in which the instruction contains a base address on page 0. That is, zero is implied as the more significant byte of the base address and need not be included explicitly in the instruction.

Zoned decimal. A binary-coded decimal format in which each 8-bit byte contains only one decimal digit.

Index

E

F

H

I

J

T

U

V

W

X

Y

Z